When All Hell Breaks Loose:

From the Ashes of Dresden to Existential Grace

A Memoir

D1516824

Manfred Bahmann

When All Hell Breaks Loose

When All Hell Breaks Loose

CONTENTS

When All Hell Breaks Loose

When All Hell Breaks Loose

For Andrea, Chris, and Daniel

When All Hell Breaks Loose

FOREWORD

Every follower of Jesus Christ has a faith journey. Mine began with the firebombing of my hometown Dresden, Germany, in the last days of World War II when I was fifteen. Literally, all hell broke loose over my head on February 13, 1945. Although my conversion began that terrifying night, it stretched over several years as I tried to move from being an enthusiastic Hitler Youth member to one whose life was based upon a sincere faith in Jesus Christ.

I struggled hard to understand my beloved Germany's Holocaust atrocities and my sense of involvement in them. Even though I was just a teenager, I did a lot of soul-searching. What had been real all those years and what was illusory propaganda? I grew up in a society that demanded total allegiance. Now, my conversion experience into a new Christianity would demand much serious reflection and a lot of research into claims made for the Christian faith. Although this conversion was not a one-time emotional event, it involved all of my emotions.

Most of this probing and soul-searching will be found in the following chapters. Because of my personal history, this can be considered in some ways a political book. I believe that a genuine faith in Jesus Christ always puts existential challenges before us. Beyond my need to come to terms with the Nazi atrocities, my allegiance to Jesus Christ as my Lord would now require me to come to terms with the different political and philosophical ideologies I would face throughout decades of change. There would be numerous times "when all hell broke loose" on a journey that involved ministries in the United States, western Canada, Latin America, and Cold-War West Berlin.

But this is primarily a religious book. During years of theological study at German universities and American seminaries, I earned an M.Div. and a Ph.D. degree in church history and have taught on the seminary level. I consider myself first and foremost a church historian. I remain firmly grounded in the practices and teachings of Martin Luther and the Lutheran church. But in 1955 I was ordained in the union Church of the Palatinate in Speyer, Germany and I have never put much weight on denominational boundaries. The decade of the 1950s was an ecumenical time when Protestant Christians sought ways of coming together, and I was heavily influenced by this. During the 1960s I rejoiced in the fresh air wafting through Pope John XXIII's Second Vatican Council, and in 1968 I was present at the birth of Latin American Liberation Theology as an ecumenical observer at the CELAM bishops' conference in Medellin, Colombia. I have cooperated closely with Roman Catholic clergy in sometimes controversial ways, as this memoir will describe, and at present I am heavily involved in Jewish-Christian dialogue and worship in Allentown, Pennsylvania.

Throughout these and other experiences, the central question for me has always been: What does it mean to be a Christian today, right now, with so many changes and faith challenges happening all around us? What is expected of me as a committed follower of Christ? Answers can and will vary. But one constant element remains for me. No matter where the search may lead, Jesus Christ was, and is, always will be there.

Dresden, 1945

1
BAPTIZED BY FIRE

"I baptize you with water; but One mightier than I will baptize you with the Holy Spirit and with fire." (Luke 3:16)

I was baptized twice. The first time was with water, the second time with fire. Both events left a profound impact on my life.

My first baptism took place under questionable circumstances. The year was 1930, three years before Hitler came to power in Germany. I was just an infant when the sacrament of baptism was "done to me," and of course I have no personal memory of the occasion. But staunch Lutheran that I am, I came to appreciate the significance of the act. It has supported me as an adult with a special sacramental strength.

My first baptism happened in the village church of Kipsdorf, a picturesque German ski resort in the Erzgebirge mountain range of Saxony near the Czech border. The officiant was a Lutheran, Pastor Mueller. He and his wife were friends of my parents. For me, they were Onkel (uncle) Walter and Tante (aunt) Anna. He and my father had joined the Nazi Party very early, in the 1920's. Both Onkel Walter and my father were kind and understanding men, as far as I can remember. I do not know whether or not they felt a hatred for Jews. I imagine their party membership was motivated by a certain amount of idealism and love for their country. Even so, both men obviously agreed that it was important for me to be baptized, and my mother was convinced of this as well. Mutti (Mama) was never a Nazi. She was a committed Christian, a regular churchgoer to the end of her life.

Whatever their motives may have been, I owe a debt of gratitude to these three adults. Because of them, I was joined to the body of Christ at the beginning of my life. Later on, the knowledge of my baptism would sustain me time and again in moments of crisis, like a protective bubble and shield. Even when I had no particular interest in religion as a child, I always knew I was somehow embraced by God's enormous grace.

My second baptism, the one by fire, was more dramatic. It happened in Dresden, where we settled after my father died in 1941 when I was eleven. In part because of his advantageous connection to the Nazi party, Vati (Daddy) had quickly advanced in the railroad bureaucracy for which he worked. First he was promoted from his post in Kipsdorf to a better position in the Saxon provincial capital of Dresden; then he moved up to a prestigious post in the German national capital of Berlin. When he died there of a stroke at the age of forty-five, I was devastated. Fearing for my health, my mother sent me to Tante Anna and Onkel Walter that summer to overcome my deep grief.

When All Hell Breaks Loose

Mutti, a well-brought-up Saxon lady, had always disliked Berlin, the sharp-edged German capital. When Vati died, she insisted we move back to the culturally more refined Dresden where she felt at home. There we lived through the city's complete devastation on February 13, 1945 when I was fifteen. The three-phase aid raid on Dresden was a totally unexpected, totally unwarranted civilian attack a few weeks before the war in Germany ended on May 8.

It was the Tuesday before Ash Wednesday. I had come home from school late in the afternoon. A strange aura lay over our city that day. Except for some youngsters running around the streets dressed as Indians or cowboys to celebrate Fasching, the German Mardi Gras, everyone was pretty depressed. People sensed that the end of the war was close at hand. The Soviet army was already on German soil just to the east of us. We wondered: When will the dreaded Russians be upon us? Nobody dared to speak about it in the apprehensive atmosphere. Certainly, not a single soul could imagine the frightful inferno that was about to engulf us that night.

My ten-year-old sister Irene and I went to bed around nine o'clock. Sirens started to wail with the air-raid alert shortly after ten. At first I did not want to get up. But when our neighbor across the hall yelled to my mother through the mail slot in our door: "Hurry up! The radio says enemy bombers are just a few hundred miles away!" that did it. I snapped out of my teenage sleepiness and dashed with Mutti and Irene down to the basement of our six-story apartment building. Through the windows T could already see the blazing flares we called "Christmas trees" lighting up the dark sky. The flares were set off by Allied scout planes to guide the bomber units that followed. Although I knew they were harbingers of death and destruction, I thought they looked kind of pretty in the night sky.

When All Hell Breaks Loose

A few minutes later, all hell broke loose above our heads. Dresden did not have real air-raid shelters as did other German cities. Our city was, and had always been, a cultural center without military installations or war industry. For this reason, the Nazis had not made the effort to build underground shelters. No one thought that Dresden would be hit. Now the harsh reality of the war caught us sharply by surprise, and we were left with only the unfortified basements of our city buildings to protect us from Allied planes.

For an hour the sky was completely covered from one end to the other by a blanket of enemy bombers. The deep droning of their engines filled the air. Bombs rained down on us without mercy, without letup. The earth heaved and vibrated with ceaseless detonations. The Americans flew daytime missions, and the British RAF came at night.

At that time, the Allies were not yet dropping napalm; this would come twenty years later with the Vietnam War. In 1945, the principal agent of destruction was phosphorus delivered in incendiary bombs. Before these were dropped, bomber squadrons threw down heavy explosives to establish air channels along the densely crowded city blocks. Once the phosphorus bombs were ignited, the fire in its thirst for oxygen pulled in air through these channels. This created firestorms that raged until all the buildings were burned out.

There was only one adult male in our basement, elderly Herr Schramm. The rest were women, young children, and teenagers, maybe thirty or forty of us in number. They cried, they whimpered, they made all sort of noises. But I could not utter a single word. I felt the blood drain from my lips and the tip of my nose was ice cold. Yet in spite of my terror, I had enough sense to find a spot under a supporting arch. I knew this was the safest place to be in case our building collapsed on top of us. As I stood hunched there, waiting wordlessly for what was to come, I stammered a silent prayer: "Herr, erbarme dich! (Lord, have mercy!)"

These words were the first heartfelt prayer of my life. My confirmation a year earlier in our neighborhood Lutheran church had been just a formality. But my desperate supplication in that basement was the real thing. From the bottom of my soul the cry went up: "Lord, have mercy!" This was the genesis of my second baptism. Thus came my baptism by fire.

Then the night around us was suddenly quiet. The early wave of the air raid was over. As we recovered from the horror of the first bombing mission, we discovered that the damage on our street was not that great. The entire center of the city seemed to be ablaze and was surely devastated, but only a few houses had been hit in our residential area.

I was too agitated to think of going back to bed. I ran outside into nearby side streets where some houses were burning, to see what could be done. With my fifteen years, I was eager to do my part. Full of youthful energy and adrenalin, I helped people drag their few possessions into the street.

Around two o'clock in the morning on Wednesday, February 14, the sirens screamed another full alert. I ran home and joined Mutti and Irene in our basement. The bombardment quickly started up again. This time, all hell broke loose right over our heads. The earth shook from the close impact of heavy explosives. I felt as if an abyss would open up and swallow us all at any moment. Again the women and children yelled and screamed, beside themselves with panic. There seemed to be no end to the horror, and I lost all sense of time.

Suddenly it was over. A deadly silence settled in; only a few people still whimpered. Mr. Schramm came over. "Come on," he summoned me, "let's look over the building!" We went from floor to floor and checked out the two apartments on each level. Debris lay everywhere. All the windows were blown out and doors were gone. A flagpole had flown in from somewhere and landed in our living room on the dining table. But although our homes were in total chaos, all in all we were lucky. We did not see fire anywhere. All the bathtubs had been filled with water as mandated by the authorities, and there were plenty of sandbags on each level.

Manfred, Age 15, 1945

After we inspected the top apartments, we climbed into the attic, where an intense heat had built up. Sparks jumped across from the burning buildings adjoining ours to the right and left. With a hand pump and pails of water, Herr Schramm and I valiantly tried to stem the fire that threatened to start in the attic at any moment. Now and then we sprayed water on each other, so that our clothes would not ignite on our bodies.

I thought we were doing quite well; hey, we might even save our house! With typical male hubris, we agreed that "If only we could mobilize those women wailing in the basement!" We shouted down at them through the stairwell, but to no avail; they couldn't hear us. We went back down the stairs, intending to organize a fire brigade for each of the six stories. But as we stood outside in the backyard looking up, we saw flames shoot out of the top floor. Had we stayed in the attic a few minutes longer, we would have been trapped--incinerated along with many thousands of others on that horrific Dresden night.

Now that our house was burning, there was only one thing to do: Get out. But how? The street was filled with burning debris. The safest route seemed to be through the connecting basements, in the hope that we would come to a less hazardous area. Following Nazi government directives, the house owners had chopped holes into adjoining cement cellar walls to provide an escape route.

We made use of this subterranean network. The thousand or so frightened residents of our city block hopped like rabbits from basement to basement in a frantic effort to get away from the fire. By some inexplicable logic they went in a clockwise direction, not knowing where they were heading. Mutti, Irene and I joined this stream of panicked humanity. For half a street block we moved slowly along together. Then the traffic began to bunch up, and stopped. The butcher on the side street had not bothered to knock the required hole into his basement wall.

It was now somewhere past three o'clock in the morning. Completely exhausted, most people slumped down on their suitcases for rest and respite. But I was uneasy. I wanted to know what was going on outside. Leaving my mother and sister behind, I pushed my way through the sullen crowd to stairs leading to the street level. Along the way I heard someone remark that this building was also on fire.

We had to get out of the trap. But as I peered through the front door into the street, I saw a ghastly sight. Fire and destruction were everywhere. Yet we had no choice. I worked my way back to Mutti and Irene and urgently insisted we must leave the deceptive shelter of the basement. Together we pushed and shoved our way back toward the stairs and up to the door. Then we darted out into the blazing street.

The scene seemed unreal. All the buildings were burning. Rafters, beams, bricks, and tiles came crashing down onto the pavement. Mutti stumbled and fell over obstacles as she ran. Flickering fires cast an eerie light on the chaos, dancing and jumping around in erratic patterns as flames ate away at the houses' upper stories. Soon they would reach the lower levels, where they would gobble up all the oxygen and suffocate the people we left behind in the basements. Their bodies would be carbonized, turned into ash by the intense heat. When they were found later by rescue squads, their seated forms would simply fall apart like powder.

We had no idea where we should go. We tried to get to the Grosse Garten, a big park nearby, but our way was blocked by burning trees. Another family from our house had come out with us; together with them, we ran down a side street until we came to a corner house that had been demolished in the first raid. Only a ruin was left. We found shelter among the jagged pieces of wall, and I took comfort in the somewhat dubious fact that since this place had already been bombed, they wouldn't drop another one here!

The darkness of night enveloped us once again. We rested and waited for some light to appear. Mutti and I began discussing where to go. She favored returning to Kipsdorf, the village where I had been baptized and my father was buried. But I disagreed. The Red Army was already in Goerlitz, less than 100 miles away. It was no longer a question; the war was lost, and the Soviets were about to overrun us. "No, Mutti, the Russians are too close now," I insisted. "Let's go west, to Tante Lilly in Hannover!" My mother did not like her sister very much, I knew. But this made eminently more sense than staying in Saxony under Russian rule. Reluctantly, Mutti saw it my way.

At long last, the first rays of sunlight broke through the thick cloud of smoke that hung over everything. It must have been around nine o'clock in the morning. It was February 14, Ash Wednesday. The family from our house wanted to return to the burned-out ruin, but we knew we had lost everything except what we carried. We had no interest in going back, so we split up with them. Mutti, Irene and I set out on our way to reach the suburbs. As we passed through a garden nursery, a Blindgaenger (an unexploded bomb) went off nearby. Again, we were lucky and were not hit.

Suddenly we found ourselves walking along a normal street. It was a real shock, unbelievable after what we had just been through. Some windows were blown out here and there, but otherwise the houses appeared to be undamaged. They still had curtains on the windows and intact doors! I could hardly comprehend the normalcy. It seemed like a fantasy. I asked myself: Where have these people been the last twenty-four hours, while we were in total hell? For them nothing is changed! How can this be?

During that horrendous night, I had been thinking fleetingly about the bomber pilots who were dropping unmitigated terror on us. I can honestly say that I did not hate them. In fact, I did not think of them as individuals at all. To me, they were instruments in the hands of an unseen devastating power. When you confront the end of the world, you no longer concern yourself with individual helpers of the apocalyptic force.

More than twenty years later, I met one of those pilots who rained death and destruction on us in that raid. It was in 1968 at a gathering of church leaders in Colombia. I was a seminary professor teaching church history in Argentina, and I represented

When All Hell Breaks Loose

the Lutheran World Federation at a conference of Latin American Roman Catholic bishops. At that meeting, I made the acquaintance of an American Methodist pastor named Dana Green, another ecumenical observer. One day he asked where in Germany I came from. When I answered: "Dresden," he looked at me startled and asked: "Were you there during the air raid in 1945?" Hearing that I was, he exclaimed: "So was I! I was one of the guys throwing bombs on you!"

Dana had been a young American bomber pilot. We went back to his room and spent hours exchanging our vastly different memories of that momentous night. He explained that before leaving on this mission from their base in England, they were briefed about its nature by what he called "this cocky major." The major informed them that this time their target would be not military installations, barracks, or factories, but defenseless civilians. Dana confided that he was sick to his stomach when he heard that. After they got back from their flight to England, he got drunk and was hung over for several weeks. Methodists are not supposed to overindulge in alcohol, of course, but at times it is hard to quiet the voice of one's conscience.

Back to that morning of Ash Wednesday 1945, Mutti, Irene and I marched along, trying to get out of the city. We were lugging a heavy suitcase filled with important documents, some 2,000 marks in cash, and other necessities for our survival. Mutti and I took turns with the carrying. I also had a knapsack with a few personal belongings, and Irene had one as well. After two hours we reached the Dresden suburb of Laubegast where Mutti had an acquaintance, a woman who had fled her home town of Cologne after having been bombed out repeatedly. Beautiful Dresden, the friend had thought, would be a much safer and more peaceful location for her little boy and herself. Unable to find an apartment in the overcrowded city, she was living in a tiny garden house. She welcomed us into her small bungalow and we gratefully took the chance to rest and wash up.

My ten-year-old sister was in pain from the heavy, putrid smoke that had badly inflamed her eyes. They needed to be cooled and washed out. I did not have this problem because I had worn a gas mask all through the night. But my jaw muscles were stiff from the pressure of the mask and needed massaging.

At around noon, the sirens sounded full alarm. Allied planes were upon us again. The previous night the British had destroyed the inner city and residential areas. Now the Americans were targeting the outlying districts. Our garden house had no cellar; there was nothing we could do except sit at the kitchen table and watch through the window as airplanes dropped their bombs. We felt the detonations all around us.

Finally the fury subsided. We had not been hit, but our hostess was beside herself with anxiety. "Frau Bahmann," she blurted out, "I can't take this anymore. It is much worse than what we went through in Cologne. I'm coming with you!" She asked me to go with her to "organize" a cart, i.e. to steal a hand wagon. I helped her willingly in this undertaking. We went to her coal merchant and she asked if she could borrow a cart, an item he would never see again. Back in the garden house, she piled her few belongings on the wheeled transport and we tied our suitcase and knapsacks on top.

We set out on our trek, joining thousands of others. On that Ash Wednesday in 1945, the beginning of the penitential season of Lent, the streets were full of people like us, marching on and on in a daze, without a clear destination, driven by only one thought: Let's get out of here. As night fell on that cold, memorable February day, we managed to find shelter in a farmer's cellar somewhere out in the countryside.

The next day was Thursday, February 15. We continued on our dreary march and got as far as Freiberg, a small Erzgebirge town.

We were exhausted and hungry. Here and there along the way, the Red Cross had set up cantines where refugees could have a sandwich and a hot drink. That evening we stayed in a school; the classrooms had been cleared of desks and straw was placed on the floors for sleeping. After a restless night, we made our way to the Freiberg railroad station. Word had it that there were trains moving people on.

The station platform that Friday morning was jammed with people desperate to get out. There was no point in using passenger carriages; all that humanity had to be transported in freight cars. Whenever a train came in, it took only a few minutes until the empty ones were overrun with clawing, frantic bodies. I saw a train pull out of the station as a little girl of about four years stood on the platform crying "Mommy, Mommy!" after the departing wagons. I often wondered what became of her.

In all the confusion, it seemed impossible to hoist our friend's loaded cart into one of these cars. We hung around and waited until evening, when the crowd had thinned out a bit. At last we could make our way onto the train. It took us free of charge to Chemnitz, soon to be renamed Karl-Marx-Stadt under Soviet occupation. Here we parted company with Mutti's friend from Laubegast. She would travel to Cologne; we were headed in a different direction, to Mutti's sister in Hannover. Our trip west in various overcrowded passenger trains was frequently interrupted. Again and again along the way, cities were being attacked by Allied bombers. The end of the war was certain. No "Hitler's Wonder Weapon" existed that could stop it.

Two questions have remained in my mind that were never answered to my satisfaction. First, why was it necessary to bomb Dresden at that late stage, since the city was not a military target? Second, how many defenseless civilians were killed by the British and American air forces in that one night? Official estimates varied widely. The Nazi media announced 300,000;

that was surely an overstatement. The Allies claimed 30,000, no doubt an understatement. The Soviets estimated 100,000, which in the end may be closer to the truth.

This was how my conversion began. First I uttered the agonized prayer: "Lord, have mercy!" as the bombs fell. Then I felt the reality of Armageddon as described so vividly in John's Revelation:

> "The seventh angel poured his bowl into the air, and a loud voice came out of the temple, from the throne, saying, 'It is done!' And there were flashes of lightning, voices, peals of thunder, and a great earthquake such as had never been since men were on the earth, so great was that earthquake. The great city split into three parts, and the cities of the nations fell, and God remembered great Babylon, to make her drain the cup of the fury of his wrath. .... And great hailstones, heavy as a hundredweight, dropped on men from heaven, till men cursed God for the plague of the hail, so fearful was that plague." (Revelation 16:17-21)

Ever since my Armageddon in Dresden, whenever a born-again Christian asks whether I have had a personal conversion, I shoot back: "What kind of conversion did you have? I have gone through Judgment Day. I have been baptized by fire!"

When All Hell Breaks Loose

When All Hell Breaks Loose

Nuremberg Trials, 1945-46

2
COMING TO TERMS WITH THE PAST

"Stumbling blocks are sure to come. But woe to him by whom they come! It would be better for him if a millstone were hung around his neck and he were cast into the sea, than that he should cause one of these little ones to stumble." (Luke 17:2)

As the Germans emerged from World War II, they did something typical for them. They invented an incredibly long word: "Vergangenheitsbewaeltigung." It means coming to terms with one's past. This is a sensible thing to do, one that is absolutely necessary for any genuine religious conversion. We have to recognize what we did wrong in order to find the opening for a new future.

In many religious conversions, such as those at revival meetings, people turn away from their personal vices—addictions, abusive behavior, unfaithfulness, and other moral shortcomings. In Germany after 1945, conversion required a more profound change. It would take more than a one-time acceptance of Jesus at an altar call. It would require a longer, more intense process of soul searching, a painful sorting out of values and priorities. Perhaps that is why the Germans came up with such an awkward, complicated term to describe the process.

When Mutti, Irene and I finally made it to Hannover after days of travel, we were received by Tante Lilly with less than open arms. Hannover, an industrial city south of Hamburg, had also suffered heavy air raids, but none as ruthless and systematic as ours in Dresden. Mutti's widowed sister had been bombed out once, and my mother was right in her reluctance to go to her for help, because Tante Lilly was clearly not happy to see us. She declared to my mother: "I'm glad you escaped that mess in Dresden, but you cannot stay with me. You must understand: I was bombed out, too. Now that I have new furniture—you know, Norma, with your two children--no, no, it just wouldn't work."

Stung, we got the message. At that moment, my aunt became a nonentity for me. Without a word we moved on. Next we tried Tante Liesel, my father's unmarried sister, a businesswoman in the charming old town of Celle not far from Hannover. Liesel Bahmann operated a "Kunstgewerbegeschaeft," a high-end boutique that specialized in expensive Danish crystal and handmade textiles. She, too, expressed relief that we survived the inferno in Dresden. But no, we could not stay with her, either. Our presence would interfere with her business, she said. This strange remark was apparently prompted by the fact, not overtly stated, that we would cramp her style in carrying on her current affair with a German army officer. Again we understood. We moved on, this time to Vati's married sister Elly, who with her husband Hans ran a similar store in nearby Braunschweig.

When All Hell Breaks Loose

By now, any appreciation I might have had for family ties was dead inside me. For the rest of my life, I could not share the faith many people have in family values. I simply do not believe in them anymore. While I do feel an intense love for my own family and am ready to do anything for them, I have never considered family to be the bedrock of human existence that gives meaning and stability to my life. These personal experiences and decades as a pastor have shown me that for many people, the reality of family life is something quite different from the extolled ideal.

We were able to stay with Tante Elly and Onkel Hans for a little while. Then Elliy drove us out into the countryside to a large estate where for years she had rented two rooms to store her merchandise. The farm, called Luederode, was owned by Frau von Wrede, a gracious aristocratic lady who readily agreed to let us move into the two rooms. Fortunately for us, they were furnished with a kitchen sink, a table, some chairs, a bed, and a kind of folding cot called a "Zieharmonikabett," an accordion bed. Except for our heavy suitcase and two knapsacks, we did not own a thing, but we had a home.

Still, the war was not over. There was more to come. It was decided that I should not stay in Luederode with Mutti and Irene but return to Braunschweig with Tante Elly to attend high school. My attendance at the local school lasted only a few days, however. Although we had managed to escape the Red Army advancing from the east, here the American army rapidly approached from the west. This was not without excitement for me as a fifteen-year-old, of course. Hans Heitmann, my uncle, a convinced Nazi like my father, was too old to serve on active military duty, but he was a major in the Volkssturm, a brigade of retired men and teenage boys cobbled together by the Nazis in the last days of the war. Onkel Hans commanded a battalion of these pathetic recruits, and he decided to use me as a courier.

This was much to my liking. Finally there was something I could do in the defense of the Fatherland. I rode a bicycle to the villages around Braunschweig carrying orders and instructions to local commanders. But that, too, did not last long. I was disappointed when Onkel Hans declared one day: "Manfred, I'm sending you back to your mother. The Americans are too close. I can no longer assume responsibility for your safety here." What a letdown! My dream of tasting military glory had come to an end. Back to Luederode it was.

There was not much fighting in our area. It was the end of March 1945, and the German troops were soon forced to pull out. With determination and speed, General Patton's tanks drove the German army into a hasty retreat. It happened so fast that the American infantry could not catch up right away.

For us German civilians, this meant that we lived in an "interregnum," the period between two rulers or governments described in history books. What an interregnum really means is that nobody is in charge. Chaos reigns supreme. This was what happened to us. Farmhands rose in revolt and ran wild, but they could not be blamed for their behavior because they were foreign slave laborers captured by the Nazis and imported from Poland, Russia, Italy, Greece, Yugoslavia, and France. Understandably these men rejoiced over their liberation. They were only too eager to take revenge on their German slave masters. Bands of fifteen or twenty men roamed the countryside and pillaged the farms. The first thing they went for was the wine cellar, so they were in high spirits as they descended on the next farm.

Luederode was set upon by one of these drunken bands. Yelling around, they searched for two individuals whom they especially hated: the foreman who bullied them all those years, and the fat female cook who served them so many meager meals. But these two had gone into hiding; the foreman escaped to the roof and held on to the chimney for dear life; the cook was lying between the railroad tracks behind the farm, hoping to avoid detection. We three, however, were not that frightened because we had nothing to lose. Mutti, Irene, and I sat at our table and played a game of Parcheesi, trying to look normal, while in the room next to us one of the drunks tried to cut off the finger of Frau von Wrede's elderly mother-in-law. He wanted the diamond ring she was wearing, but it did not slide easily off her finger. Only in the last minute was he prevented by one of his comrades.

Now I knew what an interregnum looks like. Shortly after this incident the American infantry arrived, at last. What a relief! As they moved in with their two-and-a-half-ton trucks, we children lined the roads, curious to see what our conquerors looked like. As a matter of fact, they seemed quite friendly. Many GIs marching beside the trucks passed out chewing gum and chocolate to the kids who stood eying them with great suspicion. It had been quite a while since we had seen any candy. My ten-year old sister was naturally eager to receive her share. But as Irene still recalls, I hissed at her sharply: "Don't you dare take anything from these guys! They are our enemies. Is that clear?" At fifteen, I was still a convinced member of the Hitler Youth.

Things settled down under the new military government, but at first we heard shots from a nearby village. Some of the local Nazi leaders were summarily executed after a quick trial or none at all. Then, as the excitement died out, I tried to establish a new routine for the children on the farm. Since schools were closed, I gathered them together and attempted to teach them reading and writing. I was busy with this new task when Germany finally surrendered unconditionally to the Allies on May 8, 1945.

But our little family's greatest worry was for my brother Gert, five years my senior. Gert was a lieutenant in the German navy. We had no idea where in all the confusion he might have ended up. As more and more former German soldiers came home, I looked longingly at the big entrance gate of the farm, again and again, hoping that Gert would be among the "Heimkehrer" or returnees, as the repatriates were called. But this was of course a foolish wish. My brother could not possibly know if we had survived the bombing of Dresden or where we might have found shelter afterwards. It was later that summer that an elderly family friend living in Hamburg received word from him. Gert was a prisoner of war somewhere in Russia. He would not return from the Soviet Union until 1950, five years later.

Germany was now divided into four military occupation zones. Our hometown Dresden was now in the Russian zone. Since we wound up in the northwest, we were in the British zone. South of us were the American and French zones. Communication between the western and Russian zones deteriorated quickly until it was completely cut off by the Soviets. All our financial assets in Dresden banks were appropriated by the new Communist government there. A house Mutti had inherited in rural Saxony was also confiscated. We possessed only some cash—a little over a thousand German marks—and a few clothes, nothing more.

Our legal status was completely up in the air. Since we were from the east, we should have been considered refugees. But this term was now restricted to those who escaped from the east after May 8, the official end of the war. They were entitled to certain subsidies from their fellow Germans in the west. On the other hand, we could logically have been called "bombed out." People in this category also were entitled to benefits to help them get on their feet. But once again we did not qualify; we had been bombed out in the east, not in western Germany. We ended up sitting between all the available chairs. And yet--we were alive.

Some 17.5 million people fled from the eastern German provinces. The first wave consisted of those desperately trying to escape from the feared Red Army. These were "Fluechtlinge" (refugees) in the literal sense of the word. Subsequent waves, by contrast, did not leave of their own free will but were expelled from their homes and farms when their provinces were annexed by Poland or Russia at the end of the war. They were the expellees, the "Vertriebene," and they arrived by the millions, an unbelievable flood. They came from Silesia, East Prussia, Pomerania, and the Baltic countries. Only a few stayed in East Germany; most would be absorbed by West Germany.

The farm in Luederode was not exempt from this enormous migration. Every week a new batch of people showed up with a horse-drawn cart or a farm wagon pulled by a tractor. Many were relatives or friends of our landlady. One day Frau von Wrede shared her concern with my mother: "Please, don't get me wrong! I do not want to throw you and your two children out on the street. But I first have to take care of my own family. Isn't there anywhere else you can go, Frau Bahmann?"

Mutti and I deliberated. Then we remembered the Griebelbauers. In her youth, Agnes Griebelbauer had worked as a kitchen helper in my grandfather's restaurant in Saxony. My mother was about her age, and the two young women had become friends. Later, Agnes married the dairyman on a big farm. She had stayed in touch with Mutti, and we knew that she lived near Northeim, about forty miles from where we lived. We studied a map. How could we find out if we would be welcome? The trains were not yet fully running. There was a rail connection for about 15 miles, but the rest of the way to the tiny hamlet of Uessinghausen had to be traveled on foot. Quite a challenge! But I felt up to it.

Thus, one early morning I set out on the great adventure. The first part by train was easy enough. Then came the long march. The countryside was teeming with returning German soldiers, foreign liberated prisoners, displaced persons,--I passed people of every nationality. But I was not concerned. For sustenance I had a loaf of bread and a can of "Schweineschmalz" (pork lard). That was all I seemed to need. I was possessed by a wonderful sense of liberation. What could any of these passing individuals possibly do to me? I had nothing to lose, and I intensely loved our German forests. They were my forests! I experienced that rare freedom one has when relieved of all material possessions.

Toward the end of the day, the final ten miles began to stretch out. Climbing the last hill before Uessinghausen, I no longer felt so confident that I would make it. But finally I found the Griebelbauers' house. Since postal service was not yet restored, I arrived unannounced and unexpected, just as they were sitting down to a simple evening meal of potatoes and cottage cheese. Eight people were crammed into a tiny kitchen. Besides the parents Franz and Agnes Griebelbauer, there were three teenage daughters, one farmhand, and an elderly aunt and uncle who had been bombed out. With no questions asked, they offered me a warm welcome, a place at the table, and a plate of food.

I was immediately received as part of this family who were strangers to me. Such a ready acceptance by these poor people was in stark contrast to the treatment we had received from our own well-to-do relatives. This filled me with a special affinity for poor folk, an attitude that would remain with me for the rest of my life, along with a deep mistrust of conventional family values.

When I explained our predicament, there was no discussion. Instead, Franz Griebelbauer simply said: "Why don't you join us here?" I was astonished and touched. These eight people lived in only one half of a small house. The other half was used by one of the overseers of the big estate. It was not apparent to me where we all would sleep. But our family was in need, and without any fuss we were invited to come; they would find a spot for us somehow. My middle-class upbringing had not prepared me for the spontaneous generosity so often found among the poor.

The trip back to Mutti and Irene turned out be much easier. I rode part of the way on a truck that belonged to the estate for which Griebelbauer worked. It was carrying sugar beets to town. I still had a long stretch to march, but eventually I could hop on the train. Mutti was overjoyed to see me. When I relayed the invitation, it was a simple decision. We were ready to take to the road again. Our move to Uessinghausen did not pose a big problem because we had so few belongings. Tante Elly gave us the folding accordion cot, which made a painfully narrow bed-- our first piece of furniture after the bombing raid, and a symbol of our new existence in a post-war world.

We traveled half the distance on a wagon pulled by a tractor of the Luederode farm. Griebelbauer met us there with a farm wagon from Uessinghausen and brought us to his little house. They had cleared a small room in the attic for us. The space was formerly used by one farmhand. Now it was the bedroom for the three of us. My mother and sister shared a bed with a straw mattress, while I had the privilege of sleeping on our folding cot. We ate our meals with the rest of the family. Since they were responsible for some forty cows on the farm, there was always enough cottage cheese to accompany the potatoes.

I had entered a world that was completely new to me, a city kid. I was now introduced to life on a farm. With great enthusiasm, I helped clean out the cow stable and I learned how to manage a horse-driven carriage. For the first time I saw how sugar beets are cooked out into molasses; and I watched wide-eyed as they distilled potatoes into illegal Schnapps in the laundry kitchen.

But exciting as all of this was, our personal situation seemed quite hopeless. One day I made a proposal to my mother: "Mutti, we are not getting anywhere here. I want to take off for Bavaria, to Onkel Huldreich in Passau. I could apprentice with him as a butcher." I had once spent a vacation with these relatives. They ran a butcher shop far away in southern Germany. But distance did not seem to matter. I was so hungry! I could not get the rings of fragrant, delicious sausages hanging in his store out of my mind. But my mother would not be moved. "Stop right there!"

she said firmly. "You will stay here. When school starts up, you will attend high school in Northeim!" That was the end of that.

We stayed with the Griebelbauers for more than a year. And then their little universe in the tiny house abruptly fell apart. Franz was fired from his job as dairyman. The farm administrator had caught him red-handed cutting down trees in the estate's forest to sell to his cronies. But Franz did not seem too upset by this misfortune. He just shrugged and said: "I wanted to go back to East Germany anyway; the Communists treat their people better."

But what would become of us? Help came from Frau Evers, the owner of the Uessinghausn estate and a young war widow. She asked my mother to run her farm kitchen where some twenty farmhands had to be fed. In returnwe could occupy a comfortable room in the main house and have our meals there as well.

This turned out to be a welcome change. Originally part of a medieval monastery owned by monks, the ancient mansion had enormously thick fieldstone wall, and a small chapel where the local pastor held worship services every Sunday. Having found shelter in this venerable building, things began to look up again.

Northeim, Germany

During the winter of 1945-46, the high school in the nearby town of Northeim reopened. It was a difficult start. There were not enough teachers and not enough classrooms; for a while our class met in a firehouse. Another headache was a lack of heat; the classrooms were very cold. I also faced the challenge of getting there. I had to hike three miles to the nearest railroad station, in Hardegsen. From there a commuter train brought me and other "Fahrschueler" (commuting students) to Northeim, the county seat. I was constantly fighting a cold, because the whole time I had wet feet. The rubber soles on my one and only pair of shoes had separated from the leather, so I had no protection against the rain and snow. I had only two pairs of socks; the first pair was soaked through when I reached the railroad station, and the second was equally wet by the time I reached the school.

I was joined on my daily marches by another classmate who lived in the next village. Dieter Wewerke was a farmer's son from East Pomerania. The family were expellees; they had been driven off their land by the Poles and kept as prisoners for a short while by the Russians. Dieter, too, had seen a lot of action. We teenage boys had much to share; there was a lot that we both had to digest and understand. In the process, we developed a friendship that has lasted a lifetime.

Germany was in shambles. If ever there was a point zero in history, we had reached it, both materially and spiritually. The death toll among both military personnel and civilians was staggering. Every family lost a father, mother, brother, sister, uncle, or aunt. Our major cities had been bombed into ruins by air raids. The entire infrastructure of the country was shattered. Bridges, roads, railroad tracks, telephone lines, all were either missing or in wretched condition. The economy was at a standstill. Everybody was constantly hungry and cold; there was no food, no clothing, little decent housing, and a lack of fuel to heat the buildings.

A black market had sprung up. The old German currency, of which we still had a thousand marks, was worthless. Cigarettes were now the valuable currency, and I became an expert practitioner of this new system. As a female adult, Mutti was entitled to twenty cigarettes a month on her ration card. Once I turned sixteen, I as a male was allowed forty cigarettes. This brought quite a nice sum on the black market. In addition, I received a bar of chocolate each Tuesday at school through the Hoover Feeding Program. Thus I could now do my part in "building up" the country again after the war.

We were in the grip of a bottomless cynicism. I, like so many others, no longer believed in anything. Nor did I trust anybody. All notion of good and evil had been obliterated. Like so many people and so much else, these values were casualties of the war. They did not apply to us anymore. We no longer were impressed by anybody's claim of superior justice. We had seen it all. We knew that horrendous crimes had been committed by all sides. I did not accuse anyone. But I did not want to be blamed, either.

When the first newspapers appeared in the second half of 1945, they carried many reports detailing horrors that were unearthed in the Nazi concentration camps. Such reports left me cold and untouched. After all, these papers were controlled and edited by the military governments. My reaction was: Isn't that what victors do to the vanquished? Pile dirt, shame, and guilt on them?

The war crimes trials against two dozen German leaders began in Nuremberg and lasted nearly a year, from November 1945 to October 1946. I watched the proceedings with great interest, and with deep suspicion and skepticism. I held no particular love for any of the Nazi leaders who were indicted in the war of aggression for their genocide, crimes against humanity, and other horrible acts. But it seemed to me and many others of my generation that these trials were not completely fair. Those who sat in judgment of the Nazis had also violated international law, sometimes in an outrageous manner. The western Allies had engaged in ruthless air raids against defenseless civilians. The Soviets had permitted, and sometimes encouraged, the rape of German women by their soldiers. In retrospect, I can accept the relative justice of the Nuremberg proceedings. The Nazis who were punished fully deserved the penalties for their crimes. But to this day, I maintain that it was a selective victor's justice that was meted out in Nuremberg.

What does this mean? The victors in this case were the western Allies and the Soviet Union. They had been united in a common purpose: to destroy Hitler's Nazi empire. But already then, the two sides pursued opposing agendas. There was no doubt in anybody's mind that the most heinous of the Nazi crimes was the slaughter of six million innocent civilians in a mad genocidal attempt to rid the world of Jews. This crime would stick forever in the consciousness of the world.

But it was not the only crime condemned in Nuremberg. The Soviet Russians in particular had every reason to charge Nazi Germany with unwarranted preemptive military strikes against Poland, Belgium, the Netherlands, and finally Russia. These were also ruled as crimes against humanity. Perhaps understandably, this verdict has since been overshadowed by the more vicious atrocities against the Jews, and eventually forgotten by many. Thus, when the United States launched its preemptive military strike against what President Bush termed an "axis of evil" by attacking Saddam Hussein's Iraq in 2003, few American voices were raised to protest this as a violation of international law. That is how victors often display one-sided notions of justice.

Nevertheless, the horrors of the Nazi regime continued to haunt my conscience. In school we were shown documentary films depicting the ghastly scenes encountered by Allied soldiers in the concentration camps. Our teachers were not yet personally equipped to lead a thoughtful and convincing discussion of the findings. But we talked about these events. They kept bothering and troubling us. In the end, my initial disbelief gave way to the shattering realization that unspeakable crimes had indeed been perpetrated by my own people and in my own name. It was difficult to believe. But it was undeniably true. A profound feeling of shame began to build up in some of us, a feeling of guilt as deep as our cynical sense of skepticism.

In the fall of 1945, another event took place which left an impact on me and some of my peers. A handful of German Protestant church leaders were to meet in Stuttgart with delegations from churches in England and the United States. This proposed encounter between former enemies, who were still filled with animosity from the war, created a situation of almost unbearable tension. The Americans and British insisted on a clarification of where these German clergymen stood, now that they had recently formed a new Council of the Protestant Church in Germany.

In response, the German church leaders came up with a declaration that is known as the Stuttgarter Schuldbekenntnis (Stuttgart Confession of Guilt). All of these pastors had suffered persecution by the Nazi regime. Some had been liberated from concentration camps, among them Martin Niemoeller. He had been kept for many years as a personal prisoner of Hitler in the Dachau concentration camp because of his courageous opposition to the regime. Physically he was only a skeleton now, a shadow of his former self.

The German church leaders released the following clear and unmistakable statement:

> "Through us, endless misery has been brought on many countries and peoples. It is true that for many years we have struggled in the name of Jesus Christ against the spirit which found its terrible expression in the National Socialist dictatorship. But we accuse ourselves for not having confessed with greater courage, for not having prayed more faithfully, for not having believed more

joyfully, and for not having loved more intensely" (Stuttgarter
Schuldbekenntnis of October 19, 1945).

This confession of sin provoked a storm of outrage in the German
public. The more sophisticated citizens objected to the implicit
notion of collective German guilt. For them, it meant a surrender
of an important ethical requirement of individual responsibility.
The great majority, however, felt insulted by the German church
leaders' statement for a different reason. Many had lost all their
possessions in the war, and they felt humiliated by the victorious
powers. In this declaration, insult was added to injury by their
own fellow Germans. Helmut Thielicke, a professor of theology
in Hamburg, expressed sentiments more to their liking in a short
pamphlet with the title: "The Guilt of the Others." Even years
later, those who defended the Stuttgart Declaration were still
being denounced as "Nestbeschmutzer" (nest soilers).

For us students, however, desperately struggling to come to terms
with the recent past, this confession of guilt came as an act of
liberation. It gave voice to what we felt deeply within ourselves.
We did not use it as an abstract philosophical definition of moral
guilt. It was our confession of culpability to a personal God. We
too felt a strong need to be held accountable for the unspeakable
crimes that had been done in our country and in our name. I was,
after all, a German.

When All Hell Breaks Loose

Hitler Youth

3
CAN I BE FORGIVEN?

"Then Peter came up and said to him: 'Lord, how often shall my brother sin against me, and I forgive him? As many as seven times?' Jesus said to him: 'I do not say to you seven times, but seventy times seven." (Matthew 18:21-22)
"Then turning to the woman he said to Simon: 'Do you know this woman? ... Therefore I tell you, her sins, which are many, are forgiven, for she loved much; but he who is forgiven little, loves little."' (Luke 7:44,47)

All the way from birth until the end of the war, my personal experience of National Socialism was joyous and affirming. My father had become a member in the Nazi party in the 1920s, even before Hitler came to power in 1933. Vati was a true believer. Mutti, on the other hand, had never been enthusiastic about the

When All Hell Breaks Loose

revival of our nation under Hitler's regime. She did not hold the Fuehrer in high regard. She referred to him as "dieser Kerl" (this guy). She was a devoted church member and had an unshakeable faith in God. But my parents managed to keep their ideological differences away from us children. As much as I can remember, Vati was a kind and loving family father. By the time we moved to Berlin in 1938, he had risen to be a "Zellenleiter" (cell leader), a minor official in the party. In his spare time after work, he was always on the go with some political activity or meeting.

In Berlin we lived next to the Apostles' Church in the district of Schoeneberg. Opposite our house, on the far side of the church, was the parsonage. Reverend Kurz was our pastor. He and my dad knew each other, of course, and we children were acquainted with him through "Kindergottesdienst," the German equivalent of the American Sunday School. My brother Gert, five years my senior, went to the pastor every week for instruction in Luther's Small Catechism in preparation for his confirmation. Our mother insisted on that. Gert, for his part, did not mind going to the pastor's house because he could catch a glimpse of the pastor's daughter. Barbara Kurz was a beauty in her teens. Blond, blue-eyed, and really pretty, she could have adorned any Nazi poster.

Pastor Kurz was a secret member of the Confessing Church, a Protestant faction that sharply differed from the so-called German Christians who embraced Hitler as their Fuehrer. While my dad and Pastor Mueller, who baptized me in Kipsdorf, sympathized with the Nazi-loving wing of the German church, our Berlin pastor was bitterly opposed to the Nazis. His wife, a Christian, was classified by their racial laws as a "half Jew" because her mother, who lived with them, was fully Jewish.

As a third grader I paid no attention to these details. I had more interesting pursuits. Besides, Pastor Kurz's son Eckehard, whom I called Ekke, was my best friend. We were in the same class in school and spent most afternoons playing together. One morning on our way to school we were surprised by an unusual sight. Some stores had been vandalized during the night. Broken glass littered the sidewalk, and merchandise was smashed and thrown around. We did not understand what we were seeing. It was the morning after the "Reichskristallnacht," the Night of Broken Glass, on November 9, 1938, when Nazi thugs unleashed their government-sponsored hatred against Jewish store proprietors. Our classmates reported seeing similar scenes of destruction on their way to school that day. The teacher merely quieted us down, reassuring us that although some people had gotten out of hand last night, things were now back to normal. He then directed us to a page in the textbook and our lesson continued. My questions had been answered, and obviously so had the questions of my buddy Ekke, the "quarter Jew."

One day after I turned ten, Mutti took me to a clothing store to buy my uniform for the "Jungvolk," the junior division of the Hitler Youth. She disliked the idea, but she had no choice. A teenage Jungvolk leader had shown up at our door and sternly informed her that she was in violation of the law because she failed to register me for the Nazi youth program. So I was being properly outfitted with a brown shirt and black short pants. As punishment for being a Johnny-come-lately, I was not allowed to wear a leather shoulder strap like the other boys for a while. This was a powerful inducement for me to double my efforts and "get with the program."

As a "quarter Jew," my friend Ekke was not permitted to join the Jungvolk. But this did not harm our relationship. Only after the death of my father in 1941 when I was eleven were we separated. Mutti moved us back to Dresden, and it seemed as if my parting with Ekke would be forever. I tried time and again after the war, especially during my ministerial studies in West Germany, to find out what had happened to the Kurz family and my part-Jewish friend. A pastor does not simply disappear without a trace, I thought. But none of my inquiries brought any result.

Yet the world is a small place. Twenty years later, when I was a seminary professor in Argentina, I stumbled into a sign of life from Eckehard Kurz. One Sunday afternoon my wife Marianne, an accomplished singer and pianist, invited German-speaking friends to a "Kaffeeklatsch" (coffee hour) at our home. When these fellow musicians, a delightful Jewish couple originally from Berlin, learned in which part of the city I had lived as a boy, the wife exclaimed to her husband: "Oh, that is where Ekke comes from!" Shocked as if touched by a high-voltage wire, I shot back at her: "Ekke? Ekke who?" "Ekke Kurz," she calmly replied. "Do you know him?"

We met a few weeks later, after all those many years, in Buenos Aires at the other end of the planet. Eckehard was now a pharmacist working for a big corporation. His sister Barbara also lived in the Argentine capital. Still quite attractive, she had a business as a distributor of German magazines in the Argentine capital. We sat in a restaurant and talked our heads off. There was much to catch up on. The Kurz family had survived the war in Berlin unscathed because of personal contacts Pastor Kurz had in the police department. He was warned when the next wave of persecution by the Gestapo would take place. The "Jewish" members of the Kurz family would leave the city and hide with a friend somewhere out in the country under assumed names. Thus they had escaped the Nazi terror. Good Prussian that he was, Pastor Kurz faithfully stuck it out at the Apostles' Church through all the war years until 1948. Then, when the situation began to improve, he left his charge. He was exhausted. He had had enough of Germany. He retreated to Oxford, England, and thus I was unable to find anyone in Berlin who had heard of him.

Toward the end of our long conversation, I asked these friends from my childhood how they identified themselves religiously after this long struggle: "Are you Jews, or Christians, or what?" Both spontaneously replied: "Neither one! We have had it with religion. We can do very well without it." What an extraordinary turn of events, I thought. I was amazed. The children of our pastor had become unbelievers, while the son of the Nazi official was now a professional theologian. After we left the restaurant and said our goodbyes, I roamed the streets of Buenos Aires in tremendous inner turmoil. Finally I flopped down on a park bench. Greatly agitated, I looked up at the dark sky, searching for a sign from my own father, and yelled into the night: "I hate you, Vati! I hate you! How could you have been a Nazi?" I simply had to let it out. I had to relieve the pressure in my soul.

But all the years during the war, I had not felt that way. Quite the opposite! I remembered one day in 1943 after we moved back from Berlin to Dresden, when I was summoned to the office of our high-school principal. Along with other students my age, I was ushered into the teachers' conference room. There we were greeted by a so-called "Goldfasan" (golden pheasant), the term we used to describe Nazi officials decked out in their glittering gold, brown, and yellow uniforms. The official explained that because we were the cream of the crop, the best students in the school, we were being offered a unique opportunity to enter one of the elite Nazi academies. The NAPOLAs (National Socialist Political Educational Institutes) offered a first-class education and many special privileges such as horse-back riding, flying airplanes, and more. I was elated. I ran home to convince Mutti to let me enter. I tried every trick in the book, but she would not be moved. "No," she said, shaking her head. "If they come and take you from me by force, there is nothing I can do. But if they need my signature, I'm sorry, my son. They won't get it!" Of course I was crushed. The outlook for my future looked dim indeed.

But now it was my turn to sit through confirmation class. Mutti was adamant about it. I felt this was a poor substitute for the golden opportunity presented by NAPOLA which she had denied me. I do not remember a single thing the kind pastor in Dresden taught us. I do not even recall his name. The confirmation rite left no impact on me, either. I had my mind on more exciting things. I resolved to follow in the footsteps of my older brother Gert and become a naval officer.

At the same time as my confirmation instruction, I was being prepared for the "Jugendweihe," a dedication ceremony held by the Nazi party for the Nazi Youth. The instruction was given by teenage leaders and was therefore quite forgettable. These smart young bucks in their brown uniforms had even fewer pedagogical skills than our sorely tried pastor. But we boys were veterans of classroom warfare, and several had come prepared for the session with sneezing powder. When the leader turned away, someone blew it in his direction. This made him cough and sneeze so violently that the class had to be stopped. Our young instructor, afraid that he would be held responsible for our behavior, was furious; but there was little he could do. At the end of this training, an adult party member in a "golden pheasant" uniform was assigned to apply a final polish on us before our glorious dedication ceremony. His attempt to teach was a fiasco as well. He was no educator, either, and knew nothing about the psyche of teenage boys. The session went completely by us.

Ironically, although I remember nothing about my Christian confirmation, the Nazi Youth dedication ceremony itself is still vivid in my mind. It was dramatic and impressive to a teenager. It took place in the inner court of the beautiful baroque castle called the Zwinger in the center of Dresden. One Sunday morning we assembled and marched through the inner city in full regalia and closed formation toward the castle, where we joined several hundred other Hitler Youth who had arrived in similar fashion. We were welcomed by brass choirs stationed on the balconies around the castle courtyard. Officials made rousing speeches and stirring march music was played. Together we swore oaths pledging our commitment to "Fuehrer, Volk und Vaterland" (Leader, People, and Country).

Adolph Hitler Reviewing Troops in the 1930s

After this rite of passage we were promoted to the senior division of the Hitler Youth. I had selected the sea-scout group in the hope that I might eventually make it into the navy. I was exceedingly proud to be allowed to wear a sailor's uniform. The group had a boathouse on the shore of the Elbe River, and twice every week we rowed and learned how to maneuver our craft on the river. On occasion we made longer trips for several days. We would row out to a large barge going upstream and hitch onto it, letting ourselves be pulled the rest of the day. Then we would pitch our tents on an island, build camp fires, horse around, sing folk songs, and simply hang out. When it was time to go back, we let the river carry us downstream again.

In the fall of 1944 I received my marching orders to report to a pre-military camp. I was sent to the Neusiedler Lake south of Vienna on the Hungarian border, and then transferred to a camp at Chiem Lake in Bavaria. There we were trained by regular navy personnel. We were not instructed in the use of firearms, but we learned how to manage large sailboats. When I graduated from the three-week course, I was awarded a merit badge which I proudly displayed on my navy uniform.

There must have been a fair amount of anti-Jewish propaganda in our indoctrination. But I do not remember any emphasis on this. Of much larger importance to our leaders was to instill in us a fierce sense of patriotism. In this, they succeeded beyond their expectations. We were filled with fanatical love for our nation. This was achieved not by means of abstract lectures or talks. They did it through folk songs and patriotic music, and a skillful use of ancient Germanic symbols.

To the end of my life, I will remember the words and tunes of many of these Nazi songs which so seductively expressed the vitality of our nation and the joy of belonging to our people. I rationally understand that for most people around the world, the swastika is a feared symbol of oppression and violence. But I am unable to share this emotion. This dreaded Nazi image was for me a symbol of order, light, and purity. Some of this emotion is still with me today. I know that many Americans feel the same way about the Red, White and Blue, and this sometimes troubles me. We were so imprisoned by Nazi ideology that we would gladly die for the values we thought our country embodied. We had complete faith in the loyalty of our comrades. We were elated by the thought that we were part of a victorious movement that could not be stopped by any other power in the world.

When the full extent of Nazi brutalities was revealed after World War II, my entire spiritual universe came crashing down on me. Our whole system of social and personal values came unglued and fell apart. Our nation of "Dichter und Denker" (poets and thinkers), such a source of pride to us, turned out to be a nation of "Richter und Henker" (judges and henchmen). The true character of the leaders we idolized was exposed. They were villains more despicable than common criminals. I was in freefall. There was nothing anywhere to get my head and hands around, no hold on which to preserve my sanity.

While I was in this mental fog, the desperate prayer I had uttered in our Dresden basement during the air raid came back to me. It was as if the "Herr, erbarme Dich!" (Lord, have mercy) I cried out that night was meant to haunt me. It echoed the confession of culpability by our church leaders in the Stuttgart declaration mentioned previously. Without any doubt, we all were implicated in a horrendous system of terror, whether we had actually done anything evil personally or not. Although no human court could indict me for committing any moral trespass, I still had to plead guilty before the throne of a God whose inquiry penetrates into the deepest layers of our thoughts and feelings. And yet, with all the brutal honesty that was now called for, I felt a great liberation in the Stuttgart acknowledgment of our collective German sin. I knew that I had shared in it. But a sense of God's all-seeing and incorruptible judgment also brought the recognition that this God is above all a God of mercy.

The empty void I felt within myself filled gradually with an awareness, hesitant at first, of the unfathomable grace God has declared through Jesus Christ. I was not able to find any clearer theological formulations at that time. But I began to appreciate both the stark reality of original sin and the unspeakable miracle of forgiveness through God's Christ. This paradox started to take hold in me then, and it has not left me for the rest of my years.

God's unwarranted grace is still the great paradox of my life. In spite of many years of formal theological education, I still cannot explain it satisfactorily. In the meantime, I have preached and lectured to many Jewish audiences. They are usually shocked at first to hear that anyone could have been an enthusiastic member of the Hitler Youth, as I had been. But they accept with grace my honest explanation that I did nothing morally evil or questionable as a teenager during the Nazi regime. But I always get a blank, uncomprehending stare when I confess that I feel personally implicated in the evils of the Third Reich. I do not expect my Jewish hearers to share my faith in Jesus Christ, of course. But I am always left mute when they question my sense of collective German sin before the ultimate judgment of God.

In the end, God's grace in Jesus Christ is a mystery. It cannot be explained. It reaches beyond the limits of human justice. It embraces all of my secret and unknown wrongs which no human court can detect. But if I as a Christian sincerely and honestly turn to God through Jesus Christ, my final judge will forgive the sins I have committed "in thoughts, words, and deeds by what I have done and by what I have left undone," to paraphrase the confession in the Lutheran Book of Worship.

I believe that for Christians, this acquittal through grace restores our broken relationships with God and establishes new bonds with the source of our life, even if here on earth we may be burdened with a legacy of evil deeds. It is like the mark the Lord put on Cain (Genesis 4:15), an invisible but indelible tattoo.

This is how I see my relationship to the Jewish people I meet and worship with today. I know that as a former member of the Hitler Youth, I may be met by them with a feeling of deep suspicion. And yet as one even more strongly protected than Cain, I feel completely acquitted by God and free of any guilt under the grace of Jesus Christ.

Manfred Kurt Bahmann, 1950

4
NO LOOKING BACK

"No one who puts his hand to the plow and looks back is fit for the kingdom of God." (Luke 9:62)

There can be no genuine repentance without coming to terms with one's past. But God does not wish us to get stuck in feelings of guilt. God wants us to move on with a new spirit.

As I continued my high-school studies in Northeim, I struggled to deal personally with the overwhelming problems of a lost war and horrific Nazi crimes. I also struggled with the all-important concern of what to do with my life. I was now in the second half of my teens. My future lay ahead of me. I was haunted by the question: What is the purpose of life? Is there any real meaning to all this besides bombing people to smithereens? If so, where is it? Who can show it to me?

In 1948 Mutti began to receive a widow's pension from the German railroad administration for which my father had worked. We were now financially able to move to a tiny apartment in the nearby town of Hardegsen, where I could catch the commuter train to Northeim without the long hike from Uessingshausen. Our new hometown possessed a certain charm. Hardegsen had been a market center since the Middle Ages. It boasted an ancient castle with thick, impressive stone walls. Picturesque two-story timbered houses with red-tile roofs clustered around the old fortification, lining the narrow cobblestone alleyways.

Hardegsen im Solling, Germany

Hardegsen was a favorite vacation destination for city dwellers who wanted to "take the cure" there because of its crisp, clean air. Here Mutti, Irene and I shared a small kitchen/living area where my mother and sister also slept, a basement storage unit, and a tiny room in the attic under the eaves where I could sleep. There was no bathroom—we took "bird baths" in the kitchen--and the

When All Hell Breaks Loose

ten people living in the building shared an outdoor toilet. We were cramped, but we were independent.

By now, at the age of 18, I had developed the habit of saying an evening prayer before going to sleep. I would open the little skylight in my attic space and stare out over the tiled roofs and beyond into the darkness of the night. I had no idea how to pray properly. I simply poured out my heart. At first I would begin by saying: "God, I do not know whether you are out there, or if you exist at all, or whether you hear me. But in case you do, here is what has been going on with me and in me." After a while I developed a real need to tell God what filled me on a particular day, and how I felt about the world.

Among our high-school teachers, there was one who I knew had a deeply committed Christian faith. Dr. Alex Niederstenbruch was not of the Lutheran persuasion but had a strong Calvinist belief. Among our classmates we referred to him as Alex, although we would never have called him that to his face. The greater degree of formality in the German culture did not allow for this sort of familiarity between students and teachers. But in my teenage rebellion, I managed to anger him repeatedly. I talked too much with my buddy in class. When reprimanded, I came up with some smart-alecky response. Yet secretly I respected and liked this man a great deal. In a discreet way, he exerted a powerful influence on all of us. He gave us an intelligent introduction into basic theological concepts in a course on religion, a subject that is allowed in the German school system.

It was unfortunate that my friend Dieter and I were unable to develop a meaningful relationship with our local minister. He was too set in his established ways for our taste, and he did not radiate any personal excitement. So after a while we started to visit another pastor in a neighboring village. We would bombard Pastor Kropatchek with the problems weighing us down. Of course he could not give us all the answers we so desperately needed, but he guided us. He seemed to understand us, even if we did not or could not always accept his advice.

Somewhere along the way, perhaps out of frustration, my teacher Alex urged me to read Paul's Letter to the Romans if I wanted to find the right direction for my life. "You'll find a lot in Paul that you can relate to," he said. That sounded good enough to me. I followed his advice, and this first foray into bible study whetted my appetite for more. I talked it over with Dieter, and he agreed that it would be interesting to dig deeper into the scriptures. But when would we find time for this? As it was, we had to get up at six-o'clock in the morning to catch the train to Northeim. When we came back from school in the afternoon, we were swamped with homework. We had hardly any time to ourselves.

Then I came up with an idea. Because of the train schedule, we usually arrived at the school building twenty or thirty minutes before class began. Most of the boys used these last minutes to copy their unfinished homework from a classmate. We decided we could put the time to better use by inviting others to join us in reading the bible. Of course our teacher Alex was delighted. He helped us get permission from the school authorities to use a classroom for this purpose. Before too long, even girls from the adjacent girls' school were allowed to attend. This added a distinct attraction to the undertaking, because at that time German high schools were still divided according to gender.

Keeping the bible study going was quite a challenge for Dieter and me. For a long time we were the only ones who had the courage to stand in front of our peers, read a scripture passage, and give a personal explanation of its meaning. We used some devotional aids and manuals to help us show the others why this passage was personally important for us. Even though my friend and I took turns preparing the short devotions, this added quite a load to our daily assignments. As adolescents in our late teens, we wanted to be well prepared so as not to embarrass ourselves in

When All Hell Breaks Loose

front of our peers—and even less in front of our female guests.
So we stuck with it.

Manfred's School Class, Northeim, 1950
(Manfred is in the second row, far left)

As I worked my way deeper into the bible, my appreciation grew
and my understanding deepened for what Christ accomplished for
us all according to the testimony in the scripture. Now, in my
evening prayers, I became used to calling on God as my "dear
heavenly Father." I know that this traditional form of address
does not sit well with those who reject a patriarchal order of the
world. But for me, it seemed the most natural and comfortable
way of talking to God. And it still is. One reason for this may be
that when I started my prayer life in earnest, I did not have my
dad anymore. He had been gone for almost ten years, and I hardly
remembered him. Yet I badly yearned for a father figure with
whom I could discuss the questions that were crushing me.
Apparently I chose God. Not a bad choice!

Later on, in my study of philosophy, I learned that Ludwig
Feuerbach called religion a projection of our personal needs onto

a transcendental reality we call "God." This 19th century German philosopher was convinced that an awareness of God is finally nothing but one's own self-awareness. He claimed that what appears to us as God is in reality our own spirit, soul, and heart. In his understanding, God has no independent existence or reality. God is merely man's manifest inner core or human self expressing its own distinct concepts, feelings, and actions. Thus Feuerbach prepared the way for the different theories claiming that God is dead (Friedrich Nietzsche) and religion is opium for the masses (Karl Marx).

Another insight I learned later at the university was that without relying on God or religion, modern psychology might help to explain the severe trauma I and others suffered as a result of personal experiences during and after the war, experiences that would occupy our awareness for the rest of our lives.

As I look back on those formative years, I cannot deny that I did a lot of projecting in my prayers. I piled my innermost needs upon God in heaps and bundles. Nor would I deny the fact that my war experiences transformed the innermost core of my personal self forever. As a German theology professor later said in a class: "We still have the smoke of this war in our nostrils. And we will never get rid of it."

Philosophers and such psychologists as Alexander Mitscherlich provided significant insights into human nature, especially regarding the German experience. But they could not reduce religion for me into a mere illusion. All their theories paled in comparison to the very real power of my personal faith in God. They could not drain away the effective strength I felt in God's "mighty works" (Acts 2:11) that arose through the life, death, and resurrection of Jesus Christ.

As our graduation from high school drew closer, Dieter and I decided to apply for a "Studienplatz" (study placement) in the department of theology at the nearby University of Goettingen. Although he and I were very different in our background and temperament—Dieter was a somewhat plodding farmer's son from Pomerania and I was an itchy city kid—over the last few years our friendship had grown very strong. We were battling the same problems and were looking to our faith for an answer; thus our thoughts ran along the same lines. Neither of us was sure, however, that we wanted to enter the ordained ministry. There seemed to be so many weaknesses in the organized church and institutional religion. But we had both caught a bug, or perhaps the Holy Spirit was working in us. We wanted to find out more about Christian faith and life. We wanted to learn about the Old and New Testaments, church history, the teachings of the church, and so forth, in a more systematic fashion.

In 1950, during this time of personal searching, my brother Gert came home after five years as a prisoner of war in Russia. I was preparing for my Abitur, a rigorous comprehensive examination required for graduation from high school, when Mutti received a short telegram from Berlin: "Will arrive in the next few days. Gert." Hearing this news, my emotion was so overwhelming that I failed to find adequate words for it. His return would be a drama of unspeakable joy for me.

I immediately found out when the next transport of repatriated POWs would arrive at the large camp in Friedland, just south of Goettingen. That morning I skipped school and went there by train. The camp was crowded with men, all of them released ex-prisoners. They looked alike to me. They had the same shorn hair and were swollen from malnutrition. I had not seen Gert for seven years. How could I distinguish him from all the others?

I asked an official to make an announcement through the loudspeaker asking Gert Bahmann to come to "Auskunft" (Information). Then I saw a face that looked vaguely familiar, but this fellow was shorter than I was. How could he be Gert? My brother was five years my senior and always had been taller than I was. Besides, he wore a brown uniform jacket belonging to the "Arbeitsdienst" (German Labor Service). This was wrong; my brother was a navy officer and he would be wearing a blue jacket. Still, I gave it a try. I stepped up to the stranger and said: "Gert?" He nodded: "Yes, that's me!" "I'm Manfred," I replied. He had obviously not recognized me either. After that first exchange, neither of us could say a word. Instead, I offered him a cigarette: "Care for a smoke?" All he said was: "Sure thing!"

Later that day, my brother received his discharge papers at the camp. But we could not go home yet to Mutti and Irene, who I knew were anxiously waiting for us in Hardegsen. The doctors had found some major physical problems with him, and he was transferred to the hospital in Northeim. There we argued with the medical staff until they gave him leave for a few days to visit his family. But by then the last train to Hardegsen had left. We had no choice but to start marching the ten miles toward home.

That night will always be an unforgettable experience for me. A clear moon illuminated the country roads as we walked and talked. There was so much to catch up on! We talked about life in the Russian prisoner camps; about the Dresden air raid; about the end of the war and the years since; and above all, about how to go on from here.

Gert carried a wooden suitcase he had fashioned for himself in Russia. It served as a narrow little bench when we stopped to rest. The suitcase held four hundred strong Russian mahorka cigarettes to which we helped ourselves on these brief stops. When we finally arrived at our house in Hardegsen, it was nearly 2:00 in the morning. An excited and agitated Mutti greeted us with the angry outcry: "For heaven's sake! Where have you two been horsing around for so long?"

Now our sleeping arrangements became even more crowded. But it did not matter. What counted was that we were all together again. I gladly gave Gert my bed in the attic, and I slept beside him on the narrow accordion cot. I was eager for us to exchange ideas, and it was inevitable that we would talk about religion. Gert confided to me: "Don't get me wrong! I believe in a God. But do me a favor: Leave me alone with the 'Jesus bit'. In Russia I saw how cowardly some of those so-called Christians were. I want no part of it."

Manfred and Brother Gert, 1950

I had to respect his position. But I retorted: "In that case, you must draw the consequences. Get out of the Christian church. No matter how you define 'church', it will always revolve around what you call the 'Jesus bit'." Gert agreed with me: "That's exactly what I've been thinking, too." A few days later he went to our local pastor and quit his official church membership. Mutti was horrified. "What's the world coming to!" she exclaimed. "One of you wants to become a pastor, and the other leaves the church. I don't understand anything anymore!" In later years my brother would change his stance. When he had his own family, he rejoined the church and allowed his three children to be baptized.

In the fall of that same year 1950, after successfully passing our high-school examinations, Dieter and I began theological studies at the University of Goettingen. The first requirement was to master Hebrew and Greek (we already had sufficient knowledge of the required Latin in high school). After a year we could branch out into more exciting fields such as church history, scriptural interpretation, dogmatics or systematic theology, and hands-on subjects such as the art of preaching (homiletics) and pastoral counseling.

In those years Goettingen had a number of celebrities on its theological faculty: Ernst Kaesemann and Joachim Jeremias in New Testament, Walter Zimmerli in Old Testament, Hans Joachim Iwand in Luther's theology, Otto Weber in Calvin's theology, and Ernst Wolf in church history. Two years later, when we left Goettingen for the University of Heidelberg, we again had the opportunity to hear some theological giants: Gerhard von Rad in Old Testament, Guenter Bornkamm in New Testament, his brother Heinrich Bornkamm in History of Christian Dogmas, and Edmund Schlink in Lutheran Confessional Statements.

What came as a considerable shock to me as a first-year theology student was the fact that in the German university system, no one showed the slightest interest in my personal faith. This, I later learned, was very different from the way ministerial candidates were trained in the United States. In German theology studies, the question of how one's faith in Christ might be nurtured did not enter the picture at all. The only criteria that mattered were the high academic standards that existed in these disciplines. This was very hard for me to take at first. But in the end, I was deeply grateful for this rigorous academic approach. All the doubts that can arise about God and his work would be exposed in a hard, unforgiving manner during the course of these studies. My faith had to go through a trial by fire.

At this point I would like to digress from my personal narrative to describe at some length the philosophical and theological forces that shaped my development during the university years. While I knew I had an intimate relationship with God and a strong faith in God's grace through Jesus Christ, my view of the world was utterly pessimistic, bordering on nihilism. I did not respect any absolute values. I was deeply influenced by the thought of such existentialists as Martin Heidegger and Karl Jaspers. I was fascinated by the novels and plays of French writers Albert Camus and Jean-Paul Sartre. My views were not entirely due to the devastation of the recent war. They were also the result of a thinking process that arose in the 19th century along the lines of my favorite philosopher, the Danish thinker Soeren Kierkegaard.

As with Kierkegaard, I could not embrace the optimistic romantic notion that man's destiny is determined by some reasonable force, or an Absolute Mind. For me, man's existence was defined by uncertainty and instability. Human beings are "thrown into the world," abandoned to forces that can reduce all guarantees and securities to nothing in a blink of an eye. Human existence is inescapably defined by pain and frustration, and as Kierkegaard famously put it, "a sickness unto death."

The Danish philosopher's concept of a "leap of faith" held great appeal for my generation of theological students. Faith is a "leap into nothing" with no other support but a deep trust in God. Luther had a similar concept when he described faith as "standing on the void." This mode of thinking made it possible for me to accept faith in Jesus Christ without sacrificing my intellectual integrity. The only thing that can be said about human beings with any certainty is that we exist "in relation." We are always in a relationship of inter-subjectivity, either with things or with other people. It can be in the personal interchange between two individuals in an "I–thou" relationship. Or it can be in an impersonal "I-it" relationship between a person and a thing. Absolute evil, however, results when these two relationships become mixed up and confused. If the personal "thou" of another human being is turned into the impersonal "it," the consequences are bound to be catastrophic. To treat another human being as an "it," a thing, was for my generation of students the negation of one's own humanity.

This was the mindset with which I received the message of Christ. Through my studies I felt my way into its meaning, deeper and deeper, from layer to layer. The philosophical framework of existentialism was the soil into which the seed of Christ's gospel was planted and grew in me. The great light that helped me discern my way on this journey was the Swiss theologian Karl Barth. Barth had already promoted the radical philosophy of Kierkegaard in a provocative manner right after World War I, in 1922, as part of his commentary on Romans. Now, in the years after the Second World War, Barth developed his brilliant contribution in fuller form.

Barth helped me understand that God is totally different from us humans, with all our failures and misery. God is the totally other "Thou" who is radically different from the other "thous" we may know. With a sense of hard realism, this theologian showed us that "God is in heaven, but you are on earth." Not for a minute did Barth ever lose sight of the fact that there exists an "infinite qualitative difference" between time and eternity. Human beings are separated from God by a deep chasm that cannot be bridged with the best efforts on our human side. The only way in which this profound alienation can be overcome is by the action of the all-powerful God himself. In his unfathomable mercy, God has undertaken this rescue operation. The God of whom the bible speaks is the God who has acted in human history—first with the people of Israel, and then even more convincingly and in full measure, through Jesus Christ.

According to Barth, there is only one way by which a human being can hook into this great act of salvation and become an active part of it. That is by faith, and faith alone. We humans must accept God's deeds in history and believe the promises which God has made in the course of that history. This means we have to trust that God will be faithful to his word. We must take him seriously through complete trust in him. But we have no guaranteed preparation, no education that would lead us to this trust. One's personal faith is never finished, secured, or protected. It is always—and each time anew—a jump into what is uncertain, dark, and challenging, a jump into an abyss before us. But in Jesus, God himself has become human. Through his Christ, God took our human destiny, weakness and death upon himself. In the crucifixion and resurrection of his Son, God turned our human fate around and freed us to a radically new life that is no longer determined by the forces of sin and death.

This was a radical approach to the Christian faith. Quite a few people in the church felt that Barth was extremely one-sided and without balance. They had a valid point. He upset the precarious balance between faith and reason which had been worked out so carefully by numerous 19th century theologians. Ever since the publication of his commentary on Romans, Barth had been on a militant campaign against the so-called "liberal" theology which had sprung up in the wake of the period of Enlightenment.

In the 17th and 18th centuries, Western culture unleashed the seemingly irresistible power of human reason that gave rise to a host of scientific discoveries. As new disciplines of the human mind advanced, faith seemed to be driven into retreat. As reason exposed the laws of nature in a bright light, belief in supernatural forces was relegated to unenlightened individuals who could not let go of old dogmas—or worse yet, dark superstitions. There seemed to be no point in believing anything that could not be clearly demonstrated. The 18th-century German philosopher and playwright Gotthold Ephraim Lessing spoke disparagingly of the gulf that separates the truths of human discoveries from the truths of divine revelation. He confessed: "That, then, is the ugly, wide ditch that I cannot get across, however often and however earnestly I have tried to make the leap. If anyone can help me over it, let him do it. I beg him, I adjure him."

It was this sort of harsh rationalistic attack that caused the early 19th-century theologian Friedrich Schleiermacher to mount a strong defense of the Christian faith. Retreating from dogmatism in church doctrine, he concentrated on the human experience of religion as a common awareness of our ultimate dependence, "das Gefuehl einer schlechthinnigen Abhaengigkeit." In 1799 he published his famous lectures on religion in which he made an appeal to the "educated among its despisers" ("die Gebildeten unter ihren Veraechtern"). Schleiermacher turned out to be a pioneer who influenced various branches of theological scholarship during the 19th century. Whether it was in the interpretation of scripture, or in explanations of the meaning of belief, these efforts were focused on making the various religious themes acceptable to an enlightened human mind. This, then, gave rise to so-called "liberal" theology.

Karl Barth in the first half of the 20th century declared spiritual warfare on Schleiermacher's entire theological enterprise. From Barth's commentary on Romans in 1922 and throughout the long years when he worked out the many volumes of his seminal work *Church Dogmatics*, he militated against Schleiermacher's legacy. Because of his opposition to "liberal" theology, Barth was called "neo-orthodox" in American theological literature. But this was a misnomer. Barth did not advocate a return to traditional church dogmas. He fully appreciated the great scientific achievements of the Age of Enlightenment, and he used many of its tools. But he was tired of having to apologize for his faith in Christ. He was no longer willing to accept the results of scientific research as the last word. He contended that in the end, truth cannot be claimed only for what is acceptable to the human mind. The ultimate truth for him was, first and foremost, what God wants from us. And this will of God can be known only through what God has done and said. The starting point for any valid theological reflection is God's own revelation, not the dictates of human reason.

The theological system that resulted from Barth's starting point is more properly called "dialectical," because it goes back and forth between God's revelation and human perception. Although a member of the Swiss Reformed Church, Barth combined the thought of John Calvin and Martin Luther, both of whom had made the Word of God the cornerstone of their theology.

During the early 1930s, many German church leaders were uncertain about how to react to the ideological demands of allegiance that the Nazis made on their people. Often these leaders were unsure of their own feelings about the spiritual climate created by a "liberal" theology. But Karl Barth did not suffer such scruples. He was then teaching at the University of Bonn, and with his unequivocal stand on God's action in Jesus Christ, he soon emerged as one of the leading minds of the "Bekennende Kirche" (Confessing Church) which made no secret of its opposition to the Nazi movement. He was the principal architect of the 1934 confessional declaration issued by the Barmen Convention, in which the Confessing Church pledged its allegiance to Jesus Christ and rejected the authority of Hitler as the primary "Fuehrer" or leader of all Germans.

Barth spoke a language that kindled a fire in the hearts and minds of many of us young theologians in the great confusion after World War II. The God he proclaimed was totally different from our faltering human race. Yet through his gracious acts in Jesus Christ, this God chose a people for himself who is willing to serve him fearlessly. I was ready to be part of this action.

There were other dialectical theologians besides Karl Barth. Almost all of my professors came out of this school of thought. This did not mean that they were in harmony with one another. We very much appreciated the great diversity of their views. But they were united in their rejection of religious emotion or feeling as a basis for a solid theology. Many of them would have readily agreed with the statement of Karl Marx that religion is "opium for the people," though it is also the beating heart of a suffering world. All my teachers seemed to agree that faith in Jesus Christ is not the result of our religious awareness or feeling but the work of an active God. They did not explore with us "the eager longing and groaning of creation" but sought to explain the meaning of a God who revealed himself to the human race in definite historical events (Romans 8:18ff).

Another intellectual giant was Rudolf Bultmann, who then taught at the University of Marburg. I did not hear him personally, but he spoke to us through his many followers. Most of my New Testament professors were Bultmannians. As their teacher had pointed out, knowing God's grace is not just a timeless truth or a fact of the past, but an active thing. It is about grasping the gracious action of God. This formulation shows that Bultmann was also shaped by the philosophy of existentialism. While Barth worked under the influence of Kierkegaard, Bultmann's thought was dominated by the philosopher Martin Heidegger.

The great contribution of Bultmann was the art of biblical demythologization. Under his expert guidance, our professors taught us how to dissect the Holy Scriptures in the same way a surgeon exposes the inner organs of a patient in the operating room. This was not a lack of respect for God's Holy Word. It was precisely the opposite. This manner of exploration took God's Word very seriously, by employing man's reasoning capabilities. For example, in the bible there are so-called "myths," concepts from former times that are no longer considered valid. One is the notion that the earth is flat. Our planet is not a disc floating in the waters of the oceans above an underworld or "hell," with the sky or "heaven" as a dome. The bible is full of such descriptions. Putting them aside as irrelevant, a skillful interpreter's task is to distill the kerygma (living message) of a biblical passage in a way that speaks to the people of our age in a meaningful manner.

Now in the 21st century, the question of religion requires renewed attention. In an age of instant and constant communication, our world has become much smaller. We are in immediate touch with people of diverse cultures and countries. Many have religious outlooks that are different from ours. The ecumenical exchange between different Christian groups that was strong in the last century now must expand to include more extensive dialogue between world religions. This challenge invites a deeper investigation of the elements of one's own religious experience.

When the Apostle Paul visited the Areopagus in Athens, he was confronted with a similar challenge. Walking through the streets of this Greek city, he noticed the great variety of temples that were dedicated to the religions of the ancient world. The apostle did not disparage the pluralism of religious dedication. His comment was: "People of Athens, I perceive that in every way you are very religious." He singled out one altar in particular with the inscription: "To an unknown god." Acknowledging the validity of this unknown deity, he declared in his famous speech: "In him we live and move and have our being." But then he laid all generalities aside and directed his focus in a most concrete manner to the one appointed by God to "judge the world in righteousness," the one man who has been raised from the dead, Jesus Christ (Acts 17:22, 28, 31).

In much the same way, we today honor the wealth of religious experience among all the people on our earth. But following the example of St. Paul, we Christians find the center of our focus in the revelation of God through his chosen Christ. Thus the singular emphasis of the dialectical theologians will continue to serve as a sure compass in our spiritual search.

Returning to my personal narrative, our studies at the German universities put rigorous demands on all of us. As I mentioned above, our professors were not swayed by piety or personal belief. They insisted on the highest standards of academic discipline. But although we did not have high tuition costs, we needed money for housing and food, and most of our parents were in no position to support us. In ravaged post-war Germany there were few scholarships available. The only way I could finance my years of study was to work during semester breaks in a local cement factory. It was hard labor. But that harsh necessity enhanced my education in a very significant way, as I became thoroughly familiar with the tough life of a factory worker.

This combined package of intellectual and physical stress can be captured by one incident at the University of Goettingen. I very much wanted to attend a seminar offered by Ernst Kaesemann. But so did eighty other fellow students. This world-renowned New Testament scholar, however, refused to work with so many class participants. "Twenty-five is the maximum," he declared. In order to receive one of the few coveted spots, we all appeared at the first class and were told to translate one of the most difficult passages in the original Greek New Testament without the use of a dictionary. It was an impossible assignment. But as I poured over it, I noticed that people were giving up and leaving the room. Eventually only twenty-five were left, and we who had remained were the lucky few who could attend the seminar.

In class, Professor Kaesemann asked whether we had read a list of books during semester break. I felt called upon to speak up. "How can we?" I said. "We have to slave every free minute as factory workers just to be here." This brought the wrath of the

When All Hell Breaks Loose

great man down on my head. "With that kind of attitude, young man," he roared, "you will never be a theologian worth his salt!"

Hans Joachim Iwand was another professor we held in high esteem. He gave us a brilliant introduction into the thought of Martin Luther. He was a man filled with a vibrant spirit that instilled excitement and enthusiasm in us. We were deeply saddened by the news that he would leave Goettingen for a position at the University of Bonn. Dieter and I went to see him in his private apartment. We urged him to reconsider and stay; we needed his guidance. He thanked us for the visit and then bitterly remarked: "There is no room for me here." He made a smacking noise with his lips as he continued: "This is a pool. You throw in a few stones and they cause a slight ripple in the water. Then they sink to the bottom, without leaving any permanent change."

A year after Iwand moved to Bonn, Dieter and I followed him there and stayed for one semester. Later we learned that in Goettingen he had lost some battles in the political infighting that goes on at every academic institution, usually unnoticed by the student population. He had been defeated by the powerful Bishop Hanns Lilje of the Lutheran Church in Hannover regarding some faculty appointments. This incident served to deepen our mistrust of existing church structures. We wanted to be good theologians, but we both doubted that we could function professionally in a religious institution.

It was through trials of this sort, however, that I became a firm follower of Jesus Christ. When all is said and done, there is nothing else worth living for. I have to conclude that the risen Lord took me, an uprooted and cynical teenage refugee from Dresden, firmly by the hand. As I look back, I believe that Christ was leading me into an unknown and uncertain future. Yet I was always filled with the assurance that he would go with me.

When All Hell Breaks Loose

Heidelberg Castle

5
THE PROMISED LAND

"And I have come down to deliver them and to bring them up to a good and broad land, a land flowing with milk and honey." (Exodus 3:8)

Any visitor to Israel quickly realizes that milk and honey do not flow down the street there. It is a tough land with lots of stones, requiring hard work. The same is true of any country dreamed of as "the promised land." This truth also applies to America. The United States has appealed to many people as the land of "unbegrenzte Moeglichkeiten" (unlimited opportunities), a country where fairy tales can still come true. In 1827 the aging German poet Johann Wolfgang von Goethe broke out into enthusiastic praise in the following lines:

"America, You have it better/Than our continent, the old one.
You don't have crumbling castles/Or basalt touchstones.
You aren't inwardly troubled, so far,/By useless memories
  and futile fighting.
Good luck to your use of today!
And when your children poeticize,
Take care you don't provide them
With tales of robbers, knights, and ghosts."

("Amerika, du hast es besser/Als unser Kontinent, der alte,
Hast keine verfallene Schloesser/Und keine Basalte.
Dich stoert nicht im Innern/Zu lebendiger Zeit
Unnuetzes Erinnern/Und vergeblicher Streit.
Benutzt die Gegenwart, mit Glück!
Und wenn nun eure Kinder dichten,
Bewahre sie ein gut Geschick
Vor Ritter-, Raeuber- und Gespenstergeschichten.")

My first impression of America was as a vanquished teenager in
1945. I had mixed emotions as I watched lanky, gum–chewing
GIs march into Germany. At the time I saw them as enemies who
were aggressively taking possession of my country. Given the
right opportunity and circumstances, I might even have killed
some of them.

My second encounter with America was less belligerent. But it
was still a strained experience, marked by a deep sense of
alienation. It came about almost by accident. My friend Dieter
and I wanted to broaden our theological horizons by leaving
Goettingen, and we were attracted by several professors at the
university in Heidelberg. This meant moving from the British to
the American military occupation zone. That turned out to be
quite a shock. Heidelberg not only had a magnificent castle and
one of Germany's oldest universities, but it was the seat of
USAREUR, headquarters of the U.S. Army Europe.

There were no rooms available in Heidelberg that a student could afford. We simply could not compete financially with the well heeled "Amis" and their German girlfriends. After an exhausting and unsuccessful search for several days, Dieter had enough. "If I don't find a room by the time classes start," he declared angrily, "I'll get royally drunk with the money I earned for the semester doing hard labor in the cement factory and go home. People will accommodate the streetwalkers who service the GIs, but there is no consideration for us poor students."

I was not quite ready to give up. I pointed to a large villa that had been requisitioned for American officers. "I bet there are only two guys living there," I said. "We should be able to rent a room in the attic. After all, we are studying for the ministry. It must be obvious that we are not war criminals." At the time there was still some hostility between the occupation forces and the local population. I located the military police station and got the name and telephone number of an army chaplain. I called him, and I was in luck; Reverend Grabau answered the phone himself. He was also a Lutheran, and he seemed genuinely eager to meet a couple of aspiring theologians.

We went out to the base chapel and explained our predicament to him. The chaplain listened to our tale of woe with sympathy and then said, "I'm sorry, my friends. I cannot help you. We have a non-fraternization policy in our army--we are not allowed to share living space with German nationals. If it were a matter of money, I could do something for you. But real estate is out of my reach."

It was a small opening, but I quickly seized it. I told the chaplain that with enough money we could find a room on the black market. Hearing that term, he looked at me dubiously. But when I explained the mechanics of the black market to him, he warmed up and promised to help us.

Now Chaplain Grabau made a request of us. His Sunday-morning chapel services were mainly attended by officers and their families, while evening worship was attended mostly by single enlisted men. As a good pastor, he wanted to help the young soldiers in his charge. He asked us to come out with a group of university students to the Sunday-evening services. "You see," he explained, "I do not want our boys just hooking up with German prostitutes. They should also meet people like you." So much for the non-fraternization policy, I thought. We gladly agreed.

With assistance from Pastor Grabau's discretionary fund, we soon found a small apartment in the house of a German physician behind the romantic Heidelberg castle. During the week we listened to theological luminaries in our classes. On Sunday nights, joined by a few classmates, we went to the military barracks on the outskirts of town and participated in the evening worship. I was impressed by the snappy hymns the "Amis" sang; they were much more spirited and peppy than our solemn German chorales. Any lingering feelings of awkwardness and alienation in me were dispelled by the fellowship afterwards. These friendly young men from the United States invited us to play ping pong and share Cokes© and cigarettes.

To legitimize our recruitment of fellow students, we informed the university student chaplain of our activity. One day he stopped me. "Bahmann," he said, "there are fellowships available from the World Council of Churches for a year of study in America. All costs of travel, tuition, and living are fully paid for. Are you interested? Since you and Wewerke go out to the American chapel every Sunday, I can certainly provide you both with good recommendations."

The offer took me by surprise. My friends and I had a low opinion of any theological thought that might come out of America. As far as we were concerned, the United States had not produced any brilliant philosophers or thinkers. On the other hand, a year of study without financial worries held a strong appeal. Besides, I did have a new curiosity about this strange land called America. It would be good to learn more about its people and its customs. So I filled out the lengthy application for the World Council of Churches in Geneva. Dieter, on the other hand, gave up on the paperwork.

I was interviewed along with other applicants by an extremely friendly, open gentleman named Dr. Barstow, director of the National Council of Churches in the USA. A few weeks later I was informed that I had been granted a place of study.

Thus in the summer of 1953 I found myself boarding a ship of the Holland America Line for a ten-day Atlantic crossing from Rotterdam to New York. A dozen other German seminary students were on the ship; they had also received scholarships from the World Council of Churches. In spite of a few bouts of seasickness, I enjoyed the great new adventure. But the effects of World War II were noticeable in some ways. The crew and the stewards, all Dutch nationals, made no effort to hide their dislike of us Germans. Although they were fluent in our language, they did not respond when we spoke to them in German.

What was it that actually brought me on this ship? Was it just personal curiosity? "Wanderlust?" Or was there another force at work, perhaps the providence of an all-wise God? Was the Holy Spirit using my restless impatience to propel me forward, or maybe the risen Lord Jesus Christ working through his church? Like most of the other German students, I had indicated on my application a preference among the American universities for Harvard, Yale, or Chicago. But Geneva could not send all of us to these renowned centers of learning.

At that time, ecumenical exchange between denominations was in full swing. The World Council of Churches tried to send their scholarship recipients to denominations other than their own. I was going to Dayton, Ohio, assigned to an EUB (Evangelical United Brethren) school then named Bonebrake Seminary after an important denominational leader and today called the United Theological Seminary. Other students on board were headed to different destinations across the United States.

German Exchange Students on the Gripsholm, 1953
(Manfred is fifth from the right, in rear)

I cracked jokes about this strange place called Bonebrake that I was going to; I quipped that it must be a wrestling school. But a deeper motive apparently underlay the choice. The people in Geneva purposely sent a secularized Lutheran kid to a seminary of the pious Evangelical United Brethren. As it turned out, this was not a bad idea. My new learning environment was going to be much more outspokenly religious than I had ever thought possible. I was now to experience firsthand a group of people whose strong sense of pietism no longer made them feel welcome in the established church of the Lutheran Reformation.

Upon arriving in New York, our group was warmly welcomed by our genial acquaintance Dr. Barstow in the offices of the National

Council of Churches. I was disposed to like this gentleman until he advised us in a well-meaning manner: "I hope you won't criticize everything you find in your American seminary. In the past we have had problems in this regard, particularly with our German students." His advice was based on several years of experience. But at the time I did not see it that way. In fact, I was incensed. What was the man talking about? I was a trained theologian, skilled in scientific criticism, and the first thing he tells me upon landing in his country is that I should not use my skills here? Preposterous! But I held my tongue.

The train took me from New York to Dayton. As I reached my destination and stepped out on the platform, a quite different surprise awaited. A portly, well-dressed gentleman approached me. "You must be Manfred, our student from Germany this year," the man said. "I am Dr. Roberts." He was, no less, the president of the seminary. In Germany such a welcome would have been unthinkable. There, no university president or important church leader would stoop so low as to pick up a foreign exchange student at the train station. This task would be assigned to a second- or third-year student or an office secretary. But this was not Germany. This was America!

Dr. Roberts even helped carry my luggage to his big car and brought me to the seminary campus. My roommate was not yet in the dormitory. After a quick shower, I set out to meet the "locals." I was well prepared, I thought. I had noticed in New York that cigarettes cost half the amount they did in Germany. Enthusiastically, I had bought a pack of each popular brand: Pall Mall, Lucky Strike, Camel, Chesterfield. I was in a smoker's paradise, determined always to have a ready supply at hand.

Walking around the campus, I spotted a group of students on a lawn. I introduced myself as the "student from Germany." They were a friendly lot and welcomed me warmly. Possessed by the desire to spread international goodwill among all cultures and peoples—Native Americans once shared a peace pipe on such occasions—I pulled out a pack of cigarettes and offered a smoke to my new friends. Looking bewildered and uncomfortable, they declined. Undaunted, I lit up and enjoyed my cigarette in the gorgeous August afternoon air with "the freedom of a Christian," to quote a phrase from Martin Luther.

The next morning I had an interview with the seminary dean, Dr. Bruce Behney. We went over my previous academic credits and the courses offered in the coming year. I was given a choice: either to earn the master of divinity degree (provided that I complete the required classes), or to take it easy and simply get acquainted with the church of the Evangelical United Brethren, the country in general, and its people. I chose the road of the M.Div. degree.

At the end of the interview, Dean Behney remarked: "There is one more thing, Manfred. We want you to feel completely free during the coming year. We understand that your Lutheran church has its own standards for personal behavior, and we do not want to interfere with this. But you must know that this seminary is maintained by contributions from our local church members. Frequently, these lay folk visit our campus. They would not realize that you belong to a different denomination. It could create unpleasant problems for us if they see you smoking, since our church forbids the use of alcohol or tobacco."

Once again, I was left speechless. I had never been exposed to this kind of a legalistic morality before. In hindsight, I realize that I should have been deeply grateful to these good people who so generously provided me with a full year of free studies including personal upkeep. But at the time, this did not cross my mind. Instead, once again I felt incensed. A few days earlier, I had seen the Statue of Liberty in the port of New York. This was the land that, more than any other, liked to boast of her many unique freedoms. But the first thing I heard was that I was not allowed to smoke in public. Once more, I managed to control my anger. But I was definitely not of a mind to give up smoking for a whole year. I needed a way to end this conversation with the dean. Suddenly an idiomatic expression I had recently picked up popped into my head. I declared proudly: "I'll see what I can do for you, Dr. Behney!"

From then on, I smoked mainly in the privacy of my dorm room. At the same time, I felt an inner obligation in the land of freedom to defend my personal rights, at least symbolically, against the dictates of what I saw as a narrow-minded religiosity. Each morning during a forty-five-minute break between classes, I stepped one foot off the campus, lit my pipe, and smoked. I had enough time to complete a walk around the entire seminary perimeter. I felt I owed that much deference to Karl Barth and other European theological professor, most of whom were dedicated pipe smokers. Even the immortal Johann Sebastian Bach composed a humorously wise song on the satisfying art of pipe smoking!

Luckily, my roommate Bob did not mind my smoking in our room. As a matter of fact, as time went on I had repeated visits from fellow seminarians who asked: "You wouldn't have a smoke for me, Manfred, would you?" Every time this happened, I felt vindicated. My campaign to spread peace and goodwill seemed to be working! To this day, I am convinced that legalizing morality never really works. Laws are necessary to keep the worst evils in check, but they cannot force us to do the right thing.

Before long I was in full swing with my studies at this EUB institution. Although I previously had nine years of English in school, I needed to learn some idiomatic expressions which at first hindered my comprehension. Once this stumbling block was out of the way, I threw myself unreservedly into the way people were trained for ministry in the United States.

It was a sharp contrast to what I was used to in Germany. Little attention was given to basic academic research. A knowledge of Hebrew and Greek was not required for interpreting the Old and New Testaments. But I found other elements of the instruction I received enormously helpful. The process of communication was less abstract and more concrete. The material I picked up from our teachers was eminently practical. It would immediately help in preparing a sermon or a class we might have to hold ourselves. Along with this process, our professors were also very much interested in the spiritual journey each of us was engaged in. They supported us with personal advice in matters of faith and practice. The German detached spirit of purely intellectual inquiry was replaced with a commitment to furthering the students' spiritual growth.

In the various schools of the historical-critical method my German professors introduced to us, we were trained in the art of discovering what scriptural texts actually meant. My American professors, however, were additionally concerned with the question of what these texts meant to us personally. I was no longer in a secular university dedicated only to research. This was a church seminary, the training ground for a community of believers. This contrast was not a result of differences between American Christian denominations. I would have found the same distinctive features at a Lutheran, Methodist, or any other seminary in the United States. This contrast was due to a basic difference in church culture between North America and Germany. It was an expression of the fact that Americans are far less secularized than their European counterparts.

During my German theological training in the previous two and a half years, I had not once been allowed into a German pulpit. But this was quite different in Dayton. Here I was urged to preach a sermon of my own as soon as possible. My first feeble attempt was a sermon for the seminary community one morning during the daily chapel service. I enjoyed it. It felt good to be able to express some of my deepest held views and feelings to others. It was gratifying to hear their reactions, particularly since in this case they were affirming and positive.

A Typical German Pulpit, Hardegsen, 1950

My next assignment was even more "real." I was scheduled to preach one day in a nearby state penitentiary. This was an unforgettable experience. My text was a passage from Isaiah that I had recently studied in Old Testament class. With armed prison guards lining the walls of a large auditorium, I looked out at a congregation of some one hundred inmates. I stifled an urge to tell the guards: "Why don't you go away and leave us alone?" I felt a warm affection for my listeners. That was probably just a romantic notion on my part. I literally had a "captive audience" in this setting. I had no idea how much of my sermon really reached them. But isn't that the fate of any preacher at any time?

At Christmas I was invited by one of the seminarians to visit his family. I looked forward to this opportunity to see the inside of an American home, something I had been unable to do for all the past months. I piled into a car with a group of students, and together we drove to a Pennsylvania mining area where a number of EUB congregations were located. I was welcomed warmly by my host family, and they proudly showed me off to relatives and friends in the community. They were simple people, sincere in their piety and quite ignorant of the rest of the world. Their questions about life in Germany left me dumbfounded. Above all, they wanted to know if Germans had the same sort of modern gadgets they enjoyed. I was annoyed by these questions. It did not occur to me that these poor people had just recently come into the possession of such modern household tools themselves.

I was intrigued by the fact that these miners had such a strong love for their church. This was in sharp contrast to the laborers I had come to know in the German cement factory where I worked on semester breaks. I did not make a study of this American spiritual phenomenon at the time, but later I would be reminded over and over again that a profound cultural difference exists. It seems to reside in the fact that American churches count a great many working-class people among their members, while in western Europe almost the entire working class left the church after the Industrial Revolution. The reason for this exodus, I believe, was the widespread conviction among European workers that their churches were closely allied with the rich and powerful and often served as their mouthpiece. In America, on the other hand, churches depended for their survival upon the leadership and active support of all the members, regardless of social class.

In Dayton I was occasionally invited to attend dances organized by the seminarians, many of whom had local girlfriends. I was amazed that they were already "going steady" at a rather young age. While the dictates of their pietistic church required them to avoid such indulgences as beer, wine, or smoking, I was duly impressed by the heavy necking and petting that went on at these affairs (although they stopped short of actual intercourse). At

German universities there was also a lot of heavy sexual activity at public dances; the various schools of a university—medicine, law, chemistry—were known for different degrees of wild excess. But it took me by surprise that in Dayton it was pietistic seminarians who engaged in it. I would never have expected that. Thus I completely understood President Clinton's insistence many years later that he technically "did not have sex with that woman" when it was revealed that he and Monica Lewinski engaged in oral sex. My seminarians would probably have agreed with him.

I gratefully learned many new skills from my American seminarian friends. For example, they were determined to teach me how to drive a car. In Germany I could not afford a driver's license; it was issued only after taking a series of expensive driving lessons and passing an examination. In Dayton, I was given a learner's permit without any questions. My friends were eager to be my driving instructors, even though in the process I caused them some difficult moments. I also learned a few new civic duties. In leaving a parking lot, I scratched not only my friend's car but also another vehicle. My defective moral instinct, shaped by a post-war need to survive and pride in the number of shady acts we managed to get away with, urged me to leave the scene quickly before we were found out. But my American friend had a different moral compass. He insisted on doing the right thing. He left his name, address, and insurance information on the windshield of the damaged car. I was deeply impressed by such ethical correctness.

In May 1954 I graduated from Bonebrake Seminary with a master's degree in divinity, an M.Div. I did not want to return to Germany immediately. In August the World Council of Churches would hold its plenary assembly in Evanston, Illinois. I could not pass up this opportunity. During the school year I had visited the Hamma School of Theology, a Lutheran seminary in nearby Springfield. I had gone there mainly to enjoy a beer or two with fellow Lutherans, but I also became friendly with the school's dean, Elmer E. Flack. Dean Flack took a liking to me because I had studied in Goettingen with the great New Testament professor Joachim Jeremias, whom he admired. Dr. Flack was in contact with Lutheran church officials in western Canada, who urgently needed German-speaking preachers. Thus he was able to arrange for me to do a summer pastorate in Saskatchewan.

So in the summer of 1954 I set out alone on a long, two-day trek by train, passing through Des Moines, Iowa up to Winnipeg, Manitoba. It was a dark, rainy night when I stepped out of the transcontinental Canadian train in the middle of nowhere, at a tiny Saskatchewan farming outpost named Hubbard. I was about to be introduced to the harsh, primitive beginnings that most early congregations in North America had to go through.

That morning, on a brief stopover in Saskatoon to introduce myself to the president of the local Lutheran synod, this gentleman had warned me that the German-speaking parishioners I had been assigned to did not want me to come. They recently had to endure the ministry of a rather autocratic German pastor, and they did not want to have another one. But this wise, seasoned church leader encouraged me to go anyhow. "They'll like you, Manfred," he said. "I'm sure of that!"

So now, somewhat apprehensively, I stepped out onto what was supposed to be a railroad-station platform, although there was no paving or wooden planking and I sank ankle-deep in mud. It was after ten o'clock at night and pitch dark, no lights anywhere. I was alone, engulfed in total darkness. I tried to hold my guitar and suitcase up higher, in an attempt to keep them safe. As I watched the red light of the train disappear around the curve, I thought: "Civilization, farewell!"

Then I noticed a shimmer of light a little way off. I made my way through the mud and darkness toward it. Inside a small shed, a lone individual grunted a barely understandable greeting at me. In the poor light, I could not see clearly the features of this gruff man. I inquired about a hotel and received another grunted answer, in the affirmative. He said it was too late for anyone to be awake at the hotel, so I should just walk in, take any unoccupied room for the night, and straighten out my account with the owner in the morning. I had clearly arrived in the Wild West. I was relieved that I could leave my luggage with him. Fortunately, when I arrived at the hotel, a friendly woman was still up. She cheerfully showed me a room and gave me some towels, and I collapsed into bed.

The next morning, after a much-needed sleep, I made some inquiries and was directed to the lumberyard where the council president of the Lutheran congregation worked. I had to suppress a laugh when I heard his name, Puff, which in German slang means "brothel." This plain, simple worker obviously could not know that; his German ancestors had immigrated many years before to Saskatchewan directly from the Volga district in Russia, and his command of current German was fortunately not up to date.

Herr Puff's welcome was anything but friendly, as I had been warned to expect by the synod president. "We don't want you," he bluntly told me. "But since you are here and tomorrow is Sunday, you may as well preach. I'll pass the word to the others. However, nobody will be playing the organ because our organist is having a baby. So we'll have to do without. Afterwards, we can decide how to go on." This sounded like a good plan, so I agreed. He then helped me carry my few belongings to an unpretentious wooden house which was the parsonage.

The next morning, people came in from all directions of the prairie. Their wheat fields were under water as a result of the endless rains, and they arrived in trucks and carts pulled by tractors or horses. I substituted for the pregnant organist, squeezing out a couple of hymns on the pump-pedal harmonium, hopping to and from the instrument before and after my sermon.

After the worship service, I presided over a general meeting of the congregation. No one else was ready to lead it. Only one question was on the agenda: "Do you want me to stay as your pastor for the summer, or do you prefer to have no one at all?" After a long silence, one individual voiced his opinion: "As far as I am concerned, you can stay!" I pushed and probed for more contributions from the other parishioners, either in favor or against. But it was hopeless. "Do you want to take a vote?" I asked. "We hardly ever do," someone answered. Since no one countered this response, I interpreted that as a positive decision. I said I would stay for the next three months.

After this bumpy start, I grew to appreciate these folks on the vast prairie of western Canada. I felt the joys, frustrations, and deprivations of generations of pastors as they pioneered for Christ on this endless continent. Since I was cut off from most cultural supports, I was glad to discover a radio station that brought classical music at 4:00 in the morning. I set my alarm every night for this hour. I have never appreciated the music of Bach and other composers as much as I did then, lying in my bed in the darkness and listening to their beautiful classical works.

In Saskatchewan, life moved at a slower speed than I was used to. I had time to observe the movements of a cat crossing the dirt road. I could do an enormous amount of studying and reading. I had a small confirmation class of seven teenagers. Only one, Ken, was a real problem. This farm boy could not work up any interest in Luther's catechism. When I found out he was good with horses, I struck a deal with him: "Ken, you teach me how to ride a horse, and I'll teach you the catechism." It worked. He always won the horse races we ran, and I fell from my mount several times. But now, even though the fields were still covered by water from the heavy spring rains, I could go to visit my parishioners on horseback at their widely scattered farms.

Hubbard Confirmation Class, 1954

I received a small salary, but most of my remuneration was in the form of food and other farm products. Most of these Germans had originally come from Russia, so I was treated to a lot of good Russian recipes such as pirogues, home-made sausages, and endless jars of home-canned stuffed cabbage. Yes, life was good indeed.

When I left the people of Hubbard at the end of the summer, I seriously contemplated going back there some time in the future. But I never did; life took me in other directions. The train brought me to the long-anticipated assembly of the World Council of Churches in Evanston, Illinois. What an incredible cultural contrast! After having spent the summer in a seemingly time-warped past, I was suddenly back in the 20th century. Delegates had come from all the corners of the earth. Many languages were spoken, and the speeches were simultaneously

When All Hell Breaks Loose

translated into English, French, and German. Thoughts were clear and logical and expressed with eloquent articulation. I was excited to hear Edmund Schlink, my professor from Heidelberg, deliver a major paper. I soaked it all up; I was very thirsty for renewed intellectual stimulation.

The sponsor of this conference, the World Council of Churches, was the international organization that had awarded me my American scholarship. In 1954, the worldwide churches were still under the impact of World War II. The Evanston assembly made a strong affirmation of the essential unity of all Christians in a divided world. It put major emphasis on dialogue and mutual exchange rather than differences between the participating churches. For the first time since the war, German church leaders were accorded an equal place at the ecumenical table. We students from Germany were proud that some of our professors had been invited to be keynote speakers.

It was time for me to go back to Germany. A year full of rich experiences had ended. But during that year, a dramatic change had taken place in my attitude. Although American bombs and military might had originally increased my hostility to the United States and her values, the generosity and kindness of so many individual Americans worked a miracle in my mind and heart. I developed a genuine appreciation for their country. In hindsight, I am convinced that it was the risen Lord Jesus Christ who brought about this miracle, by bringing me there and working through the lives of these great human beings. But now I had to go home. It was time.

But there was still one more surprise to come. As our group of theological students returned home on the MS Gripsholm, a diesel-powered Swedish passenger ship that had been bought by the North German Lloyd line, we shared the boat with a group of delegates from the Evanston Conference on their way back to Europe and also some American Fulbright exchange students going for a year of study in Germany. We boarded on Labor Day, although we would not leave until the next morning.

I signed up for a table in the dining room at which the other German students were sitting. I arrived late the first evening and slipped into the one chair that was still available, next to an attractive brown-haired girl on my right. I learned that her name was Marianne Schneider and that she was an American Fulbright student on her way to study voice in Germany. I was immediately hooked. There was something special about her. She was definitely out of the ordinary. Feeling the need to impress her, I asked: "How is your German?" She replied: "Oh, pretty good. I had three years of it in college." Hearing this, I flipped open the bilingual menu to the German side so that she could not read the English. It was a mean trick. The dining room steward stood over her with his pad ready to take her order. Of course she was stymied; even the best American college German class will not include words like "Ochsenschwanzsuppe" (oxtail soup), the first item on the menu. Clearly embarrassed, her face flushed. Having made my point, I opened the menu. I had certainly made an impression on her.

In spite of this rather uncomfortable start, a spark was kindled in both of us that evening. We spent eleven wonderful days on the high seas, crossing the Atlantic and falling deeply in love. We took endless walks around the decks of the ship and stood for hours at the railing, with the sharp North Atlantic wind in our faces and the taste of salt water on our lips. At night we danced in the lounge. On one occasion, still trying to impress her, I steered us while dancing directly into a mild collision with the stiff bishop of Saxony.

Yes, it was love at first sight. Incomprehensible as it was, we did not talk about it. Before leaving Des Moines, Marianne had become engaged to a Palestinian pharmacy student at their Iowa school, Drake University. But even though she seemed off limits, we had much to exchange with one another. She was the daughter of an Episcopal priest and had a vibrant Christian faith. Her great ambition was to have a career in opera. I felt sure she would not want to spend her life as a German pastor's wife in a parsonage. Although we did not think or talk about marriage at that early stage, I would not have had a problem with her on this point. I had no interest in marrying a traditional German "Pfarrfrau" (parson's wife). I wanted my future wife to have an independent life, and a head of her own.

But on the way back to Germany, the main personal question I had been wrestling with for a long time appeared to be coming to a resolution. In all my student years, I had not decided to make the parish ministry my career. I was confused; I thought that I needed a distinct call from God to enter this vocation. I had not felt such a call. On the other hand, during my pastoral activities in America, beginning with the service in the Ohio penitentiary and up to the pastorate in western Canada, I had to admit that I had a talent for this type of work. To my own surprise, I really liked it! Marianne listened patiently as I shared with her the battles I fought with myself. But I had finally reached a decision. The German churches at that time were in desperate need of pastors. They were constantly recruiting new ministerial candidates. I reasoned that the church's call might also be counted as a divine call. I was sure that if God really did not want me in this profession, he would find a way to kick me out of it.

My year-long visit to the "promised land" of America had pushed me great lengths forward in my spiritual journey. I had not only found a new continent for which I felt genuine appreciation, but I also decided to seek ordination in my home church. I was eager to return to Germany and get going with my profession. I wanted to serve the Lutheran church in which I had been baptized and raised as a child.

I also strongly considered exploring the possibility of going to a church in East Germany, behind the Iron Curtain. The Eastern congregations were particularly hard pressed because of suppression by the Communist regime. This challenge held a strong appeal for me. This could be the place where I was most needed. There, the commitment of my life might make a small but real difference.

There was, however, a serious problem with this idea. I did not see how the American girl for whom I felt such a great attraction could possibly fit into Communist East Germany. I consoled myself with the thought that in all likelihood, nothing serious would develop between the two of us. She was, after all, still engaged to this Palestinian pharmacy student in Iowa. As for my own future, I was ready to leave things in the hands of Christ who had so far guided me.

When All Hell Breaks Loose

Ramstein Air Base—Main Gate

6
NEW WINE IN OLD SKINS

"And no one puts new wine into old wineskins; if he does, the new wine will burst the skins and it will be spilled, and the skins will be destroyed. But new wine must be put into fresh wineskins. And no one after drinking old wine desires new; for he says, 'The old is good.'" (Luke 5:37-39)

I had intensely looked forward to returning to my homeland. But it turned out to be more problematic than I anticipated. I again had to go through culture shock, only this time in reverse—not going forward, but backward. I seemed to run into all sorts of problems. Mutti complained about the different clothes I was wearing: "You can't go out like that! Your pants and your jacket do not match. Those colors are too garish, anyhow. What will people say?" I did not care in the least what people would say, and I felt quite irritated. I answered her: "I dressed like that for almost an entire year. People will just have to get used to it."

My visit with our local Pastor Degenhardt was even more annoying. As I was enthusiastically rattling on to him about my experiences in America, he finally interrupted me: "That's all fine and good. But now you are back in Germany, and you must learn to tread more softly." The German phrase he used, "leise treten," was a red flag. It really means to pussyfoot. Then he quickly tried to correct himself: "I mean, take shorter steps ('kuerzer treten')." But his remark made me angry. I snapped back at him: "I heard what you said, Pastor, and I know what you really meant. I have no intention whatsoever to pussyfoot just because I am back in Germany."

These exchanges with Mutti and the pastor were innocuous enough. But underneath, a bigger struggle was brewing in me. The outward trappings of a culture often express deeper realities about the way people relate to one another in that culture. This is even more pronounced in the case of religion, where established practices are the outward vessels for deeply held spiritual truths. All too often, there is tension and even conflict between the outward form and the inner energy. This is inevitable when what has grown in the past is challenged and ultimately pushed aside by the new that is emerging.

What was the new that was emerging in me when I returned to Germany from America? Here it is necessary to take another short detour in my narrative. I want to explain the thoughts that were gathering in my head in the fall of 1954 around a new personal theology that would shape the direction of my ministry for decades.

Jesus was a Jew. No one doubts that he was also a devout Jew. But it is obvious that he did not fit smoothly into the established patterns of the traditional Judaism of his time. Different labels come to mind. Jesus could be called a deviant, a sectarian, a troublemaker, or a restless spirit.

From time to time, when God pours new wine into the seekers of truth, it is necessary to come up with new wineskins. Those who have tasted the old wine may prefer to hold on to the old skins. But new wine must be put into new containers or both will be lost, the wine and the skins. Those who opt for new wine are bound to end up either as separatist heretics—schismatics who start new systems as revolutionaries or reformers—or rebels who stay with the old system but initiate change from within.

This is the fermentation process without which new growth is impossible. New spiritual life must be caught up and put into new vessels, or else all will be lost. This is part and parcel of the incarnation. As God entered the human race, God took on human flesh and blood in the person of Jesus of Nazareth. However, the process of fermentation did not end with his ministry, death, and resurrection. As the Word of God spreads out through the human race, it gives birth to a visible body of believers. The Spirit of God becomes incarnate in a church. But in the process, it takes on the concrete form of an imperfect human organization. For those who believe that God has acted and is still acting in human history, there can never be a pure, invisible church. The spiritual community of believers cannot exist outside the frame of an impure, visible church. But the invisible reality of the spirit and its visible form will always be in tension, often struggling against each other.

This was the challenge I faced as I returned from America to Germany. By now I had reached a clear decision that I wanted to become a pastor. But I harbored deep suspicions about the church structures in which I would have to exercise my ministry. These reservations are still with me, and always will be. I treasure them. Without them, my personal growth would stop, giving way to spiritual decay and death. From the very start of my professional church career I was a skeptic, and I continue to ask critical questions about the concrete forms of "organized religion."

We do not have a lot of accurate information about Jesus of Nazareth. But some things are beyond dispute. He categorically rejected a single-minded absorption with one's self. In a manner never heard before, he challenged his hearers to an unrestricted love of God and one's fellow humans. He absolutized the love of one's neighbor: We are to take care of ourselves for the sole purpose of caring for others. His demand of love was so radical that it was to include even one's enemies. There also can be no doubt that with his message, Jesus pushed some wrong buttons and said unsettling truths. Thus, for him too, all hell broke loose. He went too far with his challenge.

On the other hand, his radical message had an irresistible appeal for many of his hearers. He attracted a large following. Thus he could not be simply shoved aside as a madman. In due time, both the religious and political leaders came to the conclusion that he had to be eliminated as a serious threat. Although the Jewish and Roman authorities had no great love for one another, in this case they came together in a rare joint decision, determined to execute Jesus as a political danger they could no longer ignore. This is why he had to die an excruciatingly painful death on a cross.

But the purpose the official authorities had hoped for was not achieved. The matter did not come to rest. Afterwards, a number of his followers reported that he had appeared to them as the risen Lord, raised by God to a new life on the third day after his death on the cross. As a result, an irresistible spiritual movement began to unfold. The first manifestations may have seemed negligible and harmless, but a powerful spirit was unleashed that could not be stopped by any human force. Spreading throughout the world, it created communities of believers in the most remote corners of the earth to form the "Body of Christ," a universal church.

As I got ready to enter public ministry, I felt a strong personal affinity to this Jesus of Nazareth. I knew from my own experience what it means when all hell breaks loose. I also knew the exhilarating feeling that comes when one is guided by the risen Lord. But the fate of Christ was a singular, unique event. As the author of the Epistle to the Hebrews is fond of pointing out, it happened "once for all" (Hebrews 7:27; 9:12). None of the Lord's followers must endure that same painful ordeal. I, too, would not and could not repeat his suffering, much as I was ready to follow in his footsteps. But like Jesus, I was a restless soul. Like Jesus, I was bound to be a troublemaker in the established church. I was not willing to accept the direction of its leaders without asking sometimes disturbing questions. At the same time, I was irresistibly drawn to the problem of authority in the visible church. This theme would engage me for the rest of my life.

The first step in my career as a Christian minister was to prove to my German church authorities that I was prepared for this profession. In a way I had done this already by obtaining the Master of Divinity degree in Dayton. Although this could have been adequate proof, I also wanted to fulfill the requirements for ordination that existed in Germany. To do so, I had to pass a comprehensive theological examination, either at one of the state universities or at the central office of a German "Landeskirche" (territorial church). In either case, the examination required a three-part academic ordeal: 1) write a research paper; 2) take four lengthy written tests, lasting half a day each, in Old Testament, New Testament, Church History, and Systematic Theology; and 3) pass a battery of oral examinations in Pastoral Theology, Preaching Skills, and Education.

When All Hell Breaks Loose

If at that time I had been interested in an academic career as a researcher and professor, it would have been advantageous to take these finals at a university. But since I wanted to become an ordained pastor, I opted for taking them at the local Landeskirche headquarters in Hannover. But when I contacted the central office, I ran into a problem. In order to be admitted for examination, I had to make a commitment to stay with this church body for 7 ½ years before I could move elsewhere. This was out of the question for me. In the back of my mind, I still entertained the thought that I might return to my native church in Saxony, behind the Iron Curtain in East Germany. And there was the problem of my personal relationship with the American girl, Marianne Schneider. I had no idea where this relationship might lead; neither of us had yet openly expressed our feelings to one another. But there was no way that I was going to tie myself down to the Hannover church for such a long time.

My friend Dieter had reservations about this kind of long commitment as well. For some time we had been receiving glowing reports from a pastor friend in southern Germany, a former university buddy named Fritz Buechner. Fritz was already ordained and served a parish in the Protestant Church of the Palatinate. In the light of the conditions set by the Hannover Landeskirche, Dieter and I hitchhiked down to visit the Palatinate church headquarters in Speyer. This Landeskirche was not strictly Lutheran but was in union with the Calvinist Reformed congregations in that area. That part of Germany had been occupied by Napoleon; thus it was exposed to certain democratic influences that were not part of the history of the more stodgy Lutheran areas up north. Another difference I noticed in Speyer was the female office receptionists and secretaries in the church headquarters—they were younger and more attractive than the ones in Hannover. This was not all that important, of course, but it was not completely ignored by us, either.

Manfred and Dieter in Speyer, 1955

We had no trouble registering in Speyer for the next round of examinations. Dieter and I spent the following months in intensive study. The theme of my research paper was an exposition of Psalm 1 including my own translation from the Hebrew original; I had to write a theological reflection and a sermon. That summer of 1955 we both passed the first examinations. This was not a trivial matter. A friend of ours, Jesko von Puttkamer, failed and was allowed to repeat the experience just one more time, a year later. Luckily he squeaked through. Had he failed the second time, he would have wasted five years of study without any realistic hope of employment. I was enormously relieved to have the ordeal behind me.

After an additional few months of practical training at a seminary of the Palatinate Church, our class was ordained in Landau on the First Sunday in Advent, November 25, 1955. A second theological examination would come in two and a half years, so we were still considered vicars under the tutelage of spiritual advisors.

When All Hell Breaks Loose

Like the rest of my class, I expected to be sent as a pastor to a local congregation in the Palatinate. I was quite surprised when I was informed by the church official in charge of our assignments, Oberkirchenrat Ebrecht: "Actually, we have different plans for you. We need a chaplain for the German Labor Service units that support the American military forces on our territory. These units are completely integrated into the life of the American bases. We need someone who is fluent in English and is also acquainted with the American way of life. Since you have a degree from a seminary in Dayton, we thought you would be ideal for this position." I was taken aback, but not for long. My outlook was mainly pacifist at the time—because of my history, I was not enamored of any military adventure—but how could I refuse this mission? Here was the challenge once again: New wine in old skins or in new ones?

I accepted Oberkirchenrat Ebrecht's offer. I would be stationed at the Army base in Kaiserslautern, called "K-Town" by the Gis. This was a hub of concentrated American power in Europe, just west of the Rhine River. Rumor had it that in case of an attack by the Soviets, the Americans would quickly withdraw behind the Rhine as a natural line of defense. "K-Town" was literally crawling with military personnel. Not far away were the sprawling Ramstein Air Base and the renowned military hospital at Landstuhl that later would receive the wounded soldiers from Iraq and Afghanistan.

I was directed to the part of town called Vogelweh. Here the buildings were occupied by the Labor Service units that were an integral part of the forces of NATO (North Atlantic Treaty Organization). In some aspects the Labor Service foreshadowed the new German army ("Bundeswehr") that was being strongly promoted by the United States. Although they were not armed, the Labor Service units were organized as military companies and battalions. The men wore uniforms with different ranks and were housed in barracks. They served as truck drivers, medics, military police, engineers, and mechanics. In addition to German companies, other units were composed of East European former soldiers who did not want to return to their countries, which were now under Communist rule—Russians, Poles, and Hungarians.

I did not care much for the military lifestyle. But I felt strong affinity with the men who had volunteered for the Labor Service. Like myself, most of them were refugees. Many had lost their families somewhere in the shuffle and had no one who really cared about them except the buddies in their unit.

My men showed no interest in religion or worship services. But once a month I was required to give a lecture on general ethical themes to each company, and their attendance was compulsory. The men were not enthusiastic about this either, of course, but they put up with it. Obviously they felt it was better than work. I disregarded the prescribed lectures the Army provided for these so-called "Character Guidance" sessions. Instead, I presented my own talks on different themes taken from contemporary life. It was always a challenge to speak for an hour to an audience of two hundred or so battle-hardened truck drivers. It was no easy task to generate even mild interest in anything at all in these listless men. For me at the age of twenty-five, it was an excellent training ground for the many challenging speaking opportunities that would come later on.

As their chaplain, I had a real opportunity to get to know some of my men personally. Several came to me for counseling, and they seemed grateful for any advice I could give them. For example, in one case where a poor fellow had gotten into trouble, I pleaded for understanding to his commanding officer, who angrily snarled at me: "Gimme a break, Chaplain! I am not Jesus Christ." "No," I replied. "But Major, we are all called to be little Christs." I do not remember if that helped any, but I was glad I could speak up for him.

At that time, in 1955, we were in the middle of the Cold War. The world was divided into two hostile camps. One half of Europe belonged to NATO, the other half to the Warsaw Pact. The dividing line ran not only straight through the middle of Germany, but also through the hearts of many Germans. Our sympathies were naturally with the western Allies; from our experience in World War II, we had a panic fear of the Russians. Two years earlier we had cheered on the East Berlin workers marching and demonstrating against the Communist regime. But the demonstration had been quickly put down by Soviet tanks.

Then a year later, in 1956, Nikita Khrushchev denounced Stalin's cult of personality. Emboldened by this unforeseen breakthrough, the Hungarians rose up and announced they would leave the Warsaw Pact. A revolt broke out in that country. At that point, all my Labor Service units were ready to rush over and assist the Hungarians in their push for freedom. But the Americans did not want to risk a nuclear confrontation. The eagerly expected marching orders were not given. In the end, Soviet tanks once again prevailed against the wishes of the people.

There was no doubt in anybody's mind that the Communist governments in the east were brutal, bloody dictatorships. But along with many of my contemporaries, I was opposed to building up a new German army. I was not completely a pacifist, yet I was convinced that German weapons had already inflicted too much suffering on the human race. I realized that capitalism and communism were in mortal combat—it was not clear to me which side was more aggressive—but I did not think that Germany should take an active role in this conflict. As I thought of the colossal carnage the Germans had inflicted on Russia in World War II, I could understand the deep-seated fear that caused the Soviets to prepare to defend themselves against another onslaught. To my way of thinking, an unarmed Germany would make a better contribution to peace in the world. But first and foremost, we had to reunite our divided country. This could happen only if Germany maintained a neutral position between the two power blocks. My semi-pacifist stance was typical for many of us for a very long time. It ended only when the Berlin Wall came down in 1989 and the country was reunited.

After crushing the barbaric rule of the Nazis, the western powers introduced my generation of Germans to a democratic ordering of society. I will always be deeply grateful for this wonderful gift. Since then, I have much treasured our democratic privileges, and I am ready to defend our freedoms of speech, assembly, and religion and the right to elect our government—if necessary, with my life. I have supported the protection of these rights by our western allies with great enthusiasm. But I also was, and still am, convinced that any defensive firepower should be used by hands that have been less sullied with innocent blood than our German ones. I do not think there was, or is, any hypocrisy in this stance. It is the result of my coming to terms with our own national past.

My year in the United States awakened in me a strong affection for the Americans. But it was not a blind love. It was rather a critical friendship. I could not accept all of their ways. We Germans feared the Russians because of their frightening military strength and brutal manner of governing. At the same time, I was apprehensive about the aggressive economic policies that Americans used to advance their own interests. In my heart I wanted there to be a middle way between communism and capitalism. I was looking for some form of humane socialism to safeguard the future of the human race. While I cherished the blessings of democracy, I was deeply convinced that my personal political freedoms were not the only values worth living and dying for. There were also other values. Even more important was the freedom before God that Christ had won for me.

There were also certain American cultural features that I not only resisted but rejected outright, and still do. A glaring example comes to mind. One year during the pre-Christmas season, the American Army colonel who was the commanding officer for the Kaiserslautern area ordered all the military chaplains to his office to tell us his plans for the Christmas celebration. They were a catastrophe. He wanted to fly an American-style Santa Claus into town with an army helicopter. This roly-poly Santa would then pass out candy to the German children who supposedly would be attracted to the scene. It was meant to foster greater friendship between the German civilians and their military occupiers.

The American chaplains took silent note of the plan. While they recognized its silliness, they did not speak up or come to my aid when I tried to squelch it. The commanding officer obviously had not the slightest understanding of German sensibilities, especially with regard to deeply felt cultural Christmas customs. This spectacle would make the Americans look even more superficial and shallow than they were already perceived by most Germans. I desperately tried to persuade the colonel that his proposal would bring about an opposite result to the one he intended. But I only succeeded in making him very angry at me. So a ridiculous and out-of-place chubby American-style Santa descended in a helicopter that year because an ignorant officer had ordered it. There were many similar occasions on which the military made Americans look very silly, and it always pained me. It reminded me symbolically of the Frankenstein monster, a giant of enormous physical strength and the small brain of a bird.

After I had served the German companies attached to the United States Army in Kaiserslautern for two years, I was asked if I would be ready for a transfer to the Labor Service units that supported the American Air Force. I agreed, and moved to the large NATO air base at Ramstein. This was quite a different environment. The secluded base was in the Palatinate countryside and strictly controlled by guards. As a base chaplain, I was completely integrated into life at Ramstein and I preached at the American services as well. Like many other officers, I had a room in the bachelor officers' quarters and was given my own office in the base chapel. Out of security concerns, I wore a Labor Service uniform and received the rank of captain.

Manfred Preaching at Ramstein Air Base Chapel, 1957

Our German troops at Ramstein were employed as military policemen and engineers. In addition, I had the responsibility of caring for similar units stationed at air bases in Hahn, Bitburg, Spangdahlem, and Wiesbaden. This larger assignment kept me constantly on the road, but I enjoyed my trips through the marvelous German forests. On each visit to these different bases, the routine was pretty much the same: low attendance or none at all of my men at scheduled worship services; a big audience of guys at the compulsory lectures on ethical issues; and finally, a few personal counseling sessions with individual soldiers. I can say that I loved all of "my men."

Surprisingly, life on these isolated American bases was not dull at all. Something new was always happening. The American Air

Force pilots excitedly described the latest fighter jet they might be flying at the time. I also enjoyed hearing the war experiences of the German commanding officer to whom I was accountable. Colonel Cieslewicz had served in World War II as a German commando under Skorceny in the SS unit that rescued Benito Mussolini in 1943 from his imprisonment at Montecassino, high in the Abruzzi Mountains of Italy. He had also engaged in other clandestine operation behind "enemy lines." At the height of the Cold War, American military authorities were not squeamish about his former affiliation with a crack unit of the Waffen SS. They needed his expertise, and they just wanted to make sure he was an efficient officer, which he was. Many such unusual friendships grew between Americans and Germans on the base. Differences in cultural habits and upbringing provided constant new topics for meaningful exchange.

I felt a particular fascination for the Jewish congregation on Ramstein Air Base. Chaplain Nathan Levinson was the rabbi. We quickly became good friends. Once when he was looking for a substitute clergyman while being away, I jokingly volunteered my services. He accepted my offer, but with a modification: "I want to be there when you preach to my congregation." What had started as friendly banter turned into an exciting adventure for me. This was the first time I would preach in a synagogue. I felt highly honored, and prepared my sermon with great care.

I chose for my text the haunting story of Cain slaying his brother Abel in Genesis 4. I applied it in a personal manner to the murder of the Jews by us Germans. I expressed not only my sorrow but also my sense of culpability before God for this disastrous genocide. Afterwards, the reaction of my new Jewish friends very much surprised me. They declared me not guilty, maintaining that I was only a boy when it all happened. While I appreciated their kindness, I did not agree with their conclusion. Obviously they had quite a different idea of our human accountability to God. While they were very exacting in their judgment of concrete human behavior, they did not share my sense of a collective German guilt before God. To me, we had all been associated with the criminal system and were accomplices to evil even if only on an emotional level. But our Christian confession "I have sinned against thee in thought, word, or deed" did not make sense to them.

I also had a good relationship with Rabbi Levinson's assistant Joachim Sommerfeld. Joachim, like me, was a native of Saxony. He had lived in Leipzig for some time under the Communists, until his family managed to get out in an adventurous way and emigrate to the United States. Joachim enlisted in the Air Force and had been assigned to our base as the Jewish chaplain's assistant.

I was fascinated by his report on life in our home province behind the Iron Curtain. One memorable night, during a bull session that dragged on into the early morning hours, Joachim made some Russian notations on the blackboard in the office as he explained the Communist youth organization Free Democratic Youth (FDJ), which every teenager was obliged to join. When we finally decided to turn in, I stopped him from erasing the marks on the board. "Let the cleaning lady take care of it," I said. Later that morning when I returned to my office, the entire chapel was in an uproar. Military police were everywhere, investigating and dusting for fingerprints. The Communist symbols that we had innocently left on the blackboard were being interpreted as signs that Soviet spies had somehow penetrated the base's tight security. I felt deeply embarrassed about my thoughtless dismissal of the writing on the board, and I confessed to the senior base chaplain. Fortunately, he had become a good personal friend and there were no repercussions.

This incident showed how much the heightened tensions of the Cold War years had everyone's nerves on edge. Although it was a silly episode of no great significance, it pointed up quite well an ongoing problem the military forces seemed to have with maintaining security. Since there were so many military secrets on the base, security was tight theoretically. If it appeared to be breached in a small matter such as ours, official reaction could border on the hysterical. Also, our German Labor Service guards complained that they were posted around the clock at completely obsolete, unused remote gates at a field where only a mouse would try to pass through at night. It was mind-killing duty.

On the other hand, in typical American fashion security was often carelessly enforced. An example was the shuttle buses that ran from the base to an American shopping center just outside the perimeter. They were there for the use of the military personnel. Without proper I.D. nobody was to be allowed entry through the main gates. Yet anyone could board these buses at the shopping center without showing I.D., and the buses were waved through the main gate without any checks. It was simply presumed that they were transporting "our own people." Any spy could have sneaked in, courtesy of the shuttle service, right up to central headquarters and its store of secrets, without showing documents or being asked a single question.

A paradox that always fascinated me about the American mindset was evident decades later in the events after September 11, 2001. Before the terrorist attacks on that terrible day, few in the United States seemed to take seriously the possibility that Fortress America, sitting between two oceans, could be penetrated. But after this tragedy, the nation overreacted. The government went after not only the Al Qaeda perpetrators in Afghanistan, but vented its anger and frustration in an irrational preemptive military strike against the "Butcher of Iraq" Saddam Hussein, who had nothing to do with 9/11.

Living in two worlds as a German who was fully integrated into the American military, I often had to do a spiritual balancing act. Time and again I was overwhelmed by the personal generosity of my American friends. But at other times, I was appalled by their cultural ignorance. Only a few knew any language other than their own, and they could display a blatant insensitivity to the feelings and ways of non-Americans. It was sometimes hard to control my anger at this. What helped me most to retain my sanity and self-control in the face of my conflicting emotions was the risen Christ present in my life. My Lord assured me that he transcends any given culture while being close to each individual believer. My faith in Christ gave me the strength to put up with the often insufferable arrogance present in every military, with their intoxicating sense of raw power and technological superiority.

Thus, while I did not feel myself beholden either to the German culture or the American way of life, Christ instilled in me a deep love for the people themselves in both countries. I remember standing on the runway of the base at Ramstein for some official act or parade, my eyes welling up with tears as our two anthems were played one after the other. When all was said and done, Christ was present in both nations.

During the winter of 1957, I was in a grim mood. My spirit was exhausted. The one bright spot of joy each week came with a light blue air-mail letter from New York. I had kept in contact with Marianne Schneider after she returned to the United States from her year of study in Stuttgart. She had broken off her engagement with the Palestinian pharmacy student at Drake, completed her Master's degree program, and moved to New York. She was working full time and studying voice with the former opera singer Rose Bampton in preparation for an operatic career. In November 1957 she made her professional debut as Mimi in Puccini's "La Boheme" in Quebec under the direction of Maestro Wilfred Pelletier. During the two years we had been separated, our correspondence had become ever more intense. We had so much to share with each other.

As Christmas approached, the American officers living in the same Ramstein bachelor officers' quarters as I did were obviously suffering from a similar melancholy. Through the open windows I could hear the blare of American Christmas carols played over and over, accompanied by the raucous voices of men who seemed to be in a constant state of drunkenness. I felt alone and miserable. I could not tear my thoughts away from Marianne. Finally I wrote her that we had to see each other again. There simply was no other way to settle the issue of our relationship.

Like many other smitten men, I was convinced that I had let Marianne know that I loved her on numerous occasions, when we were together in Germany and through my letters in the two years since then. But I had never kissed her or even held hands with her, out of respect for her engagement. While she had broken her engagement, I was not really sure how she felt about me. Particularly after her recent success in Quebec, I had no idea how she would respond to a proposal. The typical lover's dilemma! I did not feel ready to pop the question by mail. It was necessary that we meet.

We were both short of cash, but I sent her a small amount to help with a ship ticket in case she would be willing to come over. To my surprise, she answered immediately. Yes, she would come! She could get the rest of the money from her mother. At her job in New York she had become acquainted with a member of the Warburg banking family who had connections with a German shipping company. She could get cheap passage across the Atlantic on one of their freighters.

Thus, in July 1958 we met for the first time in nearly three years at my mother's place in Hardegsen. It had been an adventurous undertaking for Marianne. At the last minute she had to fly to Newfoundland to catch her freighter, which had been rerouted from Hoboken to pick up a load of zinc bound for Swansea, Wales. She was the only passenger and the only female. But as a guest of the company's owner, she was treated like royalty by the German captain and his small crew. After landing in Wales, she made her way by railroad first to London, then Hook van Holland, and eventually to Hamburg. From there it was a short rail hop to Hardegsen.

My mother was anything but enthusiastic about our meeting. Marianne had visited with us in Hardegsen on New Year's Eve in 1954, and at that time Mutti really liked the bright young American lady who spoke German. But now it was different. My mother sensed that this time we were serious about each other, and she obviously did not relish the idea. She turned taciturn and cold. But I did not care about Mutti's feelings. I had more important things on my mind.

Being with Marianne again, it was immediately clear to me that this was the person I wanted to spend the rest of my life with. But how could I say that? There seemed to be a kind of cultural barrier between the two of us. For my part, I felt it was somehow beneath our shared sense of honesty and truth to propose using what I considered a melodramatic cliché: "Will you marry me?" Later she admitted that she had actually expected more of a direct declaration from me than she received. Instead, I had expressed my deep feelings for her with a real "cool" understatement. When we were finally alone during a walk in the forest, I dryly commented: "Obviously we are going to get married. The only question is, when?" In my mind, this was not a real question but a statement of fact. Yet she agreed to go ahead with it, and we both felt, the sooner the better.

As a result, we were never formally engaged. We were in too much of a hurry. It took six weeks to assemble all the necessary paperwork required by the German and American authorities for an international marriage. Both nations had their own legal requirements. In addition, I had to present Marianne to the Landeskirche president in Speyer for approval. When we arrived for our appointment, all eyes at the church office were turned toward her. When President Stempel realized that Marianne could converse with him, he was delighted. He did not expect this young American woman to speak such fluent German with almost no accent.

On August 28, 1958 we were married in the base chapel at Ramstein. It was a very simple ceremony. All of my family were there—Mutti, Gert, and Irene. Marianne's widowed mother and brothers were not able to come on such short notice. Under the direction of the base chaplain's wife, the ladies' auxiliary of the chapel substituted for her family by providing a small but elegant reception for us in the fellowship hall.

For all its simplicity, our wedding was pregnant with a meaning that was symbolic for that time and place. All the elements of the old and new worlds with their complicated recent histories were represented. My friend Dieter, now a pastor in Kaiserslautern, and Claude Bond, an Air Force major and senior base chaplain, officiated at the bilingual service. My brother Gert held things together as my best man. My superior officer in the German Labor Service, Colonel Cieslewicz, the former SS commando, substituted for Marianne's deceased father and escorted her down the aisle. Kindhearted General Buelowius, a retired former German army general with whom I had worked in the Labor Service in Kaiserslautern, attended with his aide-de-camp, a young lieutenant who never said a word. Marianne's former landlady Frau Haeusler, a lively ex-Berliner who ran a boutique in Stuttgart with her English boyfriend Percy, also came. Marianne and I had to endure Dieter's 45-minute sermon while standing before the altar; my dear friend could not seem to find a proper way to bring his heartfelt remarks to a close, and Marianne reported afterwards that her legs were shaking.

Wedding Day at Ramstein Air Base, August 28, 1958

Later we went with my family to the Officers' Club for dinner. We all seemed to have a good time except for my mother, who clearly felt that she had lost her son to a foreign wife. But we were not deterred by her sour demeanor. After the meal we said our farewells and left for a honeymoon in Strasbourg and the wine country of the French Alsace.

Our marriage opened a whole new world for me. It also marked a definite ending in my life. It was as if the risen Christ had closed one chapter and was now leading me into an entirely new direction whose end would not yet be disclosed. Up to this point I still had considered the possibility of going back to the Saxony I left as a teenager, but I would return as an ordained pastor. Since the Communist regime in East Germany did not welcome any Christian church people, such an undertaking would have been difficult if not impossible. Now that I had an American wife, I would have to give up this idea completely. I had to turn my head in the opposite direction. Instead of going east, I would be destined to go west. But how and where? I didn't know. The living Lord would reveal the specific steps I was to take.

Manfred at St. Paul's in Grafton, West Virginia, 1959

7
A NEW KIND OF WAR

"Do not think that I have come to bring peace on earth; I have not come to bring peace, but a sword. For I have come to set a man against his father, a daughter against her mother, a daughter-in-law against her mother-in-law; and a man's foes will be those of his own household. He who does not take his cross and follow me is not worthy of me. He who finds his life will lose it, and he who loses his life for my sake will find it." (Matthew 10:34-39)

I am a war child. My whole being was shaped by World War II. But it has taken me a lifetime to learn that Christ is calling us to a different kind of war. I am still learning.

A large part of this training came after our marriage in 1958. With all the love I had for my ministry on the American military bases in Germany, the time had come for a change. I no longer wanted to be constantly on the road from Ramstein to Bitburg, Spangdahlem, Wiesbaden, and Hahn. I had a strong desire to be with my wife and enjoy marital bliss. It was time to get out of the service. The question was: Where should we go? Marianne had no objection to staying in Germany. She loves my native country. But I had no inclination to apply right away for a German parish. I had been bitten by the "American bug." I wanted to return to the States for a few years.

Above all, I was intrigued by the question: How do the churches in America finance their existence, since they do not levy a church tax on members as is the case in Germany? This may seem like a pedantic problem without great spiritual importance. But for me, it was a vital theological issue. The German church tax is collected by the state internal revenue service. In the 19th century under Bismarck's reforms, the churches had to surrender their independence to the political government in a sensitive area, the source of their economic lifeblood. The Hitler regime showed how dangerous this arrangement could be.

During the Nazi years, this method of collecting the church tax came close to strangling the German churches' spiritual life. I was deeply convinced that now our churches should sever all of their administrative ties to the government. They should assert their independence in every respect. But I was unable to arouse any enthusiasm for this position in my colleagues and friends. On the other hand, it was not clear to me either how such a financial and spiritual freedom really functioned. Therefore I wanted to live and work for a while in an American church setting that has no such religious tax collection. I wanted to find out at first hand how it worked.

My first attempts to establish contact with a Lutheran church on the East Coast of the United States were rather rudely rebuffed. One New York bishop replied that his congregations had no need for pastors with a "German brogue." Maybe he felt it was too soon after World War II and congregations were still not very fond of their former enemies.

Then a colleague at Ramstein, a genial Lutheran chaplain from West Virginia, encouraged me to contact his synod. Toby was single and we had befriended him. Some years later he left the ministry, and we learned that he was gay. According to standards prevailing then, he had to give up not only military service but a career in the church. I did not express my outrage at this violation of his basic human rights at the time, a stand I would take in the new century when ordaining gay Lutheran pastors became a burning issue. In the 1960s, I simply accepted this arbitrary rule as a fact of life. We visited Toby in his home in West Virginia a few years later, and I gratefully accepted some theological works in English that he no longer needed. I especially appreciated his multi-volume set of the bible commentary *The Interpreter's Bible*, which still serves me well over fifty years later.

Chaplain Toby was passionate in the praise of his home state. "Manfred," he assured me at the time, "those hillbillies are just as stubborn as you are. You'll get along just fine with them." He persuaded me to write to his Lutheran synodical leader asking for an assignment. I had no idea what such a pastorate would look like, but I did not care, and I knew that pastors were still in demand. Then the miracle happened; Toby's church president Rev. George Weirick invited me to come to West Virginia sight unseen for a six-month trial period. He had a vacancy in a rundown parish in an Appalachian railroad town where, as I learned later, he figured I could do no great harm.

Fortunately, I was not required to burn any bridges behind me when I left Germany. The Palatinate Landeskirche granted me leave without pay for five years. So Marianne and I got busy. We made several trips to the American consulate in Frankfurt to secure an immigrant visa for me. It was relatively easy, since

Marianne's mother (who had not yet met me) had provided an affidavit of support. I must not become a burden on American taxpayers. In the waiting room of the consulate, Marianne and I were an odd couple. The other Germans applying for immigrant visas were young war brides who had found themselves an American soldier. I stuck out in my Labor Service uniform as a German "male war bride."

So in the early spring of 1959, half a year after our wedding, we got ready to re-cross the Atlantic Ocean. My mother was devastated. Mutti was sure that she would lose her Manfred for good. I could understand her grief, but there was a greater power driving me now. It was not my American wife pulling me in this direction, as she assumed. It was a deep spiritual need inside myself. I had no doubt that Christ was calling me into this adventure.

Crossing the ocean again on shipboard revived wonderful memories of our meeting. But when we arrived back in the United States, I experienced a moment of weakness. Sudden doubts attacked me on the train ride from New York to West Virginia. What if this project ended in a big flop? We had spent all our money getting there. I had no family of my own in this country to fall back on for support. We did not even have return tickets to Germany. But my young wife laughed at my concerns and shoved them aside.

The train brought us to Aurora, a little town in the West Virginia mountains. There we were met by my new church leader, who would put us up for the night in the parsonage. Rev. George Weirick was not a bishop; in those years, American Lutherans still called the heads of their regional synods "presidents" and not "bishops." It seemed to be the proper title for this man. He was not a particularly impressive-looking individual. Short and squat, of stocky build, he spoke with a slight lisp. As I got to know him, it was clear that he was not a brilliant theologian nor an eloquent orator nor a sophisticated manager. But in his own way, this simple parish pastor who was in charge of his synod left a unique impression on me. He loved his people and knew them very well.

George Weirick could tell endless stories about his parishes. It was from him that I learned my first lesson in how to pastor an independent congregation successfully without any state support: You must earn the people's respect. It is difficult, he said. It can be a struggle. But with a twinkle in his eye, he assured me it was worth the pain and effort. He was sending me to a two-point charge, the Grafton-Newburg parish. He warned me that the people at St. Paul's in Grafton would be a particularly stubborn bunch. "They want you to move into their dilapidated parsonage, which they plan to spruce up a bit," he said. "Don't do it! That place is a pigsty. They need to find a new house for you. If you cave in on this point, you will never get any real respect from them."

So for the time being, upon arriving in Grafton Marianne and I moved into temporary quarters—a small rented apartment on the second floor of the council president's house near the center of town. Along with preaching and teaching, I began my new ministry by making house calls on all the members. I wanted to get to know them and their town as quickly as possible.

Grafton lies in a coal region that had once flourished. Formerly, coal from surrounding mines was transported on B&O railroad lines that ran through the middle of town. When we arrived, nearly all the mines were closed. With the collapse of the coal industry, the community had lost its workforce—the population had shrunk in ten years from 15,000 to 5,000 inhabitants. Most who remained behind were elderly or disabled.

The other congregation I was to serve lay five miles away in a village called Newburg that was nestled in a valley across the mountain. Coalminers and railroad workers once lived there, too, and the community had shared the same fate as Grafton. Making a go of it under such conditions would be an uphill fight. At first I labored under the misconception that all the parishioners were secretly united against me, a foreign interloper from Germany. I now know that even where a difference in backgrounds is not an issue, many new young ministers share this fear. Locals always appear to be in some kind of unstated alliance with each other. After a few years of experience, however, one realizes that people are not monolithic but individuals with whom you can connect, one by one.

Holy Trinity, Newburg, 1959

Financing church operations was a constant struggle. As we moved into our first West Virginia winter, my church treasurer Howard asked me in what seemed to be an innocuous manner: "Pastor, should I pay the church heating bill or your salary? We don't have enough money this month for both." Figuring that if the sanctuary was unheated, few people would attend and we would have even less financial resources, I said: "Go ahead and pay the heating bill." But when the problem continued for three months, I had enough. After all, the pastor and his wife had to eat. So I made a big thing of it with both church councils, and to my surprise and relief, they supported me.

Installation by George Weirick in Holy Trinity, Newburg

It was a great time of learning for me. I became acquainted with people and issues that would never have crossed my mind at a German university. In the midst of Appalachian poverty I found wonderful Christians, dedicated lay people who displayed a firmer commitment to their church than I had ever encountered among church members in Germany.

I remember especially Jim and Carol in Grafton. This married couple spent every Saturday evening preparing and running off the Sunday bulletin. Jim was a house painter by trade and both he and Carol were recovering alcoholics. I strongly suspected when visiting them that they sometimes still fell off the wagon. But they were committed Christians and solid in their support of my ministry in Grafton. They always picked up my spirits. When I was worn down by yet another point of arbitrary resistance by a member of the church council, they encouraged me: "Don't take it so hard, Pastor! We know these people. Just don't give up!"

I also remember with great fondness Theo, who lived with her retired husband in an overstuffed little house on the road to Newburg. A proud lifelong Lutheran, Theo served on several synodical committees. She had a strong interest in our youth and spent most of her summers at church camps, teaching arts and crafts. With her cheerful outlook, she was always an inspiration to me. And then there was Marge, a mother hen with a large brood of teens and preteens. Her commitment to organized religion was shaky, and the family did not have much interest in formal schooling—they preferred hunting, fishing, and sports— but she had a generous spirit and an open heart. They were the typical "hillbillies" my chaplain friend Toby in Ramstein had told me about. In her rough, unkempt way, Marge turned out to be a warm friend of the Grafton congregation and a person on whom one could depend.

In comparing our regular Sunday offerings with the weekly collections in German churches, another surprise awaited me. Although we had difficulty making our budget, the generosity of many American churchgoers was simply astounding. Christians in the United States put their European fellow believers to shame. The struggle to balance the church books literally "paid off." In those years, a strong sense of ownership prevailed among the lay members. These Christians knew it was "their" church because they paid for it out of their own pockets. I began to appreciate this basic truth of American church life.

While I was grateful to individual members for digging deeper into their pockets when a special need arose, I also had to confront the hard fact that because of diminishing numbers, we were not always able to balance the congregational books. Unfortunately, my parish did not have a tradition of regular giving. Older members remembered fondly "how it had always been done." They still preferred holding bake sales and covered-dish dinners to make up a budget shortfall. They had never done regular pledging and resisted new approaches to responsible stewardship. I felt I had to come up with a novel approach to break the log jam.

Without consulting anyone, I invited the 25% of our members who were strong contributors to a private meeting. This group was already carrying nearly 75% of our church expenses. I informed them about the state of our financial affairs. I told them point blank: "Your small group can make or break our church. The decision is in your hands. We want to move forward in a certain direction. Are you ready to support a new stewardship plan by making a generous formal pledge? With your example, others will follow." Although many seasoned church people would criticize this method, in our situation it worked. While I was there, we not only kept the ships of our two congregations afloat but could even regard the future with some optimism.

There was still the unresolved problem of the dilapidated parsonage. Marianne and I continued to live in the small rented apartment, and following George Weirick's advice, I refused to approve spending any money or effort to renovate the rickety structure next door to the Grafton church. When a modest brick home on the outskirts of town came on the market for a good price, I made my move. I obtained the consent of the more reasonable parishioners in the smaller Newburg congregation to go into debt in order to purchase a new parsonage. The big stumbling block would be several diehards at St. Paul's in Grafton who could not be moved by gentle persuasion. I would have to use blackmail on them.

I had passed my six-month trial period and was well settled into my ministry when help came through a form letter of inquiry sent by the pastor of a large congregation in York, Pennsylvania. He wondered whether anyone would be interested in being his associate pastor. The offer was quite tempting. In spite of my affection for my congregants, putting up with the primitive conditions of Appalachian poverty—and especially the mindset of many that went with it—was a daily struggle. The congregation in York could provide a more civilized, cultured setting. After a quick visit there and an interview with the pastor, I received an invitation to take on the associate position.

But God had different plans. I still had things to learn in the hill country of West Virginia. At the decisive meeting of the Grafton congregation on the purchase of a new parsonage, I simply told my people about the offer from the church in Pennsylvania. I told them to vote as their consciences dictated. But if they rejected the opportunity to provide a new parsonage, we would move on to York. This was, of course, crass coercion, and I am not so sure that it was completely ethical or good church leadership. But my mind was made up. To move the congregation forward, it had to be done this way. As a result, even the diehards in Grafton gave their grudging consent rather than lose their pastor.

The parish bought the attractive little house, and it became our home for nearly two years. In spite of the frictions and nasty arguments that arose, I was convinced that direct personal involvement by lay people in the running of their church affairs builds a more solid faith community. This simply does not happen in the impersonal German church structure, where paid staff rather than volunteers run parish programs and the believer in the pew is just a nameless cog in the bureaucratic machinery.

I was so inspired by this insight that I convinced my good friend Dieter to come and join me in this exciting adventure. President Weirick placed him in a small vacant rural congregation as a supply pastor for half a year. While Dieter was grateful for this experience, when his time was up he returned to Germany. My friend had quite a struggle with the English language, and ties to

When All Hell Breaks Loose

his family back home proved to have a stronger pull.

By now Marianne and I had become accustomed to life in a small town. We were grateful for the strong support and affection coming from the majority of our parishioners. It was time to start a family. In January 1961 our little "hillbilly" was born at an excellent hospital in nearby Philippi; a beautiful baby girl we named Andrea. The event was so exciting that even my Mutti overcame her deep resentment that Marianne had "abducted" her Manfred to America, and came to see her new granddaughter. As it turned out, Mutti liked what she saw of the United States so much that one day she admitted: "If I were younger, I could see myself coming here." Yet when I brought her to the airport and we said goodbye, she pressed my hand and pleaded with me: "Manfred, bleib deutsch!" (Manfred, never give up being German!)

With Marianne's Mother in Grafton, 1959

Marianne's mother Miriam Schneider also came from Iowa for occasional visits. I had a very easy, uncomplicated relationship with her. She was still teaching school in Des Moines at that time; Marianne's father, deceased for ten years, had been an Episcopal priest. Mother Schneider still played the organ in their church. I was grateful that although she had never seen me and could not attend our wedding in Germany, she had readily sponsored my immigration visa. From the first time we met, I found myself on the same wave length as this intelligent and generous mother-in-law. As the widow of a pastor, she fully understood our parish trials and struggles.

There were two aspects to the presence of the Risen Christ manifested in the American church that I wanted to get more deeply involved with. One was the unique witness of Lutheranism in America that differed from other Protestant denominations. Lutherans had arrived over the centuries from a variety of non-English-speaking cultures. They had originally worshiped in Swedish, Norwegian, Slovak, German, Hungarian, Danish, Finnish, or Latvian, so they naturally had formed different church bodies. In the 20th century, having largely left their original languages behind, many of these culturally based groups initiated a series of mergers, and by 1950 they were making plans to come together as one united church body. Just prior to my immigration, in 1958, eight of these churches formed the LCA (Lutheran Church in America). At that time there was a strong hope that eventually the LCA would merge with two other church bodies of about the same size, the American Lutheran Church and the Lutheran Church-Missouri Synod, in order to present a unified Lutheran witness in the United States.

This last expectation was unfortunately not fully realized. But at the time I was excited about the opportunity to be part of this significant step forward in North American Lutheranism. I had the responsibility of introducing in my parish the red SBH (Service Book and Hymnal) which was specifically issued for the new LCA. Of course there was grumbling among some old-timers who missed one or two of their favorite tunes in the previous hymnal. But gradually both congregations in Grafton and Newburg learned and sang the new liturgies and hymns with vigor and even joy.

This success was a bit of a surprise. Generally, the parishioners I would minister to did not like innovation. Most people were not adventurous, always preferring the tried and the familiar. This backward-looking attitude was quite a challenge, and it always made me uneasy because I am convinced that those who refuse to look ahead will eventually not have a future. I frequently felt frustrated with them on this point. No matter how hard I tried in my preaching to convince them to let go of the past, over and over I seemed to hit a brick wall. There was stony silence. Many times I would come home after church and angrily mutter to myself Jesus' unkind comment: "Do not cast pearls before swine, lest they trample them under foot and turn to attack you" (Matthew 7:6).

Unfortunately, in spite of all my efforts, my fears about Grafton's future were realized over the long term. Both the town and their Lutheran congregation slid further and further downhill after we left in the fall of 1962. When Marianne and I returned for a visit forty years later, we were shocked to find the church closed, the property overgrown, and the building in ruins. Most of the roof was gone and the stained-glass windows were broken. We saw birds flying in and out of the sanctuary. On Main Street, all the former small businesses were boarded up. Grafton was a county seat, but except for the courthouse it resembled a ghost town. We learned that the remaining Lutherans had joined the Presbyterians years before and had sold the church building to a fundamentalist group, who had eventually abandoned it.

But another important reason why I needed those years in Grafton and Newburg to grow was my initial dismissive attitude about non-Lutheran church groups. Apparently my three-year apprenticeship with God in West Virginia was not only about finances. On one level, because of my theological training and my year with the Evangelical United Brethren in Dayton, I believed strongly in the ecumenical movement and supported efforts to bring the different Christian traditions together. But up until now, this had been a theoretical exercise. The concrete reality I saw in West Virginia was a different story.

I was at first bewildered by the religious pluralism that existed in the United States. Where did it come from? When I attended the monthly meetings of the ministerial alliance in Grafton, a duty I felt was part of my official obligations, I always felt alienated from most of the other pastors I met there—Baptist, Pentecostal, Methodist—although I did feel some mild affinity with the Episcopalians and Presbyterians. I considered all of them to be fine human beings, and certainly they were all good Christians. But I simply could not accept some of these pastors as colleagues in ordained ministry. They were driven by a different spirit. There was only one way to resolve my confusion. I simply had to learn more about them.

Occasionally people had suggested that with my training and background, I should work on a doctoral degree. But I always turned down the idea. I just wanted to be a good pastor. I sometimes liked to quote Martin Luther, who remarked: "I preach for Jack and Jane ('fuer Hans und Grete'). If the learned doctors do not like it, there's the door!" But now my concrete encounters with clergy from unfamiliar backgrounds began to work on my mind. I gradually realized that most of the American Protestant denominations were Calvinist; they came from England and Scotland, not the European mainland. This apparently had an influence on their historical diversity and lack of cohesion. At the same time, I discovered that my knowledge about the history of Christianity in England was woefully inadequate. In our German universities, we had only lightly touched on this subject without any real depth, considering it relatively unimportant.

So I decided to go back to school. With the help of my friend Dr. Flack, dean of Hamma Divinity School in Springfield, Ohio, I applied and was accepted as a graduate student at the Hartford Seminary Foundation in Hartford, Connecticut.

My goal was a Ph.D. degree in the history of the Protestant reformation in England. I very much looked forward to these new studies. But in spite of all the struggles we had gone through together, leaving my two fragile congregations tore me apart. I really had come to love these difficult people. As our little family left Grafton for Hartford in the fall of 1962, with 19-month-old Andrea sleeping in the back seat of our VW beetle, I was so overcome with emotion that I was unable to drive. Marianne had to take the steering wheel. Yet once again I was sure that Christ, my risen Lord, had new and important challenges waiting for me.

When All Hell Breaks Loose

When All Hell Breaks Loose

The Hartford Seminary Foundation, 1962

8
GETTING THE RIGHT ARMOR

"Put on the whole armor of God, that you may be able to stand against the wiles of the devil. For we do not fight against flesh and blood, but against the principalities, against the powers, against the world rulers of this present darkness, against the spiritual hosts of wickedness in the heavenly places." (Ephesians 6:11-12)

The year was 1962. After three years in West Virginia, Hartford was a great relief. It felt as if I were back in civilization. Instead of ramshackle houses perched between barren rocks on steep hills, there were tree-lined streets with nice villas and lots of shade. Once again I was surrounded with well-educated people who could engage in coherent, interesting dialogue. We were in New England, one of the oldest parts of the country, settled by

the Puritans. Connecticut is called the Constitution State, and Hartford is rightfully proud of the state's long history.
The formerly upscale West Hartford neighborhood in which the seminary is located has in recent years "gone bad," as some people call it. Many low-income African Americans live there now, bringing with them signs of obvious poverty. The same is true for that part of New Haven in which Yale University is situated. Both have taken on the elements of other inner-city neighborhoods. But not all of us consider this phenomenon as a deterioration. In any case, West Hartford now displays the special appeal of an urban culture.

In the fall of 1962, when the seminary was at the height of its academic reputation, our personal financial situation was once again precarious. It was fortunate that as a graduate student I did not have to pay tuition. But other than that, we were on our own financially. We had very little furniture—our main possessions were a baby-grand piano and my collection of books. Thus, Marianne's brother Bob could help transport our household goods in a U-Haul trailer. The seminary provided a cramped but furnished student apartment in an ancient residence called Tyler Hall, since torn down.

Marianne had sent inquiries to several dozen colleges about music teaching openings, without success. Then she learned of a full-time position for a reference librarian at the municipal library. Although she had no library experience, she was hired. At that time there was a shortage of trained librarians, so they would hire anyone with a graduate degree and provide basic reference training. I found part-time work at a local Lutheran church as assistant pastor to an authoritarian, old-school pastor who needed help with youth work and confirmation classes. The pay was miserable, but we needed every penny. On the Sundays when I was not occupied at Grace Church, I did supply preaching at vacant pulpits in the area. Thus we scraped by.

Our toddler daughter Andrea was too young for the seminary day-care center, so a social worker recommended a certified caregiver she called "Auntie" Paquette. Mrs. Paquette lived nearby and babysat several toddlers. She agreed to look after Andrea in her home as needed. Usually I would drive Marianne early in the morning to the library and then either stay home with Andrea or bring her to "Auntie." I was often plagued by a guilty conscience; I felt that I was jeopardizing the inner health of our child by handing her over to a stranger at such an early age, just to satisfy my desire for an advanced academic degree.

Manfred Returning From Preaching, 1964

But we were living and working in an optimistic environment. In the fall of 1962, a positive spirit prevailed in the United States. Looking back from the vantage point of today to the first half of the 1960s, I realize that those were the last years of the American economic Golden Age after World War II. Today, people are so bitterly divided over all kinds of issues that benign English words like liberal and conservative have lost their innocence. They are no longer normal descriptions but battle cries. In the combative air prevailing now at the beginning of the 21st century, civil discourse between people of differing opinions is next to impossible. Quite a contrast to earlier times! Forty years ago, our country could still bask in the sunshine of winning a just war against Hitler and liberating Europe from his despotic rule. Yes, there was the pressure of the Cold War; but the Soviet Union was an external threat against which the American people stood firmly united in spite of growing internal issues. In 1962, we still had the luxury of a clear international conscience. We were not yet politically divided by the scruples that arose after 1965 as the conflict in Vietnam deteriorated. Now, America is still seen by many across the world as an international bully because of our unwarranted invasion of Iraq.

Although the uncertainties of a budding civil rights movement were appearing on the horizon, I personally enjoyed the generally upbeat outlook of those years. But then President Kennedy sent American soldiers as "military advisers" to the regime in South Vietnam, and my critical European mind rebelled. "How are the G.I.s supposed to tell the difference between 'good' and 'bad' Vietnamese?" I scoffed. Yet even so, I had come to appreciate this young American president. In the Cuban missile crisis, I felt he displayed great courage when he called the bluff of Russian Premier Nikita Khrushchev. And after his dramatic challenge to the Soviets at Berlin's Brandenburg Gate with the declaration: "Ich bin ein Berliner," I simply loved the man, as did most Germans. There was a moment when I had to smile at myself in disbelief. How I had once looked down on the Americans as total strangers! But now I had to admit: "I have become one of them."

As a resident alien I was not allowed to vote. But in 1962 I was initially against putting a Roman Catholic in the White House. Like most of my Protestant colleagues at the time, I was unsure about which loyalty such a president would answer to. But after

Kennedy was elected, my misgivings quickly dissipated. When this charismatic leader was assassinated the following year, one week after our son Christoph was born, I grieved for our dead president as if he were a relative.

For two and one-half years I threw myself into my studies with complete enthusiasm. The Hartford Seminary Foundation was originally affiliated with the Congregational Church. It was a natural place to dig into the rich history of Congregationalism in the New World, which was such a strong force in Connecticut and particularly Hartford.

But I was there to find out about the Protestant reformation in England, and my academic supervisor was just the right man for this. Dr. Robert Paul, an Englishman, was a Congregational minister who specialized in the history of Oliver Cromwell, the Lord Protector. He brought me to a deeper understanding of the inner historical dynamics of the church in England.

Here I must once again digress from my personal narrative. I need to explain in some detail what so captivated my interest in English Protestantism. The situation in the British Isles at the time of the reformation was completely different from the German experience. In England, Protestantism did not get its start from a German professor/monk bent over the bible in serious research. Rather, it had its beginnings in the political exigencies of England at the time. King Henry VIII desperately needed a male heir for his throne. But the harshness of his measures still remain incomprehensible. Why did he have to behead those who stood in his way, or keep them in dungeons?

Yet one can sympathize to a degree with the king's dilemma. After long civil unrest, he was convinced that only a male successor would keep the country together. Eventually his desperate attempt to satisfy this perceived need forced him to break his bonds with the pope in Rome. Only after that would events move from the political arena to impassioned theological confrontation. Once the gospel had free rein, it was inevitable that the good news of God's grace in Christ would conquer the hearts of many English people and dominate their convictions.

But then all hell broke loose. In the turmoil that followed, some religious seekers sought orientation for themselves and their beliefs on the European mainland, particularly in the new theological centers of Wittenberg and Geneva. Here they would be charged up even further by the ferment that was created by the European reformers Luther, Zwingli, and Calvin. These influences became especially intense in the years 1553-1558, when with severe persecutions Mary Tudor forced the English church back into communion with Rome. Nearly three hundred former spiritual leaders were burned at the stake as heretics.

Now the sentiments of the English people turned bitterly against the pope. The spirits of many became inflamed with unwavering hostility. When Mary's half-sister Elizabeth I sought to restore inner balance to her kingdom by seeking the support of regional bishops, she ran into strong resistance from Calvinist Protestants who were unwilling to conform to the new order of the emerging Church of England. These separatists increasingly pursued their own reformist paths by adopting a congregational church polity. Under Elizabeth's successor James I, they suffered harsh discrimination. Ironically, this also applied to the few Roman Catholic believers who had managed to survive those violent years. Not surprisingly, many separatists sought to establish a new life for themselves in the territories of America, once they had a chance. The first religious pilgrims to survive the perilous crossing of the Atlantic Ocean settled in the Massachusetts Bay Colony. New England was the cradle of American Protestantism.

I wanted to be a good neighbor to the array of different churches in the New World, so it was imperative that I become familiar with their histories and also with the American past. To a large extent, I could do that on my own. But it was just as important to understand their origins in England. This gripping story could only be passed on to me by Professor Robert Paul, who had a scholar's knowledge of the church reforms in his home country.

Dr. Ford Lewis Battles, renowned for his English translation of John Calvin's *Institutes*, was another church historian at Hartford. He was an outstanding Calvin scholar. I benefitted greatly from his classes and seminars, especially since I had arrived with a rather one-sided view of Calvin. Dr. Battles helped me appreciate him as more than just a Frenchman with a sharp legal mind, as I had been led to assume. He opened up for me another side of this great reformer, who was apparently a warm-hearted believer with a fondness for the psalms. He introduced me to the spirit of mysticism which also can be found in Calvin.

Today, relations between Calvinists and Lutherans are cordial. We enjoy altar and pulpit fellowship; American ministers from the Presbyterian and Reformed traditions may cooperate with Evangelical Lutherans and vice versa without any problem. But in the 1960s this was not yet so. Then, the suspicions and fears of "otherness" kept Christians from recognizing Christ's living presence in their cousins of a different Protestant persuasion. Dr. Battles helped to open my eyes in this regard.

As a future historian, I was required to take a course entitled "Historical Method," taught by Dr. Paul Leser, a German native who came to the United States as a fugitive from the Hitler regime. He was not a theologian; he may not even have been a Christian. But it did not matter. He was a good professor and historical researcher; he knew his stuff.

My experience in Dr. Leser's class deserves a wider description. He began our first session by handing out a questionnaire that asked nonsensical questions such as: "What is 3x5?" "Who is the President of the United States?" "When did World War I end?" and so on. It seemed totally ridiculous. Then he lowered the boom. After we responded to each innocuous question, he would ask: "How do you know?" Our stumbling answers only brought us into one predicament after another. In witty fashion, our teacher forced us to think through the different sorts of logic one needs to use in the interpretation of historical records. He wanted us to focus our attention completely on the analysis of written texts which are the primary sources for historical research.

With biting irony and sharp wit, over the course of the semester Paul Leser disabused us of the grand notion that a competent historian is one who can establish sweeping connections between significant events of history. "Not so!" he insisted. "A good historian is a scholar who carefully works on the minutiae of primary sources and through painstaking research establishes their authenticity as credible witnesses." In my previous studies at German universities, I had absorbed the various schools of historical-critical analysis in the interpretation of the bible. But now for the first time I was challenged to engage in the actual nitty-gritty of assessing the value of one historical source as more authentic than another, when compared to claims that had less validity. This was for me an enlightening exercise.

In order to be admitted to the doctoral program, I was required to learn one more language. In addition to the classical languages of Latin, Hebrew, and Greek and my command of German and English, it was necessary for me to learn French so that I could handle all the literature in my field of study. This was fun. I had always admired French for its beauty and elegance. Our teacher was a New England spinster in her late sixties, small and wiry with a knot of white hair. Miss Flora Shepherd was a tough taskmaster who did not allow any digression from her appointed goals. But her austere exterior concealed a warm affection for us students as her "children." I quickly acquired an acceptable fluency in the required language, although in future years my capacity to use French was practically destroyed when I had to teach in Spanish for five years in Latin America.

I eagerly absorbed my courses at the Hartford Seminary. They were all tools I would need to function as a full member of Christ's household in the new world I had adopted as my home. They were essential parts of God's armor for me in the bewildering pluralism of the American environment. But of course not everything was perfect harmony. I had hoped to start work immediately on a doctoral dissertation about the English reformation. But this was met with an absolute "No." I was informed that I first had to fulfill the requirements for a Master of Sacred Theology degree before I could enter a Ph.D. program. The fact that I would be allowed to do this at a German university did not help. This upset me. But I had to live with it.

The main theme I planned to explore in a doctoral thesis was the authority of the church in the midst of different denominational splits in the English reformation. This topic had really captured my spirit. Confronted with the requirement to obtain an S.T.M. degree first, I decided to research the same topic as it applied to the Lutheran reformation in Germany. Fortunately, the proposal for my master's thesis, entitled "The development of Luther's principle of ecclesiastical authority (1512-1530) in the German reformation," was accepted by the seminary authorities.

Yet I still smarted. It galled me that once again, as had been true in Dayton when I was not allowed to smoke on campus, my freer—or wilder—German spirit was put under a tight control. I had landed against my best intentions with the theme of Martin

Luther instead of the more interesting religious panorama that developed in England at that time. Little did I know that this theme would become a strong weapon in my armor of God.

The seminary library contained the German Weimar Edition of Luther's collected works, which was a tremendous advantage. I immersed myself in Luther's lectures on the Psalms. They dealt with his inner personal struggles, with the political forces in Germany at that time, with the Peasants' Revolt and the Turkish threat, with the personal ambitions of the territorial princes. My advisor Dr. Paul kept after me with admonitions to polish my English writing style. He held up as an example Dr. Peter Berger, a renowned star on the seminary faculty who was originally from Austria and had written several bestsellers on the sociology of religion.

Let me digress once again for a moment of explanation. As I developed Luther's concept on the unity of the church, I sensed a growing tension between some of my Hartford professors and me. This was most palpable in my dealings with George Riggan, the professor for systematic theology. It is true that in my effort to recreate Luther's basic positions, I was under the spell of Karl Barth, the reformed Swiss dogmatician who captured Luther's ideas so well. Unfortunately, Barth was not very popular in America at that time.

Most American thinkers in the 1960s pigeon-holed Karl Barth as "neo-orthodox." Those who read him felt alienated. They did not want to be associated with any sort of orthodoxy, for fear of losing touch with the ongoing trajectory of historical events. The dominant stance at American Protestant seminaries was one of so-called "liberal theology." It tried to establish links between Christian statements of faith and the American culture. Barth and his European colleagues, on the other hand, called themselves "dialectical theologians." They used the pessimistic analysis of

such existentialist philosophers as Soren Kierkegaard to understand the human situation. This radical view, bordering on nihilism, did not sit well with most Americans.
Already at the end of World War I, Europeans had begun to reject any comfortable bonding between the Christian faith and the surrounding culture. These convictions were intensified through the years of struggle against Nazi ideology and on into World War II. Barth in particular put strong emphasis on the great divide that separated God the creator from us the created beings. He called God "the one who is totally other." There is no natural bridge leading from us to the creator. Our knowledge is not capable of encompassing divine reality. We can know God only through his coming to us and revealing himself to us. This pessimistic idea was foreign to the American experience in those years, when the general population felt understandably proud as victors and were filled with an unbounded optimism.

While the so-called "neo-orthodox" elements in my dissertation did not win high praise from the professors on my committee, they tolerated them with benevolent smiles at my backwardness. In fact, when I presented the finished product of nearly 300 pages to them in the hope of being awarded the S.T.M. degree, I was surprised to be told that I could jump over that requirement on one condition: that I expand my thesis into a full-length Ph.D. work under the supervision of the well-known Luther scholar Roland H. Bainton, who was teaching at Yale University in nearby New Haven. Of course I leapt at the invitation!

In addition to this good news, I was offered a teaching assistant position at the seminary. This was an important breakthrough. Along with my research, I now taught courses in church history to other seminarians, and it was a thrilling experience. The stipend was modest, but it allowed Marianne to quit her library job and stay at home. We could even afford to have another child, and in November 1963 our son Christoph was born. Now we had not only a West Virginia hillbilly in the family but a Connecticut Yankee.

With Andrea and Christoph in Hartford, 1964

Whenever I had a free hour, I bundled up the children and took off for the paths and playgrounds in Elizabeth Park, not far from the seminary. It was during this period that, against my best intentions, I became thoroughly Americanized. I fully blended into the local scene as a happy father. One day I said to myself with a touch of irony: "Hey, Manfred, now you are one of 'them'!" I remembered how strange and foreign those "Amis" had looked when I first saw them straggling down the road in 1945 behind Patton's tanks. How much had happened to me since then!

On the other hand, as I worked on Luther's understanding of the church, I mounted a vigorous defense of the theological legacy I had received in Germany. I was not willing to yield an inch on the basic convictions of my faith. Yet in actual practice, I still preferred the structure of American church life over the German centralized model. This difference became clear in an incident during a visit to Hartford Seminary by the Lutheran theologian and concentration camp survivor Pastor Martin Niemoeller. One morning our seminary president asked me: "Do you want to pick up our German guest from the train station?" Of course I was overjoyed; Niemoeller was one of my idols. He had courageously challenged Hitler's arrogant claims to absolute leadership, and for that crime he was held for years at the Dachau concentration camp as "Hitler's personal prisoner." He had always symbolized for us young theologians what was good and honorable in our German church.

At the time he came to visit Hartford, Niemoeller was president of the Hessen Landeskirche. On the way from the train station he asked me: "So, what are you doing in the United States?" I explained my study program, and he commented: "But can't you do that just as well in Germany?" I replied: "I do not really like being there anymore. Actually, I am opposed to the compulsory church tax." My great hero shook his head in disagreement. "Herr Bahmann," he said, "all this fighting over the church tax is nothing more than a pointless struggle over the emperor's beard!" At that moment it dawned on me how far I had inwardly moved away from the German church structure. To this day, over fifty years after that conversation, I remain convinced that the church tax is an umbilical cord that threatens the genuine spiritual life of a faith community.

In 1964, during my second year of study, I received a letter from the headquarters of the Landeskirche in Speyer informing me that my five-year leave of absence had ended. If I wanted to retain my position as a tenured pastor in that church, with the claim to a full pension after retirement, I had better come home. But I had my answer ready. I replied that I was involved in a doctoral program that was more important to me than a guaranteed church pension. Thus I cut my last official ties to the church in Germany.

When All Hell Breaks Loose

That fall, as I greeted worshipers leaving the sanctuary after a service at Grace Church, a man asked to speak with me privately. He was a church official serving on the LCA board that oversaw our Lutheran missions in Latin America. He informed me that they needed a professor for church history at the Lutheran seminary outside Buenos Aires. He asked me if I would consider going to Argentina. Taken aback, I could only indicate a mild interest. Undeterred, the official saw to it that Marianne and I were invited to repeated visits with our Lutheran Board of Global Missions at 231 Madison Avenue in New York. We were wined and dined. Each time the officials found more reasons to entice us, including an intensive Spanish language course that would prepare me well enough to teach church history in that language. Marianne also was intrigued by this adventure. One day as we drove home from New York to Hartford, I asked her: "What do you think?" She replied: "It could actually be quite interesting!" I slammed on the brakes and pulled the car over, surprised and somehow delighted by her response. We talked about it, we thought about it, and we prayed over it. In the end, we decided to accept the challenge.

Instead of attending the usual two-year training period at a Lutheran missionary institute in Chicago, we would be sent to a Roman Catholic missionary training center for American and Canadian monks, nuns and priests in Cuernavaca, Mexico. There we would immerse ourselves in Spanish-language instruction for four months. In Argentina I would have to write the final version of my doctoral dissertation on Luther. But when it was finished, the board would pay for my trip to Hartford to defend my thesis.

As we prepared for our departure from Hartford, the problem of our different nationalities arose. I was still a German citizen, while Marianne and the children were Americans. I did not like the idea of our family traveling on different national passports. I asked myself: "Manfred, have you now become American?" In all honesty I had to say: "Well--not really!" But then I had an insight. I realized that one's nationality is a political confession and not necessarily a cultural affirmation. By becoming an American citizen, I would only need to swear allegiance to the United States Constitution, not the American Way of Life. I would not be obliged to uphold Coca Cola©, white bread, and all the other cultural atrocities the Americans managed to produce. Once this was settled in my mind, I applied for my naturalization papers at the federal courthouse in Hartford.

It was summertime, apparently a slow period for bureaucratic action. The federal court was closed for vacation. When it opened again in fall, there would be a waiting period of several weeks before I could be sworn in as a citizen. This would be long after the start of our training course in Mexico. I was ready to give up the whole idea, particularly since I still had nagging doubts about becoming a naturalized American in the first place.

The situation was saved at the last minute by one of our Hartford professors. He was a good friend of a federal judge, and he could persuade this official to come downtown and open the court in the middle of the summer so that I might become a proper citizen before leaving for Mexico. Of course I could not turn my back on such generous hospitality. Once again the free and open spirit of this nation captured my heart and mind. On the appointed day the press appeared and a reporter and photographer recorded the special swearing-in. A picture of the judge and myself appeared with an article in the Hartford Courant the next day. It was not bad publicity for the accommodating judge.

As we left the city in New England that had been so friendly to us, I asked the risen Lord to help me deal with the next culture shock that was bound to come. For several years I had tried to juggle the two different cultures of the Old European World and the New American World. I was very conscious of the fact that now I was adding another world to the game. From here on out, I would have three balls in the air: Europe, North America, and

When All Hell Breaks Loose

Latin America. Would all hell break loose once again in my life? Or would my Lord Christ be there to help me not drop the balls?

CIDOC Institute at Hotel Chula Vista, Cuernavaca, 1965

9
YANKEE GO HOME! BUT I NEED YOU!

"But to what shall I compare this generation? It is like children sitting in the market places and calling to their playmates, 'We piped to you, and you did not dance; we wailed, and you did not mourn.' For John came neither eating nor drinking, and they say, 'He has a demon'; the Son of man came eating and drinking, and they say, 'Behold, a glutton and a drunkard, a friend of tax collectors and sinners!'" (Matthew 11:15-19)

As the Braniff 747 airplane carried me and my small family to Mexico City, I could not imagine the full extent of the adventure awaiting us. Personally I was looking forward to learning another language, and I was wondering what life in a Latin culture might be like. But it did not occur to me that I was about to discover a new presence of Christ. I would meet people who shared with me a deep and authentic faith in Jesus, yet had to live out their faith in concrete situations that would often seem totally strange and at times even threatening.

I would be living and working within the Latin American reality of the risen Lord. And I would be introduced into the living reality of Christ in the Roman Catholic Church. On that point I felt absolutely confident about my identity as a Lutheran. There could be no question that Luther was my great hero. I was also absolutely sure how I felt about the "Catholics." While I accepted them as fellow Christians, there was simply no possibility that I could ever be one of them.

The administrators of the Lutheran Board of Global Missions in New York must have sensed this strong conviction in me. In our interviews they had told me: "We have been approached several times about sending our missionaries for language training to CIDOC (Centro Intercultural de Documentación), a Roman Catholic institute in Cuernavaca. We were not sure about taking the risk with other candidates. But with you it is different. With your strong theological foundation, we do not have such concerns. Afterwards, we would like you to write a report about your experience at the institute, so we can decide whether CIDOC is appropriate for Lutheran missionary personnel."

So here I was, on my way to gain a deeper understanding of Catholicism than I ever had, or even cared to have, before. There could not have been a more fortunate time for such a mission. It was 1965 and the Second Vatican Council was coming to an end in Rome. The Catholic Church would soon go through a radical transformation in all aspects of its life.

The late 1960s was also a period when America entered a new chapter in its own history. However, at the time neither I nor anyone else was fully aware of the great national changes that would take place while we were away. The United States had emerged on the world stage as one of the victors of World War II, but the globe was growing increasingly smaller. At the same time, it was sharply divided between East and West, between socialism and capitalism. There were now only two superpowers, the Soviet Union and the United States. Each had at its disposal enormous economic and military power. The blocks of nations they controlled were called the First World and the Second World. The unaligned countries that formed the Third World were mainly in the southern hemisphere. Still developing their own power, they either tried to maintain a certain neutrality or to play out the two superpowers against each other.

In the Vietnam War period, when the French could no longer defend their former colony against the advances of communism, America assumed leadership in a big way. In hindsight we know that while this policy was inspired by good intentions, it was fatally flawed, something that at the time was not immediately obvious to everyone. In addition, large American corporations had begun to flex their economic muscle in the Third World, overpowering local competition. Already in those years, strident voices were raised in the Third World with the call: "Yankee, go home!" This sentiment was strong throughout Latin America.

Yet there was a strange twist to this anti-Americanism. As has often been the case in recent history, while the actual presence of the Americans was intensely disliked, the local populace did not really want them completely out. There seemed to be the same ambiguity that Jesus encountered in his fellow Jews when they compared him to John the Baptist. His countrymen found fault with both of them, but for different reasons. Nothing satisfied them. I once ran into a telling comment by an American missionary to India that captured this lingering discontent very well: "I know that I am not wanted," the missionary said. "But I also know that I am needed. And therefore, I mean to stay."

Upon our arrival in Mexico, I discovered the rich diversity of the Roman Catholic Church at close hand. I learned that there is no such thing as "the Catholics"—one monolithic block—as I had been brought up to believe. There are "many Catholics" who differ individually from one another. In the fall of 1965 there were two strong separate strands among them. There were the traditionalists who wanted to preserve the church as they had always known it. And then there were the progressives who followed the call of Pope John XXIII and were eager to bring their church up to date, or as it was put at the Second Vatican Council, to bring about "aggiornamento." In Mexico I would encounter both kinds of Catholics.

On our first Sunday in the new country, we wanted to attend a worship service in English. We could not find a Protestant one, and in the Catholic churches mass was naturally celebrated in Spanish. The exception was the local cathedral, where mass was said in English at one service on Sunday for the benefit of "gringo" tourists. This suited us just fine. That was where we went, and I enjoyed both the liturgy and a fine sermon given by the priest. But there was one strange element. During the service, several elderly dark-skinned women in poor clothing moved slowly past us up the center aisle on their knees toward the altar, silently mouthing their rosaries.

I was puzzled as I watched them inch forward. What were these tiny Indian women doing in this English worship service? With the gringo mentality of a newcomer, I suspected that they were sizing up the tourists in the sanctuary in order to more effectively beg for alms when we left the church. I had it all wrong. These devout old women had no such intentions. I learned later that they had preferred the mass when it was spoken in unintelligible Latin. Then they could tune out and give themselves completely to their personal prayers and adoration of God without being disturbed. Since Vatican II, this mystical form of worship was disrupted as the priests abandoned Latin and said mass in Spanish. The fact that they could now understand what was being said distracted these women from their meditations. Since the

Latin mass was no longer available, they had substituted the unintelligible English mass as the next best thing.

Cuernavaca, about one hour's drive from Mexico City, has been called "the city of eternal springtime" because of its year-round temperature of seventy-two degrees. Spanish conquistador Hernán Cortez chose Cuernavaca as his vacation residence, and it was easy to see why. The city is charming and picturesque. It is built on a series of hills that are connected by narrow cobblestone alleys and winding streets lined with high whitewashed walls. Behind these walls, one can glimpse beautiful private gardens and charming ironwork balconies.

Cuernavaca, 1965

The language and cultural institute CIDOC was established to prepare Roman Catholic missionaries serving in Latin America. At that time it was housed on one of the hills in the former Hotel Chula Vista. In spite of its pretentious name, Chula Vista was a charming place. We were immediately captivated by the rich vegetation—bushes, trees, and flowers blooming in luxuriant shades of red, purple, and blue—planted around lush green lawns. A large swimming pool, sparkling under the bright sun, stood on a lower level behind the Spanish-style main building.

The institute, founded in 1961, was run by American theologian and educator Ivan Illich. By 1965 this charismatic and prophetic priest was still a monsignor. Years later he would renounce his official position in the Catholic hierarchy. Illich was a brilliant scholar with a complete mastery of the teachings of his church. He spoke seven languages fluently. He was also outspoken in his progressive views.

New York's Cardinal Spellman had managed to get rid of this fiery troublemaker in his diocese by assigning him to train missionaries in Mexico. Fortunately for Illich, the venerable Bishop of Cuernavaca Mendes Arceo, who resided in a former Franciscan monastery next to the cathedral, supported him and was a frequent visitor to the center. The bishop was himself a progressive force in the Vatican II reforms which were turning the Roman Catholic Church upside down. He well understood the spiritual fire that burned behind Ivan Illich's flashing dark eyes.

Upon the arrival of our little Lutheran family—Andrea was four years old, Christoph almost two—we were warmly greeted by Illich himself. I was convinced that he did not intend to convert us to Roman Catholicism. Rather, he saw our presence as a hopeful sign for the reconciliation of our divided church bodies.

We would be attending the fall language course with about 120 priests, monks, and nuns from the United States, Canada, France, and Belgium. Mexico's anti-clerical dress code forbade the wearing of religious garb in public, so each course participant had been instructed to bring one or two secular outfits. Most of the nuns adapted quickly. They established a communal clothes closet in their dormitory, sharing their meager wardrobes with each other to provide some variety during the four months' stay. In addition to skirts, shirts, nylons, and even makeup, the women adopted new hairdos, arranging each other's short-cut hair into a reasonable semblance of style.

Illich apologized that he could not offer us accommodations suitable for a family. He explained: "The others are of course all celibates. One side of the dormitory is for the men, and the other side for the women. Could you look around in the neighborhood for a place to rent? Brother Jerry will help you."

We were happy to do that. Living for four months so closely together with monks, nuns and priests, we were sure we would want some private space. With the help of Brother Jerry, an affable American monk fluent in Spanish, we soon found an adorable little house with a small swimming pool in the front yard. It was about a five minutes' walk down the hill from the institute. From the street, you had to descend 160 steps past a lush tropical garden to get to the house, which sat halfway down the hill. It was well away from the busy street above, and thus seemed ideal for a family with two active small children. We moved in immediately.

We ate our main meal of the day at noon with the other course participants in a large chandeliered dining hall at the institute. The kitchen was run by a strict Swiss woman who served normal American meat-and-potato meals instead of the local Mexican fare. We had to make a special request for milk for Andrea and Christoph. Our Swiss chef was not used to feeding children in this celibate environment, and Mexican children apparently did not drink milk. This strange American custom awakened some amused curiosity in the local busboys.

The noon meal was part of our language training. We ate together with our instructors at large round tables, and we were allowed to converse only in Spanish. This rule provided a strong incentive for us to begin using simple words like bread, water, milk, glass, or potatoes in sentences. Nobody likes to eat in complete silence, so we soon overcame our inhibitions and employed the Spanish words and phrases we were learning in actual conversation.

Our course ran for only four months. In that short time, we would have to master enough basic Spanish to carry out our respective ministries in the various Latin American countries to which we were headed. In my case, it meant teaching church history on a seminary level, a rather bold challenge. Because Marianne had to care for the children, she had an individual tutor who took her through the same course at home. We memorized dialogues and phrases, repeated sounds and sentences, absorbed rules of grammar, and repeated correct pronunciation all day long, over and over, without using a word of English. It was the most demanding learning program either of us had ever experienced. But because of this discipline, politely but rigorously enforced by our young Mexican teachers, a student could achieve the desired level of proficiency.

It took only a couple of weeks before our idyllic garden house turned into an attraction for some of our fellow students. Since it was an easy five-minute walk from the institute, we had a steady stream of visitors. The nuns in particular liked to visit us, and not just because they enjoyed the children. In spite of the progressive thought emanating from the Second Vatican Council, there was one barrier which even Ivan Illich could not cross. This was the use of the hotel's large swimming pool by both priests and nuns. In order to avoid any confusion, the pool was declared off limits to the nuns. Our tiny pool in the front garden of our house could not compare with the gleaming wonder behind the hotel, but it offered the nuns privacy and refreshing coolness under the burning Mexican sun. We declared it unrestricted. As a result, we hosted those nuns who did not mind donning bathing suits.

Every morning in class we were treated to a major lecture designed to prepare us for the concrete situations we would encounter in our ministries in Latin America. While the language instruction was done in small groups of three participants with one Mexican university student as instructor, the lectures were given to the full assembly. All one hundred and twenty of us gathered in a large hall that resembled the auditorium of a university. The speakers were prominent scholars or active leaders in their fields. Juan Luis Segundo, a Jesuit from Montevideo, explained to us the new theological impulses he saw emerging in Latin America. A few years later he was recognized as a leading Liberation Theologian. Another Catholic theologian with a similar outlook was José Severino Croatta, a New Testament scholar. Then there was Daniel Berrigan, an American Jesuit who became famous for his militant opposition to the Vietnam War and the draft. Berrigan, I later learned, had been banished to Latin America for his political actions and was sent to CIDOC for a period of time before going farther south. Our grown children still remember him for the candy he carried in his pockets and shared with them when they were small.

I was particularly drawn to the lectures of Dr. Antonio Donini, an Argentine Jesuit and a religious sociologist. We would become lifelong friends. One day he confided to me that he planned to leave religious orders to get married. Later on, I was able to help him find a teaching post in the United States.

On the days when we had no outside speakers, Illich would take over the lectures. He gave us an unforgettable introduction to the Latin American reality. I will never forget the morning when he stood before us in the crowded hall and yelled like a raging madman: "I hate Yankees!" He wanted us to have a taste of the anti-Americanism we would soon encounter. His approach deeply offended some of the American nuns. They were unable to take this hostile attack on their patriotic loyalties. Illich's method of preparing them for the realities they would face was too much, and they left to go back to their mother house in Maryland. This was probably a good idea. I admired Illich's wisdom in not trying to persuade these good sisters to stay. He knew that if they could not take his offensive speech, they would not be able to handle the greater offenses awaiting them as Americans in Latin America.

Our family quickly settled into a regular daily routine. I spent most of the day at the institute. Our four-year old Andrea attended a German-language kindergarten group several mornings a week while Marianne stayed at home with nearly two-year old Christoph and followed the course with her tutor Maria. When I came home, the children and I would splash around in the pool while Marianne prepared a light supper. One evening as I gave the children their after-swim shower, Chris slipped on the wet floor of the bathroom and fell. He began to scream in pain, and one of his legs stuck out at a grotesque angle. A doctor was called, and as it turned out, our son had broken his thighbone. The doctor was very sympathetic but said that with Christoph's thin bones, he would be taking a risk if he tried to set it. He recommended taking him to the Children's Hospital in Mexico City in the morning. "I know he will have a terrible night because he hurts very badly," he said. "But in the long run it will be better that way. Trust me!" We trusted him, and we all had a bad night. The little fellow was crying in pain the whole time.

In the morning, my Jesuit friend Donini—"Father Donini or FaNini" as the children called him—came with his Volkswagen beetle. We placed our small patient on some pillows in a desk drawer and laid him in the back seat. Then this Argentine Jesuit drove Chris and me to the capital. The visit to the children's hospital was an eye-opener. I became acquainted with a different form of health care. I had expected to deliver my sick child to the clinic and then return to Cuernavaca the same day. Far from it! That was not the way things were done in Mexico. In the United States I would have been told by the medical personnel: "Leave your child to us and get out of the way." Instead, I was given a friendly and reassuring look by the nurse who received us and said: "As his father you will, of course, stay with the boy until he goes home."

I was not prepared for this. While Father Donini returned to Cuernavaca, I went to a drugstore and bought a toothbrush and shaving kit. In Chris's room there was a cot that could be rolled under his hospital bed. I would sleep on it. It was a perfect arrangement. When my boy came out of the operating room with his leg properly set and bandaged, he clutched my finger with his little fist for comfort and at long last fell peacefully asleep.

I felt like a victor coming home after a major battle when Donini brought us back a day later. Marianne had told me over the telephone that Andrea had been bitten by a blond scorpion during our absence. But what was that in comparison to our successful outcome, I thought with male pride. Little did I realize that what happened while we were gone was much more shattering.

That night when Chris and I were at the hospital in Mexico City, a fierce thunderstorm came down on Cuernavaca. Such a storm could be terrifying. It felt as if a fearsome Aztec god had emerged out of the nearby volcano Popokatepetl and raged in anger: "Go back where you came from, foreign invader!" The electricity went out, and Andrea became frightened in the dark. It had been a traumatic day with Chris in the hospital and Daddy gone. She jumped out of her bed and ran over to Marianne for protection. On the way in the darkness she stepped on a blond scorpion. As she cuddled in bed with Marianne, she complained that her foot hurt. Marianne, knowing nothing of scorpions, tried to calm her and get her back to sleep again. Fortunately, the light came back on again and Marianne could see the scorpion on the floor by the bed. She managed to kill it with her shoe. Not knowing what to do, or even how to say "scorpion" in Spanish, she wrapped it in a tissue, warned Andrea not to move from the bed, and ran out into the pouring rain up the hill to the institute. In halting Spanish she showed the insect to the Mexican night clerk and exclaimed: "La nena, la nena! (The girl, the girl)."

The clerk blanched. He recognized the danger. Blond scorpions can be especially deadly for children. Time was of the essence. He shouted "Alagran!" and called the emergency services while institute staff was alerted. Andrea was rushed with Marianne by her side to the hospital, but they did not have the anti-venom serum on hand. It had to be gotten from a pharmacy. Meanwhile our little girl was slipping in and out of consciousness, coughing as her lungs started to fill with mucus from the poison. Brother Jerry was by her side, telling her jokes and stories and trying to keep her awake in any way he could think of. Another institute staff member, an elegant American woman named Feo, made the necessary trips to the pharmacy and kept company with Marianne through the long dark night. It took six hours and four injections of serum before the antidote took effect. The quick action of our new friends had saved Andrea's life. Thank God!

Our little girl looked puffy and swollen when Chris and I arrived back in Cuernavaca the next day. Although she had survived, my strong and brave Marianne was terribly upset. She knew that our little house was probably infested with scorpions. She was adamant: "Unless you get us out of here, the children and I are going back to my mother's house in the United States!" Nothing I could say would change her mind. Finally I consulted with Illich. He fully understood our predicament. Without a lot of trouble, he arranged for us to occupy two adjoining guest rooms on the ground floor of the institute.

As shattering as these two accidents of our children were, they proved to be a godsend. Although we now lived in cramped quarters, we quickly became fully integrated into the life of the others. This was a real blessing. I began to attend the evening worship services held in a tastefully appointed chapel in the main building. Since I did not want to intrude on the liturgy, I kept myself in the back of the room. Yet night after night I heard these people praying for my children by name. This deeply affected me. I simply had to recognize that these Catholics were my sisters and brothers, in spite of our doctrinal differences. They felt exactly the same way about me and my family. Many of them began dropping by for a brief visit, and both priests and nuns offered to babysit any time, as if we were their own family.

Chris had his broken leg in a clumsy, heavy cast and could not walk. Still, I wanted to go out with my two children and explore the neighborhood. We had found a stroller somewhere, and I pushed the little guy up and down the cobblestoned alleyways in that vehicle for six weeks, Andrea at my side with her favorite doll in her arms. Wherever she went, the doll went too.

Mexican Children With Andrea in Cuernavaca, 1965

On these outings, we got acquainted with some of the local culture. I could try out my little bit of Spanish on the Mexican children we met along the way. They were intrigued by our two little blondes and wanted to chat with us. But through their eyes we were given an insight into the grim reality of life in Latin America. Time and again I was shocked to learn that ten-year old Maria or eleven-year old Josefina would rather be in school than in the street. But she could not afford it. Why? "Because I have to take care of my little brothers" was the standard answer. Her mother was somewhere at work, and the father was long gone. I shuddered at these conditions. I knew that this appalling poverty was passed on from one generation to the next in a never-ending spiral. I was especially touched when one of the little girls asked Andrea: "May I touch your doll? Just once?" She could not dream of owning such a beautiful object herself. But just to touch someone else's doll brought her joy and made her eyes shine.

On Columbus Day we joined a crowd of people gathered in the town's central square. For the Mexicans, October 12 was not a day to remember Columbus but an opportunity to celebrate their own heritage. They called it "Día de la rasa" (Day of the race). And celebrate they did, with abandon! We stood tightly pressed together as brilliant fireworks burst over our heads in the pitch-dark night. What a marvelous sight! We chimed in with all the "oohs" and "aahs" around us. It was, however, a pleasure not without risk. One of the rocket coals came like a fiery missile down on me, hitting my chest and burning a hole in my shirt. It was not a serious injury, but it was a reminder that violence was somehow always in the air.

Just before Halloween, Father Donini said: "Come with me! I want to show you something you will not believe." He drove me out to a local cemetery. There was an incredible hustle and bustle as droves of children crowded in on us, begging: "Let me carry water for you!" It soon became apparent what was going on. Everywhere people were washing and scrubbing tombstones or planting flowers on graves. But it was not a sad scene. Far from it! These were happy people. Hilarity was in the air. They were getting ready for All Saints Day. Here in Mexico, however, it was called "La Fiesta de la Muerte"--a celebration of death. In their homes they had built altars adorned with skulls and coffins made out of white sugar, along with fruits and an abundance of flowers. Now they fixed up the graves of their loved ones for the fiesta.

In the past they had held raucous all-night parties in their cemeteries, consuming copious amounts of tequila as they stood watch at grandma's tomb. Now the authorities had put a stop to this practice. But it was still a festive occasion. I heard one mother warn her teenage son: "If you don't straighten out this minute, you will not come to the cemetery tomorrow!" I could not imagine any German or American teenager considering this a terrible punishment. My Argentine friend Donini who introduced me to this scene grinned at my display of mixed emotions. Then he reassured me: "Don't worry! You will not see this behavior in Buenos Aires!"

It was perhaps inevitable that the closeness and intimacy that grew between us and our Catholic friends after we moved into the main building fostered many confidential exchanges. The liberating reforms of the Second Vatican Council had raised the hope in some people that before too long, Catholic priests might be able to marry. It did not come as a complete surprise when a young priest from Canada wanted to find out from us what the life of a married pastor is like. He had fallen in love with one of the lay social workers and saw in our marriage a model for himself and his love. But I had to dampen his enthusiasm. I told him that I did not believe the Vatican would relax the rules for priestly celibacy for a very long time. Shortly thereafter, the two of them left the program and returned to Canada.

Far from giving up my Lutheran heritage, these few months in Cuernavaca filled me with an even more sincere appreciation of what Martin Luther had accomplished. But they also gave me a new appreciation for the church that expelled him as a heretic.

How do I explain this contradiction? Yes, there are divisive church doctrines—clashes of teachings and opinions, mutually opposing approaches and probings. But beyond our human divisions, there is the presence of the crucified and risen Christ in both. Christ time and again calls all believers into communion with himself and then with one another.

Something happened toward the end of my stay that made me particularly aware of a change in my attitude. The conclusion of the Second Vatican Council in Rome in December 1965 nearly coincided with the end of our language course. Upon his return from Rome, Cuernavaca's bishop Mendez Arceo decided to celebrate an open-air mass in the monastery court on the steps of the cathedral. It was a balmy Mexican night. Bright spotlights illuminated the altar that had been set up in front of the massive church door, providing dramatic contrast to the deep darkness surrounding us. It was a reminder that "The light shines in the darkness, but the darkness has not overcome it" (John 1:5).

In his outdoor sermon that night, the bishop addressed us as his "carísimos hijos" (beloved children). He then tried to explain the concluding statement of the Vatican Council, which reaffirmed the role of the Virgin Mary as the Mother of the church. This was always hard for us Protestants to swallow. "You all have heard what the fathers of the Council said about Mary," the venerable church leader explained in his deliberate, solemn voice. "And they are right. Mary is the mother for all of us. But ..." Now the bishop's voice gathered full strength as he shouted: "Mary is also our sister in the faith. Let us never forget that!"

I stood there mesmerized. With my strong Lutheran convictions fully intact, I had to agree wholeheartedly with this statement. The man was right. Suddenly it hit home with me. In our protest against the dictates of Rome, heirs of the Protestant Reformation rail against the concept of Mary as "our heavenly Mother." But in the process we have expelled Mary as "our sister in the faith" from our church communities. In the end we were the losers. We have impoverished the practice of our own faith by dismissing Mary. After many long years of study, I am sure that Martin Luther would agree with me.

Just before Christmas 1965, we left the sun of Mexico and flew for a vacation in sub-zero temperatures to Marianne's mother in Iowa. We were not expected in Argentina until March. I was not only equipped with a basic knowledge of Spanish, but a wall of resistance had crumbled within me. A new comprehension of Christ's Body in this world had been allowed to emerge. This was not the last time that would happen. As I walked with Jesus into a future prepared for me by God, there were more such stubborn walls that had to come down. Sometimes, when all hell once again threatened to break loose, they would keep on crumbling.

When All Hell Breaks Loose

Lutheran Seminary in José C. Paz, Argentina, 1966

10
GOD'S RADICAL CALL

"When he opened the sixth seal, I looked, and behold, there was a great earthquake; and the sun became black as sackcloth, the full moon became like blood, and the stars of the sky fell to the earth; ... The sky vanished like a scroll that is rolled up, and every mountain and island was removed from its place. ... And he who sat upon the throne said, 'Behold, I make all things new.'" (Revelation 6:12-14; 21:5)

Buenos Aires, the "Capital Federal" of Argentina, is a vibrant city. It displays great elegance. It has a distinctly French flair, reflected in the architecture of its public buildings and the layout of its self-contained residential neighborhoods. Buenos Aires has rightly been called the Paris of the South.

"Porteños" or natives of this port city have a highly cultivated sense of beauty. They are proud of its broad avenues with historically significant names like the Avenida de Mayo and Avenida de Nueve de Julio. The "Subte" or subway system may not be the swiftest in the world, but it is a lot cleaner than the New York subway, and visually more polished. The Subte is a vital lifeline in this metropolis of twelve million people, half of Argentina's total population.

There is a strong Italian influence in the country. The percentage of Italian immigrants is higher than that of the Spanish. As a result, Argentines speak Spanish with a distinct cadence that is softer and more musical than in the rest of Latin America. They call their language "castellano," although according to linguists it resembles Neapolitan Italian more than the Spanish of Castile. One sociologist called the Argentine culture a "transplant" brought over from Europe. This is how we also felt after we arrived there in February 1966.

Out in the backlands, in the vast middle of the country, the scenery changes drastically. There is not a hill or mountain in sight. In the wide expanse of the pampa you see only flat, windblown grasslands--and herds of roaming cattle that are overseen by self-assured, almost pompous gauchos in loose white shirts, baggy black pants and wide-brimmed black hats. Once in a while you see an Indio, a descendant of the native population, but nearly all the original Indios were wiped out by the Spanish conquerors' diseases. Generally, the Argentines are white-skinned Europeans from diverse backgrounds..

The Capital Federal seems to be on a different planet from the rest of the country. The Teatro Colón has had an international reputation for over one hundred years as one of the finest opera houses in the world. Many other halls and venues offer a rich fare of cultural events.

But make no mistake, you are not in Europe. There are many differences that disorient someone from the north, and not only cultural ones. There is, for example, the tilt of the earth. At night you will search the sky in vain for the constancy of the North Star and the familiar Big Dipper. You are in the southern hemisphere. You will have to get used to a moving night sky. The Southern Cross travels slowly across the heavens as the night progresses. Like the unfamiliar stars and the oddly tipped moon, the seasons are turned upside down. Easter come in the fall and Christmas at the height of summer. Ironically, in spite of the heat Argentine Christmas ads and decorations feature Santa in a heavy red suit lined with white fur. He must feel the urge to jump into a swimming pool.

We landed at Ezeiza International Airport in late summer. A bright, hot sun bore down. Dr. Bela Lesko, president of the Lutheran seminary in José C. Paz, a town about a forty-minute ride from the capital, picked us up in his white Argentine-made Ford Torino. He was in a foul mood, and he let me know it. Classes would not start for another three weeks, he informed me, and he had not expected us so soon. Our arrival had forced him to interrupt his summer vacation. Also, workmen were still making repairs on the house we were to live in. During the ride from the airport, he thawed only a little. It was not a warm welcome.

But when we reached the campus, I was immediately taken in by the charm of the seminary grounds. The attractive colonial-style main building glistened pale pink in the sun. The compound was ringed on three sides with shady eucalyptus trees that hid a high wall. In the backyards and around the lawns, orange, lemon, and grapefruit trees abounded. There were in fact so many grapefruit lying on the ground that the students played football with them. Every morning when I went outside, cool breezes filled the air

When All Hell Breaks Loose

with the strong aroma of eucalyptus mingled with the smell of fresh soil from the pampa. It would become an intoxicating perfume that made me face each day with eager anticipation.

It was an ideal setting for a family. Our two small children, aged five and going on three, could run around and ride their tricycles without fear because the campus was protected by the high wall. There were four spacious brick homes for faculty families. We had the use of one half of a two-story double house. By local standards we would be considered part of the upper-class elite in our accommodations, which included four bedrooms, polished hardwood floors, and all amenities.

The other half of the house was occupied by an Argentine family, the seminary business administrators Albor and Luisa Casal and their two pre-teen children. They were a charming family, and in no time we became good friends. Marianne appreciated the practical shopping advice she got from Luisa. There were no supermarkets in the town at that time, just individual shops and a small grocery store selling canned goods. When she went to buy meat for the first time, for example, she found that the butcher down the street had half a cow hanging from the ceiling on a large hook. Innards such as liver, heart and kidneys were displayed on the marble counter. Customers told him what cut they wanted, and he obliged. Of course Marianne did not know the Spanish words for meat cuts, so she asked Luisa to make her a list of names. Argentine beef, the best in the world, was dirt cheap in its own country. Sirloin steak and filet mignon became our daily fare for a while. Then, unbelievably, I was the one to complain: "Do we always have to eat steak? Why don't you make some of your delicious vegetable soups!"

Bela Lesko, who had picked us up from the airport, was my immediate superior as president of the seminary. He lived with his wife and three teenage children in the largest of the four faculty houses on the other side of the campus green. He had

When All Hell Breaks Loose

been born in Hungary, and his wife Eva was a gracious lady from Sweden. Anders Ruuth, also a Swede, taught practical theology; he and his family lived next door to the Leskos. On our side of the campus, the other faculty house was occupied by the family of Heinz Joachim Held, called HeiJo, a fellow German who taught systematic theology. The Held family had four small children about the same ages as ours. It was not long before Spanish became the common language of the children, and over the years our families developed a strong friendship. Between our house and the Helds was the residence of Don Andres, the Argentine caretaker, and his extended family.

We seemed to have landed in a perfect little universe. In 1966, all the buildings were still new at our address: Gaspar Campos 6151, José C. Paz. They had the sheen of freshness and modernity. But the outward appearance was deceiving. The funds that built and maintained this upscale Lutheran outpost came from Europe and America. The Argentine economic reality was quite different. A visitor venturing out from the glitz and elegance of downtown Buenos Aires would be confronted by "villa miserias" or slums that surrounded the metropolitan area on all sides. At first I could hardly believe my eyes. Riding the commuter train to and from the city, I saw the terrible misery of families living beside the tracks in flimsy shacks pieced together from wood planks, pieces of tin, corrugated metal sheets, or whatever they could find. They had no running water or toilet facilities. They were lucky if there was a clean water source somewhere not too far away.

Who were these unfortunate people? Most of the villa miseria dwellers came from the countryside when they could no longer feed their families as small tenant farmers because agro-business corporations had taken over the land. Attracted by rumors of jobs among the bright lights of the big city, they came hoping to find work. Usually no job materialized. But they stayed, living on public or unused private land in huts nailed together out of scrap, scrounging around in the huge garbage dumps for anything edible or saleable. Their youth often became involved in drug dealing. Although the police knew what was going on, they themselves were involved in a struggle of authority between federal and local police units. They were susceptible to graft because their small policemen's salaries were not sufficient to raise a family.

Very quickly I found myself in an enormous personal conflict. I loved the charm of our new country and our own comfortable living conditions. But I also was overwhelmed by the appalling squalor I saw everywhere. How was I supposed to reconcile these glaring contrasts?

One day in June 1966, a few weeks after the start of classes, regular radio and television programming was interrupted by a bulletin informing the populace that the government had been deposed in a "golpe del estado," a coup d'etat. A group of generals surrounded the Casa Rosada, the presidential palace, with tanks and informed the democratically elected president Dr. Arturo Illia that he had to go. Illia protested at first, of course. But he was a cultivated elderly figurehead and wanted to avoid bloodshed, so he complied with the wishes of the military and stepped down.

I was speechless, in a state of shock. The radio was broadcasting Strauss waltzes interspersed with assurances that everything was under control. They seemed to be right. Our everyday routine proceeded without the slightest change or further disturbance. I asked some of our students for an explanation, but they shrugged their shoulders. They said this happened every so often. It was just a part of life.

My classes were going well, although I had to write out my first lectures in longhand, laboriously, until I felt comfortable with the Spanish. Then one day an unexpected visitor arrived on campus and said he wanted to meet the new professor for church history. His name was Leopoldo Niilus. He was a young lawyer and an active Lutheran. His family had come to Argentina as displaced persons from Estonia after World War II. He was an insistent, provocative fellow. He said he had only one question to ask me: "Do you believe in revolution or in evolution?" He wanted to know whether I believed that the solution to the problems of his adopted country would come about through gradual development or radical upheaval.

Niilus's question could have applied to all of Latin America. Was there a way to bring relief to this troubled sub-continent without a radical overthrow of the firmly entrenched rich and powerful? I did not want to be forced into such an extreme position. I wanted to avoid having to choose between absolute alternatives. I tried to explain to Niilus that as a historian, in any conflict I must always take both sides into account. I argued that some historical change comes slowly, by degrees, and other change can happen quite abruptly. It would be arbitrary and dogmatic to cast an exclusive vote for either evolution or revolution. But the more I argued and discussed this point with him and others, the more I became dissatisfied with my own logic. To this day, fifty years later, I still struggle with it. When I think of Latin America, I am haunted by the question: Evolution or revolution? Although no definitive answer has emerged that applies in all cases, I know that behind this alternative lurks God's radical call to serve our brothers and sisters in need without any reservation whatsoever.

This was on my mind one afternoon when, as I was taking a steaming hot bath, a thought suddenly struck me. "Manfred," I told myself, "you are getting increasingly redder. And not just from the hot water on your skin. You came down here with some lingering pride in your German culture and education. You also value your American citizenship and a Ph.D. from an American seminary. But what help are these advantages down here? What do such achievements have to do with the dilemmas that must be faced in Latin America?"

I realized that neither my fellow Germans nor my fellow Americans in business here had a consuming desire to help the Latin Americans suffering from severe poverty and injustice. They came to pursue trade interests in the most advantageous way possible, without any regard for the damage they could be causing to the local population. I slowly began to appreciate the necessity of revolutionary change over the failed example of gradual improvement in the conditions I saw around me. From then on, I favored a "red" or progressive outlook over a "black" or reactionary position on the economic front. Any sort of dynamic change had to be better than the present state of human exploitation.

Two years after the visit by Niilus at our Lutheran seminary, I would learn that many dedicated Roman Catholics had reached the same conclusion. In 1968 I was present at the birth event of Latin American Liberation Theology at a bishops' conference in Medellín, Colombia. This theological initiative that later spread throughout the world and strongly influenced the current pope, originated in Latin America's grass-root church communities. Roman Catholic believers would became convinced that Christ identifies most personally with the suffering poor.

Latin American Liberation Theology opened up new ways of experiencing the presence of the risen Christ. For example, it celebrates God's "preferential option for the poor." It seeks to redress the wrong that has been done to them. This is the central theme that liberation theologians discovered in the bible. This theology calls for a drastic reordering of the rewards in our societies. Since in most cases the rich and powerful are not ready to relinquish their privileges to the poor voluntarily, some of these changes will in the end have to be forced upon them. Rejecting the incremental changes of a gradual development, this provocative theology stakes its hope on the complete reversal of values which God expects from us. It is a desperate cry for help that has come out of the very soul of Latin America.

As I thought about the implications of the stark contradictions and harsh realities I saw every day, I realized that they were also evident in the implanted presence of our Lutheran seminary. Even though we spoke Spanish, and our students were all Latin American young people, our attractive school was set up as a foreign body, a transplant from the north, protected by a gate and a high wall. It had little in common with the local community.

Our Facultad Luterana de Teología (Lutheran Theological Seminary) was established after World War II with funds from North American Lutheran churches and the Lutheran World Federation. During my tenure there, from 1966-70, it still received its operating budget from these two sources. In fact, my salary was paid in dollars by the Board of Missions in New York. But there was no effective oversight of the seminary's financial operations. I learned that our president Bela Lesko enjoyed a gentlemen's agreement with a prominent Lutheran leader in the United States: Whatever funds the president requested, he would receive from the Board in New York. No questions asked.

Bela himself had been a war refugee. He had great personal sympathy for other refugees. Thus he provided those clergy and academics who had landed in Argentina with all sorts of teaching assignments, regardless of their credentials or the seminary's needs. As a former refugee myself, I certainly respected his generosity in this regard. But since I had been a parish pastor in the United States, I also knew at first hand how hard it was to raise those American dollars from individual church members and congregations. Many were struggling financially themselves. It was hard to see these funds dispensed with such unthinking largesse in the mission field. I felt it was a kind of exploitation in reverse. Care for the gifts of the other must also be part of our stewardship.

I was happy that we as a Lutheran school could supply churches on the whole sub-continent with our unique contribution. Luther's special notion of Christian freedom and the sense of evangelical joy unleashed by his reforms in the 16th century are needed in Latin America. They have never been fully realized in the Roman Catholic cultures there. As Lutheran educators, we have an important message and a significant mission. But those who acknowledge God's preference for the poor will also understand that it must be done in an appropriate way.

None of the other faculty shared my concern about our lack of seminary budget oversight. My European colleagues were used to the fact that their salaries arrived out of some fund or other, paid by an impersonal bureaucracy. My Argentine colleagues, on the other hand, were glad to have an income from "rich gringos" in the United States. Why should they care? Why get worked up over finances? Yet I knew that many American contributions came from missionary societies that were kept alive by dedicated senior citizens and normal churchgoers, hardly "rich gringos," and I felt outraged.

We had an enrollment of twenty ministerial students. We had about the same number of teachers, both full- and part-time. In addition to core professors needed for biblical studies, systematic theology, church history, and the practical disciplines such as preaching, counseling, and educational skills, there were all sorts of adjunct faculty members teaching anything under the sun, from church architecture to photography. In addition, we had the same number of about twenty support staff—gardeners, cooks, secretaries, and cleaning personnel. Forty employees for twenty students—it was a crazy setup.

Night after night I wandered around the dark campus, troubled in my conscience, trying to make sense of it all. I was particularly bothered by the fact that I seemed to be the only one who was really concerned. I began to doubt my own sanity. I told myself: "If everyone else is happy with the way things are, and only one always complains, watch out for the malcontent! He must be the crazy one." By this logic, I was the problem.

Argentine Seminarians With Manfred, 1966

Yet I did enjoy my students. In the 1960s there were hardly any women preparing for the ordained ministry. We had only men, most of them young. With rare exceptions, they had German names like Weiss, Blatezky, Knoblauch, or Schaad. But they all were proud of their Spanish first names: Juan, Carlos, Ernesto, or Pedro. They were first and foremost Argentines. Sons of German immigrant families, they all spoke some German. But their real language was Spanish. In class they would rattle it off like machine-gun fire. Particularly in my first year, I had enormous problems keeping up with them. But I managed. It helped that I seldom had more than four students in any given class. While most came from middle-class backgrounds, they all had first-hand knowledge of the shocking poverty in their nation.

Our Andrea was now five years old and attending a Spanish-speaking school connected to our local Lutheran parish. She had picked up the language in no time. Christoph, whose name was changed on official Argentine documents to Cristóbal, was nearly three years old. For months after we arrived he was quiet with strangers, speaking to no one but us. Yet I saw that he listened intently to the new sounds spoken around him. My students had dubbed him affectionately "el filósofo" (the philosopher). Then one day, out of the blue, our son began to speak perfect Spanish with an Argentine inflection. Apparently he had figured it out.

Marianne and I were fortunate to enlist the help of an excellent language tutor, an attractive single "porteña" (Buenos Aires native) woman named Adelina Cantarella, to continue upgrading our still-rudimentary Spanish. She turned out to be a perfect choice. As a porteña, Adelina had a deep affection for her city, her country, and her mother tongue. Her father, now deceased, had been a physician. She lived with her widowed mother in an old but elegant downtown apartment building and was an active member of a Methodist congregation.

Beyond the weekly lessons in grammar, pronunciation, and vocabulary, Adelina introduced us to the refined but different ways of the Buenos Aires upper class. We experienced this for the first time when we were invited to her home one evening for dinner. We arrived punctually at six o'clock, the time we had been told, bearing a bouquet of flowers. We wanted to present ourselves in the most favorable light. But we did not do the correct thing, obviously. The flowers were all right, but we had arrived much too early. I am afraid we created an embarrassment for our hostess and her gracious mother, who were still in their bathrobes getting ready for the evening. A maid ushered us into the living room and served us some drinks. The invitation had been for six, but dinner did not begin until after eight o'clock. We learned later that nine o'clock was the usual dinner hour.

Spanish is a beautiful language. It can enrapture you. Adelina was an engaging teacher, explaining the special cadences of the language, its rise and fall. Although I worked at it for over five years, I never learned to use it in all its grandeur. But maybe that was not such a bad thing. Shortly after our arrival, I attended a worship service at which the venerable Lutheran church president Jonás Villaverde preached. I was overwhelmed by his mastery of elegant Spanish rhetoric. Yet as I left the church, I was at a loss to remember any message. I felt that instead of the compelling Word of God, "Palabra de Dios," I had heard a lot of enchanting words of God, "palabras de Dios."

The occasion for Villaverde's sermon was the annual assembly of pastors and lay delegates of the Argentine Lutheran Church. Their number was not impressive, perhaps fifty delegates. They fit comfortably into the modest sanctuary of the main synodical congregation in Villa del Parque, a district of Buenos Aires. What was lacking in numbers, however, was made up for by the wild, undisciplined nature of the proceedings. There was no order of speakers. Nobody raised a hand to ask for the privilege of the floor. Instead, people jumped up from their seats and interrupted one another with their impassioned arguments. I was appalled by the bedlam. I felt completely out of place. I must have come across as a wooden, lifeless "gringo" to the other participants.

But unlike these public proceedings, I could maintain a certain continuity and order in my own classes, which were small. As I worked my way through the centuries of church history, my goal was to bring my students to a genuine appreciation of world history. On the whole, they had received a provincial, even nationalistic, outlook in their schooling. I felt it was important to make them aware of the wider world out there. Some leading Latin American thinkers complain that this kind of international emphasis turns their youth into "phony Europeans." If so, it was a risk I was quite ready to take. For better or worse, much of our world—and theirs—has been turned spiritually into a European or American colony. I may regret my choice. But this is the world we live in, and if we want to change it, we must begin there!

Above anything else, I wanted my students to make Luther's joyful message of God's love in Jesus Christ their own, the core of their thinking and their beliefs. They especially had to learn how to distinguish between the law and the gospel. They had to understand what had happened in their own culture and country. I tried to show them how church and state became entangled in a system of tyrannical domination that cruelly exploited the people. From Luther they could learn that when the liberating news of Jesus Christ is turned into oppressive laws, the idea of a good and generous God is replaced by an idea of God as a vengeful judge.

Luther called God's loving concern for the human race God's "opus proprium" (proper work). But God's punishment, which at times is also needed, he defined as God's "opus alienum" (alien work). When these two aspects are entangled, the gift of God's free love can be overcome by the imposition of a harsh order on human beings who will not stop fighting each other. The only way out of this mess is a return to the free gift of God's grace, offered in Jesus Christ and joyfully accepted by believers.

Luther's concept of a Christian's freedom was what I practiced in my classroom. I took great pains to stay away from any sort of Lutheran indoctrination or party line. My aim was to enable my students to develop free and independent positions as a result of their own research. I instructed them in a responsible use of the bible and other sources. I compared our situation to a courtroom in which the students had to act as lawyers in interpreting the historical texts, while the rest of the class acted as a jury on the validity of their arguments. One student later confided to me: "It was in your church history class that we learned how to work in a scientifically responsible manner." This was high praise for me. He had obviously captured my intent. This student later earned his own doctorate in Germany.

Nearly all of our students came from two of the three Lutheran church bodies present in Argentina. The Evangelical Church of the River Plate (Iglesia Evangélica del Río de la Plata, or IERP) consisted of German-speaking immigrant congregations. Our second participating church body, the United Evangelical Lutheran Church (Iglesia Evangélica Luterana Unida, or IELU), was founded by North Americans as a mission project among Spanish-speaking Argentines. The third Lutheran body, which was associated with the Missouri Synod, did not cooperate with us. Both participating church bodies now used Spanish in their worship, although the River Plate Church also continued to offer German services.

Our seminary president asked me to write a history of the more recent IELU, which was smaller in numbers and struggling for survival. I could see the value of such a chronicle, but I never got around to it, mainly because I felt it was more important to bring out a Spanish edition of Martin Luther's principal writings. Levon Spath, an American Lutheran pastor who had previously served in Argentina, spearheaded this ambitious project. Fortunately, he had important contacts to publishers and financial sources. My German colleague and good friend HeiJo Held was ready to get involved as well, and some native Spanish speakers were hired as translators.

When everything was arranged, work on the first volume of the *Obras de Martín Lutero* (Works of Martin Luther) could begin. HeiJo and I carefully scrutinized the first-draft translations of Luther's German texts and fine-tuned them both linguistically and theologically. I wrote a long introductory chapter on the historical background of Luther's writings and how to read them. It was laborious and time-consuming, but full of excitement for me. What a joy when in 1967 the first volume of Luther's works appeared in Spanish under the Paidos imprint !

Still, Niilus' question of "development or revolution?" continued to haunt me. I was unhappy that we were training young men to serve as pastors for Latin Americans living in poor circumstances while spoiling them with a relatively luxurious life style during their seminary years. As I analyzed this reality, my critical German spirit—dedicated to relentless probing—wrestled with the generous American spirit—a sovereign self-confidence that enables it to put up with inconsistencies and imperfections. Both spirits struggled within me. Time and again I found my personal balance only by holding on to the risen Christ who triumphs over different cultures and nationalities.

In 1967, during our second year in José C. Paz, I received an important call from the Hartford Seminary Foundation. I was summoned to come back for the oral defense of my Ph.D. dissertation on Martin Luther. By then I had become deeply immersed in the problems and events in Argentina, and the summons felt like a call from a long-forgotten world.

I flew back to Hartford. Once there, I felt like a stranger. Everything seemed so different. About a dozen professors had come together, and each of them was allowed to take pot shots at me. I was not brilliant in my oral defense. The first question came from my main adviser Robert Paul, a specialist in the history of the Congregationalists in England. Out of nowhere, he asked me about the influence of Ernst Troeltsch on my research. I was totally unprepared for this question. In the early 20th century, Troeltsch had combined religion and society in a way that was similar to Schleiermacher's approach. Although in the 1960s he still enjoyed a fair reputation at Hartford, by then he was all but ignored at German universities. I was not influenced by him at all. Dr. Paul obviously thought that we must have something in common since we were both Germans, but Troeltsch had nothing to do with my area of study. I mumbled some vague generalities and felt sufficiently humbled.

I did better with the next question, from George Riggan. This systematic theologian knew how much my outlook had been shaped by Karl Barth, the Swiss theological giant who implied that the truth of theology is superior to the insights of philosophy. In an attempt to poke into this dichotomy, Riggan wanted to know how I would defend my thesis against the charge that it expressed an ideology rather than theology. This was a clever tack to take. But I was ready for him. I told him that in my present context of Latin America, an important distinction between ideology and theology does not exist. The basic question is whether an argument is good and useful or abstract and bad. Riggan beamed with approval.

Then a New Testament professor wondered why I had not used any contributions from the extensive Luther research happening in Scandinavia. This was an easy one. I shot back: "Why do you ask this? I used material from Regin Prenter throughout my thesis. He is a Scandinavian from Denmark!" The professor apologized: "I didn't know that. I thought he was a German." Thus I survived the ordeal, and was granted my degree.

It felt good to get back to Ezeiza Airport. I was greeted by Marianne and our children as well as by a group of enthusiastic students who seemed as proud of my achievement as I was relieved. Following an academic tradition, they came prepared

with a pair of scissors and sliced off half the necktie of one more
freshly baked Ph.D.

The Union Seminary At Camacuá 282, Buenos Aires

There was a general Protestant seminary in Buenos Aires called
Facultad Evangélica de Teología (Evangelical Theological
Seminary). It reminded me of Union Seminary in New York City.
Usually referred to simply as Camacuá, the seminary was located
in the middle of the city at Camacuá 282. Its ecumenical faculty
trained ministerial students from Methodist, Baptist, Episcopal,
Presbyterian, Disciples of Christ, and Waldensian backgrounds.
While this seminary lacked the confessional unity we had in our
Lutheran school, because of its denominational diversity it could
put greater emphasis on the serious social problems of our Latin
American context. These two orientations are connected. The
more a religious body is occupied with its own inner life, the less
energy it has for the social context in which it exists. The less
emphasis it places on its own inner cohesion, the more interest it
can take in the pressing needs of the surrounding society. I felt a
certain envy that this general Protestant school was much more

Latin American in character than our suburban Lutheran enclave in José C. Paz.

During my second year the president of the Facultad Evangélica at Camacuá, José Mígues Bonino, approached me with a request. Mígues Bonino was an Argentine Methodist, a fine theologian who had participated in the Roman Catholic Second Vatican Council in Rome as an ecumenical observer. Now he asked for my help. Their professor for church history had returned to the United States, and he had no replacement in sight. Could I step in? Of course I jumped at the chance to bring our two seminaries into closer contact.

Without asking permission from my Lutheran colleagues, I took on the chair for church history at the union seminary in addition to my Lutheran classes. With our low number of students in Jose' C. Paz, my teaching load was light enough that I could easily find the extra time for it. Sometimes when the Facultad Luterana enrolled only three or four students in a class, I simply loaded them into my car and drove us downtown to the other seminary, where they could attend the same class with a much larger group of fellow students. When he found out about this, our seminary president Lesko was greatly distressed; he thought that our Lutheran kids would be theologically contaminated by contact with the Methodists, Waldenses, and Disciples. But I did not share his concern. To the contrary, I was deeply convinced that they would be enriched by the experience.

Soon thereafter my friend HeiJo Held, our Lutheran dean for academic affairs, was called to be president of IERP, the German Evangelical Church of the River Plate. My Lutheran colleagues elected me to take his place. Now, as the academic dean, I was in a position to actively promote a fusion of the two seminaries. After getting to know the union seminary, I was convinced that in our specific situation unity with them would make visible the presence of the risen Christ in our theological efforts. Thus

whenever I could do so in a responsible way, I used my authority
to combine our Lutheran students with those from the seminary
in Buenos Aires.

Bela Lesko could now barely contain his anger at me. But I had
the support of my friend HeiJo, the new German IERP church
president, as well as other colleagues who had cool heads along
with a deeply committed faith in the risen Christ. Gradually we
were able to merge the classes of our two schools, and the outline
of a new joint institute for theological studies began to take
shape. It would be located at Camacuá 282 in the city. We came
up with a somewhat bombastic-sounding name that is still in use
today: Instituto Superior Evangélico de Estudios Teológicos
(ISEDET), the Graduate Evangelical Institute of Theological
Studies. Best of all, we were able to persuade Lesko to give up
his fierce opposition to the merger by promising him the position
of president with its grandiose title. Somewhat mollified, he
accepted, and in 1969 ISEDET was born.

I felt very much at home in our new institute. It was there that I
found my closest academic friends. José Mígues had become a
trusted ally in the effort to create our joint school. Ricardo
Chartier, an American Baptist with a superb mastery of Spanish,
was a flamboyant professor of social ethics who was extremely
popular with the students. Lambert Schuurman taught systematic
theology. A cheerful individual from Holland, he was a member
of the Dutch Reformed Church who had specialized in Luther's
doctrine of the Two Kingdoms. I felt a particularly close affinity
with Andrew Kirk, an Anglican New Testament professor from
England, who shared my views in most of our seminary affairs.
Juan Litwiller, a Presbyterian from the United States, was also a
good friend.

At the merger, I relinquished my post as Lutheran dean so that
Litwiller could take over as academic dean in the combined
seminary. The faculty also included an older New Testament

professor, Rudolf Obermueller, a fellow German who had lived in Buenos Aires since the 1930s. I suspected that at one time he had sympathized with the Nazi movement, but we never talked about it.

All in all, life at the downtown seminary was varied and exciting. After class I would hang out with the students and drink beer in the neighborhood bars. I began to come home later and later. This pattern stretched out until it gave rise to our second marital crisis. The first crisis occurred when Marianne refused to return to our scorpion-infested little house in Cuernavaca. Now she gave me an ultimatum: Come home at a decent hour if you want to save your marriage. Shocked and chastened, I saw the light.

As a result of the seminary merger, many of our Lutheran clergy developed a resentment against me. I was sharply attacked by the Argentine pastors in the IELU, our United Lutheran Church, who complained that "Bahmann is selling us out to the Methodists." While our Lutheran faculty families still lived on the campus in José C. Paz, all classes were now held at ISEDET in Buenos Aires. For the time being, the academic buildings in which the older ordained pastors had received their theological education stood empty and unused, awaiting a new purpose.

When I returned for a visit in 1998, a number of these Argentine pastors still complained about my actions. They had always suspected some nefarious purpose. The truth is that I only wanted the best possible education for "my" students, and that is what the merger gave them. During the following years the compound at Gaspar Campos 6151 in José C. Paz began to be used in various new ways. It was a center for political refugees during the brutal reign of Chilean General Pinochet in the 1970s; later it housed a school for adult education and other social programs.

My classes and lectures were probably monitored occasionally by secret government agents. But our affiliation with the Argentine

Protestant churches gave us some protection, even though we were not part of the one "correct" Roman Catholic Church. But I had been able to develop personal connections with the Jesuit college in San Miguel, a town near José C. Paz. On one occasion, these Jesuit friends invited me to attend a clandestine meeting they had arranged with leaders of the outlawed Communist Party. It was held in a convent out in the country. As I rang the doorbell, an apple-cheeked nun welcomed me with a friendly smile: "Oh, you must be with the Reverend Fathers." I nodded "Yes" and was led to a room tucked away in the back of the convent. My friends were already there, along with some simple worker types who were the Communist leaders. They had brought along a few teenage youth, apparently in the hope of imparting ideological instruction. These leaders were serious but totally uninspiring. It was all rather dull and lifeless. I actually felt sorry for them and their young charges.

It was hard to hold out much hope for the political future of Argentina, or even for Latin America as a whole. My local Lutheran parish pastor Raúl Denuncio was a prime example of my concern. He was a fiery Argentine of Italian heritage and a dynamic preacher. I liked him a lot. But one day, as we were discussing the political situation, he told me: "We Argentines need a fascist government that can keep us under control!" I was deeply annoyed and very disappointed by his remark. Yet I realized that this sentiment was strongly felt by a large part of the population. While they liked to call themselves Peronistas after Juan Domingo Perón, whom most of them adored, hardly anyone could articulate a clear unified platform for the Peronist Party. Peronist positions reached from extreme fascism on the right to complete socialism on the left. My conclusion was: "They don't know what they want or how to get there!"

During much of our time there, Argentina was ruled by the military. After the ouster of the elected president Arturo Illia in 1966, General Carlos Onganía established a rigid right-wing regime. He dissolved the legislature, banned all political parties, and placed the national universities under government control. But although he enjoyed support from the business community, he could not stop a further decline in the already miserable economic situation. Unrest in the country spread and found expression in increasingly violent terrorist activities.

As we got ready to return to the United States in December 1970, opposition to General Onganía's government had grown so strong that the military leaders decided to replace him with another general, Roberto Levingston. A year later they put in another one, Alejandro Lanusse. The debacle of installing successive generals as president ended in the brief return of Perón from his exile in Madrid. When he died in 1974, he was succeeded by his widow. But Isabel Perón was deposed two years later.

Then in 1976, things in Argentina became really ugly when a murderous dictatorship was established by General Jorge Videla. For the next five years he carried on a "dirty war" against all who were suspected of undermining the government. Thousands of citizens disappeared. Many of these "desaparecidos" were never found. Others were subjected to horrendous torture. Yet because they were considered tough warriors against communism, these generals enjoyed strong support from the American government. In the end, as is usually the case, Videla overreached. When the government tried to retake the Falkland Islands (Islas Malvinas) from the British in 1981, their iron grip on Argentina ended in the fiasco of a war they had no chance to win.

For people living in the United States or Europe, it is easy to place the entire blame for their continued plight on the Latin Americans themselves. There is no doubt in my mind that they must shoulder the largest part of the responsibility for issues they so often have neglected in the past. But a burden of responsibility lies also on the shoulders of others who live outside the southern sub-continent.

Most of Latin America's major industries are owned or controlled by foreign corporations who do not honor the same obligations to the public good as they are obliged to do in the First World. It is true that graft and benign neglect often play a role in such issues. But it is also true that those who refuse to see the unfairness of their situation are guilty of blaming the victim rather than the perpetrator. The fact remains that masses of people in Latin America are sinking deeper and deeper into poverty while those at the top benefit handsomely from their cheap labor. The question of Niilus still haunts me: "What will bring about change—revolution or evolution?"

Christ says to his disciples: "In the world you have trouble. But be of good cheer! I have conquered the world" (John 16:33). We can be cheerful indeed, because the conquest of the world belongs to our risen Lord. He does not conquer with military might, and that is a reason to rejoice. Yet along with his loving reassurance, the risen Lord puts before us God's radical call: "Behold, I make all things new." This means we have to change our ways. As we look at the struggles of fellow believers in Latin America, those of Christ's followers who are comfortably situated in the First World must ask ourselves some disturbing questions. "If anyone says, 'I love God', and ignores his brother or sister, he is a liar; for he who does not love his brother and sister whom he has seen, cannot love God whom he has not seen" (1 John 4:20).

When All Hell Breaks Loose

Pope Paul VI in Bogotá, August 1968

11
A PREFERENCE FOR THE POOR

"Listen, my beloved friends. Has not God chosen those who are poor in the world to be rich in faith and heirs of the kingdom which he has promised to those who love him?" (James 2:5)

In 1967, two years into my five-year professorship in Argentina, I received an important letter from Geneva. I was busy preparing my classes on church history and revising translations of Luther texts for the Spanish edition when the Lutheran World Federation asked me to represent them at an upcoming conference of Latin American Roman Catholic bishops (CELAM). I sensed that this conference could be significant, but I had no idea how true this would turn out to be. This bishops' conference would point my life and my theological outlook in a completely new direction.

The Second Vatican Council of the Roman Catholic Church had already left a strong impact on my faith. I began to use some of the Council's statements in my own teaching. As I saw it, the Second Vaticanum took up significant evangelical elements that Luther had stressed in his reformation, and made them her own. This was more like the church Luther always wanted to be part of but had not encountered in his lifetime. Nowadays, one can hear more biblical preaching in some Roman Catholic parishes than in many Lutheran churches. In Vatican II, the entire Christian Church as the visible Body of Christ entered a new era.

The Second Vatican Council concluded in 1965 with the understanding that the reforms it had initiated should be fleshed out in concrete detail on a worldwide scale by regional bishops' conferences held around the globe. This "fleshing out" was the purpose of the assembly I was asked to attend in Latin America. It was now customary for such a significant church meeting to include representatives from other religious bodies as partners and ecumenical observers. Thus the Roman Catholic bishops from Latin America would include me as "Mr. Lutheran."

The conference met in August 1968 in Medellín, Colombia. In those years Medellín was still a charming city. It had not yet become a world center for the drug trade. The theme of the assembly was impressive: "The Church in the Present-Day Transformation of Latin America in the Light of the Council." Given the history of Latin America, it was not surprising that the conference would be held "in the light of the Council." But the boldness with which the "transformation" of an entire continent was its stated aim expressed the unbounded hope that reigned in those years. It was the same kind of optimism that inspired the first human beings to land on the moon in July 1969.

I fully shared this optimistic outlook at that time. I felt confident in the firm foundations of my faith in Christ as they were laid down by Luther. I rejoiced over the new life in Catholicism, all the while humming along with the Beatles tunes that in those years brought a new sophistication to rock music. Life was definitely good.

But I was not prepared for the jolts that would break open my thinking and reveal new dimensions in my understanding of Christ. A solid faith is the basis, that much I knew. But to be alive, faith must support a passionate love and concern for the poor. This was the part I still had to grasp.

I was filled with excitement as the plane carried me from Buenos Aires to the Colombian capital Bogotá. In preparation for the bishops' conference, I studied the papal encyclical "Humanae Vitae" that Pope Paul VI, who was installed in June 1963 after the death of Pope John XXIII, had just published. This encyclical took an unambiguous position against any form of artificial birth control. The baby pill was out! While the papal directive was addressed to all Roman Catholics throughout the world, its release just a few weeks before the Medellín conference was obviously timed to have a particular impact on Latin America.

As I sipped Scotch on ice, compliments of the airline, and smoked the cigarette which was then still permitted, my heart sank as I read. I knew the impact this encyclical would have on the upcoming deliberations. I thought: "If that's the way my Catholic friends want to play it, they are not going to effect any sweeping transformation of this continent. I may just as well return to my classes and save the Lutheran World Federation the rest of my travel allowance." Of course I did not do that; I traveled on. In Bogotá the Council of Catholic Bishops had made arrangements for me to stay with an extremely wealthy family, and they turned out to be very gracious hosts.

The hopefulness in the air during those years was underscored by a powerful and unique event: For the first time in history, a Roman pontiff would visit this most Catholic of continents. Never before had a pope set foot on Latin American soil. What a

momentous occasion! the pope would take part in a Eucharistic
Congress in Bogotá, after which he would open the CELAM
bishops' conference in the Bogotá cathedral on August 24. I had
the good fortune to be present on both occasions.

In a vast field outside Bogotá, a huge throng awaited the arrival
of the pope. I stood in the midst of a crowd that had come from
all over Latin America. They represented different ethnic groups.
Many wore colorful native costumes. A boisterous, joyful mood
permeated the air. As a representative of Lutheranism, I wore a
black clergy suit and white pastoral collar, indistinguishable from
the garb of many priests who were waiting and watching. I struck
up a casual conversation with one of them standing next to me.
We had a friendly exchange until he noticed the wedding band on
my left hand. Concerned, he looked up and asked: "My God,
what is this?" I smiled at him: "Soy casado! I am married!" He
was horrified; had they really removed the celibacy requirement
after Vatican II? My companion was visibly relieved when I
confessed my Lutheran identity.

Waiting for the Pope, Bogotá, 1968

A few minutes later, a helicopter appeared above our heads. It was carrying the pope. A tumultuous joy broke out in the crowd. Everybody seemed to go crazy. I, too, the Lutheran heretic, was unable to resist the emotion that filled the air. I whipped out my white handkerchief and waved it, shouting along with everybody else: "Viva el Papa! Viva el Papa!"

But while I was excited about building new ecumenical relations, I still had some unanswered questions. In the Bogotá cathedral a few days later, I sat in the spacious choir section beside the altar for the solemn celebration that would open the CELAM bishops' conference. I felt a bit overwhelmed by the opulent splendor of this venerable sanctuary. Pope Paul VI was only a few feet away from me. As he began his inaugural address, I heard his first sentences of greeting but then the sound was gone. We saw only the movement of his lips. The pontiff seemed unaware that the microphone was on the blink. I shook my head and thought: "O, my dear Latin American friends, you knock yourselves out with such enthusiasm when the pope comes to visit for the first time in history. And at the critical moment, the mike doesn't work!"

I wondered what to do. All around me were splendidly robed cardinals, archbishops, and bishops. They sat impassively, heavy gold pectoral crosses resting on their chests. My eyes were drawn to the crucifix above the altar. As I meditated on this cross, I heard the words of Martin Luther admonishing me: "Forget about the splendor! Begin with the wounds of Christ! God comes to us not in his glory but in his humanity." Yes, I agreed. But what was I to do in this situation? A thought took hold of me: "If you truly accept the simple humanity of your God, then you should do what decency requires of you. Get up, take the few steps to the pope and tell this nice elderly gentleman from Italy that the mike is on the fritz!" Of course courage failed me. I consoled myself with the thought that I was only a guest, not a full member of the household.

Then I noticed the worn, lined face of a man sitting across the aisle opposite me. He was wearing a simple alb and a wooden cross. Finding some comfort in his weathered features, I realized that this must be Dom Hélder Cámara, the renowned Archbishop of Olinda and Recife in northeastern Brazil. Because of his committed struggle for the rights of the poor, he was known to some as "the red bishop"—not much better than a Communist. Meanwhile, someone had gone forward and advised the Holy Father of the situation. As we waited for the public address system to be repaired, we sang a Te Deum until the pope could continue his discourse.

The following day I settled in to study the full text of the pope's sermon. I tried to sort out my impressions of him as a human being. Yes, I liked him. But he seemed so different from his predecessor—the popular, down-to-earth John XXIII. Paul VI was more of an aristocrat, more ascetic. He impressed me as a deeply spiritual man who was given to reflection on many issues. One year earlier he had written a papal letter full of strong hope regarding the development of the peoples. His encyclical "Populorum Progressio" of March 26, 1967 had been received with great enthusiasm by many in the Third World. Although warning against the dangers of totalitarian ideologies and violent revolutions against "injustices that cry out to heaven," the pope gave a strong endorsement of the reforms that were needed to lift the underdeveloped countries out of their misery and poverty. And yet—just prior to this visit he had fired off his "Humanae Vitae" against artificial birth control.

Again my heart sank as I delved into his message of the previous day in the Bogotá cathedral. He had obviously tried to set the direction in which the bishops' conference should go in the next two weeks. He wanted to make three major points:
    1) The Catholic Church should be a bold part of the social changes that were transforming Latin America, seeking to

"raise up the poor and all who live in conditions of human
and social inferiority."
2) In doing so, the church should steer clear of "atheistic
Marxism, systematic revolt, and blood and anarchy."
3) He declared once again an intransigent and absolute
prohibition of any artificial birth and population control.

I was dismayed and perplexed. This package made no sense. I
had lived long enough in Latin America to know that such a
program would never work in that reality. With some luck, one
might be able to combine any two of the pope's three points with
some success. But not all three. One might perhaps be able to
improve the lot of the poor without bloodshed and anarchy. But
then a way had to be found to control the population explosion,
an impossibility without the pill. On the other hand, one could try
to promote the well-being of the poor without contraception. But
this would invite violence and bloodshed. Trying to have all three
demands together was like trying to have your cake and eat it too.

While I was attempting to digest this sermon, Paul VI returned to
Rome. That afternoon I was taken with the church leaders to the
modern, comfortable buildings of a seminary in the provincial
city of Medellín. As we were traveling in the bus, I wondered:
How will these guys respond to the direction the Holy Father set
for them in his sermon? Will they go for all three points? How
wide will these prelates throw open the windows of their
cathedrals? How much sharp wind from an often hostile world
will they allow to blow into their venerable edifices?

I was in for a surprise. When the bishops' conference opened on
Monday, August 26, 1968 with the theme "Preference for the
Poor," I became privy to a completely new and unexpected
method of interpreting Roman Catholic documents. It was at that
moment and in that atmosphere that Latin American Liberation
Theology was born. As an eye-witness to this spectacular birth, I
was compelled to record my impressions in a book entitled *A*

Preference For the Poor, published in 2005 by University Press of America. Some of that account is repeated here.

What method did the bishops use? Although they often quoted the pope, my Protestant mind told me that their use of his words did not reflect his meaning. They massaged the message. After a polite reference to the Holy Father, they would take off in another direction, one more to their liking, ending up with conclusions that were not at all implied in the papal pronouncements. In the flash of a few short days, I received a valuable education in how the Roman Catholic Church functions on the inside. At the same time, I saw how each discrepancy between the pope's words and their application by the prelates opened a free space in which the Holy Spirit could move and work. Fascinated, I watched this process unfold. It occurred to me that by slavishly clinging to the words of a written text, we Protestants often tend to fill up many such spaces prematurely.

An indomitable spirit was at work in Medellín, a spirit every bit as joyfully infectious as the one I had experienced while waiting for the pope in the field outside Bogotá a few days earlier. I caught my breath as Avelar Brandao Vilela, the Archbishop of Teresina in Brazil and one of the conference's co-presidents, called for a new outpouring of the Holy Spirit upon Latin America. With great passion he demanded that the bishops' conference "become a new Pentecost." His call was seconded by the Argentine Bishop Eduardo Pironio, who later became a cardinal and then general secretary of the Episcopal Council. Pironio boldly asserted that they had come together "in the communion of the Spirit that assures and manifests the saving event of a new Pentecost for Latin America." For a moment I was not sure whether I was listening to staid Catholic bishops or fiery Pentecostal preachers.

Medellín was contextual theology. It sounded an urgent message that came straight out of the crying needs of daily life. During the first week, the conference remained in the firm grip of so-called "experts" who confronted the participants with a clear-eyed, scientifically documented presentation of the harsh realities that dominate Latin America. This upset some of the older, more formidable prelates. They fumed that they were being kept captive by younger scientists and theologians. "What is all this nonsense?" they protested. "I have lived all my life here. What are they trying to tell me?" The younger "experts" who made them so angry were Franciscans and Jesuits, and some social scientists. Using slides and statistical reports, they presented irrefutable evidence of the appalling living conditions in Latin America. They left no doubt as to the abject poverty of the masses, the widespread illiteracy and unemployment, the lack of decent housing and medical care, the flight of millions of families from the countryside to the burgeoning slums ringing every metropolitan area, and other ills.

It was during the second week that the prelates themselves could speak their minds. They divided into working groups around such themes as Peace, Justice, Family, Education, Youth, Pastoral Care of the Masses, Concern for the Elites, Lay People, Priests, and the Religious. As an ecumenical guest I had no vote in the assembly. But in every other way I was treated as an equal—I had the right to speak and express my opinions. It was up to me which working group I wanted to join. I chose the commission on Justice. Immediately I was elected by the rest of the group to be the secretary of our commission. For the rest of the conference, I furiously took notes of the deliberations and sometimes heated arguments, all in Spanish. Every evening I worked hard to compose a faithful set of minutes which had to be approved by the rest of our group the following morning. A number of my summaries made their way into the final version of the Medellín document on Justice. This was ecumenical cooperation in the best sense. On one occasion I was even asked to lead the whole assembly in their morning devotions. I had them sing Martin

Luther's hymn "A Mighty Fortress is our God," which they did with great gusto.

Medellín has been criticized by some because it failed to produce a single coherent document. It is true that the conference ended with only a loose collection of statements on different urgent needs. To my way of thinking, this was inevitable. Latin America does not exist as a coherent, orderly system of cultures. Instead, it seethes with unrest, constantly bubbling and changing underneath a seemingly smooth veneer. But those who can catch this restless spirit will hear how these bishops spoke with one voice.

On the issue of justice, the bishops declare that "the misery that besets large masses ... in all of our countries ... as a collective fact expresses itself as injustice which cries to the heavens." They recognize the "almost universal frustration of legitimate aspirations that creates the climate of collective anguish in which we are already living." They are firmly convinced of the need for radical change:

> "All of us need a profound conversion so that 'the kingdom of justice, love and peace' might come to us. ... We will not have a new continent without new and reformed structures, but, above all, there will be no new continent without new men, who know how to be truly free and responsible according to the light of the Gospel."

The most penetrating statements to come out of Medellín are from the commission on Peace. Perhaps this is because Dom Hélder Câmara, the progressive Brazilian bishop, worked with this group. Here one finds the provocative statement on "institutionalized violence." Without mincing words, the bishops declare: "Violence constitutes one of the gravest problems in Latin America." In other words, there is no realistic way to avoid violence, so terribly inflamed is the general situation. Thus the bishops urge the powerful and rich in their countries

> "... not to take advantage of the pacifist position of the Church in order to oppose, either actively nor passively, the profound

transformations that are so necessary. If they jealously retain their privileges, and defend them through violence, they are responsible to history for provoking 'explosive revolutions of despair.'"

An indomitable spirit was unleashed at Medellín. The bishops faced the hopeless living conditions on their continent without flinching and with great courage. But they did not despair. They were possessed by an even greater spirit of joy and faith. I did not doubt that they were equipped with a special strength through God's Holy Spirit. But this joyful strength seemed to dissipate when they dealt with the overwhelming disaster of the population explosion. The statement on Family and Demography is one of their weakest documents. In a wooden, uninspired manner, it merely regurgitates what the papal encyclical "Humanae Vitae" had already pronounced: "The teaching of the Magisterium forbidding the voluntary use of artificial means that thwart the conjugal act is clear and unmistakable."

This was a great disappointment to me. "Good luck!" I muttered to myself. In the future, whenever I pointed out that a peaceful and orderly transformation of Latin America will be impossible without allowing the free use of the pill, my warnings would be brushed aside by my Catholic colleagues as the remarks of an outsider who does not understand the Latin American soul. Some radical leftists among my friends even welcomed the explosion of the population bomb ticking away on their continent. They considered it to be additional fuel for the radical revolution they were waiting for.

There could be no doubt that in spite of an optimistic spirit, revolutionary unrest was in the air. You could smell it with every breath you took. The Catholic seminary compound in which the bishops held their conference was tightly sealed off to the outside world for security reasons. Mounted police patrolled our hill, keeping a watchful eye out for any unauthorized intruder. Similarly, no illegal material was permitted on the premises.

One day I was approached by an acquaintance from Argentina and informed that a woman named Clelia Luro needed to talk to me urgently at a house in downtown Medellín. Clelia was the wife of Monseñor Jeronimo Podestá, bishop of the fictional Argentine diocese of Orrea de Animico. I knew this couple quite well. Actually, the two were not legally married. By accepting the holy sacrament of marriage with Clelia, Podestá would have lost the validity of his status as a priest which had been conferred on him through the sacrament of ordination. Having sex with someone would not have invalidated his priestly vows. But marrying someone would have caused a conflict between these two sacraments and would have defrocked him on the spot. Therefore, the two preferred living together "in sin" without being formally married. In this way, Podestá could continue functioning as a valid priest although he lost his position as the bishop of Avellaneda. He was now assigned to a diocese which existed only in name, Orrea de Animico. It was one of those crazy situations in a church that sometimes seemed to go crazy.

When I met Podestá in Buenos Aires, I had taken an immediate liking to him. He was a charismatic individual with a free spirit, yet he also had a genuinely catholic piety. In spite of his intense difficulties with the hierarchy, he was deeply devoted to his church. Since he seemed to integrate in his own life so many qualities I had found in Luther, I frequently asked him to come to one of my classes and speak to our students.

When I went to see Clelia in Medellín, she showed me a carton of books and implored me to smuggle them past the security controls into the conference. Podestá had recently published a small volume under the title *La Violencia del Amor* (The Violence of Love) in which he had gathered up his sermons, lectures, and articles that explained his unique position. The provocative title expressed both the burning impatience that spurned him on to battle for long-overdue reforms, and the authentic passion he felt for his people. There was no way to distribute openly copies to the assembled bishops.

Perhaps because of my own spirit of freedom in Christ, I accepted the mission to find a clandestine way to transport a carton full of *La Violencia del Amor* into the seminary. As an ecumenical observer, I seemed to be an ideal courier. Nobody would suspect a staid Lutheran clergyman of illegal mischief. For the Catholics, this was strictly a dispute within their own family; it had no connection to a non-Catholic.

The operation worked just fine. I carried my smuggled cargo past the security check without incident. The priest to whom I was to deliver the forbidden publication inside the seminary did not betray me, and over one hundred copies of Podestá's volume reached the hands of the gathered bishops.

As is the custom on such occasions, the Medellín conference was to conclude with an elaborate celebration of mass. This raised an intriguing opportunity for our group of about a dozen ecumenical observers. In addition to my Lutheran presence, there were an Anglican, a Methodist, a Presbyterian, a Baptist, a Pentecostal, and some others, including an Orthodox priest and a member of the Taizé community in France. We had gotten to know each other quite well in the last two weeks. Now we were united by a desire to receive the sacrament of holy communion together with our Roman Catholic friends.

But there was a delicate problem. Bound by its own dogmatic laws and restrictions, the Roman Church did not allow a free sharing of Christ's body and blood. We were, however, a pretty savvy bunch. One of us in a brilliant inspiration remembered that Roman Catholic canon law in most cases permits an exception if there is an emergency. We wanted to address the three prelates who were the presidents of the conference in a formal manner, by presenting to them a joint petition as a group. In our petition, we stated that we would like permission to receive the sacrament of holy communion together with them because we found ourselves in an emergency: We felt driven by the love of Christ.

Ecumenical Observers at Medellín, 1968

It worked. The presiding prelates informed us that we were free to participate in holy communion. There was but one condition: We should not make a spectacle out of it. This was how each one of us also felt. Genuinely motivated by the love and unity with which the Risen Christ bound us together, we had no interest in a publicity performance for the benefit of the press.

Shortly before the beginning of the mass, I was approached by a savvy-looking reporter from a Dutch TV channel. He revealed himself to be an ex-priest, and he had obviously maintained excellent connections to the hierarchy. He told me: "I understand you are about to do something revolutionary during the service." He hinted that he had been tipped off. When I asked: "Who told you?" he just smiled. "Never mind," he said. "Let's just say that a little bird flew into my room and let me in on it."

Then the reporter pressed his case: "Will you go through with it if I train my TV camera on you?" "Hey, look," I retorted, "there will be nothing for you to film. We are just doing together what Christian believers have done for nearly two thousand years. I don't care what you do with your camera. As for me, I will do what I resolved in my heart to do."

I was glad that I had been warned, however. As I lined up with the communicants during the mass, I suddenly was caught in the blinding light of a TV camera. It was an act of brutal aggression. Although I knew who did it and why, anger still welled up in me. How did the press dare inject itself into both my worship of God and my personal relations with my fellow believers?

At that moment, I suddenly thought about the fact that the same glaring floodlights are standard equipment in the interrogation and torture of victims by all sorts of brutal oppressors. Since Christ suffers along with all of these victims, I reassured myself that blinding floodlights can have a legitimate place when we commemorate Christ's sacrifice. As I received the body of Christ on that occasion, I felt with all my being that I, too, was part of Christ's living body in our world today.

The joint worship service had a lasting impact on me. It also had brief repercussions. A few days after I returned to Argentina, I received a telegram from Geneva, Switzerland from the Lutheran bishop who headed the Lutheran World Federation. Obviously "my" Dutch reporter had done an outstanding job covering the events in Medellín for European viewers. The telegram read: "Urgently need an explanation on receiving holy communion at a Mass." Clearly, my ecumenical friends and I had upset not only some Roman Catholics. We had also ruffled a few Lutheran feathers. I sent a lengthy explanation of our action to the bishop, which apparently pacified him. The matter was laid to rest.

When we returned to the United States in December 1970, I was a changed individual. In large part, I felt Latino. I thought and reacted like a Latin American. I would bristle and get defensive when a disparaging remark was made about "my" South America or one of its countries. I also referred to "North America" and "South America" instead of just "America." Latin Americans consider them to be two distinct continents, not one.

Above all, I now understood better the reality of Roman Catholicism. I was still a firm disciple of Martin Luther, no doubt about that, and certain features of Catholic piety will always remain strange to me. But in some ways I could feel for the first time what it is like to be a Roman Catholic. I had experienced the vitality of a renewed Roman Church, a church that was renovated by the Second Vatican Council and then in Latin America by the Medellín Conference. This had happened in such a radical way that I could envision Martin Luther as a cheerful member of it.

Coming back to the United States in December 1970, as far as the visible church was concerned, I was an unbridled optimist. I felt that we would never go back into a dark past age. Things could only get better, more or less in a straight line. It was a heady time to be an active participant in Christ's global ministry.

Manfred in Parkersburg, 1971

12
HOMEWARD BOUND

"Then I will gather the remnant of my flock out of all the countries where I have driven them, and I will bring them back to their fold." (Jeremiah 23:3)

It was December 1970. We were on our way home for a sabbatical year in the United States. As we rode the shuttle from JFK to LaGuardia to catch a plane to Ohio, snow and ice covered the ground. Our children stared out of the bus window with curiosity and excitement. After five years in Argentina, Andrea and Chris did not remember a thing about their native land. They had been born in the United States, but that seemed so long ago. "How come people here are all so old?" Andrea blurted out.

Marianne's mother and stepfather were waiting at the airport in Dayton to pick us up. They had driven from Des Moines with a load of household items for our furlough home in Springfield, near the Wittenberg University campus. The temperature was below freezing, and they quickly bundled us into the heavy winter jackets, hats, and scarves they had brought along. We arrived at our new quarters, a comfortable two-story home provided for missionaries on furlough. After a couple of days to get reacquainted and catch up, our relatives said goodbye and returned to Iowa.

I had been invited to spend my furlough year at the Hamma Divinity School, a Lutheran seminary connected with Wittenberg University. The seminary president Dr. Fred Wentz was on the Board of Missions and had attended a conference I arranged in Buenos Aires. Through him, I was invited to teach at Hamma as a guest professor.

Although our children had completed the Argentine school year, we enrolled them in the local elementary school in the grades they had just finished. They spoke good English, but at this point they still felt more at home in Spanish. We decided it would not hurt them to review the same material in English in their new environment. Chris on his first day at school was astonished to discover that there were children who actually spoke English. Apparently that possibility had not occurred to him. Andrea had already commented on the shuttle bus from JFK, observing the drivers we passed on the freeway, that the United States is full of old people compared to Argentina.

We were coming home, yes. But it would not feel like a real homecoming. We did not return to the same country we left in 1965. I did not sense the "womblike warmth of America" so bitingly satirized by Norman Mailer in his book *The Naked and the Dead*. When the Israelites returned from exile in Babylonia, they found a Jerusalem that was vastly different from the one they remembered. So it was with me. I returned to a country profoundly different from the United States we had left.

In December 1970 the Vietnam war was roaring along in full furor. I had followed events from a distance in the Buenos Aires evening news and daily papers. But now I could see with my own eyes how this conflict had divided our people into two hostile camps. The bitter polarization that would accompany American political life for decades had begun. War supporters on the one side and resisters and draft dodgers on the other were unable to come to an agreement. Most could not even speak to each other.

Moreover, the country had been turned upside down by a cultural revolution that culminated in Woodstock in 1969. The norms of a straight-laced society were being challenged by the provocations of a new counter-culture. People resisted all sorts of authority. Long hair and a refusal to shave were visible male symbols of this rebellion. Student demonstrators paralyzed the operation of academic institutions, demanding participation in giving grades and running their schools. Marriage also had come under attack. Unbounded free love was to replace lifelong monogamous commitment between sexual partners. Drugs would supposedly create a feeling of personal liberation. The philosophy that underlay these experiments seemed to be: "Enjoy yourself! Be happy! Don't be so uptight!"

Frequently these two movements, the war protesters and the cultural rebels, made common cause. Together they had grown into a powerful political force that affected everybody. Even those in the middle who tried to keep out of the controversies could not escape their impact. Eventually the war in Vietnam would come to an ignominious end. The troops coming home felt humiliated and the whole country was demoralized. But there was one thing on which everybody agreed: Such a disaster should never occur again.

This was the context into which we stepped from Argentina. As I began to teach, I was impressed by the good faculty at Hamma. I felt a genuine respect for my colleagues. Most became good friends. But I could see that the seminary was floundering in the new cultural context. The varied, apparently mutually exclusive theories and focuses among the faculty made them unable to come up with a clear direction they all could subscribe to.

Of course we were all wrestling with the same issue of how to bear a truthful witness to Christ's presence in our teaching. But the emphases differed. At that time TM, or Transcendental Meditation, was the "in" thing in American pop culture. I felt it was a watered-down form of a lay person's understanding of psychology. But now, TM methods began to pop up in seminary courses. No matter what the subject—systematic theology, New Testament, counseling, church history—the faculty would be constantly asking whether we were talking as "adults" or if "the child in us" was coming out. It was ridiculous.

The seminary president Fred Wentz simply could not get a handle on this frazzled mess. I was convinced that a clear and more solid theological view was badly needed at Hamma. In order to do my share, I offered him my expertise as a scholar of Luther's theology and reformation history. I would have been delighted to teach classes in these neglected areas. But I was brushed aside. There was no interest in such an approach. I was told that these subjects were woefully out of touch with the times.

Rather, I was supposed to contribute my knowledge of Latin American churches and Liberation Theology. Some of the new thinking that emerged in Medellín had already made its way to the United States. I was profoundly pleased about this widespread interest. When a leading Lutheran theologian made disparaging comments about the new trend, I sharply confronted him, to the delight of our assembled seminary community. I vigorously defended the demand that the church has to give a clear and

intentional preference for the poor in today's world. The eminent
visiting theologian was Dr. William Lazareth, who became a
friend years later when he was my bishop in New York City.

At the same time, I was aware of the danger of this mandate for
the poor. It should not be turned into the one foundation on which
the Church of Christ is built. Without being firmly anchored in
the saving acts of Christ himself, the faith community will lose its
sense of direction. In the twinkling of an eye, the church can
change from being the Body of Christ into the charitable service
department of any ideology that comes down the road.

This was evidently happening at Hamma. We no longer imparted
a clear witness to Christ to our students. One example: When
applying for a vacant position in an Ohio parish, one of our
graduates was asked to explain his understanding of the
sacraments. Apparently not equipped to deal with this basic
question, the young man coolly declared to the members of the
search committee: "This is not where it's 'at' for us. We are
beyond sacraments."

I was of course concerned about Hamma's future, but as a guest
professor I had limited influence. There was not much I could do
to avert the impending crisis. When I arrived, President Wentz
was already in a deadly struggle with the bishop of the Ohio
synod over the seminary's direction. Hearing disturbing feedback
from the congregations such as the incident described above, the
bishop was ready to pull the financial plug on Hamma. By
stopping the synod's support, he could let the school die. This is
what finally happened. Hamma eventually had to close its doors;
it was merged with Trinity Lutheran Seminary in Columbus.

Before this inevitable outcome materialized, I decided that I
would have to move on. The question was: Where? The original
plan was, of course, that after my furlough year we would return
to Argentina. My heart and all our worldly goods were still in

Buenos Aires. But an issue had arisen regarding my salary that was important to me. I told the board that I would gladly continue to serve in Latin America under one condition: That they pay me in Argentine pesos, not dollars.

This was part of my personal theology of liberation. The Presbyterians had already made such a change on their mission fields. They recognized that the economic injustice exemplified by missionaries who received dollars but paid their bills in devalued pesos had erected a wall of alienation between the Argentine religious personnel and the missionaries. I was tired of being dismissed by my colleagues as a well-paid "gringo." With the galloping local inflation, my income increased substantially every month that I was paid in American dollars.

At stake was not some supposedly irrelevant administrative detail. I really felt it was necessary to correct this policy of the Board of Missions which affected my credibility on the field. For their part, our board officials in New York refused to change established policy on all the mission fields just because of me. Consequently, I decided to quit. I said I would be happy to consider returning, if and when they changed their payment policy. Some years later, they did so. But by then my life had moved on.

I kept my eyes open for a teaching post after my year in Springfield was over, but none was available. In reality, I had never thought of myself exclusively as a teacher. As much as I enjoyed doing research and standing in front of a class, I always loathed the internal power struggles that seemed to haunt academic settings. My thoughts turned back to my primary profession, the parish ministry. It briefly occurred to me that perhaps it was time to return to Germany. My friend Dieter was now a pastor in Berlin, and he urged me to come. Fritz, who had suggested we come to the Palatinate in 1955, was also in Berlin and knew of an attractive parish vacancy there. But I felt such a move would be unfair to our children. Andrea and Chris had lived for five years in Argentina and were still strangers in their own country. For their sake, we had to stay put for a while longer in the United States.

I had remained on the Western Pennsylvania/West Virginia Synod's clergy roster of the LCA (Lutheran Church in America). My synodical president responded quickly when I told him about my interest in a vacant ministry position. Very soon I received a conference call from two gentlemen on the pastoral search committee of First Lutheran Church in Parkersburg. They were in need of a new pastor. I knew about that congregation; it was the largest and most prestigious Lutheran church in West Virginia.

One of the callers informed me by way of introduction that he was the owner of a well-known bread factory. Then he said that before pursuing the issue of my qualifications any further, he first wanted to know if I was a "revolutionary." I thought I knew what was on his mind. I told him: "It all depends on what you mean with 'revolutionary'. I am just coming from Latin America where they have real revolutionaries who are armed and occasionally kill people. I can assure you that I am not one of those." I sensed that the caller on the other end of the line was a bit impatient with my answer. "No, I am not talking about anything like that," he interjected. "Just tell me: Do you have a beard?" On that score, I could put his mind at ease. "No," I replied. "At the moment I have no beard."

This exchange was not entirely silly. Having long hair or a beard was a definite message in 1971. It identified those who promoted the values of the counter-culture as opposed to the established culture. At the same time, I was taken aback by the shallow superficiality with which this wealthy factory owner probed into the qualifications of his future pastor. But this did not deter me from accepting a call to his congregation.

When All Hell Breaks Loose

My ministry in Parkersburg was a definite challenge. There seemed to be a steady clash of personal values among the members themselves, not just with me. Quite a few church supporters were financially well off, but it was mainly "new" money. To me, the interests and cultural values of these people seemed unrefined and impractical, without much thought behind them. For example, there was the modern parsonage they had bought in an upscale neighborhood at the edge of town. The brick ranch-style house was surrounded by an extensive lawn that had to be mowed every week in order to keep a suburban close-cut look. Looks were important to my parishioners. The parsonage property, house and lawn, looked like an ad in a magazine.

Marianne was not comfortable in this setting. Although she loved the natural beauty of the state, she did not care for the pretentious vibe she felt in this river town bordering West Virginia and Ohio. She worried about the effect it would have on our young children. She saw how easily Andrea was drawn into the prestige of her role as the pastor's daughter in this tight-knit community, and she did not want her to grow up in an atmosphere of ingrown values.

West Virginia, 1972

I, on the other hand, persuaded myself that I could put up with this culture shock. It is all part of Christ's incarnation, I thought. When the Word became flesh, it also took on the values of ordinary people. I as their pastor should be able to take them on as well. In this sense, the parish ministry is always a demanding practice of the theology of incarnation. Whether we are in North America, Germany, or Latin America, parish pastors must work with the values of their parishioners, even when they do not personally share them.

In 1972, the second year of our stay in Parkersburg, the basement wall in our picture-book parsonage developed a serious crack. The wall abutted a small hill, and to avoid future water damage, the cost of a permanent repair would be substantial. At that time, pastors were just beginning to receive housing allowances instead of parsonage living quarters. My immediate recommendation to the church council was to sell the house. I explained that if they would provide me with a monthly housing allowance from the parsonage sale proceeds, I could begin to build equity on my own. The response was unenthusiastic. No one wanted to get involved in such a new project.

Thus, on my own, I found a potential buyer willing to put up a hefty down payment, even with the crack in the basement, because of the house's prime location and the price I quoted. Released from the need to do urgent and costly repairs on the parsonage, the congregation could not refuse the offer. After the sale, I was given a modest housing allowance that enabled us to buy an old two-story house closer to the center of town. Our children reacted to this further change in their environment by informing us that the house we bought was haunted by ghosts. Maybe so. At least it was within walking distance of the church.

I spent a lot of time in local hospitals. One of my predecessors, a certain Pastor Schwegler, was remembered by many with great love although he was an autocrat of the old school. Schwegler, I learned, had a sleeping problem. He would get up between four and five o'clock in the morning, and not knowing what to do with himself, would begin calling on as many sick people as he could rouse in the hospital at this early hour. He would bring each one a copy of last Sunday's church bulletin. Although a few complained to me that he had interrupted the last hour of sleep they were able to snatch in their hospital bed, the general opinion was one of admiration. Unaware of his insomnia, they praised his tireless efforts as "such a dedicated pastor."

I felt I was under pressure to live up to the almost impossible visitation standard set by Pastor Schwegler. I did not disturb the early morning routine in our hospitals, but I made it a point regularly to visit our sick and to bring communion to all of our homebound people. It was a long list and quite a work load. There were occasions when I wondered whether I spent enough time with the healthy in our congregation.

First Lutheran Church had a strong Sunday School program. Dr. Bob, a local physician, was its devoted superintendent. Robert Fankhauser was a good family doctor and in many respects an ideal Christian. He had a deep love for his Lord Jesus that was rivaled only by his deep love for our children and youth. He wanted to keep them out of trouble at any cost. With his simple pietism, Dr. Bob used the Sunday School to warn our young people against the dangers of sex. He insisted on teaching the high-school class himself. With his solid background in medical education, he was an excellent resource and taught our teens a lot. However, in his good-natured naivité he never suspected the real reason for the fact that his class was always so well attended. It was obvious to me as an observer that our youngsters were learning from him how forbidden acts are done, without getting into trouble by having to experiment themselves.

1972 was the year of the Watergate break-ins. Senator George McGovern of South Dakota was running as the Democratic candidate in that year's presidential election, attempting to drive the incumbent President Richard Nixon out of the White House. It was a vitriolic struggle. Both sides fought with fierce determination. On June 17, five men were arrested for breaking into the offices of the Democratic National Committee in the Watergate office complex in Washington, D.C. The president immediately distanced himself from this debacle, denouncing it as a botched and unprofessional crime by some misguided individuals. He declared that an investigation would have to wait until after the November election. I was incensed, and I did not understand the equanimity with which most Americans accepted this blatant disregard of democratic due process. I felt as if someone had just slapped me in the face.

The issue about which people fought most bitterly in the 1972 election was the Vietnam War. This tragic conflict had ballooned into a controversy of great ethical proportions. McGovern urged voters to bring the troops back with the message: "Come home, America!" Nixon supporters called McGovern a wimpy coward and mocked him with the slogan: "George, come home to America!" Similar arguments would be used later against the Democratic candidates in 2004 and 2006 during the Iraq war.

Some things never change, it seems. The futility of the Vietnam bloodbath was painfully evident every night on the evening news, where the senseless sacrifice of human lives, both American and Vietnamese, was shown. I tried very hard to practice self-control in my preaching, although I felt more than once like shouting from the pulpit: "Stop this senseless massacre!"

I felt particularly desperate on Christmas Eve 1972, when Nixon widened the circle of violence by ordering the bombing of Cambodia. For me there was no question as to what our crucified and resurrected Prince of Peace expected from us. How could I preach "Peace, peace, peace" in this circumstance? On the other hand, I did not want to spoil the family celebrations of a joyful

Christmas for my congregants, either. I contented myself with preaching a traditional Christmas sermon. But I felt like an Old Testament prophet who had the word of God burning like fire in his guts. On the Sunday after, I no longer could hold it in. The text of the first scriptural reading was a strong passage on peace from Isaiah. I used it in my sermon to criticize the insane war. One of the congregants responded by sending me a communion card on the offering plate with the scribbled words: "Please do not criticize President Nixon or his foreign policy. I, like many Americans, voted for him." I was not unhappy about this comment, and I would have loved to talk personally with the individual. Since I had no way of knowing who it was, I opened my sermon the next Sunday with the following sentence: "I do not think we have a foreign policy that can be rationally discussed at this time." Then I concentrated on exploring the meaning of the text appointed for that day. That seemed to take care of it for the most part.

In these struggles, however, I experienced time and again the presence of the living Christ. At First Lutheran in Parkersburg, the Lord continued to unite us in spite of our political and ideological differences, through his good news and through his sacraments. My life was greatly blessed by unusual friendships we could form with some wonderful people. Again and again, our common worship proved to be a vital source of strong renewal.

Some of my new acquaintances were real surprises. This is always a great reward of parish ministry. A pastor meets all sorts of strange individuals, and we often come to love them even though they seem altogether weird. I fondly remember a couple named Martin and Ruth who, after an absence of many years, came back to join our congregation again as full members. "We want you to know," they said, "that we are members of a charismatic group. We have met the Lord Jesus personally. We now speak in tongues." Out of respect for me, they asked: "Is this a problem for you?" I answered that I had no objection to their

When All Hell Breaks Loose

new spiritual adventures. I said: "I myself do not speak in tongues, and I do not believe that I am missing out on a vital spiritual gift. But I rejoice for you in the encouragement you seem to receive from it. We will gladly welcome you as members of our community on one condition. You must not assume that your spiritual gifts are superior to those of the rest of the congregation, just because you pray to God in tongues." They consented, and became faithful members of our church. I always enjoyed seeing Martin in front of me with his bible open while I preached. He was my most attentive hearer, checking every bible reference I made. If he did not agree with any of my points, I could be sure that he would insist on discussing them with me.

The rock musical "Jesus Christ, Superstar" had just become a big hit. I was riveted by it. For me, it pulled together all the deeply conflicting forces of those tumultuous years. Nixon was reelected on November 7, 1972 in a landslide. The war in Vietnam raged on with unabated fury. The full truth about the scandal of the Watergate break-ins was stuck somewhere; it did not seem to come into the open. Along with my strong faith in Christ, the sarcasm expressed in this new musical was one way I, and many others like me, could honestly react to this unbelievable situation.

Produced in 1970, Tim Rice and Andrew Lloyd Webber's immensely popular musical tells the story of Jesus' final week in Jerusalem up to his crucifixion. Like many earlier Passion narratives, it does not bear witness to Christ's resurrection. I had no serious problem with ending the story of Jesus in this stark manner. With my Lutheran theology of the cross, I could let myself go and fully identify with the texts and melodies by Rice and Webber.

"Jesus Christ, Superstar" highlights the political and interpersonal struggles between Judas Iscariot and Jesus. Judas is depicted as a conflicted, tragic figure. But here he is a thoroughly believable human being rather than the demonic tool of the devil he has been traditionally portrayed as. Twentieth-century attitudes and sensibilities pervade the lyrics. A lot of contemporary slang is used, and ironic allusions to the political power struggles of the times are scattered throughout. This is how the author and composer had gotten their hooks into me.

This musical was followed the next year by a second rock opera, "Godspell," by Stephen Schwartz and John Michael Tebelak. "Godspell" opened off Broadway on May 17, 1971 and quickly became popular. But it was "Jesus Christ Superstar" that really attracted the wrath of fundamentalist Christians on the religious right. They were scandalized that Jesus had been depicted as a man, not as God, and that the resurrection was ignored. Precisely these features appealed to my Lutheran sensibilities. I used some portions of this musical in my 1973 Lent services. It was the first time that guitars were heard in First Lutheran's sanctuary, an "abomination" that former Pastor Schwegler had vowed never to permit. Except for some minor grumbling by a few elderly members, I survived that transition into the new era as well.

One Sunday afternoon in the spring of 1973, as I was waking up from a nap, Marianne asked: "Have you seen this ad in the new 'Lutheran' magazine? A congregation in California is searching for a pastor. That's unusual for the 'Lutheran.'" I grumbled a sleepy reply: "What do you mean, an ad for a pastor? That's against the rules! Vacancies go through a process." But there it was. University Lutheran Church at Stanford University had an ad for an experienced and innovative "spiritual leader" as they called it (avoiding the term 'pastor', I noticed). This intrigued me. At Marianne's urging, I answered the maverick ad. I knew how anxious she was to get out of Parkersburg, but I had no intention of leaving so soon; we had been there barely two years.

A short time later, I received a detailed list of questions from California. This was apparently sent to all applicants for the position. I loved the questions. They were so timely and to the point that I felt a need to respond to them. Later, I found out that I was one of around sixty applicants for the dual position of Lutheran campus pastor at Stanford University and pastor of University Lutheran Church in Palo Alto. Some telephone conference calls followed, after which I was asked to come to Palo Alto for a job interview.

A couple named Doug and Gisela picked me up at the San Francisco airport. This was again a different world. The palm trees everywhere reminded me of Mexico. The brilliant, glaring sun almost blinded me. As we sped along the bumpy Highway 101 in a Volkswagen bus, I was overpowered by the strong colors of the flowers and bushes along the road.

Doug was a young Stanford engineering professor. Gisela was an attractive, petite blonde originally from Hamburg. It felt good to speak fluent German again with her. They had three sons, and they were strong members of the congregation. I would stay in their home in Mountain View, a town just south of Palo Alto.

That evening I held a brief vesper service in ULC's modern round sanctuary, after which they had a potluck dinner in the parish center. The participants were mainly graduate students with young families. There were also some townspeople, a few undergraduate students, and two or three professors. It was a lively, interesting group, and they had a lot of questions for me. I was particularly struck by the simplicity of the foods they had brought. The array of salads with hardly any meat dishes was in stark contrast to the casserole–heavy potluck meals served at First Lutheran in Parkersburg. It was certainly a healthier selection than I had been used to.

University Lutheran, or ULC, was affectionately called "Uni Lu" by most members and "Luni U" by a few. Although it was across the street from the campus, the congregation was not officially connected with Stanford University. Its ministry was heavily subsidized by the national Lutheran church. As a congregation with an ever-shifting membership, it had difficulty making ends meet. They constantly had to scrape around for money, in contrast to my wealthy, stable Parkersburg congregation. It would mean a life of limited means, if not outright poverty, for our family in a very expensive area. The young people at Stanford may have had few financial resources, but they definitely had the spirit, and this Lutheran campus ministry post was one of the most prestigious in the country. When I was chosen by "Uni Lu" to be their next pastor, I could not resist. With Marianne's relieved blessing, I accepted the call.

In the summer of 1973, after only two years in Parkersburg, we said a regretful goodbye to a somewhat shell-shocked First Lutheran Church and drove across the country to California. As so many had done before us, we were on the long trek west. I was firmly convinced that this was what Christ expected from me. Of course I wondered where the future might ultimately take us, and I was deeply worried about the inner makeup of the United States. Nixon continued undisturbed in the White House. There seemed to be no one who would, or could, get him out. I did not understand how the Americans could go about their business so calmly and confidently. This is the one question that many a foreign-born observer will raise: "Why don't the Americans rise up and do something about it?"

After several days on the road we came to Salt Lake City. Here, the vastness of this land really hit home. As I was swimming with our children in the motel pool, it finally dawned on me. I thought: "The people of this country move in their own direction as they see fit—perhaps slowly and in a clumsy manner, but they do it with or without their presidents. This is indeed a huge country. Surprisingly, they usually manage somehow to end up on the right track ." I was coming home. I had begun to discover the unique secret in the soul of the average American.

When All Hell Breaks Loose

Manfred at University Lutheran Church

13
NO LASTING CITY

"For here we have no lasting city, but we seek the city which is to come." (Hebrews 13:14)

First there was the fantastic climate. Moving from West Virginia to Palo Alto, California in July 1973, we discovered a world where the sun was always shining. Seldom did it rain. The scenery in the Bay area was breathtaking, with a wide variety of shade trees and brightly colored flowers. Every evening a blanket of fog rolled in from the Pacific Ocean across the San Andreas mountains, cooling everything down.

Stanford University's main-quad architecture—beige arcades and red tile roofs—blends harmoniously with the yellow hills of the aptly named Golden State. The main entrance to the campus is

Palm Drive. It extends an elegant welcome to visitors, leading up to the Romanesque-style Memorial Church, designed and built by Mrs. Leland Stanford in memory of her husband. The Hoover Tower, visible from far and wide, is a monument to Stanford's most famous alumnus Herbert Hoover. Besides the Hoover Archives, the tower houses the Hoover Institution of War and Peace, a conservative think tank.

Stanford is one of America's elite universities. It thinks of itself as the "Harvard of the West." It has world-famous medical and business schools. It houses superb research institutes, and it is a leader in many of the sciences. As a result, the people you meet there are usually fascinating individuals. Most are endowed with an exceptional IQ. In the fall of 1973, just as the Silicon Valley technology revolution was beginning to change the world forever, I found myself in an academic paradise. I had made it to the top level in scholarly America.

University Lutheran Church was right across the street from the campus. The round sanctuary had a hexagonal roof topped with a tall sky-lit steeple. My first pastoral act was to move the altar from one side of the room to the center. I rearranged the moveable chairs in circular rows around it, so that people could see each other. The organ and piano remained to one side. The sanctuary walls were clear glass, allowing the congregation to see the lush plantings of bushes and flowers around the building.

A roofed walkway led from the sanctuary past a central lawn to a seminar building housing a lounge, a large meeting room with a stone fireplace, a full kitchen, and two offices. A small parking lot was adjacent to the lawn. The property provided an attractive and gracious setting, inviting visitors to come in and worship a friendly God. Afterwards they could chat with the pastor and congregants over coffee and cookies in the seminar building.

My congregants were a talented and spirited bunch. It was an unusual worshiping community. Besides the graduate students, many of them married with young children, we had a number of professors and quite a few local professionals, mainly engineers who had graduated from Stanford years ago and stuck around to work in the new computer-related industries that were springing up everywhere. On Sunday morning our graduate students were hungry for a break from their lectures and the high-pitched, highly competitive environment they had to endure. Our weekly eucharistic celebrations were joyful events. Occasionally someone would bring in a lively new hymn or song and we would run with it. Members wrote liturgies and formed a jazz combo to accompany our so-called "Blues Mass," brought to us from the University of Illinois by a transfer student.

Already in those days there was a lot of wealth in the Bay Area. This was a challenge to my faith. I met and made friends with a Methodist minister named Joe Hardegree who was a convinced Marxist. Joe's theological and ideological convictions were quite out of the ordinary, and he had given up his pulpit to drive a taxi. One day he told me that as a campus pastor at Stanford, I was "in the belly of the beast." I found no fault with his analysis; in fact, I had to agree with him. I was at the nerve center of what made America tick. But different from Joe's ideological stance, I was confident that my strong faith in the risen Christ would support me even in this setting. I knew for certain that even in "the belly of the beast" we do not have "a lasting city."

I was hankering for the opportunity to teach a seminar on campus in Latin American Liberation Theology. But my inquiry resulted in a harsh rebuff from William Clebsch, chair of the religion department. He informed me that established policy precluded any religious practitioner—any active priest or pastor—from teaching a Stanford class. There was no room for "outside proselytizers" (his words). As a parish pastor, I was not allowed entry into the exclusive circle of the faculty. The pat rejection was unfair and it hurt. I clearly had no place in this closed academic hierarchy.

What I did not fully appreciate at the moment was that the risen Lord did not want me as a teacher in this sophisticated context, but indeed as what I was, a "practitioner." I had run into one of those roadblocks that force us in a direction we do not anticipate. This happens to the best of us. We need only to consult the scriptures for examples. As the Apostle Paul traveled through Phrygia and Galatia, his original plan was to go north from there (Acts 16:6). But "they were held back by the Holy Spirit from speaking the word in the province of Asia." Christ had different designs on them. Instead, they were sidetracked into making a jump to Macedonia. This is how they brought the gospel from Asia to the European mainland. I believe that something of this sort happened to me at Stanford. The Lord had plans for me which differed from my own inclinations at the time. I was needed as a pastor, to be engaged in concrete action in some specific situations.

The decade of the 1970s was a bewildering time. At the beginning, once again "all hell broke loose." Although the war in Vietnam was winding down, student anti-draft protests were still a familiar feature of campus life across the country. Every night Walter Cronkite concluded the bad news from Vietnam with his famous "And that's the way it is on this ..." (giving the broadcast date). The handwriting was on the wall. Soon it would be over, one way or another.

I was still filled with optimism. After the military fiasco in southeast Asia ended, I hoped that North American journalists would be smart enough to train their cameras on the unspeakable living conditions in Latin America. It was time to challenge the nation not to another military adventure but an all-out war on poverty. I was naive enough to assume that the American people with their generous nature would respond to the call for such a peaceful campaign. I failed to understand the depth of the ideological obsession on the part of many people about the struggle against communism. It was apparently more than just a political war. It was a sacred duty. The fight against the "evil empire" of darkness had become a religious obligation transcending any political, economic, or other reason. It summoned their personal commitment on an emotional level that cannot be rationally explained.

Because of this fixation, the Vietnam War had ripped open a deep rift in the American soul that produced an irreconcilable hostility between the peace-lovers and the warrior-types. With the latter, I sometimes encountered sentiments I was familiar with in the fascists of my youth. I recognized these pseudo-religious forces as dangerous, and I resolved to fight them as a pastor. It was unfortunate that these poisonous tensions never really healed. Long after the war in Vietnam was over, animosity between the "doves" and "hawks" flared up again during the war in Iraq.

When we arrived at Stanford in the fall of 1973, revelations about the Watergate scandal were shaking the moral foundations of America to the core. Two weeks after I started as the new Lutheran pastor on campus, a protest march made its way from the Inner Quad, the serene center of the university, down beautiful Palm Drive and on to City Hall in downtown Palo Alto. The protesters called for the impeachment of President Nixon. All the university groups, student clubs, political and social organizations took part, both professors and students.

I was happy to march along with the rest. But then I noticed a young man walking all by himself. He was apparently shunned by the others. He was a skinny little guy wearing a blond wig. What he lacked in height was compensated for by the enormous size of the sign he carried. "GPU FOR IMPEACHMENT" it said. I had no clue what to make of it. I was, however, put off by the way people kept their distance from him. I thought: "Aren't we in this together? Don't we all want to see Nixon impeached?" I stepped up to him and asked: "So, what is GPU?" He explained: "Gay People's Union." Now the light went on. It was obvious why the other marchers were avoiding the strange little fellow. I was, however, still offended by this lack of solidarity, so I finished the march walking by his side in my clerical collar.

That is how I met Joel Roberts. Through him I was introduced to a new chapter in the great drama of human liberation. In due time I was to learn that our gracious God wants to free us from the hateful prejudices too many people harbor against our gay and lesbian fellow humans. This is a special form of "racism" that has to be overcome in the same way as the disgust some feel against Blacks, Jews, or independent women.

Those were heady years in many ways. The Vietnam War, the Watergate scandal, resistance to the draft, civil rights for the Blacks, and feminist liberation, all were dominant themes. In each of these struggles, one could sense a great optimism in the people. "We shall overcome," that glorious song of the civil rights movement, became the hymn used by everyone, whatever their cause might be. My cause, or call, was to preach the joyful news of Jesus Christ to those caught up in this American turmoil.

The air during our worship services was charged with the many tensions arising from these conflicts we were all facing. But I felt a strong encouragement coming from this university crowd. I felt they wanted me to take bold and provocative positions in my preaching on the different controversies. And I did. I tried very hard to make sure, however, that the joyful gospel of Jesus Christ was not drowned out by the war, the protest against apartheid in South Africa with its demand to cut our investments, the feminist struggle, or whatever else agitated our minds. Since I could not be sure that I always succeeded in getting this message across, I developed a new style of delivery. I ended each sermon with a time for questions and opposing views from my hearers. Besides being a way to break up the boredom of a long sermon, it allowed the assembled believers to take an active role in proclaiming God's saving word.

This worked extremely well. Among these articulate individuals there were always some who gladly made use of this opportunity. Problems only arose when someone turned the after-sermon period into a soap box from which to launch a diatribe on an unrelated issue. And then there was Dr. Willy Hermanns, a retired German professor who possessed a quaint charm in many respects, but was unfortunately prone to abuse the feedback period by reading lengthy poems he had written. Another troublesome case was Larry Hendrickson. Larry, a doctoral student in audiology, frequently used the occasion to unload his personal depression on the rest of the community. Aside from such self-centered derailments, however, we managed to have lively exchanges where the participants brought Christ's message into their personal lives, or conversely, their lives to Christ.

It was natural that my preaching would be rejected by some. One example was a professor from South Africa who was working on a project in the Hoover Institution. His wife was German. After a few visits to our worship, they stopped coming. When I asked why, the wife with typical German bluntness let me have it. "During the Hitler regime," she declared, "the Nazis came into our churches in full uniform with their swastika flags. They used our worship for party propaganda. You are doing the same thing, except from the opposite side of the spectrum."

That was not a fair accusation. We had neither uniforms nor flags. Nor did we engage in partisan politics. But unintentionally, this lady had hit upon an important truth in my life. There was a big flaw in my theology. Since I came to a strong faith in Christ by rejecting the ideology of fascism, I had never found a way to apply Christ's command of "loving our enemies" to the Nazis. This strong anti-fascist prejudice was bound to show up in my preaching. I felt no need to hide it or apologize for it. People who are put off by that are not necessarily themselves fascists. But I suspect that they want a neutral God who takes no sides in any of the conflicts between good and evil. They have not yet come to an understanding of what God's prophets are all about.

On Sunday mornings I engaged in structured teaching as well as preaching. After worship and a short coffee hour, I would conduct a bible study. At first we worked our way through the twelve minor prophets. Then, as an expression of the great turmoil being felt by all of us, our students insisted on a study of John's Revelation. They wanted to know: Is this book a prediction of the end of times that we are experiencing now? What else can we make of the wild symbols and images portrayed by John?

This was a great learning opportunity for me. For the first time in my life, I realized that the obscure author of Revelation had been through a situation very similar to mine when all hell broke loose. In my case, it was when Dresden went up in flames. In his case, it was captivity in a Roman camp for political prisoners on the isle Patmos. In the chaos of a world breaking apart, he encountered the liberating presence of the living, risen Christ. This was the story of my life, too.

Joel, my gay acquaintance from the impeachment rally and parade, had turned into a regular visitor at our services and participated in our activities. His religious affiliation was not neatly defined—his background was Jewish, but he confessed to being something of a Buddhist. He appreciated the fact that our congregation accepted his sexual orientation without misgivings, and as we became better acquainted, he introduced me to the Gay People's Union, where I met a number of other homosexuals. At first I needed to overcome some emotional barriers that I myself did not fully understand. But as I got to know these students personally, I realized that most of them were very fine human beings.

One day Joel had a challenge for me. "I have to ask you for a big favor," he said as he came barging into my office. "We want to do a Gay Pride Week this summer with workshops, discussions, and seminars. I think we also should have a religious service. Will you help us?" "Of course," I replied, without hesitating. "At my ordination I made a solemn vow to preach the Gospel of Christ to anybody who is ready to hear it. Your people are no exception! How many attendees do you expect?" Joel answered: "Several hundred." I was taken aback. "Where are you going to put them?" I asked. "Our chapel does not hold more than a hundred." Joel corrected me: "That's where you come in. You have to get Mem Chu for us!" He was referring to Stanford Memorial Church. This beautiful sandstone building with wide marble steps leading up to a high domed altar is the nondenominational university church, centrally located next to the university president's office.

Stanford Memorial Church

My friend Robert Hamerton-Kelly, a native of South Africa and a Methodist, was the dean of Mem Chu. He swallowed hard as he listened to my unusual request to use his elegant sanctuary for a Gay Pride worship service. "You have to understand," he observed, "I could not personally take part in such an event because of my official position at the university. But I do not want to turn down the request of a fellow pastor. Sure, go ahead. But you will have to be in charge."

The Gay Pride service was a deeply moving experience for all of us who participated. Several other campus pastors took part, and the founder of the predominantly gay Metropolitan Community Church preached an excellent sermon. I had volunteered to be in charge of the confession and absolution. In order to dramatize the weight of our sins, I dragged a heavy iron chain on my shoulder to the altar and let it drop unceremoniously on the marble steps with a loud clang. A number of gay attendees told me afterwards how much they had been affected by this symbolic action.

Some weeks after this experience, my friend the dean remarked: "By the way, Manfred, your gay service cost Stanford University a million dollars. As news of it got out, some of our conservative donors stopped their financial support." But I felt no remorse. My only comment to him was: "If anyone has to lose a million bucks, let it be Stanford. They are rich enough. They can absorb the loss." Bob Hamerton-Kelly laughed. I had the feeling that he silently agreed with me.

Because I occasionally dropped in at the Gay People's Union, I became known in the gay community as a clergy person who didn't have "hang-ups about homosexuals." Time and again, lesbian and gay couples with no affiliation to our congregation came and asked me to marry them. I appreciated them as intelligent, sensitive human beings, and I certainly understood their desire to be united with their life partners in a formal way. I hated to disappoint them, but at that time I had to tell them: "I cannot help you with what you want—a marriage that is respected and honored in our society." On the other hand, I recognized that Holy Scripture does not reject faithfulness between people who love each other. Much to the contrary, God's Word promotes and supports such faithfulness. So, after discussing the issue with my church council, I devised a series of liturgies similar to our standard weddings and performed them for couples at my discretion. However, I always made it clear that these were not marriages but "covenants of fidelity."

"Uni-Lu" did not have a parsonage, and we had found ourselves looking for housing in one of the richest neighborhoods in America. As a result of the new electronics boom in Silicon Valley, real estate was already soaring out of sight. (Joe Hardegree was right, we were sitting in the belly of the beast.) For the first year we rented a small house in Palo Alto while we looked for a place to live that we could afford on a pastor's salary. With a loan from the National Campus Ministry in Chicago and proceeds from the sale of our Parkersburg house, we managed to pull together a down payment on a small older home near the Hewlett-Packard firm. This depleted all our financial resources. Marianne was able to land a half-time job as a library assistant in the university archives; later she worked full-time as a specialist in the music library. This was a financial life-saver during our nine-year stay.

Our humble home in Barron Park on Georgia Avenue had two distinctive and unexpected features that we could put to good use in my pastoral ministry. One of the former owners had been a cement contractor with an apparent distaste for yard work. He had paved over all the outside areas, front and back, and built an in-ground swimming pool in the rear yard. In addition, behind the house there was a large circular barbeque pit made of stone and cement. I immediately saw the potential here. For a student congregation where most people lived in cramped quarters,

swimming and grilling in our backyard could provide an
additional opportunity for ministry.

Thus, every Monday evening we held open house. We invited
everyone to a swim and a Latin American "asado" (cookout).
Each one brought the grill item of his or her choice and a
beverage. Very quickly this became a highly popular event. All
sorts of individuals showed up: students and professors, straight
people and gay, harried professionals and worried job-seekers,
gifted artists and ordinary folk. The four-foot-wide grilling area
held every imaginable source of protein: hamburgers, hot dogs,
veggie burgers, fish, kabobs, various cuts of steak. While I kept
things sizzling over the coals, people cooled down in the pool or
just sat and talked. The small children of graduate-student parents
came in and out for short intervals, dripping wet, while the adults
got into issues that troubled their minds. Topics ranged from deep
theological concerns to travels in the world, from problems in
personal relations to the shifting sands of politics. In the free flow
of ideas we were able to do a surprising amount of ministry with
one another. It was a lived fellowship, a true example of
Christian community.

All during this time, I continued to search for new ways of
reaching out to the diverse Stanford population. It was a tricky
proposition. For the most part, they were fast-paced individuals
with widely diverging interests. On occasion I would put on my
clerical collar, swing myself onto my bike, and ride over to the
campus. I would "hit on the dorms" unannounced. I knocked on
doors in the undergraduate dormitories, interrupting surprised
students at their computers. I would introduce myself and simply
invite them to our University Lutheran Church.

I also established a visible presence at the Stanford Coffee
House. This remarkable establishment was located in the middle
of campus and served the best European-style coffee available at
that time in the area. In my clerical garb, I would place myself at

one of the long wooden tables and nurture a cup of delicious Viennese brew. This was to indicate that I was "open for business." I was not exactly swamped with comers, but it was always a pleasant surprise when one or the other found his or her way to sit down with me. In this non-threatening environment, people could join me for just a friendly chat or, at other times, to unload a troubling concern. On a few occasions I enjoyed some friendly theological sparring with physics Nobelist William Shockley, who also frequented the coffee house to enjoy its superb coffee and occasionally attended our worship service.

An opportunity to continue teaching in a regular classroom setting finally came when I was invited to give courses in Latin American Liberation Theology at the Pacific School of Religion in Berkeley, across the San Francisco Bay. A number of theological seminaries were located in Berkeley, including our Pacific Lutheran Theological Seminary as well as Roman Catholic and Episcopal schools of divinity. In a genuinely ecumenical venture, they had formed a new institute for graduate studies called the Pacific School of Religion. It was an ideal teaching venue for me. With my background in ecumenical relations in Argentina, I fit right in.

It was something of a paradox that Berkeley was also the home of the free-spirited University of California. There, people looked down on what they considered the "starchy conservatism" of Stanford. They reveled in their reputation as "Berkeley-Beserkley." During the Vietnam crisis, its students had famously staged even wilder anti-war riots than the Stanford kids. I enjoyed the freer spirit across the Bay, even as it allowed me to return to a more disciplined classroom style. In the course of my work among the seminarians there, I met several fascinating persons. One who stood out was Ellen Barrett, the first openly confessed lesbian to be ordained into the Episcopal priesthood by Bishop Paul Moore of New York. She was a gifted student and a delightful individual.

Back at Stanford, I maintained cordial relations with my Roman Catholic colleagues. Rev. John Duryea was the pastor of St. Ann's Church in Palo Alto and served as the university's Catholic chaplain. We quickly became good friends. This thin, aristocratic-looking priest was an enthusiastic backwoods hiker and exuded a dynamic charisma. One day he shocked the entire Palo Alto world when he announced from the pulpit that he would marry Eve, a divorced woman with two daughters. With great eloquence and compelling theological reasoning, he justified this unusual step using arguments from documents of the Second Vatican Council. In no time, of course, John was relieved of his church responsibilities. All his church benefits and pension claims were canceled. But his spirituality remained vibrant as he accepted the personal losses confidently, without any complaint. I admired him for his courage. There was no question in his mind whatsoever—he would continue his ministry as a Catholic priest even though separated from Rome and the local bishop. Along with a number of former parishioners who followed him from St. Ann's, he established a new ministry he named the Angelo Roncalli Community after Pope John XXIII.

I gave strong support to John Duryea in his revolutionary break with the hierarchy. It bore so many characteristics reminiscent of Martin Luther. I would gladly have accepted him and his people into the fellowship of Uni-Lu. But John was convinced that God still wanted him to be a "Catholic Priest." However, he gratefully accepted our invitation to use our facilities as the new spiritual home for his Angelo Roncalli Community. I was welcome to be with them as a guest preacher at any time, and we subsequently lived out our ecumenical commitment to the fullest. Until John's death 35 years later, this faith community continued to hold its worship at Uni-Lu every Sunday afternoon.

After the remarkable Gay Pride service at Mem Chu in the summer of 1974, Joel Roberts continued to be a permanent

presence in our community. He never became a Lutheran; he had
no use for justification by grace through faith or any other
abstract doctrine. His line was the Buddhist demand: "Be present
here and now!" He was for years our paid sexton, and he did far
more than take care of the grounds and buildings. He was also
our interior designer. Like a good housewife, he made our parish
rooms more livable by adding flower pots and other accessories.
Unfortunately, during the time of Joel's employ we lost one
congregational treasurer because he insisted on being paid "under
the table." This was more than that proper Palo Alto professional
could stomach.

One day Joel brought in an unkempt, wild-looking young man he
had picked up somewhere. His name was John Trauner. John was
a homeless alcoholic and drug addict who could no longer take
care of himself. Joel had taken him on as a legal ward. At first I
assumed there must be a sexual connection between them. But
this proved to be wrong. John was interested in women while Joel
was not. What motivated Joel, I felt strongly, was his altruistic
desire to take care of someone who was totally rejected by
everyone else, as Joel had been when his own father threw him
out at age fourteen. For Joel, it was genuinely what the bible
calls "agape."

Joel Roberts (right) and John Trauner

A problem surfaced for our faith community, however. Joel had assumed that we as confessing Christians would simply join him in this rescue operation without question. And gradually, but with reluctance, some members of our congregation did so. But during the week our parish rooms were being used by a day-care center, and I refused to permit John to sleep in the buildings. So people came up with creative concepts. First we permitted him to pitch a tent on the property. Then we acquired a wooden shed which we moved onto the parking lot. John was quite content to live there, particularly since Joel always provided him with bottles of cheap wine. Finally Joel could move him into an apartment elsewhere in the Bay area.

Marianne and I suspected that one of our regular worshipers, a man in his forties, was a pedophile trying to ingratiate himself with our younger boys. We sat down with our son Chris, now in junior high school, and explained the situation to him in detail. I did the same with our young mothers. I told one of them: "You are wise to stay alert. But to protect your two sons, be completely open with them. Tell them about pedophiles and warn them about the danger signs while they are still under your care. That is the best protection you can give them. This is what we are doing with our Chris. You know that he is the same age as your Tom." She was grateful for this advice, and the family stayed with the congregation. Chris, for his part, told us with obvious glee about the cat-and-mouse aspect of our pedophile member's ham-handed attempts to win his attention.

At this point, I think it is important to digress for a moment and reflect on my state of mind during that period in my life. When I began my ministry at Stanford, I was looking for concrete ways of how to transport Latin American Liberation Theology into

North America. In my weaker moments, I would secretly dream about the possibility of a socialist economy along the lines of Sweden, one that might bring the continent's north and south together into a profitable partnership for both. Had I ended up as a classroom professor, I would most likely have pursued this dream for many years. As it was, God steered me in a different direction. While the masses in Latin America need above all a just, broad-based economic liberation, people in the north need above all to free themselves from other enslaving forces. God showed me that after the hard-fought struggles for the civil rights of Blacks and women in our country, the time for justice and liberation from sexual discrimination and oppression has come. That is the main struggle now as I write in the second decade of the new century.

In the fourth and fifth centuries of the Christian era, theological leaders of the ancient church spent their efforts on the question: "Was Jesus God? And how could this be?" At best they could answer it only in part. But they gave us the Nicene Creed and some important doctrinal guidelines. In the Middle Ages, the leading question was turned upside down. Anselm of Canterbury wondered: "Why did God become man? (Cur deus homo?) And how could this be?" Again, some helpful doctrines were developed which can still serve as guidelines. But they only partially answer the question.

For faith in our times, the important question is: Was Jesus right? And why is he right for us? Does the story of Jesus reflect our own relationship with God? That is why Jesus simply tells us: "Follow me!" In the gospels, our Lord does not invite people into an ontological speculation about his being, i.e., whether he is God or man. Rather, he tells us to do the straightforward thing: to get up and follow him. In his Small Catechism, Martin Luther captures this dynamic by saying in his explanation to the second article of the Creed: "I believe that Jesus Christ, true God begotten of the Father, and true man born of the Virgin Mary, is my Lord." We simply have to follow Jesus as our Lord. Then things fall into place for us as believing Christians. As I tried to follow Jesus as my Lord, I was being led in ministry to some of society's most rejected human beings in the elegant setting of Stanford University.

The San Francisco Bay area is one of the most desirable locations in the United States. Marianne and I felt completely at home in its cosmopolitan atmosphere. The surrounding countryside with its magnificent redwood forests and dramatic Pacific coastline is breathtakingly beautiful. When we had been in Palo Alto for nine years, we seriously considered the possibility that we would stay there for the rest of our active lives. I could understand why some of my colleagues in ministry declared: "I'm ready to serve God anywhere in the world, as long as it is the Bay Area."

I hoped to make University Lutheran Church totally independent financially, if at all possible. As a constantly changing campus congregation made up of perpetually strapped members, "UniLu" had to be subsidized by the national Lutheran Church. To gain complete financial freedom would be a steep, perhaps impossible challenge. But it was a challenge that could excite me. "Sitting in the belly of the beast, but cutting the umbilical cord that connects us financially to that beast?" This held a strong appeal for me. And indeed, after a strong financial campaign, we were able to burn the mortgage held by the ELCA on August 17, 1980.

But by then, things in my personal life had begun to flip around in an unexpected manner. In the summer of 1978, our family had made a month-long visit to Germany. It was a dramatic return for me. I was especially touched by the joyful way my children had related to their cousins, aunts and uncles, and their German Omi (Grandma). I was also surprised at the warm reception I received from my former schoolmates in Hardegsen and Northeim, most of whom were now also established professionals. It had been twenty years since I spent any length of time in my home country. After we returned to California, I was suddenly gripped by a massive attack of homesickness.

During more than two decades of traveling filled with many exciting projects, I had not greatly missed Germany or felt the need to make frequent visits there. But now it hit me with full force. Was I homesick, or was it a midlife crisis? I was nearly fifty years old when out of nowhere, a strong elemental need arose that paralyzed the functioning of my mind. After two weeks of silent pain and grief, I couldn't hold it inside anymore. I poured out my heart to Marianne as we sat on a tree-shaded hillside above the San Andreas fault overlooking the long, narrow lake. It was a spot we often visited in the early evening. My sensible, emotionally balanced wife listened quietly, and then stilled the torrent of my tears and sobs with the simple statement: "If that's how you feel, maybe it's time to go back to Germany."

Immediately I realized the sense of this. "O.K., let's do it!" I responded, wiping my eyes. Then I added: "But I want to go to West Berlin. I want to be in the middle of things. I want to live in the city where the Wall shows the rupture that divides Germany and also the rest of the world." After nine years in the rarefied atmosphere of an elite university, I decided that this time I would seek a working-class parish. I needed a complete change. And as the Holy Spirit would have it, that is what I got.

When All Hell Breaks Loose

St. Thomas Church at the Wall, West Berlin, 1982

14
NO FUTURE, NO HOPE

"The hand of the Lord was upon me, and he brought me out by the Spirit of the Lord, and set me down in the midst of the valley; it was full of dead bones ... And he said to me, 'Son of man, can these bones live?' And I answered, 'O Lord God, thou knowest.' ... Then he said to me, 'Son of man, these bones are the whole house of Israel. Behold, they say, 'Our bones are dried up and our hope is lost; we are clean cut off.'" (Ezekiel 37:1, 3, 10).

I got off the train at Bahnhof Zoo (Zoo Station). It was New Year's Day--Friday, January 1, 1982. I had come with the "Interzonenzug," the train running through communist East Germany that connected West Germany with West Berlin. After Helmstedt there was a rigorous passport control by the "Vopos" ("Volkspolizei" or People's Police) when we crossed the border into what formerly was called the East Zone, now proudly

proclaiming itself to be the German Democratic Republic or
GDR, the State of Workers and Farmers.

The weather was gray and nasty. A cold drizzle fell, and piles of
dirty snow lay here and there. I was picked up at the railroad
station by two members of the church I would serve for nine
months on a sabbatical leave from ULC, St. Thomas in the
bohemian district of Kreuzberg 36. My chauffeur was Irmela
Mukurarinda, a member of the church council. She had brought
along Christiane Briesenick, the office secretary. Irmela was the
daughter of a Lutheran pastor in the GDR. She had left the East
after marrying an African from Uganda with whom she now had
three children; she was studying for the ministry in West Berlin.
Christiane was a divorcee with a teenage daughter.

We drove through the crowded streets of West Berlin in Irmela's
beat-up VW Beetle to my apartment in the parish building of St.
Thomas Church. Marianne had been forced to remain behind in
Palo Alto because of job obligations; she would join me in June.
Until then, I had to fend for myself.

I was definitely in a different world. I sensed that the American
code of morality did not apply here. Apparently a looser set of
norms shaped interpersonal relations. The provocative vibes
coming from red-haired Christiane made it clear that it would not
be hard to have sex with her that first night in town. She was
definitely open to an adventure. I wondered if anybody would
even raise an eyebrow. Still, I probably would have ruined my
ministry right then and there, before it even got off the ground.

As I walked the streets in those first days of 1982, everything
seemed to have a sharper, more aggressive edge. People
impressed me as being not just jaded and tired but edgy and
jumpy. I, however, felt elated. The wide sidewalks with their
worn paving stones brought back childhood memories of
Schoeneberg, the Berlin district where we lived when my father

was alive. I delighted in the sounds of the German language all around me, especially when it came from the light voices of children. In many ways, I was home again. But Thomas Wolfe had it right: "You can't go home again." West Berlin was now a foreign city to me.

The first thing I wanted to do was establish contact with the squatters in my parish area. I was not sure how many illegal houses there were, but Kreuzberg 36 was the center of West Berlin's alternative scene. I had found out from Irmela that the Mariannenstrasse 48 was a squatter building. So on that first evening of the New Year 1982, I decided to start there.

It was pitch dark as I stood in front of the squatter house, looking for a way to enter. The massive old oak door was tightly locked, and the house looked completely deserted except for some light on the fifth floor. There was no bell or buzzer. The five-story building seemed to be an impenetrable fortress on that cold wintry evening. Not knowing what else to do, I picked up some pebbles from the gutter and threw them at the one lit window with loud shouts of "Hello! Hello!" Finally it opened and a young man shouted down to me: "What's the matter? What do you want?" I yelled back: "I'm Manne" (a Berlin nickname for Manfred), "I'm the new parson down the street at the Mariannenplatz. I want to talk with you guys." He shot back at me: "Let me see! I've got to talk with the others first." Then the window went shut. After a moment he was back: "All right. Come on up!" He threw down a large brass key on a piece of string; it landed with a clank on the sidewalk.

After fumbling with the old lock, I pushed open the heavy door. I groped my way up a dark staircase littered with debris. A young man held open an apartment door on the fifth floor. Here I found a group of about fifteen men and women in a large common room. They were in high spirits, celebrating the birthday of one of their comrades. I was invited right away to share in the plum cake with bowls of whipped cream they were enjoying, and we quickly got acquainted with each other. They were intrigued by the fact that I had just arrived from the United States, and impressed that my first pastoral act was to visit them. Walter, whose birthday it was, became a good friend from then on.

The district of Kreuzberg has a character all its own. In 1982 it was a chaotic scene. Nothing seemed to fit or work as it properly should. The streets were populated with youthful punks sporting tattered clothes and outlandish Mohawk haircuts, as well as by Turkish women shrouding their plump figures in long shawls. Berlin-Kreuzberg had turned into "Little Istanbul" teeming with the families of Turkish guest workers. It also was home to a German alternative youth culture that literally believed in nothing anymore. They held this view with a passion. Their statement of faith was: "No Future, No Hope." Part of my mission was to be a Lutheran pastor for this motley crowd. I did not yet know how to do that. But the challenge of such a ministry had attracted me to this particular church.

The Berlin Wall was everywhere. It ran right through the parish territory of St. Thomas. The barrier was built in 1961 by the GDR government in order to stop the massive exodus of East Germans fleeing the glories of the Socialist revolution. One corner of our church building was just a few yards away from the ten-foot-high cement wall. High-spirited young people used the western side of the Wall as a screen for their creative and artistic urges. The entire construction was covered with spray-painted art. Some graffiti depicted surrealistic figures and symbols. Others consisted of clever slogans. My favorite was: "May we have another wall, please? This one is full."

Many of the original residents had fled the divided district years before, leaving behind abandoned stores and apartment buildings. With their departure, big construction firms took an interest in the properties left behind. The plan was to tear down the solidly built

When All Hell Breaks Loose

19th-century structures and replace them with "modern" housing units, i.e. flimsy buildings with amenities like elevators and central heating, but with smaller apartments and considerably higher rents. This project to destroy Kreuzberg's historic character had the blessing of the West Berlin Senate, which wanted to change the working-class district into an upscale one and attract more affluent residents.

St. Thomas Church at the Berlin Wall

This is what provoked the "Berliner Haeuserkampf" (Berlin house wars) of the 1970s and 1980s. In order to save Kreuzberg from destruction, young Germans moved into empty apartment buildings slated for demolition and occupied them illegally. The squatters were called "Hausbesetzer" (house occupiers). Filled with idealism, they followed the example of the Dutch Kraakers who pulled off similar illegal actions in Amsterdam, rescuing old buildings and neighborhoods from the rapacious appetite of corporate developers. Certain provisions in Germany's more liberal laws made it impossible for corporate owners to simply evict the youthful rebels. Thus, when I started out in January 1982, I faced a significant challenge: Twenty-five buildings in my parish area were illegally occupied by squatters.

Once again, all hell seemed to have broken loose. But this time it was not because my hometown Dresden was being devoured by an inferno. Now a historical West Berlin district was in danger of being destroyed because of the political upheavals of our times. In spite of all its youthful energy, Kreuzberg 36 had become a spiritual wasteland covered with dry bones. I felt like Ezekiel when he was asked: "Can these bones live?" Here I faced young Germans who had lost any hope for the future. Like Ezekiel, I felt like stammering: "O Lord God, thou knowest!" And yet, I wanted to be right there. With every fiber of my being, I wanted to be in the midst of all these "dry bones." No matter how scraped bare those bones appeared to be, I was convinced that this was where the risen Christ called me to be at that moment. I felt that all my previous experience was a preparation for this challenge.

Everyone in the district lived closely together with the Turkish families. They were Muslim "guest workers" employed in West Berlin factories. Most of them spoke little if any German and avoided assimilation. Surrounding these implanted elements of punks, squatters, and Turks were the "regular" working-class Germans who had remained when the Wall went up. Of course they were filled with bitter disappointment at the way things had gone in their district. I knew of no established precedents for this ministry, no proven methods of what should be done. There were no guarantees anywhere. Maybe there were no solutions at all. Perhaps the alternative punks had it right when they categorically declared: "No Future, No Hope!" The only force I had to go on was my faith in the resurrected Lord.

In addition to the outward social problems in my parish, St. Thomas was stuck with a colossal church building that nobody needed or wanted anymore. When the Wall went up in 1961, the congregation had been split in two and never regained its former strength. By the time I arrived in 1982, nobody had any idea what to do with the enormous brick structure with two bell towers and a round dome that rose some six stories into the air. Sitting majestically at the end of the Mariannenplatz, a large grassy square, the church dominated the whole neighborhood. It had been built by the Kaiser in the 19th century to seat three thousand worshipers; it looked more like a cathedral than a parish church. Now it sat unused during the week, and on Sundays there were at best twenty worship attendees. During cold weather, services were held in a large seminar room in the parish center, to save the cost of heating the high-domed sanctuary.

Although membership had shrunk drastically in recent years, St. Thomas was still a two-pastor parish. As I began my ministry, the first pastor Verena Janzen was in a psychiatric clinic. She had collapsed with a complete nervous breakdown just before Christmas. Originally she and I had agreed that I would assist her for nine months while I was on sabbatical leave from my campus ministry at Stanford University. But when she became ill, she left word that I should take over all her parish duties including the administration. She also gave firm instructions that she did not want to see me, a weird directive since I had to consult with her about handling the parish affairs. My response was: "Nuts! I want to see her. I have come too far for such treatment."

On the second day of January, a Saturday, I visited my ill colleague in the clinic. She was in a deplorable condition and summarily brushed me off. Subsequent visits confirmed my first impression that it would not be possible for me to work at her side. It was not just that she was being treated for alcoholism and agoraphobia. She had broken a promise to me that she would not resume a sexual relationship with a female member of our church council. I did not see how I could possibly develop any kind of a credible cooperation with her in these circumstances. Ministering to the demoralized and chaotic neighborhood was one thing. But being tied to an emotionally disturbed fellow pastor in addition seemed more than I could handle. With a heavy heart, I informed our district superintendent Gustl Roth: "Either Verena goes, or I go." Gustl's decision was immediate: "You stay, Manfred. I'll find another parish for Verena when the time comes."

This decision did not sit well with my new church council when they were told. Verena was not only popular with her lesbian lover, but also with her hand-picked council members. All had been faithful supporters of her ministry for years, and I was an unknown quantity. In order to find out whether I should in fact stay with them or return to Stanford University, I asked the council for a vote of confidence. I received an extremely weak nod. For the time being, they realized they had no other choice.

This disappointing reaction was not a great surprise. These lay leaders were representatives of an established German religious institution called the "Volkskirche" (people's church). It was supposed to take care of the basic religious needs of the population, but in reality most of my council members did not have strong spiritual concerns. They seldom attended worship services, and they had no spiritual preparation for the deep conflicts on our troubling scene. Their service was strictly of a political nature; they felt an obligation to represent and guard the interests of "normal" neighborhood residents in church affairs. The current social situation in the district left them in a state of total confusion.

At my first worship service on Sunday, January 3, 1982, not one member of the church council showed up. But as a result of my visit to their house on New Year's Day, three squatters from the Mariannenstrasse 48 came to worship. I was delighted. It looked like a hopeful sign for a new spiritual beginning.

Undeterred by the lack of support from my council, I charged ahead with whatever parish programs still functioned. On Tuesday afternoons a round of more or less 20 seniors gathered for coffee and cake in the seminar room of the parish building. They were loyal churchgoers. After prayers and a simple meditation, we would sing through the hymns for the coming Sunday. In addition, on one evening each week I met with a group of teenagers, usually all boys, in the parish hall. These savvy kids had no interest in a structured youth program; they just wanted to "hang out" and talk. They even began to show up more often than planned, usually when they felt bored at home, which was most of the time. The ringleader Freddy organized a crew to get castoff furniture for my bare pastoral apartment. They were delightful kids. I loved to share my faith with them.

Teaching Luther's Small Catechism in this environment was another new adventure. I had about a dozen confirmands. They, too, were bright, street-smart youngsters. A typical exchange at our first session went as follows: I asked, "What are we trying to do in confirmation class?" One of the urchins replied: "Pastor, don't get any wrong ideas! I for one do not believe in God." I then insisted: "So, what are you doing here?" The little smart aleck enlightened me: "I am here just for the moolah." At first I was stumped, until I learned that on the day of their confirmation, these youngsters could expect to receive an amazing amount of money from their various relatives in spite of the general poverty in our area. Their aunts and uncles lacked the imagination to come up with a meaningful present for the confirmands and gave them cash instead. The total amount could easily exceed one thousand D-Marks. The kids did the math, dividing this amount by the number of hours they had to sit it out with the pastor. That translated into more than 25 D-Marks per hour. It would be a long time before they earned an hourly wage as high as this.

Thus, these bright little devils willingly showed up for an hour of instruction each week. Of course their parents never came to church, although this was contrary to the vows they had made at their children's baptism. Yet, more than once I was told by an authoritarian father: "Just let me know if he causes you any problems, Pastor! I'll straighten him out with the belt." This was, of course, the exact opposite of the educational methods I had in mind. I was challenged to use all my creative instincts to come up with a teaching style that could crack open the hard crust of the petrified materialistic outlook held by both children and parents. In a few cases, I believe I even managed to succeed.

Manfred and his St. Thomas Confirmation Class, 1984

One of my confirmands, Claudia, was a lovely girl of about fifteen. She was deeply spiritual. At the end of our catechetical course, she came and asked me to be excused from the actual confirmation. She explained: "Afterwards we would have a big party with my family, and my dad will get drunk again and start beating up on my mother." What could I say? I did not press her.

The day of confirmation presented quite a spectacle. The families of the confirmands appeared in full force with all the aunts and uncles. It was obvious by their comportment that none of these adults were churchgoers. They felt clearly uncomfortable in the strange sanctuary environment and made up for this discomfort by engaging in loud talk. Some even rolled up the printed programs with the liturgy and hit each other over the head with them. Here you saw the Volkskirche at its worst. It had nothing to do with the worship of God. The confirmation service was not an affirmation of their children's baptism. It was simply a rite of passage by which the teenagers took a big step into adulthood.

This sad commentary on the reality of the "People's Church" really got to me. After this experience, I let out my anger in one of the pastor's columns in our parish newsletter. I went after those who use the church as a personal "Beduerfnisanstalt" (toilet). I said: "They do their business and satisfy their needs; then they walk away without giving it another thought." Of course my diatribe did not do much good and some parishioners were upset by my comment. But I felt better afterwards.

In our worship life, I looked for ways to introduce the unique style of preaching I had developed at Uni-Lu in California. My desire was to practice the same kind of dialogical sermons with my Kreuzberg congregation that I had with the Stanford students. I hoped to take up provocative and challenging positions while providing them with an opportunity in the middle of the service to respond with their own opinions. I sensed that these Berliners would be open to such a spontaneous approach. But I felt it could not be done effectively in our large sanctuary. What had seemed natural in the intimacy of our Stanford chapel was unfeasible in the enormous, echoing nave of St. Thomas Church.

So I came up with an alternative. I found a catchy, though long, German name for it: "Predigtnachgespraech" (after-sermon discussion). I preached provocative sermons, and immediately after the service everybody was invited to a coffee hour in the parish center. There we would discuss the message I had given and how it related to events taking place in our city or around the world. After-church coffee hours were a novelty there at that time, and the result was astounding. We had lively discussions that often stretched into the afternoon. It was gratifying to see that we were attracting a growing number of new churchgoers, many of them young professionals and university students.

Before long, the after-church meetings became so popular that we decided to add a second session on Wednesday nights. The purpose was not to react to the previously preached sermon, but rather to take a look at the upcoming texts. We used another humongous German word to describe the Wednesday sessions: "Bibelgespraechskreis" (bible-study group). We studied the lectionary readings proposed for the next Sunday and then argued with each other about its meaning in our given situation.

This method came straight out of liberation theology. In exactly the same manner, the "comunidades de base" (base communities) in Latin America studied the bible in order to analyze and understand their political and social situation. They wanted to find tools for overcoming the forces that oppressed them, using God's Word. In the same manner, I wanted to create a Christian base community of committed believers at St. Thomas through the after-church and Wednesday-evening discussions.

To my delight, it worked very well. After a few weeks, we were joined by a bearded young man in blue overalls who introduced himself simply as Christian, a mechanic. But he surprised me time and again with surprising contributions to the discussions that betrayed a sharp analytical sense of theology. When I confronted him with my suspicion that he was more than a toolmaker, Christian Herwartz admitted that he was a Jesuit worker-priest employed in a nearby factory.

In good liberation-theology fashion, I preached God as the champion of the poor and oppressed. This emphasis was appreciated by the people in my budding "base community." The depressing conditions in our neighborhood made them realize that they were also engaged in a struggle for liberation. This viewpoint agreed well with Martin Luther's theology of the cross, which emphasizes the joyful news of God's grace for "losers" rather than a show of success for "winners." Occasionally my radical sermons would bring a mild rebuke from my good wife Marianne. With her Episcopal distinction between discipleship and priesthood, she often complained that I as a Lutheran put far too much emphasis on Christ's cross and not enough on the Easter message.

Although I tried hard, in spite of all my efforts I failed miserably to gain any support for the revolutionary ideas of Karl Marx. The brutal reality of the East German form of socialism was too close for most of our members. They were simply overwhelmed by it. People had no patience for the finer points of Marx's philosophy. Even the young punks in our neighborhood had absolutely no interest in such tedious political analyses. These kids were anarchists. As such, they passionately rejected any structure or discipline, from the right or from the left.

I did find a few older socialists, however. Sieglinde Haferung and her husband Emilio Molina were long-time communists. Emilio had fought against General Franco and the fascists in his native Spain. Later he was picked up by the Germans in France and survived the brutality of Buchenwald concentration camp. Since the Communist Party was outlawed in West Berlin, Emilio and Sieglinde had joined the SEW, the socialist "Einheitspartei West." Sieglinde, however, was also a strong Christian. Different from most of our established church members, she was staunchly regular in her church attendance. It was no surprise to me when in due time she was elected to the new church council I was trying to put together. This caused some consternation among local people who knew of her party affiliation. "What's going on in the church?" they would complain. "How can you have a communist on your council?"

I was struggling to adjust to the unmovable nature of our established church structure. In my heart I rebelled against the high-sounding claims of a state-based Volkskirche. In actual fact, the church had lost contact with the "Volk," the people it was to serve. In my opinion, it had turned into a bureaucracy that simply carried out its functions in order to maintain itself. It seemed to have lost a sense of purpose and mission.

But there was one function of the Volkskirche that I personally treasured. It was the large number of funerals that I held every month. St. Thomas had 4,200 nominal members, many of whom were elderly, and I would often conduct two or three funerals in any given week. Although this sometimes meant traveling an hour or more to reach the city's far-flung cemeteries, it was a pastoral service I really loved. I often did not know the deceased member personally, but as a pastor I could accompany the family and friends through this period of grief. I could bring them the message of hope and light which the risen Christ holds ready for us. I always felt enriched by the life stories of these people, many of whom were refugees from the former eastern provinces that were now a part of Poland. I listened closely to their experiences in the hard times of war, as well as their subsequent achievements and successes. It was by sharing the story of Christ with them in these circumstances that I was able to appreciate the established Volkskirche as a genuine force of real life.

I could feel how my parish was seething with pent-up human conflicts and tensions. It was just a question of time before an explosion occurred. On the wall of one house, someone had sprayed in bold letters the anarchist slogan that so many people in the neighborhood ascribed to: NO GOD--NO STATE—NO SLAVERY! It was in part a manifesto, in part a statement of fact. It was what they had experienced and felt in their bones. As they saw it, God had not helped them with their personal problems. Neither had the state. The only thing left was the drudgery of a slave. The youthful punks with their chains and outlandish Mohawk hairstyles proclaimed the same creed with their defiant declaration: "No Future No Hope."

I managed eventually to gain entry into all the illegal squatters' houses. Each community was different, both in size and outlook. In some of them, dozens of young people lived together. In others, there were perhaps only fifteen or twenty. The people in

Leuschner Damm 9 called their commune "Der Turm" (The Tower). I learned that the son of a Berlin pastor lived with them. Rumor had it that they were linked to an underground terrorist organization called the Red Army Faction which carried out abductions and killings. A house in Manteuffelstrasse called the "Bauhof" (construction yard) was a talented lot. Along with a few university students, nurses, and a doctor, they had a lot of skilled craftspeople in their group. They functioned as a sort of "Home Depot" for the rest of the squatters.

It did not take long for me to become accepted by these young people as their pastor. Many of the squatters were gainfully employed tax-paying members of my parish, and thus official congregants. Several of the houses appreciated my help in establishing legal contact with the power company. Since they were illegal occupiers, their signatures were not accepted for the signing of legal documents. That is where I had to step in. The first time I became a signatory for one of the houses, I wondered if it would be worth the risk. If these anarchists did not pay their electric bill, I could well be stuck with it. What a lack of faith on my part as their spiritual leader! They kept their promise and paid every bill on time.

Riskier by far was another maneuver I was asked to perform periodically for "my" squatters. They loved to hold street fairs. There had to be two every year, at a minimum. These were involved affairs that stretched out over several blocks. The streets and sidewalks were lined with vendors and food stands of all sorts, and they had street performers and musicians. It was always a colorful and lively scene, with people from all over the city attending. Again, as squatters with no legal address the "Hausbesetzer" could not be official organizers. It was up to me to go to the police station and sign the necessary papers. My biggest problem was how to bring the festivities to a close on time. Usually the police permit gave us only until nine or ten o'clock in the evening. No matter what the permit said, however, people were never ready to disperse. Time always seemed to be up just when the festive mood was at its peak.

Squatter-Occupied House

I remember a big block party I organized on the Oranienplatz one warm summer night. The police lieutenant on duty called me over. "Pastor," he warned, "your party is already a full hour beyond the limit. I have several units of riot police on hand. Are you going to stop this affair, or do you want me to bring in my troops? It's up to you!" On that occasion, I just barely managed to ward off a street battle between the police and the drunken, uncooperative revelers.

Another time one of the vendors, an Egyptian selling glassware, refused to be curtailed by me. He was already quite inebriated and built like a gorilla. When I warned him to cool down, he simply scooped me up into his enormous arms and smashed me down onto the pavement. I was knocked out for a few moments. When I got up, I had a horrendous headache and was bleeding from my left arm. A nurse living in the Bauhof squatter house on the Manteuffelstrasse treated me and bound up my wounds. She was from England, a lovely girl, and I felt some relief in the fact that I could talk with her at that moment in English.

The eruption of violence I expected happened on June 17, 1983. It was the 30th anniversary of the 1953 uprising of East German workers in Berlin against the Communist government. The revolt was brutally put down by Soviet tanks. In commemoration of this event, a group of nationalistic "super-patriots" were bussed in from West Germany to deliver a twofold message to our divided city: 1) The Turkish guest workers should all be sent back to Anatolia; and 2) The illegal squatters should all be evicted and sent to hell. With this propaganda, the West Germans planned to march through the center of the city and stage some rallies.

Of course the West Berliners resented this meddling in their affairs. The next day a massive counter-demonstration by10,000 construction workers, students, trade unionists, hospital workers, secretaries, church people, and others assembled at the city hall to send a message of their own: "'Wessies,' go home!" As luck would have it, the West Germans' parade was canceled because the majority of the bussed-in participants, mostly young people, had disappeared upon arrival to go shopping and sight-seeing. Rather than disperse, the West Berlin counter-demonstrators formed a long column and marched from city hall through the streets to Kreuzberg. The parade of 10,000 ended up at the "U-Bahn" (elevated) station Kottbusser Tor in the heart of my parish.

Several hundred riot police were already in position in tank-like "Wannen" (police minibuses).They were decked out in helmets, shields, and batons. When I saw that they had on sneakers instead of the usual police boots, I knew there would be trouble. These guys had come prepared to do a lot of running. I said to a friend: "Let's get out of here before it is too late!"

As we shoved our way out of the narrow square, more and more people were pressing into the space under the elevated tracks. Then, as the marchers milled around, "it" started. Nobody knew by whom. Rumor had it that someone threw a water bottle in the air. Perhaps one of the anarchists tossed a stone at the police. Did a nervous young cop discharge the first canister of tear gas? It did not matter. In no time the whole neighborhood became a battle scene. Streets were barricaded by protesters setting fire to trash containers. Parked cars had their windshields bashed in. The police were everywhere, running across the Mariannenplatz and chasing after troublemakers. Tear gas wafted down the streets. Many people, some of them women and children, rushed to our parish building and sought refuge in the stairwell. Once again, all hell had broken loose. We were in a war.

That Saturday was my sister's birthday. When I called her in the evening, I could see from my third-floor study window clouds of smoke from countless fires rising over the rooftops. I decided to tell our worshipers the next morning to stay close to home for a day. I was sure that the battle in the streets would continue. It usually did.

On Sunday morning the dewy grass on the Mariannenplatz in front of our church sparkled in the sun. It was going to be a glorious summer day. The world seemed as perfect as it could be. Unlocking the heavy portals of my church, I noticed some punks from the dilapidated squatter house "Besetza-Eck" (squatter corner) at Oranienstrasse 198 coming toward me. They looked glum. My cheerful "Good morning" was met with a gruff "What's good about it?" Then came the bad news: "We were evicted last night!" they said. Senator Heinrich Lummer, West Berlin's Interior Minister who was in charge of the police, had used the turmoil of the previous day's events to throw this illegal community of fifty mostly alcoholic punks out on the street. They must have annoyed him for some time.

"Where are you now?" I asked. "Some of us are still in jail," they replied. "The others are sitting over there on the grass. We have nowhere to go." Obviously something had to be done. Thinking quickly, I told my young friends: "I first have to hold a worship service and baptize some babies. Wait there, and then I'll come and talk with you."

After the church service I found the group still sitting in the middle of the Mariannenplatz. Some were half naked; they could not get at their clothes because the house had been sealed off by the police. I knew they were a wild bunch. Several sported Mohawk hairdos in shades of purple or green. Many had dogs at which they yelled commands. One had a pet rat chained on her shoulder. They were in their late teens or early twenties, and most were either alcoholics or drug addicts. On that bright Sunday morning, some already seemed a bit high and empty beer bottles were strewn around. They had "No Future No Hope" written all over them. No wonder Senator Lummer did not like them.

I offered them a choice: "You can stay tonight either in the sanctuary or in the parish building," I said. "Which do you prefer?" They opted for the parish building. The sanctuary's marble floor would be cold, and in addition they had their dogs with them. Our day-care center across from the parish house had a kitchen where they could do cooking. This was crucial; I was concerned that they get solid food into them. I did not want these punks roaming the streets of our neighborhood drunk and on empty stomachs, with all the pent-up rage they had inside them.

Listening to them, I felt rising in my gut the angry determination of an Irish priest. I sternly warned these unruly youngsters: "But give me your word that you'll stay inside tonight and not get involved in the street fights that will be going on." They gave me their promise and kept it. But I had an uneasy night's sleep.

The following day I was able to borrow ten large army tents from the West Berlin senator in charge of youth and sport programs. The punks established a tent city as their temporary home. With a sense of irony, they called their establishment "Lummer Reisen 1983" (Lummer Tours 1983), named for the city senator who ordered their eviction. It was a colorful and dramatic scene. The large white tents sat wedged between the barricade of the East German Wall and the high towers of the cathedral-like church-- historical contradictions coming together in a prism!

Our worship life went through some radical changes. Since they were being roused from sleep on Sunday mornings by the ringing of the church's mighty bells over their heads, the tent dwellers inquired: "Manne, we want to come to your services. What are we allowed to do in your church and what not?" Aware of their addiction to alcohol, I answered: "You should not bring beer. You can refrain from drinking for an hour." They came back at me: "What about smoking?" I replied: "Well, I'm a strong smoker myself. If you can't give it up for an hour, at least sit in the balcony." But their next question pushed me too far: "How about our animals? Can we bring them along?"

Tent City By the Church, Summer 1983

This I could not swallow. "No way!" I blurted out, using language they would understand. "Keep your "Scheisskoeter" (shit mongrels) out of my church service!" They acted hurt at my response, but they kept pushing. "How dare you call our beautiful animals 'shit mongrels', Manne?" they complained. "Don't you know that they were also created by God?" I answered: "All right, maybe your theology is better than mine. Your dogs were indeed created by God. They may even get into heaven before I do. But into my church service they will not come!"

As the punks straggled into church on Sunday morning, some of our regular worshipers were taken aback and even shocked. They had not counted on that. But they did not complain, at least to me. As could be expected, my harsh instructions were ignored by the kids. One or two brought their dogs along. They headed straight for the high rear balcony, the area of choice because I had said they could smoke. Mr. Piechottka, our organist, was the only other person up there with them. He did not like it, of course, but he had to be where the organ was. Every so often during the service I caught the sickly sweet aroma of marijuana wafting down into the sanctuary. It was a new worship experience.

Although there was a lot wrong with these kids, I felt a strong affinity with them as rejects of our German society. Their deep pessimism about any human convention reminded me of Martin Luther's rejection of human efforts to achieve salvation. The punks did not hold out great hope for the human race. In like manner, Luther did not put his ultimate trust in any human being. These young Germans, considered the dregs of their own society, symbolized for me the depths to which that secularized nation had fallen. A new beginning would have to start with them. As "the least of Christ's brothers and sisters," they came in as the last. Precisely for this reason, I felt they deserved to hear the message of Christ's good news.

And the punks did listen. Very carefully! More so, it seemed to me, than the average churchgoer. On one occasion, when in my sermon I drew a general contrast between "old and young, poor and rich, a hard-working laborer and a punk," they left the church muttering: "Today Manne preached shit!" They felt offended by this negative comparison. In the after-church coffee hour, they insisted that they were as hard-working as any other laborer.

As the summer progressed with no end in sight for the tent city, there was some on-going grumbling among our regular church members but no serious protest. My church council had raised concerns, but they felt that they must go along with this new style of ministry. Most of our active worshipers seemed to sense that we were doing what was expected of us by Christ's gospel. The only overtly hostile critique came to me from people who never bothered coming to church. I therefore refused to take their complaints seriously.

But I continued to worry about drug abuse in the tents. In spite of my stern warnings, I knew these kids continued to use drugs such as marijuana and hashish. All it would take was one raid by the police, and their tent city would be blown away like chaff in the wind. But the raid never came. Apparently the police brass assumed, mistakenly, that the ground on which the tents stood belonged to the congregation. (It was actually city property.) The last thing they wanted was a fight with the institutional church. I felt no obligation to enlighten them.

One of Kreuzberg's important official allies was a local pharmacist who was the district's elected representative for building and construction. I got to know Werner Orloski very well. His friendship meant a lot to me. We shared an affection for the Hausbesetzer. He belonged to the AL or Alternative Party, the green environmentalist party. Like so many intellectuals in secularized Germany, he had quit the church long ago. Although he admired my style of Christian ministry, this was not enough reason for him to come back to church.

The BesetzaEck Squatters

But the tent city at St. Thomas was a major point of interest for journalists, politicians, tourists, film-makers, and other curious spirits from all over West Germany. As the summer progressed, I became heavily involved with an initiative called STATTBAU that was formed to settle the squatter issue in a legal and socially conscious manner. In the course of negotiations with the city, I had occasion to meet with Berlin's Lord Mayor Richard von Weizsaecker. The mayor was an impressive individual and a deeply committed Christian, open to listening to all sides. At first he declared: "I do not accept the political propaganda about the squatters. Most are young West Germans who have other living alternatives. There is no need for them to occupy illegally any of the houses in our city." I challenged him: "I cannot speak for all of them. But I can assure you as one Christian to another: My punks living in tents at St. Thomas have nowhere else to go. It is our sacred obligation as a church to give them a roof over their heads." He was a great guy. He responded: "I did not know that. Let me check more deeply into this!"

Mayor von Weizsaecker kept his word. Three months after the start of "Lummer Tours 1983" in June, we were notified that our Besetza-Eck punks could return to their house. It seemed like a miracle. It was the first time that any squatters had been allowed to repossess their building. Not only that; in response to demands by many, the remaining illegally occupied buildings in Kreuzberg 36 were deeded over to the squatters themselves, under the close supervision of the STATTBAU corporation. The newly legalized squatters were contracted to restore their houses within five years with their own labor and with financial subsidies from tax funds. Along with some architects, social workers, and representatives of other public institutions, I was appointed to STATTBAU's board of directors.

In the fall of 1983, after the punks had returned to their house, I accepted an invitation by the West German government to go on a six-week lecture tour through Central America. It was the 500th anniversary of Martin Luther's birth. Since I was one of only a few Luther scholars who could speak Spanish, I was given the privilege of lecturing about our German reformer to university and church groups in Puerto Rico, Mexico, Nicaragua, Costa Rica, Cuba, and Ecuador. It was a rare opportunity for me to visit Cuba, which was still off limits to American citizens at that time. In the wake of Ronald Reagan's recent invasion of Grenada, I was exposed to a lot of antagonism against the United States at all these Latin American centers of learning. Afterwards, in my report on this trip in the "Kiez Depesche," a monthly Kreuzberg counter-cultural publication, I did not hold back on relating these biting anti-American comments.

My church council reacted with unexpected harshness. They were unable to understand how their American pastor could be so anti-American. They sharply accused me of mixing politics and religion. I think the controversial article was probably just the straw that broke the camel's back, after a number of events had taxed their patience with my ministry. They stripped me of my power as administrative head of the congregation and appointed a council member named Wilfried Wolter as parish administrator.

The reprimand really hurt. In addition, confidential sources at our church headquarters revealed to me that Wilfried had a history of financial and other irregularities at several other congregations. Since I was unable to share this information, I could not prevent him from running as a candidate for my church council. He had slipped into our governing body as a bone fide member, against my wishes. Although I did not hold his sexual orientation against him, I knew that Wilfried was in many ways a slimy character. He had studied for the ministry in East Germany but had flunked the necessary exams, and was somehow able to come west. He now busied himself with sundry occupations, among them running a secret brothel in our neighborhood with a friend . His outward sanctimonious manner effectively served to beguile the rest of the council. This episode was not just a serious setback for my ministry but a congregational concern that required my continued vigilance. I simply had to live with it.

At that time I had the privilege of being elected to the synod council, the highest legislative level of the Berlin territorial church called the "Landeskirche." It was an honor and a rare experience that afforded me a closer look into the inner workings of this body. I was particularly struck by the openly political forces that operated in this august body, in clear contrast to the way American church bodies behave.

We were 120 representatives, almost exclusively academics and professionals. After the opening worship and a shared meal, the synod council split into three political caucuses. They were unapologetically identified as "the leftist," "the rightist," and the "centrist" wings. My jaw dropped. Such a frank announcement would have been unthinkable in our American synod councils.

Time and again during my four years in West Berlin, I had a strong desire to see the "socialist paradise" on the other side of the obscene Wall. As an American citizen living in the still-occupied American zone of the divided city, I had no trouble getting a visa to visit the so-called "Capital of the GDR." On a short visit back to California in 1984, I met and exchanged cards with an East German communist official who was giving a lecture at Stanford. Eventually Dr. Rainer Hagen and I became friends, and we sparred good-naturedly over the role of religion in society on my occasional visits to his office in East Berlin.

One Christmas he invited us to a concert given by the Dresden Kreuzkirche boys' choir at the refurbished East Berlin State Theatre. My friend Rainer and all the other officials in the auditorium proudly wore Communist Party pins in their lapels. I was surprised when the audience insisted on hearing "Silent Night, Holy Night" as the final encore of the evening. When I questioned Rainer's enthusiasm for this hallowed Christian carol on ideological grounds, he replied somewhat defensively: "Well, it is part of our folkloric tradition." At that time, no one had the slightest inkling that the Wall between us would be torn down in just a few years.

The fact that my slippery new council member Wilfried Wolter was running the affairs of St. Thomas turned out to be a minor blessing in the end. It was a relief not to have to bother with the tedious details of everyday administration. This must have been how the apostles felt when the first deacons were appointed: "It is not right that we should give up preaching in order to serve tables" (Acts 6:2). I was happy to let Wilfried handle the daily chores such as opening the mail. Now I could use my energies and time in an effort to secure the second pastoral position for our parish. This was a tricky operation. The number of clergy a parish could have was clearly defined by the number of members in the parish. With 4,200 souls, St. Thomas was right on the cusp between one and two ministers. I tried to plead our case with the church officials, pointing out the special ministry we carried on to the alternative community. While I was still at St. Thomas, we could maintain the precarious balance. But after my departure, the parish lost its right to a second pastor.

During my tenure, I always enjoyed having a female colleague at my side. In my first two years it was Anke Wolf, who did her internship with me as her mentor. After that it was Irmela Mukurarinda, who had picked me up in her VW beetle when I first arrived on New Year's Day in 1982. After completing her theological examinations, Irmela had returned to St. Thomas as a newly ordained pastor. I truly enjoyed working with these gifted theologians. Anke had spent time in Holland, and her experience there brought a healthy shot of reformed theology and a special love for the Old Testament into our parish life.

Anke had a sharp intellect. But at times she also annoyed me with a certain legalistic rigidity and coldness. Once she had fulfilled her share of official duties, she could turn a deaf ear to my requests for additional assistance. Irmela, on the other hand, was warmer and had an excellent instinct for the needs of simple people. She could have inherited this gift from her father, a clergyman, or have picked it up from her former socialist environment in East Germany. In any case, this quality made Irmela a good pastor. She had some problems, however, in her theology. As she confided to me, she did not have a full grasp of Christ's resurrection and thus had reservations about the sacrament of the eucharist. Nevertheless, she was highly popular with the folks at St. Thomas. I was pleased that she became my successor when the time came for me to leave.

We were given enthusiastic encouragement by our Roman Catholic sister church, St. Michael's. The close ecumenical bond

we had was a source of great spiritual strength. Godehard
Puender, the parish priest, was a Jesuit like Christian Herwartz,
the worker priest who was a regular at our bible discussions.
Since Godehard had worked for years in Brazil, we shared a love
for Latin America and a passion for liberation theology. I felt that
he was my spiritual brother. Burdened with the administration of
the Catholic parish, he lived in tension with his Jesuit brother the
worker-priest Herwartz, who had the freedom to take the most
radical Christian positions as a secularly employed mechanic.

Occasionally St. Thomas and St. Michael's would combine
worship services on "low" church holidays like Easter Monday,
which we were required to observe. Most of our congregants
enjoyed these joint ecumenical experiences. We took meticulous
care to stay away from any con-celebration of the sacrament so as
not to exceed limits set by the Catholic hierarchy. But on one
occasion when I preached the sermon at St. Michael's wearing
my black Protestant robe, Godehard received a sharp reprimand
from Archbishop Meissner, the conservative head of the Berlin
Catholic diocese.

With all the conflicts we had to face, both Lutheran and Roman
Catholic, I felt we had a good time together. My ministry to the
squatters had made a impact on our Catholic sisters and brothers
as well. We were not mere social engineers tinkering around with
the gears of society. Nor were we irresponsible hotheads looking
for trouble. What burned in both our Catholic and Lutheran
spirits was the desire to erect a signal of Christ's resurrection in
our section of town. We were convinced that we could bring a
new life of hope and joy to people who were drowning in despair
after having lost their hope in the future. In this mission we were
fully confident that the risen Lord Christ was walking with us on
every step of our road.

As we prepared for Easter in April 1984, the tent city had been
long gone. The punks were back in their building and renovating

it. The Oranienstrasse 198 was now a veritable construction site. I was deeply moved when they approached me with a request: "Manne, we don't hear your church bells anymore, and we don't come to your service because it is too early for us. But we don't want to miss Easter. So could you come to our house and hold a service for us?" How could I turn them down?

Thus on the afternoon of Easter Sunday 1984, with my youth director Karl-Otto on the guitar and Marianne to lead the singing, I held a eucharistic celebration in the dusty courtyard behind the Oraniensstrasse 198. We put boards on a sawhorse to serve as a makeshift altar. As dogs roamed among the seated worshipers, wagging their long tails, I passed out the words of some snappy new Christian songs like the German version of "Lord of the Dance." Waving at the sheet dismissively, one of the punks complained: "I don't know any of these hymns. What happened to 'Praise to the Lord, the almighty, the king of creation'? Can't we sing that?" So we did. They sang the old hymn lustily—they must have learned it during confirmation class back home--and it turned into a real celebration of Christ's resurrection.

There was no doubt in my mind that I was doing what the Lord had singled me out to do. And I was willing to continue doing it until retirement. But then I was called from a different corner. Although I was convinced that all of my previous experience had been a preparation for my ministry in Kreuzberg, I was again suddenly pulled into an unexpected direction. The pull came from our children Andrea and Chris, who had not moved with us to Berlin. When they decided to stay in California in 1982, I believed that we had cut the umbilical cord. It is always a painful separation when parents must release their offspring into the world as independent adults. It is true that for the longest time I had a guilty conscience. I accused myself of leaving Chris behind at too early a stage. He was eighteen when I saw him slump grief-stricken onto our piano after I told him that Marianne and I would be going to Berlin. This picture stayed with me and was haunting me. But Chris seemed to have settled into an independent life in the Palo Alto area as a rock/pop musician, and in his job at a Bay Area pharmaceutical research company.

But now both of our children let us know in no uncertain terms how badly they missed and needed us. Andrea had finished her undergraduate studies at a Jesuit college in Santa Clara and had begun a three-year graduate program at New York University's Tisch School of the Arts. She had insisted in a tearful phone call: "When are you guys coming back to America? I don't know if I can take New York much longer by myself."

My first reaction was negative. Like many another grumpy dad, I snorted: "They know where to find me. If they want to see me, they can come here. After all, I pay for their flights anyhow." Thank God, my good wife had greater wisdom. Marianne put the pressure on me: "Come on, Manfred, you don't want to stand as a stranger before your children in ten years!"

It turned out that Marianne herself felt the need to return to the good ole USA. The cultural hubris and anti-Americanism in Germany had worn her out. She also felt that as time went on, I had not given her the emotional support that she in fact needed. It was a similar marital crisis to the one in Argentina, when I spent many nights drinking beer with students in Buenos Aires rather than coming home at a decent hour. After bitter tears, intense conversations, deep prayer, and reflection, I had to relent. I finally agreed to gather my widely scattered family from the four winds across nine time zones—California, Berlin, and New York—and bring them together again.

In 1986, I made the decision to leave my beloved Berlin and go back to America. This would be my fourth return. I exchanged several letters with Bishop Graefe of the New York Lutheran synod, who recommended me to a struggling German-speaking congregation named Zion-St. Mark's Lutheran Church on the

Upper East Side of Manhattan. The council president Wilfried
Spalholz, a native German from Gelsenkirchen and a carpenter,
paid us a brief visit in Berlin. In return, Marianne and I flew to
New York where I held a trial service. We also visited Andrea,
who shared a house in Brooklyn with other students and very
much looked forward to our coming.

If we had stayed in Kreuzberg, we would have had front-row
seats watching the great miracle of November 8-9, 1989, when
the Wall fell. But it did not turn out that way. On March 31,
1986, we set out for the beginning of yet another new life. This
time it would be in New York City.

When All Hell Breaks Loose

15
LADY LIBERTY

"Keep, ancient lands, your storied pomp! cries she
With silent lips. Give me your tired, your poor,
Your huddled masses yearning to be free,
The wretched refuse of your teeming shore,
Send these, the homeless, tempest-toss'd to me,
I lift my lamp beside the golden door!"
                              Emma Lazarus

New York: the Super City. Where to begin, and where to end, in
one's praise of this fabulous place?

Musicians from all over the world vie for an opportunity to
perform at the Metropolitan Opera or in Carnegie Hall. The
Metropolitan Museum of Art, the Guggenheim, and the Museum

of Modern Art outshine most other galleries of their kind. Research done at Columbia University, New York University, or the Memorial Sloan-Kettering Cancer Center is of the same excellence as the work done at institutions in Cambridge, Oxford, Heidelberg, Berlin, or Paris. Two exquisitely designed botanical gardens attract schoolchildren as well as biologists from all over the world. At night, the dark sky over Times Square sparkles with a dazzling array of brilliant light. The Trump Tower on Fifth Avenue proudly displays the glitter of newly acquired wealth, while the Waldorf and Plaza hotels wear the elegance of old money. In the midst of it all, Central Park is a green oasis inviting everyone to slow down for quiet reflection. For a long time in the past, the Empire State Building was the tallest structure in the entire world.

The city pulsates with a quick life that never stops. Today, its spirit is captured best by the insistent rhythm of rap music. Black teenagers from Harlem do their wild acrobatics on Union Square to the sound of it.

Here beats the heart of American capitalism. Its core is Wall Street. On September 11, 2001, international terrorists knew where to strike at that heart. Their vicious, brilliantly executed attack hit the twin towers of the World Trade Center. In a manner more eloquent than words, the memorial at Ground Zero bears witness to what was once the vital center of worldwide commerce.

Manhattan is an island. Here America opens herself to the Atlantic Ocean. Winds carry the fresh ocean air into the crowded streets, and Lady Liberty extends her welcome to the newcomer. The excitement of this place is unlimited. Yes, abject poverty is visible in many streets. There are signs of intense human pain. The huddled masses, the homeless, and the wretched are to be found there. And yet, the city pulls itself together again and again with tough determination. Its resilience never dries up.

We landed on a sunny afternoon at JFK airport from Berlin. It was the Monday after Easter 1986. My personal start in New York was anything but glamorous, however. I did not detect any sparkle anywhere. Yet I still felt the joyful message of Christ's resurrection deep within myself, and I was grimly resolved to meet whatever challenges lay ahead. Once again, all hell would break loose. My faith was about to be put to severe new tests.

Considering my personal outlook on the flawed values of capitalist societies, it was ironic that we would be living in one of Manhattan's most desirable zip codes. The parsonage of Zion-St. Mark's Lutheran Church on East 84th Street was a four-story brownstone house only a few blocks from the mayor's elegant residence Gracie Mansion. The parsonage had been owned by this German-language congregation since the 1920s, and it badly needed repair.

Many of our neighbors were millionaires. Next door to us lived Ben with his fashionable wife Christine and their two young sons. I was filled with envy as I looked at their beautifully kept house and garden. No expense had been spared. Not for a moment did I suspect that 19 years later, in 2005, Ben would kill his beautiful wife, who was 17 years younger than himself, with a steak knife in a domestic quarrel. At the time of our arrival, he was busy installing expensive new sandstone sills in his windows. By contrast, in our brownstone we were unable to take showers because there was no hot water coming through the ancient pipes in our run-down bathroom. Our fenced-in back garden was the same size as Ben's. But ours was no more than an unkempt junk yard. The previous occupant had tossed bottles, cans, and old electric parts into the uncut weeds.

Zion-St. Mark's church building was in the middle of the next block. The sanctuary was upstairs on the second floor; you had to climb steep carpeted steps to get there. When the building was constructed in the 1880s, elderly people with arthritic knees were not taken into account. Now they made up the majority of the membership. Entering the ground-floor parish hall from the street, you were greeted in the foyer by a long wall painting on one side depicting an idealized German forest scene in garish greens and browns. It was hopeless kitsch, but it expressed the homesickness felt by many immigrants who were part of this congregation over the years. While I understood their feelings, this painting was definitely not the Germany I represented, and I felt disgusted by it.

Difficulties over difficulties! Wherever I looked, I found another daunting challenge. The biggest problem at first, however, was my own kind of homesickness. My heart was still in Kreuzberg. I could not stop thinking about the ministry I had left behind at St. Thomas. I was my own worst enemy, unable to commit fully to the new reality of New York. I was putting an unbearable burden on Marianne, who had to live with me. She must have gone through hell. I definitely drank too much Scotch. I went to bed too late, and I did not feel like getting up in the morning. It was bad. I may not have been aware of it at the time, but my inability to focus clearly also got me into a lot of trouble with my sermon preparation. I was distracted and could not find the central point I needed to drive home in my sermon.

Still, with a lot of hard work and stubborn determination I began to make progress. Although the people welcomed us with sincere warmth, the small congregation was a spiritual jungle. It badly needed weeding. Except for a few men and one family, the German Sunday worship service was attended almost entirely by elderly women.

Although reaching out to the English-speaking community was part of my call, many in the congregation let me know that they did not like my efforts to start an English service. As for the parish administration, there had been no accountability for a long time. The drawers in a filing cabinet in my office were stuffed with unopened mail, some of it years old, that often contained uncashed checks. There were no regular church council meetings. Important decisions were made as needed by three men, two of them brothers, in impromptu conclaves after church.

I had to put an end to this anarchy if we were to get anywhere. I stirred up considerable confusion by insisting on establishing regular parish governance. But we quickly held elections, and I had a functioning church council already that first summer.

An elderly synodical leader, knowing the enormity of the task that was before me, advised: "Manfred, there are close to 100,000 people living in the blocks around your church. This is your potential. This is your mission field." He was right. People kept moving into the changing neighborhood, occupying the high-rise luxury apartments and condominiums that were going up on every corner. The elderly Germans who had lived for decades in rent-controlled tenement apartments were dying out, replaced by affluent young English-speaking professionals who could pay triple the rent. When we arrived, two forty-story apartment buildings were under construction on our street, replacing the brownstone houses that had been emptied and demolished.

I had an almost pathological desire to invite all New Yorkers to our church. How could I attract these newcomers? Our English worship services would begin in September. Marianne and I had decided to schedule them at 5:00 p.m., as far away as possible from the German service at 11:00 a.m. The afternoon hour was not ideal, but we wanted to calm the suspicions of our German members that we planned to do away with the German worship.

With the financial help of the synod, we designed attractive brochures and sent out a thousand letters of invitation to new residents in our 10028 zip code. All summer I leafleted the neighborhood apartment buildings. I could make friends with many of the doormen. I walked the streets in my clerics, handing out brochures and introducing myself to everyone I met. I joined the East 84th Street Neighborhood Association and attended the meetings of the local auxiliary police. I went to every public event I heard about. Often I did not know what I was doing there,

Zion-St. Mark's Lutheran Church, East 84thStreet

but I wanted to be present if only as a human billboard. I hoped that if people saw me in my clerical outfit, they would become aware of our little church sitting between 1st and 2nd Avenues.

This problem of reaching people kept bugging me throughout all my years in New York. There was no fool-proof method. While I continued to put church brochures in the high rises, banks, and shops, perhaps the most important thing was my involvement with the East 84th St. Neighborhood Association. I was elected to the board of directors and became our block president, in charge of replacing the sick trees lining the street in front of our church.

Over time I served as something of a neighborhood priest.
Although most of our neighbors did not worship with us, some
wonderful friendships could develop from these contacts. And in
the end, these efforts bore some fruit. Gradually the afternoon
English worship service grew to an average attendance of twenty-
five, with about forty coming to the German morning worship.

For our German members, the heart and soul of congregational
life was not their worship service but our four annual German
Fests. These events had no religious importance whatsoever.
They were held to celebrate spring, strawberries, harvest home,
and Christmas. They were essentially pagan in character. More
than a hundred Germans would assemble for them, coming in
from all over the five boroughs. The Fests always followed the
same routine. With Marianne at the piano, everybody first sang
German folk songs. Then came a mediocre cultural presentation
in the form of a German poetry reading or some vocal solos.
Finally, the long-awaited "Kaffee und Kuchen" (coffee and cake)
appeared, served by members of our "Frauenverein" (women's
auxiliary). During the coffee hour the crowning event took place:
it was a "Tombola" (raffle) with a bountiful supply of colorfully
wrapped prizes.

My role as the pastoral host at these fund-raising affairs was to
open them with a prayer and keep things moving. I performed my
role as master of ceremonies grudgingly. I was convinced that
many attendees considered these parties a valid substitute for
going to church. This was all the religion they needed. I felt only
disdain for the Fests. To me, they exemplified what I liked to call
"Bratwurst Deutschtum" (Bratwurst Germaness). A lot of the
older immigrant Germans still lived in a nostalgic fairyland that
had never existed: a land of oom-pah-pah bands, Bavarian-style
dirndls, and lederhosen. They were not interested in exploring the
need for "Vergangenheitsbewaeltigung," i.e., coming to terms
with the past, dealing with the legacy of Nazi atrocities that so
profoundly shaped my generation of Germans.

In that first summer of 1986, evil visited our church. The Captive
Nations Committee was a local ideological group representing
nations still under Communist rule--Poles, Hungarians, East
Germans, Czechs, and others. This right-wing organization was
led by Germans and held a special German-language worship
service annually. They wanted to do it this year at Zion-St.
Mark's on Sunday, July 20. They had held events in our church
before I arrived. But unwittingly, in 1986 they chose the very
date on which a bold attempt on Hitler's life had been made by
the German resistance in 1944. I knew that their purpose was
supposedly to stage a propaganda demonstration against the
Soviet Union. But I felt that the plan was evil because they veiled
their true nationalistic and right-wing political agenda under a
high-sounding guise of freedom from communism rather than
dealing with the crimes of the Nazis, their own legacy.

Refugees from Latvia, Estonia, Hungary, and Afghanistan came
into our sanctuary dressed in their national costumes and carrying
the flags of their countries. One bold banner proclaimed: "Danzig
bleibt Deutsch!" (Danzig/Gdansk will remain German!). I almost
exploded when I saw it. Many of the Americans present did not
understand why I was so upset. In my sermon on that anniversary
date of Hitler's failed assassination attempt, I pointed out how the
committed Christian faith of Colonel Claus von Stauffenberg and
other conspirators in the July 20 plot against Hitler profoundly
influenced this action. I also sharply attacked the resurgence of
fascist ideas in our days. There was a palpable tension in the air
as I spoke from the pulpit. It was clear that most of my audience
did not agree with me. But I could not care less.

Afterwards, at the next meeting of my newly formed church
council, I could persuade them that in the future these Captive
Nations people should hold their nationalistic service in some
other church. In protest, the extremely upset couple who had
organized the event resigned their church membership with us.

But it was no great loss. Horst Uhlich was an unreformed Nazi, as he openly admitted. He was proud of his three first names: Horst Adolf Hermann, in honor of Horst Wessel, Adolf Hitler, and Hermann Goering. While the three men who had made all the important congregational decisions prior to my coming did not openly object to these developments, I could feel some resistance growing against the new pastor.

Another Nazi member of our church was Charlotte Tschanter, a wealthy single woman in her eighties. At one time she admitted to being totally puzzled by me. She said: "You did not care for Adolf Hitler, Herr Pastor? Why not?" My answer was beyond her comprehension. But for some reason she had decided to like me, and we developed a cordial relationship. As a sign of her trust, she insisted that I help her with bank affairs she could not handle anymore.

There were a number of incidents involving Frau Tschanter. For example, at our Fests she was fond of reciting German poetry and always came prepared. Then there was her method of quieting down the loud buzz of conversation. In order to attract everyone's attention, she would bang her carved wooden cane on the table and yell: "Ruhe, Ruhe!" (Silence, silence!) That formidable cane was more than a walking support; she wielded it as a weapon. One day when she tried to leave her apartment house, she found her way blocked by a young woman named Jennifer sitting on the steps to the street. Without a moment's hesitation, she whacked the unfortunate girl several times with her cane. But since this was not Nazi Germany, Jennifer went to the police and sued her for damages. That was when I became involved. Eventually I could work out a reconciliation between the two.

After a while Frau Tschanter and Jennifer even became good friends. Jennifer took pity on the old lady and looked in on her. One day the young woman called me in desperation. Frau Tschanter did not respond to her knocks at the door; could I come without delay? Together we were able to open the apartment door, but we could not unhook the security chain inside, so we called the paramedics. They came in no time; but surprisingly, now the old woman let us in. She fiercely resisted the attempts of the paramedics to check her out, yelling: "Schweine, Schweine" (pigs, pigs). One of the men, an orthodox Jew with a knowledge of Yiddish, reacted with enormous kindness and succeeded in calming her down. I did not say anything. But I thought: If only you knew what an incorrigible Nazi she is, would you have been so nice to her?

We attracted to our various congregational events a liberal young Jew I met at a German-language literary club. Elliot Juenger was a born American, but his parents were German Jews. He was simply in love with Germany, in spite of it all. He spoke perfect German, and whenever he showed up at our church affairs, he was tolerated by the others. When he finally made a trip to Germany, I printed his impressions and concerns in our newsletter. This was too much for a rich butcher's widow named Dora Halder. Dora let me have it. "I've had enough of this," she shouted at me. "I lost three brothers in the war fighting against the Russians. I do not want to hear another thing about what the Nazis did to the Jews."

These were challenges, indeed! But that's what I wanted and needed when I had to leave Berlin behind.

To be fair, there were several exceptional individuals attending our German worship services as well. We had a delightful pair of elderly sisters from England with a perfect command of German. During the war they suffered through attacks by the Luftwaffe in the London blitz. One of them had even driven an ambulance during those frightful nights. But this did not kill their genuine appreciation for the German people and culture. They regularly worshiped with us and became vocal members of our church council. For years these two aged spinsters, Ina and Helen Dietz, were in charge of our financial records and kept them meticulously up to date.

Then there were John and Ruth Barto. Although they had long been members of the prestigious Madison Avenue Presbyterian Church, they gradually moved over and became part of our struggling congregation. Initially Ruth had held a deep grudge against our church because her beloved brother was killed in combat in France. For a long time she looked at all Germans as his murderers. But over time, and through our mutual concern for the neighborhood, we became close friends and eventually she was elected to our church council. Ruth had been the art editor of school textbooks and a high-school art teacher in Harlem. She gave us expert advice and made the necessary connections when we had to restore the stained-glass windows in our sanctuary.

Other unusual members of our budding English congregation deserve mention. Louise Schalow, a former nurse, had taught in China in her younger years. She, along with Flora O'Rourke and Florence Becker, worshiped with us every Sunday afternoon although they were active members of our large sister church Immanuel Lutheran on Lexington Avenue. Marie-Louise Barbir, also a nurse, had lived for many years in Lebanon and taught nursing at the American University in Beirut. Her daughter Nadine enriched our services with her beautiful soprano voice. Kathy Jolowicz came to us with her mother Ruth from Trinity Lutheran Church on Central Park West. She organized and ran a successful German language school for young American professionals in our parish rooms.

James Bess, a retired television producer and a long-time member of St. Peter's Church at the Citicorp Center, found a home with us and became very active. Even though his conservative politics were completely contrary to my progressive tendencies, James was a regular worshiper and a generous giver. We became good personal friends. James was an exceptional driver who negotiated his way calmly through the harrowing streets of New York. He enjoyed chauffeuring me in his car to whatever visits I needed to make outside the city. Paul Knight, a young investment banker from Nebraska, had recently moved with his new wife into one of the new high-rise apartments on our street. After joining with us, he served for years as our church council president.

The move to New York became a time of great blessing for us as a family. We had a lot of catching up to do with Andrea and Chris. All four of us needed quality time with each other. Now, finally, we could speak and to enjoy each other's company again. Upon our arrival, Andrea took over the fourth floor of the parsonage, which had been converted into a small apartment years before. She continued with her rigorous graduate theatre program at NYU's Tisch School of the Arts and received her master's degree in June 1988. She was very grateful for all the support she received from Marianne and me in defining and achieving the goals for her life.

In June 1986, Chris visited us from California where he was working full time and playing in a band he had formed with a friend. During our time in Berlin, I had been plagued by a bad conscience for having abandoned our son in Palo Alto when he was eighteen. Now on his first trip to New York, he intended to stay for a short time. But already on his second day, Chris was hooked. The Super City New York did not let him go. He called Suzi, a girl he had recently met in California, and managed to persuade her to come for a few days as our guest. Suzi turned out to be a delightful young woman. Together they explored the city, and at the end of their vacation, the two Californians went back to their jobs. However, in February 1987, Chris joined us in New York for good. A year later Suzi followed suit and moved in with us permanently. Shortly thereafter, Andrea moved to Astoria with her new boyfriend Dan while she worked as a waitress and auditioned for acting jobs. Chris and Suzi had been sharing an extra bedroom; now in 1988 they could move upstairs to Andrea's vacated fourth-floor apartment. Although they were not married, no one in the congregation raised any public objection to Chris and Suzi living "in sin" in the parsonage, especially since they now worked as the church sextons.

Our first summer of 1986 had been a happy time, with lots of sun and many good memories. We worked to clear out the filthy mess of bottles, rusty metal parts and other junk in the weeds behind the house, and started to reclaim the yard. With the help of Ruth and John Barto, we established a garden and pruned back the grapevine on an arbor just outside the rear door. When things were presentable, we repeated our Palo Alto ministry of grill parties and good conversation with church members and friends from the neighborhood. Once again, our backyard served to bring people together.

The Refurbished Parsonage Garden

During our eleven years in New York City, we had a steady stream of visitors from California and Germany. Lots of young folk liked to visit New York. When word got around that we had a cot bed on the back porch behind the kitchen, young friends and friends of friends found their way to us for a night or two. But most important during the first few years was the time we had for intense conversations in the circle of our own family. Marianne and I treasured our extended breakfasts with our children. We took long strolls on the promenade along the East River in Carl Schurz Park, by Gracie Mansion. There was so much we had to work through with each other and digest.

One concern felt by Marianne was that we had no place to call our own. What if something happened to me and she had to vacate the parsonage? Where would she go? As much as we enjoyed living rent-free on the Upper East Side of Manhattan, the parsonage belonged to the congregation. She was right. We had to consider this possibility.

When Andrea graduated from the University of Santa Clara in 1984 and Chris was living on his own, we had been able to sell our home in booming Palo Alto for a much inflated price. We had banked most of the profit and fortunately could invest in a new venture. We began looking in areas close enough to the city that we could go there on my days off. Like many New Yorkers, we first thought of upstate New York, north of the city. We rented cars and drove there numerous times, looking for property we could afford. But we learned that we would have to travel at least three hours before finding any real estate within our means.

Seeing our frustration, Andrea came up with a novel idea: Why didn't we consider Pennsylvania? I was extremely skeptical. "I know Pennsylvania is your home state," I said to Marianne. "But we would first have to drive all the way across New Jersey where housing is also too expensive. It would take three hours before we see anything we could afford." But at the insistence of my wife and daughter, I agreed to give it a try.

Marianne had heard about the beauty of the Pocono Mountains from her parents. So we checked in the newspapers and picked up a couple of the Poconos real estate booklets that were available around the city. My jaw dropped in amazement when I saw the price of properties on the other side of the Delaware River. They were half the cost of similar homes we had seen upstate.

Thus, on a snowy morning in January 1987, we drove up to Pocono Lake to look at properties. One of the homes we were shown was a small cedar chalet on a wooded lot in a private development called Locust Lake Village. After seeing several other houses, we went for lunch at a German restaurant called the Edelweiss. Suddenly I noticed Marianne was crying. "What's the matter?" I asked. She confessed: "I really fell in love with that little house on Fox Trail. I know you said you wanted more evergreen trees on your property, and that's why you probably won't go for this one. But I really related to it. I find it absolutely charming. But whatever you want to do ..."

Of course this clinched the deal for me. We bought the romantic little chalet in the Pocono mountains, nestled deep in the woods and surrounded by beech trees, visited by deer and squirrels and occasionally a black bear.

I now had the privilege of living in two worlds. My real life was in the city, with the congregation and all the challenges of the city's hustle and bustle. But just two hours away, I could escape with Marianne to a mountain retreat for a day or two when time permitted and the pressures became too much. Incorrigible city slicker that I am, I always went through a kind of culture shock when we got into the mountains. I found it hard to believe that there was a place where you did not hear a sound when you went to bed at night.

Locust Lake Village was near several well-known ski areas: Camelback, Jack Frost, Big Boulder. Our little cedar chalet had been built as a rental for weekend skiers. It had a cathedral ceiling in the great room with a wall of windows that gave light and a feeling of generous space to the interior. We had a small kitchen and dining area, and two tiny bedrooms and full bath, on the ground floor. A finished upper balcony area under the pitched roof provided quarters for several more sleepers. We converted that into a third bedroom with a desk and a computer hookup.

We modified the fieldstone fireplace by installing a catalytic wood-burning insert that in no time heated the entire building. I had no shortage of wood from our own trees and those of our neighbors. Thick branches broke off every winter, and I collected more all year round. I cut them up with an electrical saw and then split them with a neighbor's log splitter. I thoroughly enjoyed this rustic way of life, so different from my existence in the city.

211 Fox Trail, Locust Lake Village

We had fabulous neighbors across the road. Orlando Cortez was a delicately built native of the Philippines. He had retired from a bank job in Philadelphia some years before and could give me many fine tips on how to live in a forest environment. His wife Judy was a large red-haired American lady from Philadelphia who had worked in a bank while raising four boys. She was warm and generous but quite disorganized. Judy was also a pack rat. Her living-room table was always a mass of junk mail, bills, notices, and journals. But she had a heart of gold. Judy and Orlando were long-time members of the local Methodist church, and we often worshiped with them when we were there for a midweek service. At first we had no car, so Judy would pick us up at the bus stop and take us back to the bus when we went home. In the summer and during vacations, we shared grill parties and meals with them and their extended family.

Tom Cortez, one of their four grown sons, lived with them. He was even larger in size than his mother. Tom was also a pack rat. Their garage was jammed full with motorbikes, snow-blowers, and assorted spare parts. Tom ran a lawn-maintenance business in the summer and plowed driveways in the winter. I was happy that I could rely on him when I needed to fix broken equipment. Occasionally Tom dropped off a load of logs in my driveway with his pickup, and he shoveled us out when it snowed. For ten years, until I retired and we moved into the chalet, the Cortezes kept an eye on our house and were helpful with any emergency or need that arose. Marianne and I will always be grateful for that.

In February 1987, on one of our early visits to our mountain retreat, I rented a car and managed to convince our son Chris, on his first visit from California, to come along. Chris had spent most of his life in California and Argentina. He had experienced real winter weather only during two years as a child in West Virginia. As I drove us up into the mountains, a gentle snow started to float down silently and softly through the crisp, clean air. Our son became completely still. It was as if he had been transformed. Not a sound came out of him. This same sense of wonderment always filled us when we approached our house in the Poconos. It was like being in a kind of fairy tale.

Meanwhile, my ministry in Manhattan was keeping me very busy. There was always something cooking in our bilingual congregation. Early on, Marianne had begun an informal choir of

Germans and Americans, both members and non-members, who loved to sing. It was not a regular church choir that sang anthems during Sunday worship, but a seasonal group that performed twice a year—at Christmas, and then again in the spring. They developed many friendships among themselves as they rehearsed. They gave a number of fund-raising concerts, the first of which enabled us to buy a grand piano for the sanctuary. Their programs included German folk songs, old English tunes, selections from Bach, Brahms, Handel, and Haydn, and sing-alongs in both German and English.

In 1992 we commemorated Zion's 100th anniversary with a series of events. Prominent among them was an abbreviated version of German composer Engelbert Humperdinck's opera "Haensel und Gretel," with performances in both German and English. We were able to put together two good casts of singers from our two worshiping congregations and friends, as well as from Marianne's choir. Joyce Lynn, a singer with the New York City Opera chorus, volunteered to be the production's director. A large number of non-singing church members became involved as actors (myself included), stage hands, set designers and helpers. Others worked on costumes and makeup, and several contributed their talents to build an impressive cookie house and witch's oven. The unusual production turned out to be a great success. It attracted a lot of attention for Zion-St. Mark's.

But while we were indeed getting to be known in our part of town, with one hundred thousand people in our mission field, this was, I felt, only a small gain. No matter how hard I tried, we were unable to grow enough to solve the problem that dogged us: a persistent lack of money. We did not have a satisfactory means of financing the ministry of our church. When I arrived in 1986, the congregation had a small endowment fund which was projected to last two years. But when that ran out, they would not be in a position to pay my full salary and benefits, and Sunday offerings were completely inadequate.

As part of their agreement with the Metropolitan New York Synod to call me, the congregation had agreed to rent out the large social hall during the week to Gymboree, an exercise program for small children. Unfortunately, neither Gymboree nor the well-to-do young parents they served had any interest whatsoever in our worship life or regular church activities. The program itself was an inconvenience because of the vast amount of toys, mats, balls, and other equipment they stored on our premises. But we had no choice. We had to put up with them, since we desperately needed the money.

This precarious financial situation changed dramatically in 1989, when I was offered the opportunity to be the Lutheran campus pastor at New York University. While it was a part-time position, it would mean a considerable increase in my work load. But I did not hesitate for a moment and accepted. I received a half-time salary from the campus ministry department of the ELCA. Of this amount, I kept a portion to bring my income package up to the generally accepted level, and passed the rest on to the treasurer of Zion-St. Mark's. This supplemental income, together with several bequests from wills, enabled me to leave the congregation ten years later on a much more secure financial foundation with $350,000 in reserves.

New York University is located in Greenwich Village. Most of its buildings are clustered around Washington Square. This is one of the oldest parts of Manhattan. A lot of artists prefer that part of the city. They and others in the Bohemian alternative culture have left their imprint on this part of town. It was an eye-opener for me. They were quite different from the business types and professionals I lived with on the Upper East Side. I cherished the opportunity to discover these nuances in the human layers of the great city. Whenever my schedule would permit, I walked the three miles from our parsonage on East 84th Street all the way to Washington Square. I wanted to be able to absorb these many faces of New York. At other times, I would walk north into Spanish Harlem and the real Black Harlem on 125th Street, to add also these tastes to the mixture. I was beginning to feel at home in the Big Apple. New York was now as much home for me as Berlin had been.

I thoroughly enjoyed my work with the students and faculty at NYU. It was good to be back in an academic environment. The young people were a source of great joy for me. Our daughter Andrea was no longer among them; she had graduated with her Master of Fine Arts the year before. I did not relate only to the Lutheran students; the first thing I did was to change the name of my ministry from Lutheran to Protestant. Although there were small unofficial religious groups on campus, I was the only officially recognized pastor at NYU for the entire Protestant constituency.

I established two permanent events for each week. On Tuesdays I conducted a bible study, and on Thursdays I held a service of holy communion. It was obvious that the students preferred the bible study by far. Because of the manner in which I led it, they had a chance to interact with each other and get involved in wide-ranging discussions. But the service of holy communion was very important to me personally. I wanted to give my students the firm foundation of a sacramental presence which went to a deeper level, beyond verbal exchanges. Some of them began coming uptown to attend our Sunday afternoon English worship at Zion-St. Mark's, and I could baptize one of these students into the body of Christ during one of our services.

The university provided me with an office that was adequate for our normal weekly activities. However, we also wanted to host special events such as films and larger debates on campus. In order to do this, it was necessary for us to register as a student club. To qualify, we needed five students ready to sign on as officers. This was not as simple as it sounds. Most of my regulars were undergraduates who were not ready to commit to such a permanent responsibility. Finally out from under their parents' control, they wanted to be unburdened. I really had to cajole and convince in order to find five student officers among my kids.

The university held a student club festival at the beginning of each academic semester: one in fall, and another in spring. There were at least fifty student clubs for all sorts of different interests, from sports to religious preferences, or with various political and social inclinations. At these festivals, our club had an information table with brochures and programs. Large numbers of incoming students passed by this array of offerings, looking for soul mates with whom they would feel comfortable associating. These were always crucial times for me. I sat at our table in my clerical collar with a student, trying to catch the eye and the interest of as many potential new members as I could.

I found quick and easy access to my Roman Catholic campus ministry colleagues. They were fortunate that the New York archdiocese owned half a city block in the middle of the NYU campus. The Catholic Church had established an attractive chapel and parish center there, with many facilities. They had a sizable staff with a priest, a nun, and several aides. I liked to joke that while I could offer only two fixed programs on two days, they were able to invite their students every day to different kinds of masses, with pasta and without. They had a full program all week long.

At the other end of the scale were the unofficial Pentecostal and Evangelical Christian groups, led by students. Some were called Campus Crusaders and others Seekers. Their goal was to cultivate a religious awareness filled with a strong emotional commitment. I took them quite seriously. These groups were a real competition, because some of the young people who were drawn to my ministry also felt an attraction to such an uncritical, spontaneous approach to religion.

When All Hell Breaks Loose

While I wanted my students to have a strong belief in God, I also challenged them to use their brains to examine the intellectual implications of their faith. I emphasized the spiritual freedom we inherited from the reformers of the 16th century. We showed a whole spectrum of religious films, for example, that included "The Last Temptations of Christ" (banned by the Catholic Church) and "The Life of Brian" which was considered scandalous from a moralistic point of view by the Evangelicals.

I did a fair amount of counseling. I loved working through the problems my students wrestled with: their religious orientation, their future plans, relations with their parents, and so on. The kids were always glad when we arranged retreats for them in the Poconos. The group was always small enough that they could bring sleeping bags and stay in our mountain home. They also came for grill sessions in the backyard of the parsonage, a good chance to get away from campus for discussion and reflection.

NYU Students with Manfred in the Parsonage Garden

* * *

When All Hell Breaks Loose

Let me make another short digression here. I want to mention a problem that concerned me deeply during my years in New York. These were the Reagan years. Ronald Reagan was being hailed as one of the great American presidents by many people. He still is beloved by a surprising number of Americans. Perhaps I should have given him more credit for his part in bringing the Cold War to an end. But I was appalled by the brutal way in which he drove the Soviet Union into an armaments race. I was probably not being totally fair when I felt that Michael Gorbatchev made a more valuable contribution to stop the insanity between East and West with his innovative concepts of Perestroika and Glasnost.

However, what I most deeply resented was the way Reagan tried to undo the inner communal structure of life in the United States. I did not understand how he was able to get away with his brazen attacks on organized labor, or how he undermined the economic foundations of the middle class with his mantra: "Do not look to the government for solutions! Government is not the answer; government is the problem." This chaotic principle violates the biblical understanding of sound government as an agent of God. Bette Dewing, a reporter for the small New York newspaper "Our Town" who occasionally worshiped with us, called these measures "capitalism gone berserk." I agreed with her.

In the end Reagan's deregulation policies, which were applied for over two decades, led to economic disaster in 2008, the last year of George W. Bush's presidency. His philosophy of totally unfettered capitalism started a process of freeing business from any accountability. Thirty years later, the financial system spiraled completely out of control and collapsed.

We were nearing the end of 1989 when the Berlin Wall finally cracked open. November 9 was a day of great liberation. That

When All Hell Breaks Loose

night our parsonage was packed with people from all over town. I had no idea how the news spread so quickly among so many young Germans that we were having a party. But I was happy to celebrate with all of them. I would have loved to see them at our worship services. But this was not one of their interests.

For us as a family, 1989 had been an eventful year. Andrea married Dan McCook on Christmas Day, December 25. Andrea and Dan had met when they were both working in the Beach Café, a restaurant in our area. We had the ceremony in our church and the reception in our parish hall; both spaces were festively decorated for Christmas. It was a very special affair because many relatives and friends took an active part. Marianne's elderly mother and her second husband flew in from Des Moines. Our faithful church member James Bess baked two turkeys. Others brought special foods or did presentations. Afterwards Andrea and Dan lived for a while in Astoria and then moved south to Florida, where Dan had personal connections. Andrea is now an assistant professor for theater at Flagler College in St. Augustine, while Dan runs the college radio station. They have a son, Daniel, who is our only grandchild.

Meanwhile, by 1989 our son Chris had set out on a path that none of us was able to follow. After taking some college courses in California and in New York City, he had dropped out with the comment that the professors did not know what they were talking about. He also stopped coming to church, contemptuously calling worship an ordeal that offered him nothing. I was beside myself. He seemed to trample underfoot the two institutions that filled my life with meaning: education and the church. At the time I did not realize that my son had to do this. He needed to protest a father who in his mind often tended to be authoritarian. We had reached a stage of alienation which made it impossible for us to talk to each other. It was extremely painful.

Only later did I learn that Chris had been breaking forth into a new world of discovery of his own. He was being pulled deeper and deeper into an exploration of Buddhism. If I had been more astute as a church historian, I should have foreseen that my son is much more of a mystic than I will ever be or come to understand. He is much more in tune with his own and other people's feelings than I am, much less bound to the hard facts on which I try to establish my personal views. And yet, he is dedicated to the task of probing for deeper meaning in this unproven field. We now have come to appreciate these personal differences between us, and we enjoy our time together when we can share with each other our different perspectives.

Chris and I were still estranged in 1997 when I decided to retire and leave New York. He and Suzi had to vacate the parsonage, and they returned to California. They were both in good health, and Marianne and I told them that we would not support them; they were on their own. As long as Chris did not go to school, we felt no financial obligation to help him. We knew they would go through very rough patches, and at times they must have been hungry. That was hard on us, but they had to learn to make their own way.

One day Chris called with the news that he had been hearing a persistent voice telling him to go back to college. Such a thing would never have happened to me. I do not have voices talking to me. Nevertheless, when he enrolled in a community college, we started to help with their rent. Chris then received scholarship aid from the University of California in Santa Barbara and graduated in East Asian studies with outstanding grades. His excellent record resulted in his acceptance with tuition aid at the Harvard Divinity School. After completing his M.Div. degree there, he began his career as a chaplain at the Dana Farber Cancer Institute and as a meditation professional in the Boston area. He also began teaching as an adjunct instructor at the divinity school.

When All Hell Breaks Loose

When I retired in July 1997 from Zion-St. Mark's Church, I had been their pastor for eleven years. In one way, it was a success story. The English-language part of the congregation was now strong enough to take a decisive lead in running the church. But in another way, it was a story of failure. There were still those in the German-speaking part who actively resented the growing influence of the Americans. We had tried a number of ways to overcome this tension. We held combined church council retreats. We even used the services of a professional conflict manager sent by the bishop. But in the end, it all failed. A German business woman who was on the council rallied the original German leaders behind herself and blocked all attempts at cooperation. Before we would allow this unfortunate situation to make us sick, Marianne and I decided to say good-bye to our friends at the church and move to Pocono Lake. After all, at 67 I was above retirement age.

After we left, the German leaders of the council quickly called a younger pastor directly from Germany. This was done without input from the bishop or the synod. The new man used an authoritative style to reassert the preeminence of the German side of the congregation, with an afternoon English service tolerated for financial reasons. By yelling, threats, and intimidation, he pushed out anyone who spoke up or questioned him in any way. He fired the German language school director who had built this successful program from scratch, and established his wife in that position. Apparently he was using Zion-St. Mark's as a stepping stone to bigger things; during the week he spent his time on his computer studying for an on-line law degree. When that was finally accomplished, he moved to Arizona and then established himself as a legal expert on immigration affairs in California.

Since this pastor left, no other permanent pastor has been called. As I write, the congregation barely functions with a rump council of three persons. They are renting out the vacant parsonage for a hefty sum, and they are not accountable to anyone. Visiting preachers receive a per diem to hold one Sunday service with a German liturgy and an English sermon. A worship attendance of fifteen or twenty with no follow-up or parish administration has caused nearly all previous activity to fall by the wayside.

When I retired to Pennsylvania in July 1997, I was not ready to give up my ministry in New York completely. I wanted to continue my part-time service as the campus pastor at NYU for a few more years. The commute was not difficult, and I looked forward to keeping my hand in the active life of this exciting city as long as possible. I could keep this up until 2000. I also was part of some ecumenical groups and remained on the board of the German Seamen's Mission at the International Seafarers House on Irving Place.

On Monday, September 10, 2001, I went in to Manhattan for a meeting that would be held the next day at the Episcopal center near Wall Street. I stayed that night at the apartment of my brother-in-law Vincent Schneider on the Upper West Side. Vincent and his wife Sally were not there; they were at their regular home upstate in Kingston.

Tuesday was a splendid morning. The day was so inviting that I set out to march downtown. On Broadway I saw a diner that advertised oatmeal for breakfast. That sounded good. I walked in and found a totally weird scene. It was deathly silent in there. Everyone—both the clients and the staff—stared at a TV screen as if mesmerized. The fellow behind the counter looked like the owner; he appeared to be numb. I asked him: "What's going on here?" He murmured in a low voice: "A plane just flew into the World Trade Center." I thought he was crazy. I sat down and ordered my oatmeal. Then I looked at the TV and saw with my own eyes the second plane crashing into the other tower. Now I became as numb as the others. Wordlessly I finished breakfast, paid, and continued my walk down Broadway.

At 42nd Street, crowds of people stood quietly watching the news ticker flash above Times Square: "Terrorist attacks on the World Trade Center." It was incomprehensible.

When I reached 23rd Street, people were crowding around a car radio that brought more detailed news. Mayor Giuliani had cordoned off the lower part of Manhattan. Nobody could go below 14th Street. The emergency crews needed unhindered access. I would have to curtail my plan to walk down to Wall Street. The meeting would probably not be held, anyway. As I crossed over to Seventh Avenue, I could see clouds of smoke rising from where the Twin Towers had been.

All along the way, I was enormously impressed by the collective calm with which the New Yorkers reacted to this horrible event. Except for a few hysterical nuts, we kept our outrage under firm control. But there was a definite feeling of solidarity in the air. We all were in this incredible attack together. We needed the combined strength from each other. I found a Presbyterian church that was open and sat down in the cool sanctuary to rest. Yes, my feet were tired. But more than that, I needed to pray to God. There was such a turmoil of anger, confusion, and helplessness within me.

The rest of the day, Manhattan was completely cut off. Nobody could leave or enter the island. It was an eerie feeling, as if we were in a war zone. At least I could finally get through to Marianne on the phone and reassure her that I was all right. That evening I met with a friend, a young German doctor, in a Chinese restaurant. As we ate, we listened to President Bush's address. I was proud of him as he warned the nation against any form of hatred and animosity against Islam. The next morning we were still under martial law, unable to leave. I tried to go to Ground Zero, but I could not get through. The rescue workers had their hands full; they did not need onlookers. However, I managed to get to Washington Square, my former campus-pastor territory at

NYU. Coming around one street corner, the wind blew biting smoke from the smoldering fires right in my face. That's when I lost it. I broke down and started to cry. I had to think of the innocent victims: the receptionists and secretaries, the bankers and lawyers, the fire fighters and police, and all the rest, who lost their lives in this terrible catastrophe. At the same time, I remembered the thousands of innocent civilians who were incinerated in the firebombing of Dresden.

As I walked through Washington Square, I came to a large group of student gathered at one of the fountains. I listened as they poured out their hearts to each other over the horror they had just experienced. Apparently some of their fellow students were among those killed. Some were crying. One girl admonished the crowd about how much they needed each other now. A young man reported:" I'm just coming from St. Vincent's Hospital. I wanted to give blood, but there were so many donors before me that mine wasn't needed right then." The young people all insisted: "Let's stay positive and not give in to hatred!" One confessed: "I'm scared of those who shout that we should bomb Afghanistan to smithereens!"

One student pointed to the big arch at the entrance to the square and read aloud its inscription by George Washington: "Let us raise a standard to which the wise and honest can repair. The event is in the hand of God." A young woman from India told us: "I am not a Christian. I am a Hindu. But I want to sing a song about Jesus to you." And she did.

I was deeply moved by all this. I could not restrain myself any longer. Feeling that I was still the pastor to these young folk, I pushed my way into the center and spoke to them. I said: "It is good that we are here together. This is a day of great infamy, just like Pearl Harbor. Then they attacked military installations. But this is much worse. This time they attacked defenseless civilians right in the heart of America.

"But I want you to know that this is not the first time such a thing has happened. Other people and other nations have gone through similar terror attacks. I myself am a survivor of the firebombing of my hometown Dresden in Germany in WWII. In one night, upward of 60,000 defenseless civilians were burned, incinerated by phosphorous bombs. I am not complaining about it, because we Germans did similar atrocities in Coventry, Rotterdam, and London. But be assured that we have the whole world on our side right now, ready to support and help us."

That is how it really was after September 11, 2001. Even French newspapers declared: "Nous sommes tous Americains!" (We all are Americans!) For a while everyone was united in a spirit of unity. Our churches were packed with people eager to support one another. But then the feelings of fear and revenge took over. Our politicians started to portray the United States as the only true victim of such horror in recent history. Members of the Bush administration used the country's fear of further attack to "go it alone" in an unfortunate foreign policy that destroyed much good will and sympathy we had built up from other countries. Using half truths and propaganda, the administration's "neocons" paved the way for war in Afghanistan and Iraq. In the end, we would be once again divided.

Fox Train, Locust Lake Village

16
TWILIGHT

"I am hard pressed between the two: my desire to depart and be with Christ, for that is far better; but to remain in the flesh is more necessary for you." (Philippians 1:23-24)

As I moved toward the end of my public service, there were some moments when I shared with St. Paul the desire to depart and be with Christ. But this desire was never strong enough to overcome the wish to remain in the flesh. I like to think that I am ready to die. But I feel like Woody Allen who stated: "I am not afraid to die. I just don't want to be there when it happens."

After I left Zion-St. Mark's Church in 1997, I discovered the rich variety of ways that retirement offers for the exercise of ministry.

For the next two years I continued my part-time campus ministry at NYU. Having the good fortune to be able to sleep at my brother-in-law's Manhattan apartment, I spent three days each week in the city. I continued to hold holy communion services and bible studies with my students. But I kept weekends free of NYU commitments, just as before.

This was a great arrangement. I had the benefit of enjoying two worlds. During the week I was "in the city." But my weekends were spent "in the country." I was free to serve as a substitute preacher in congregations without pastoral care. There was not a single Sunday when my services were not needed. I preached in Lutheran churches from Pennsylvania to New Jersey to upstate New York. This was a great experience. I met a lot of wonderful people. It gave me a good idea about what was going on in our Evangelical Lutheran Church in America.

In the summer of 1998 I went back to Argentina for a visit with my old friends. My former students were now important church leaders. We had wonderful opportunities to exchange our views. My principal interest was to find out what had happened to Latin American Liberation Theology on its home turf. I could speak with those who had welcomed this bold theological initiative thirty years ago, like my friend Jose Miguez Bonino, and also with those who had been adamantly opposed to it. The fires of passion had now died down on both sides. But I was happy to discover that this theology had indeed left an imprint on the churches in Latin America. They had come to understand that God does show a clear preference to the poor. The trip left me with a strong urge to work through the complex issues of this theological contribution. So I wrote a little book entitled *A Preference for the Poor*, which was published in both English and German.

Working on this publication brought me a big breakthrough. We now had a computer which Marianne used for a number of her own writings. It would be necessary for me to learn how to get along with this new technological device if I wanted to publish my book. I was deeply grateful to have my wife as a competent teacher. In my many confusions I would cry out time and again: "Marianne, Marianne, help! What am I supposed to do now?" She showed infinite patience. In time I was able to master the rudimentary basics of "computer speak."

In 1999 I substituted on Sundays at St. Paul's Lutheran Church in Albrightsville, Pennsylvania which was seeking a pastor. After much consideration they persuaded me to accept once again a full-time call for ministry in their congregation. However, this meant the end of my service as campus pastor at NYU.

There were two reasons why I made this sacrifice: a) Personal curiosity. Although we had owned our Pocono chalet for 12 years, I still felt more like a New Yorker at that time. I was curious about what made the people living on these mountains tick. I wondered how I would get along with them. And b) The warmth of the church members. I was impressed with the sincerity and genuine warmth coming from the people on the search committee. So I promised them that I would serve St. Paul's for the next five years, God willing and health permitting. As it happened, I stayed with them for nearly eight years until we moved to Allentown..

St. Paul's is a white wooden country church sitting amid fields on the 2000-foot-high Pocono Plateau. It stands alone close to a crossroads which is the village of Albrightsville. A few members were old-timers who still lived in the homesteads in which they were born. But the majority were transplants from the cities. Some were permanent residents, while many others had second homes in the new housing developments that had mushroomed in the rock-strewn forests of the plateau. Our own home was in such a development, Locust Lake Village, about fifteen miles from the church building.

Hundreds of such modern developments had sprung up in the last decades as more and more urban dwellers in Philadelphia and New York had the means to buy or build a vacation home. But as soon as they could, many of these nomads moved their entire existence out into the woods where they could enjoy the high mountain air all week. For them, the long commute was worth it.

Most of my parishioners were hard working and thoroughly honest, although they were not exactly "forward-looking." They liked to stick with what they knew, the "tried and proven." They were hesitant to try experiments such as a new liturgy or a newly released hymnal. Very few had held positions of leadership in industry, business, or the community.

We desperately needed to increase our church membership in order for the small congregation to survive. But my people did not have the skills to reach out to strangers in friendship. If a new face showed up in our pews, there was barely a handshake and no follow-up mechanism except perhaps a postcard. The rest was up to me. If new visitors came more than twice, I made it a point to see them in their homes and ask if they might be interested in joining us as full members. I did an enormous amount of personal visitation. But the effort gradually paid off. We were able to receive 159 new church members during my pastorate.

Across the street from the church, the congregation had built a huge pavilion furnished with a full kitchen for the preparation of cookouts. It came replete with picnic tables for 100 people. Every summer, barbeques were organized as fundraisers and people came from far and wide for baked chicken or roast pig. These events were extremely popular. Some were combined with cake walks that awarded around 80 home-made cakes as the large wheel turned to the playing of a local band. Apparently many people felt that this was all they wanted from their church; we never saw them at worship. In this respect, they reminded me of the equally popular German "Fests" put on by our women at Zion-St. Mark's Church in Manhattan.

We had a well-attended Sunday School, however, of children who lived nearby. In an attempt to interest the parents of these children in worshiping with us, I decided to change its schedule. They were used to holding classes an hour before the worship service. The parents would drop off their children and then return to pick them up an hour later when the service was about to start. Neither the parents nor the children ever stayed for church. With the approval of the church council, I now had Sunday School start at the same time as worship. The children stayed in the sanctuary for the opening liturgy. After the children's sermon they went down to the parish hall for their lessons while the worship service continued. This worked much better and gave our worshipers a chance to get to know the kids. At the same time, it gave the children some exposure to a worship service. And occasionally a young mother would even stay for worship.

A number of the "imported" members told me that years ago when they first began attending St. Paul's, they did not feel welcomed by the "old families." This had apparently not improved much over time. We had to change that attitude in order to become a "friendly" congregation. This had to take place in the style of our worship. But the church council had little interest in our liturgical practices. Their discussions concentrated rather on the pavilion events and picnics. So I managed to gather together a hand-picked worship committee of alert individuals with whom we could create a new climate in our services. We started using the "Celebrate" insert and increased the use of lay readers and assistant ministers. Instead of serving the eucharist in separate tables, we now received the sacrament in the form of a "continuing communion." Against some heavy opposition, we were finally able to replace the red Service Book and Hymnal with the green Lutheran Book of Worship and the blue "With One Voice." All of this helped to create more joyful and spirited services. It now was "fun" to worship in our church. Still, I could not generate any enthusiasm for a truly contemporary style of worship, and we had no instrumentalists in any case.

My beloved St. Paul's Church in the mountains did not show a strong interest in the issues of the day, either. This was the time when The Evangelical Lutheran Church in America was studying the question of whether gay and lesbian candidates who live with their partner in a committed relationship can be ordained and called to serve as pastors. Under the guidance of Bishop David Strobel, our Northeastern Pennsylvania Synod called on all local congregations to discuss this theme. When I brought up the ticklish subject, the president of the church council did not want to touch it. He told me: "Our congregation is not interested in this sort of thing." But after much persistence and a tough struggle on my part, we could have at least one informed and intelligent discussion on this controversial issue. Apparently most of the congregation had no problem with gays and lesbians, as long as the synod would not force them to call such a pastor.

To be fair, I also was able to gather a group of very solid friends because of the sometimes controversial positions I held. There were strong and committed Christians in that congregation. Even though they did not always agree with my views, I could count on their personal support whether a conflict was about the liturgy, a social concern, or some other issue. During my ministry in Albrightsville, I took many long walks in and around our development, thinking about my ministry and the people I was serving. I would hike through the woods and up the hills for two to three hours. It was my time for personal prayer and reflection.

St. Paul's Church always had a close relationship to the local fire department. Whenever the congregation celebrated a major event, we were able to use their big social hall. The husky volunteer firefighters, many of them sons of the congregation, never came to our worship services except for a funeral or the wedding of a

friend or relative. But in time I got to know them all. They treated
me as their local clergyman, and after a while I became their
official volunteer chaplain. Besides offering prayers at their
programs, I would join them in the kitchen after one of their large
community meals and scrub the greasy pots and pans. I always
liked to wash dishes, and it was my personal specialty to attack
the cookware and the huge ovens.

In 2007, 10 years after my "official" retirement, I left St. Paul's
and we moved to Allentown. Our life in the Pocono mountains
had been basic and uncomplicated and also very satisfying. The
rough simplicity with which we lived with the woods and hills
and deer was healthy. At the same time, we enjoyed spiritual and
intellectual stimulation through our congregation and our writing
activities. But as we advanced in years—I was 77 and had five
heart bypasses in 2000--we realized that we needed to be in a
living environment where help would be more easily available if
needed. After looking at several senior resident communities, we
finally decided on Luther Crest which was founded in 1983 by
the Lutherans. We are very happy with our choice. I call it our
"Princely Residence" for elder citizens. It is a three-level senior
community with about 300 independent-living people and 100 in
the assisted-living, memory support, and health-center units. We
had to pay a large entrance fee which consumed the proceeds
from the sale of our Pocono chalet. But Luther Crest makes a
reassuring promise: Once you are accepted into the community,
you will never be dismissed for a lack of funds.

The monthly maintenance fee includes one major daily meal.
Luther Crest has a well-deserved local reputation for excellent,
upscale cuisine. We eat this meal with the others in a large dining
room with wait staff always ready to help as needed. Marianne
has thus been liberated from the daily grind of spending lots of
time in the kitchen. We have a comfortable apartment with a nice
living room, two bedrooms, two full baths, a small kitchen, and a
balcony overlooking a grassy courtyard with a gazebo. Of course

before moving in, we had to get rid of even more stuff than we had when we left Manhattan. It was a relief for me!

Marianne now pursues interests that are close to her heart. She always was an outstanding musician, and now she also proved herself to be a gifted writer. She has published two books. *West Berlin Journal*, written under her pen name Eloise Schindler, is an account of the years we spent in Berlin-Kreuzberg. The other book, *Coping With the Limelight,* is a manual on stage fright, something that had always plagued her as a soloist. She is active in the Luther Crest writers' group and contributes articles to two publications, "News Notes" and "Crest Chronicle." She has a singing group of ten women called the Melodiannes who give a spring concert every year.

I had the good fortune to be called as a part-time pastor to St. Joseph's Lutheran Church here in Allentown. This small congregation was across the Lehigh River in the less desirable eastern part of town, while our "princely" residence for seniors is in the more affluent west. After several hard blows that depleted their membership, the congregants had seriously considered closing the doors of their sanctuary. But they were running an important after-school program for elementary school children on Thursday afternoons called Village Partner, in conjunction with Mosser Elementary School up the street. This ministry, along with some funds from a former member's trust, kept them going.

As their pastor I had the advantage to look at Allentown from two opposite perspectives. The seniors at Luther Crest are financially secure. There is not a single one who did not get a college education.. East Allentown around my church, on the other hand, was always a working-class area. There were not many college degrees around. Everybody struggled extremely hard to get by. Most of the congregation's old families were brought over from the Austro-Hungarian Burgenland to work at Bethlehem Steel. When the corporation went bankrupt in 2005, East Allentown declined and so did the church. Now this part of town is to a large extent populated by transient residents who stay for a few months or a year and then move on.

When I was called in 2007, Sunday worship was attended by about thirty people, most of them elderly. I did not see any realistic hope for a long-term future growth because of the unstable population. It was unfortunate also that the church had no parking lot, discouraging the participation of members who had moved away. Some years prior to my coming, the church had suffered another blow when the pastor entered into a relationship with the married organist who happened to be Roman Catholic. This scandal depleted the membership even further.

I am only half joking when I say that many of our immediate neighbors lived with one foot in jail. A young father renting the house next to the church was caught by the police hiding over ten pounds of marijuana in his home. He was sentenced to several years in jail. His two adorable kids had been coming to our Sunday School, and their young mother occasionally found the strength to bring them to our worship service. But one day they were gone. The house next door now sits vacant.

Those few who remained faithful to St. Joseph's were open to change and this was a source of spiritual strength for me. During my pastorate the congregation willingly accepted and quickly learned two contemporary liturgies to liven up our worship life. One was an arrangement by Marianne of traditional spirituals set to the words of the liturgy. The other used portions of composer David Haas's lovely communion setting "Do This in Memory of Me," brought to our attention by daughter Andrea.

A special theological challenge arose in 2009. By this time, the debates about homosexuality had grown highly divisive for the Lutheran church. In that year's church-wide assembly, the issue of whether homosexuals living in a committed relationship with a life partner can be ordained was to be decisively settled. I was taken aback by the intensity of emotions kicked off among many Lutherans on this subject. Some were beside themselves at the thought that any kind of homosexual could be authorized to instruct their children. I was particularly disturbed by the clumsy reactions coming from many of my fellow pastors. They did not seem to have the theological equipment or preparation to handle problems of such explosive power.

I shared my concern with our Bishop Zeiser. Reminding him of my training as a church historian with emphasis on the Protestant reformation, I offered to hold a few workshops in which I would show how Martin Luther interpreted the bible. I felt this could be helpful in a conflict of such powerful dimensions.

The bishop went along with me. But he insisted that a theologian who held the opposite view be given equal opportunity to present his reasoning at these workshops. I met with the young pastor he suggested, Brett Jenkins, and we worked out a reasonable method of presenting our contradictory positions. Together we held three workshops in our synod--in Allentown, Reading, and Scranton-- with fairly good success.

In Scranton my lecture "With a Bound Conscience" was received with particular enthusiasm by a group of dedicated Lutheran lay attendees. In it, I explained Luther's basic distinction between Law and Gospel. Somehow this struck a particular chord with these Christians. They wanted to hear more from me. They also had a particularly strong interest in Dietrich Bonhoeffer and they wanted me to come back.

With the help of their local pastors, this group brought together a diverse audience of about thirty people who indicated an interest. Most were Lutherans. But there also were a few Jews, a Muslim, some Catholics, Baptists, and others. Dick Yost, a Lutheran from Clarks Summit, emerged as the principal organizer.

When All Hell Breaks Loose

So, I went to work. Beginning in 2010, I developed a series of presentations for this group which I called "Pocono Lectures." After my initial presentation on Luther's hermeneutics, I gave them three separate talks under the title "Theology Backwards." The first lecture was on Dietrich Bonhoeffer and his early theology as it is expressed in his important work *The Cost of Discipleship*. I called it "From Bonhoeffer to Luther." In the second one, I dealt with Luther's understanding of Christian Freedom. In the third lecture, I went back to Bonhoeffer and showed how he went beyond Luther in the development of his theology in its final stage. By this time, my audience was ready to hear my personal confessions as a Hitler Youth. I entitled this talk "Encounter with Evil." After that, I gave a critical analysis of the spiritual forces in present day America under the title "The Land of the Free."

At the time, I was studying many diverse Jewish authors for my own enrichment. I was particularly impressed with the work of Pamela Eisenbaum in her book *Paul was not a Christian*. I did not agree with all of her arguments, but she convinced me to a large degree. So I wrote a critical assessment of it in my next Pocono Lecture, taking her title for my own but adding a question mark: "Paul was not a Christian?"

At first I was reluctant to agree with Marianne's insistence that I give a lecture on Martin Luther and the Jews. But then I gave in. It was hard work. But in the end, this research proved to be personally gratifying. I followed it with a presentation entitled "Bonhoeffer and the Jews." Then my Scranton audience asked for a lecture comparing Bonhoeffer and Martin Luther King, Jr. My knowledge of Dr. King being severely limited, I made liberal use of *Bonhoeffer and King* by J. Deotis Roberts, a renowned Black theologian. Thus I could fulfill the wish of my friends.

At the time of this writing in 2014, with the support of our Luther Crest chaplain Dianne Kareha I have been able to repeat the

Pocono Lectures to a larger audience. They are held at Luther Crest and open to the public. My research into Jewish authors has brought me to admire greatly the thought of Irving Greenberg, an Orthodox rabbi with a unique insight into the relationship of Judaism and Christianity. With a particular focus on his work *For the Sake of Heaven and Earth*, I have written several lectures on him which I hope to present in Scranton and Allentown. The first of these is called "A New Encounter" and is introductory in nature. The other three lectures are under the title "The Failed Christ," a provocative term used by Greenberg.

Our move to Allentown brought us great spiritual enrichment. Although this county seat was always a town of hard-working laborers with a Lutheran church on every other corner, it also has a healthy presence of Jewish residents and several synagogues. One of them is Keneseth Israel, a Reform congregation located next to Muhlenberg College. For many years Marianne and I have attended an interfaith clergy colloquy held there. The colloquy is sponsored by the Institute for Jewish-Christian Understanding, affiliated with the college. We are good friends and admirers of Dr. Peter Pettit, its accomplished director.

For years while we were in the Poconos, we drove down the mountain every month to meet with this group of mainly Christian ministers and one or two rabbis. It became a wonderful opportunity to reach a new understanding of Jewish history. We learned that the Jews have a wonderful freedom in the way they keep the 613 mitzvoth, or commandments, that are taught in the Torah, the Pentateuch. We discovered that they are less legalistic in their understanding of the Torah than most Christians. Since they were chosen by God in his grace through the covenant with Abraham, they live less encumbered and breathe more freely.

Dr. Pettit consistently drove home his main argument: that many Christians have made a caricature of Judaism through countless instances of supercessionist interpretation. We came to appreciate that Jews and the early Christians were at first two parallel sides of one religion. With the destruction of the temple in Jerusalem in 70 C.E., they separated more decisively. One side developed rabbinical Judaism in the tradition of the Pharisees, while the other side developed orthodox Christianity through the followers of Jesus. Their separation became definite in the 4th and 5th centuries. After Christianity rose to be the dominant religion in the Roman Empire, the Jews became the victims of a permanent persecution.

Now that we were living in town, I enjoyed frequent contact with friends at Keneseth Israel, especially their rabbi at that time, Rob Lennick. Rob was not interested in Pettit's clergy dialogue. He was dedicated to a single-minded defense of Judaism. I was impressed with the unapologetic presentation of his theology. Before too long, we became good friends. Aside from the fact that Rob did not believe in Jesus as the Christ, our shared belief in God was equally strong and very similar in many respects. It therefore was not surprising that occasionally we exchanged our pulpits. Several times Rob preached on Sunday mornings at St. Joseph's, and I preached in his synagogue on Friday night. Rabbi Rob was an engaging preacher, and my Lutheran congregants were delighted to have a change of pace.

Unfortunately, serious internal tensions had developed within the synagogue. Rob was fighting with his cantor Ellen Sussman and asked me for advice. It was a situation that could have existed also in a Lutheran congregation. Even after he was able to get rid of her and hire a new cantor, the problems continued. Finally in the summer of 2012, Rob was fired by his board of directors in spite of an ongoing contract; he was given a large settlement to leave immediately. It was handled in a secretive manner that I found highly questionable. I now have a very good relationship with the new rabbi Seth Phillips, a former Navy chaplain with extensive interfaith experience. I continue to worship with this Reform Jewish congregation on most Friday evenings. It is good for me to confess with them: "Hear, O Israel! The Lord our God is one!" Their prayers give me real personal strength

I am struggling hard to come to a better comprehension of Judaism. In the process, this synagogue has become a spiritual home for me. At first it seemed as if the people of Keneseth Israel paid no attention to my presence at their worship. It was quite different from a typical Christian congregation. Nobody made it a point to greet me or welcome me. Nobody wanted to find out who I am or what I am doing. You might say that it felt cold and impersonal. But this was not the actual reality. These people were not ignoring me at all. They just left me in peace. Now that I am a regular participant, many individuals greet me as a matter of fact. When I was in the hospital for an operation, someone called on the entire congregation to pray for me. But they have a different spirit. They do not push me or try to coax me into anything. They exhibit a distinct form of freedom, one that maintains a certain personal distance out of respect for the other. I had to learn this at first, and now I truly appreciate it.

Ever since we found out about the horrors of the Holocaust, we Christians have made great efforts to get rid of our prejudices. But during these last years I have become aware of the many ways in which we still carry around a secret supersessionism in us. With a deep sense of gratitude we recognize that most of God's great promises were fulfilled for us in the coming of Jesus as God's Messiah. This is a part of my faith that I will never surrender. But in my Jewish friends, I encounter people with an equally strong conviction although they do not share this part of my belief. Their faith in God is just as passionate as my own. But they have no need to accept Jesus as a unique agent sent by God with a special assignment for all of us. It was Marianne who first opened my eyes on this point. She declared: "The Jews don't need God's saving grace in Christ. They had it already through the covenant with Abraham!"

This seems so obvious. But when looking more closely at this declaration, we discover serious implications. I have had tough personal struggles with some of these. It is second nature for us Christians to claim for the church what was first promised to the people of Israel. It is true, thanks to the merits of Christ, that we are also God's legitimate people. But where does this leave the Jews? Are they now out of the picture? Or are they a different people of God? I have come to accept a theological pluralism as expressed by Michael S. Kogan in his book *Opening the Covenant*: "Christ for Christians, Torah for Jews, presumably other paths for other religions, all of them established by God--a plurality of life-giving revelations to humanity."

Out of a deep gratitude for what Jesus as the Christ has done for us, Christians are in danger of short-changing Israel by skipping across the richness of gifts God has given to his first people of selection. Such Christians downgrade God's faithfulness to his original promises. But as St. Paul reminds us, "God has not rejected his people whom he foreknew" (Romans 11:2). Where this warning is ignored, there can be no appreciation for the passion with which Jews affirm the values of their faith: "Torah, Israel, and the radical unity of God" according to Kogan. Where these values are embraced, however, a view opens up for the wealth of grace which God poured out upon this people.

This grace can be seen in several of the covenants which God has established with Jews. He made an enormous promise to Abraham: "I will make you a great nation, and I will bless you, and make your name great, so that you will be a blessing" (Genesis 12:2). This declaration is fundamental to Jewish existence: "I will bless you, and you will be a blessing."

In Genesis 17:4, 8, God said to the forefather Abraham: "You shall be the ancestor of a multitude of nations. And I will give you and your offspring the land where you are now alien, all the land of Canaan, for a perpetual holding, and I will be their God."

After having shown his readiness even to sacrifice his son Isaac, Abraham is told by the Lord: "By myself I have sworn, says the Lord: Because you have done this and have not withheld your son, your only son, I will indeed bless you. By your offspring shall all the nations of the earth gain blessing for themselves, because you obeyed my voice" (Genesis 22:16,18).

These promises to the forefather Abraham are reinforced by the covenant God made with Israel at Mount Sinai. God called Moses to tell the Israelites: "You shall be my treasured possession out of all the peoples. Indeed, the whole earth is mine, but you shall be for me a priestly kingdom and a holy nation" (Exodus 19:5).

Amy-Jill Levine, a Jewish professor of New Testament Studies at Vanderbilt University in Nashville, Tennessee, came up with a fortunate picture to describe the present relationship between Judaism and Christianity:

"Today church and synagogue have different canons, different vocabularies, different understandings, and different practices. [But] synagogue and church may be pictured as railroad cars traveling on parallel tracks. The cars look the same from a distance: they both have wheels marked 'Genesis' and 'Isaiah'; they both have dining areas; they both have conductors. On closer inspection, the differences become more apparent. The synagogue also has wheels marked Talmud and midrash, and the church has wheels inscribed Gospels and Letters. The dining car of the synagogue has matzo-ball soup, whereas the specialty of the house for the church is ham. The conductors for the synagogue include Rashi and Maimonides; for the church, Augustine and Aquinas share driving duties. And the conductors drive on parallel, but separate tracks. They and the passengers are aware that if one car gets derailed, the other will be damaged. But this is only the immediate view. If we follow those parallel tracks back to the horizon, we see that they meet. Skeptics call this an optical illusion; theologians call it God's-eye view. In that far past, there was only one track, that of Jesus and Hillel, James and Akiva, for all the passengers were Jews. They might have sat in separate rows, but they were all on the same track. There was no distinction between 'Christian' and 'Jew'; there were only Jews. If we look then to the other horizon, we see that the tracks meet once more. As different as they are, church and synagogue have the same goals, the same destination, whether called olam habah, the kingdom of heaven, or the messianic age. The two cars pull into the same station, and they have the same stationmaster there to welcome them" (Levine, *The Misunderstood Jew: The Church and the Scandal of the Jewish Jesus,* HarperOne, 2006, p. 213).

When All Hell Breaks Loose

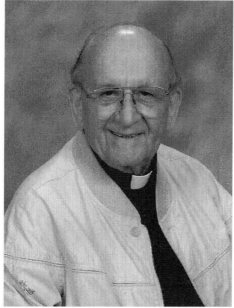

Manfred, 2013

18
EPILOGUE

"But we have this treasure in clay jars, so that it may be made clear that this extraordinary power belongs to God and does not come from us. We are afflicted in every way, but not crushed; perplexed, but not driven to despair; persecuted, but not forsaken; struck down, but not destroyed; always carrying in the body the death of Jesus, so that the life of Jesus may also be made visible in our bodies. For while we live, we are always being given up to death for Jesus' sake, so that the life of Jesus may be made visible in our mortal flesh.) (2 Corinthians 4:7-11)

The teenager who miraculously escaped from the inferno of the firebombing of Dresden turned into an angry young man. I had to struggle very hard to come up with a coherent view of the world I live in. More than anything else it was a sense of defiance that filled me. I was proud that somehow I had survived this horrible catastrophe. I was determined to say: "Whatever other evil you may have, bring it on. Keep it coming! I can take it!"

In the end, I failed. I was never able to bring a coherent view of this world together. Today I know that I was probably suffering from post traumatic stress, PTSD. At that time the phenomenon was not yet widely known. This knowledge came after the wars in Vietnam, Afghanistan, and Iraq.

Some might maintain that I am still in the grips of this mental disorder. They have a point. Just take a look at the disorganized pattern in which my entire life unfolded. You do not see the steady development of a respected and successful career. It is a journey that took me to different countries. It forced me to confront and come to terms with several different cultures. It made it necessary for me to learn different languages in order to express myself. It exposed me to a great variety of different audiences. It threw me into doing battle with conflicting political ideologies, as well as with unruly and unfounded religious convictions. You may well come to the conclusion: "What a confusion! What a mess!"

It was absolutely necessary for me to be thrown into complete despair. This happened not only at the end of World War II. It also happened to me time and again through the rest of my life. Whatever sound and sane method I found of looking at life was ground down into bits and pieces. It seems that I needed to be broken down and opened up, time and again, so that new life impulses were given a chance to thrive and bear fruit in me.

I was broken down so that God would have an opening to pour in the energies of a new life. I had to be made low so that God might be grand in me again and full of majesty. This happened in my life over and over. My anger had to be overcome by the greater strength of God's power of forgiveness. My personal defiance had to be disarmed by God's superior force of mercy and grace. God did this for me through the life of Jesus and through his shameful death on the cross and through his final resurrection to a new life. This is what I call the gospel—the good news of Jesus Christ.

God appointed Jesus as our Christ. He died because of all the wrong that takes place among us. But he was also raised from death. This double event, cross and resurrection, occurred so that our massive wrong might be forgiven and be replaced with a new life. Through this deed God has placed the power of forgiveness as the central focus into our world. The act of forgiving is the vehicle by which dissentions among us are overcome and wounds can be healed which we have inflicted upon one another.

As I went through the devastating experience of seeing my hometown consumed by fire, I had the sensation of experiencing the end of the world. I always feel an immediate, very personal reaction when I hear any serious talk about the total destruction and disappearance of our world. For me this is not an outlandish nightmare. It is a real possibility.

Documents about this fearsome idea are called "apocalyptic." The Greek word "apocalypse" is translated as "revelation." This literature deals with events that must be "revealed" because they cannot be comprehended with our normal senses. They are passed on through visions, dreams, and imaginings that are often filled with grotesque pictures. This type of literature has always held a certain attraction for me.

In the same way, I have a quick personal connection with individuals who went through similar harrowing blows in their own lives. They seem to be more interesting and creative than their normal, paler contemporaries. I have to make a special effort to relate to people who do not stand out in any particular manner, who just seem to exist. And yet, it is such human beings who keep this life moving forward, even if their pace sometimes seems sluggish. They are the ones who raise families. They grow our food and provide us with clothing. They build our houses and make it possible for us to communicate with each other. They move us to the places we have to go. We cannot do without them.

While for me it can be difficult to relate to them at times, in their quiet heroism the simple folk whom I have often tended to ignore turned out to be my best teachers. When as a student I worked in a cement factory on semester break, I learned from my rough fellow workers the beauty of comradery. In Latin America I was deeply impressed by the quiet endurance and steady persistence of the simple people there. In North America I am struck time and again by the realization that this is essentially a country of unsophisticated individuals who have had the good fortune to build a strong middle class. American churches have traditionally run on the personal commitment of time and energy of laypeople who do not require great theological insights.

As I look at the turning points in my personal journey, I discover that I have actually carried on a rather passive existence. I have lived reactively. That is, I did not have the urge to pursue or initiate any grand ideas. Rather, I reacted to circumstances and alternatives that presented themselves in a concrete situation. It was up to me to decide between one or the other. This often led me down paths that did not present a clear or obvious end result, but rather a new set of alternatives. Eventually a direction would usually emerge. This is how I have been guided throughout my life. I am convinced that God steered me through these diverse stages of my journey.

That is how I ended up as a pastor. As a young man, I did not hold this occupation in high regard. Other careers seemed far more glamorous. But I passionately wanted to study theology and the bible because of my intense involvement with the story of Jesus Christ. I had no interest in the clergy. I thought they were out of touch with reality and seemed to belong to the past. But as a result of my studies and a number of personal experiences, I changed my tune. I eventually responded to the call of the church which at that time was urgently in need of pastors, and I was ordained.

A similar thing happened in my relationship to America. Originally I had no desire to go there. What could they teach me, a German theologian, about religion? Nothing about the country or its population greatly pulled me. But my involvement in Heidelberg on Sunday evenings with young GIs prompted our university student pastor to tell me about study scholarships in the United States. Out of these two seemingly insignificant self-interests—a way to get affordable housing in Heidelberg, and a year free of economic need in America—grew a lifelong commitment.

In 1955 after I returned from this year abroad, I was ordained and assumed I would be assigned to a regular pastorate in Germany. Having experienced war at first hand, I never considered becoming a military chaplain. But once again, because of my personal involvement with Americans, the church superiors put pressure on me to carry out a ministry among the new German Labor Service units serving with NATO forces at Kaiserslautern, Ramstein, and other military bases in the Palatinate area. So I donned the chaplain's uniform with the rank of captain.

After my marriage to Marianne in 1958, it was definitely a wish of mine to spend at least a couple of years in America. I wanted to examine more closely some features of church life there which differed from our German Volkskirche setup. I had no intention whatever of turning this into a lifelong affair. Yet once we were there, one thing led to another. I discovered that in order to understand what I was seeing in American religious life, I needed a more solid background in the English reformation. This realization led to an interest in doing postgraduate studies. Through another personal fluke—I had renewed an exchange-year acquaintance with the dean of the Lutheran Hamma School of Theology and he supported my proposal—I received a fellowship for doctoral studies at the Hartford Seminary Foundation.

Before beginning serious work on English church history in Hartford, the school insisted that I first obtain another master's degree. I could do nothing to change their minds, so I decided to work on Martin Luther's concept of the church. The rather lengthy dissertation that resulted prompted the faculty committee to allow me to enlarge it into a Ph.D. dissertation. Thus, through no prior intention of my own, I emerged not as an authority on the English reformation but as a Luther scholar. This would then become my professional identity as a theologian.

Apparently it was still not the time to return to Germany as I had originally planned. Through another coincidence—a member of our Lutheran mission board was in Hartford on vacation and happened to hear me preach one Sunday—I was tapped for a position as professor for church history at our seminary in Argentina. Although by now Marianne and I had two young children, we were willing to go. For almost six years we lived as missionaries in a surprisingly and wonderfully different environment. Our experiences on this sub-continent opened new cultural vistas and profoundly changed us.

When we came back to North America, after three years of teaching and ministry in Ohio and West Virginia I became the Lutheran campus pastor at Stanford University in California. This was another rich and marvelous adventure. By now, my time for catching up with some features of North American church life had stretched out to more than twenty years. I had to go home again. I accepted a position in West Berlin and had a fascinating ministry for over four years in the counter-culture district of Kreuzberg. I would have loved to stay as pastor of the Thomas

Church until retirement. But as happened so often before, my expectations were not decisive.

Marianne and I were physically separated from our children by thousands of miles and multiple time zones. When it became necessary for family reasons to return to America in 1986, I was at first very homesick for Germany. But once again, new doors opened as I worked for eleven years to build a viable German-English congregation on the Upper East Side of Manhattan. At the same time, my outreach as a campus pastor at NYU helped me discover the metropolitan Big Apple as the world-famous "Super City" it is.

When we retired to the Pocono mountains of Pennsylvania in 1997, pastors were still in demand. After substitute preaching for some months, I came to know the pains and joys of being a full-time pastor in a small American country church. Now that we live in a retirement community in Allentown, I have maintained a strong worshiping connection with a Jewish congregation. As God has guided me here, I cherish the valuable new opportunities available in the Lehigh Valley to grow in my understanding of Judaism.

While living and working in Pennsylvania, I returned to visit Dresden several times. The most moving experience was in 2005, when I accompanied Bishop David Strobel of our Lutheran synod in Northeast Pennsylvania to the rededication of the Frauenkirche (Church of our Lady), an impressive baroque church that turned into a pile of rubble after the 1945 bombing. The Communist government established in that part of Germany had no interest in rebuilding this religious structure, so the ruin was left standing in the center of the city. For sixty years it was used by the local population as the focal point for an annual commemoration of the destruction on February 13. While at that time churches were allowed to hold worship services, the official government doctrine was atheism and gradually the number of believing

Christians had fallen to below 25% of the population. Nevertheless, on these occasions hundreds of people chose to gather before the ruined Frauenkirche to hold their prayer vigils and demonstrate for peace.

After the collapse of communism in 1989, the stark pile of rubble continued to serve as a strong symbol for peace, and I agreed with those who opposed its reconstruction. Yet determined Dresdeners succeeded in raising several hundred million Euros from private sources around the world. The architects salvaged and identified original stones that were usable. Adding new ones, and using plans that were still available from the original construction, the church was completely restored to its former magnificence.

The rededication in 2005 was a gala affair. It was attended by politicians and church leaders from everywhere. I was fortunate to accompany my Pennsylvania bishop David Strobel to Dresden on this occasion, as his interpreter. German Chancellor Angela Merkel worshiped with us, as did a member of the British royal family. It was a deeply moving experience. What touched me the most was an altar cross fashioned from long medieval nails that had been in the roof of England's demolished Coventry Cathedral. The citizens of these two cities, Dresden and Coventry, went through similar experiences. As Dresden was the victim of senseless destruction at the end of the war in 1945, Coventry had been senselessly bombed in the early war years of 1940-41. A strong bond of understanding and friendship had grown over the years between the residents of the two cities. On the occasion of the rededication in Dresden, Coventry furnished the cross of nails that now stands on the altar of the Frauenkirche as a powerful symbol of reconciliation. It is on the cover of this memoir.

In 2011 I returned to Dresden once again, this time with the newly elected bishop of our synod Samuel Zeiser, successor to

When All Hell Breaks Loose

David Strobel. Our small delegation was hosted by the Lutheran Church of Saxony, our partner synod, for the Evangelischer Kirchentag, or Protestant Church Rally, held every two years in a different German city. More than 150,000 Lutherans came from all over Germany, taking over my hometown for a week. It was astonishing to see in this formerly East German setting such a rich variety of offerings including religious services, discussions and lectures, as well as artistic performances. The programs covered religion, political and ethical themes, the arts, and cultural interests. They were presented in many different venues– –churches, schools, sport stadiums, concert halls, and factories.

Huge assembly areas had been established on both banks of the Elbe River, where some of the major events took place. The speeches and music were transmitted through huge loudspeakers that broadcast their sound all through the town. It seemed as if, for this one week at least, the secularized city of Dresden was soaked with the Christian faith.

On the last day of the rally, our theme was the petition from the Lord's Prayer: "Thy Kingdom Come!" As our group came down off a bridge crossing the Elbe, our way was blocked by a man holding a bicycle. He was apparently not a Christian, but his curiosity had been aroused by the messages blasting from the loudspeakers. He looked at me intently and asked: "What is this about your kingdom? Is it real, or is it just an idea? Tell me more about it!"

Although I did not know the guy, I loved him for his question. I would have enjoyed so much the chance to sit down with him in a restaurant over a beer or two. I would have loved to dig deep with him into our faith as believers in Christ. But I was unable to stay and answer. I had to go on with the group. I was their translator, and we were in a hurry to get to another meeting.

When All Hell Breaks Loose

So that is what happened when all hell broke loose and God came to me in my town, sixty years ago. And sinner that I was, I answered his call.

El factor humano

Seix Barral Los Tres Mundos

John Carlin
El factor humano

Nelson Mandela
y el partido que salvó una nación

Traducción del inglés por
María Luisa Fernández Tapia

Diseño original de la colección:
Josep Bagà Associats

Título original:
Playing the Enemy

© John Carlin, 2008
www.johncarlin.eu

Derechos exclusivos de edición
en español reservados
para España:
© Editorial Seix Barral, S. A., 2009
Avda. Diagonal, 662-664 - 08034 Barcelona

© Traducción: María Luisa Fernández Tapia, 2009

ISBN 13: 978-84-322-0910-9
ISBN 10: 84-322-0910-4

Editorial Planeta Colombiana S. A.
Calle 73 No. 7-60, Bogotá

ISBN 13: 978-958-42-2141-4
ISBN 10: 958-42-2141-8

Primera reimpresión (Colombia): abril de 2009
Impresión y encuadernación: Editorial Linotipia Bolívar
Impreso en Colombia - Printed in Colombia

Para mi hijo, James Nelson

«No hay que apelar a su razón,
sino a sus corazones.»

NELSON MANDELA

INTRODUCCIÓN

La primera persona a la que propuse hacer este libro fue Nelson Mandela. Nos vimos en el salón de su casa de Johanesburgo en agosto de 2001, dos años después de que se retirase de la presidencia de Sudáfrica. Después de intercambiar unas cuantas bromas, cosa que se le da muy bien, y algunos recuerdos comunes sobre los tensos años de la transición política en Sudáfrica, que yo había cubierto para un periódico británico, le hice mi propuesta.

Empecé por exponer los temas generales y le dije que, en mi opinión, todas las sociedades aspiran, conscientemente o no, a utopías de un tipo u otro. Los políticos comercian con las esperanzas de la gente de alcanzar el cielo en la tierra. Como no es posible, las vidas de las naciones, como las de las personas, son una lucha perpetua por hacer realidad esos sueños. En el caso de Mandela, el sueño que le sostuvo durante sus veintisiete años de cárcel fue el mismo que el de Martin Luther King Jr.: que un día, a la gente de su país, se la juzgara no por el color de su piel sino por su carácter.

Mientras hablaba, Mandela seguía sentado, inescrutable como una esfinge, como hace siempre que la conversación se vuelve seria y él es el oyente. Uno no está seguro, mientras parlotea sin parar, de si le está prestando atención o está perdido en sus propios pensamientos. Sin embargo, cuando cité a King, asintió, los labios cerrados, con un brusco movimiento de barbilla.

Animado, le dije que el libro que pensaba escribir trataba sobre la pacífica transferencia de poder de la minoría blanca a la mayoría negra en Sudáfrica, el paso del apartheid a la democracia; que el libro iba a cubrir diez años, empezando por el primer contacto político que tuvo él con el gobierno en 1985 (me pareció ver que asentía también a eso), cuando todavía estaba en prisión. En cuanto al tema, era una cuestión que podía tener importancia en cualquier lugar en el que surgen conflictos debidos a la incomprensión y la desconfianza que van de la mano del tribalismo congénito de la especie. Cuando dije «tribalismo», me refería al sentido más amplio de la palabra, aplicada a la raza, la religión, el nacionalismo y la política. George Orwell definió el término como esa «costumbre de suponer que a los seres humanos se les puede clasificar como a los insectos, y que es posible aplicar a bloques enteros de millones o decenas de millones de personas la etiqueta de "buenas" o "malas"». Nunca desde el nazismo se había institucionalizado ese hábito deshumanizador de forma tan completa como en Sudáfrica. El propio Mandela describió el apartheid como un «genocidio moral»: sin campos de la muerte, pero con el cruel exterminio del respeto de un pueblo por sí mismo.

Por ese motivo, el apartheid fue el único sistema político que, en el apogeo de la guerra fría, muchos países —Estados Unidos, la Unión Soviética, Albania, China, Francia, Corea del Norte, España, Cuba— estuvieron de acuerdo en considerar, según la definición de Naciones Unidas, «un crimen contra la humanidad». Sin embargo, de esa injustica épica nació una épica reconciliación.

Le conté a Mandela que, en mi trabajo de periodista, había conocido a mucha gente que luchaba para lograr la paz en Oriente Próximo, Latinoamérica, África, Asia: para esas personas, Sudáfrica era un ideal al que todos aspiraban. En la industria de la «resolución de conflictos» que floreció tras el final de la guerra fría, cuando empezaron a estallar conflictos locales en todo el mundo, el manual a seguir para alcanzar la paz por medios políticos era la «revolución negociada» de Sudáfrica, como alguien la llamó una vez. Ningún otro país había hecho la transición de la tiranía a la democracia mejor ni con más compasión. Reconocí que ya se había escrito mucho sobre los mecanismos internos del «milagro sudafricano». Pero lo que faltaba, en mi opinión, era un libro sobre el factor humano, sobre lo milagroso del milagro. Lo que yo tenía en mente era una historia desinhibidoramente positiva que mostrase los mejores aspectos del animal humano; un libro con un héroe de carne y hueso; un libro sobre un país cuya mayoría negra debería haber exigido a gritos la venganza y, sin embargo, siguiendo el ejemplo de Mandela, dio al mundo una lección de inteligencia y capacidad de perdonar. Mi libro iba a estar habitado por un amplio repertorio de personajes, blancos y negros, cuyas historias transmitirían el rostro viviente de la gran ceremonia de redención sudafricana. Pero también, en un momento en el que, si observábamos a los líderes mundiales, la mayoría nos parecían enanos morales (la esfinge ni se inmutó al oírlo), mi libro iba a tratar sobre él. No sería una biografía, sino un relato que ilustrase su genio político, el talento que desplegó al ganarse a la gente para su causa a base de apelar a sus mejores cualidades; al sacar a relucir, en palabras de Abraham Lincoln, a «los ángeles buenos» de su naturaleza.

Le dije que quería situar el libro en torno al espectáculo dramático de un acontecimiento deportivo concreto. El deporte era un poderoso instrumento de movilización de masas y agudizaba las percepciones políticas (también aquí hizo un rápido y seco gesto de asentimiento). Cité varios ejemplos: los Juegos Olímpicos de Berlín en 1936, que Hitler utilizó para promover la idea de la superioridad aria, aunque el atleta negro estadounidense Jesse Owens desbarató sus planes al ganar cuatro medallas; Jackie Robinson, el primer negro que jugó en la liga de primera división de béisbol y ayudó a poner en marcha el cambio de actitud que desembocaría en una gran transformación social en Estados Unidos.

Luego recordé a Mandela una cosa que él había dicho uno o dos años antes, en la entrega de un premio a la labor de toda una vida a la estrella del fútbol brasileño Pelé. Había dicho, según las notas que llevaba conmigo, que «el deporte tiene el poder de transformar el mundo. Tiene el poder de inspirar, de unir a la gente como pocas otras cosas... Tiene más capacidad que los gobiernos de derribar las barreras raciales».

Para resumir, le conté a Mandela cuál iba a ser el corazón narrativo de mi libro y por qué iba a necesitar su apoyo. Le dije que había habido una ocasión deportiva que había superado a las demás que acababa de mencionar, en la que se habían unido todos los temas de los que le acababa de hablar en la conversación; una ocasión que evocaba de forma mágica la «sinfonía de la fraternidad» de los sueños de Martin Luther King; un acontecimiento en el que se plasmó todo aquello por lo que Mandela había luchado y sufrido en su vida. Me refería a la final del...

De pronto, su sonrisa iluminó la habitación y, con sus grandes manos unidas en señal de reconocimiento, terminó la frase por mí: «¡La final de la Copa del Mundo de rugby en 1995!» Mi propia sonrisa confirmó que había adivinado, y añadió: «¡Sí, sí, por supuesto! Entiendo perfectamente el libro en el que está pensando —dijo con voz firme, como si no tuviera ochenta y dos años sino cuarenta menos—. John, tienes mi bendición. La tienes de todo corazón.»

Animados, nos dimos la mano y acordamos volver a vernos pronto. En esa segunda entrevista, con la grabadora encendida, me explicó que la primera vez que se había hecho una idea del poder político del deporte había sido en la cárcel; que había utilizado la Copa del Mundo de rugby de 1995 como instrumento en el gran objetivo estratégico que se había propuesto para sus cinco años como primer presidente elegido democráticamente de Sudáfrica: reconciliar a los blancos y los negros y crear las condiciones para una paz duradera en un país que, sólo cinco años antes, cuando él salió de prisión, contenía todos los elementos para una guerra civil. Me contó, entre risas, lo que le había costado convencer a su propia gente para que apoyara al equipo de rugby, y me habló con respeto y afecto de François Pienaar, el rubio y grandullón hijo del apartheid que capitaneaba la selección sudafricana, los Springboks, y del manager del equipo, otro afrikaner gigantesco, Morné du Plessis, a quien Mandela calificó, en ese estilo medio británico, elegante y anticuado que tiene, como «un caballero excelente».

Después de que Mandela y yo nos viéramos aquel día, todo tipo de gente aceptó hablar conmigo para el libro. Ya había acumulado gran parte del material para mi relato durante los seis apasionantes años que trabajé en Sudáfrica como corresponsal del *Independent* de Londres, entre 1989 y 1995, y había vuelto al país varias veces como periodista durante los diez años posteriores. Pero no empecé a entrevistarme con personas pensando específicamente en este libro hasta después de hablar con Mandela, y lo hice con una estrella de los Springboks de aquel campeonato llamado Hennie le Roux. Uno no espera sentirse afectado y sentimental después de hablar con un jugador de rugby, pero eso es lo que me pasó, porque Le Roux se emocionó mucho al hablar de Mandela y del papel que a él, un afrikaner decente pero poco versado en política, le había tocado desempeñar en la vida nacional de su país. Pasamos juntos unas dos horas en una planta de un edificio de oficinas vacío, mientras caía la tarde, y en tres o cuatro ocasiones tuvo que interrumpirse mientras hablaba para reprimir los sollozos.

La entrevista con Le Roux marcó el tono que iban a tener las docenas de conversaciones más que mantuve para este libro. Hubo muchas ocasiones en las que a mis interlocutores se les humedecían los ojos, sobre todo cuando se trataba de alguien del mundo del rugby. Y en todos los casos —ya fuera el arzobispo Desmond Tutu, el general afrikaner Constand Viljoen, nacionalista de extrema derecha, o su hemano gemelo Braam, más bien de izquierdas—, revivieron la época de la que hablábamos con un entusiasmo que a veces rayaba en la euforia.

Más de una vez, la gente comentó que el libro que iba a escribir parecía una fábula, o una parábola, o un cuento de hadas. Resultaba curioso oírlo de boca de quienes habían sido los protagonistas reales de una historia política llena de violencia, pero era cierto. El hecho de que ocurriera en África y tuviera que ver con un partido de rugby era casi lo de menos. Si hubiera sucedido en China y el elemento dramático hubiera consistido en una carrera de búfalos de agua, el relato habría podido ser igualmente ejemplar. Porque cumplía las dos condiciones esenciales de un buen cuento de hadas: era una gran historia y contenía una lección eterna.

Otras dos cosas me impresionaron cuando empecé a revisar todo el material que había acumulado. En primer lugar, el genio político de Mandela. La política, reducida a sus elementos esenciales, es persuasión, ganarse a la gente. Todos los políticos son seductores profesionales. Viven de cortejar a la gente. Y, si son listos y hacen bien su trabajo, si tienen talento para conectar bien con el pueblo, prosperan. Lincoln era así, y Roosevelt, y Churchill, y De Gaulle, y Kennedy, y Martin Luther King, y Reagan, y Clinton y Blair. También lo era Arafat. E incluso Hitler. Todos ellos se ganaron a su gente para la causa que defendían. En lo que les superó Mandela —el anti-Hitler— fue en el alcance de su ambición. Después de ganarse a su propia gente —ya suficiente proeza, porque era gente muy diversa, formada por todo tipo de creencias, colores y tribus—, se propuso ganarse al enemigo. Cómo lo hizo, cómo consiguió ganarse a personas que habían aplaudido su encarcelamiento, que habían querido verle muerto, que habían planeado declararle la guerra, es de lo que trata principalmente este libro.

La segunda cosa de la que me di cuenta fue que, además de un relato, incluso además de un cuento de hadas, esta historia podía acabar siendo una parte más del enorme canon de obras de autoayuda que ofrecen a los lectores modelos para prosperar en su propia vida. Mandela domina, más que ninguna otra persona viva (y seguramente muerta) el arte de hacer amigos e influir en la gente. Da igual que procedieran de la extrema izquierda o de la extrema derecha, que al principio hubieran temido, odiado o admirado a Mandela: todas las personas a las que entrevisté dijeron haberse sentido renovados y mejores gracias a su ejemplo. Todos ellos, al hablar de él, parecían brillar. Este libro pretende, humildemente, reflejar un poco la luz de Mandela.

Capítulo I
DESAYUNO EN HOUGHTON

24 de junio de 1995

Se despertó, como siempre, a las 4:30 de la mañana; se levantó, se vistió, dobló su pijama e hizo su cama. Había sido un revolucionario toda su vida y ahora era presidente de un gran país, pero no había nada capaz de hacer que Nelson Mandela rompiera con los rituales establecidos durante sus veintisiete años de prisión.

Ni cuando estaba en casa de otra persona, ni cuando se alojaba en un hotel de lujo, ni siquiera cuando pasaba la noche en el palacio de Buckingham o la Casa Blanca. Con la suerte de que nunca le afectaba el jet lag —le daba igual estar en Washington, Londres o Nueva Delhi—, siempre se levantaba a las 4:30 y se hacía la cama. Las personas encargadas de limpiarle la habitación en todo el mundo se quedaban siempre estupefactas al ver que el dignatario que les visitaba les había hecho la mitad del trabajo. Sobre todo, la señora a la que le tocó limpiar su suite del hotel en el que se alojó durante una visita a Shanghai. Le trastornaron las individualistas costumbres de Mandela. Cuando los ayudantes de éste le contaron que la camarera se había quedado molesta, él la invitó a su habitación, le pidió disculpas y le explicó que hacer la cama era como limpiarse los dientes; era algo que no podía evitar hacer.

La misma fijación tenía con una rutina de hacer ejercicio que había comenzado ya antes de la cárcel, en los años cuarenta y cincuenta, cuando era abogado, revolucionario y boxeador aficionado. En aquellos tiempos, corría durante una hora antes de que amaneciera, desde su pequeña casa de ladrillo en Soweto hasta Johanesburgo y vuelta. En 1964 ingresó en prisión en Robben Island, una isla junto a la costa de Ciudad del Cabo, y permaneció en una celda diminuta durante dieciocho años. Allí, a falta de otra alternativa, corría sin moverse del sitio. Todas las mañanas, durante una hora. En 1982 le trasladaron a una cárcel en tierra firme en la que compartió celda con su mejor amigo, Walter Sisulu, y otros tres veteranos de la lucha contra el apartheid en Sudáfrica. La celda era grande, aproximadamente del tamaño de media pista de tenis, y allí podía dar unas vueltas cortas. Lo malo era que, cuando emprendía aquellos medios maratones de interior, los demás estaban todavía acostados, y se quejaban amargamente de que todas las mañanas les sacaran de su sueño los vigorosos e implacables pisotones sexagenarios de su, por lo demás, querido camarada.

Tras su salida de prisión en febrero de 1990, a los setenta y un años, aflojó un poco el ritmo. En vez de correr, empezó a andar, pero con paso rápido y, como antes, todas las mañanas, durante una hora, antes de que amaneciera. Solía hacerlo en el barrio de Houghton, en Johanesburgo, donde se fue a vivir en abril de 1992 tras el fracaso de su segundo matrimonio, con Winnie. Dos años después llegó a la presidencia y, a partir de entonces, tuvo dos magníficas residencias a su disposición, una en Pretoria y otra en Ciudad del Cabo, pero siempre se sintió más a gusto en su casa de Houghton, un refugio en los barrios acomodados y, hasta hacía poco, sólo para blancos, del norte de la metrópolis más rica de África. A un habitante de Los Ángeles le llamarían la atención las semejanzas entre Houghton y Beverly Hills. Los blancos se habían cuidado bien durante la larga estancia de Mandela en la cárcel, y él pensó que también tenía derecho a un poco de buena vida. Le gustaba el carácter tranquilo y señorial de Houghton, el espacio y la frondosidad de sus paseos mañaneros, las charlas con sus vecinos blancos, a cuyas fiestas de cumpleaños y otras ceremonias asistía de vez en cuando. En los primeros tiempos de su presidencia, un chico judío de trece años se presentó en casa de Mandela y entregó al policía de guardia en la puerta una invitación para su *bar mitzvah*. Los padres se quedaron asombrados al recibir una llamada telefónica del propio Mandela, unos días después, para que le dijeran cómo llegar a su casa. Y se quedaron aún más asombrados cuando le vieron aparecer en su puerta, alto y sonriente, el gran día de su hijo. Mandela se sentía bienvenido y cómodo en una comunidad en la que, durante la mayor parte de su vida, sólo habría podido vivir si hubiera sido lo que en la Sudáfrica blanca llamaban —independientemente de la edad— un «chico de jardín». Se aficionó a Houghton y siguió viviendo allí durante todo su mandato, sin dormir en sus mansiones oficiales más que cuando el deber lo exigía.

En aquella mañana concreta, en pleno invierno del

hemisferio sur, Mandela se despertó a las 4:30, como siempre, se vistió y se hizo la cama... pero entonces, con un comportamiento asombrosamente fuera de lugar en una criatura tan de costumbres como él, rompió la rutina; no fue a dar su caminata matutina. Fue al piso de abajo, se sentó en el comedor y desayunó. Había pensado el cambio de planes la noche anterior, con lo que había tenido tiempo de advertir a sus sorprendidos guardaespaldas, la Unidad de Protección Presidencial, de que a la mañana siguiente podían quedarse una hora más en la cama. En vez de llegar a las cinco, podían entrar a trabajar a las seis. Les iba a hacer falta ese descanso extra, porque el día iba a ser una prueba para ellos, casi tanto como para el propio Mandela.

Otra señal de que aquél no era un día cualquiera fue que Mandela, normalmente poco dado a los nervios, tenía un nudo en el estómago. «No sabes lo que pasé aquel día —me confesó—. ¡Qué tenso estaba!» Una confesión curiosa, en un hombre con su historia. No era el día de su liberación en febrero de 1990, ni su toma de posesión como presidente en mayo de 1994, ni siquiera la mañana de junio de 1964 en la que se despertó en una celda, sin saber si el juez iba a condenarle a muerte o, como al final fue, a cadena perpetua. Era el día en el que su país, Sudáfrica, iba a enfrentarse a la mejor selección del mundo, Nueva Zelanda, en la final de la Copa del Mundo de rugby. Sus compatriotas estaban tan nerviosos como él. Pero lo extraordinario, en un país que había dado bandazos históricos entre crisis y desastres, era que los nervios que sentían todos se debían a la perspectiva del inminente triunfo nacional.

Hasta entonces, cuando había una noticia que dominaba los periódicos, casi siempre significaba que había ocurrido o estaba a punto de ocurrir algo malo; o que se refería a algo que una parte del país interpretaría como bueno y otra como malo. Esa mañana, había un consenso nacional sin precedentes en torno a una misma idea. Los 43 millones de sudafricanos, blancos, negros y de todos los matices, compartían la misma aspiración: la victoria de su equipo, los Springboks.

O casi todos. Había al menos un descontento en aquellas últimas horas antes del partido, uno que deseaba que perdiera Sudáfrica. Se llamaba Justice Bekebeke y aquel día era la encarnación del espíritu de contradicción. Se atenía a lo que él consideraba sus principios, pese a que no conocía a nadie que compartiera su deseo de que ganase el otro equipo. Ni su novia, ni el resto de su familia, ni sus mejores amigos de Paballelo, el distrito negro en el que vivía. Todos sus conocidos estaban con Mandela y los Boks, a pesar de que, de los quince jugadores que iban a vestir esa tarde la camiseta de rugby sudafricana, verde y dorada, todos eran blancos menos uno. En un país en el que casi el 90 % de la población estaba formado por gente de color de distintas razas, Bekebeke no quería tener nada que ver con aquello. Se mantenía en sus trece y se negaba a unirse a aquella casi borrachera de camaradería multirracial que extrañamente se había apoderado incluso de Mandela, su líder, su héroe.

A primera vista, tenía razón y Mandela y los demás no sólo estaban equivocados sino que se habían vuelto locos. El rugby no era el deporte de la Sudáfrica negra. Ni Bekebeke, ni Mandela, ni la gran mayoría de sus compatriotas negros se habían criado con él ni eran especialmente aficionados. Para ser sincero, Mandela, de pronto un gran hincha, habría tenido que reconocer que le había costado entender varias de las reglas. Como Bekebeke, Mandela había sentido la mayor parte de su vida una clara antipatía hacia el rugby. Era un deporte blanco y, en especial, el deporte de los afrikaners, la tribu blanca dominante en el país, la raza superior del apartheid. Los negros habían considerado a los Springboks, durante muchos años, como un símbolo de la opresión del apartheid, tan repugnante como el viejo himno nacional y la vieja bandera de los blancos. Y la repugnancia debía ser aún mayor para alguien que, como Bekebeke y Mandela, hubiera sido encarcelado por luchar contra el apartheid; en el caso de Bekebeke, durante seis de sus treinta y cuatro años.

Otro personaje que, por motivos muy distintos, quizá podía estar en la misma línea que Bekebeke aquel día era el general Constand Viljoen. Viljoen estaba retirado, pero había sido jefe del ejército sudafricano durante cinco de los años de enfrentamientos más violentos entre los activistas negros y el Estado. Había derramado mucha más sangre defendiendo el apartheid que Bekebeke luchando contra él y, sin embargo, nunca había ido a la cárcel por lo que había hecho. Debería haber estado agradecido por ello, pero, por el contrario, había dedicado parte de su retiro a tratar de movilizar un ejército que se levantase contra el nuevo orden democrático. Sin embargo, esa mañana, se levantó de la cama en Ciudad del Cabo en el mismo estado de tensión y excitación que Mandela y el grupo de amigos afrikaner con los que iba a ver el partido en televisión por la tarde.

Niël Barnard, un afrikaner con el curioso mérito de haber luchado tanto contra Mandela como contra Viljoen en diferentes momentos, estaba todavía más tenso que sus dos antiguos enemigos. Barnard, que se disponía a ver el partido con su familia en su casa de Pretoria, a 1.500 kilómetros al norte de Ciudad del Cabo y a 40 minutos de autopista de Johanesburgo, había dirigido el Servicio Nacional de Inteligencia sudafricano, el SNI, durante el último decenio del apartheid. Era el hombre más cercano al implacable presidente P. W. Botha y estaba considerado como un personaje demoniaco y siniestro tanto por la derecha como por la izquierda, así como por mucha gente más allá de las fronteras de su país. Defensor del Estado —independientemente de la forma que adoptase ese Estado— por profesión y por temperamento, había librado una guerra contra el Congreso Nacional Africano (CNA) de Mandela, había sido el cerebro que dirigió las conversaciones de paz con ellos y después había pasado a defender el nuevo sistema político contra los ataques de la derecha, a la que pertenecía originalmente. Tenía fama de ser aterradoramente frío y clínico. Pero cuando se dejaba ir, se dejaba ir. El rugby era su válvula de escape. Cuando jugaban los Springboks, se deshacía de todas sus inhibiciones y se convertía, como él mismo reconocía, en un animal gritón. En este día, cuando iban a jugar el partido más importante de la historia del rugby sudafricano, se despertó hecho un manojo de nervios.

El arzobispo Desmond Tutu, sobre cuya vida privada solía guardar Barnard detallados expedientes, se encontraba en un estado de aprensión similar, o se habría encontrado si no hubiera sido porque estaba inconsciente. Tutu, que había sido el suplente de Mandela en los escenarios mundiales durante los años de cárcel de éste, era seguramente el más exuberante de todos los premios Nobel, y había pocas cosas que pudiera disfrutar más que estar presente en el estadio durante el partido, pero se encontraba en aquel momento en San Francisco, pronunciando discursos y recibiendo premios. Después de una búsqueda ansiosa, había encontrado la noche anterior un bar en el que podía ver el partido por televisión al amanecer, hora de la costa del Pacífico. Se había ido a la cama con una sola inquietud: su desesperado deseo de que, a la mañana siguiente, los Springboks rompieran los pronósticos y vencieran.

En cuanto a los propios jugadores, habrían sufrido suficiente tensión si ésta hubiera sido una final de la Copa del Mundo como cualquier otra. Pero ahora tenían una carga añadida. Antes de que empezara la Copa, quizá uno o dos de aquellos campechanos deportistas habría dedicado algún pensamiento fugaz a la política, pero nada más. Eran como otros hombres blancos sudafricanos y como la mayoría de los hombres en todas partes, en el sentido de que pensaban poco en la política y mucho en el deporte. Sin embargo, cuando Mandela había ido a verles un mes antes, el día antes de que comenzara el campeonato, les había asaltado una idea nueva: que se habían convertido literalmente en actores políticos. En la mañana de la final, comprendieron con impresionante claridad que la victoria contra Nueva Zelanda podía permitir algo aparentemente imposible, unir a un país más polarizado por la división racial que ningún otro en el mundo.

François Pienaar, el capitán de los Springboks, se despertó con el resto de su equipo en un hotel de lujo situado en el norte de Johanesburgo, cerca de la casa de Mandela, en un estado de concentración tan profunda que tuvo que hacer un esfuerzo para comprender dónde estaba. Cuando salió a correr a media mañana para desentumecerse, su cerebro no tenía ni idea de dónde le llevaban las piernas; no pensaba más que en la batalla de la tarde. El rugby es como una partida gigante de ajedrez que se juega a gran velocidad y con gran violencia, y los Springboks iban a enfrentarse a los grandes maestros del deporte, los All Blacks de Nueva Zelanda, el mejor equipo del mundo y uno de los mejores de la historia. Pienaar sabía que los All Blacks podían ganar a los Boks nueve de cada diez veces.

La única persona con una responsabilidad mayor que los jugadores de los Springboks aquel día era Linga Moonsamy, miembro de la Unidad de Protección Presidencial. Tenía asignada la tarea de ser el guardaespaldas «número uno» de la UPP y debía estar a un paso de Mandela desde el momento en el que saliera de casa para ir al partido hasta su vuelta. Moonsamy, antiguo guerrillero en el CNA de Mandela, era muy consciente, como profesional, de los peligros físicos que iba a afrontar su jefe ese día y, como antiguo combatiente por la libertad, del riesgo político que estaba asumiendo.

Agradecido por la hora extra de sueño que le había concedido su jefe, Moonsamy llegó en coche a la casa de Mandela en Houghton, al puesto de policía situado a la puerta, a las seis de la mañana. No tardó en llegar el equipo de la UPP que iba a proteger a Mandela durante todo el día, dieciséis hombres en total, la mitad de ellos ex policías blancos y la otra mitad antiguos combatientes por la libertad como él. Hicieron un círculo en el jardín delantero, como hacían todas las mañanas, en torno a un miembro del grupo llamado el oficial de planificación, que les transmitió las informaciones recibidas del Servicio Nacional de Inteligencia sobre posibles amenazas a las que tenían que estar atentos y los detalles de la ruta hacia el estadio, los puntos vulnerables del trayecto. Uno de los cuatro vehículos del equipo se fue a examinar el trayecto y Moonsamy se quedó allí, junto con otros, para comprobar sus armas, examinar el Mercedes-Benz blindado de color gris de Mandela y hacer el papeleo. Como formalmente estaban a sueldo de la policía, siempre tenían formularios que rellenar, y aquél era el momento ideal para hacerlo. Si no ocurría nada inesperado —y ocurría muchas veces—, tenían varias horas que matar hasta el momento de salir, así que disponían de amplias oportunidades para conversar antes del partido.

Pero Moonsamy, consciente de la responsabilidad especial que tenía ese día —porque la identidad del guardaespaldas número uno cambiaba de un día para otro—, estaba tan atento a su gran tarea como François Pienaar a la suya. Moonsamy, un hombre alto y ágil de veintiocho años, se enfrentaba en aquel momento al reto más grande de su vida. Pertenecía a la UPP desde que Mandela había llegado a la presidencia y ya había acumulado unas cuantas aventuras. Mandela insistía en hacer apariciones públicas en lugares impensados (por ejemplo, en bastiones de la derecha rural afrikaner) y le encantaba sumergirse de forma indiscriminada en las multitudes para disfrutar del contacto no filtrado por su gente. También le gustaba hacer paradas imprevistas, pedir de pronto a su chófer que se detuviera en una librería, por ejemplo, porque acababa de acordarse de una novela que deseaba comprar, y entraba en la tienda sin preocuparse por la conmoción que provocaba. Una vez, en Nueva York, cuando su limusina estaba en un atasco de camino a una cita importante, Mandela salió y bajó a pie por la Sexta Avenida, para asombro y delicia de la gente que pasaba por allí. «¡Pero, señor presidente, por favor...!», rogaban los guardaespaldas. Y Mandela respondía: «No, mirad. Vosotros hacéis vuestro trabajo y yo hago el mío.»

En este día, el trabajo de la UPP iba a ser distinto a cualquier otro que habían hecho o harían jamás. El partido de aquella tarde, o la participación de Mandela en él, iba a ser, en opinión de Moonsamy, como cuando Daniel entró en el foso de los leones, salvo que se trataba de 62.000 leones presentes en el estadio Ellis Park, un monumento a la supremacía blanca no muy lejos del amable barrio de Houghton. El 95 % de los espectadores serían blancos, en su mayoría afrikaners. Rodeado por aquella muchedumbre tan inusual (Mandela no había aparecido nunca ante una multitud así), iba a bajar al campo a dar la mano a los jugadores antes del partido y luego, al final, a entregar la copa al capitán vencedor.

La escena que imaginaba Moonsamy —masas del viejo enemigo, afrikaners barrigudos con camisas de color caqui, rodeando al hombre al que, durante casi toda su vida, se les había enseñado a considerar el mayor terrorista de Sudáfrica— tenía cierto tono surrealista. Sin embargo, englobaba el propósito realista y completamente serio que se había fijado Mandela. Su misión, como la de todos los sudafricanos negros políticamente activos de su generación, había sido sustituir el apartheid por lo que el CNA llamaba una «democracia no racial». Pero todavía tenía que alcanzar un objetivo que era igual de importante y no menos difícil. Ya era presidente. Un año antes se habían celebrado las primeras elecciones en la historia de Sudáfrica según el principio de «una persona, un voto». Pero todavía quedaba mucho por hacer. Mandela tenía que asegurar los cimientos de la nueva democracia, tenía que hacerla resistente a las peligrosas fuerzas que aún estaban al acecho. La historia demostraba que una revolución tan total como la sudafricana, en la que el poder pasa de la noche a la mañana a manos de los rivales históricos, provoca una contrarrevolución. Aún había en circulación muchos extremistas fuertemente armados y con formación militar; muchos resentidos afrikaner, los «bitter enders», la versión sudafricana, más organizada, más numerosa y más armada del Ku Klux Klan estadounidense. En esas circunstancias, como había aprendido Moonsamy con sus lecturas de textos políticos, era esperable que hubiera terrorismo de derechas, y el terrorismo de derechas era lo que más deseaba evitar Mandela como presidente.

La mejor forma de hacerlo era conseguir que la población blanca aceptara su voluntad. Desde el principio de su presidencia valoró la posibilidad de que la Copa del Mundo de rugby le diera la oportunidad de ganárselos para su causa. Por eso se había empeñado en convencer a sus propios partidarios negros de que abandonaran el justificado prejuicio de siempre y apoyasen a los Springboks. Por eso quería demostrar ese día a los afrikaners en el estadio que aquél era también su equipo, que iba a compartir con ellos el triunfo o la derrota.

Pero el plan estaba lleno de riesgos. Los extremistas podían disparar contra Mandela o hacer estallar una bomba. O el propio acto podía volverse contra ellos. Una mala derrota de los Springboks no ayudaría. Todavía peor era la perspectiva de que los hinchas afrikaners la emprendieran a abucheos al oír el nuevo himno nacional, tan querido de los negros, o que ondearan la vieja y odiada bandera naranja, azul y blanca. Los millones de personas que vieran el partido en los distritos negros se sentirían humillados e indignados y preferirían apoyar a la selección de Nueva Zelanda, con lo que el consenso que Mandela había conseguido crear en torno a los Springboks se haría añicos, y surgiría la consiguiente posibilidad de desestabilización.

Sin embargo, Mandela era optimista. Estaba convencido de que las cosas iban a salir bien, como estaba convencido (como una pequeña minoría) de que los Springboks iban a ganar. Por eso, aquella mañana invernal y luminosa de sábado, se sentó tenso pero de buen humor a consumir su acostumbrado y copioso desayuno. Tomó, por este orden: media papaya, gachas de maíz seco, al que añadió frutos secos, pasas y leche caliente; una ensalada verde y luego, en plato aparte, tres rodajas de plátano, tres rodajas de kiwi y tres rodajas de mango. Después se sirvió una taza de café, que endulzó con miel.

Mandela, impaciente por que empezara el partido, comió aquella mañana con especial apetito. No se había dado cuenta hasta entonces, pero toda su vida había estado preparándose para ese momento. Su decisión de entrar en el CNA cuando era joven, en los años cuarenta; su liderazgo desafiante en la campaña contra el apartheid en los cincuenta; la soledad, la dureza y la callada rutina de la cárcel; el exhaustivo régimen de ejercicios al que se sometía tras las rejas, siempre seguro de que un día saldría y desempeñaría un papel fundamental en la política de su país; todo eso, y mucho más, había construido la plataforma para el empuje definitivo de los diez años anteriores, un periodo en el que Mandela había asumido sus batallas más difíciles y sus victorias más improbables. Hoy era la gran prueba, la que ofrecía las posibilidades de recompensa más duradera.

Si salía bien, llevaría a una conclusión victoriosa el viaje que, con una ambición propia de una epopeya clásica, había emprendido en la última década de su largo camino hacia la libertad. Como el Odiseo de Homero, había avanzado de obstáculo en obstáculo y había vencido cada uno de ellos, no porque fuera más fuerte que sus enemigos, sino porque era más listo y más seductor. Unas cualidades que había forjado tras su detención y encarcelación en 1962, cuando comprendió que la vía de la fuerza bruta que había intentado, como jefe y fundador del brazo militar del CNA, no servía para nada. En la cárcel pensó que la forma de matar el apartheid era convencer a los blancos de que lo mataran ellos mismos, de que se unieran a su equipo y se sometieran a su liderazgo.

Fue también en la cárcel donde aprovechó su primera gran oportunidad de llevar a la práctica su estrategia. En aquella ocasión, el adversario fue un hombre llamado Kobie Coetsee, cuyo estado de ánimo en la mañana del partido de rugby era de excitación nerviosa, como el de todos los demás; cuya claridad de ideas sólo se veía nublada por la duda de si ver el partido en su casa, a las afueras de Ciudad del Cabo, o sumergirse en la atmósfera de un bar cercano. En este día, Coetsee y Mandela estaban en el mismo bando hasta un punto que habría sido impensable cuando se conocieron, diez años antes. Entonces tenían todos los motivos para sentir mutua hostilidad. Mandela era el preso político más famoso de Sudáfrica; Coetsee era el ministro de Justicia y Prisiones. La tarea que se había propuesto Mandela, que llevaba cumplidos veintitrés años de su cadena perpetua, era ganarse a Coetsee, el hombre que controlaba las llaves de su celda.

Capítulo II

EL MINISTRO DE JUSTICIA

Noviembre de 1985

1985 fue un año de esperanza para el mundo, pero no para Sudáfrica. Mijail Gorbachov llegó al poder en la Unión Soviética, Ronald Reagan tomó posesión como presidente para un segundo mandato y los dos líderes de la guerra fría celebraron su primera cumbre, el indicio más firme en cuarenta años de que las superpotencias podían convencerse mutuamente de aparcar sus estratagemas para la destrucción recíproca asegurada. Mientras tanto, Sudáfrica avanzaba en la dirección opuesta. Las tensiones entre los militantes antiapartheid y la policía estallaron en la escalada más violenta de hostilidades raciales desde que los casacas rojas de la reina Victoria y los regimientos del rey Cetshwayo se aniquilaron mutuamente en la salvaje carnicería de la guerra anglo-zulú de 1879. La dirección del CNA, en el exilio, animaba a sus partidarios en el interior a que se alzaran contra el gobierno, pero también llevaban a cabo su ofensiva en otros frentes: a través de los poderosos sindicatos, las sanciones económicas internacionales y el aislamiento diplomático. Y a través del rugby. El CNA llevaba diez años de campaña para privar a los sudafricanos blancos, especialmente a los afrikaners, del rugby internacional, la gran pasión de su vida. En 1985 fue cuando consiguieron sus mayores triunfos, al frustrar una gira prevista de los Springboks por Nueva Zelanda. Fue doloroso. El recuerdo reciente de aquella derrota inyectaba aún más fuerza a los musculosos brazos de los antidisturbios afrikaner cuando golpeaban con sus porras las cabezas de sus víctimas negras.

La única perspectiva que había ese año en el horizonte parecía ser la guerra civil. Un sondeo de opinión nacional llevado a cabo a mediados de agosto descubrió que el 70 % de la población negra y el 30 % de la blanca creían que el país se encaminaba en esa dirección. Pero, si las cosas llegaban a ese extremo, el vencedor no sería el CNA de Mandela, sino su principal adversario, el presidente P. W. Botha, más conocido en Sudáfrica como «P. W.» o, por los amigos y enemigos en quienes despertaba temor, *die groot krokodil*, el gran cocodrilo. A mediados de 1985, Botha, que gobernó Sudáfrica entre 1978 y 1989, anunció el estado de emergencia y ordenó que 35.000 soldados de la Fuerza de Defensa Sudafricana, FDSA, entrasen en los distritos negros segregados. Era la primera vez que se pedía al ejército que ayudase a la policía a sofocar lo que el gobierno consideraba una rebelión cada vez más organizada. Tales sospechas se confirmaron cuando la dirección del CNA en el exilio respondió a la medida de Botha con un llamamiento a la «guerra popular» para hacer que el país fuera «ingobernable», lo que hizo que los blancos huyeran en masa del país —a Gran Bretaña, a Australia, a Estados Unidos—. 1985 fue el año en el que los espectadores de televisión de todo el mundo se acostumbraron a ver Sudáfrica como un país de barricadas humeantes en el que los jóvenes negros lanzaban piedras contra policías blancos armados de fusiles, en el que los vehículos blindados de la FDSA avanzaban como naves extraterrestres sobre muchedumbres negras aterrorizadas. De acuerdo con las normas del estado de emergencia, las fuerzas de seguridad disponían de poderes prácticamente ilimitados de búsqueda, incautación y detención, además de la tranquilidad de saber que podían atacar a los sospechosos con impunidad. En los quince meses anteriores a la primera semana de noviembre de ese año, 850 personas murieron en actos de violencia política y miles fueron encarcelados sin cargos.

En ese clima, ese año, Mandela lanzó su ofensiva de paz. Convencido de que las negociaciones eran la única forma de acabar definitivamente con el apartheid, decidió afrontar el reto solo y, como se vio después, con las manos atadas. A principios de año, los médicos habían descubierto que tenía problemas de próstata y, temiendo que fuera cáncer, decidieron que necesitaba ser operado con urgencia. Habían hecho el diagnóstico en la cárcel de Pollsmoor, donde había sido trasladado desde Robben Island tres años antes, en 1982. Pollsmoor, en tierra firme, cerca de Ciudad del Cabo, fue la cárcel en la que compartió la gran celda con Walter Sisulu y otros tres presos veteranos a los que ponía furiosos con sus carreras antes de amanecer. La operación, llevada a cabo el 4 de noviembre de 1985, fue un éxito, pero Mandela, que tenía ya sesenta y siete años, tuvo que permanecer bajo observación. Los médicos ordenaron que convaleciera en el hospital durante tres semanas más.

Durante ese interludio, la primera estancia de Mandela fuera de la cárcel en veintitrés años, comenzaron sus diez años de intentos de ganarse a la Sudáfrica blanca. Por una coincidencia histórica extraordinaria, fue el mismo mes en el que se reunieron Reagan y Gorbachov. Igual que el presidente estadounidense se disponía a emplear su encanto para ganarse al líder soviético, Mandela se preparaba para utilizar la suya con Kobie Coetsee, el hombre que ocupaba el cargo con el título más contradictorio del mundo: ministro de Justicia de Sudáfrica.

Si la cumbre de las superpotencias en Ginebra fue un espectáculo mediático, la reunión sudafricana se llevó a cabo en el mayor de los secretos. La prensa no se enteró de ella hasta cinco años después pero, aunque la hubiera conocido en su momento, incluso si la noticia se hubiera filtrado, habría sido difícil encontrar a alguien que se la creyera. El CNA era el enemigo, los instigadores de un «ataque total» de inspiración soviética, en palabras de P. W. Botha, y contra quienes las fuerzas de seguridad del Estado habían lanzado lo que él llamaba una «estrategia total». No había nada más inconcebible que la idea de que el régimen de Botha negociase con los «terroristas comunistas», y mucho menos con su líder encarcelado.

Aun así, si algún miembro del gobierno debía contactar con el enemigo, ése tenía que ser Coetsee, cuya cartera no sólo abarcaba la Justicia sino también los Servicios Penitenciarios, es decir, el sistema de prisiones. Además, Botha escogió a Coetsee para ser su emisario secreto porque era de una lealtad ciega: uno de los pocos miembros de su gabinete en el que Botha podía confiar para que se comportase con discreción. Por otra parte, era Coetsee quien había recibido, como sus predecesores en el ministerio de Justicia, las largas cartas de Mandela solicitando la entrevista. Con dichas solicitudes, Mandela no hacía más que continuar una tradición infructuosa del CNA, desde su fundación en 1912, de intentar convencer a los gobiernos blancos para que se sentaran a debatir con ellos el futuro del país. Pero ahora, por fin, iba a suceder: las primeras conversaciones entre un político negro y un miembro destacado del gobierno blanco. El motivo de Botha para aprobar el encuentro era, en parte, la curiosidad; el CNA había lanzado en 1980 una campaña para liberar a Mandela y éste se había convertido ya en el preso más famoso y menos conocido del mundo. Pero a Botha le impulsaba sobre todo la situación cada vez más volátil en los distritos segregados y las presiones crecientes del mundo exterior. Tenía la sensación de que había llegado el momento de tantear las posibilidades de reconciliación, de aventurarse a intentar probar si, un día, podría ser posible la convivencia con la Sudáfrica negra. Como explicaría Coetsee posteriormente: «Nos habíamos metido nosotros mismos en un rincón y necesitábamos encontrar la forma de salir.»

Lo curioso era que, aunque Mandela había sido el solicitante, era Coetsee el que se sentía incómodo. Se trataba de una mezcla de culpabilidad y miedo; culpa porque iba a ver a Mandela como emisario del gobierno que estaba matando a su gente; miedo porque había leído el expediente de Mandela y le inquietaba la perspectiva de ver cara a cara a un enemigo aparentemente tan despiadado. «La imagen que me había formado de él —dijo durante una entrevista en Ciudad del Cabo pocos años después de dejar el gobierno—, era la de un líder decidido a hacerse con el poder, si llegaba la oportunidad, sin importarle el coste en vidas humanas.» Del expediente de Mandela, Coetsee debió de extraer también la imagen mental de un ex boxeador de los pesos pesados que, diez meses antes, había tenido la temeridad de humillar a su adusto y malhumorado jefe, P. W. Botha, delante de toda la nación. Botha se había ofrecido públicamente a dejar en libertad a Mandela, pero había exigido unas condiciones previas. Mandela tenía que prometer abandonar la «lucha armada» que él mismo había iniciado al fundar el brazo militar del CNA, Umkhonto we Sizwe (Lanza de la Nación), en 1961, y tenía que comportarse «de manera que no haya que detenerle» con arreglo a las leyes del apartheid. Mandela respondió con una declaración leída por su hija Zindzi durante una concentración en Soweto. Desafió a Botha a renunciar a la violencia contra los negros y ridiculizó la idea de que él podía quedar en libertad cuando, mientras existiera el apartheid, todas las personas negras seguían viviendo cautivas. «No puedo y no voy a hacer ninguna promesa cuando ni vosotros, el pueblo, ni yo somos libres —decía la declaración—. Vuestra libertad y la mía no pueden estar separadas.»

Coetsee tenía dudas comprensibles sobre la reunión, pero la balanza se inclinaba a su favor. Al fin y al cabo, Mandela era el preso, y Coetsee el carcelero; Mandela estaba delgado y débil tras la operación, vestido con ropa de hospital —bata, pijama y zapatillas— mientras que Coetsee, de traje y corbata ministeriales, derrochaba salud. Y Mandela tenía mucho más que perder en la reunión que Coetsee. Para Mandela era una oportunidad a vida o muerte que quizá no se repetiría; para Coetsee era un encuentro exploratorio, casi un acto movido por la curiosidad. A ojos de Mandela, era la oportunidad que había buscado, desde que se inició en la política cuatro décadas antes, de tener una conversación seria sobre la dirección que iba a tomar el país en el futuro, entre la Sudáfrica blanca y la Sudáfrica negra. De todos los retos que afrontaría posteriormente con sus poderes de seducción política, ninguno estaría tan lleno de peligros. Porque, si hubiera fracasado, si hubiera discutido con Coetsee o si no hubiera habido química entre ellos, aquél habría podido ser el principio y el fin de todo.

Pero, desde el momento en el que Coetsee entró en la habitación del hospital de Mandela, las aprensiones por ambas partes se evaporaron. Mandela, un anfitrión modelo, mostró su sonrisa espléndida e hizo que Coetsee se sintiera a gusto y, casi al instante, para sorpresa discretamente contenida de ambos, preso y carcelero se encontraron charlando de forma amigable. Cualquiera que les hubiera visto sin saber quiénes eran habría pensado que se conocían bien, como un consejero real conoce a su príncipe o un abogado a su mejor cliente. En parte, porque Mandela, que mide 1,83 metros, empequeñecía a Coetsee, un tipo menudo y pizpireto con grandes gafas de montura negra y pinta de abogado urbanista. Pero, sobre todo, por una cuestión de lenguaje corporal, por el efecto que la actitud de Mandela tenía en la gente con la que hablaba. En primer lugar, su postura erguida. Luego, su forma de dar la mano. Nunca se agachaba, ni inclinaba la cabeza. Todo el movimiento lo hacía con la articulación del brazo y el hombro. Si a eso se añadían el enorme tamaño de su mano y su piel curtida, el resultado era majestuoso e intimidatorio. O lo habría sido de no ser por su mirada cálida y su inmensa sonrisa.

«Tenía un don natural —recordaba Coetsee, entusiasmado—, y me di cuenta desde el momento en que lo vi. Era un líder nato. Y también afable. Estaba claro que el personal del hospital le tenía simpatía y, pese a ello, le respetaba, aunque sabían que era un preso. Y no había duda de que dominaba su entorno.»

Mandela mencionó a gente de los Servicios Penitenciarios que ambos conocían; Coetsee le preguntó por su salud; charlaron sobre un encuentro casual que Coetsee había tenido con la mujer de Mandela, Winnie, unos días antes en un avión. A Coetsee le sorprendieron la disposición de Mandela a hablar en afrikaans y su conocimiento de la historia afrikaans. Fue todo muy cordial. Sin embargo, los dos eran conscientes de que la importancia de la reunión no residía en las palabras que intercambiasen, sino en las que se quedaran sin decir. El hecho de que no hubiera ninguna animosidad ya era una señal, transmitida y recibida por ambos, de que había llegado la hora de explorar la posibilidad de un cambio fundamental en la forma de relacionarse políticamente la Sudáfrica negra y la Sudáfrica blanca. Fue, como diría Coetsee, el comienzo de una nueva práctica, «hablar en vez de luchar».

La ausencia de cámaras, el tranquilizador entorno del hospital, el pijama, la afabilidad sin consecuencias de la charla, todo disimulaba la realidad de que Mandela había conseguido llevar a cabo la proeza aparentemente imposible por la que el CNA llevaba luchando setenta y tres años. ¿Cómo lo había hecho? Como todos los que son muy buenos en su trabajo —sean atletas, pintores o violinistas—, había trabajado mucho y durante largo tiempo para desarrollar su talento natural. Walter Sisulu había vislumbrado al líder en él desde el día en el que se conocieron, en 1942. Sisulu, seis años mayor que Mandela, era un veterano organizador del CNA en Johanesburgo; Mandela, que tenía veinticinco años, acababa de llegar del campo. Mandela era un paleto en comparación con la sofisticación urbana de Sisulu, pero el astuto activista que era este último, al observar al joven que se mantenía erguido ante él, vio algo que podía serle útil. «Me impresionó más que cualquier otra persona que había conocido —dijo Sisulu más de medio siglo después de aquel primer encuentro—. Su aire, su simpatía... Yo buscaba a gente de cierto calibre para ocupar puestos dirigentes y él fue un regalo de los dioses.»

Mandela solía decir en broma que, si no hubiera conocido a Sisulu, se habría ahorrado muchas complicaciones en la vida. La verdad es que Mandela, cuyo nombre en xhosa, Rolihlahla, significa «alborotador», hizo lo indecible para buscar esas complicaciones y demostró tener talento para adoptar gestos de valor político durante el movimiento pacífico de resistencia en los años cuarenta y cincuenta. Había que organizar actos públicos que crearan conciencia política y dieran ejemplo de audacia a la población negra en general. Mandela, «voluntario jefe» de la «campaña de desafío» de aquel periodo, fue el primero que quemó su documento de identidad de hombre negro, conocido como «carnet de paso», un método humillante que impuso el gobierno del apartheid para asegurarse de que los negros no entrasen en las zonas blancas más que para trabajar. Antes de quemar el carnet, escogió el momento y el lugar que podían causar el máximo impacto en los medios. Las fotografías de la época le muestran sonriendo para las cámaras mientras infringía aquella ley fundamental del apartheid. En el plazo de unos días, miles de personas negras seguían su ejemplo.

Como presidente de la Liga Juvenil del CNA en los años cincuenta, destacó como un individuo extraordinariamente seguro de sí mismo. Durante una reunión de la máxima dirección del CNA, un acto de etiqueta en el que se presentó con un pulcro traje marrón, sorprendió a todo el mundo con un discurso en el que predijo que él sería el primer presidente negro de Sudáfrica.

Tenía algo del desparpajo del joven Mohamed Alí, y no sólo por el hecho de que boxeaba para mantenerse en forma, una forma física que le gustaba exhibir. Varias fotografías le muestran posando para las cámaras, desnudo de cintura para arriba y en posturas clásicas de boxeo. En las fotografías en las que aparece con traje, tiene un aire de estrella romántica de Hollywood. En los años cincuenta era ya el rostro más visible de la protesta negra, y vestía de forma impecable: el único hombre negro que se hacía los trajes en el mismo sastre que el hombre más rico de Sudáfrica, el magnate del oro y los diamantes Harry Oppenheimer.

Cuando el CNA emprendió la lucha armada en 1961, en gran parte a instancias de Mandela, y él se convirtió en comandante en jefe del brazo militar, Umkhonto we Sizwe, abandonó los trajes y se pasó al *chic* revolucionario, tomando como modelo a uno de sus héroes, el Che Guevara. En el último acto público al que asistió antes de ser detenido en 1962, una fiesta en Durban, apareció vestido de guerrillero, con uniforme de camuflaje. En aquel momento era el hombre más buscado de Sudáfrica, pero era tal la importancia que daba a mantener una actitud desafiante y tal el placer que le producía el destacar en una multitud, que rechazó el consejo de sus camaradas de que se afeitase la barba que se había dejado para imitar al Che y con la que aparecía en los carteles de búsqueda de la policía.

Si su vanidad supuso, al menos en parte, su caída, también supo utilizarla. En la cárcel, acusado de sabotaje, decidió que en su primera aparición ante el tribunal iba a volver a acaparar toda la atención. Entró en el juzgado con una lentitud y una autoridad deliberadas, vestido, como correspondía a su categoría en el clan xhosa en el que se crió, con el elaborado atuendo de un alto caudillo africano: una piel de animal sobre el pecho, cuentas en torno al cuello y en los brazos. Mientras caminaba hacia su silla, la sala cayó sumida en silencio; incluso el juez tuvo que hacer un breve esfuerzo para encontrar su voz. Se sentó, y, luego, a un gesto del juez, se levantó, y examinó lentamente la sala antes de comenzar un discurso electrizante. Empezó: «Soy un hombre negro en un tribunal de hombres blancos», y consiguió exactamente el objetivo nacional que buscaba, crear un espíritu incólume de desafío negro.

Fue un descubrimiento importante. La cárcel podía servir también de escenario político; también desde detrás de las rejas podía causar impacto. Aquello cambió su forma de ver la sentencia que le aguardaba y, a partir de aquel momento, aprovechando la experiencia que había adquirido como abogado defendiendo a clientes negros en los tribunales blancos durante los años cincuenta, utilizó la cárcel como campo de entrenamiento, un lugar en el que prepararse para la gran partida que le esperaba al salir. Refinó su talento natural para el teatro con el fin de lograr sus fines políticos y ensayó su papel ante sus guardianes y ante otros presos para afrontar el destino triunfante que tenía la temeridad de creer que le aguardaba fuera.

El primer reto era conocer a su enemigo, una tarea que emprendió con el mismo rigor que dedicaba a su ejercicio físico. Disponía de dos herramientas: libros —en los que aprendió sobre la historia de los afrikaners y estudió su lengua— y los guardias afrikaners de la prisión, unos hombres sencillos que ocupaban el estrato inferior en el gran sistema laboral que daba prioridad a los blancos. Fikile Bam, que compartió cárcel con Mandela durante algún tiempo, recordaba con viveza la seriedad con la que, desde el principio de su condena, Mandela se propuso comprender la mentalidad afrikaner. «En su opinión —y era lo que nos predicaba a los demás—, el afrikaner era africano. Pertenecía a la tierra, y cualquier solución que se encontrara para los problemas políticos iba a tener que contar con los afrikaners.»

En aquel tiempo, la postura oficial del CNA era que el poder afrikaner era una versión actualizada del colonialismo europeo. Hizo falta mucho valor para que Mandela se opusiera a esa opinión, que declarase que los afrikaners tenían tanto derecho a ser llamados africanos como los negros con los que compartía la celda. Y tampoco disimuló su nueva pasión por aprender cosas del pasado de los afrikaners. «Tenía un gran interés por los personajes afrikaners históricos, entre ellos los líderes afrikaners durante la guerra de los bóers —explicaba

Bam—. Sabía de memoria los nombres de los distintos generales bóers.»

En la cárcel, Mandela se inscribió en un curso de lengua afrikaans durante un par de años, y nunca desperdició la oportunidad de mejorar su dominio del idioma. «No tenía absolutamente ningún reparo en saludar a la gente en afrikaans ni en probar su afrikaans con los guardias. Otros presos tenían sus dudas e inhibiciones, pero Nelson no. Quería conocer de verdad a los afrikaners. Y los guardias le eran muy útiles para su propósito.»

Y no sólo para aprender el idioma. Mandela vio a aquellos hombres, el rostro más visible e inmediato del enemigo, y se marcó un objetivo: convencerlos para que le tratasen con dignidad. Si lo lograba, pensó, habría muchas más probabilidades de poder hacer lo mismo, un día, con los blancos en general.

Sisulu le había observado fuera de la cárcel, le observó en la cárcel y —como el entrenador que descubre al joven boxeador que luego se convierte en campeón de los pesos pesados— se felicitó por la astucia de su elección. Sisulu siempre estuvo, porque lo prefería, a la sombra de Mandela, pero éste le pidió consejo sobre asuntos personales y políticos toda su vida. Fue Sisulu, por ejemplo, el que mejor comprendió cómo ablandar los corazones de los carceleros blancos. La clave, como explicaría mucho después, era el «respeto elemental». No quería aplastar a sus enemigos. No quería humillarlos. No quería pagarlos con la misma moneda. Sólo quería que les tratasen con respeto.

Eso era precisamente lo que querían también los hombres blancos que controlaban la prisión, duros y de escasa educación, y eso es lo que Mandela se esforzó en darles desde el principio, por muy horrorosa que le hicieran la vida. Su celda, su casa durante dieciocho años, era más pequeña que un cuarto de baño. Medía 2,5 × 2,1 metros, o tres pasos por dos y medio de Mandela, y tenía una pequeña ventana con barrotes, de 30 cm^2, que daba a un patio de cemento en el que los presos se sentaban durante horas a romper piedras. Mandela dormía sobre un colchón de paja, con tres mantas muy finas que eran su única protección contra el frío viento de los inviernos del Cabo. Como los demás presos políticos, que contaban con menos privilegios que los presos comunes del ala lujosa de la isla, estaba obligado a llevar pantalón corto (los largos sólo se los daban a los presos indios o mulatos, no a los africanos negros), y la comida era escasa y deprimente: unas gachas de maíz aderezadas, los días buenos, con cartílago. Mandela empezó pronto a perder peso, y la falta de vitaminas hizo que su piel se volviera amarillenta, pero, aun así, se veía obligado a trabajar duramente, o con un pico en la cantera de cal de la isla o recogiendo algas que se exportaban a Japón como fertilizante. Para lavarse, les daban cubos de agua fría del Atlántico.

Dos meses después de la llegada de Mandela a Robben Island, su abogado, George Bizos, tuvo la primera oportunidad de ver lo que la cárcel le estaba costando. Mandela estaba mucho más delgado e iba vestido de forma humillante, con aquellos pantalones cortos y zapatos sin calcetines. En torno a él, formando una caja, había ocho guardias elegantemente uniformados, dos delante, dos detrás y dos a cada lado. Sin embargo, desde el momento en el que Bizos vio a su cliente, se dio cuenta de que Mandela se movía con un aire distinto al del típico preso. Cuando salió del furgón penitenciario con su escolta, fue él, y no los guardias, el que marcó el paso. Bizos se abrió paso entre los dos guardias de delante y abrazó a su cliente, para confusión de los funcionarios, a los que nunca se les había ocurrido la idea de que un hombre blanco pudiera abrazar a uno negro. Los dos charlaron brevemente y Mandela le preguntó a su viejo amigo por la familia, pero de pronto se interrumpió y dijo: «George, perdona, no te he presentado a mi guardia de honor», y le nombró a cada uno de los agentes. Los guardias se quedaron tan asombrados, recordaba Bizos muchos años después, «que se comportaron verdaderamente como una guardia de honor y me dieron la mano con todo respeto».

No siempre era así. Los guardias y los jefes de la prisión rotaban, inevitablemente, y algunos regímenes fueron brutales, mientras que otros fueron relativamente benignos. Mandela, reconocido por los demás presos políticos como líder desde el primer día, perfeccionó el arte de manipularlos a todos, independientemente de su carácter. Se esforzó en convencer a los presos de que, en el fondo, todos los guardias eran seres humanos vulnerables, que era el sistema el que había convertido a muchos de ellos en animales. Pero eso no quería decir que, cuando la ocasión lo exigía, Mandela no supiera defender activamente sus derechos. La única vez en la isla que un guardia estuvo a punto de golpearlo, Mandela, abogado y boxeador, se mantuvo firme y le dijo: «Como me ponga la mano encima, le llevaré ante el más alto tribunal del país. Y, cuando acabe con usted, será tan pobre como una rata.» El guardia refunfuñó y gruñó, pero no le pegó y se alejó humillado.

En la mini Sudáfrica que era la isla, los presos negros se enfrentaban al régimen carcelario blanco como lo habían hecho ante el gobierno cuando eran libres. La desobediencia civil era el principio general, y se manifestaba en huelgas de hambre, huelgas de celo y el hábito de mantener toda la dignidad que podían. Los guardias con los que se encontró Mandela cuando llegó a la isla estaban acostumbrados a que los presos les llamasen *baas*, «jefe». Mandela se negó y, aunque sufrió intimidaciones por ello, nunca cedió.

Las condiciones penitenciarias en el pequeño feudo de la isla, antiguamente una colonia de leprosos y un manicomio, dependían mucho de la personalidad del oficial que estuviera a cargo en un momento dado. En 1970, un hombre discreto y afable llamado Van Aarde fue sustituido por el coronel Piet Badenhorst, el personaje más temible que Mandela iba a conocer durante sus años tras las rejas. Badenhorst y los nuevos reclutas que llevó consigo a la isla crearon un reinado de terror que duró un año. Badenhorst era incapaz de abrir la boca sin soltar tacos, y se acostumbró a dirigir los peores insultos a Mandela. Sus guardias seguían el ejemplo del jefe: zarandeaban a los presos de camino a la cantera, sometían sus celdas a registros inesperados y confiscaban sus preciados libros, entre ellos las obras de Shakespeare y los clásicos griegos que eran los favoritos de Mandela y Sisulu. Un día de mayo de 1971, por la mañana, los guardias de Badenhorst entraron en la galería política, sección B, borrachos. Ordenaron a los presos que se desnudasen mientras registraban las celdas. Una hora después, uno de los presos se desvaneció y, cuando otro protestó y arremetió contra ellos, le dieron tal paliza que su celda acabó salpicada de sangre.

Mandela mantuvo la calma y, bajo su dirección, los

presos recuperaron las lecciones que habían aprendido fuera, en la lucha política. Pidieron ayuda más allá de su microcosmos de la isla. Enviaron mensajes a través de visitantes y la Cruz Roja internacional. También llegó ayuda de la política progresista más conocida en el parlamento sudafricano, Helen Suzman, que visitó a los presos en la isla y, por indicación de ellos, habló con Mandela, al que habían elegido de forma unánime como portavoz.

El momento decisivo se produjo cuando tres jueces visitaron la cárcel a finales de 1971. En presencia de Badenhorst, se entrevistaron con Mandela, que no se contuvo y denunció el duro trato que les propinaba el coronel. Habló de la pobre dieta y los duros trabajos, pero se detuvo, sobre todo, en el incidente de los guardias borrachos que habían desnudado y golpeado a los presos. Badenhorst le hizo un gesto con el dedo y dijo: «Ten cuidado, Mandela. Si hablas de cosas que no has visto, te vas a meter en un lío, ¿me entiendes?» Mandela aprovechó el error de Badenhorst. Se volvió, triunfante, a los jueces, como si volviera a ejercer de abogado en un tribunal, y les dijo: «Caballeros, ya ven ustedes el tipo de hombre que tenemos como comandante. Si es capaz de amenazarme aquí, en su presencia, pueden imaginarse lo que hace cuando no están.» Un juez se volvió hacia los otros dos y dijo: «El preso tiene mucha razón.»

Mandela había domado a su torturador. Después de la visita de los jueces, la situación en la cárcel mejoró y, al cabo de tres meses, llegó la noticia de que iban a trasladar a Badenhorst. Pero la historia no se quedó ahí. Todavía estaba por llegar lo más interesante, porque tendría un efecto en Mandela que influiría en su actitud respecto a los «opresores» afrikaners el resto de su vida y fue decisivo cuando, por fin, pudo entablar el combate político con ellos.

Unos días antes de que Badenhorst se fuera, el comisario nacional de prisiones, un tal general Steyn, visitó Robben Island. Se entrevistó con Mandela en presencia de Badenhorst. Al terminar la entrevista y cuando Steyn ya no podía oírle, Badenhorst se acercó a Mandela y, con una voz extraordinariamente cortés, le informó de su inminente partida. Luego dijo: «Sólo quiero desear buena suerte a su gente.» Mandela se quedó momentáneamente sin saber qué decir, pero luego se recobró lo suficiente como para darle las gracias y desearle también buena suerte en su nuevo puesto.

Mandela reflexionó sobre ese incidente y examinó las enseñanzas que podían sacarse de él, cómo un hombre al que había considerado cruel y salvaje, al final, había revelado tener una luz más suave. Aparcó esas reflexiones, pero también encontró formas de utilizarlas enseguida. Aplicando las estrategias que había desarrollado durante sus siete años en Robben Island, utilizó toda la ayuda que pudo de gente como Helen Suzman y el sistema judicial para hacer que la cárcel fuera un lugar más habitable. A finales de los setenta, no sólo había mejorado mucho la calidad de la comida, la ropa y las camas respecto a 1964, no sólo se habían terminado la recogida de algas y los trabajos forzosos en la cantera, sino que se habían añadido todo tipo de lujos inimaginables. Los presos podían ver películas, oír la radio en un sistema de altavoces por todas las instalaciones y, lo mejor de todo, hacer deporte. Incluido el tenis, curiosamente. También el fútbol, el pasatiempo favorito de la Sudáfrica negra. A insistencia de las autoridades, se añadió a la lista el rugby. Las normas eran que una semana se jugaba al fútbol y otra al rugby, siempre de manera alterna. Los presos más jóvenes jugaban al rugby y oían retransmisiones de partidos importantes en la radio, aunque todos ellos apoyaban ruidosamente a los equipos rivales.

Eso llegaría mucho más tarde. Antes se produjo la conversión de Kobie Coetsee, aquel día de noviembre de 1985.

Cuando Mandela fue dado de alta en el hospital, el 24 de noviembre de 1985, Botha coincidió con Coetsee en que no debía volver a la amplia celda que había compartido los tres años anteriores con sus cuatro viejos camaradas. Permanecería en Pollsmoor pero iba a estar en una celda propia, en una parte vacía de la cárcel. No era un castigo, sino un primer paso hacia la libertad. Se trataba de mantener los nuevos contactos entre Mandela y el gobierno en el máximo secreto posible, incluso ante los demás presos. Mandela agradeció el hecho de tener el espacio que necesitaba para ordenar sus ideas y elaborar su estrategia. Además, Coetsee se encargó de proporcionar a Mandela, en su celda solitaria, un trato de favor como ningún *baas* le había dado jamás a un hombre negro en Sudáfrica. Su comida mejoró y empezó a recibir periódicos, una radio y acceso a un invento desconocido en Sudáfrica cuando él ingresó en la cárcel, una televisión.

Tenía asimismo la compañía de un guardia llamado Christo Brand que había sido trasladado con él desde Robben Island y que le adoraba. Criado en una granja, Brand había tenido su primer contacto con la electricidad a los diez años y había abandonado la escuela a los quince. Era un hombre que tenía la mitad de años que Mandela, amable, que consideraba a su preso casi como un padre. Mandela cumplía su papel: entre otras cosas, escribía cartas a la esposa de Brand para quejarse de que su marido no hacía lo suficiente para mejorar; que era muy inteligente y, si se le convencía para que estudiara, podía hacer algo más con su vida. El hijo de Brand, Riaan, que nació en 1985, se convirtió también en una especie de nieto postizo de Mandela. Brand metió a Riaan clandestinamente en Pollsmoor cuando tenía ocho meses para que Mandela pudiera cogerlo en brazos. Mandela lo hizo y los ojos se le humedecieron; llevaba veintitrés años sin poder tocar a ninguno de sus seis hijos. A medida que Riaan fue creciendo, Mandela nunca dejó de preguntar cómo le iba en el colegio, y le escribió puntualmente cartas cada año por su cumpleaños.

Los altos jefes de Pollsmoor, más distantes, eran más difíciles de abordar que Brand. Mandela tuvo que mantener agudizados sus sentidos para ganárselos. El oficial a cargo del ala C de la cárcel, de máxima seguridad, era un tal comandante Van Sittert, un hombre que, como contó después Brand, se sentía más a gusto tratando con presos comunes que con los políticos. «El comandante solía visitar las celdas una vez al mes —contaba Brand—. Los presos políticos le parecían una molestia: se quejaban y pedían cosas con mucha más frecuencia que los presos comunes; además, el comandante no hablaba inglés muy bien, y también por eso se sentía incómodo con ellos.» Mandela era ya famoso en todo el mundo, una auténtica celebridad. Y eso irritaba todavía más al comandante Van Sittert, hacía que estuviera más incómodo en su presencia.

Mandela se lo pensó mucho. Había sometido a todos los demás jefes, pero el picajoso e inseguro Van Sittert iba a poner verdaderamente a prueba sus poderes de seducción. Habló con Brand para intentar encontrar algún punto flaco. Y gracias a él lo encontró. Sittert era un fanático del rugby. Así que Mandela, que no era especialmente aficionado a ese deporte, se propuso aprender celosamente todo lo relacionado con él antes de la visita mensual del comandante. Por primera vez en su vida, leyó las páginas de rugby de los periódicos, vio los programas deportivos en televisión y se propuso estar al tanto de las últimas noticias para poder hablar con el comandante sobre su gran pasión de forma más o menos creíble.

Mandela tenía otro incentivo además de la satisfacción política de hacerse con una nueva presa blanca. Tenía una necesidad concreta, una petición que quería hacer, que afectaría su bienestar inmediato y que sólo el comandante podía conceder. No quería esperar otro mes para tener una oportunidad de lograr lo que necesitaba, así que tenía que aprovechar el momento cuando surgiera. Mandela se entrevistó con el comandante Van Sittert por primera vez en el corredor, delante de su celda. Y, aunque la vestimenta volvía a situarlo en desventaja, como había ocurrido el día en que conoció a Kobie Coetsee, porque él iba vestido de preso y el comandante como un oficial del ejército, Mandela volvió a dominar la situación. Recibió al comandante como si fuera un invitado en su casa. Y, sabiendo lo poco que le gustaba a Van Sittert hablar inglés, se dirigió a él en afrikaans.

«Mandela estuvo muy educado, como de costumbre —recordaba Brand—. Le saludó con una gran sonrisa e inmediatamente se puso a hablar de rugby. ¡Me sorprendió muchísimo! Ahí estaba, diciendo que tal jugador lo estaba haciendo muy bien, pero que aquel otro no estaba dando el máximo rendimiento y había decepcionado en el último partido, y que quizá había llegado la hora de dar una oportunidad a no sé qué jugador joven, porque parecía muy prometedor, y así sucesivamente.» Cuando el comandante superó su propio asombro, se animó y se mostró de acuerdo con Mandela prácticamente en todos sus argumentos. «Podía verse cómo al comandante se le iban despejando todas las dudas», terminó Brand.

Después de tender la trampa, Mandela atrajo al comandante hacia ella. Le llevó lentamente a su celda, mencionando como de casualidad que tenía un pequeño problema, que estaba seguro de que el comandante no querría que tuviera que aguantar un hombre de rugby como él. Le dijo que estaba recibiendo más comida para el almuerzo que para la cena y que, por ese motivo, había adoptado la costumbre de guardarse parte del almuerzo para la tarde. Lo malo era que, para entonces, la comida se había enfriado. Pero había una solución, dijo Mandela. Había oído hablar de una cosa llamada calientaplatos. Le parecía que era la solución para su dilema. «Comandante —dijo—, ¿sería posible que me ayudara a obtener uno?»

Para sorpresa de Brand, Van Sittert capituló sin resistencia. «¡Brand —ordenó—, vaya y consígale a Mandela un calientaplatos!»

Obtuvo todo eso y más cuando volvió a reunirse en secreto con Kobie Coetsee, esta vez en su casa. El ministro, deseoso de otorgar a Mandela la dignidad que consideraba que merecía, dispuso que las autoridades de la prisión le pusieran una chaqueta por primera vez en veintitrés años y que le llevaran, no en un furgón, sino en un elegante coche. En ese segundo encuentro, el contenido de la discusión fue más explícitamente político. Coetsee, satisfecho, informó a Botha de que la cárcel parecía haber suavizado a Mandela, que ya no era el agitador y terrorista y parecía dispuesto a estudiar un acuerdo con los blancos.

Mandela obtuvo más privilegios. Brand y Van Sittert se sorprendieron al recibir órdenes de que pasearan a Mandela en coche por Ciudad del Cabo. Un pequeño comité formado por personas de confianza de Botha, que sabían de las conversaciones secretas (Coetsee, Niël Barnard, jefe del Servicio Nacional de Inteligencia, y uno o dos más), temía que, si se enteraba todo el gobierno de las negociaciones, alguien podía acabar filtrando el asunto a la prensa. No obstante, les parecía tan importante que Mandela empezara a aclimatarse a la vida fuera de la cárcel que incluso autorizaron a sus guardias a dejar que saliera a dar pequeños paseos por su cuenta, a mezclarse con la población local desprevenida. En una ocasión, Christo Brand se lo llevó a su casa y le presentó a su mujer y sus hijos. Otro día, dos guardias le llevaron en coche hasta una ciudad llamada Paternoster, a 100 kilómetros al norte de Ciudad del Cabo, en la costa del Atlántico. Mientras Mandela paseaba solo por la prístina playa blanca de la ciudad, apareció de pronto un autobús lleno de turistas alemanes. Los dos oficiales se asustaron y temieron que le reconocieran. No tenían que haberse preocupado. Los turistas, extasiados ante la salvaje belleza de la zona, hicieron fotos e ignoraron al hombre negro de cabello gris que andaba por allí cerca. Mandela podría haberse precipitado hacia

ellos y haber subido al autobús en busca de asilo político, pero todavía no quería salir de la cárcel, pese al clamor que se había ido formando en todo el mundo por
su liberación. Le parecía que podía hacer más cosas si se
quedaba dentro y negociaba.

Capítulo III
SERVICIOS SEPARADOS

Justice Bekebeke era un joven negro airado en noviembre de 1985, uno entre millones. Alto y delgado, como una escultura africana, tenía unas maneras educadas y una relajante voz de barítono que indicaba una sabiduría penosamente adquirida muy por encima de sus veinticuatro años. Bekebeke vivía en Paballelo, un distrito segregado sin árboles a 750 kilómetros al norte de la cárcel de Mandela en Ciudad del Cabo y a otros tantos al oeste de Johanesburgo, en el límite del desierto de Kalahari, en los últimos confines de la tierra. En Sudáfrica había un distrito negro junto a cada ciudad blanca. Pero, aunque los distritos negros siempre tenían muchos más habitantes, en los mapas sólo aparecían las ciudades blancas. Los distritos eran las sombras negras de las ciudades. Paballelo era la sombra negra de Upington.

Upington era una cruda caricatura de una ciudad del apartheid. Un visitante poco curioso quizá no habría notado en Johanesburgo los más burdos límites racistas del sistema. Pero en Upington esos límites eran ineludibles: letreros de «*Slegs Blankes*» («Sólo blancos») en aseos públicos, bares, fuentes, cines, piscinas públicas, parques, paradas de autobús, la estación de ferrocarril. Toda esa insensatez, exigida legalmente por la Ley de Servicios Separados de 1953, generaba, a veces, humor de dudoso gusto. Una mujer negra que llevara en tren al bebé blanco de su «señora», ¿tenía que viajar en la sección de «sólo blancos» o en la de «no blancos»? Un visitante japonés que entrara en un aseo público de «sólo blancos», ¿estaría infringiendo la ley? ¿Y qué tenía que hacer el conductor de un autobús sólo para blancos si ordenaba a un pasajero de piel oscura que se bajara y él se negaba e insistía en que era un hombre blanco muy bronceado?

Era frecuente que, entre los blancos progresistas de Johanesburgo o Ciudad del Cabo, estos detalles legales fueran ignorados. En lugares como Upington, en el corazón del territorio afrikaner, se obedecían con un rigor calvinista. Paballelo era un lugar más pobre, más sucio y estaba más abarrotado que Upington, pero era menos asfixiante. Allí uno podía escapar de las restricciones más mezquinas del apartheid. Podía comer, comprar o sentarse donde quisiera. Para ir a Paballelo desde Upington había que recorrer kilómetro y medio hacia el oeste, por la carretera a Namibia, hasta llegar al matadero municipal. Allí había que girar a la izquierda y entonces uno se encontraba con un letrero roñoso que decía «Bienvenidos a Paballelo». El contraste entre uno y otro lugar, como siempre que se cruzaba del mundo blanco al mundo negro en Sudáfrica, era estremecedor, como si se hubiera retrocedido un siglo o se hubiera pasado directamente de una zona residencial de Marbella a Burkina Faso. Una zona era un laberinto seco y amontonado de casas como cajas de cerillas en una llanura de matorrales; la otra era un oasis artificial de sauces llorones, jardines con césped de campo de golf, cuidadas rosaledas y grandes casas cuyos dueños no se habían contenido a la hora de tomar agua del cercano río Orange. Upington habría sido casi elegante si no fuera tan poco natural, si el verdor no oliera a falso adorno en medio del calor abrasador y la sequedad del desierto, si no hubiera sido un sitio en el que los blancos llamaban constantemente a los negros por el más humillante de los nombres, *kaffir*, la versión sudafricana de *nigger*.

Tres recuerdos infantiles iban a tener un efecto duradero en Justice Bekebeke. El primero se remontaba a su niñez, cuando visitó Ciudad del Cabo con su familia. Mientras contemplaba el océano Atlántico, vio un puntito de tierra no muy lejos de la costa. Su padre, que apenas sabía leer pero sabía cuáles eran sus convicciones políticas, le dijo que aquél era el lugar en que estaban «nuestros líderes». El punto era Robben Island. Justice pidió a su padre una moneda para echarla a uno de los telescopios costeros y poder ver a sus dirigentes. No lo consiguió, porque la isla estaba a 11 kilómetros de distancia, pero sí vio las siluetas de los edificios en los que estaban las celdas, lo suficiente para elaborar una fantasía mental de que había estado realmente en la isla. Volvió a casa y contó esa fantasía como si fuera verdad, y logró impresionar tanto a sus amigos en el colegio que, cuando se quiso dar cuenta, se había convertido él mismo en un líder en Paballelo, alguien a quien sus jóvenes colegas acudían en busca de orientación política.

Gracias a ese episodio, y gracias a la influencia de su padre, Justice se alió desde muy joven con el Congreso Nacional Africano de Mandela, y no con su rival, el

Congreso Panafricanista, más radical. El CPA era un partido abiertamente racista y vengativo que tenía eslóganes como «una bala, un colono» y «arrojar a los blancos al mar», y que casi se convirtió en la fuerza dominante en la política negra durante los años sesenta. El CPA era el Hamás de Sudáfrica.

Imaginemos a Yasir Arafat convenciendo a Hamás de que se rindiera a su liderazgo para que el pueblo palestino se uniese bajo la bandera de Al Fatah, y nos haremos una idea de lo que consiguió Mandela con sus bases, mucho más pobladas y con más diversidad tribal. En la Sudáfrica negra había zulúes, había xhosas, había sothos y otros seis grupos tribales, todos con distintas lenguas maternas y la mayoría con algún tipo de animosidad histórica respecto a los otros. Mandela, de quien todo el mundo sabía que pertenecía a la realeza xhosa, acabó por ganarse a más del 90 % de los sudafricanos negros.

El segundo recuerdo decisivo de Bekebeke quedó sellado cuando tenía diez años. Oyó hablar de un hombre negro que había discutido con un policía blanco. La disputa se caldeó cada vez más hasta que el policía sacó la pistola y disparó al hombre, que, mientras caía, asestó una puñalada al policía y le mató. Justice no conocía al hombre negro, pero le pareció que la historia tenía la fuerza de una parábola. «Me encantó aquel hombre —se indignaba, con la misma energía de su juventud, cuando contaba la historia, muchos años después—. Me pareció un héroe por enfrentarse al policía blanco, por defenderse.»

Si ese recuerdo indica el reto que iba a afrontar Mandela al tratar de convencer a su gente para que aceptara el fin negociado del apartheid, el tercer gran recuerdo de infancia de Justice mostraba lo difícil que iba a ser convencerles para que apoyasen a los Springboks. Hablamos de un partido de rugby jugado en Upington en 1970, también cuando tenía diez años.

Como a la mayoría de los niños negros, el rugby le interesaba poco. Era el entretenimiento salvaje y extraño de una gente salvaje y extraña. Pero, esa vez, la curiosidad y la perspectiva de disfrutar con una derrota poco frecuente de sus vecinos blancos le animaron a ir al estadio local. La selección de rugby de Nueva Zelanda estaba de gira por Sudáfrica y había ido a Upington a jugar contra el gran equipo de la provincia, el North West Cape. El estadio era pequeño, con una capacidad de 9.000 espectadores, y espacio —donde pegaba más el sol— para sólo unos cuantos centenares de negros. Sin embargo, Justice fue con la esperanza de que el equipo local, el orgullo de la Upington afrikaner, recibiera una buena paliza.

Los afrikaners, que son en su mayoría de ascendencia holandesa y hablan una lengua que casi todos los holandeses actuales podrían entender, constituían el 65 % de los cinco millones de blancos en Sudáfrica. El otro 35 % hablaba inglés en casa, era sobre todo de ascendencia británica (aunque había unos cuantos portugueses, griegos y judíos lituanos) y dominaban el mundo de los negocios, en especial el de las grandes empresas, que, en Sudáfrica, quería decir las minas de oro, diamantes y platino. El poder político, sin embargo, estaba en manos de los afrikaners. Gobernaban el Estado —todos los ministros, todos los generales del ejército, todos los jefes de los servicios de inteligencia eran afrikaners— y eran los que poseían y cultivaban las tierras. La relación entre los afrikaners y la tierra era tan total que la palabra *boer*, que quiere decir «granjero» en afrikaans, era prácticamente un sinónimo de afrikaner. No era extraño, dado que 50.000 agricultores blancos eran dueños de doce veces más tierras de labor y de pastos que los 14 millones de negros rurales del país.

Al ser quienes controlaban los alimentos y las armas, los afrikaners eran los protectores del resto de la Sudáfrica blanca. O, como dijo en una ocasión P. W. Botha: «La seguridad y la felicidad de todos los grupos minoritarios en Sudáfrica dependen de los afrikaners. Da igual que hablen inglés, o alemán, o portugués, o italiano, o incluso hebreo, no hay diferencia.»

Botha era torpe pero tenía razón. Los afrikaners eran los señores y protectores del apartheid. Por eso el joven Justice vitoreó como loco aquel día a los neozelandeses, un equipo formado sólo por blancos pero llamado, para confusión y delicia de Justice, los All Blacks (todos negros), un nombre derivado de sus uniformes. Y tuvo mucho que celebrar. Dirigidos por un jugador calvo y robusto llamado Sid Going, los visitantes derrotaron a North West Cape 26-3. Justice, al evocar aquel recuerdo de infancia, se frotaba las manos con alegría mientras hablaba de cómo los de Nueva Zelanda «asesinaron» a los bóers de Upington; aquellos gigantes sobrealimentados que les humillaban a él, a su familia y a sus amigos a diario, que insistían siempre en que los negros los llamaran *baas*. A partir de aquel día, Justice se convirtió en un aficionado al rugby, aunque sólo fuera de la manera limitada y estrictamente vengativa en que lo eran los sudafricanos negros. Sólo le gustaba cuando los rivales extranjeros eran buenos y vencían a los bóers.

Justice pasó a ser un adolescente atento a la política, que comprendía la importancia que tenía el rugby para los afrikaners; que era lo más parecido que tenían, fuera de la iglesia, a una vida espiritual. Tenían su cristianismo de Antiguo Testamento, llamado la Iglesia Holandesa Reformada; y tenían su religión laica, el rugby, que era para los afrikaners lo que el fútbol para los brasileños. Y, cuanto más de derechas eran los afrikaners, más fundamentalista su fe en Dios, más fanática era su afición al deporte. Temían a Dios, pero amaban el rugby, sobre todo cuando llevaba camiseta de los Springboks.

Las sucesivas selecciones nacionales sudafricanas habían adquirido, a lo largo del siglo XX, la fama de ser los jugadores de rugby más duros del mundo. En su mayoría eran afrikaners, aunque, de vez en cuando, algún «inglés» (como les llamaban los afrikaners cuando querían ser educados) especialmente voluminoso, o duro, o rápido, se colaba en el equipo nacional. Y, al ser afrikaners, en su mayoría eran hombres de huesos grandes, hijos de granjeros de manos callosas que, de pequeños, habían aprendido a jugar descalzos y en campos duros y secos en los que, si uno se caía, sangraba.

Como metáfora de la arrolladora brutalidad del apartheid, los Boks cumplían muy bien su papel. Por eso su distintiva camiseta verde se había vuelto tan detestable para los negros como la policía antidisturbios, la bandera nacional y el himno nacional, *Die Stem* (La llamada), cuya letra alababa a Dios y celebraba la conquista blanca de la punta meridional de África.

En tales humillaciones pensaba Justice durante aquel fatídico mes de 1985. Mientras Mandela, cosa inconcebible, se reunía en secreto con Kobie Coetsee, Justice se encontraba menos dispuesto a hacer concesiones que nunca. Le llenaba la oscura indignación de un hombre que sabía que, por haber nacido negro, nunca podría aprovechar su talento natural hasta el límite. Siempre había sido un estudiante especialmente brillante, que, a los quince años, estaba muy por delante de sus colegas y sus padres (su madre nunca aprendió a leer). Pero las autoridades de Upington, que administraban Paballelo, no permitían la escolarización de niños negros a partir de esa edad. Se atenían al pie de la letra a lo dictado por el principal arquitecto del apartheid, Hendrick Verwoerd, que, en 1953, como responsable del Departamento de Asuntos Nativos, elaboró un plan de estudios diseñado, según él, para «la naturaleza y las necesidades de las personas negras». Verwoerd, que después sería primer ministro, decía que el objetivo de su Ley de Educación Bantú era impedir que los negros recibiesen una educación que pudiera hacerles aspirar a puestos por encima de los que les correspondían. El auténtico propósito era sostener el gran elemento del sistema del apartheid, la protección encubierta de los puestos de trabajo de los blancos. El padre de Justice, decidido a hacer lo que fuera para esquivar el sistema, le envió al otro extremo del país, a la provincia del Cabo Oriental, a una escuela metodista llamada Healdtown en la que había estudiado el propio Mandela.

Justice pasó los diez años siguientes yendo y viniendo entre Upington y el Cabo Oriental, 900 kilómetros a través del país, en el intento, a menudo frustrante, de lograr una educación que le ayudara a alcanzar su sueño de ser médico. Empezaba a aproximarse, había aprobado todos los exámenes necesarios para que le admitieran en Medicina, cuando, a finales de 1985, sucedió el desastre. Se enamoró de una chica y la dejó embarazada. Tenía veinticuatro años, pero a la institución educativa cristiana en la que se encontraba le pareció intolerable. Le expulsaron y volvió a Paballelo en la primera semana de noviembre, consumido por la frustración.

El regreso de Justice coincidió con el primer episodio grave de lo que las autoridades del apartheid llamaron «disturbios negros» en el distrito. Estaba ocurriendo en todo el país, pero era un fenómeno nuevo en un lugar atrasado como Paballelo, en el que, hasta entonces, la resistencia política había sido siempre clandestina. Durante el primer fin de semana de Justice en casa, el domingo, 10 de noviembre, el distrito estalló. Los «disturbios» siguieron la triste coreografía que tan bien conocían ya los telespectadores en todo el mundo, salvo en Sudáfrica, donde las imágenes estaban censuradas. Unos cuantos negros se reunieron en un espacio abierto de Paballelo para denunciar la última letanía de injusticias sociales. La policía local temía desde hacía tiempo que sus negros, hasta entonces bastante domesticados («nuestros negros», solían decir, sin darse cuenta de las ideas rebeldes que se arremolinaban en sus cabezas), pudieran seguir el violento ejemplo de sus primos con ínfulas de Johanesburgo y Ciudad del Cabo. Convencidos de que había llegado el temido día, siguieron la pauta de sus colegas metropolitanos y arrojaron gas lacrimógeno contra la pequeña muchedumbre de manifestantes. Justice no estaba presente aquel día, pero no faltaron otros jóvenes negros airados que respondieron tirando piedras a los policías, que, a su vez, cargaron contra la multitud, lanzaron a sus perros contra los que arrojaban piedras, les persiguieron y golpearon con porras a los que atrapaban.

La policía no estaba preparada para hacer frente al caos desencadenado, en el que los manifestantes quemaron casas y vehículos de aquellos a quienes consideraban colaboradores de los blancos, gente como los concejales negros pagados por el régimen para darle una pátina de respetabilidad democrática. La policía abrió fuego y mató a una mujer negra embarazada. Después dijeron que les había arrojado piedras. Pero todo el mundo en Paballelo sabía que, en realidad, estaba saliendo de su casa para ir a comprar el pan.

La revolución había llegado por fin a Upington. Durante dos días, lunes y martes, los residentes de Paballelo se enfrentaron sin cesar a la policía, esta vez con Justice en primera línea.

El martes por la tarde, llegaron refuerzos policiales de Kimberley, la ciudad más próxima, a 270 kilómetros. Al frente estaba un tal capitán Van Dyk, que propuso negociaciones de paz. Esa tarde, Justice y otros líderes locales se reunieron con él en el distrito. No se alcanzó ninguna solución, pero acordaron volver a verse a la mañana siguiente, en esta ocasión con toda la comunidad presente, en el polvoriento campo de fútbol local. La idea, que el capitán Van Dyk aceptó, fue que los residentes de Paballelo expusieran los motivos de queja que habían ocasionado todos los disturbios en primer lugar. Si el capitán de la policía podía dar algún tipo de satisfacción, alguna sensación de que los problemas planteados se iban a abordar a nivel político, tal vez los ánimos se calmarían y podría evitarse el violento enfrentamiento que se avecinaba. A Justice y los demás líderes les pareció prometedora la actitud de Van Dyk. Era distinto a los policías zafios con los que estaban acostumbrados a tratar en Upington.

A la mañana siguiente, el 13 de noviembre, acudieron miles de personas al campo de fútbol. Una vez más, la coreografía siguió una pauta conocida y reprodujo el desarrollo de otros miles de concentraciones de ese tipo en todo el país. Bajo la mirada de una falange de fuerzas antidisturbios de uniforme gris y azul y una columna de voluminosos vehículos blindados con enormes ruedas llamados *Casspirs*, una ordenada muchedumbre negra se reunió en el centro del campo. El acto comenzó, como siempre, con el himno oficial de la liberación negra, el *Nkosi Sikelele iAfrika*. La letra, en xhosa, la lengua de Mandela, decía:

> *Dios bendiga a África*
> *Que su gloria sea elevada*
> *Oye nuestros ruegos*
> *Dios, bendícenos*
> *A nosotros, tus hijos*
> *Ven, Espíritu*
> *Ven, Espíritu Santo*
> *Dios, te pedimos que protejas a nuestra nación*
> *Intervén y pon fin a todos los conflictos*
> *Protégenos*
> *Protege a nuestra nación*
> *Que así sea*
> *Por siempre y para siempre.*

Era generoso, triste, desafiante, y tenía la fuerza reiterativa de una ola en el océano. Para los sudafricanos negros y los que simpatizaban con su causa, era un llamamiento al valor. Para las autoridades del apartheid y, en especial, para los jóvenes policías blancos a quienes iba inmediatamente dirigido el himno, era una expresión amenazante de la vasta marea negra que podía alzarse y devorarlos.

Después del *Nkosi Sikelele* se rezó una oración cristiana. Mientras los miles de asistentes se dirigían a Dios con la cabeza inclinada, y antes de que nadie hubiera ni empezado a hablar de política, un oficial de la policía local, el capitán Botha, arrebató el mando al capitán Van Dyk. Botha era de Upington.

Para consternación de Van Dyk, Botha cogió un megáfono y anunció, en un grito con el que estaban familiarizados todos los veteranos de las protestas negras en Sudáfrica, que la muchedumbre tenía «diez minutos para dispersarse». Lo único peculiar del anuncio fue que lo hiciera tan pronto, antes incluso de que hubieran terminado los rezos. El capitán Van Dyk quizá habría llegado a la misma conclusión, pero habría observado las cortesías religiosas un poco más y tal vez habría simulado por lo menos buscar un acuerdo negociado.

El capitán Botha no esperó a que transcurrieran los diez minutos. Antes de que pasaran dos, ordenó a sus tropas que dispararan gas lacrimógeno y balas de goma y que soltaran a los perros. Algunos de los negros más jóvenes arrojaron piedras, pero la mayoría de la gente salió corriendo, con los gritos de las mujeres ahogados por el temible ruido de los acelerones de los *Casspirs* que les perseguían. Casi todas las vías de salida estaban bloqueadas por policías que llevaban armas, acariciaban sus porras o golpeaban sus *sjamboks*, unos gruesos látigos de cuero, contra el suelo pedregoso. Justice vio un hueco, llevó a un grupo de unas 150 personas —hombres y mujeres, jóvenes y viejos— por Pilane Street y dejó atrás a los policías blancos.

De pronto, de una de las pequeñas casas de ladrillo gris de la calle, salieron unos disparos. Un niño cayó al suelo gravemente herido. Entonces salió corriendo de una casa un hombre con una pistola sobre la cabeza. El hombre que había disparado, se lanzó hacia la ira, el miedo, el caos. Se llamaba Lucas Sethwala. Era un elemento peculiar en la Sudáfrica del apartheid, un policía negro; uno de esos «colaboradores» que habían sido el blanco de los disturbios el domingo por la noche. En algún rincón del cerebro de Justice, como motor que le impulsaba, estaban las imágenes que le habían inspirado, Robben Island y el sufrimiento de «nuestros líderes», la alegría fugaz de ver a los All Blacks masacrar al equipo de rugby de Upington, la Ley de Servicios Separados, las Áreas de Grupo, la escolarización que se acababa a los quince años, el ejemplo emocionante del héroe que había matado a puñaladas al policía blanco... todos esos recuerdos y más le carcomían. Sin embargo, en aquel momento, cuando se lanzó a correr solo en pos del agente de policía Lucas Sethwala, la principal sensación fue una locura frenética; el único propósito era la venganza.

«No tuve tiempo de pararme a reflexionar. No fue una decisión racional. Fue pura emoción», recordaba Justice.

El hecho de que Sethwala todavía tuviera su arma en la mano y Justice no tuviera ninguna, que Sethwala se volviera mientras corría y disparase contra Justice, demuestra lo alocada que fue la reacción de este último. Pero los tiros fallaron y Justice le atrapó, le arrebató el arma y le golpeó en la cabeza con ella. Le golpeó sólo dos veces, pero fueron suficientes. Se quedó quieto, muerto. Justice se levantó y siguió corriendo, pero el grupo que iba detrás de él, que había celebrado con un grito la captura de Sethwala y los golpes, hizo lo que las muchedumbres sudafricanas hacían entonces, con demasiada frecuencia, en esas situaciones. Empezaron a dar patadas al cuerpo inerte de Sethwala y alguien corrió en busca de una lata de gasolina. Justice no lo vio; se lo contaron después. Alrededor de cien personas se reunieron en torno al cadáver, dando vítores de alegría. Era una victoria, por fin, o algo que, en la locura del momento, se parecía mucho a una victoria para Paballelo. Rociaron el cuerpo de gasolina, encendieron una cerilla y le prendieron fuego.

Justice huyó al otro lado de la frontera, a Windhoek, la capital de Namibia. Pero entonces Namibia no era aún un país independiente; seguía perteneciendo a Sudáfrica. Seis días después, el 19 de noviembre, le detuvieron y le devolvieron a Upington, donde él y otros veinticinco fueron encarcelados y acusados de asesinato. La llamada Ley del Propósito Común permitía procesar no sólo a la persona o personas directamente responsables de un crimen, sino también a todos los que podían haber compartido el deseo de cometerlo, que habían prestado apoyo moral. Con una definición tan vaga, la policía podría haber detenido a dos, cinco, diez, veinte o sesenta y dos personas. Optaron por veintiséis, a las que acusaron del asesinato de aquel hombre. Entre los acusados estaba un matrimonio de sesentones que tenían once niños y ningún remoto antecedente penal ni político. Los investigadores no hicieron ningún esfuerzo para distinguir entre el grado de culpabilidad del viejo matrimonio y el de Bekebeke. No sabían que él era el que había propinado los golpes decisivos. Ni lo iban a averiguar durante el largo juicio posterior. Si se les declaraba culpables, los «26 de Upington» recibirían la misma sentencia para la que se había preparado Mandela cuando ocupó el banquillo en Pretoria veintiún años antes: la muerte en la horca.

Capítulo IV
EL COCODRILO ATRAPADO

1986-1989

Kobie Coetsee se había rendido más rápido de lo que podían esperar él o Mandela. Pero éste dudaba de que su siguiente objetivo fuera a ceder con tanta facilidad. Para alcanzar su meta suprema —una entrevista con el propio Botha—, antes tenía que ganarse al hombre que guardaba la puerta presidencial, el jefe del Servicio Nacional de Inteligencia, Niël Barnard. Barnard, que había estudiado política internacional en la Universidad de Georgetown, en Washington, D.C., se había ganado, a los veintitantos años, fama de genio precoz. Botha oyó hablar de él por primera vez cuando Barnard era profesor de Ciencias Políticas en la Universidad del Estado Libre de Orange. De manera impulsiva, Botha lo sacó de la universidad y lo contrató para que dirigiera, con treinta años, el SNI. Era el 1 de junio de 1980. Barnard permanecería en su puesto hasta el 31 de enero de 1992, después de haber servido a Botha durante casi diez años y a su sucesor, F. W. de Klerk, durante dos.

Nadie, en el aparato del apartheid, estaba más enterado de lo que ocurría en la política sudafricana que Barnard, que disponía de informadores en todas partes, algunos en el corazón del CNA. Era astuto y discreto, funcionario hasta la médula y con un fuerte sentido del deber. Durante los doce años que fue jefe del SNI, una organización que se ganó el respeto —aunque no el afecto— de otras como la CIA y el MI6 británico, su rostro fue tan desconocido para el gran público como el de Mandela lo había sido en la cárcel. No había nadie en quien Botha confiara más.

Barnard era un tipo alto, delgado, de cabello oscuro y sin sentido del humor. Un Mr. Spock afrikaner, que hablaba de manera monótona y cuyos rasgos eran tan inexpresivos que, si uno se lo encontraba por casualidad al día siguiente de haber hablado con él, seguramente no lo reconocería. Pero los mecanismos de su mente eran claros, y años después, aunque hablaba de forma un poco acartonada, recordaba con agudeza el ambiente político y las luchas dentro del gobierno durante los años ochenta.

«Algunas personas, sobre todo en el ejército, pero también en la policía, en el fondo creían que teníamos que luchar contra ello de una u otra forma —recordaba—. En el SNI pensábamos que ésa era una manera equivocada de abordar la situación. Nuestra opinión era que un acuerdo político era la única respuesta a los problemas del país.» No hay duda de que era un mensaje muy difícil de vender al aparato oficial de Sudáfrica. Barnard no se hacía ilusiones. «Pero lo importante era que P. W. Botha, que prácticamente había nacido y se había educado en la estructura de seguridad, creía firmemente que, de una u otra forma, teníamos que...

cómo lo diría... estabilizar la situación sudafricana y, a partir de ahí, tratar de encontrar algún tipo de solución política.»

Un día de mayo de 1988, Botha convocó a Barnard a su despacho y le dijo: «Doctor Barnard, quiero que se reúna con el señor Mandela. Intente descubrir si es cierto lo que propone usted desde hace tiempo. ¿Es posible llegar a un acuerdo pacífico con el CNA; con ese hombre, Mandela? Trate de averiguar qué opina sobre el comunismo... y luego trate de averiguar si Mandela y el CNA están interesados en un acuerdo pacífico. Porque también tenemos graves dudas acerca de sus objetivos.»

La primera entrevista de Barnard con Mandela se celebró en el despacho del comandante de Pollsmoor. Según recordaba Barnard, de forma parecida a las primeras impresiones de Kobie Coetsee, «Mandela entró y vi inmediatamente que, incluso vestido con un mono y unas botas, tenía una presencia y una personalidad dominantes.» Los dos hombres se sentaron, conscientes de que el verdadero objetivo de aquella reunión era conocerse, desarrollar una relación que pudiera sostener las negociaciones políticas que pudieran producirse con posterioridad. Hablaron de naderías —Mandela le preguntó de qué parte de Sudáfrica era y Barnard se interesó por su salud— y acordaron volver a verse.

Sin embargo, antes de eso, Barnard ordenó, como Coetsee, que vistieran a Mandela con ropas más propias de alguien de su categoría. Como explicaba Barnard, «hablar sobre el futuro del país vestido con un mono y unas botas, evidentemente, era inaceptable. Acordamos con Willie Willemse, el comisario de los Servicios Penitenciarios, que, a cualquier reunión futura iría vestido de manera correspondiente a su dignidad y su orgullo como ser humano». Y la ropa no fue lo único en lo que Barnard decidió que había que dar facilidades a Mandela. También pidió un lugar más apropiado para los encuentros. «En cualquier reunión futura, Mandela tenía que estar a la misma altura, como igual, eso lo tenía muy claro. Recuerdo que Willie Willemse y yo dijimos que nunca podíamos volver a tener una de esas reuniones dentro de la cárcel. Así era imposible tener una situación de igualdad.» A partir de entonces, Barnard y Mandela se reunieron en casa de Willemse, en el recinto de Pollsmoor, y no en su insulso despacho.

Empezaron a hacerlo en la segunda entrevista, una cena a la que Mandela acudió con chaqueta. «Fue un invitado maravilloso», recordaba Barnard, que abandonó su reserva natural al hacer memoria. En las reuniones, la mujer de Willemse hacía unas cenas deliciosas, corría el vino y los dos hombres hablaban durante horas sobre cómo poner fin pacíficamente al apartheid.

Por su parte, Kobie Coetsee llegó a la conclusión de que mantener al preso en la cárcel era impropio y tan poco útil para el propósito general de las negociaciones como vestirlo con el uniforme. No es que en Pollsmoor le trataran mal. En comparación con la claustrofobia que había aprendido a soportar en Robben Island, su celda de Pollsmoor le parecía el mar abierto. Pero el sitio al que fue a parar era una especie de transatlántico de lujo.

Cuanto peor trataba el régimen de Botha a los negros en la calle, mejor trataba a Mandela. Él podía haber protestado. Podía haberse enfurecido con Barnard, haber amenazado con interrumpir las conversaciones secretas. Pero no lo hizo. Entró en el juego porque sabía que, aunque su capacidad de intervenir en los hechos que estaban ocurriendo fuera en aquel momento prácticamente inexistente, sus posibilidades de influir en el futuro de Sudáfrica podían ser inmensas. Por eso, cuando, en diciembre de 1988, el general Willie Willemse le informó de que le iban a trasladar de su gran celda solitaria en Pollsmoor a una casa dentro del recinto de una prisión llamada Victor Verster en una bonita ciudad llamada Paarl, a una hora al norte de Ciudad del Cabo, en el corazón de las tierras del vino, Mandela no puso ninguna objeción.

Cambió su celda por una espaciosa casa bajo la supervisión —o, más bien, el cuidado— de otro Christo Brand, otro guardia afrikaner que le había acompañado en Pollsmoor y Robben Island. Se llamaba Jack Swart y su trabajo era cocinar para Mandela y hacerle de mayordomo, con deberes como abrir la puerta a sus invitados, ayudarle a organizar su agenda y mantener la casa limpia y ordenada. La cocina era amplia y estaba bien equipada, e incluía electrodomésticos impensables cuando Mandela entró en la cárcel. Le permitían recibir visitas de otros presos políticos aún encarcelados. Uno de ellos fue Tokyo Sexwale, un agitador de Umkhonto we Sizwe que había pasado trece años en Robben Island acusado de terrorismo. Sexwale pertenecía a un pequeño grupo de *jóvenes turcos* del CNA que habían intimado con Mandela en la isla y que no sólo hablaban con él de política sino que se relajaban con él jugando a Escaleras y Serpientes y al Monopoly antes de que le trasladaran a Pollsmoor. Sexwale se reía al recordar aquella visita a Mandela en Victor Verster. «Vimos un televisor en la casa. Ya era fuerte aquello. Pero luego vimos otro. ¡Dos televisores! ¡Aquélla era, pensamos, la prueba definitiva de que se había vendido al enemigo!»

Con una gran sonrisa, Mandela les aseguró que no era un televisor. Explicó a sus boquiabiertos invitados que era una máquina para hervir el agua. Cogió una taza llena de agua y les hizo una demostración: puso la taza dentro y apretó un par de botones. Al cabo de unos momentos, sacó la taza de agua hirviendo del microondas, un aparato que sus invitados no habían visto jamás.

Siempre con Jack Swart presente, Mandela invitó a cenar en su nueva «casa» a gente tan variada como Barnard, Sexwale y su abogado, George Bizos. Antes de que llegaran los invitados, Swart y Mandela discutían aspectos de etiqueta como cuál era el vino apropiado. En cuanto a las verduras, algunas procedían del propio jardín de Mandela, que incluía una piscina y una vista de las grandiosas montañas escarpadas que rodeaban los fértiles valles y viñedos de El Cabo. Y el paraíso no habría sido completo para Mandela sin un gimnasio, dotado de bicicleta estática y pesas, en el que hacía ejercicio diligentemente todas las mañanas antes del alba.

Se trataba, según Barnard, de facilitarle la transición, después de lo que ya eran veintiséis años de hibernación, a un mundo nuevo de microondas y ordenadores personales. «Nos dedicamos a crear una atmósfera que permitiera a Mandela vivir en un entorno lo más normal posible», explicaba Barnard. El propósito de fondo, según él, era ayudarle a prepararse para gobernar y para desempeñar un papel en el escenario mundial. «Le dije muchas veces: "Señor Mandela, gobernar un país es un trabajo difícil. No es, con todos los respetos, como sentarse en un hotel de Londres a beber cerveza Castle importada de Sudáfrica y hablar del gobierno (era una pulla de Barnard contra los líderes del CNA en el exilio)." Le dije: "Gobernar es un trabajo duro, tiene que entender que es difícil."»

Barnard también se encargó de otra tarea más delicada, la de preparar al presidente Botha, el *krokodil*, para entrevistarse con Mandela. La presión inicial para que se celebrara ese encuentro surgió del propio Mandela, que empezó a expresar cierta impaciencia por la lentitud de los avances.

Quería que las conversaciones abriesen la puerta a un proceso de negociaciones en el que participasen el CNA, el gobierno y todas las demás partes que lo quisieran, con el fin de acabar con el apartheid por medios pacíficos. Al llegar 1989, tras más de seis meses de reuniones entre preso y espía, Mandela se hartó. «Está bien tener conversaciones preliminares con usted sobre los aspectos fundamentales —le dijo a Barnard—, pero comprenderá que no es un político. No tiene la autoridad ni el poder necesarios. Tengo que hablar con el propio Botha, lo antes posible.»

En marzo de 1989, Barnard entregó a su jefe una carta de Mandela. En ella, Mandela alegaba que la única forma de conseguir una paz duradera en Sudáfrica era mediante un acuerdo negociado. Decía que, por otra parte, la mayoría negra no tenía intención de rendirse. «El gobierno de la mayoría y la paz interna —escribió— son dos caras de la misma moneda, y la Sudáfrica blanca tiene que aceptar que no habrá paz ni estabilidad en este país hasta que no se aplique plenamente ese principio.»

Quizá más importante que esa carta fue el hecho de que Mandela ya había convencido a Barnard del argumento que contenía. Barnard podía convencer a su jefe, aunque la carta no lo consiguiera.

«Sí... —contaba Barnard, con una nota de afecto en la monotonía metálica de su voz—, el viejo —se refería a Mandela— es uno de esos individuos extraños que te cautiva. Tiene ese carisma peculiar. Te das cuenta de que quieres escucharle. De modo que, sí —continuaba Barnard—, en nuestra mente, desde una perspectiva inteligente, nunca tuvimos la menor duda. Éste es el hombre; si no podemos llegar a un acuerdo con él, no habrá ningún acuerdo.»

Eso es lo que le dijo a Botha. Pero había también otros argumentos sobre los que recomendó pensar al presidente. El mundo estaba cambiando a toda velocidad. El movimiento anticomunista de Solidaridad había obtenido el poder en Polonia; en la plaza de Tiananmen había manifestaciones para exigir reformas en China; el ejército soviético había puesto fin a sus nueve años de ocupación de Afganistán; el Muro de Berlín se tambaleaba. El apartheid, como el comunismo, pertenecía a otra era.

Los argumentos de Barnard influyeron en Botha, pero el presidente podría haber seguido titubeando, irritándose y dando vueltas en su fortaleza mental si el destino biológico no hubiera intervenido. En enero de 1989 sufrió una apoplejía que inyectó un nuevo sentido de urgencia en sus actuaciones.

Más que quererle, los miembros de su gabinete le respetaban y algunos incluso le temían. Sus enemigos dentro del propio Partido Nacional percibían, por fin, señales de debilidad, y se disponían a dar el golpe de gracia. Barnard, una de las pocas personas que sí sentía afecto por Botha, presentía que su jefe tenía los días contados en su cargo y que tenía que actuar rápidamente. «Recuerdo que le dije que era el momento perfecto para entrevistarse con Mandela, lo antes posible. Si no, íbamos a desperdiciar, quizá, una de las oportunidades más importantes de nuestra historia. Mi postura, que le transmití a Botha, era: "Señor presidente, si se entrevista con Mandela y eso se convierte en la base, el fundamento de la evolución futura de nuestro país, la historia siempre le reconocerá como el hombre que inició este proceso necesario. En mi opinión meditada, es una situación con todas las de ganar."»

Era una forma educada de decir que Botha se encontraba tal vez ante la última oportunidad de ser recordado no sólo como un enorme reptil aterrador. Botha lo comprendió y Barnard volvió a Mandela con la feliz noticia de que el presidente había aceptado reunirse con él. «Pero le advertí: "Mire, ésta es una reunión para romper el hielo, no para tratar de temas fundamentales. Venga a saber algo de él. Hable de las cosas fáciles en la vida. Y no toque el tema de Walter Sisulu... Si vuelve a mencionar la puesta en libertad de Walter Sisulu, el señor Botha dirá que no. Le conozco. Y si dice no, es no... Deje eso a un lado. Hay otra forma de abordar la cuestión. Además, no hable de temas espinosos, no es el objeto de la primera reunión."»

Mandela escuchó cortésmente, pero no tenía la menor intención de seguir los consejos de aquel joven inteligente, descarado y algo raro, al que llevaba más de treinta años. Los dos habían hablado mucho sobre la posible liberación de Sisulu, que llevaba en prisión veinticinco años, y, si a Mandela le parecía oportuno, pensaba sacar a relucir el tema con Botha. Lo que no rechazó, en cambio, fue la oferta de Barnard de hacerse ropa especial para la ocasión. Por cortesía del SNI, un sastre le midió para un traje. Cuando se lo enviaron hecho, Mandela se miró en el espejo y el resultado le gustó. Era la reunión más importante de su vida y estaba deseando crear el ambiente adecuado. Como un actor a punto de salir a escena, repasó las notas que había estado preparando durante varios días, ensayó sus frases y se metió en el papel. Iba a entrevistarse con su carcelero jefe de igual a igual. Dos caudillos que representaban a dos pueblos orgullosos.

La mañana del 5 de julio de 1989, el general Willemse recogió a Mandela en Victor Verster para hacer con él el trayecto de 45 minutos desde Paarl hasta la majestuosa residencia presidencial conocida como Tuynhuys, en Ciudad del Cabo, un monumento del siglo XVIII al poder colonial blanco. Justo antes de entrar en el coche, Willemse, que había adoptado momentáneamente el papel de Jeeves de Jack Swart, se aproximó a Mandela y le ayudó a ajustarse la corbata. Mandela, tan elegante antes de entrar el cárcel, había perdido el toque.

Aproximadamente una hora después, cuando Mandela acababa de salir del coche y se disponía a entrar en las oficinas de Botha, Barnard, que le aguardaba, hizo una cosa extraordinaria. Ansioso por que su protegido causara buena impresión, se arrodilló delante de Mandela y ató bien los cordones de los zapatos del señor mayor.

Mandela se detuvo, sonriente, en el umbral de la guarida del cocodrilo, con la sensación de que, si daba con el tono adecuado y escogía sus palabras con prudencia, el triunfo para el que llevaba preparándose un cuarto de siglo podía estar, por fin, al alcance de su mano. Sabía que la decisión de Botha de entrevistarse con él era un reconocimiento de que las cosas no podían seguir como hasta entonces. Por eso no le había causado ninguna angustia pensar si estaba bien o no sentarse a hablar con los gobernantes más violentos que había conocido Sudáfrica desde la instauración del apartheid en 1948.

Para empezar, Mandela entendía, como no podían entenderlo los Justice Bekebeke que estaban en primera línea de fuego, que la violencia que había desencadenado Botha contra la población negra en los cuatro años anteriores era un signo de debilidad y desesperación crecientes. La fantasía de legitimidad se había desvanecido y el único instrumento que quedaba para mantener vivo el apartheid era el cañón de una pistola. Si Mandela había aprendido algo en la cárcel, era a mirar todo el conjunto. Y eso significaba no dejarse distraer por los horrores que estaban ocurriendo y mantener la vista firmemente puesta en el objetivo distante.

Y había algo más. Tras tantos años de estudiar a los afrikaners, su lengua y su cultura, había aprendido que, por encima de todo, eran supervivientes. Habían llegado de Europa, se habían asentado en África y la habían convertido en su hogar. Para ello, habían tenido que ser duros, pero también pragmáticos. Había dos P. W. Botha. Estaba el matón despiadado y estaba el hombre que en una ocasión había advertido a los afrikaners, en un famoso discurso, que tenían que «adaptarse o morir».

Barnard llamó a la puerta del presidente, la abrió y entró en el lujoso salón, decorado con tapicerías versallescas. Mandela recuerda ese momento en su autobiografía, *El largo camino hacia la libertad*: «Desde el lado opuesto de su enorme despacho, P. W. Botha se acercó. Tenía la mano extendida y una gran sonrisa y, la verdad, desde aquel primer momento, me desarmó por completo.» Kobie Coetsee, que presenció la reunión junto con

Barnard y que observó con asombro cómo Botha le servía una taza de té a Mandela, creía más bien que el desarme fue mutuo. Mandela consiguió que el viejo y áspero cocodrilo se relajara, le tranquilizó con su sonrisa franca y su aire solemne, y hablando con él en afrikaans. «Creo que, cuando se vieron por primera vez, sintieron casi alivio», explicó Coetsee.

Botha mostró un respeto incondicional por Mandela. Éste fue también todo cortesía, pero la ventaja que tenía sobre el presidente era la astucia de sus artes de seducción. Para ponerle las cosas fáciles, habló de las analogías entre la lucha actual del pueblo negro por su liberación y el combate similar de los afrikaners casi cien años antes, en la guerra de los bóers, para sacudirse el yugo imperial británico. A Botha, cuyo padre y cuyo abuelo habían luchado contra los británicos en aquella guerra, le impresionó que Mandela conociera la historia de su gente.

Cuando consideró que había ablandado suficientemente al presidente, Mandela desobedeció las instrucciones de Barnard y mencionó el tema de la liberación de su amigo Sisulu. Era de una importancia crucial, afirmó, tanto por motivos políticos como por motivos personales, que Sisulu, cuya salud no era muy buena, saliera a la calle. «Curiosamente —recordaba Barnard una década después—, Botha escuchó y dijo: "Señor Barnard, usted sabe los problemas que tenemos. Supongo que se los ha explicado al señor Mandela, pero creo que debemos ayudarle. Creo que hay que hacerlo. Quiero que preste atención a eso." Y yo contesté: "De acuerdo, señor presidente."»

No todo fue fácil entre los dos hombres. «Hubo momentos de gran sinceridad —recordaba Coetsee—, y las dos partes se mostraron muy firmes en sus posturas.» Mandela debió de tener que morderse la lengua cuando Botha, según recordaba Coetsee, empezó a hablar de «criterios y normas, civilización y las escrituras», que era la forma figurada que tenían los políticos del Partido Nacional de contrastar los méritos de su cultura con la barbarie ignorante del mundo habitado por los negros. Por su parte, a Botha no debió de gustarle que Mandela volviese a decir que el Partido Comunista era un viejo aliado y que no iba a «deshacerse ahora de socios que han estado con el CNA a lo largo de toda la lucha».

Sin embargo, los dos hombres se despidieron con la misma afabilidad que a la llegada. La química que había percibido Coetsee había funcionado, porque Botha confirmó de inmediato una de las impresiones que había tenido Barnard: Mandela era un hombre de sólidas convicciones y no temía manifestarlas. «Mandela fue muy sincero, incluso muy directo a veces —dijo Barnard—. A los afrikaners les gusta eso.» Botha observó al líder de la Sudáfrica negra y prefirió ver una versión idealizada de su propia brusquedad. Al apelar a su vanidad y su orgullo afrikaner, Mandela había conquistado al *krokodil*. «Mandela —dijo Barnard— sabía cómo utilizar su poder con sutileza. Es como comparar las antiguas fortunas y los nuevos ricos. Sabía cómo manejar su poder sin humillar a sus enemigos.»

Una declaración oficial tras la reunión dejó clara la victoria de Mandela, en un lenguaje anodino: los dos hombres habían «confirmado su apoyo a la evolución pacífica» de Sudáfrica. En otras palabras, Botha se había comprometido al plan que Mandela había elaborado en sus veintisiete años de prisión: la paz a través del diálogo. Los preparativos para unas negociaciones completas entre el CNA y el gobierno, ahora con la bendición del máximo mandatario afrikaner, iban a seguir adelante. Y estaba el regalo añadido de los aparentes avances en cuanto a la liberación de Walter Sisulu y otra media docena de presos veteranos, que se produjo tres meses después, si bien, para entonces, Botha había abandonado ya su cargo y había sido sustituido por F. W. de Klerk.

Ambos dejaron aquella reunión de Tuynhuys más satisfechos de sí mismos y del mundo que al entrar. Mandela, en especial, se fue con una discreta sensación de triunfo. Como escribió en su autobiografía, «el señor Botha llevaba mucho tiempo hablando de la necesidad de cruzar el Rubicón, pero no lo hizo hasta aquella mañana en Tuynhuys. Entonces sentí que habíamos llegado a un punto sin retorno».

Aquél fue el final del trabajo político de Mandela tras las rejas. Se había ganado a sus carceleros inmediatos, como Christo Brand y Jack Swart; después, a los jefes de la prisión, el coronel Badenhorst y el mayor Van Sittert; luego a Kobie Coetsee, Niël Barnard, y, contra todo pronóstico, nada menos que al viejo cocodrilo. El siguiente paso era salir de la cárcel y empezar a ejercer su magia con la población en general, ampliar su ofensiva de seducción hasta que abarcase a toda Sudáfrica.

Capítulo V
PLANETAS DIFERENTES

El mundo en el que Mandela se encontró viviendo en 1989 estaba muy lejos, en el tiempo y en el espacio moral, de las dificultades cotidianas en Sudáfrica, sobre todo la Sudáfrica negra. Mientras se arreglaba para cenar en casa del simpático matrimonio Willemse, mientras jugaba con su horno microondas, hablaba de vino con su mayordomo, se bañaba en su piscina y admiraba las vistas desde su jardín, los hombres más poderosos del país —los mismos con los que se sentaba a tomar esas refinadas tazas de té— se escabullían por la puerta trasera y se colocaban sus trajes de vampiro para descargar su furia sobre la gente a cuya libertad había dedicado Mandela su vida.

Aparte del caos habitual que creaba la policía antidisturbios en los distritos negros, los escuadrones de la muerte de la policía y el ejército cuya creación había aprobado Botha se dedicaban a quitar de en medio a activistas a los que consideraban especialmente peligrosos para el Estado. Y Kobie Coetsee seguía presidiendo un sistema judicial que condenaba a muerte a más gente que Arabia Saudí y Estados Unidos (aunque menos que China, Irak e Irán) y que dictaba una sentencia injusta tras otra. En abril de 1989, dos granjeros blancos declarados culpables de matar a golpes a uno de sus empleados negros fueron condenados a una multa de 1.200 rand (unos 500 dólares de entonces), más una pena de seis meses de cárcel, suspendida durante cinco años. Ese mismo día, otro tribunal declaró a tres policías culpables de matar a golpes a un hombre negro pero no encarceló más que a uno de ellos, casualmente el que era negro, durante doce años.

Pero nada podía compararse con lo que la gente de Coetsee estaba preparando en un tribunal del centro de Upington. De las 26 personas acusadas del asesinato de Lucas Sethwala, el policía negro que había disparado contra la muchedumbre, se las habían arreglado para declarar culpables a 25. Lo que todavía estaba por decidir, a mediados de 1989, era si los 25, que llevaban en la cárcel desde finales de 1985, iban a sufrir la obligatoria condena a muerte.

Paballelo seguía con pasión todos los detalles del juicio. Sin embargo, para los blancos, era como si se celebrase en Borneo, por lo que les interesaba. Salvo los policías de servicio, no apareció ni un solo blanco durante los tres años y medio que duró el proceso. Para cautivar, un drama necesita que el espectador tenga una condición humana común con los protagonistas. Para Upington, Paballelo era un mundo paralelo, poco iluminado, habitado por una especie distinta; más valía dejarlos solos.

Sería injusto insinuar que Upington tenía el monopolio del racismo blanco. El juicio que allí se celebraba y las circunstancias que lo rodeaban podrían haber sucedido en cualquiera de otras muchas ciudades de Sudáfrica. Upington, en medio del desierto, ofrecía una imagen muy nítida del apartheid, de las líneas claramente dibujadas que mantenían separadas a las distintas razas. Pero los habitantes blancos locales no estaban solos, ni mucho menos, ni eran sustancialmente distintos de la mayoría de sus compatriotas de piel clara. Y, aunque eran objeto de sátiras y críticas en todo el mundo, había que preguntarse si el ciudadano medio de Estados Unidos, Canadá o España, si hubiera nacido en la Sudáfrica del apartheid, se habría comportado de manera muy diferente. Vivían en la misma órbita general que la gente más privilegiada del mundo occidental. Sus vidas consistían en el hogar y el trabajo, en disfrutar de una existencia tranquila y confortable. La política no solía interesarles. La diferencia estaba en que vivían al lado de unas personas que estaban entre las más pobres y peor tratadas del mundo, y en que su buena suerte, la razón por la que los sudafricanos blancos tenían seguramente el mayor nivel de vida del mundo y, desde luego, la mejor calidad de vida, dependía de la desgracia de sus vecinos negros.

Pensemos en una familia de los estratos económicos más bajos de la Sudáfrica blanca. Por ejemplo, la familia de François Pienaar, que acabaría siendo el capitán Springbok en la final de la Copa del Mundo de rugby en 1995. El padre de Pienaar era un trabajador en la industria del acero. Su familia no vivía bien, en comparación con el nivel medio de la Sudáfrica blanca. Para ellos, la vida era una lucha continua. Pienaar se avergonzaba del coche familiar, viejo y abollado, de los regalos que recibía en Navidad, menos extravagantes que los de otros chicos. Sin embargo, la familia Pienaar tenía una casa lo suficientemente grande como para incluir a dos criadas negras internas, que llamaban a François y a sus tres hermanos pequeños *klein baas*, «jefecitos». Aquel tipo de relación entre niños de seis años y criadas lo bastante mayores como para ser sus madres o sus abuelas era normal en las casas de los blancos, y lo había sido desde hacía mucho tiempo. En una ocasión, P. W. Botha describió al *New York Times* su relación con los negros cuando era niño. «Mi padre me enseñó a ser estricto con ellos —dijo—, pero justo.»

Pienaar creció en una ciudad industrial al sur de Johanesburgo y a 750 kilómetros al este de Upington, llamada Vereeniging. La Vereeniging blanca tenía la misma relación con el distrito segregado más próximo, Sharpeville, que la Upington blanca tenía con Paballelo. Sharpeville ocupaba en la mente de la familia Pienaar un espacio casi tan poco significativo como Selma, Alabama. Por el contrario, Vereeniging tenía gran peso en la mente de los residentes de Sharpeville. Era el lugar desde el que se había acercado a visitarles la muerte en una ocasión famosa. Sharpeville sufrió en una ocasión la peor atrocidad de la era del apartheid; en 1960, las fuerzas de policía dispararon a unos manifestantes negros desarmados que huían y mataron a 69.

Seguramente había más odio concentrado hacia los blancos en Vereeniging que en ningún otro lugar de Sudáfrica. Sharpeville era el distrito en el que el CPA —el de «un colono, una bala»— tenía su base de apoyo más sólida. Pero Pienaar, de niño, no tenía idea de que los negros le consideraban su enemigo mortal, ni sabía nada de la existencia de Sharpeville, y mucho menos de su historia. Los negros se movían en la periferia vagamente borrosa de su conciencia infantil. Como reconocería más tarde: «Éramos una típica familia afrikaner de clase obrera, con escasa conciencia política, que nunca hablaba de ello y se creía por completo la propaganda de entonces.»

Lo mismo pasaba prácticamente con todos los que crecieron en el mundo de Pienaar. Ni se les ocurría poner en duda la justicia de que los blancos tuvieran casas más grandes, mejores coches, mejores colegios, mejores instalaciones deportivas, o el derecho ancestral a saltarse la cola por delante de los negros en la oficina de Correos. Todavía más remota le resultaba a Pienaar, como a la gran mayoría de los afrikaners de su clase social, la idea de que los blancos hubieran adquirido esa vida privilegiada de forma sospechosa y un día pudieran arrebatársela por las malas. En su adolescencia, pensar que los negros pudieran organizarse como una fuerza que mereciera el nombre de «enemiga» habría parecido rocambolesco. El enemigo, para alguien que jugaba al rugby como François, eran «los ingleses», que también jugaban al rugby, aunque nunca tan bien como los afrikaners, a los que la población de habla inglesa llamaba «los holandeses». El joven Pienaar estaba muy orgulloso de que, durante toda su trayectoria escolar, su equipo no perdiera jamás contra un colegio cuyo idioma predominante fuera el inglés.

La diferencia entre la pasión de la familia Pienaar por el rugby y su falta de interés por la política quedó patente en la gira que hicieron los Springboks en 1981 por Nueva Zelanda. Este país, normalmente uno de los más plácidos del mundo, se dividió peligrosamente en dos con la gira, por los apasionados sentimientos de la mitad del país, que compartía la ciega devoción al deporte de los afrikaners, y la otra mitad, que aborrecía el gran «crimen contra la humanidad» de Sudáfrica. Nunca había estado tan polarizada la población del país isleño. La gira duró ocho tumultuosas semanas y, en todos los lugares a los que fueron los Springboks, les recibieron manifestantes enloquecidos, policía antidisturbios con sus cascos, soldados y alambradas. Los estadios estaban siempre llenos, pero en las calles había otros tantos manifestantes que los cercaban. El último partido de la gira en Auckland se vio interrumpido por una avioneta que arrojó bombas de harina sobre el terreno. Con las imágenes de policías aporreando a manifestantes vestidos de payasos, el resultado fue un magnífico espectáculo televisivo. Los Pienaar estaban viéndolo y se quedaron francamente asombrados.

Arnold Stofile llamaba al rugby «el opio de los bóer». Stofile, un hombre negro que, como Bekebeke, no había dejado que las indignidades del apartheid coartaran su poderosa personalidad, se crió en una granja, se unió a una organización tapadera del CNA a principios de los sesenta, se convirtió en profesor de Teología en la Universidad de Fort Hare (donde había estudiado Mandela), fue ordenado ministro presbiteriano y jugaba al rugby, un fenómeno menos infrecuente entre los negros de su nativo Cabo Oriental que en otras partes del país. Pero no dejaba que su pasión personal por el deporte nublara su visión del panorama político general. Se convirtió en uno de los organizadores más activos de boicots de competiciones deportivas internacionales. «Siempre definimos el deporte como una muestra de apartheid con chándal —decía Stofile—. Era un elemento muy importante en la política exterior de este país, y las figuras del deporte eran embajadores de facto de Sudáfrica, un elemento clave de los esfuerzos para hacer que el apartheid no fuera tan inaceptable. En cuanto a la política interna, el deporte era la barrera que separaba a los jóvenes blancos de los negros; por eso contaba con un enorme apoyo del gobierno y las grandes empresas tenían grandes rebajas fiscales por patrocinarlo. Era el opio que mantenía a los blancos en una ignorancia feliz; el opio que tenía adormecida Sudáfrica.»

Impedir que Sudáfrica consumiera la droga feliz y que el gobierno tuviera sus «embajadores» fue la misión a la que Stofile dedicó casi veinte años de su vida. «Una huelga de trabajadores, incluso una bomba, afectaba a un grupo pequeño —explicaba—. Esto afectaba a todos, todos los hombres blancos, todas las familias, en un país apasionado del deporte, cuyo máximo motivo de orgullo ante el resto del mundo eran sus hazañas deportivas.»

Niël Barnard, que sufrió la ofensiva de Stofile, estaba de acuerdo. «La política del CNA de aislamiento deportivo internacional, especialmente el aislamiento del rugby, nos resultó muy dolorosa a los afrikaners. Desde el punto de vista psicológico era un golpe cruel, porque el rugby era un campo en el que sentíamos que, a pesar de ser un país pequeño, podíamos tener la cabeza alta. Impedir que jugáramos al rugby con el resto del mundo acabó siendo un instrumento de influencia política increíblemente eficaz.»

El éxito más espectacular de Stofile se produjo en 1985, el año trascendental en el que pareció ocurrir prácticamente todo en Sudáfrica. Salió ilegalmente del país y consiguió llegar a Nueva Zelanda, con ayuda de un antiguo miembro de los All Blacks que era alto comisario de su país en Zimbabue. Una vez allí, prestó todo su peso, de forma decisiva, a una campaña para impedir que los All Blacks llevaran a cabo una gira prevista por Sudáfrica.

Nueva Zelanda estaba tan dividida y tan furiosa que toda la cultura del rugby, la pasión y el orgullo del país, corría peligro. Los sentimientos del bando opuesto a la gira eran tan fuertes que los padres se negaban a dejar que sus hijos jugaran al rugby en el colegio y les amenazaban con impedir que volvieran a jugarlo jamás. Stofile recordaba con satisfacción que se lanzó a una ofensiva de propaganda: habló ante muchedumbres, apareció en la radio y la televisión, elevó el debate nacional más allá de unos conceptos abstractos de blanco y negro y dio a la causa un rostro y un nombre. Cuando llegó a nueva Zelanda, el apoyo al boicot deportivo estaba en un 40 %. Tres semanas después, esa cifra había subido al 75 %. No obstante, la junta directiva del rugby neozelandés decidió hacer la gira, pero entonces intervinieron los propios jugadores y un grupo de ellos llevó la cuestión a los tribunales. La aparición de Stofile como testigo fue decisiva. Un tipo fornido, que amaba el rugby tanto como el neozelandés corriente, Stofile, alegó que lo que estaba en juego era más importante y ofreció un elocuente relato de primera mano de las burdas injusticias que sufrían los negros, con especial énfasis en la Ley de Servicios Separados y lo que significaba para su vida diaria. Concluyó recordando al tribunal que un país con la admirable tradición democrática de Nueva Zelanda debería avergonzarse de colaborar con un régimen que tenía el descaro de describir a un equipo —los Springboks— extraído de sólo el 15 % de la población como los auténticos representantes de toda Sudáfrica. «Fui el segundo testigo —contó Stofile, sonriendo al recordar—, y, cuando acabé, habíamos ganado el caso. La gira se canceló. Fue una gran victoria.»

Al volver a su país, Stofile fue detenido y condenado a doce años de cárcel. La Sudáfrica negra celebró su triunfo igual que había celebrado, cuatro años antes, las escenas de disturbios en el país de las antípodas que tanto habían confundido a la familia Pienaar.

Para Pienaar, el rugby era sólo un deporte, su principal entretenimiento de niño, junto con las peleas. Su vida, desde muy pequeño, había sido violenta, pero nunca con intención criminal o política, como en los difíciles distritos segregados; era violencia porque sí. Cuando Pienaar tenía siete años, los miembros de una banda rival le colgaron de un árbol. Si no hubiera pasado en ese momento un adulto, habría muerto. Aun así, la cuerda le dejó profundas marcas en el cuello. Más tarde, cuando estaba en la universidad, más o menos en la misma época en la que Bekebeke mató a Sethwala, Pienaar estuvo a punto de hacer lo mismo —o temió haberlo hecho— con un extraño con el que se cruzó delante de un bar en una calle de Johanesburgo, a altas horas de la noche. Durante una pelea de borrachos, derribó al hombre, que aterrizó de cabeza en el suelo con un ruido seco. Entre esos dos incidentes, rompió más costillas y más dientes, dentro y fuera del campo de rugby, de los que podía recordar.

Desde la perspectiva del mundo de Justice Bekebeke, en el que las diversiones eran el fútbol y el baile, el rugby era un deporte extrañamente salvaje, en el que los jugadores salían del campo en camilla, como soldados después de una batalla; en el que los espectadores, inevitablemente grandes e inevitablemente borrachos, en sus uniformes de guardabosques bóer, con camisa y pantalón corto caquis, calcetines gruesos y botas, devoraban con entusiasmo sus tradicionales salchichas *boerewors* y bebían su bebida favorita, coñac con coca cola. En cuanto a los niños, a ojos de los negros, parecían seguir el ejemplo de sus padres. Sus vidas consistían en peleas sangrientas sin fin en las que estaban constantemente golpeándose con sillas en la cabeza, cuando no estaban colgando a sus amiguitos de los árboles.

La horca estaba muy presente en la mente de un afrikaner llamado J. J. Basson la mañana del 24 de mayo de 1989. Basson, el juez que había dictado el veredicto sin precedentes en el caso de Upington, llevaba casi seis meses escuchando los argumentos de los abogados de la defensa, sobre todo Anton Lubowski, para que tuviera en cuenta circunstancias atenuantes que pudieran mitigar las condenas a muerte de Justice Bekebeke y los otros 24 asesinos convictos.

Lubowski era un afrikaner de treinta y siete años, alto, atractivo, criado en Ciudad del Cabo, cuyo aspecto parecía, como su nombre, el de un seductor conde polaco. Era un activista profundamente inmerso en la lucha política contra el apartheid y pertenecía a ese menos del 1 % de la población blanca que no sólo veía Sudáfrica con los mismos ojos que el resto del mundo, sino que actuaba de acuerdo con esa opinión; que se había arriesgado y había tomado la decisión consciente de nadar contra la feroz corriente de la opinión ortodoxa entre el *volk*. Era una de esas escasas personas blancas que de verdad conocían su país, todo su país; que pasaba tiempo en los distritos segregados, haciendo amigos y conspirando; que se esforzaba por aprender unas cuantas palabras de la lengua negra.

Los periodistas que cubrían el juicio se hicieron amigos de Lubowski en aquellos primeros meses de

1989. Justice Bekebeke no era entonces más que un rostro al otro lado de un juzgado repleto. Sin embargo, años más tarde, era Bekebeke el que hablaba de aquella época. «Anton era uno de los nuestros —decía, con una solemnidad afligida—. Él y nosotros éramos uno. Le llamábamos "número 26", como si fuera otro acusado más. Era mucho más que nuestro abogado.» Dentro de los juzgados de Upington había una sala especial de consultas en la que los abogados se reunían con sus clientes. «Pero él no quería hablar con nosotros allí. Quería vernos en nuestro entorno, así que venía a las celdas. Decía que se sentía más cómodo allí. Era nuestro camarada. No veíamos su piel blanca, que era un afrikaner.»

Lubowski iba a las celdas situadas bajo el tribunal, cantaba con ellos canciones de protesta y bailaba con ellos sus bailes desafiantes. Y luego los representaba, alto e impresionante en su toga negra de abogado, en el calor desértico del tribunal, donde las ventanas estaban abiertas de par en par con la esperanza de atrapar alguna pizca de brisa pasajera. Se enfrentaba a Basson, discutía con él en un tono legal y discreto o, cuando todo lo demás fallaba, con muestras de indignación. Mandela habría estado más dispuesto que Lubowski a perdonar a Basson, habría estado más dispuesto a ver su crueldad como consecuencia del mundo en el que se había educado. Pero Mandela también habría visto que Lubowski era una imagen de ese mundo mejor que quería crear en Sudáfrica y que, en gran parte, gracias a los Lubowski sudafricanos podía él tratar de convencer a sus compatriotas negros de que, no porque una persona fuera blanca, tenía necesriamente que ser mala.

A primera hora de la mañana del 24 de mayo, el día

que Basson iba a dictar su veredicto, Lubowski confesó en el desayuno que lo máximo a lo que podían aspirar era un rayo de paternalismo benevolente que iluminara el gélido corazón de Basson. Lubowski tenía las mayores esperanzas para el matrimonio de sesentones, Evelina de Bruin y su marido Gideon Madlongolwana. «No creo que ni siquiera Basson pueda estar tan loco como para ahorcarlos a ellos», dijo. Tenían once hijos, dos todavía en edad escolar. Evelina era una criada doméstica regordeta que cojeaba un poco al caminar. Gideon había trabajado fielmente para los ferrocarriles sudafricanos durante treinta y seis años. Ninguno de ellos tenía antecedentes penales. Lubowski pensaba que iban a salvarse. El acusado para el que no tenía ninguna esperanza era Justice Bekebeke, que en aquella época tenía veintiocho años y era el miembro del grupo más elocuente y militante.

Si hubieran querido dar ejemplo con él y hubieran perdonado al resto, eso habría tenido cierta lógica. «El verdaderamente culpable era yo —decía después Justice—. Hacia el final de la fase de atenuantes del juicio, Anton vino a las celdas a decirnos cuáles eran nuestras posibilidades. Yo les dije a todos que, en mi opinión, tenía que confesar, por el bien del grupo. No me dejaron prácticamente terminar. Saltaron todos, furiosos. Me dijeron: "Antes te mataríamos nosotros que dejar que te maten ellos." No querían que confesara ante aquel juez blanco. Era cuestión de dignidad y de solidaridad, y comprendí inmediatamente que no había posibilidad de más discusión. Anton estaba presente, y dijo: "Muy bien, sabéis qué, yo no he oído esto. Esta conversación no ha tenido lugar."»

Los compañeros acusados de Bekebeke hicieron un tremendo sacrificio, porque el juez Basson sobrepasó las peores expectativas de Lubowski. Dictó que los atenuantes sólo valían para once de los acusados; que, además de Justice Bekebeke, Evelina de Bruin y Gideon estaban entre los catorce para cuyo comportamiento no veía excusa, cuyo propósito, el 13 de noviembre de 1985, consideraba que había sido el asesinato.

Gritos de dolor, asombro e ira llenaron el tribunal, mientras los acusados y sus familiares se tapaban el rostro con desesperación e incredulidad, porque aquello no era lo que sus abogados les habían dicho que debían esperar. Evelina de Bruin se inclinó sobre su marido y lloró. Basson, impasible, pospuso la sentencia definitiva hasta el día siguiente. Pero las emociones que había desencadenado en el tribunal se extendieron a la calle. Se agruparon 40 o 50 mujeres, jóvenes y ancianos, bajo la mirada de un número igual de policías fuertemente armados. Lloraron, luego rompieron a cantar canciones protesta como las que se oían en toda Sudáfrica en funerales, manifestaciones y juicios políticos.

Un adolescente se separó del grupo y emprendió un *Toi Toi*, una danza de guerra que simbolizaba la resistencia airada contra el apartheid. Mientras siseaba «¡¡Zaaa!! ¡Za-Zaaa! ¡Zaaa! ¡Za-Zaaa! ¡Zaaa! ¡Za-Zaaa!» y daba pisotones tan fuertes que las rodillas rebotaban hasta la barbilla, daba vueltas y más vueltas, como en trance, moviendo los brazos y apretando los puños hasta hacerlos palidecer. Pero no llevaba ninguna lanza, y los policías tenían armas y perros que mostraban sus fauces, y una videocámara le enfocaba.

Las mujeres lo miraban y meneaban la cabeza. Temblaban por él. Tenían razón. Esa noche, la policía enloqueció. Es difícil saber exactamente por qué. Quizá porque la madres de los condenados habían alterado el recatado y prístino equilibrio del centro de la Upington blanca al reunirse allí a derramar sus lágrimas y cantar sus tristes cantos. Quizá porque, en un momento de alivio dentro de un día de penas, las mujeres negras que se encontraban ante los juzgados rompieron a carcajadas y aplausos cuando un coche de policía chocó de forma accidental contra el costado de un Toyota que pasaba. Quizá fue simplemente porque Upington no había saciado todavía del todo su sed de venganza, seguía indignada por la intrusión de las protestas negras en las cómodas certidumbres de sus vidas en el apartheid.

Fuera por lo que fuese, el caso es que, al anochecer de aquel jueves, un escuadrón antidisturbios salió por la parte del matadero a las afueras de la ciudad, giró a la izquierda hacia Paballelo y atacó a todo el que se les puso a tiro. Por lo menos veinte personas recibieron palizas graves. Algunos acabaron inconscientes. Algunos fueron pisoteados. Algunos recibieron en el abdomen patadas hasta sangrar. De los veinte que tuvieron que ser hospitalizados, cinco tenían trece años y cuatro tenían quince.

Al día siguiente, el último día del juicio de Upington, el tribunal volvía a parecer un horno. Pero el juez J. J. Basson, envuelto en su toga roja ritual, no sudó ni una gota. Iba a dictar unas condenas a muerte, pero su voz tenía un tono ausente —como un burócrata impaciente por irse a casa tras una larga jornada— cuando invitó a cada uno de los acusados a dirigirse brevemente al tribunal, tal como permitía la ley.

Los catorce condenados habían pedido a Justice que hablara en su nombre. Él había pensado escribir algo, pero al final no pudo. Se limitó a hablar con el corazón en la mano:

«En un país como Sudáfrica —comenzó, dirigiéndose a Basson—, me pregunto cómo puede aplicarse verdaderamente la justicia. Yo, desde luego, no la he encontrado. Pero me gustaría pedir, señoría, que olvidemos nuestro odio racial. Busquemos la justicia para toda la humanidad. Luchamos para que todos los grupos raciales vivan en armonía. ¿Pero es posible, en nombre del Señor? ¿Es posible en un país así?... Me gustaría que el Señor le conceda muchos años para que un día pueda verme a mí, un hombre negro, caminando por las calles de una Sudáfrica libre... Y, señoría, que el Señor le bendiga, señoría.»

Al acabar sus palabras, un hombre menudo que estaba de pie al fondo de la sala musitó: «¡Amén!» Estaba erguido, apoyado en un bastón de madera con el puño de marfil, impecablemente vestido con traje de tres piezas y corbata. Era el padre de uno de los acusados y la imagen —tenía más o menos la edad de Mandela— de un anciano distinguido. Pero cuando el juez Basson anunció sus veredictos, el hombre se sentó muy despacio y se derrumbó con la cabeza entre las manos. Había ordenado la muerte en la horca para Justice Bekebeke y los otros trece condenados. Basson hizo el anuncio con voz seria y luego suspendió la sesión por última vez. Los presos fueron a las celdas de debajo del tribunal, y Lubowski fue con ellos. Estaba destrozado. «Nosotros le consolábamos a él», recordaba Bekebeke.

Se llevaron a los «catorce de Upington», como pronto se empezó a llamarlos, a un gran furgón amarillo de la policía para transportarlos a la cárcel central de Pretoria, la prisión de máxima seguridad más conocida entonces en Sudáfrica como Corredor de la Muerte. Sus dedos morenos se aferraban a las rejas de metal del vehículo. Dirigidos por Bekebeke, los condenados iban cantando el *Nkosi Sikelele*, el único gesto de desafío que les quedaba.

Llegaron al Corredor de la Muerte al día siguiente por la tarde, un sábado, y el lunes, al amanecer, ahorcaron a una mujer que estaba allí presa. Durante el resto de 1989, más presos murieron ejecutados, semana tras semana. Desde 1985, Sudáfrica había llevado a cabo 600 ejecuciones legales. Al preso le anunciaban su muerte con una semana de adelanto y luego le colocaban en una celda llamada «la olla», a dos celdas de distancia de donde se alojaba Justice Bekebeke. Antes de cada ejecución, Justice oía a los condenados llorar toda la noche. Oía a los carceleros que abrían la celda al amanecer, oía las oraciones, oía cómo se llevaban al preso lloroso por las escaleras hasta el cadalso. Cuando dejaba de oírse el llanto, sabía que el preso había muerto. «Al horror que era todo aquello —contaba Justice—, había que añadir el saber que la semana siguiente podía tocarte a ti.»

Pero no fue él. Fue Anton Lubowski. Los catorce de Upington soportaron muchas penas en el Corredor de la Muerte, pero ninguna como la que sintieron al oír en la radio el 13 de septiembre de 1989, dos meses después del té de Mandela con Botha en Tuynhuys, que la noche anterior habían matado a tiros a Lubowski a la entrada de su casa en Windhoek, Namibia. Justice nunca olvidó aquel momento. «Aquella mañana estábamos en mi celda seis de los de Upington. Al principio reaccionamos con incredulidad. No podía ser verdad. Luego, a medida que pasó el tiempo, comprendimos la realidad y nos quedamos destrozados, desolados, inconsolables. Sabíamos quién lo había hecho. Por supuesto que lo sabíamos. Era el Estado.»

Capítulo VI
EL AYATOLÁ MANDELA

1990

Después de años de travesía del desierto, el mito se hizo hombre; el patriarca, envejecido, volvió a ser visible para su pueblo y prometió darle la libertad. Era la encarnación de la virtud revolucionaria y en todas partes le recibían enormes multitudes extasiadas. «Golpearé con mis puños las bocas del gobierno», gritó el día en que volvió de su largo exilio, y diez días después, el 11 de febrero de 1979, el Estado se había derrumbado y sus milicias controlaban las calles. En medio de aclamaciones de felicidad, el ayatolá Jomeini se proclamó jefe de un nuevo gobierno revolucionario.

Exactamente once años después, el 11 de febrero de 1990, Nelson Mandela puso fin a su exilio, al salir de la cárcel. El gobierno sudafricano no dejó de advertir la coincidencia en las fechas. Temían que, al dejarlo en libertad y al permitir que el CNA actuara en la legalidad después de una prohibición de treinta años, fueran a desencadenar lo que, en momentos de pánico, llamaban entre ellos «el factor ayatolá». Niël Barnard no estaba tan inquieto como la mayoría. Pero incluso él estaba preocupado, en algún rincón de su escéptico corazón de espía, por la posibilidad de que Mandela le hubiera tomado el pelo, le hubiera engañado. La pesadilla de las autoridades era que, después de salir en libertad en Ciudad del Cabo, Mandela iniciara una larga marcha hacia el norte, al centro político de Johanesburgo y Soweto. «Iría cobrando impulso —explicaba Barnard—, y recorrería el país, llegaría a Johanesburgo y sería casi como el ayatolá, un movimiento imparable... cientos de miles de personas arrasando todo, disparando y matando. Lo que nos angustiaba era si íbamos a poder superar las primeras 24, 48, 72 horas sin un gran levantamiento popular, sin una revolución.»

Si el precedente iraní había hecho dudar al gobierno, fue otro episodio extranjero más reciente lo que empujó al nuevo presidente, F. W. de Klerk, a continuar con urgencia la labor que había iniciado P. W. Botha. La caída del Muro de Berlín, apenas dos meses antes, dio motivos para creer que, ocurriera lo que ocurriera en Sudáfrica, el comunismo nunca volvería a ser viable, ni en Europa del este ni en Sudáfrica. Además, si el apartheid había sido una vergüenza hasta entonces, ahora era ya insostenible ante la comunidad internacional. Fue una suerte para De Klerk que su predecesor hubiera tenido la prudencia de preparar el terreno para la liberación de Mandela y el inicio de las negociaciones.

Pero ese día, el 11 de febrero de 1990, De Klerk se detuvo menos a pensar en su buena suerte que en los riesgos que podían acechar en torno a la liberación de Mandela. No contribuyó a tranquilizar su ánimo ni el de los otros miembros del gobierno que la liberación de

Mandela, por razones que De Klerk, viéndola en la televisión, no comprendió al principio, no se produjera, ni mucho menos, según el horario previsto. En la entrada de la cárcel de Victor Verster había una batería de cámaras de televisión y millones de personas seguían el acontecimiento en todo el mundo, pero, dos horas después del momento anunciado para su aparición, seguía sin suceder nada.

Cuando Mandela apareció, por fin, saliendo con paso decidido por la puerta principal de la prisión bajo el sol reluciente de media tarde, su sonrisa triunfante de felicidad, como un soldado que volviera de la guerra, ocultaba el hecho de que, un rato antes, se había mostrado furioso. La razón era su mujer, Winnie, que aparecía un poco menos contenta a su lado. El retraso se debía a ella, que había llegado tarde esa mañana de Johanesburgo porque había acudido a una cita con su peluquera. Una de las consecuencias fue una severa reprimenda de Mandela; otra fue que, mientras tanto, la tensión empezó a aumentar peligrosamente en la Parade, la gran plaza abierta de Ciudad del Cabo en la que Mandela debía pronunciar su primer discurso como hombre libre. Se había reunido una enorme muchedumbre bajo el sol ardiente, incluidos muchos jóvenes negros que tenían pocos motivos para tener buenos sentimientos respecto a la falange de policías blancos colocados para vigilar al ayatolá. Hubo algunas escaramuzas, gas lacrimógeno, algunas piedras arrojadas. No fue un baño de sangre ni nada parecido, pero sí bastó para hacer que la gente saliera disparada en todas direcciones.

A Mandela y su séquito, que se encontraba en una caravana de coches, les hicieron saber que era mejor que esperasen a que las cosas se hubieran calmado un poco. No era un comienzo muy prometedor, pero la cárcel le había enseñado a Mandela paciencia. Su gente de seguridad le dijo que lo más prudente era detener el convoy y esperar, y él se mostró de acuerdo. Decidieron aparcar a las afueras de la ciudad, en un elegante barrio blanco, políticamente progresista, llamado Rondebosch, en el que vivía un joven médico llamado Desmond Woolf con su mujer, Vanessa, y sus pequeños gemelos, Daniel y Simon.

Los Woolf estaban siguiendo los acontecimientos del día por televisión con la madre de él. El doctor Woolf y su mujer pertenecían a un pequeño sector de la sociedad blanca, políticamente sensible, que estaba decididamente a favor de la liberación de Mandela. Incluso habían discutido entre ellos la posibilidad de unirse a la muchedumbre en la Parade. Ahora, en cambio, se trataba de saber si el propio Mandela iba a poder llegar. Por lo que decían en televisión, nadie parecía saber exactamente dónde estaba.

De pronto llamaron a la puerta. Era una amiga de Vanessa Woolf, para decirles que Mandela estaba sentado en un coche delante de su casa. «¡Venga ya, no seas ridícula!», dijo el doctor Woolf. «No —respondió la amiga—. Está aquí. ¡Salid, rápido!»

El matrimonio salió con sus dos hijos y la madre del doctor Woolf, y vieron delante de ellos una fila de cinco coches aparcados. «Y allí estaba él —contaba el doctor Woolf—, sentado en el coche de en medio. Nos detuvimos... y le miramos asombrados. La atención del mundo entero estaba centrada en él y él estaba allí, delante de nuestra casa, cuando se suponía que debía estar en otro sitio. Y nos quedamos mirándolo y él bajó la ventanilla, nos hizo un gesto para que nos aproximáramos y dijo: "Por favor, acérquense."»

El doctor Woolf se presentó, Mandela se presentó, y se dieron la mano. El doctor Woolf llevaba a Simon, que tenía sólo un año, y Mandela estiró la mano para tocar la del niño y luego pidió permiso a su padre para cogerlo y meterlo por la ventanilla en el coche. «Lo hizo botar en su rodilla y le preguntó cómo se llamaba. Luego quiso saber por qué le habíamos puesto Simon, si el nombre tenía algún significado especial. Pareció gustarle mucho poder tener a un niño en brazos.» Luego se presentó Vanessa Woolf y Mandela cambió a Simon por Daniel. Después se acercó a saludar la madre del doctor Woolf y así se completó aquella alegre escena de domingo por la tarde.

Otro residente de Rondebosch, Morné du Plessis, también había estado dudando antes si ir o no a la Parade y, al final, había decidido ir. Era uno de los personajes más famosos de aquella multitud —desde luego, el blanco más famoso— y, para los afrikaners, era una especie de dios.

Du Plessis había sido capitán de los Springboks durante los malos tiempos, como su padre lo había sido antes que él. Felix du Plessis encabezó el equipo sudafricano de rugby que obtuvo cuatro famosas victorias sobre Nueva Zelanda en 1949, el año posterior a la primera victoria electoral del Partido Nacional, que afianzó el apartheid en la vida sudafricana para los siguientes cuarenta años. Morné, que nació ese mismo año, acabó mejorando el récord de su padre, puesto que no sólo infligió un castigo similar a los All Blacks sino que se retiró en 1980 con un historial internacional de 18 victorias en 22 partidos. Con él de capitán, Sudáfrica ganó 13 partidos y perdió sólo dos. Durante los nueve años que jugó en la selección fue un héroe nacional afrikaner y, como tal, la expresión más visible de la opresión racial que simbolizaba la camiseta verde de los Springboks para los sudafricanos negros. Pero él, a diferencia de algunos de sus compañeros de equipo, era capaz de verlo. Nunca olvidó que, en partidos verdaderamente importantes, como contra los Lions británicos en 1974 y los All Blacks neozelandeses en 1976, los pocos negros que había en el estadio eran, en palabras suyas, «fanáticos partidarios del otro equipo».

Por eso no fue demasiado sorprendente —Du Plessis era seguramente el más alto de las decenas de miles de personas reunidas en la Parade— que un hombre negro, aparentemente borracho, se acercara a él esa tarde, le insultara y le dijera que se fuera, que aquélla era una ceremonia en la que él no pintaba nada. «Pero lo que me impresionó no fue la actitud amenazante de aquel tipo —contaba Du Plessis—. Fue el hecho de que otro negro se apresuró a amonestarle. Entonces se unieron otros, enfadados por que me hubiera tratado así, y se lo llevaron.» Era gente pobre que hablaba en xhosa, la lengua de Mandela, pero Du Plessis comprendió que tenían la sutileza política suficiente para saber que, a cuantos más blancos pudiera convencerse de participar en las celebraciones de la liberación de Mandela, mejor para todos.

Du Plessis había ido aquel día porque sentía con toda la fuerza la importancia histórica del momento y quería formar parte de él. Pero la razón profunda se remontaba al primer hombre que había marcado la dirección que iba a tener su trayectoria política, su padre. Felix du Plessis fue capitán de los Springboks durante la primera euforia del poder del Partido Nacional, pero siempre fue partidario del Partido Unido, más moderado, más progresista —o, por lo menos, menos intransigente—, al que el Partido Nacional había derrotado en 1948. Además luchó en la Segunda Guerra Mundial con los aliados, otro factor que le hizo oponerse a la postura antibritánica, y en algunos casos ambiguamente pronazi, de los Nacionales. La madre de Morné era una sudafricana blanca de habla inglesa y, en todo caso, más contraria todavía al Partido Nacional que su padre. Eso no quería decir que estuvieran a favor de un gobierno de la mayoría. El Partido Unido se oponía al apartheid porque consideraba que tenía un racismo burdo, pero los padres de Du Plessis nunca pusieron en duda la conveniencia fundamental del poder blanco.

Tampoco la ponía en duda su hijo, que nació en la misma ciudad que François Pienaar, Vereeniging, una coincidencia asombrosa dado que no sólo ambos acabaron siendo capitanes Springbok sino que, exactamente cinco años después de la liberación de Mandela, Du Plessis se convirtió en manager del equipo de Pienaar en la Copa del Mundo. Sin embargo, la coincidencia se quedaba ahí, sin incluir el relativo progresismo político de la familia Du Plessis —más acomodada—, aunque, la verdad, la política tenía casi tan poca importancia en la vida del joven Morné como en la del joven Pienaar.

Sin embargo, en 1970, Du Plessis se encontró con un hombre que dio el empujón necesario a esas brasas de rebelión que le habían encendido sus padres. Se llamaba Frederik van Zyl Slabbert. Profesor de sociología en la Universidad de Stellenbosch, en la que estudiaba Du Plessis, Slabbert era un pensador progresista, de gran brillantez académica pero sospechoso a ojos del aparato afrikaner, que además era un buen jugador de rugby a nivel provincial. La combinación de esos dos factores —un jugador de rugby que estaba a favor del principio una persona, un voto— fue un descubrimiento que abrió los ojos a Du Plessis y le hizo ver que era posible admirar a alguien que pensaba que el apartheid era perverso.

Si Slabbert dio un ligero empujón a Du Plessis, su debut con los Springboks en una gira por Australia en 1971 fue una brusca revelación. Desde el punto de vista deportivo, fue todo un éxito. Sudáfrica derrotó a Australia en los tres partidos que jugaron y Du Plessis se convirtió en un auténtico héroe en casa, la nueva estrella rutilante del rugby. Pero la alegría de Morné se vio empañada por el hostil recibimiento de una buena parte del público asutraliano al equipo. «Fue abrumador ver tanta furia en personas tan lejanas —recordaba—. Las imágenes de aquellos rostros australianos indignados, el odio que parecían tenernos, nunca se me olvidó.»

Empezó a tomar cuerpo en Du Plessis la idea de que pasaba algo «grave» en su país. Pero una cosa era sentirse incómodo y otra dejar que la política le distrajera de su carrera en el rugby. Durante sus nueve años como estrella de los Springboks, nunca adoptó una postura pública, cosa que podría haber hecho y habría causado sensación. Nunca habló sobre sus dudas ni de su apoyo al Partido Federal Progresista, al que pertenecía Helen Suzman, la vieja visitante de Mandela en la cárcel, y al que se incorporó Slabbert, que se convirtió en miembro del parlamento en representación de Rondebosch a mediados de los setenta y poco después asumió el liderazgo del partido. Los «progres», considerados como librepensadores estrambóticos en el pequeño mundo aislado de la Sudáfrica blanca, en realidad eran conservadores, en comparación con el resto del mundo. Representaban a una población de habla inglesa, en general acomodada, ansiosa de criticar el duro trato que daban los bóers a los negros pobres pero poco dispuesta a visitarlos en uno de sus distritos; no obstante, el PFP tuvo el mérito de ofrecer una voz pública legal de oposición al apartheid dentro de Sudáfrica y un puente para facilitar la transición hacia los cambios que iban a llegar posteriormente. El propio Slabbert sería un intermediario crucial en los primeros contactos secretos entre el gobierno y el CNA en 1987, poco después de las primeras reuniones de Mandela con Kobie Coetsee en la cárcel.

Morné du Plessis, con todo lo valiente que era en el terreno de rugby, no asumió ningún riesgo político fuera de él. Hasta aquella tarde del 11 de febrero de 1990, en la Parade de Ciudad del Cabo. Fue porque confiaba, como Joel Stransky, en que la liberación de Mandela curase a un país que, como sabía desde hacía tiempo, estaba enfermo. Stransky siguió la puesta en libertad de Mandela en televisión, desde un café en Francia. No era tan impresionante como ir a la Parade, pero era prueba de más interés que el mostrado por la mayoría de sus futuros camaradas en el equipo Springbok, cuya actitud resumió uno de los gigantescos delanteros del equipo, Kobus Wiese. Al preguntarle, mucho después, cuál había sido su reacción ante la liberación de Mandela, contestó con sinceridad: «No estaba prestando mucha atención, la verdad.» En cambio, Stransky recordaba haberse sentido «absolutamente entusiasmado».

La vida de Stransky estaba totalmente dedicada al deporte, pero no tanto como para que no experimentara dos efímeros momentos de despertar político. El primero llegó tras un acontecimiento del que apenas si debió de tener noticia: el levantamiento de unos escolares no mayores que él en Soweto, en 1976. Como consecuencia, sus padres empezaron a sospechar que alguien podía prender fuego al colegio de su hijo. «Recuerdo que mi padre tuvo que ir a hacer guardia a nuestro colegio por la noche, durante los disturbios y los motines. No estoy seguro de si sabía exactamente lo que pasaba porque los adultos no hablaban verdaderamente de ello, pero, a partir de ese momento, tuve muy claro que las cosas no estaban bien en este país.»

El segundo conato de despertar político de Stransky llegó en 1981, cuando tenía catorce años, durante la tumultuosa gira de los Springboks por Nueva Zelanda. Se dio cuenta de que tenía que haber una buena razón para que la mitad de Nueva Zelanda estuviera indignada con sus compatriotas. Stransky fue un ejemplo del efecto que Arnold Stofile y otros activistas anti-rugby del CNA querían provocar entre la población blanca. Al negarles su droga feliz, pretendían despertarlos de su sopor. Estaban creando las condiciones para el cambio político. En algunos hallaron un público más receptivo que en otros. En Stransky se encontraron con la reacción perfecta, porque, cuando Mandela salió en libertad, él se emocionó.

Stransky sospechaba también que la liberación de Mandela quizá podía ser positiva para su carrera en el rugby. Ya estaba considerado como uno de los mejores jugadores del país. A los veinte años se había convertido en un jugador fundamental para la provincia de Natal, uno de los cuatro mayores equipos del país. Como no era del tipo corpulento, fuerte y arrollador, tenía que tener el valor y la resistencia necesarios para soportar una paliza de rivales del tamaño de Pienaar una docena de veces en cada partido. Pero Stransky ocupaba la única posición en un equipo de rugby que no exige una velocidad ni una dimensión sobrenaturales: medio apertura. El equivalente, en el fútbol, sería el medio centro organizador, el que decide el juego, para el que es fundamental tener cerebro y habilidad con el balón. Además, chutaba de maravilla.

Y era ambicioso. Por eso, cuando terminó la temporada sudafricana de rugby en octubre de 1989, al empezar la primavera, se fue a Francia a jugar. El rugby que se jugaba allí no era tan intenso como en Sudáfrica, pero le permitió mantenerse en forma durante el verano sudafricano, de modo que, cuando comenzó la nueva temporada, en abril de 1990, pudo empezar fuerte desde el principio, en buena forma física y rindiendo a un alto nivel. La jugada salió bien. Al regreso de Stransky de Francia, la provincia de Natal acabó ganando el campeonato nacional. Y la liberación de Mandela también iba a ser positiva para él, tal como había esperado. Para Stransky, la libertad de Mandela significaba acabar con el boicot internacional a los Springboks. Sentado en aquel café francés, imaginó que un día iba a poder jugar al rugby vistiendo los colores de su país.

Estaba previsto que Mandela llegara a la Parade alrededor de las tres de la tarde, pero era tal el caos que, al final, acabó llegando casi cinco horas después, al atardecer. Y, para contribuir a la extraña sensación de anticlímax que enturbió los históricos acontecimientos del día, pronunció un discurso que no cumplió las expectativas, que no emocionó a nadie.

A la mañana siguiente, la primera en la que se había despertado como hombre libre desde hacía veintisiete años y seis meses, tuvo que someterse a una prueba que parecía todavía más dura: una rueda de prensa ante medios de todo el mundo. Había 200 periodistas, muchos de ellos presentadores de televisión célebres en sus países. Sudáfrica no tenía televisión cuando Mandela entró en la cárcel. Él había aparecido ante una cámara de televisión sólo en una ocasión, en una entrevista cara a cara con un periodista británico un año antes de su detención, en 1961. En 1990, todos los políticos habían tenido que aprender a manejarse ante las cámaras. Pero he aquí que Mandela, que era tan famoso como falto de experiencia en la era de los medios de masas, estaba a punto de enfrentarse a lo que más temían los políticos de cualquier lugar, una rueda de prensa sin condiciones. No podía saber lo que le iban a preguntar los periodistas. Y su discurso de la noche anterior, tan poco carismático, había suscitado dudas sobre el nivel de su actuación esa mañana. Al fin y al cabo, tenía setenta y un años y había pasado casi tres décadas en prisión. ¿Hasta qué punto podía estar bien? ¿Cuánta agudeza podía tener?

La rueda de prensa se celebró a primera hora de la mañana en el jardín de la residencia oficial en Ciudad del Cabo del jefe de la Iglesia anglicana en Sudáfrica, el arzobispo Desmond Tutu, que, hasta ese momento, como ganador del premio Nobel de la Paz en 1984, había sido el rostro más visible de la resistencia al apartheid en todo el mundo. La mansión, con el típico tejado a dos aguas del estilo holandés de El Cabo, se encontraba en la boscosa ladera de Table Mountain, el monolito cuyo perfil rectangular veía Mandela desde Robben Island. Dado que Mandela se levantaba siempre a las cuatro y media de la mañana, las cosas tenían que empezar temprano: los periodistas debían estar allí a las seis y media. Cuando salió de la casa con su mujer, Winnie, a su lado, todavía había rocío sobre las hojas. Mandela y su esposa sonrieron y saludaron mientras bajaban los escalones de piedra hasta donde aguardaba la prensa. Tutu, dando brincos de alegría, feliz de no tener que seguir desempeñando el papel de máxima celebridad antiapartheid del mundo, encabezaba la marcha. No hubo más que un sobresalto, cuando Mandela se detuvo en la mesa y observó una artillería de objetos de peluche que estaban colocados ante él. Uno de sus ayudantes le susurró algo al oído, y Mandela respondió con una señal y un «Ah, ya entiendo...». Los objetos de peluche eran micrófonos.

A partir de ese momento, todo fue como la seda. Aplacó a sus propios partidarios y a los demás líderes del CNA al reafirmarse en su compromiso simbólico con la lucha armada y la vieja política (que el CNA pronto iba a abandonar) de nacionalizar la riqueza mineral del país. Al mismo tiempo, indicó su determinación de ser un líder fuerte al dar el audaz paso de calificar al presidente F. W. de Klerk —que llevaba veinte años en el gobierno del apartheid y que acababa de llegar al poder en otra elección «general» sólo para blancos— como «un hombre íntegro»; y tendió una mano tranquilizadora a la Sudáfrica blanca en cada oportunidad que se le presentó.

Tuvo palabras de reconocimiento para los más amables de sus carceleros —los Christo Brand, los Jack Swarts y los Willem Willemses— cuando le hicieron la gran pregunta que no tenían más remedio que hacerle, si tenía algún resentimiento tras sus veintisiete años y medio de cautividad. También reconoció, de forma pasajera pero enérgica, lo que había aportado la cárcel a la formación de su estrategia política. «A pesar de los tiempos difíciles en prisión, también tuvimos la oportunidad de pensar en programas... y en la cárcel ha habido hombres que eran muy buenos, en el sentido de que entendían nuestro punto de vista e hicieron todo lo que pudieron para hacernos lo más felices posible. Eso —dijo Mandela con énfasis, como si subrayara la frase al pronunciarla— borra cualquier resentimiento que pudiera tener un hombre.»

Al preguntarle lo que más le había asombrado en su regreso al mundo, declaró que estaba «completamente sorprendido» por el número de personas blancas que le habían recibido en la calle el día anterior. Y lo más importante, Mandela dijo que la vía hacia una solución negociada era una fórmula que parecía muy sencilla: la conciliación de los miedos blancos con las aspiraciones negras. «El CNA está muy preocupado por abordar la cuestión de las inquietudes que tienen los blancos sobre la exigencia de una persona, un voto —dijo—. Insisten en... garantías... para asegurarse de que la plasmación de esta exigencia no desemboque en la dominación de los blancos por los negros. Entendemos esos sentimientos y el CNA quiere abordar el problema y encontrar una solución que convenga tanto a los blancos como a los negros de este país.»

Al oír en público esas palabras que había oído tan a menudo en privado, Niël Barnard suspiró aliviado. Aquello no era el lenguaje de la insurrección. No era un ayatolá pegando puñetazos en la boca a la gente. Cuando terminó la rueda de prensa, 45 minutos después de empezar, todas las angustias previas parecían ridículas. Mandela había transformado lo que se había anunciado como su primer interrogatorio público en el amable equivalente externo a una charla junto a la chimenea. Había plantado la semilla, entre algunos sudafricanos blancos, de la idea de que un hombre negro podía llegarles al corazón. François Pienaar, que seguía sin ser, ni mucho menos, un animal político, se sintió sorprendentemente conmovido al ver a Mandela en televisión. «No puedo recordar ninguna emoción más que tristeza —me dijo—. Me sentí triste por el tiempo que había pasado en la cárcel y, aunque tenía el rostro lleno de orgullo, me dio pena que hubiera perdido tanto tiempo.»

Otros telespectadores blancos seguramente sintieron menos simpatía, y muchos debieron de gruñir. Una parte importante de la opinión de derechas pensaba que el aparato blanco se había equivocado al no ahorcar a Mandela, cuya influencia como fuente de inspiración para los revolucionarios negros había sobrevivido a su cautiverio. Esa gente contempló la liberación de Mandela en televisión y no sintió más que amargura y desprecio por De Klerk y el que consideraban su gobierno traidor por haber vendido a la Sudáfrica blanca, por dejar suelto en la calle al terrorista supremo.

Muy distinto fue el efecto que causó entre los periodistas que estaban en el césped del arzobispo Tutu la mañana del 12 de febrero de 1990. No hicieron falta más que 45 minutos para que Mandela atrapara a los medios de todo el mundo en su astuto abrazo. Los periodistas no se habían dado cuenta, porque también ellos estaban aturdidos, pero, con el tiempo, comprenderían que Mandela era un estratega brillante, un genial manipulador del sentimiento de las masas. Su talento para el teatro político era tan sutil como el de Bill Clinton o el de Ronald Reagan. En aquella rueda de prensa, Mandela logró dar un golpe que tanto Clinton como Reagan habrían envidiado. La sesión terminó con los 200 periodistas reunidos haciendo algo que no habían hecho jamás. El ser humano que había dentro de ellos se impuso al periodista y de pronto se vieron, con gran confusión y sorpresa por su parte, rompiendo a aplaudir de manera espontánea.

Ganarse a la prensa afrikaner no fue tan sencillo. Los blancos en general, y los afrikaners en particular, se sentían inseguros y temerosos ante las consecuencias de la liberación, por lo que se aferraron a las cosas más alarmantes que dijo —la política de nacionalización, la «lucha armada», la lealtad del CNA a sus aliados del Partido Comunista— y no se fijaron en el aprecio que había manifestado por sus carceleros ni su deseo de alcanzar un acuerdo aceptable para todos. Un reto similar fue el que tuvo que afrontar con su propia gente, tanto entre los dirigentes, entre los que había habido algunas quejas sobre su decisión unilateral de emprender negociaciones secretas con el gobierno, como entre la masa de la población, para la que Mandela era un mito poderoso pero, como líder de carne y hueso, una figura por descubrir.

Con el fin de abordar estos dos problemas, Mandela voló a Johanesburgo, a dos horas de distancia, la misma mañana de la rueda de prensa, y de allí fue en coche a Soweto, donde, esa tarde, Arrie Rossouw fue a verlo a la casita familiar de la que había salido para entrar en prisión. Era una de esas anodinas cajas de cerillas que llenaban, en filas interminables, todos los distritos segregados de Sudáfrica, casi idéntica al lugar en el que había vivido Justice Bekebeke antes de ir a la cárcel. Rossouw era el principal corresponsal político de *Beeld*, el periódico del aparato afrikaner. Era uno de los cinco periodistas afrikaner invitados a la casa de ladrillo rojo desvaído para mantener una entrevista colectiva con el hombre al que sus periódicos habían mostrado durante décadas a los lectores como la encarnación del *swart gevaar*, el «peligro negro». Rossouw estaba bastante más enterado que el promedio de los *volk*. Había tenido contactos con el CNA en el exilio, era consciente de la necesidad de que la Sudáfrica blanca llegara a un acuerdo con la Sudáfrica negra y conocía la imagen del apartheid que había en todo el mundo lo suficiente como para sentirse incómodo cuando viajaba al extranjero; es decir, estaba muy por delante de la mayoría de sus lectores, del mismo modo que Niël Barnard estaba muy por delante de la gente que votaba al Partido Nacional. No obstante, Rossouw tenía motivos para estar nervioso. Era demasiado pronto para declarar terminada la alerta sobre el ayatolá (para el día siguiente se había preparado lo que el CNA llamaba una concentración de masas en Soweto).

Pero Mandela hechizó a Arrie Rossouw como había hechizado horas antes a sus colegas extranjeros en la rueda de prensa de Ciudad del Cabo. «Allí estaba, en el pequeño salón de su casita de ladrillo, y nos saludó como un rey, el rey más encantador imaginable —dijo Rossouw—. Se presentó, nada menos. "Hola, soy Nelson Mandela ¿cómo está?" Y entonces me presenté yo, y él sabía todo sobre mí. Sabía exactamente quién era. Dijo que me había leído con gran interés desde hacía tiempo, y se acordaba de artículos que había escrito hacía meses.»

Los afrikaners fueron el primer grupo de periodistas con el que habló Mandela en *petit comité*, antes que con la prensa negra, la prensa blanca progresista y la prensa internacional. «Nos escogió de forma deliberada para transmitir el mensaje de que todos los sudafricanos iban a tener un lugar en el futuro de la nación; sobre todo, que no salía de la cárcel pensando en la venganza. Comprendió, desde luego, que los afrikaners eran la clave para lograr una paz duradera y trató, a través de nosotros, de afrontar sus temores desde el primer día, literalmente.»

Rossouw era lo bastante astuto como para comprender que Mandela estaba haciendo lo que quería con él. Pero se lo tragó de todas formas. «Se veía que sabía cómo llegar a los afrikaners. Lo que nos dijo fue, en esencia: "Miren, les conozco a ustedes y a su gente, han hecho mucho por este país, y conozco sus miedos, pero vamos a hablar de ellos y a ser amigos." Y mientras hablaba, se reía de sí mismo, de forma que uno no se sentía intimidado por él, sino a gusto. De pronto, me sentí tremendamente privilegiado de estar en su presencia. Me vi allí, sentado, viendo a aquel hombre, y recordé que había rumores de que estaba enfermo, gravemente enfermo, y pensé: "¡Por favor, Dios, que no sea verdad!" Porque comprendí la enorme importancia que iba a tener aquel hombre para el bienestar de nuestro país.»

Una diferencia entre los sudafricanos blancos políticamente astutos como Rossouw y el sudafricano negro corriente era que este último no tenía que procesar la liberación de Mandela racionalmente para comprender la feliz enormidad del momento. Salvo un peligroso reducto de zulúes conservadores y anacrónicos al este del país, nadie discutía el derecho automático de Mandela al liderazgo. Ni siquiera Justice Bekebeke, que habría podido sentirse olvidado o amargamente fuera de honda. A pesar de llevar nueve meses y cuarenta ejecuciones en el Corredor de la Muerte, él también suspendió la razón, se olvidó de sus circunstancias y celebró la liberación de Mandela como si hubiera sido la suya propia. «Teníamos una hora de ejercicio diaria, pero ese día nos quedamos todos en las celdas para escuchar la radio. Pusieron una canción mientras esperábamos y esperábamos. *Release Mandela*, de Hugh Masekela. Todos cantamos y bailamos. Cuando la radio anunció que estaba saliendo acompañado de Winnie, aquel momento fue la libertad para nosotros. Nos olvidamos de dónde estábamos.»

En todos los lugares a los que iba Mandela se reunía una muchedumbre. Sin embargo, él no hablaba el lenguaje de la muchedumbre. En las semanas inmediatamente posteriores a su liberación, emprendió una larga marcha por toda Sudáfrica, y en todos los lugares a los que fue aparecía mucha gente, ansiosa por verlo, soñando con que les dedicara una sonrisa, con tocar la punta de sus dedos cuando tendiera las manos —desde el principio fue una pesadilla para los guardaespaldas— a la multitud. La Sudáfrica negra reaccionaba ante él como si fuera una mezcla de Napoleón y Jesucristo. Pero, aunque cristianos como el arzobispo Tutu interpretaban el mensaje subliminal de lo que decía como una exhortación a «amar a tu enemigo», sus argumentos eran duros.

Para convencer a los militantes que proporcionaban

al CNA su energía política, tenía que apelar a algo más que a la moralidad; tenía que usar el lenguaje duro de la necesidad política y dejar que algunos sectores de su público creyeran, si querían, que no había nada que le gustase más que una revolución como la de Castro. Así que hablaba de que llegar a un acuerdo con la Sudáfrica blanca era necesario, no de que fuera deseable, y lo hacía en un lenguaje inflexible que convencía a los militantes, al reiterar que los principios básicos no eran negociables. Recordó al gobierno que, si no accedían a la democracia plena de «una persona, un voto», si pensaban —como pensó De Klerk durante un tiempo— que podían inventarse algún compromiso legalista que siguiera afianzando los privilegios de los blancos, entonces se encontrarían con una batalla. Ninguno de los millones que vieron u oyeron a Mandela en aquellos primeros días de libertad pudo confundirle con un pacifista gandhiano.

Mandela había sido un famoso sin rostro durante muchos años, pero ahora su imagen se conocía ya en todos los rincones del mundo, y en Sudáfrica daba la impresión de estar en todas partes al mismo tiempo. Su larga marcha parecía una fiesta gigantesca, un desfile real de ciudad en ciudad. La primera de las concentraciones masivas se llevó a cabo dos días después de su liberación en el estadio de Soccer City, la «ciudad del fútbol», en Soweto, con 120.000 personas. Fue la coronación de Mandela como rey de la Sudáfrica negra. A partir de ese momento, en cada parada se repitió la misma ceremonia. En Durban, la mayor ciudad de la provincia de Natal, le rindió homenaje un número similar de zulúes. En Bloemfontein, la sede del tribunal supremo de Sudáfrica, acudieron 80.000. En Port Elizabeth, capital de la provincia del Cabo Oriental, en la que nació Mandela, 200.000.

En cada caso se daba una mezcla del frenesí de un concierto pop con la pasión de una final deportiva y el fervor de una misa solemne. Su primera aparición en el escenario, acompañado de Sisulu y otros sumos sacerdotes de la lucha, provocaba arrebatos. Pero luego el acto se sumía en un orden extraño y se desarrollaba una liturgia cuyos rituales conocía todo el mundo.

Lo primero era el grito del maestro de ceremonias sobre el estrado, «¡Amandla!», que significa «poder» en xhosa. La multitud reunida respondía «¡Awethu!» —«¡para el pueblo!»—, repetido cuatro o cinco veces, *in crescendo*.

Luego llegaba el que los líderes negros habían considerado siempre el himno nacional, el *Nkosi Sikelele*, en cuyas cadencias fúnebres el público introducía ahora, con el puño levantado, un tono triunfante que antes no se oía. Cantaban el himno con la pulcritud de un coro profesional, como si hubieran estado ensayando para ello durante toda su vida, cosa que, en cierto sentido, habían hecho, en todas las concentraciones de protesta a lo largo de los años. No sólo se sabía todo el mundo, las 120.000 o 200.000 personas, la letra, sino que los hombres sabían cuándo callarse y dejar que cantaran las mujeres, y las mujeres sabían cuándo dejar que se oyeran las voces profundas de los hombres.

Luego, más «¡Amandla! ¡Awethu!», luego «¡Un agravio a uno!», que provocaba la respuesta «¡Es un agravio a todos!», seguida de «¡Viva el CNA, viva!», «¡Viva!», «¡*Viva** el CNA, viva!», y luego «¡Larga vida a Nelson Mandela!», «¡Larga vida!».

* En castellano en el original.

Después había más cantos y luego bailes, como una discoteca gigantesca, después más «¡Larga vida a Nelson Mandela!» y luego, por fin, se levantaba él, con aspecto de ser todavía más alto que sus 1,83 metros, alzaba el puño derecho y los cuellos y los rostros extasiados se volvían hacia él en adoración, y él gritaba «¡Amandla!» y en respuesta recibía el «¡Awethu!» más sonoro, y la gente le señalaba y gritaba, porque le había visto, por fin, a lo lejos, y para eso había ido todo el mundo. Y después empezaba a hablar. No era un buen orador, su voz tenía un carácter monótono y metálico que nunca cautivaba a sus oyentes como la del histriónico arzobispo Tutu. Al cabo de un rato, la muchedumbre empezaba a agitarse, como durante los sermones en la iglesia, pero, cuando acababa, todos volvían a la vida y volvían a gritar los «¡Amandlas!» y los «¡Vivas!» hasta iniciar de nuevo un canto increíblemente conmovedor del *Nkosi Sikelele*, y luego todo el mundo se iba a casa, con la coronación terminada. Pero el sentimiento duraba mucho más allá del fermento de la concentración. Mandela encarnaba el destino de todos los sudafricanos negros. En él tenían depositadas todas las esperanzas y las aspiraciones; se había convertido en la personificación de todo un pueblo.

Capítulo VII
EL REY TIGRE

«¡Colgad a Mandela!», «Mandela, vete a casa, a la cárcel», «De Klerk traidor»: éstas eran algunas de las pancartas más educadas que se veían en una concentración de la derecha blanca en Pretoria cinco días después de la liberación de Mandela. El escenario era la Church Square, un cuadrángulo en el corazón de la capital de Sudáfrica, dominado en su centro por una estatua gris y salpicada de pájaros del patriarca bóer Paul Kruger, elegantemente vestido con la banda presidencial, abrigo, sombrero de copa y bastón. Asistían unas 20.000 personas, un porcentaje de la población blanca tan grande como lo habían sido de la población negra las 120.000 personas reunidas en Soweto.

Los sentimientos eran tan intensos como en el estadio de Soccer City cuatro días antes, pero el ánimo no podía ser más diferente. En Soweto, se había respirado un aire de victoria; en Church Square, se percibía una callada desesperación bajo la actitud desafiante. Aquella gente temía estar a punto de perderlo todo. Eran burócratas del gobierno que tenían miedo de perder sus puestos de trabajo, pequeños empresarios que tenían miedo de perder sus empresas, granjeros que tenían miedo de perder sus tierras. Y todos ellos temían perder su bandera, su himno, su lengua, sus escuelas, su Iglesia Reformada Holandesa, su rugby. Y, latente, tiñéndolo todo, el temor a una venganza equivalente al crimen.

Se habían reunido en la capital sudafricana a instancias del Partido Conservador, el brazo político del extremismo de derechas. El PC, el principal partido de la oposición en el parlamento blanco, era vástago del Partido Nacional, del que se había escindido ocho años antes porque sus dirigentes consideraban a P. W. Botha sospechosamente de izquierdas, y ahora consideraban que De Klerk era el mismo demonio.

La derecha afrikaner tenía su liturgia, aunque no tan elaborada o practicada como la del CNA. Empezaron por cerrar los ojos, abrir las manos en gesto de súplica, inclinar la cabeza y rezar una oración. Luego cantaron *Die Stem*, el lúgubre himno nacional oficial, que alaba a Dios y celebra los triunfos de los bóers cuando avanzaron en sus carretas hacia el norte en la Gran Marcha de mediados del siglo XIX, durante la que fueron quedándose con las tierras negras por el camino. Unos hombres vestidos con camisas pardas se entremezclaban con la multitud, como bravucones de colegio. Eran miembros del Afrikaner Weerstandsbeweging (el movimiento de resistencia afrikaner), el más famoso de una colección fragmentada de grupos de extrema derecha. Más conocidos como AWB, su enseña rojinegra estaba formada por tres sietes colocados de forma que recordaba a la esvástica nazi.

Pero en esta ocasión no fueron los camisas pardas los que definieron el acto. Lo más siniestro, y una medida más pesimista del reto que le aguardaba a Mandela, era la aparente normalidad de la mayoría de la gente, una muestra variada del espectáculo humano como la que se podía ver cualquier día de la semana en el centro de Upington, o Vereeniging, o cualquier otro lugar de la Sudáfrica blanca. Había jóvenes con vaqueros y camisetas de los Springboks, parejas jóvenes y entusiastas con bebés, hombres barrigudos con pantalón corto caqui y calcetines largos, viejos señores con chaquetas de *tweed* y señoras vestidas como si fueran al baile anual del club de bolos. Eran la clase media blanca de cualquier lugar de Europa o Estados Unidos. Y no querían que los negros gobernaran sus vidas. Todos ellos tenían en común la pesadilla de una mano negra saliendo de debajo de la cama en mitad de la noche, de pandillas de jóvenes maleantes negros irrumpiendo en sus hogares.

Si se examinaba la situación con detalle, se veía algo que nunca aparecía a primera vista, un fondo de blandura y vulnerabilidad en la Sudáfrica blanca, tanto entre los afrikaners como en la gente de habla inglesa, los de la ciudad como los del campo, los ricos como los pobres. La diferencia era hasta qué punto conseguía disimularlo cada uno. Pero, como en la dura imagen de supervivientes que preferían tener de sí mismos, sobre todo los afrikaners, no encajaba reconocer esa vulnerabilidad, algunos se esforzaban para disfrazar sus temores tras la retórica de la resistencia. Eso no quiere decir que no creyeran lo que decían. El miedo les volvía peligrosos. Aquel día, en la concentración de Church Square, el doctor Andries Treurnicht, el líder del Partido Conservador, obtuvo el mayor aplauso del día cuando gritó: «¡El afrikaner es un tigre amistoso, pero no hay que meterse con él!» Las certezas claras y sencillas del pasado empezaban a resquebrajarse, pero ahí tenían una verdad en la que preferían creer y en la que ni Mandela ni los ya legalizados «comunistas» del CNA podían jamás hacer mella. El afrikaner era un tigre y cualquier animal que se mezclara con él estaba condenado. «Mientras el CNA actúe como una organización militante, les atacaremos con toda la fuerza que podamos —rugió Treurnicht, teólogo y antiguo ministro de la Iglesia Reformada Holandesa—. Por lo que a nosotros respecta, es la guerra, sin más.»

En el CNA, algunos seguían convencidos de que podían derrotar al tigre. Mandela sabía que no. El enemigo tenía todas las armas, la fuerza aérea, la logística, el dinero. El gran principio de actuación política de Mandela era el que había comprendido hacía mucho tiempo en la cárcel: que la única forma de vencer al tigre era domesticarlo. Aquella gente que protestaba a la sombra de la estatua de Paul Kruger era la misma a la que había sometido a su voluntad en Robben Island.

La primera prioridad de Mandela era evitar una guerra civil, y no sólo entre blancos y negros, sino entre blancos y blancos también. Los liberales como el doctor Woolf, que habían llegado a donde estaban después de nadar audazmente contra las corrientes de la ortodoxia blanca, iban a estar en el punto de mira de los guerreros de la derecha. Ya lo estaban. El propio doctor Woolf había recibido amenazas de organizaciones de derechas después de que se publicara en un periódico de Durban la historia del encuentro de su familia con Mandela. Lo habían incluido en una lista de condenados a muerte. Y los Arrie Rossouw de la prensa afrikaner también habían pagado un precio por adelantarse a su tiempo. A las oficinas de su periódico, *Beeld*, en Johanesburgo, llegaban correos envenenados, y la centralita telefónica estaba bloqueada por llamadas insultantes. En una concentración de derechas en el Estado Libre de Orange, dos semanas después de la liberación de Mandela, dieron una paliza a un fotógrafo blanco de *Beeld*.

No había dos personas que encarnasen mejor la división entre los blancos sudafricanos que los gemelos Viljoen. La historia de Braam y Constand Viljoen no es exactamente la de Caín y Abel, ni la del hijo pródigo, pero tiene elementos de ambas. Los dos hermanos, físicamente idénticos, habían emprendido caminos radicalmente opuestos en su adolescencia y estuvieron sin apenas comunicarse durante cuarenta años. Cuando volvieron a hacerlo, el destino tuvo mucho que ver. Si los hermanos no hubieran hecho las paces, Sudáfrica podría haber acabado envuelta en una guerra.

Nacidos en 1933 en una familia afrikaner de clase alta rural cuyas raíces se remontaban a los colonos del siglo XVIII, de los primeros en llegar de Europa a la punta meridional de África, los Viljoen (se pronuncia «Filyun») tenían razones no sólo políticas para vivir separados. Juntos, corrían el riesgo de que se les considerase unos gemelos de comedia, mientras que, por separado, resultaban imponentes. Eran hombres serios, que se tomaban en serio a sí mismos y sus papeles en la sociedad, y a los que tomaban en serio los demás. Las otras dos cosas que tenían en común eran su devoción religiosa y su amor a la agricultura, a la que Constand se dedicaba de forma intermitente en la granja familiar de Transvaal Oriental y Braam —más a menudo— en otra granja a casi 370 kilómetros de distancia, en Transvaal Septentrional.

En cuestión de temperamento y de concepción del mundo, no podían ser más distintos. Braam, el reflexivo, emprendió carrera en la Iglesia. Constand, el hombre de acción, entró en el ejército. Pero, aunque una trayectoria podía parecer más pacífica que la otra, fue Braam el que luchó y, desde el punto de vista estrictamente profesional, fracasó, mientras que Constand, con una suavidad admirable, ascendió hasta la cima de su profesión. Si Braam se enfrentó al sistema y perdió, Constand no sólo se incorporó al sistema, sino que se *convirtió* en él. Llegó a ser no sólo general, no sólo jefe del ejército, sino comandante supremo de la Fuerza Sudafricana de Defensa, que incluía la marina y la fuerza aérea. P. W. Botha le designó para el cargo cuando tomó posesión como primer ministro, en 1980. Viljoen permaneció en él, la última línea de defensa del apartheid, hasta su jubilación, en 1985. Dirigió las fuerzas sin las cuales el apartheid se habría venido abajo de la noche a la mañana. Arriesgó su vida y quitó la vida a otros en apoyo de un sistema político basado y definido en tres de las leyes más perversas jamás creadas: la Ley de Servicios Separados, la Ley de Áreas de Grupo y la Ley de Inscripción de la Población, todas aprobadas en el parlamento cuando él y su hermano tenían diecisiete, dieciocho y diecinueve años, cuando estaban decidiendo qué rumbo emprender en la vida.

La Ley de Servicios Separados era la que prohibía a las personas negras entrar en las mejores playas y los mejores parques, y a las niñeras negras viajar en los compartimentos blancos de tren con los bebés blancos de las «señoras» para las que trabajaban. Las otras dos leyes que aplicaba Constand Viljoen eran tan injustas y absurdas como ésta.

La Ley de Inscripción de la Población compartimentaba a los grupos raciales. Había cuatro categorías principales. En orden descendiente de privilegios, eran: blancos, mestizos, indios y negros. Una vez que cada sudafricano estaba en la casilla racial correspondiente, se derivaban todas las demás leyes del apartheid. Sin la Ley de Inscripción de la Población, por ejemplo, habría sido imposible aplicar la Ley de Inmoralidad, por la que era ilegal no sólo que alguien se casara con una persona de otra raza, sino que tuviera cualquier cosa parecida a un contacto sexual. En parte para adaptarse a la incontinencia amorosa de una pequeña minoría de almas moralmente débiles y en parte para satisfacer el deseo de la gente de mejorar en lo material, el gobierno incluyó en la Ley de Inscripción de la Población una cláusula que concedía a las personas el derecho, biológicamente asombroso, a intentar cambiar de raza.

Para ello había que presentar una solicitud ante un organismo de Pretoria llamado Junta de Clasificación de Razas y estipular de qué raza a qué raza deseaba cambiarse uno. Se llevaban a cabo varias entrevistas y, en los casos más difíciles, los solicitantes comparecían ante la junta, formada por hombres y mujeres, todos blancos. Los miembros de la mesa pedían a los aspirantes que se pasearan delante de ellos para poder examinar sus posturas y la forma de sus nalgas. Si la cuestión seguía sin resolverse, la forma científicamente más fiable de disipar las dudas era la prueba del lápiz. Se metía un lápiz en el pelo de la persona: cuanto más enganchado se quedaba, más oscura era su clasificación. Las cifras del Ministerio del Interior de 1989 muestran que

573 mestizos pidieron ser blancos y, de ellos, 519 lo consiguieron, y que 369 negros solicitaron ser mestizos y, de ellos, lo lograron 327. En estos casos, el motivo para solicitarlo era claramente el deseo de mejorar las condiciones materiales. Pero en los archivos se ve también que 14 blancos pidieron ser mestizos, y 12 lo consiguieron; que tres blancos pidieron ser indios y dos, chinos, y los cinco lo lograron. Evidentemente, esos milagros no fueron posibles gracias a un frío razonamiento, sino a la simpatía de la Junta de Clasificación de razas por los impulsos admirablemente sacrificados y románticos de los solicitantes.

La Ley de Áreas de Grupo era la que prohibía que los negros y los blancos vivieran en las mismas zonas de las ciudades, la que hacía obligatoria la separación física entre la ciudad blanca y el distrito segregado negro. Pero para los ideólogos del apartheid, era más que eso. Era una ley de inspiración divina. Los *volk* temerosos de Dios nunca habrían establecido un sistema de tanto alcance, que condenaba a la gran mayoría de los habitantes de su país a ser ciudadanos de cuarta clase, si no hubieran estado seguros de que tenían una justificación bíblica para lo que estaban haciendo. Como otros fundamentalistas anteriores y posteriores, hurgaron en el Antiguo Testamento y encontraron argumentos teológicos para arrojar a los negros a la oscuridad exterior. Según un libro titulado *Biblical Aspects of Apartheid*, publicado en 1958 por un eminente teólogo de la Iglesia Reformada Holandesa, la legislación sobre las Áreas de Grupo también era válida en el más allá. El libro reconfortaba a los sudafricanos blancos que podían temer que iban a tener que mezclarse con los negros en el Cielo. No había que preocuparse. *Biblical Aspects of Apartheid* les garantizaba que el Libro Sagrado decía que había «muchas mansiones» en «la casa de nuestro Padre».

Constand Viljoen dedicó su vida a defender esas leyes contra las fuerzas dirigidas por su principal enemigo, Nelson Mandela. Braam Viljoen, que, desde muy pronto, pensó que las leyes del apartheid eran una abominación, se convirtió en uno de los soldados de a pie extraoficiales de Mandela.

Si el problema de Constand era que pensaba muy poco, el de Braam era que pensaba demasiado. Unas cuantas afirmaciones desde el púlpito de que las leyes del apartheid eran obra de Dios, y Constand se apresuraba a salir alegremente en defensa de la patria. Braam, un adolescente de ideas asombrosamente independientes para un afrikaner criado en una granja a más de 200 kilómetros de la ciudad más próxima, oía decir al *dominee* local de la Iglesia Reformada Holandesa las mismas palabras que su hermano y le parecían profundamente inquietantes. Al ir a la Universidad de Pretoria a estudiar teología, con el propósito de hacerse él mismo *dominee,* le interesó el trabajo de un pequeño grupo subversivo de teólogos que ponían en tela de juicio las ortodoxias dominantes. Eso, a su vez, le hizo interesarse por el CNA. Leyó con gran atención su Carta de la Libertad («Sudáfrica pertenece a todos los que viven en ella, blancos y negros») cuando se hizo pública, en 1955, el año en el que su hermano terminó la universidad y se convirtió en oficial del ejército.

Mientras Constand ascendía con facilidad e impresionaba a sus superiores, a Braam le impresionó la seriedad cristiana del antecesor de Mandela en la dirección del CNA, Albert Luthuli. A principios de los sesenta, cuando ya era profesor de teología, Braam firmó una declaración que afirmaba que era una herejía identificar el apartheid con la voluntad de Dios. La declaración estaba redactada de forma solemne y respetuosa. En privado, Braam estaba furioso. «Llegué a detestar la ingenua e infantil justificación bíblica del apartheid, que se basaba en una interpretación literal del Génesis —explicaba después—. Odiaba también aquella forma fundamentalista de pensar, de afirmar ciegamente que ésa era la palabra de Dios, de no admitir ningún debate. Como es natural, eso me supuso un conflicto con mi familia. Con mi hermano, que era ya comandante en la FDSA, dejé de hablar de política, por las buenas.» Y también le supuso un conflicto con la Iglesia Reformada Holandesa, que le calificó de disidente y le impidió ganar el sueldo que le correspondía como *dominee* con las cualificaciones teológicas necesarias. Siguió impartiendo clases en la universidad hasta los años ochenta, pero, por motivos económicos, se vio obligado a volver a la agricultura a tiempo parcial.

En la granja, intensificó su actividad política cuando empezó a comprender lo que significaba el apartheid para los que ocupaban el estrato más bajo de todos: las personas negras en las áreas rurales. A principios de los ochenta, cuando las protestas negras se incrementaron en todo el país, él se involucró en lo que empezó a llamar «la lucha por la libertad» y conspiró con los mismos dirigentes políticos a los que su hermano, como jefe de la FDSA, se había comprometido a derrotar. También estaba metido hasta el cuello en las actividades del Consejo Sudafricano de Iglesias, un organismo que las fuerzas de seguridad consideraban una tapadera de los terroristas del CNA. Cuanto más poderoso se volvía su hermano, más consciente era Braam de los métodos brutales que aprobaba el jefe de Constand. Antes sabía que el sistema era perverso, pero hasta entonces no se había dado cuenta de lo criminal que podía ser. «Estaba escandalizado y horrorizado. ¡La gente que trabajaba con mi propio hermano mataba y torturaba a otros!» En realidad, Braam tuvo suerte de que no le torturaran y le mataran a él. Después de la liberación de Mandela, descubrió que había estado en la lista de objetivos de una unidad de los servicios secretos militares que había asesinado a Anton Lubowski.

«No creo que mi hermano estuviese al tanto», insistía, convencido. Pero Constand debió de sospechar que pasaba algo. «Me envió un mensaje, a través de nuestra madre —recordaba Braam—, en el que me aconsejaba que, "si sabía lo que me convenía", dejase los comités del Consejo Sudafricano de Iglesias.»

Braam no hizo caso. A lo largo de los años ochenta siguió trabajando con el consejo eclesiástico. En 1987 fue con otros 50 intelectuales afrikaner liberales a Dakar, Senegal, para una reunión sin precedentes con la dirección en el exilio del CNA. Uno de los personajes clave de esa reunión fue Frederik van Zyl Slabbert, el primer héroe político de Morné du Plessis. Cuando Braam Viljoen regresó de Dakar, el SNI de Niël Barnard le interrogó, pero él siguió actuando como siempre. Ese mismo año se incorporó al pequeño pero valiente Partido Federal Progresista (otro elemento en común con Morné du Plessis, puesto que era el partido que Morné apoyaba). Incluso fue candidato parlamentario por el PFP, antes de unirse a un *think tank* anti-apartheid casi ilegal, llamado Instituto para la Democracia en Sudáfrica, que había creado, después de dejar la política activa, Van Zyl Slabbert.

A pesar de sus profundas disparidades («vivíamos en

mundos distintos», explicaba Braam), Braam y Constand tenían muchas cualidades en común. Ambos eran honrados y estaban escrupulosamente dedicados a su trabajo. Constand era un soldado de soldados, recto, sensato, que pasó su vida profesional dentro de una burbuja moral, convencido de que pertenecer a las FDSA era tan honorable como estar en el ejército de Nueva Zelanda. Era muy admirado por los que estaban a sus órdenes, así como por los millones de sudafricanos blancos que le conocieron durante su prolongado mandato como jefe del ejército y después de todas las fuerzas armadas. Consolidó su reputación a mediados de los setenta, cuando fue el oficial al mando de la fuerza expedicionaria sudafricana en la guerra de Angola, que luchó del lado de Jonas Savimbi y sus guerrilleros de UNITA contra el gobierno marxista del país, en uno de los numerosos conflictos regionales que había en todo el mundo durante la guerra fría. El gobierno angoleño recibía ayuda de Cuba y la Unión Soviética y UNITA de Estados Unidos. Sudáfrica entró en combate porque sus gobernantes eran tan anticomunistas como los de Washington y porque el gobierno angoleño ayudaba al CNA.

Al ser nombrado jefe de la FDSA en 1980, Constand se vio obligado a prestar más atención al CNA, que actuaba en países vecinos como Zambia y Mozambique, y a las organizaciones que actuaban en su nombre en Sudáfrica, cada vez más rebeldes, y con las que se relacionaba su hermano. Un año antes, un documento del gobierno había dicho que la amenaza política y militar contra Sudáfrica estaba aumentando «a un ritmo alarmante». Decidido a formular la guerra contra el CNA en términos geopolíticos que resultaran más del agrado de la comunidad internacional, el documento afirmaba que «la ofensiva total» del enemigo era parte de un plan de Moscú para utilizar Sudáfrica «como punto de partida para la conquista del mundo». El lenguaje convenció a los conservadores estadounidenses y a la primera ministra británica Margaret Thatcher, que se mostró públicamente de acuerdo con el presidente Botha en que el CNA era una organización «terrorista» de inspiración comunista. Animado, Botha ordenó que el ejército entrase en los distritos segregados. Como consecuencia, Viljoen se convirtió en el primer comandante en jefe de las fuerzas armadas sudafricanas que vio cómo sus competencias rebasaban la protección del país frente a un enemigo exterior e incluían la protección del Estado contra su propio pueblo. El ejército, de pronto, tuvo que actuar codo con codo con la Policía de Seguridad, con incursiones conjuntas en países vecinos como Mozambique, Botsuana y Lesotho que causaron la muerte de tantos civiles inocentes como miembros del CNA.

Constand nunca se sintió a gusto en ese papel. Su visión moral quizá no era tan abierta como la de su hermano, pero tenía sus escrúpulos. En mayo de 1983, una incursión de la FDSA en Mozambique confundió varios hogares particulares, una guardería y una fábrica de zumos de frutas con unas instalaciones de misiles, un centro de entrenamiento y una base logística del CNA. Murieron seis personas, ninguna de ellas perteneciente al CNA, y la acción provocó un furioso memorándum interno de Viljoen al jefe del ejército en el que se declaraba no sólo decepcionado, sino escandalizado. «Si tuviéramos que analizar nuestra eficacia operativa y hacer públicos los resultados, nos avergonzaríamos», escribió.

Los resultados no se hicieron públicos y, con la ayuda de una prensa complaciente, se publicitaron las hazañas de la FDSA con la mejor luz posible. Una incursión en Gaborone, la capital de Botsuana, en la que los soldados sudafricanos mataron a un niño de seis años y un hombre de setenta y uno, se describió en los periódicos sudafricanos en términos gloriosos; un diario encabezó el relato épico con el titular «Los cañones de Gabarone». Cuando Constand se jubiló, después de una carrera militar de treinta y un años, se había convertido en una leyenda viva —en la imaginación popular afrikaner, casi un Mandela blanco— y, sobre todo, en un general valiente, de principios, sensato, en la tradición bóer decimonónica de políticos-soldados como Andries Pretorius y Paul Kruger: en otras palabras, el antídoto perfecto al hombre ladino, escurridizo, claramente poco bóer que era el pactista F. W. de Klerk. La decisión de Constand Viljoen de seguir la tradición bóer y volver a su granja sólo sirvió para aumentar la devoción de sus admiradores. En 1985, creyó que su vuelta a la tierra era definitiva. Cinco años después, mientras sufría viendo en televisión la puesta en libertad de Mandela, no podía imaginar que los *volk* pronto iban a llamarlo para que abandonara su granja y les dirigiera en su última gran guerra de liberación.

Capítulo VIII
LA MÁSCARA

1990-1993

Mandela estaba de nuevo en la cárcel al mes de haber salido. Esta vez, por propia voluntad, visitó el lugar al que en 1964 había temido ir a parar, el Corredor de la Muerte en Pretoria. Fue a ver a los 14 de Upington y a otros presos que estaban encarcelados, en su opinión, por motivos políticos. Justice Bekebeke se lo perdió. Por una serie de circunstancias desafortunadas, relacionadas con una inoportuna visita familiar, no pudo ver a Mandela. «No quería morir en el Corredor de la Muerte, pero quería suicidarme», decía después Justice medio en broma. Mandela aseguró a los de Upington que, con su salida de la cárcel, las cosas habían cambiado definitivamente en Sudáfrica. No sólo iba a convencer al gobierno para que aceptase una moratoria sobre las ejecuciones, sino que iba a hacer todo lo posible para conseguir su libertad. Ellos le creyeron. Para los fieles negros, Mandela podía hacer milagros. «Aunque no estuve con él, compartí el entusiasmo de los demás —me dijo Justice—. Supimos ahora con certeza que íbamos a salir.»

Sudáfrica había emprendido un rumbo nuevo y, aunque De Klerk era formalmente quien gobernaba, era Mandela quien controlaba la situación. Comenzaron las negociaciones entre el CNA y el gobierno. El proceso que había iniciado en secreto Mandela en la cárcel siguió adelante, ahora de manera abierta. La derecha gruñó, pero el CNA y el gobierno empezaron a conocerse bien, cada uno descubrió, para su sorpresa, que el otro —como dijo un dirigente del CNA— no tenía cuernos, y entre los dos empezaron a crear la confianza mutua de la que depende siempre el avance en unas negociaciones. «El proceso», como lo llamaron los entendidos, comenzó formalmente en mayo de 1990 y progresó todo lo razonablemente bien que podía esperar Mandela. Una de las principales concesiones que Mandela obtuvo enseguida fue la que había prometido a los 14 de Upington, el cese de todas las ejecuciones legales. Los presos políticos empezaron a salir poco a poco como parte del toma y daca de las conversaciones. Pero el grupo de Upington, ninguno de cuyos miembros pertenecía oficialmente al CNA, no entraba en esos cálculos. La ley seguiría su curso y tendrían que esperar a las apelaciones para quedar libres.

Las delegaciones del gobierno, el CNA y otros grupos más pequeños se reunían de lunes a viernes en habitaciones llenas de humo, como abogados en litigio, en un edificio de congresos cercano al aeropuerto de Johanesburgo y denominado, con una grandiosidad exagerada, World Trade Centre. Al cabo de un tiempo, algunos de los delegados se llevaban tan bien que empezaron a preguntarse si no estaban adelantándose demasiado a sus bases; si podían surgir problemas, sobre todo para el gobierno, cuando llegara la hora de pedir a la gente que aprobaran los acuerdos a los que habían llegado. El negociador jefe del CNA, un antiguo líder sindicalista llamado Cyril Ramaphosa, y el negociador jefe del gobierno, el ministro de Defensa Roelf Meyer, se hicieron tan amigos que, muchas veces, discutían los temas los fines de semana, mientras se iban de pesca. Mandela y De Klerk nunca llegaron a llevarse tan bien pero, aunque tenían momentos de tensión, mantenían un contacto permanente y a veces se reunían hasta altas horas de la noche. Ya no había ninguna necesidad de pedir una cita: el antiguo preso podía conseguir que el presidente se pusiera al teléfono en cualquier momento.

En este clima de rápida transformación, en mayo de 1991, el tribunal superior de apelaciones de Sudáfrica revocó 21 de las 25 condenas por asesinato originales en el caso de Upington y desestimó las 14 sentencias de muerte. Bekebeke fue uno de los cuatro cuyas condenas fueron confirmadas. Iba a salir del Corredor de la Muerte, pero el tribunal había dictado que tenía que cumplir una condena de diez años. Aceptó la noticia de buen talante y abrazó al anciano Gideon Madlongolwana, que, con su mujer Evelina, había quedado en libertad. Al cabo de ocho meses, después de haber pasado un total de seis años, un mes y quince días en prisión, también Bekebeke salió a la calle. El 6 de enero de 1992 se reunió con su familia y sus amigos y con su novia, Selina, en Upington. Fue un momento feliz, pero Bekebeke se sentía impaciente. Tenía mucho tiempo que recuperar y una promesa que cumplir. Se la había hecho a sí mismo y a sus compañeros de cárcel el día del asesinato de Anton Lubowski.

Hasta entonces, había tenido muy clara la ambición de su vida. Quería ser médico. «Pero ese día cambiaron mis planes. A partir de ese día, sólo quise ser una cosa: abogado. Iba a empuñar su lanza. Iba a seguir sus pasos. Iba a llenar el vacío que él había dejado. Iba a convertirme en otro Anton.»

Era una cosa sorprendente en la boca de un joven militante negro como Bekebeke, pero la cárcel le había suavizado como había suavizado a Mandela. Dos semanas después de salir, había llevado a la práctica su retórica grandilocuente. Se disponía a empezar, a los treinta y un años, sus estudios universitarios en Ciudad del Cabo, el lugar en el que había tenido su ilusa inspiración infantil de visitar a Mandela y los demás «líderes» en su cárcel de la isla. Bekebeke fue un alumno brillante en la Universidad de Western Cape. Consiguió las mejores notas en sus exámenes y obtuvo una beca. Era, en sus propias palabras, un estudiante poseso. «Siempre me guió el espíritu de Anton; sabía que, por muy duro que fuese, nunca iba a amilanarme, nunca iba a fallarle. Había dicho a mis camaradas del Corredor de la Muerte que iba a hacer aquello. Había hecho una promesa, y la cumplí.»

Mandela iba camino de cumplir su propia promesa de llevar la libertad a Sudáfrica, pero aún le aguardaban tormentas, fenómenos de carácter político que no había previsto y que, al principio, escaparon a su control. Mientras las negociaciones en el World Trade Centre avanzaban a paso tranquilo, la derecha había emprendido ya su batalla para echarlas por tierra. Era una batalla que adoptó diversas formas, y una de ellas, la más sangrienta, tenía rostro negro. Porque en Sudáfrica no había sólo una derecha blanca, sino también —mucho más difícil de entender desde fuera— una derecha negra. Y sus intereses coincidían.

El movimiento zulú de derechas Inkatha y sobre todo su líder, Mangosuthu Buthelezi (del que un embajador extranjero dijo que estaba «loco como un zorro»), tenían tanto miedo como la derecha blanca de que, si el CNA llegaba al poder, quisiera ejercer una venganza temible contra ellos. Buthelezi había aceptado el apartheid, y sólo había fingido que no en alguna ocasión, cuando le había parecido necesario. Su retórica, muchas veces, imitaba la del CNA, llena de ataques contra el racismo del gobierno y esas cosas, pero la verdad era que se había apuntado al sistema. El plan del «gran apartheid» de Hendrick Verwoerd había sido dividir Sudáfrica en una serie de patrias tribales que deberían ser reconocidas internacionalmente como Estados soberanos. Verwoerd, el doctor Strangelove del apartheid («nunca me asalta la duda de que quizá esté equivocado», declaró en una ocasión), preveía que cada uno de los nueve grupos tribales de Sudáfrica tuviera su propio mini-estado, mientras la tribu blanca se quedaba con la parte del león, la zona rica en minerales y agricultura, incluidas las grandes ciudades. Buthelezi secundó el plan y aceptó un pequeño feudo financiado totalmente por Pretoria y llamado KwaZulu. En él llevaba una gran vida como «ministro principal», con un gabinete de ministros y una fuerza de policía encabezada por un general de brigada afrikaner (en ese terreno mandaba Pretoria) que había sido jefe en la Policía de Seguridad de la Sudáfrica blanca.

El mini-Estado de Buthelezi habría podido resultar cómico si no hubiera sido un instrumento de la contrainsurgencia de Botha. Guiado por el general residente enviado por Pretoria, Buthelezi envió a sus fuerzas *impi* («batallón», en zulú) contra la mitad de la población zulú y partidaria del CNA, en unos combates entre los dos bandos que produjeron miles de muertes. El CNA y sus seguidores llegaron a odiar a Buthelezi tanto como a Botha, si no más. Buthelezi temía que, si Mandela llegaba alguna vez al poder, él perdería los privilegios políticos y económicos derivados de su complicidad con el Estado del apartheid. Asimismo temía una venganza sangrienta, igual que la derecha blanca, por lo que ninguno de los dos veían ninguna ventaja en un proceso de negociación cuyo fin era el gobierno de la mayoría.

A los seis meses de la liberación de Mandela, los guerreros de Inkatha habían extendido su guerra más allá del territorio zulú, a los distritos segregados de los alrededores de Johanesburgo, con ataques contra la comunidad en general, porque sabían que, en su gran mayoría, apoyaba al CNA. Cada mes morían centenares de personas, a tiros, atravesadas por lanzas y cuchillos o quemadas. En sus ataques, que se prolongaron durante los tres primeros años posteriores a la salida de Mandela, los matones de Buthelezi contaban con la ayuda descarada de la policía uniformada, cuyos coches blindados escoltaban a los *impis* de Inkatha en sus pogromos. Otros elementos de la Policía de Seguridad y los servicios de inteligencia militares proporcionaban armas a los terroristas de Inkatha de forma clandestina. El objetivo estaba muy claro: provocar al CNA para que entrase en una serie de miniguerras en los distritos y, de esa forma, hacer que el nuevo orden previsto fuera ingobernable.

A pesar de toda su serenidad y todo su encanto, Mandela tuvo momentos de enorme indignación, en la mayoría de los casos causada por las matanzas y por De Klerk, a quien lamentaba haber llamado «un hombre de integridad» y al que acusaba de complicidad pasiva con la violencia. Tokyo Sexwale, el antiguo preso de Robben Island y ahora miembro del máximo organismo del CNA, el Comité Ejecutivo Nacional (CEN), decía que hubo un momento el que Mandela quiso romper las relaciones con el gobierno. «Así que nos quejamos. "Si hacemos eso, ¿entonces qué? ¿Volvemos a la lucha armada?" Mandela estaba muy enfadado, pero teníamos que vencerle, y lo conseguimos. Pero le afectó mucho por la cantidad de sangre que estaba derramándose en todo el país.» Mandela se desahogó criticando a De Klerk. «Si fueran blancos los que mueren —proclamó—, sé que él estaría tomándose mucho más interés en la cuestión.»

Buthelezi, que era consciente de que la impunidad que le garantizaba el Estado del apartheid no incluía el derecho a matar gente blanca, se vio cada vez más próximo al derechista Partido Conservador y sus variopintas tropas de asalto, que jaleaban a los *impis* de Inkatha, celebraban sus matanzas y aguardaban con ansiedad el día en el que pudieran forjar una alianza zulú-bóer contra el CNA. Mientras tanto, Mandela recibía cada vez más informaciones de sus servicios de inteligencia y de gobiernos extranjeros amigos que hablaban de movilización de la derecha.

A principios de 1992 no había señales de que disminuyeran las matanzas en los distritos segregados y todo indicaba que la extrema derecha iba a jugar sus bazas más violentas. El peligro acechaba, y Mandela tenía que disiparlo. Necesitaba calmar los temores de los blancos, darles algún incentivo para aceptar el nuevo orden que se avecinaba. En una reunión del comité ejecutivo de su partido surgió la idea de convertir el palo político que había constituido el deporte en una zanahoria: ofrecerse a relajar o incluso a abandonar por completo el boicot al rugby. Arnold Stofile, el hombre encarcelado en 1985 por su papel en la interrupción de la gira de los All Blacks, participó activamente en el debate. «No es una zanahoria corriente la que estaríamos ofreciendo a la Sudáfrica blanca —dijo el efervescente Stofile a sus colegas, muchos de los cuales no comprendían la importancia del rugby para el afrikaner—. Esto no es política. Esto no es ideología. Es algo mucho más poderoso y primitivo, mucho más personal. Ofrecernos a reinstaurar los partidos internacionales de rugby es decir a los blancos: "Si cooperáis con nosotros, podréis ir a Europa, Estados Unidos y Australia a visitar a vuestros amigos y que, cuando os comprueben los pasaportes en el aeropuerto, no os miren como parias." Y verán que además es bueno para los negocios y, sobre todo, que supondría volver a caer bien a la gente. Eso es lo importante. Eso significará muchísimo para ellos. Podrán exclamar: "¡Nos quieren! ¡Nos quieren!" En resumen, camaradas, los blancos sudafricanos podrán volver a sentirse seres humanos, ciudadanos del mundo.»

Un miembro del comité ejecutivo que entendía a la perfección lo que quería decir Stofile era Steve Tshwete, un antiguo preso de Robben Island que había sido jugador de rugby. Tshwete había defendido la opción de utilizar el deporte como instrumento de cambio positivo desde la puesta en libertad de Mandela. Arrie Rossouw, el periodista político del diario en afrikaans *Beeld*, contaba que, a principios de 1990, voló a Zambia, la base del CNA en el exilio, y tuvo largas charlas hasta altas horas de la noche con Tshwete, que ya por entonces era el más deportista de la organización. «Tshwete entendió desde el principio que el reestablecimiento de los partidos internacionales de rugby haría que los afrikaners revisaran sus prejuicios sobre el CNA —explicaba Rossouw—. Era apasionado partidario de utilizar el rugby como instrumento de reconciliación.»

Stofile y él defendieron su argumento ante el comité. Las opiniones estaban divididas entre los pragmáticos, que creían que había llegado la hora de tender una inmerecida mano amistosa, y los que consideraban que la idea de recompensar la perfidia de los bóers era indignante. Fueron los pragmáticos los que lograron convencer a Mandela. La idea de utilizar el rugby como incentivo para que los afrikaners se subieran al tren de la democracia coincidía plenamente con la estrategia que había ensayado en la cárcel, especialmente con el comandante Van Sittert en el encuentro del «calientaplatos», y que había desplegado desde entonces con tan valiosos efectos políticos. Los blancos tenían mucho pan, pero se les había negado el circo. El CNA iba a devolvérselo; iba a permitir que los Springboks volvieran a actuar en el escenario mundial.

En agosto de 1992, Sudáfrica jugó su primer partido internacional serio en once años contra Nueva Zelanda, en el estadio Ellis Park de Johanesburgo. Las autoridades de rugby y el CNA llegaron a un acuerdo previo. Les permitimos el partido, dijo el CNA, mientras ustedes impidan que se utilice el encuentro «para promover los símbolos del apartheid». Sin embargo, había un problema intrínseco: la camiseta verde de los Springboks, que seguía siendo un poderoso símbolo del apartheid para los negros y, en la mente de los blancos, estaba inevitablemente asociada a los otros dos símbolos a los que se refería el CNA al fijar sus condiciones: la vieja bandera sudafricana, que seguía siendo la bandera oficial, y el viejo himno nacional, *Die Stem*, que seguía siendo el himno nacional. Pedir a los aficionados al rugby que separasen un símbolo de los otros, dado el inevitable estado de ebriedad en el que se encontraban muchos ya al entrar en el estadio y dada su falta de sensibilidad política, parecía pedir demasiado y demasiado pronto.

Efectivamente. Las banderas del apartheid ondeaban en todo el estadio y Louis Luyt, el grandullón y descarado presidente de la Unión Sudafricana de Rugby, desobedeció las normas de manera escandalosa cuando ordenó que se interpretase el himno blanco. La muchedumbre entonó el canto como un grito de guerra y convirtió lo que el CNA había esperado que fuese un ritual de reconciliación en una ceremonia de desafío. *Rapport*, el periódico en afrikaans más anclado en el pasado, hacía un derroche de sentimentalismo al describir «las suaves lágrimas de orgullo» que habían derramado los *volk* en Ellis Park, y luego pasaba al relato heroico, en el que aplaudía su espíritu inflexible. «Éste es mi canto, ésta es mi bandera —se extasiaba *Rapport*—. Aquí estoy y aquí entonaré hoy mi canto.»

Los afrikaners progresistas como Arrie Rossouw, el negociador principal del gobierno, Roelf Meyer, y Braam Viljoen, el hermano del general, agacharon la cabeza desesperados. Los dirigentes del CNA se apresuraron a expresar su indignación. Arnold Stofile se sintió traicionado. «Nunca fuimos dogmáticos en la cuestión del aislamiento —explicaba—. Convertimos el palo en una zanahoria dulce y jugosa. Pero no todo el mundo se la comió. Así que, cuando los aficionados nos decepcionaron de aquella forma, cantando el himno del apartheid y todo lo demás, nuestra gente se enfadó verdaderamente.»

Sin embargo, después de que pasara la tormenta de Ellis Park, Mandela defendió enérgicamente en las reuniones del CEN las ventajas de seguir utilizando el rugby como instrumento de persuasión política. Era una postura difícil de defender ante un grupo de gente decidida y harta de sufrir indignidades a manos de los blancos. Pero lo hizo. «Hasta ahora, el rugby ha sido la aplicación del apartheid en el deporte —dijo a sus colegas del CNA—. Pero ahora las cosas están cambiando. Debemos utilizar el deporte para ayudar a la construcción nacional y promover todas las ideas que creemos que contribuirán a la paz y la estabilidad en el país.»

La respuesta inicial fue «muy negativa», recordaba Mandela. «Yo entendía la ira y la hostilidad de los negros, porque habían crecido en una atmósfera en la que el deporte era un brazo del apartheid, en la que apoyábamos a los equipos extranjeros cuando jugaban contra Sudáfrica. Ahora, de pronto, yo había salido de la cárcel para decirles que debíamos apoyar a esa gente. Comprendía muy bien su reacción y sabía que me iba a costar mucho.» La dirección del CNA discutió el asunto en varias reuniones. El argumento más poderoso de Mandela era que el rugby equivalía, en palabras suyas, a varios batallones. «Mi idea era asegurarnos el apoyo de los afrikaners, porque —como no dejaba de recordarle a todo el mundo— el rugby, para los afrikaners, es una religión.»

En enero de 1993, sólo cinco meses después del desastre en el partido contra Nueva Zelanda, Mandela dio a la Sudáfrica blanca el mayor, mejor y más inmerecido regalo que podía imaginar: la Copa del Mundo de rugby de 1995. No sólo se iba a permitir a los sudafricanos competir por primera vez, sino que Sudáfrica iba a ser el país anfitrión. Walter Sisulu encabezó una pequeña delegación que se reunió en la sede del CNA en Johanesburgo con los máximos dirigentes del Consejo Internacional de Rugby. Todos salieron del encuentro proclamando su «júbilo» por la decisión del CNA de apoyar incondicionalmente una propuesta impensable sólo tres años antes, cuando Mandela aún estaba en la cárcel.

Pero, en vez de responder con la gratitud que esperaba Mandela, la derecha blanca intensificó su retórica de resistencia y sus planes de guerra. Vieron que las negociaciones entre el CNA y el gobierno estaban preparando el camino hacia la democracia. De Klerk había anunciado unas semanas antes que tenía ya una fecha para celebrar elecciones con la participación de todas las razas, abril de 1994. Los temores que despertaba esa perspectiva pesaban más que los incentivos deportivos de Mandela.

A los pocos días del anuncio sobre el rugby, en los círculos políticos sólo se hablaba de guerra civil. Incluso el presidente De Klerk, un abogado que, en general, intentaba apaciguar los ánimos, se sintió obligado, por las informaciones de los servicios de inteligencia, a declarar que la alternativa a las negociaciones era «una guerra devastadora». Un miembro de su gabinete dijo: «Estamos preocupados por los acontecimientos en Yugoslavia, mucho más de lo que la mayoría de la gente piensa.» También lo estaba el CNA. Mandela y sus lugartenientes se mostraban claramente inquietos por la posibilidad de que sus sueños de democracia «se ahogaran», como dijo el propio Mandela, «en sangre».

Estuvieron a punto el 10 de abril de 1993. Del variado grupo de gente que constituía la extrema derecha surgió una extraña pareja que cometió lo más parecido a un regicidio que había visto Sudáfrica desde el asesinato de Verwoerd en 1966, pero con consecuencias incalculablemente más peligrosas. Verwoerd había muerto apuñalado por un mensajero parlamentario medio loco. Fue un espanto para su familia y sus seguidores, pero no para el sistema político, que siguió adelante como si no hubiera pasado nada. El asesinato de Chris Hani fue una cosa completamente distinta.

Hani era, junto a Mandela, el mayor héroe de la Sudáfrica negra. Si Mandela no hubiera existido, o si hubiera muerto en prisión, Hani habría sido el líder de la Sudáfrica negra por aclamación. Como en el caso de Mandela, su mito le precedía. Después de vivir en el exilio durante casi treinta años, su rostro era desconocido para el gran público hasta que se levantó la prohibición sobre el CNA y él volvió a su país, poco después de que Mandela saliera en libertad. El mito se basaba en dos argumentos fundamentales: había dirigido las dos organizaciones a las que más temía el régimen blanco, Umkhonto we Sizwe y el Partido Comunista de Sudáfrica. La regla general, entre los militantes negros, era que, cuanto más odiado por el gobierno era un dirigente del CNA, más se le admiraba. Hani, heredero de Mandela como «terrorista jefe» para los blancos, había sido una leyenda cuyas dimensiones se veían agrandadas por las historias que llegaban a los distritos segregados sobre proezas e intentos de asesinato a los que había sobrevivido; por el rumor —totalmente cierto— de que había nacido en medio de una extrema pobreza, en la zona negra y rural del Cabo Oriental.

Las fotografías e imágenes televisivas del 10 de abril de 1993 presagiaban grandes problemas: el ídolo caído, tumbado boca abajo en un charco de sangre, las manifestaciones espontáneas en todo el país y los bosques de puños negros alzados con ira, las barricadas ardiendo, los coches quemados, los policías blancos de las fuerzas antidisturbios que apretaban los fusiles contra el pecho, en un gesto protector. La dimensión del peligro quedó patente en las palabras que el arzobispo Tutu empleó para contener a los negros e impedir que hicieran lo que exigía la justicia natural. «No dejemos que los asesinos de Chris triunfen en su siniestro propósito de hacer que nuestro país arda en llamas —rogó Tutu—, porque ahora podría arder en llamas con gran facilidad.»

El asesino de Hani, el hombre que le mató a tiros delante de su casa en el barrio de Dawn Park, una zona de clase obrera, antes sólo blanca, a las afueras de Johanesburgo, era un inmigrante polaco, un soldado de a pie del movimiento blanco de resistencia, un miembro del AWB llamado Janusz Walus cuyo celo anticomunista sólo se equiparaba a su deseo de ser aceptado por la derecha bóer. El compañero de armas de Walus, lo más parecido al cerebro que ideó el plan, compartía la necesidad del polaco de que los *volk* le aceptasen. Se llamaba Clive Derby-Lewis y tenía exactamente el aspecto y la forma de hablar que uno podría esperar de alguien con un nombre como ése. Miembro del parlamento por el Partido Conservador del doctor Treurnicht, vestía chaquetas azules y corbatas, lucía un bigote exuberante y hablaba inglés con acento aristocrático e incluso pijo: parecía un actor interpretando al tópico golfo británico.

Estos dos aspirantes a bóers empujaron a Sudáfrica más cerca que nunca de una guerra entre razas. *Beeld* lo entendió a la perfección. El periódico del aparato afrikaans advirtió: «Un estallido apresurado en este momento, una bala perdida, un acto de venganza puede derribar la delicada estructura de las negociaciones y desatar fuerzas satánicas.»

Mandela recibió la noticia por teléfono en Qunu, la aldea del Transkei en la que nació, junto al Cabo Oriental. Richard Stengel, que colaboró con Mandela en su autobiografía, estaba con él en aquel momento, mirando cómo se tomaba su típico desayuno de gachas, fruta y tostadas. El rostro de Mandela se volvió de piedra o, como decía Stengel, congelado «en la mueca de la tragedia». Se quedó destrozado. Sentía un cariño paternal por Hani como hombre y un enorme respeto por él como heredero político. Sin embargo, sopesó de inmediato la gravedad del momento y vio que no podía permitirse el lujo de dejarse llevar por sus sentimientos. Se apresuró a cambiar de padre apenado a político calculador.

«Colgó el teléfono —recordaba Stengel—, y su mente ya estaba maquinando y trabajando, pensando qué iba a ocurrir. ¿Qué iba a suponer aquello para la nación? ¿Qué iba a suponer para la paz? ¿Qué iba a suponer para las negociaciones? Empezó a hacer una serie de llamadas a sus colaboradores e inmediatamente vio que aquello podía ser la chispa que iniciara el incendio, la revolución, Dios sabía qué. Mantuvo por completo el control del momento político. Y yo casi tenía la sensación de que podía ver el interior de su cerebro, ver todo el engranaje. Se comportó como un consumado animal político, pensando en todas las consecuencias de aquello y lo que significaba.»

Lo que significó fue que en aquel momento tuvo más poder que nunca para definir el rumbo que iba a emprender su país. La opción más fácil habría sido la guerra. La difícil era llamar a la contención, pedir a las masas airadas que dejaran de lado las emociones en favor del objetivo fundamental.

Jessie Duarte, su secretaria personal, era la que le había dado la noticia por teléfono, y fue quien le recibió esa tarde, después de que fuera al pueblo de Hani a ofrecer sus respetos a la familia, cuando llegó al cuartel general del CNA en Johanesburgo. «Estaba muy triste —recordaba Duarte—. Quería verdaderamente a Chris. Pero también sabía que no podíamos perder tiempo, que no era el momento de dejarse llevar por sus sentimientos personales. La conclusión a la que llegó fue que las posibilidades de que estallara la violencia en respuesta a la muerte de Chris eran inmensas y, a pesar de que era un momento muy difícil para todo el mundo, su responsabilidad era calmar a la gente.»

Duarte trabajó con Mandela cuatro años. Compartían un despacho y casi nunca viajaba a ningún sitio sin ella. Era una mujer de corta estatura, intensa, llena de energía, cuyo feroz activismo político le había ganado la fama de joven airada en los círculos del CNA. Pero Mandela le despertaba su lado alegre y ella se convirtió, entre muchas otras cosas, en una especie de hija adoptiva. Como tal, era una de las pocas personas a las que él dejaba ver su tristeza, ante las que, de vez en cuando, se quitaba la máscara impertérrita del político. Jessie Duarte era una de las personas que mejor sabía que su vida era más feliz, más rica y, en general, más satisfactoria en la política que en el plano personal, que había estado lleno de fracasos, decepciones y tragedias.

Duarte estaba a su lado el día de abril de 1992 en el que anunció su separación de su segunda esposa, Winnie. Le impresionó el aura negra que cubrió a Mandela cuando se dio cuenta de la enorme desilusión que había supuesto Winnie. Ella tenía un amante mucho más joven al que había seguido viendo incluso después de que Mandela saliera de la cárcel, nunca compartía el lecho con él cuando él estaba despierto, utilizaba un lenguaje vulgar que a Mandela le repugnaba y bebía de forma grosera y excesiva. Como declaró él en el juicio del divorcio tres años más tarde, al describir cómo habían sido los dos años de matrimonio que vivió tras salir de prisión, «era el hombre más solitario», más aún por la ilusión del amor que le había sostenido en la cárcel y que ella había ayudado a alimentar con sus visitas. Una carta que él le escribió a ella a poco de entrar en prisión revelaba el anhelo y su percepción de que era necesario no dejar que los que le rodeaban descubrieran esa vulnerabilidad. «Mi querida Winnie —escribió Mandela—, he sido bastante capaz de ponerme una máscara tras la que añoro a mi familia a solas, sin apresurarme a mirar el correo hasta que alguien dice mi nombre. Me esfuerzo por reprimir mis emociones mientras escribo esta carta.»

Anunció el fin de su matrimonio en la sede del CNA en Johanesburgo. En una sala demasiado pequeña para la ocasión y atiborrada con más de 100 periodistas de todo el mundo, Mandela se sentó ante una mesa, con Walter Sisulu al lado, se colocó las gafas de cerca y leyó una breve declaración. Luego alzó la vista, más canoso y más serio de lo que nunca se le había visto, y dijo: «Señoras y señores, estoy seguro de que comprenderán lo doloroso que es esto para mí. La conferencia se ha terminado.» Normalmente, un anuncio de tal magnitud empuja a los periodistas a hacer una avalancha de preguntas con la esperanza de provocar una respuesta espontánea que pueda proporcionar una buena cita. Sin embargo, mientras él se levantaba despacio y con rigidez y se volvía hacia la puerta con el rostro dolido, los periodistas permanecieron callados, sin excepción.

Nunca habían tenido ni volverían a tener un atisbo tan desgarrador de la pena que sentía por su fracaso como hombre de familia. Fue la única vez que dejó deslizarse la máscara, que permitió que el mundo viera la tristeza escrita en su rostro; la tristeza acumulada durante decenios, porque se sentía responsable de las penalidades que había sufrido Winnie durante su estancia en la cárcel y por los ebrios actos de delincuencia a los que había acabado viéndose reducida, incapaz de hacer frente por sí sola a la combinación de fama y persecución policial implacable a la que estaba sometida. Mandela se sentía asimismo responsable de la rebeldía y, en algunos casos, el rencor hacia él, que mostraban varios de sus hijos (dos con Winnie y cuatro —dos de ellos habían muerto— con Eveline). «Nunca pudo quitarse la idea de que, si no hubiera ido a la cárcel, toda su familia habría sido gente muy distinta», decía Jessie.

Pero ése era el riesgo que asumió conscientemente el día de 1961 en el que fundó Umkhonto we Sizwe. Había tomado entonces la decisión de ser padre de la nación primero y *paterfamilias* después. En parte para ocultar el dolor de la decisión que había tomado, en parte como medida de lo completa que había sido su dedicación a la causa, la máscara política se convirtió en su verdadero rostro; Mandela el hombre y Mandela el político se convirtieron en uno mismo.

La muerte de Hani le causó a Mandela un dolor equiparable al del divorcio. Entonces había perdido a una esposa; ahora había perdido a un hijo. Pero esta vez no podía permitirse el lujo de quitarse la careta. La audiencia, en directo y en *prime time*, era todo el país, a través de los canales estatales de la South African Broadcasting Corporation. De Klerk podría haberse opuesto, pero no lo hizo porque comprendió que, ante la catástrofe que se avecinaba, él era impotente, irrelevante. Tenía tantas posibilidades de influir en las masas negras indignadas como Mandela de influir en el AWB, o quizá incluso menos. El guardián de la paz era ya Mandela, no De Klerk. Cuando se dirigió a la nación aquella noche a través de la radio y la televisión, lo hizo como un jefe de Estado *de facto*.

«Fue un padre hablando de un hijo al que acababan de asesinar y pidiendo a la gente que guardara la calma», explicaba Jessie Duarte sobre la aparición de Mandela. Presentado de esa forma, ¿cómo iba a desobedecer nadie? Si el propio padre no clamaba venganza, ¿qué derecho tenía nadie más a buscarla? Por una vez, el estilo oratorio monótono de Mandela encajó a la perfección con el mensaje que pretendía transmitir. En esa ocasión, el reto no era ganarse a los blancos; era convencer a su propia gente. Para ello tenía que redirigir el río de su ira, que se encaminaba directamente hacia el enfrentamiento hostil con la Sudáfrica blanca. Para conseguirlo, tenía que apelar no a su resentimiento, sino a lo que quedase de su generosidad. Por eso, en su discurso televisado, llamó la atención de los espectadores sobre el hecho de que, en medio de la tragedia, la heroína había sido una afrikaner. Janusz Walus fue detenido casi inmediatamente gracias a una mujer afrikaner, una vecina de Hani, que había tenido la presencia de ánimo de anotar el número de matrícula del coche en el que había huido.

«Un hombre blanco, lleno de prejuicios y odio, vino a nuestro país y cometió un acto tan repugnante que toda nuestra nación se encuentra al borde del desastre —dijo Mandela—. Una mujer blanca, de origen afrikaner, arriesgó su vida para que pudiéramos conocer y llevar ante la justicia al asesino.»

Si Mandela exageró el heroísmo de la mujer, lo hizo con un propósito político claro. «Éste es un momento trascendental para nosotros —dijo—. Nuestras decisiones y nuestras acciones determinarán si utilizamos nuestro dolor, nuestra pena y nuestra indignación para avanzar hacia lo que es la única solución duradera para nuestro país, un gobierno elegido por el pueblo... Hago un llamamiento, con toda la autoridad de la que dispongo, a toda nuestra gente para que permanezca en calma y honre la memoria de Chris Hani comportándose como una fuerza de paz disciplinada.»

Salió bien. En todo el país hubo manifestaciones masivas, pero la gente no dejó que su pena se transformara en furia violenta. «Aquellos días de 1993 fueron verdaderamente críticos —reflexionó mucho después Tutu—. Lo que sé con seguridad es que, si [Mandela] no hubiera estado presente, el país se habría desgarrado. Porque lo más fácil habría sido dar rienda suelta a los perros de la guerra. Eso era quizá lo que muchos jóvenes turcos querían. Fue uno de los momentos más desoladores, y la ira se podía palpar. Si Nelson no hubiera hablado en televisión y radio como lo hizo... nuestro país habría estallado en llamas.»

Capítulo IX
LOS «BITTER ENDERS»

1993

Para el general Constand Viljoen, que seguía los acontecimientos desde su granja, el espectáculo era exasperante. No importaba cuántos obstáculos se interpusieran en su camino, la máquina de Mandela seguía adelante. No es que Viljoen hubiera participado en la conspiración para asesinar a Chris Hani. No pertenecía al ala asesina de la FDSA. Pero, como miembro de los *volk* y como obstinado estudioso de la guerra contra la insurgencia, había dado por sentado que el asesinato de Hani iba a hacer que se tambalease el proceso de cambio democrático. Bill Keller, entonces jefe de la oficina de *The New York Times* en Sudáfrica, describió el sorprendente efecto estabilizador del discurso de Mandela y el hecho de que el gobierno lo hubiera transmitido por radio y televisión como señales «de la relación implícita que se ha desarrollado entre el gobierno y el Congreso Nacional Africano». Keller continuaba: «Es una relación conflictiva pero extraordinariamente duradera, que equivale casi a un gobierno informal de unidad nacional. Como consecuencia, el proceso de cambio pacífico se ha convertido en algo, si no inexorable, al menos asombrosamente resistente.»

Viljoen lo sabía tan bien como Keller, pero no le gustaba nada. Peor aún, él y el resto de los *volk* de derechas prefirieron interpretar el funeral de Hani —un acto masivo que terminó con un emocionante llamamiento de Desmond Tutu a la paz y la unidad— como una presentación en sociedad de los negros vengativos. En vez de prestar atención a las palabras de Mandela y Tutu al llamar a la calma, se fijaron en los mensajes de discordia emitidos desde el estrado por miembros jóvenes y de tercera categoría del CNA que hicieron justo lo contrario de lo que siempre pretendía Mandela y apelaron a los instintos más bajos de la multitud con una canción que era muy popular entre la juventud airada de los distritos. El estribillo, al ritmo del tambor y repetido en un hipnótico *crescendo*, decía: «¡Matad al bóer! ¡Matad al granjero! ¡Matad al bóer! ¡Matad al granjero!»

Este sentimiento estaba siempre presente entre los jóvenes activistas negros. Lo más lógico habría sido aprovechar su energía y transformarla en una revolución de tierra quemada, al estilo del ayatolá. El miedo, los prejuicios y la culpa que llenaban el corazón de los blancos eran tan grandes que a muchos les resultaba imposible pensar en los cambios que tenía planeados Mandela más que como una venganza.

Los gritos de «Matad al bóer», que Mandela toleró como forma de dejar que los jóvenes desahogaran su indignación, fueron una nota al margen, no el centro del acto. Constand Viljoen no lo comprendió y decidió que llevaba ya demasiado tiempo callándose su indignación en la granja y que había llegado el momento de responder al llamamiento del deber nacionalista. El 7 de mayo de 1993 entró en la refriega y acudió a la mayor concentración realizada hasta entonces por la derecha, en Potchefstroom, una ciudad a 110 kilómetros al suroeste de Johanesburgo. Allí se representó un mini-Nuremberg, con banderas, insignias que imitaban la esvástica, desfiles, guerreros bóer resentidos, los «bitter enders», con sus barbas y sus camisas pardas, y oradores desaforados como Eugene Terreblanche, del AWB. Se juntó una gran y variada multitud de descontentos, unidos en su miedo a que, el día que los negros llegaran al poder, tratasen a los blancos como los blancos les habían tratado a ellos. Allí estaban un grupo derivado del AWB, llamado Movimiento Bóer de Resistencia (Boere Weerstandsbeweging, o BWB), una organización llamada Resistencia contra el Comunismo, el Movimiento Monarquista Afrikaner, la Fundación para la Supervivencia y la Libertad, Blanke Veiligheid (Seguridad Blanca), Blanke Weerstandsbeweging (Movimiento Blanco de Resistencia), el Ejército Republicano Bóer, Boere Kommando, Orde Boerevolk (Orden del Pueblo Bóer), Pretoria Boere, Volksleër (Ejército del Pueblo), Wenkommando (Comando de la Victoria), los Lobos Blancos, la Orden de la Muerte e incluso el Ku Klux Klan. Se les podría haber considerado un puñado de chalados con disfraces si no hubieran sido 15.000 y si aquella no hubiera sido la ciénaga mental de la que había salido el asesino de Hani, Janusz Walus.

Los primeros patriotas bóer que vieron llegar a Constand Viljoen le recibieron con veneración. En el momento culminante del acto, le hicieron subir al escenario y le invitaron a asumir la dirección de los *volk*.

Hizo lo que le pedían, mientras Eugene Terreblanche le acompañaba al escenario y declaraba que estaría «orgulloso, orgulloso» de servir como «cabo» a las órdenes de un héroe bóer como Viljoen. Éste, como correspondía al espíritu reinante, denunció la «infame alianza» que se había forjado entre Mandela y De Klerk y se declaró dispuesto y deseoso de dirigir los batallones bóer. «El pueblo afrikaner debe estar listo para defenderse —gritó el general—. Cada afrikaner debe estar preparado. Cada granja, cada escuela es un blanco. Si atacan nuestras iglesias, nadie está a salvo. Si nos quitan nuestra capacidad defensiva, acabaremos destruidos. Es inevitable un conflicto sangriento que exigirá sacrificios, pero haremos esos sacrificios de buena gana porque nuestra causa es justa.»

La muchedumbre rugió su aprobación. «¡Dirígenos, nosotros te seguiremos! ¡Dirígenos, nosotros te seguiremos!», clamaron. Terreblanche tenía gran sentido del espectáculo, pero el serio Viljoen, que aún contaba con todo el respeto de los oficiales de la FDSA, era el redentor al que los *volk* habían estado esperando. Los líderes del AWB, el BWB, el Wenkommando y todos los demás grupos prestaron, como había hecho Terreblanche, juramento de lealtad al general, al que allí mismo se nombró líder del nuevo «Ejército Popular Bóer».

Aquel día se creó asimismo un brazo político, el Afrikaner Volksfront, una coalición formada por el Partido Conservador y todas las demás milicias. El programa del Volksfront consistía en la creación de un Estado afrikaner independiente —un *Boerestaat*— en un territorio dentro de las fronteras de Sudáfrica. «Un Israel para los afrikaners», lo llamó Viljoen, que prácticamente llegó a exponer de forma explícita la visión que tenía de sí mismo —compartida por sus entusiasmados seguidores— como el Moisés bóer.

Los periodistas, a veces, sentían la tentación de burlarse de aquellos críticos que recurrían al Antiguo Testamento. Pero la llegada de Viljoen, que arrastró a otros cuatro generales como ayudas de campo, hizo que la derecha blanca se convirtiera en una amenaza seria. Dos días después de la concentración de Potchefstroom, De Klerk hizo la advertencia más dura que había lanzado hasta la fecha y declaró que había aumentado la posibilidad de desembocar en «una sangrienta guerra civil como la de Bosnia».

Viljoen emprendió su nueva misión con la dedicación y la meticulosidad que habían caracterizado sus operaciones militares en Angola. Al cabo de dos meses, sus generales y él habían organizado y dirigido 155 reuniones clandestinas en todo el país. «Teníamos que movilizar psicológicamente a los afrikaners, iniciar nuestras campañas de propaganda —explicaría más tarde Viljoen—. Pero también era muy importante construir una enorme capacidad militar.» En aquellos dos primeros meses, el Volksfront reclutó para la causa a 150.000 secesionistas, de los cuales 100.000 eran hombres de armas, prácticamente todos con experiencia militar.

Eso quería decir que quedaban otros tres millones y pico de afrikaners, y un total de cinco millones de sudafricanos blancos si se incluía a los «ingleses», que no estaban claramente alineados con la causa separatista. ¿Dónde estaban? Había una minoría como Lubowski que apoyaba activamente al CNA. Había otra minoría importante, alrededor del 15 % de los blancos, de perso-

nas que quizá no votarían por el CNA en unas elecciones pero tenían la suficiente conciencia política para ver
lo que era realmente el apartheid y daban su apoyo al
Partido Demócrata, el nuevo heredero del Partido Federal Progresista por el que se había presentado Braam Viljoen en las elecciones de 1987. Aproximadamente el
20 % de los blancos, sobre todo afrikaners, aceptaba en
silencio las ideas generales del Volksfront, o al menos sus
temores. Y luego estaba el resto, el gran sector de la clase media blanca sudafricana al que pertenecían François
Pienaar y su familia, que, en un 60 %, solía creer que podía confiar la defensa de sus intereses al Partido Nacional, que llevaba tantos años en el gobierno. De vez en
cuando, esas personas despertaban de su sopor, pero
sólo cuando sucesos como el asesinato de Hani saltaban
a primer plano y entonces se les ocurría que sus vidas
cotidianas podían sufrir las consecuencias.

Sin embargo, ese mismo sector era susceptible a los
llamamientos de Mandela. Sus opiniones no eran ina-
movibles y sus identidades dependían menos de antiguos prejuicios que las de los fieles del Volksfront; por
eso, para ellos fue una agradable sorpresa que Mandela
elogiara a la mujer afrikaner que había anotado la matrícula del asesino de Hani. Y les gustó su actitud respecto al rugby, cuyos primeros frutos saborearon el 26
de junio de 1993, cuando los Springboks comenzaron
sus largos y deliberados preparativos para la Copa del
Mundo —para la que aún quedaban dos años— jugando un encuentro contra Francia en casa. Fue el partido
en el que debutó con los Springboks François Pienaar.

Al enterarse de que había sido seleccionado, Pienaar, que entonces tenía veintiséis años, reaccionó como
si viviera en un país normal. En su autobiografía, *Rain-*

bow Warrior, no menciona el tenso contexto político en el que alcanzó la «ambición primordial» de su vida. Los asesinatos que seguían produciéndose en los distritos, los preparativos de la derecha para la guerra, la posible inminencia de las elecciones con participación de todas las razas; ninguna de esas cosas ocupaba seriamente sus pensamientos, todas tenían tan poco que ver con su vida como lo habían tenido los negros de Sharpeville durante su infancia. En el rugby sudafricano se estaba iniciando una nueva era y el equipo nacional necesitaba un nuevo capitán. Pienaar se sintió abrumado al enterarse en su primera sesión de entrenamiento de que en su primer partido iba ya a dirigir el equipo contra Francia, algo sin precedentes en ningún deporte. El encuentro iba a celebrarse un sábado en el estadio King's Park de Durban. El jueves anterior, Pienaar hizo que sus padres fueran a Durban, el primer vuelo en avión de sus vidas, y por la tarde les llevó al hotel en un Mercedes-Benz que los patrocinadores de los Springboks le habían prestado. Mientras posaba para una serie de fotografías familiares vestido con su uniforme Springbok, en forma y listo para la batalla, se sintió más feliz que ningún otro afrikaner.

Esa misma tarde, miles de soldados del Volksfront limpiaban sus armas en preparación para la primera acción militar desde que el general Constand Viljoen había sido designado jefe de los del final amargo. En una operación logística bien organizada, se dirigieron por carretera a Johanesburgo a lo largo de la noche, con el propósito de llegar al amanecer a las puertas del World Trade Centre, la sede de las negociaciones entre el CNA y el gobierno. Llegaron de toda Sudáfrica, del Cabo Occidental y el Cabo Septentrional, de Transvaal Oriental y Transvaal Septentrional. Eddie von Maltitz encabezaba un contingente de Ficksburg, en el Estado Libre de Orange, a cinco horas de distancia. «Organizamos un autobús y nos apiñamos en él, sólo hombres fuertes y muy bien armados —recordaba después—. Esperábamos sangre. No teníamos que detener sólo al CNA, teníamos que detener a De Klerk. Teníamos que interrumpir las negociaciones. Estaban llevándonos al Apocalipsis. Era una nueva toma de la Bastilla; el comienzo de una revolución, pensamos.»

El autobús de Von Maltitz estaba ocupado sobre todo por miembros del AWB, al que se había unido en el agitado año de 1985. ¿Por qué entró en aquel grupo? «Dios me habló —explicaba—. Me instó a luchar para impedir que los comunistas se apoderasen de mi país.» Cristiano devoto, Von Maltitz era de origen alemán pero se consideraba bóer honorario. El manifiesto del AWB le tocó muy de cerca. Según él, la misión del movimiento de resistencia era «garantizar la supervivencia de la nación bóer» que «había nacido por la Providencia Divina». Con tal fin, proponía la secesión y la creación, dentro de las fronteras sudafricanas, de «una república cristiana libre».

Pero el mayor atractivo para la mayoría de los camisas pardas del AWB no era el manifiesto, sino su líder, Eugene Terreblanche, cuyos discursos contenían perlas como «¡Allanaremos la grava con Nelson Mandela!» y «Nos gobernaremos a nosotros mismos con nuestros genes blancos superiores». Pero mejor aún era cómo lo decía. El fornido Terreblanche, con su barba blanca, era un orador que enardecía. Se podía contar siempre con él para agitar las pasiones de los bóers, ansiosos por ocultar sus miedos bajo una actitud bravucona y desafiante. Era bueno, en parte, porque era un actor nato, cuyo accesorio más preciado era el caballo blanco que montaba, en parte porque tenía un sentido rico y poético de las cadencias del lenguaje, en parte porque la afición a la bebida le soltaba la lengua y en parte porque, durante su juventud, se había asegurado de estudiar las técnicas oratorias de Adolf Hitler.

Von Maltitz era menos demagogo que Terreblanche, pero estaba tan motivado como él. Su celo hizo que ascendiera rápidamente en el AWB hasta convertirse en el principal lugarteniente de Terreblanche en el Estado Libre, el corazón geográfico de Sudáfrica. Aunque no era bóer de nacimiento, lo era en espíritu. Su abuelo había luchado junto a los afrikaners en la guerra contra los británicos, pero, más importante, sentía un amor a la tierra tan puro y apasionado como cualquiera de los *volk*. Criado en la granja familiar, que heredó de su padre, se consideraba un auténtico hijo de África, orgulloso de haber ordeñado su primera vaca a los tres años. Desde el punto de vista militar, opinaba que aportaba a las fuerzas de los bóers cierto grado de profesionalismo prusiano del que carecían algunos de los fanfarrones de Terreblanche. Había hecho el servicio militar en un regimiento de paracaidistas de élite, sabía manejar todo tipo de armas y era cinturón negro de kárate.

Sin embargo, se sentía cada vez más decepcionado con Terreblanche, en particular con su forma de beber. (En más de una ocasión, el líder, borracho, se cayó de su caballo blanco, para delicia de periodistas y transeúntes negros.) Terreblanche, avisado de que era posible que perdiera a su mejor hombre en el Estado Libre, le llamó una noche por teléfono y le dijo: «Herr von Maltitz, ¿está conmigo o contra mí?» Von Maltitz respondió de manera ambigua: «Estoy con usted en la causa.»

Poco después (esto ocurría en 1989), Von Maltitz se fue y formó un grupo al que dio el nombre de Movimiento Bóer de Resistencia, BWB, que al poco tiempo dejó para formar otro grupo más que se llamó Resistencia Contra el Comunismo. De aspecto erguido y nervioso, con fuertes manos de agricultor, siempre salía de casa vestido con uniforme militar de camuflaje y con el arma en la cadera. Von Maltitz estaba convencido de que Dios hablaba con él —a menudo—, lo cual podría haber resultado divertido si, como reacción a la liberación de Mandela, no hubiera convertido su granja en un campo de entrenamiento militar junto a su uso habitual. Al menos una vez a la semana, reunía a soldados cristianos que pensaban como él y les preparaba para lo que llamaba la «plena resistencia militar» contra el CNA. «El enemigo llama ya a mi puerta trasera. Debo combatirlo», era el razonamiento que hacía. Llegó a entrenar simultáneamente hasta a 70 aspirantes a *kommandos* en el uso de fusiles y pistolas Magnum y en la guerra de guerrillas.

Von Maltitz figuraba en la lista de los radicales de derecha vigilados por el Servicio Nacional de Inteligencia de Niël Barnard. Para los agentes de dicho servicio y para el puñado de periodistas que seguía las actuaciones de la extrema derecha, el nombre de Eddie von Maltitz adquirió una resonancia siniestra.

Los guerreros bóer irrumpieron en el World Trade Centre la mañana del 25 de febrero de 1993. En el edificio de cristal y hormigón, de dos pisos, se habían reunido dos personajes destacados, Joe Slovo, líder legendario del Partido Comunista, y el ministro de Exteriores Pik Botha. Antes del ataque, unos 3.000 miembros armados del Volksfront se encontraron frente a la policía antidisturbios que había formado un perímetro de protección alrededor del edificio. Un bando iba de marrón y el otro de azul grisáceo, pero, por lo demás, eran la viva imagen el uno del otro. Hablaban el mismo idioma, tenían los mismos apellidos, les habían impartido la misma propaganda supremacista blanca todas sus vidas, habían aprendido a odiar y temer al CNA. Los policías del batallón antidisturbios eran los encargados por el apartheid de aplastar los movimientos de protesta negros. Aquel día, en el World Trade Centre, se enfrentaron a algo nuevo y extraño. El descontento blanco. Su entrenamiento —su educación— no les había preparado para aquello. ¿Qué debían hacer? ¿Habría alguno en sus filas que siguiera el ejemplo del soldado que vigilaba la Bastilla, que se negó a disparar contra su pueblo y volvió el arma contra su oficial? Y en ese caso, ¿qué pasaría?

El pulso duró cuatro horas, con los dos bandos situados a 100 metros uno de otro, sin que ninguno se atreviera a dar el primer paso. El gobierno era consciente de que, si moría alguien, si se creaban mártires bóer, las consecuencias podían ser catastróficas. El CNA contaba con numerosos seguidores, pero pocos estaban armados. Esta gente, en cambio, estaba armada hasta los dientes, y en Constand Viljoen tenía a un líder capaz de desgarrar el país. Por consiguiente, se ordenó a la policía que actuara con la máxima contención, que no respondiera con la fuerza habitual en un entorno que dominaban mejor, el de una muchedumbre de jóvenes negros arrojando piedras. Además, el respeto de las autoridades por Viljoen les permitía confiar en que la contención suscitara una reacción razonable por parte de sus adversarios y la situación no acabara en un baño de sangre.

No está claro si Viljoen apoyó la orden de atacar. Pero la acción comenzó cuando Terreblanche ordenó a sus tropas de asalto, la unidad de «élite» del AWB, que avanzaran. Estos soldados, conocidos como la *Guardia de hierro*, se diferenciaban de los demás gracias a sus uniformes negros, parecidos a los de las SS. Eran una treintena. La policía se apartó lentamente y les dejó pasar. Eddie von Maltitz, con su uniforme de camuflaje, se unió a ellos y trotó junto a un *bakkie* (un tipo de camioneta) de cuatro ruedas y del tamaño de un carro de combate que se dirigió hacia la entrada del edificio, atravesó el cristal y abrió una brecha por la que cargó Von Maltitz. «Yo encabecé el primer grupo que entró —recordaba, triunfante—. Teníamos chalecos antibalas y estábamos listos para disparar. Yo tenía una ametralladora RI.»

En un instante, había 400 guerreros armados dentro del edificio, después de pasar al lado de unos policías armados que no sabían cómo reaccionar. En un momento dado, un grupo de cuatro miembros del Volksfront rodeó a un periodista negro de la agencia de noticias Reuters. Iba vestido con chaqueta y corbata, y eso pareció enojarlos especialmente. «Es un *kaffir* lleno de ínfulas», musitó uno. Mientras decidían si hacerle algún daño, intervino un periodista blanco. «Eres una vergüenza para la raza blanca», le dijo uno de los asaltantes armados. De pronto apareció Eddie von Maltitz. «Dejad tranquilo a este hombre —gritó—. No tenemos ningún problema con el hombre negro. El problema es nuestro gobierno blanco. Vamos a disparar contra esos traidores. Vamos a disparar contra Pik Botha.»

Posteriormente, Von Maltitz presumía de haber «evitado un baño de sangre». Viljoen impidió uno más grande aún. El general entró por la puerta rota y fue al piso de arriba, flanqueado por una guardia solemne de miembros del AWB, para hablar con los delegados del CNA y el gobierno y con los oficiales de policía al mando. Había dejado claro lo que quería. Como un terrorista que coloca una bomba pero luego llama a la policía para que la desactive, había demostrado la capacidad de su gente para hacer daño. Lo único que quería en ese momento era que les dejaran salir y que no se detuviera a ninguno de sus hombres al volver a casa. Se aceptaron sus condiciones y, salvo unas cuantas pintadas groseras en las paredes, algo de orina en las alfombras y mucho cristal roto, no pasó nada. Por segunda vez en dos meses, Sudáfrica había coqueteado con la catástrofe pero había logrado evitarla.

La vida real seguía adelante con independencia de todo aquello. A menos de un kilómetro del World Trade Centre, la gente seguía trabajando en sus oficinas y sus fábricas como siempre. Dos kilómetros más allá, los pasajeros se embarcaban en el aeropuerto de Johanesburgo y los aviones seguían despegando y aterrizando sin interrupción. La ciudad bullía como de costumbre, los semáforos se ponían en rojo y en verde, los cafés estaban llenos. Y los Springboks de Pienaar se entrenaban ferozmente a 500 kilómetros de distancia, en Durban, para el partido del día siguiente contra Francia.

El CNA tenía ya motivos suficientes para decir:

«Basta ya, vamos a quitaros la zanahoria y nunca más os la vamos a devolver.» Sin embargo, no lo hizo. Una vez más, Mandela, con el apoyo de Steve Tshwete, se impuso con el argumento de que no era a la gente como Viljoen, como Terreblanche y como Von Maltitz a quien había que apelar, porque por ahora eran casos perdidos, sino a los afrikaners normales y corrientes. Como toda la gente normal de cualquier país que se encuentra entre la guerra y la paz, esas personas ponían la seguridad y la prosperidad por delante de la ideología, observaban de qué lado soplaba el viento y trataban de ver qué opción favorecía más los intereses de sus familias. Para esas personas, el rugby seguía siendo un incentivo; quitárselo les haría daño, les haría estar más tentados de aproximarse al bando de Viljoen. Mandela sabía que el rugby era el opio del apartheid, la droga que adormecía a la Sudáfrica blanca para que no viera lo que hacían sus políticos. Quizá era útil tener a mano una droga que anestesiara a esa Sudáfrica blanca ante el dolor de perder sus poderes y sus privilegios.

El partido contra Francia, una potencia en el rugby mundial contra la que Sudáfrica no había podido jugar desde hacía trece años, fue el momento de más orgullo en los veintiséis años de vida de François Pienaar. Desarrollado ante un estadio repleto, 52.000 espectadores, el encuentro eclipsó en la imaginación popular los sucesos ocurridos 24 horas antes en el World Trade Centre. El resultado final fue un empate 20-20, pero para Pienaar, y para la mayor parte de los blancos sudafricanos, tuvo sabor a victoria.

1. Mandela, el primero de los miles que quemaron su «carnet de paso» del apartheid durante la campaña de desafío del CNA en 1952. *(Eli Weinberg, UWC-Robben Island Museum Mayibuye Archives.)*

2. Mandela, activista político y abogado, luciendo uno de los trajes hechos para él por el mejor sastre de Johanesburgo, en 1958. *(Jurgen Schadeberg.)*

3. Nelson y Winnie Mandela en los primeros y felices días de su matrimonio. *(Eli Weinberg, UWC-Robben Island Museum Mayibuye Archives.)*

4. Mandela en su pose de boxeador aficionado y fanático de la forma física. *(Eli Weinberg, UWC-Robben Island Museum Mayibuye Archives.)*

5. Mandela vestido con la túnica tribal, en casa de un amigo, cuando estaba huido de la policía, en 1961. *(Eli Weinberg, UWC-Robben Island Museum Mayibuye Archives.)*

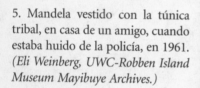

6. Mandela en prisión, en 1977, en actitud hosca, mientras un fotógrafo partidario del apartheid tomaba una instantánea de él en Robben Island. Esta foto fue la primera fotografía que se tomó de Mandela desde su ingreso, 15 años antes. *(South African National Archives. Cortesía de la Fundación Nelson Mandela.)*

7. Kobie Coetsee, el ministro de Justicia que inició las negociaciones del gobierno del apartheid con el prisionero Mandela, en su despacho. *(Terry Shean, Sunday Times/Picture-NET Africa.)*

8. Mandela se reúne en secreto con el presidente P. W. Botha en Tuynhuys, la residencia presidencial en Ciudad del Cabo. Están presentes, empezando por la izquierda: el general Willie Willemse, comisario de los Servicios Penitenciarios; Mandela; Niël Barnard, jefe del Servicio Nacional de Inteligencia; Botha; y Kobie Coetsee, ministro de Justicia. *(Ters Ehlers.)*

9. Nelson Mandela sonriente en su despacho de la sede del CNA en 1992, mientras proseguían las negociaciones con el gobierno y el país se debatía entre la paz y la guerra. *(Gisèle Wulfsohn.)*

10. Mandela en su toma de posesión como presidente en Pretoria, el 10 de mayo de 1994, con su hija Zenani a la izquierda; a la izquierda de ella el vicepresidente F. W. de Klerk y, a la derecha de Mandela, el otro vicepresidente, Thabo Mbeki. El hombre alto de uniforme detrás de Mandela y Zenani es Georg Meiring, jefe del ejército surafricano. *(David Sandison, Sunday Times/PictureNET.)*

11. Mandela dirigiéndose a una muchedumbre en la Parade de Ciudad del Cabo, entre escenas de júbilo desenfrenado, el día de su salida de prisión, el 11 de febrero de 1990. (*Chris Ledochowski.*)

12. El ejemplo de Mandela y la insólita ascensión de los Springboks contribuyeron a que Justice Bekebeke dejara de ser un ejemplo perfecto de joven resentido —en prisión por asesinato— para convertirse en un abogado muy respetado. (*Independent Electoral Commission South Africa.*)

13. Después de unas conversaciones secretas con Mandela, el general Constand Viljoen decidió renunciar a la lucha armada y participar en las primeras elecciones democráticas de Suráfrica. Aquí aparece durante la apertura del nuevo parlamento, el 24 de mayo de 1994. (*Shaun Harris/Picture-NET.*)

14. Mandela saluda a los jugadores de los Springboks por primera vez en su campo de entrenamiento. Aquí le da la mano a James Small, el miembro más emotivo del equipo. *(Getty Images.)*

15. Morné du Plessis, el mánager del equipo Springbok, que trabajó mucho para despertar la conciencia política de los jugadores, en un partido de la Copa del Mundo de rugby, en junio de 1995. *(Sunday Times/PictureNET.)*

16. Chester Williams, el único jugador no blanco del equipo Springbok, marca durante un partido de la Copa del Mundo, en el camino hacia la final. *(Paul Velasco/PictureNET.)*

17. ARRIBA: Mandela, vestido con la camiseta Springbok, saluda a la multitud antes de que comience la final de la Copa del Mundo de rugby en Ellis Park, Johanesburgo, el 24 de junio de 1995. Detrás de él, con gafas negras, está su guardaespaldas «número uno», Linga Moonsamy; a su derecha, de perfil, está la máxima autoridad del rugby, Louis Luyt. *(Paul Velasco/PictureNET Africa.)*

18. DERECHA: François Pienaar, el capitán Springbok, alza la Copa del Mundo, victorioso, en el terreno de juego de Ellis Park. *(John Parkin, AP Photo/PictureNET.)*

19. François Pienaar celebra con el jugador que marcó todos los tantos de los Springboks en la final, Joel Stransky. *(Paul Velasco/PictureNET Africa.)*

20. Aficionados surafricanos al rugby, exultantes tras la victoria de los Springboks. *(AP/PictureNET.)*

21. Nelson Mandela, a los ochenta y nueve años y retirado de la política, vuelve a saborear la victoria con los Springboks cuando obtuvieron la Copa del Mundo de rugby en 2007. *(Getty Images.)*

Capítulo X
LA SEDUCCIÓN DEL GENERAL

En 1838, el general bóer Piet Retief encabezó un millar de carretas de bueyes cargadas de hombres, mujeres y niños hasta el corazón del territorio zulú. Dingaan, el rey zulú, miró a los expedicionarios con aprensión. Le habían llegado informaciones de que se quedaban con todas las tierras por las que pasaban, pero también había oído que habían infligido pérdidas terribles a las tribus negras que habían intentado oponerse a ellos. El primer instinto de Dingaan fue mantenerse firme y luchar. Al fin y al cabo, los zulúes eran los guerreros más valientes, disciplinados y temidos de todo el sur de África. Generaciones anteriores de su pueblo habían barrido todo lo que encontraban a su paso, como parecía que estaban haciendo ahora los bóers. Pero este enemigo tenía caballos y rifles, y el rey zulú pensó que más valía tratar de llegar a un acuerdo que enviar a los lanceros de sus *impis* contra ellos. Así que mandó a unos emisarios a ver al general Retief y le invitó a su *kraal* real, con la propuesta de buscar una fórmula que les permitiera convivir en paz.

Retief, de quien los libros de historia dicen que era un hombre honorable, aceptó la invitación, pese a las advertencias de parte de su gente de que no se fiara del rey zulú, que había ascendido al trono después de asesinar a su medio hermano, Shaka. Pero Retief calculó que Dingaan no sería tan imprudente como para hacer lo mismo con el líder de un gran contingente de hombres blancos fuertemente armados.

El 3 de febrero, Retief llegó a la capital zulú de uMgungundlovu, que significa «el lugar secreto del elefante», con un grupo de 69 hombres y ofrendas de ganado y caballos para Dingaan. Las cosas fueron bien. Antes de que acabara el día siguiente, las dos partes acordaron un tratado por el que Dingaan cedía grandes franjas de tierra a los pioneros bóer. Para celebrar el pacto, el rey invitó a Retief y su grupo a una fiesta dos días después, con danzas tradicionales zulúes. Les dieron instrucciones de dejar sus armas fuera del *kraal* real, y así lo hicieron ellos. Entraron, se sentaron y, cuando la danza alcanzaba su frenético clímax saltarín, Dingaan se levantó de golpe y gritó: «*¡Bambani aba thakathi!*» («¡Matad a los magos!») Los guerreros del rey dominaron a Retief y sus hombres y los llevaron a una colina cercana en la que los masacraron.

La historia de Piet Retief y Dingaan la conocían todos los niños sudafricanos blancos en edad escolar. Para los tradicionalistas como Constand Viljoen, que vivían rodeados del folklore bóer y se consideraban seguidores de la orgullosa tradición de héroes bóer como Retief, el recuerdo de la traición de Dingaan era siempre un aviso de lo que podía ocurrir si se confiaba en el hombre negro.

En opinión de los fieles del Volksfront, eso era lo que Mandela estaba haciendo con F. W. de Klerk. Braam Viljoen, el hermano gemelo de Constand, comprendía la forma de pensar de la extrema derecha prácticamente mejor que nadie, teniendo en cuenta que se alineaba más o menos con el CNA. Lo que la derecha había preferido aprender de la historia era que «nuestros negros» no respondían a una persuasión racional, sino a la intimidación y la fuerza. Braam Viljoen escribió un documento para IDASA, el *think-tank* para el que trabajaba, que influyó en Mandela y el CNA e hizo que empezaran a tomarse a la extrema derecha tan en serio como se la tomaba desde hacía tiempo De Klerk, que poseía mejores informaciones. En su informe, Braam decía que el nuevo tipo de dirección había «transformado la actitud de la derecha de catástrofe inevitable en activismo militante, y había permitido que los grupos afrikaner más variados se unieran bajo el nuevo paraguas del Volksfront». Braam, que no excluía la posibilidad de que sectores importantes de la FSAD respondieran al llamamiento de su hermano, advertía de que era necesario oír a la extrema derecha. «A veces pienso que están coincidiendo los elementos clásicos de la tragedia: el pasado que determina de forma ineludible el futuro, el heroísmo y el valor que se mezclan extrañamente con la estupidez absoluta para provocar el desastre supremo e inevitable.»

Para averiguar si la extrema derecha podía tolerar la «audiencia» que proponía, es decir, conversaciones con el CNA, Braam decidió que había llegado la hora de romper el hielo con su hermano. Cuatro meses antes de cumplir sesenta años, a principios de julio de 1993, Braam y Constand Viljoen se sentaron a hablar de política por primera vez que recordaran ellos.

Braam empezó haciendo a Constand una pregunta sencilla y directa. «¿Cuáles son vuestras opciones?»

«Me temo —respondió Constand— que no tenemos más que una opción. Vamos a tener que resolver esto mediante la acción militar.»

Braam, que contaba con que dijera eso, prosiguió: «Quizá exista otra opción. ¿Qué te parecería una reunión bilateral de alto nivel con el CNA, como último intento de evitar una guerra civil?»

Constand reflexionó un instante y dijo: «Lo consultaré con mi consejo en el Volksfront.»

Unos días después, Constand respondió a su hermano. Constand estaba familiarizado con la guerra, quería evitarla. Era partidario de reunirse con Mandela, y la dirección del Volksfront, unos militares que obedecían por naturaleza a su jefe, se habían mostrado de acuerdo. «La respuesta es sí —dijo Constand a su hermano—. Estamos dispuestos a reunirnos con el CNA.» Braam se puso a trabajar de inmediato. Contactó con un antiguo alumno suyo de teología llamado Carl Niehaus, que se había convertido en uno de los afrikaners de más renombre en el CNA. Dirigía el día a día en el departamento de comunicaciones de la organización.

Braam Viljoen le dijo a Niehaus que, desde que su hermano había sido nombrado jefe del Volksfront, había estado viajando por todo el país animando a los fieles a la guerra. Aspiraban a desbaratar el proceso de negociaciones e impedir que se celebraran elecciones con participación de todas las razas. Constand, en colaboración con altos oficiales de la FSAD que simpatizaban con su causa, estaba pensando seriamente en organizar un golpe de Estado. «Braam me dijo que eran capaces de romper la lealtad de la FSAD al proceso de negociación y apartar al gobierno del poder con un golpe clásico —recordaba posteriormente Niehaus—. Me dijo que estaban convencidos de tener suficiente potencia de fuego y suficiente gente para lograrlo.»

Braam le dijo a Niehaus que el Volksfront no iba a participar, como habían hecho muchos grupos políticos pequeños, en las negociaciones del World Trade Centre. Para ellos, sentarse con el CNA ya era malo, pero sentarse con el gobierno de De Klerk era impensable. La única remota posibilidad de encontrar una salida pacífica a la crisis inminente estaba en tener conversaciones directas entre el CNA y la dirección del Volksfront. ¿Creía Niehaus que era factible?

Niehaus se apresuró a hablar con un responsable de inteligencia del CNA, Mathews Phosa, y le preguntó si había que tomarse en serio los rumores de golpe. Phosa confirmó que, según sus fuentes, había que tomárselos muy en serio. Phosa era partidario de una reunión con el Volksfront, igual que otros personajes del CNA con los que habló Niehaus. «Cuando Nelson Mandela se enteró de la propuesta, no lo dudó. Inmediatamente comprendió el valor del encuentro —recordaba Niehaus—. Creía en el contacto personal, y estaba convencido de que podía conectar con Constand Viljoen y convencerlo de que se lo pensara mejor.»

Niehaus transmitió la respuesta positiva del CNA a Braam, que informó a su hermano. Constand dijo que le parecía bien que se celebrara la reunión, pero que tenía dos condiciones previas esenciales. Tenían que dar garantías absolutas, primero, de que la delegación del Volksfront iba a estar segura y, segundo, de que la reunión se iba a hacer en absoluto secreto. Constand, que quizá tenía en mente a Piet Retief, estaba siguiendo, sin saberlo, el ejemplo de Mandela. A finales de los ochenta, habría sido desastroso para el prisionero Mandela que las bases del CNA se hubieran enterado de que estaba hablando con el enemigo. La confusión habría dado paso a dañinas divisiones en las filas. Viljoen tenía miedo de que ocurriera eso mismo, o algo peor, si sus soldados descubrían que iba a reunirse con Mandela.

Braam tranquilizó a su hermano en nombre del CNA y, el 12 de agosto de 1993, sólo cuatro días después del primer contacto con Niehaus, Braam y Constand Viljoen atravesaban la puerta principal de la casa de Nelson Mandela en Houghton. Él mismo les esperaba allí, con la mano tendida y su sonrisa abierta. Fue un encuentro que dejó asombrados a las dos partes. Mandela era mucho más alto que los dos hermanos, con una imponente presencia física. Y se mostró muy cálido con ellos, aparentemente encantado de verlos. Por su parte, él miró a uno y otro hermano y vio a dos hombres de altura media y peso normal, con las mismas narices protuberantes, las barbillas prominentes, las cabezas cubiertas de una cabellera blanca pero juvenil y los ojos solemnes de color azul marino. Sólo cuando les hizo un gesto para que entraran y les vio caminar advirtió una diferencia entre el paso rígido y marcial del hermano militar y el más desgarbado del hermano teólogo.

Constand había ido acompañado de los tres generales retirados que constituían el alto mando de su Volksfront; Mandela tenía a los dos máximos responsables de los brazos militar y de inteligencia del CNA. Braam y Carl Niehaus, los mediadores, completaban el grupo. La persona más relajada durante las incómodas presentaciones fue Mandela, que daba la impresión de estar recibiendo a un grupo de embajadores europeos. Pero lo que había allí eran dos grupos de personas que estaban a punto de dar la vuelta a una relación de décadas, sin dejar de mantener la misma rivalidad violenta. Viljoen estaba haciendo lo que había hecho Mandela en 1961: establecer un movimiento de resistencia armada para intentar cambiar de forma violenta el statu quo. Mandela quería dar a los aspirantes a terroristas la alternativa pacífica que a él no se le había ofrecido hasta casi treinta años después de fundar Umkhonto.

Mientras las dos delegaciones se observaban, sin tener claro si estar fascinados u horrorizados de encontrarse todos en la misma habitación, Mandela invitó amablemente al general Viljoen a sentarse junto a él en el salón. Las discusiones formales en torno a una gran mesa de conferencias iban a empezar enseguida, pero antes Mandela quiso rendir a P. W. Botha el homenaje de reproducir con Viljoen las elegantes maneras que el gran cocodrilo le había mostrado cuatro años antes en Tuynhuys. Ofreció a Constand una taza de té y se la sirvió él mismo. «¿Quiere leche, general?» El general dijo que sí. «¿Le gustaría un poco de azúcar?» «Sí, por favor, señor Mandela», respondió el general.

Viljoen removió su té en un estado de silenciosa confusión. Aquello no era en absoluto lo que esperaba. Unos estereotipos largamente arraigados se venían abajo. Lo que no comprendía en aquel momento —y no podía comprender, por su educación— era que, en términos políticos, no estaba a la altura de su interlocutor. Mandela, que era un hombre de mundo y no uno de los *volk*, tenía una capacidad de penetrar en las mentes de personas culturalmente distintas a él de la que el general carecía. Sabía cuándo halagar y aplacar (Niël Barnard hablaba del «instinto casi animal» de Mandela «para llegar a las vulnerabilidades de una persona y tranquilizarla»); sabía también cuándo podía pasar al ataque sin ofender, con lo que transmitía una impresión de hombre directo que sabía que le iba a gustar al general, como le había gustado a P. W. Botha. Años después, Mandela dijo: «He trabajado con afrikaners desde que hacía prácticas de abogado, y me han parecido siempre sencillos y francos. Si a un afrikaner no le caes bien, te dice *"gaan kak"* —«lárgate», sería una traducción cortés del original bóer—. Pero, si le caes bien, entonces está de acuerdo contigo. Tienen la capacidad de continuar lo que empiezan.»

Mandela —cortés pero sin pelos en la lengua— se esforzó en caer bien a Viljoen. «Mandela empezó diciendo que el pueblo afrikaner les había hecho mucho daño a él y a su gente —recordaba el general Viljoen—, y que, sin embargo, sentía un gran respeto por los afrikaners. Dijo que quizá era porque, aunque era difícil de explicar a la gente de fuera, el afrikaner tenía mucha humanidad. Dijo que, si el hijo de un peón en una granja de un afrikaner se ponía enfermo, el granjero afrikaner le llevaba en su *bakkie* al hospital, y llamaba para preguntar por él, y llevaba a sus padres para que lo vieran, y se portaba muy bien. Al mismo tiempo, el granjero afrikaner trataba duramente a su peón y esperaba que trabajase mucho. Era un jefe exigente, dijo Mandela, pero también era humano, y ese aspecto era algo que a Mandela le impresionaba mucho.»

Viljoen estaba asombrado por la capacidad de Mandela de ir más allá de las caricaturas superficiales y comprender con tanta profundidad, en su opinión, el verdadero carácter del afrikaner. Otra cuestión es cuántos peones de granja negros habría encontrado Mandela que confirmaran su opinión del *baas*. Lo importante era que Mandela sabía que su descripción del afrikaner como un cristiano rudo y curtido se ajustaba perfectamente a la visión que Viljoen tenía de su propio pueblo.

Viljoen se quedó tan intrigado como se había quedado Botha cuando Mandela empezó a destacar las similitudes entre la historia de los negros y la de los afrikaners, dos pueblos que habían librado guerras de liberación. Y, por supuesto, Mandela estaba haciendo algo que Viljoen no se esperaba. Estaba teniendo la cortesía de hablar con él en su propio idioma.

Mandela había valorado muy bien la atmósfera y le había dejado claro a Viljoen que era un hombre con el que podía hablar y del que podía esperar que le entendiera. Pero el auténtico meollo de la reunión llegó al final de su conversación en torno a las tazas de té. Braam y Niehaus estaban escuchando justo en ese momento.

«Espero que comprenda lo difícil que les resulta a los blancos confiar en que las cosas van a ir bien con el CNA en el poder —dijo Constand Viljoen, y añadió—: No estoy seguro de si se da usted cuenta, señor Mandela, pero esto puede detenerse.»

«Esto» quería decir la transición pacífica hacia el gobierno negro. No lo dijo con todas las letras, pero claramente estaba indicándole a Mandela que iba a haber una intervención militar y que la derecha, con la ayuda de la FSAD, podía hacerse con el poder si no se daba a los afrikaners una franja de territorio soberano dentro de las fronteras sudafricanas.

Mandela, muy serio, respondió: «Mire, general, sé que las fuerzas militares que puede reunir usted son poderosas, bien armadas y bien entrenadas; y que son mucho más potentes que las mías. Militarmente, no podemos luchar contra ustedes; no podemos ganar. Sin embargo, si va usted a la guerra, le aseguro que tampoco ganará, no vencerá a largo plazo. Primero, porque la comunidad internacional estará por completo de nuestro lado. Y segundo, porque somos demasiados, y no pueden matarnos a todos. Así que, dígame, ¿qué tipo de vida va a tener su gente en este país? Mi gente se irá al campo, las presiones internacionales sobre ustedes serán enormes y este país se convertirá en un infierno para todos nosotros. ¿Es eso lo que desea? No, general, si entramos en una guerra no puede haber vencedores.»

«Es verdad —replicó el general Viljoen—. No puede haber vencedores.»

Y ahí acabó la cosa. Aquél fue el entendimiento sobre el que la extrema derecha y el movimiento negro de liberación construyeron su diálogo. Aquella primera reunión en Houghton sentó las bases para tres meses y medio de negociaciones secretas entre delegaciones del CNA y el Volksfront. El Volksfront quería establecer el principio constitucional de un Israel afrikaner, a lo que el CNA nunca dijo totalmente que no y nunca dijo totalmente que sí; su principal preocupación era conseguir que la gente de Viljoen siguiera en las conversaciones y para ello les tentaron con la posibilidad de futuras conversaciones sobre la constitución de su anhelado *Boerestaat*.

Aquellos contactos siguieron adelante pese a una serie de acontecimientos que podían haber sido desestabilizadores y que se produjeron durante los tres últimos meses de 1993. El primero fue el anuncio, por parte de los negociadores del World Trade Centre, de que las primeras elecciones sudafricanas con participación de todas las razas se celebrarían el 27 de abril de 1994. Luego crearon un comité encargado de escoger un nuevo himno nacional y una nueva bandera. Entonces, Mangosuthu Buthelezi descubrió sus cartas al formar una coalición con la extrema derecha blanca, un organismo del que formaban parte el Volksfront e Inkatha y que se llamaba la Alianza para la Libertad. (Los seguidores de Viljoen, impresionados por la disposición de Inkatha a respaldar su retórica con la fuerza, celebraron el hecho.) Después, los asesinos de Chris Hani, Janusz Walus y Clive Derby-Lewis, fueron condenados a muerte. Luego, una mujer negra fue coronada Miss Sudáfrica por primera vez. Y, para echar más sal en la herida, Mandela y De Klerk recibieron el premio Nobel de la Paz. Y, lo más importante de todo, Mandela y De Klerk presidieron una ceremonia en la que quedó solemnemente aprobada la nueva constitución de transición del país. El resultado de tres años y medio de negociaciones fue un pacto por el que el primer gobierno elegido democráticamente sería una coalición que iba a compartir el poder durante cinco años: el presidente pertenecería al partido mayoritario pero la configuración del gabinete debía reflejar la proporción de votos obtenida por cada partido. Las nuevas disposiciones ofrecían asimismo garantías de que ni los funcionarios blancos, incluidos los militares, iban a perder su trabajo, ni los granjeros blancos iban a perder sus tierras. Tampoco habría ningún juicio al estilo de Nuremberg.

Aunque era con De Klerk con quien había llegado a ese acuerdo histórico, Mandela siempre sintió más respeto personal por Constand Viljoen —e incluso por P. W. Botha— que por el presidente que le había puesto en libertad. Para Mandela, Viljoen era, como él, un líder patriarcal que, dentro de los límites de su simplista naturaleza bóer, tenía un gran corazón. Mandela veía reflejadas en Viljoen algunas de sus propias cualidades —honradez, integridad, valor— que más le gustaban.

En De Klerk, por el contrario, Mandela veía pocas cosas que quisiera emular. Nunca le perdonó lo que consideraba su desprecio por la pérdida de vidas negras en los distritos segregados y consideraba que el presidente era un abogado mezquino y sibilino que se perdía en los detalles y carecía del temperamento y la convicción propios de un verdadero líder. Era una opinión que incluso muchos de sus propios colegas en el Comité Ejecutivo Nacional del CNA consideraban injusta, pero, si había algo que el probo caballero victoriano que era Mandela odiaba, era el sentimiento de que alguien había traicionado su buena fe.

Pese a ello, fue con De Klerk con quien Mandela recibió su premio Nobel conjunto. La concesión le indignó, no porque le pareciera prematura, que lo era, puesto que nadie sabía aún cuál iba a ser el resultado de la carrera entre la paz y la guerra, sino porque, según su viejo amigo y abogado George Bizos, creía que De Klerk no lo merecía, que el premio debería haber ido a parar a Mandela y el CNA en su conjunto. «Cuando De Klerk pronunció su discurso de aceptación —contaba George Bizos, que viajó a Noruega con la delegación del Nobel—, Mandela esperaba que reconociera que se había cometido una injusticia con las crueldades del apartheid contra la gente de Sudáfrica. Pero De Klerk no incluyó ninguna referencia de ese tipo.» Como si se creyera la propaganda, como si se creyera la media verdad tácita del acto de que se había ganado una posición de igualdad moral con Mandela, lo único que dijo De Klerk fue que ambas partes habían cometido «errores». «Miré a Mandela. Él se limitó a menear la cabeza.»

Esa noche, Mandela y De Klerk presenciaron junto a la catedral de Oslo una procesión de antorchas. Parte de la ceremonia consistía en una interpretación del *Nkosi Sikelele*. Mandela notó que, mientras cantaban el himno de liberación, De Klerk charlaba distraídamente con su esposa. La paciencia de Mandela llegó al límite durante la cena, organizada por el primer ministro de Noruega y con 150 invitados, miembros de su gobierno y el cuerpo diplomático. Cuando Mandela se levantó para hablar, Bizos se quedó tan asombrado como todos los demás ante el veneno que destilaron sus labios. «Dio los detalles más horribles de lo que habían sufrido los presos en Robben Island —recordaba—, incluido cómo habían enterrado a un hombre en la arena dejándole sólo la cabeza fuera y cómo habían orinado sobre él... Contó la historia como ejemplo de lo inhumano que había sido el sistema, aunque no llegó a decir: "Aquí están las personas que representaban a ese sistema."»

Es evidente que Mandela guardaba cierto resentimiento hacia sus carceleros, al contrario de lo que había asegurado en la rueda de prensa al día siguiente de su liberación y a la imagen que los admiradores de todo el mundo deseaban tener de él. Después de todo no era un santo.

Capítulo XI
«HAY QUE APELAR A SUS CORAZONES»

1994

Una dieta sencilla y baja en grasas, mucho ejercicio, el fresco aire de mar, suficientes horas de sueño, horarios regulares, prácticamente nada de estrés: la cárcel tenía sus compensaciones. Eso ayudaba a entender por qué los médicos de Mandela confirmaban lo que decían quienes le habían visto en acción durante aquel año tan repleto de acontecimientos espectaculares: a los setenta y seis años, tenía la constitución de un hombre de cincuenta en buena forma. Mil novecientos noventa y tres fue un año cargado de acontecimientos; 1994 prometía ser todavía más difícil. Mandela se levantaba todos los días a las 4:30 no sólo por costumbre, sino por necesidad. La derecha blanca y la derecha negra seguían negándose a presentarse a las elecciones y amenazaban con la guerra si se llevaban a cabo sin contar con ellas. En el caso de que sí se celebraran las primeras elecciones multirraciales el 27 de abril, según lo previsto, Mandela tendría que ocuparse de una campaña electoral, y, si vencía, tendría un país que gobernar, un país con los problemas habituales en todas partes, más la certidumbre de que el problema fundamental de la estabilidad, la perspectiva del terrorismo contrarrevolucionario, no iba a desaparecer.

Lo bueno era que Constand Viljoen estaba perdiendo su entusiasmo por la guerra. Desde su llamamiento a las armas en Potchefstroom, había desarrollado —con la ayuda de Mandela— una conciencia más clara del baño de sangre que podía desencadenar y estaba empezando a ver que un gobierno dirigido por negros podía no ser tan apocalíptico como había pensado al principio. Sin embargo, seguía exhortando a su gente a movilizarse para la guerra. «Si quieres discutir con un lobo, asegúrate de tener una pistola en la mano», era su lema. El problema era que ya no estaba completamente seguro de si el lobo era un lobo, o un perro que podía domesticarse. Mandela le caía bien, pero tenía sus dudas sobre el CNA; le preocupaba que los dirigentes con los que se reunía, como el astuto número dos de la organización, Thabo Mbeki, pudieran estar abusando de su buena fe y engañándole para que vendiera a su gente. Y había otra cosa. Si el CNA estaba poniendo en práctica un juego retorcido y engañoso, si lo que en realidad quería era convertir Sudáfrica al comunismo y llevar a cabo una terrible venganza contra los blancos mientras fingía lo contrario, los altos jefes de la FDSA se lo habían creído por completo. El general Georg Meiring, sucesor de Viljoen como jefe de las fuerzas armadas, había pronunciado justo antes de la Navidad de 1993 un discurso en el que prometía su apoyo a la nueva constitución (uno de los incentivos para hacerlo fue la amenaza, por parte del progresista jefe de las fuerzas aéreas, de que estaba dispuesto a bombardearle si volvía al ejército en contra del nuevo orden). Viljoen sabía que, si el Volksfront declaraba la guerra, seguramente se enfrentaría al poderío del mismo ejército en el que él había servido con tanto orgullo y distinción. Todavía era posible contar con que algunos sectores de la FDSA lucharían junto a la resistencia bóer, pero, de no producirse un golpe de mano —que cada vez era menos probable— en la cúpula, la institución parecía estar alineada con Mandela y De Klerk.

El general Viljoen no se había sentido nunca tan inseguro e incómodo. A medida que las posibilidades de victoria del Volksfront se volvían más remotas, sus soldados clamaban en voz más alta pidiendo la guerra. Mandela también oía esos gritos, y simpatizaba con Viljoen. Sabía que las bases del general necesitaban lanzar vítores. Los demás dirigentes del CNA no lo tenían tan claro. En una reunión del Comité Ejecutivo Nacional a principios de 1994, se discutió qué postura debía tener el nuevo gobierno sobre la delicada cuestión del himno nacional. El viejo himno era claramente inaceptable. Una parte de *Die Stem*, una lúgubre melodía marcial, era una aceptable y neutral súplica a Dios para que «proteja nuestra amada tierra»; pero otra —y ésa era la parte que oían los negros— celebraba los triunfos de Retief, Pretorius y el resto de los «expedicionarios» en su marcha hacia el norte a través de Sudáfrica en el siglo XIX, una marcha en la que aplastaron la resistencia negra y sus «carros chirriantes dejaron sus surcos en la tierra». El himno extraoficial de la Sudáfrica negra, el *Nkosi Sikelele*, era la sentida expresión de un pueblo que había sufrido mucho tiempo y anhelaba la libertad.

La reunión acababa de empezar cuando entró un

ayudante para informar a Mandela de que tenía una llamada de un jefe de Estado. Salió de la sala y los treinta y pico hombres y mujeres del órgano supremo de decisión del CNA siguieron debatiendo sin él. Hubo un consenso abrumador en favor de eliminar *Die Stem* y sustituirlo por el *Nkosi Sikelele*. Los miembros del comité ejecutivo estaban felicitándose por su decisión y lo que simbolizaba para la nueva Sudáfrica cuando regresó Mandela. Le dijeron lo que habían decidido y él respondió: «Pues lo siento. No quiero ser grosero, pero... creo que debo expresar lo que pienso sobre esta propuesta. Nunca pensé que personas experimentadas como vosotros podían tomar una decisión de tal magnitud en un tema tan importante sin ni siquiera esperar al presidente de vuestra organización.»

Y entonces Mandela expuso su punto de vista. «Esta canción que despacháis con tanta facilidad contiene las emociones de muchas personas a las que todavía no representáis. De un plumazo, decidiríais destruir la misma —la única— base de lo que estamos construyendo: la reconciliación.»

Los hombres y mujeres del Comité Ejecutivo Nacional del CNA se sintieron abochornados. Mandela propuso que Sudáfrica tuviera dos himnos que serían interpretados, uno después de otro, en todas las ceremonias oficiales, desde las tomas de posesión presidenciales hasta los partidos internacionales de rugby: *Die Stem* y el *Nkosi Sikelele*. Los luchadores por la libertad, rápidamente convencidos por la lógica del argumento de Mandela, cedieron de forma unánime. Jacob Zuma, que había presidido la reunión, dijo «Bueno, creo... creo que la cosa está clara, camaradas. Creo que la cosa está clara.» No hubo objeciones.

El comité capituló ante el enfado de Mandela porque sus miembros comprendieron que su solución para el problema del himno era la mejor desde el punto de vista táctico. Había amonestado al comité sobre la necesidad de ganarse a los afrikaners y mostrar respeto por sus símbolos; sobre la conveniencia de hacer todo lo posible, por ejemplo, para decir unas palabras en afrikaans al principio de cada discurso. «No hay que apelar a su razón —explicó—, sino a sus corazones.»

En el caso de Constand Viljoen, Mandela se dirigió al cerebro y el corazón, pero al final fue el corazón el que ganó. Ayudó enormemente el hecho de que, el 11 de marzo, el Volksfront sufrió su Waterloo, y eso movió al general en la dirección hacia la que Mandela había estado empujándole con suavidad.

A apenas seis semanas de las elecciones, Viljoen respondió a una llamada de uno de sus aliados negros en la Alianza por la Libertad. En esa ocasión no era Buthelezi, sino el líder de otro de los pequeños Estados tribales que el ideólogo jefe Hendrick Verwoerd había ideado como parte de su estrategia del «gran apartheid», un hombre llamado Lucas Mangope, cuyo poder en Bophuthatswana estaba amenazado por la mayoría de sus ciudadanos, partidarios del CNA y ofendidos por su dependencia de Pretoria. Viljoen movilizó una fuerza de más de mil hombres para ir a la capital de «Bop», una ciudad llamada Mmabatho. La cosa acabó en desastre cuando el AWB de Eugene Terreblanche entró en la refriega y emprendió lo que los periódicos afrikaans describirían más tarde como un *kaffirskietpiekniek,* un pícnic de tiro al *kaffir.* Las fuerzas de seguridad de Mangope se rebelaron y dirigieron sus armas contra los miembros del Volksfront, y cuando, horas más tarde, llegó la FSAD en una columna de vehículos blindados, las tropas de Viljoen abandonaron el campo de batalla en medio del caos.

Suele decirse que lo que ocurrió en Mmabatho fue la única razón por la que Viljoen decidió abandonar la lucha de resistencia bóer. Pero él reconoció que había más factores. Una vez librado del elemento vándalo del AWB, habría podido seguir dirigiendo una campaña «militar» eficaz, aunque todos los demás lo habrían llamado terrorismo. «Teníamos un plan. Podríamos haber impedido que se celebraran las elecciones, y no con la FSAD, sino nosotros solos. Teníamos los medios, teníamos las armas, teníamos la táctica y teníamos la voluntad. No de hacernos con el poder, no de derrotar a la FSAD, pero sí de impedir que se celebrasen las elecciones, no me cabe ninguna duda.»

Arrie Rossouw, al que, cuatro años después de la liberación de Mandela, se consideraba un peso pesado del periodismo afrikaner y que posteriormente sería director de *Beeld* y de *Die Burger*, estaba de acuerdo. «No hay duda de que podía haber hecho un daño terrible a este país —afirmaba—. Muy fácilmente podía haber colocado a 400 ex miembros de los regimientos de Reconocimiento [fuerzas especiales], perfectamente entrenados, a sus órdenes y, con ellos, bien dotados de armas, podría haber hecho estallar aeropuertos, estaciones de tren, estaciones de autobús, podría haber asesinado a gente. No habrían conseguido derrocar al gobierno —eso lo aprendieron en Mmabatho—, pero sí habrían podido paralizar la economía y causar un caos político total. Y habrían podido mantenerlo durante años y años.»

En otras palabras, podrían haber hecho lo que el IRA hizo en Irlanda del Norte durante treinta años, pero con unos efectos mucho más catastróficos. En parte, porque disponían de más armas y más hombres con experiencia militar, pero, sobre todo, porque Sudáfrica estaba construyendo su democracia con una economía quebradiza, vulnerable al caos y el derrumbamiento como no lo habían sido jamás Irlanda ni Gran Bretaña. Lo alarmante fue que no era un colectivo, sino un solo hombre, el que debía decidir qué vía iban a emprender, la paz o la guerra.

«Sí, fue una decisión completamente mía. Completamente —confirmó Viljoen en tono solemne—. Durante aquellas últimas semanas antes de las elecciones, en el Volksfront afrikaner había división de opiniones, entre una mitad que quería la opción violenta, impedir las elecciones y todo el proceso democrático en Sudáfrica, y la otra que quería una solución negociada.» Sufrió con la decisión. «Siempre me pareció que la guerra y la violencia no son opciones fáciles. Yo sabía lo que era la guerra. Así que les dije a mis partidarios que asumía la responsabilidad de decidir si luchar o no. Fue la decisión más difícil de toda mi vida. En el ejército, tiene que entenderlo, antes de tomar una decisión en un asunto como éste, sopesamos todos los factores, evaluamos, reflexionamos, y sólo después de un largo proceso nos decidimos. Pensé que la mejor opción eran las negociaciones y participar en las elecciones. Me pareció que era lo mejor para el país y lo mejor para el pueblo afrikaner.»

El factor decisivo para Viljoen no fue ni la chusma del AWB, ni el fiasco de Mmabatho, sino otra cosa. «El carácter del oponente, si se puede confiar en él, si uno cree que está verdaderamente a favor de la paz. Lo importante, al sentarse a negociar con el enemigo, es el carácter de los interlocutores al otro lado de la mesa y si cuentan con el apoyo de su gente. Mandela tenía las dos cosas.»

Había pocos capaces de resistirse al encanto de Mandela; ni siquiera De Klerk, ni siquiera cuando estaban en plena campaña, uno contra otro, antes de las elecciones del 27 de abril, y ni siquiera después de que se enfrentaran en un debate en vivo en televisión como los de Estados Unidos. De Klerk, lo bastante joven como para ser hijo de Mandela, se mostró más despierto y mejor preparado que su adversario. Pero entonces, cuando el debate se aproximaba a su fin, Mandela tendió la mano y estrechó la del presidente, y le ofreció el elogio de que era «un auténtico hijo de África». De Klerk, atónito, no tuvo más remedio que aceptar el apretón y puso su mejor sonrisa, aunque sabía que en ese momento Mandela estaba dándole un golpe decisivo.

«Tenía la sensación, y la tenía todo el mundo, de que yo estaba ganando los puntos —recordaba posteriormente De Klerk—. Pero él se recuperó cuando, de pronto, me elogió y me dio la mano delante de todas las cámaras. Quizá estaba planeado de antemano. Quizá fue una medida política. Pero creo que sus triunfos mediáticos, en general, eran producto de una reacción instintiva por su parte. Creo que tiene un talento extraordinario para ello.» Pocos días después del debate, el propio De Klerk hizo una cortés declaración pública. Durante su última rueda de prensa antes de las elecciones, le pidieron su opinión sobre su rival. «Nelson Mandela —replicó De Klerk, con las manos extendidas como si se rindiera— es un hombre predestinado.»

Como parte de la campaña electoral, Mandela acudió a un programa nocturno de entrevistas en la emisora Radio 702 de Johanesburgo, para responder a preguntas de los oyentes en directo. Eddie von Maltitz, el primer guerrero del Volksfront que había entrado en el World Trade Centre durante el asalto, estaba en su granja con varios de sus *kommandos* y estaba escuchando el programa. Cuando sus camaradas le instaron a que llamase y le dijera unas cuantas cosas al *kaffir*, Von Maltitz accedió. Dedicó nada menos que tres minutos a despotricar y protestar contra Mandela: el comunismo era tal, los terroristas cual, la destrucción de nuestra cultura, las normas civilizadas, las reglas. Acabó con una amenaza brutal y directa. «Este país se verá inmerso en un baño de sangre si usted sigue de la mano de los matones comunistas.»

Después de una tensa pausa, Mandela respondió: «Bueno, Eddie, me parece que es usted un sudafricano digno de tal nombre y no me cabe duda de que, si nos sentásemos a intercambiar puntos de vista, yo me aproximaré a usted y usted se aproximará a mí. Vamos a hablar, Eddie.»

«Eh... bueno, vale, señor Mandela —murmuró Eddie, confuso—. Gracias —añadió y colgó.

Tres meses después, en su granja, aunque seguía llevando ropa de camuflaje, botas de cazador y una pistola de 9 mm al cinto, Eddie era otro hombre. Había dejado de entrenar a sus *kommandos*; había abandonado sus preparativos para la guerra. La charla en Radio 702 había cambiado todo. «Aquello fue lo que me hizo pensar», explicó después. El nuevo primer ministro del Estado Libre de Orange, en el que vivía, un hombre del CNA, fue el que le hizo dar el paso decisivo. Se llamaba *Terror* Lekota, un sobrenombre que le habían dado por su capacidad letal de marcar goles en el terreno de fútbol. Lekota, que había estado en Robben Island durante los últimos años de Mandela allí, tenía muchos instintos muy parecidos a los de él. Decidió que su primera misión, al llegar al poder, era ganarse a los granjeros afrikaner del Estado Libre. Si lo conseguía con Von Maltitz, tendría mucho más fácil hacerse con los demás. Llamó personalmente a Von Maltitz y le invitó a su fiesta de cumpleaños en su residencia en la capital del Estado, Bloemfontein. Von Maltitz dijo que no, pero Lekota insistió. «Por favor, Eddie, me gustaría verdaderamente que viniera.» Von Maltitz dijo que consultaría con sus hombres y luego le daría una respuesta. «Hablamos y pensamos que no teníamos nada que perder —recordaba después Von Maltitz—. De modo que, cuando volvió a llamar, le dije que sí.»

Von Maltitz acudió a la que llamaba «la gran casa» en Bloemfontein totalmente armado. «No quería ser un Piet Retief con Dingaan», explicaba. Entró en la casa y se unió a la fiesta, en la que predominaban los negros, sin que nadie le registrase. «*Terror* Lekota me vio desde el otro lado de la sala, se acercó y me dio un gran abrazo. Debió de notar mis pistolas, pero no dijo nada. No dejó de sonreír. Me cayó bien. Era sincero. Como el señor Mandela, un hombre sincero. Así que pensé: Vamos a darles una oportunidad; se la merecen.»

¿Por qué? Porque Mandela y su nuevo amigo *Terror* le habían tratado con respeto, con el «respeto elemental», de Walter Sisulu. «Nunca obtuve ese respeto de De Klerk y el Partido Nacional. En cambio, del señor Mandela, sí. Creo de verdad que debemos darles una oportunidad.»

El CNA había ganado las elecciones con casi dos tercios de los votos nacionales y casi el 89 % del voto negro. Del resto, el 1 % fue al CPA, claramente antiblanco, cuyo lema de «un colono, una bala» fue despreciativamente transformado por los partidarios del CNA en «un colono, uno por ciento», y el 10 % fue a parar a Inkatha (abandonado por Viljoen, el jefe Mangosuthu Buthelezi no tuvo más remedio que incorporarse al proceso electoral). El Partido Nacional obtuvo el 20 %, que significaba cuatro puestos en el gabinete, incluida la vicepresidencia para De Klerk, en el nuevo gobierno de coalición que iba a presidir Mandela. Y el partido de Viljoen, que se llamaba Frente por la Libertad, consiguió el 2 % de los votos, que significaba nueve respetables escaños en el nuevo parlamento multicolor.

En cuanto se conocieron los resultados, John Reinders, jefe de protocolo presidencial con De Klerk y P. W. Botha, se puso en contacto con sus antiguos patronos, el Departamento de Servicios Penitenciarios. Botha le había sacado de la burocracia carcelaria en 1980, cuando tenía el rango de comandante, pero ahora se encontró, para su tranquilidad, que todavía tenían un hueco para él.

Su última tarea antes de irse fue organizar la toma de posesión de Mandela como presidente, el 10 de mayo de 1994. Fue una pesadilla logística en comparación con la de De Klerk, a la que no había acudido ninguna delegación extranjera, salvo los diplomáticos destacados en el país. Esta vez, las cosas iban a ser muy diferentes. Cuatro mil personas se reunieron en la sede del poder en Pretoria, un conjunto de edificios de principios del siglo XX llamado Union Buildings y situado sobre una colina que dominaba la ciudad. Entre los invitados estaban personas a las que era difícil imaginar en una misma habitación, como Hillary Clinton, Fidel Castro, el príncipe Felipe de Inglaterra, Yasir Arafat y el presidente de Israel, Chaim Herzog. Se interpretaron los dos himnos nacionales —*Nkosi Sikelele* y *Die Stem*— uno detrás de otro, mientras ondeaba la nueva bandera nacional. Era la bandera más multicolor del mundo, una especie de colcha de retazos en negro, verde, oro, rojo, azul y blanco, una combinación de los colores asociados con la resistencia negra y los de la vieja bandera sudafricana. Mandela prestó juramento ante un juez blanco, flanqueado por su hija Zenani y rodeado de antiguos presos negros y generales blancos de la FSAD en posición de firmes y uniforme de gala. («Unos años antes, me habrían detenido», bromeaba después.) La ceremonia se cerró con el espectáculo de los reactores de la Fuerza Aérea Sudafricana volando por encima y pintando los colores de la nueva bandera en el cielo.

Francamente aliviado de que la ceremonia hubiera transcurrido sin ninguna catástrofe, John Reinders llegó a su despacho de los Union Buildings a primera hora de la mañana siguiente, 11 de mayo, con un par de grandes cajas de cartón bajo el bazo. Era un hombre alto y corpulento, pero tenía la actitud respetuosa de alguien más menudo y el sentido común suficiente para saber cuándo iba a ser derrotado.

«Esa mañana llegué pronto para recoger mis cosas —recordaba Reinders—. Todos los blancos habíamos solicitado empleo en otros sitios, porque estábamos seguros de que nos iban a pedir que nos fuéramos. Bastantes tenían previsto ir a trabajar para el señor De Klerk en la vicepresidencia.»

Reinders estaba empaquetando sus recuerdos de los diecisiete años que había pasado dirigiendo la oficina de la presidencia, organizando ceremonias, conociendo a gente famosa en viajes oficiales, cuando, de pronto, le sacó de sus reminiscencias una llamada a la puerta. Era otro madrugador. Mandela.

«Buenos días, ¿cómo está?», dijo, mientras entraba en el despacho de Reinders con la mano extendida.

«Muy bien, señor presidente, gracias. ¿Y usted?»

«Bien, bien, pero... —continuó Mandela, confundido—, ¿qué hace?»

«Estoy recogiendo mis cosas para irme, señor presidente.»

«Ya veo. ¿Y puedo preguntarle dónde va a ir?»

«De vuelta a los Servicios Penitenciarios, señor presidente, donde trabajaba antes.»

«Mmm —dijo Mandela, apretando los labios—. Yo estuve allí veintisiete años, ya sabe. Fue horrible —sonrió mientras repetía—, ¡horrible!»

Reinders, estupefacto, le devolvió una media sonrisa.

«Bueno —continuó Mandela—, me gustaría que pensara en la posibilidad de seguir con nosotros. —Reinders examinó los ojos de Mandela con asombro—. Sí, hablo en serio. Usted conoce este trabajo. Yo no. Yo vengo del campo. Soy un ignorante. Si se queda conmigo, sería sólo para un mandato, nada más. Cinco años. Luego, por supuesto, sería libre de marcharse. Ahora, compréndame: esto no es una orden. Sólo me gustaría que se quede si desea quedarse y compartir sus conocimientos y su experiencia conmigo.»

Mandela sonrió. Reinders sonrió también, esta vez con más confianza.

«Así que ¿qué dice? —preguntó Mandela—, ¿se queda conmigo?»

A pesar de su asombro, Reinders no lo dudó. «Sí, señor presidente. Me quedo. Sí. Gracias.»

Entonces, su nuevo jefe le encargó su primera tarea: reunir a todo el personal de la presidencia, incluidos los limpiadores y los jardineros, para una reunión en la sala del consejo de ministros. El presidente se paseó entre ellos, estrechó la mano y dijo unas palabras a cada uno del centenar aproximado de personas, en afrikaans cuando correspondía. Luego habló dirigiéndose a todos. «Hola, soy Nelson Mandela. Si alguno de ustedes prefiere acogerse al convenio, es libre de marcharse. Váyanse. No hay problema. Pero se lo pido, ¡quédense! Cinco años, nada más. Ustedes conocen esto. Necesitamos esos conocimientos, necesitamos esa experiencia que tienen.»

Todos y cada uno de los miembros del personal de la presidencia se quedaron.

Dos semanas más tarde, el 24 de mayo, 400 delegados recién elegidos se reunieron en Ciudad del Cabo para la apertura del primer parlamento democrático de Sudáfrica, en el mismo edificio de la Asamblea Nacional en el que antes se reunía el parlamento reservado a los blancos. Hasta entonces, había sido un lugar lúgubre, pesado, monocromático. En la mañana de mayo en la que la cámara abrió sus puertas a la democracia no racial de Mandela, la escena se transformó en una imagen de tecnicolor. La imagen desde lo alto de la galería de invitados era una mezcla entre la Asamblea General de Naciones

Unidas, un concierto pop y una fiesta universitaria de fin de curso. Un vistazo a la lista de nuevos miembros del parlamento lo decía todo. Antes se llamaban Botha, Van der Merwe y Smith. Ahora tenían esos nombres, pero también Bengu, y Dlamini, y Farisani, y Maharaj, y Mushwana, y Neerahoo, y Pahad, y Zulu. Y un tercio de los parlamentarios, incluida la nueva presidenta, Frene Ginwala, eran mujeres. Más impresionante todavía era la proporción de diputados que habían estado en la cárcel o huidos de la policía. Prácticamente todos los representantes del CNA habían infringido la ley; ahora iban a ser ellos quienes la elaborasen, dirigidos por el preso más antiguo de todos, el último hombre en llegar ese día: Mandela.

Cuando se corrió la voz de su llegada, los parlamentarios se pusieron en pie y el murmullo dejó paso a un rugido, cantos de libertad y rítmicas danzas entre los miembros más jóvenes y exuberantes del contingente del CNA. En medio de la mezcla variopinta de la Nación Arcoiris, el general Viljoen era una figura anómala. Serio como siempre, de traje gris y corbata, estaba de pie en el centro de la cámara ovalada, en la parte inferior, como correspondía al líder de la honorable oposición del Frente por la Libertad. Mandela apareció, también por la parte inferior, sonriente y erguido, entre los vítores de la asamblea.

Viljoen miraba a Mandela con una mezcla de admiración y afecto. Al verlo, Mandela rompió el protocolo parlamentario, cruzó hasta él, le dio la mano y dijo con una gran sonrisa: «Me alegro mucho de verle aquí, general.»

Algunas voces desde la galería gritaron: «¡Dele un abrazo, general! ¡Vamos, dele un abrazo!»

Al recordar el momento, Viljoen esbozó una ligera sonrisa, asintió y luego recuperó la solemnidad. «Pero no lo hice. Soy un militar y él era mi presidente. Le di la mano y me puse firme.»

Y ahí podía haber acabado la cosa: el orden reestablecido, los viejos enemigos reconciliados, el buen rey coronado, todos los actores salen —de forma exuberante— por la izquierda del escenario. Pero no fue así. Todavía no se había terminado, ni para Mandela ni para el general Viljoen. Todavía quedaba un acto por representar para que Viljoen pudiera colgar la espada con el espíritu tranquilo, una última serie de obstáculos que superar para que Mandela pudiera considerar completada la odisea de su vida.

Como indicaba Viljoen, «el 40 o el 50 por ciento de mi gente no participó en las elecciones.» Durante la semana anterior a las elecciones, algunos colocaron bombas en paradas de autobús y otros lugares en los que los negros se reunían en gran número. También pusieron una bomba en el aeropuerto internacional de Johanesburgo. Murieron 21 personas y más de 100 resultaron gravemente heridas. Los discursos de Mandela durante su primer mes de mandato eran siempre optimistas, porque intentaba crear una atmósfera positiva y llena de energía. Pero no pudo resistirse a señalar, al cerrar aquella primera sesión del parlamento, que las fuerzas de seguridad iban a permanecer en plena alerta. «El problema de la violencia de origen político sigue estando con nosotros», dijo.

Mandela tuvo mucho de lo que ocuparse durante sus cinco años en el cargo: proporcionar casas y escuelas, agua y luz a los negros. Pero su máxima prioridad fue sentar las bases de la nueva democracia, construirla a prueba de bombas. Sabía que iba a haber intentos de subvertir el nuevo orden, inevitablemente frágil. No era posible que toda la Sudáfrica blanca cediera sus viejos poderes, y no pocos privilegios, sin luchar.

En cuanto al general Viljoen, se debatía como se había debatido Niël Barnard cuatro años y medio antes, la mañana de la liberación de Mandela. A pesar de haberse entrevistado con Mandela 60 veces en la cárcel, Barnard no podía desechar por completo la señal de alarma que sonaba en el fondo de su cerebro para advertirle, aunque fuera irracional, sobre el peligro del factor ayatolá. Viljoen tenía dudas similares, como si no pudiera acabar de creerse que la vida podía ser tan buena como hacía parecer Mandela, como si no hubiera sido capaz de librarse de toda su desconfianza ancestral respecto al hombre negro. Una parte de él estaba preocupada, mientras estaba sentado allí el día de la apertura del parlamento y durante todo el año posterior, por la posibilidad de que hubiera actuado conforme a sus intereses —Mandela siempre había tenido la puerta abierta para él y siempre le había tratado con respeto—, pero no conforme a los intereses de su pueblo. Confesó después que le había remordido la conciencia. «Estaba preocupado. Muy preocupado —dijo—. Se habían dicho muchas cosas muy bonitas, pero ¿dónde había una prueba que pudiera enseñar a mi gente de una vez por todas?»

La solución era que Mandela demostrase a la gente de Viljoen que también era su gente; que ampliara su acogida, más allá de Constand Viljoen, John Reinders, Niël Barnard y Kobie Coetsee, a todos los afrikaners. El asesor legal y confidente de Mandela en la oficina presidencial, un abogado blanco llamado Nicholas Haysom, que había estado en prisión tres veces durante los años de la lucha contra el apartheid, definió la misión en términos épicos muy apropiados.

«Lo llamamos la construcción nacional. Pero Garibaldi tiene una frase que lo ilustra de manera más elocuente —explicaba Hanson, con una referencia a Giuseppe Garibaldi, el patriota soldado que unificó Italia a mediados del siglo XIX—. Al acabar su misión militar, Garibaldi dijo: "Hemos hecho Italia, ahora debemos hacer italianos."» En realidad, el reto que aguardaba a Mandela era más difícil que el de Garibaldi. «Italia estaba dividida pero era homogénea. Sudáfrica, en 1994, era un país dividido histórica, cultural y racialmente, y en muchos otros aspectos —añadió Haysom—. Por muchos discursos, negociaciones, constituciones que hubiera, no bastaban por sí solos para "hacer sudafricanos". Hacía falta algo más que uniera a la gente. Era necesario que Mandela hiciera lo que mejor sabía hacer: elevarse por encima de nuestras diferencias, ser más grande que todos esos factores que nos separaban y apelar a lo que nos unía.»

Capítulo XII
EL CAPITÁN Y EL PRESIDENTE

1994-1995

«Al contemplarlo —dijo Mandela, recordando su primer encuentro con François Pienaar—, si se tenía en cuenta de dónde venía, lo que se veía era un afrikaner típico.»

Mandela tenía razón. Si los ideólogos del apartheid hubieran tenido la misma afición a poner el arte al servicio de la política que sus homólogos soviéticos, habrían escogido a Pienaar para representar el espécimen ideal de la virilidad afrikaner. Con 1,92 metros de altura, llevaba sus 120 kilos de músculo con la gracilidad escultural del David de Miguel Ángel.

Si además, como decía Mandela, se tenía en cuenta su origen, uno se imaginaba a un niño que había crecido hasta hacerse adulto en Vereeniging en los años setenta y ochenta y veía, casi con claridad cinematográfica —como hizo Mandela—, una fiel representación del 90 % de los *volk* afrikaner: unos hombres condicionados por el periodo y el lugar en el que les había tocado nacer, que les obligaba a ser unos individuos francos, sencillos, trabajadores, duros, secretamente sentimentales, devotos y fanáticos del rugby, que se relacionaban con sus numerosísimos vecinos negros con una mezcla de desdén, ignorancia y miedo.

Ahora bien, si había algo que Mandela había aprendido en sus tratos con los afrikaners era que no había que fiarse de las apariencias. «No me pareció en absoluto el producto típico de la sociedad del apartheid —decía Mandela—. Le encontré muy simpático y tuve la sensación de que era progresista. Y había estudiado. Era licenciado en Derecho. Era un placer sentarse a charlar con él.»

El placer era lo último en la cabeza de Pienaar el 17 de junio de 1994, mientras se detenía en las escaleras de piedra de los inmensos Union Buildings y se disponía a entrar para asistir a una reunión a la que le había invitado el presidente Mandela. Pienaar, que tenía en aquel momento veintisiete años pero de pronto se sintió mucho más joven, confesó a los periodistas presentes que no había estado tan nervioso en toda su vida; que la perspectiva de entrevistarse con el presidente era más aterradora que cualquier partido de rugby.

Vestido con traje oscuro y corbata, Pienaar entró por una pequeña puerta situada en el ala oeste de los edificios, pasó por un detector de metales y se presentó ante dos policías que le aguardaban en una mesa tras una ventana de cristal verde a prueba de balas. Ambos eran afrikaners y en seguida comenzaron una animada conversación sobre rugby con él. Uno de ellos le llevó a un patio y por un pasillo decorado —aunque apenas se dio cuenta de la anomalía— con acuarelas de escenas de la Gran Marcha, carros de bueyes y hombres a caballo sobre un fondo de *veldt* pardo y amarillento. El policía le dejó en una pequeña sala de espera, desnuda salvo por unos sillones de cuero, en la que entró la ayudante personal de Mandela, una mujer negra, alta e imponente, llamada Mary Mxadana, que le pidió que se sentara y esperase un momento. Permaneció solo durante cinco minutos; las manos le sudaban. «Estaba increíblemente tenso a medida que se acercaba el momento de conocerle —recordaba—. Me sentía verdaderamente intimidado por él. No dejaba de pensar: "¿Qué digo? ¿Qué le pregunto?"»

Entonces volvió Mxadana, le preguntó si quería té o café —él dijo que café— y le pidió que la acompañara. Salió de la sala de espera al pasillo con los cuadros de las carretas, se detuvo ante una puerta alta de color marrón oscuro, llamó con un golpe seco y entró. Mantuvo la puerta abierta para Pienaar, cuyo miedo escénico no hizo más que empeorar al ver la amplia sala, que le pareció tremendamente vacía hasta que cruzó el umbral y vio, a la derecha, a un hombre alto y de pelo gris que se levantaba de un salto. Mandela tenía setenta y seis años pero se acercó a Pienaar con la rapidez de un rival de rugby que fuera a hacerle un placaje; la única diferencia era que él estaba erguido, tenía una gran sonrisa y la mano tendida. «¡Ah, François, qué bien que haya venido!» Pienaar musitó: «No, señor presidente, muchas gracias por invitarme.» Mandela le dio la mano de manera efusiva y Pienaar advirtió, para su sorpresa, que el presidente era casi tan alto como él. «¿Y cómo está, François?» «Oh, muy bien, señor presidente, ¿y usted?» «Ah, muy bien. ¡Muuuy bien!»

Mandela, sin dejar de sonreír, claramente contento de tener a ese joven bóer grandullón en su nuevo despacho, le hizo ademán de que se sentara en un sofá situado en ángulo recto con el suyo y le felicitó por la victoria de los Springboks contra Inglaterra, un convincente 27-9, en un partido celebrado en Ciudad del Cabo seis días antes.

Llamaron a la puerta y apareció una señora con una bandeja de té y café. Era una mujer blanca, de mediana edad, que llevaba un vestido de flores con hombreras. Mandela la vio aparecer en la puerta, al otro lado de la habitación —una distancia seis veces mayor que la celda que había sido su hogar durante dieciocho años— e inmediatamente se puso de pie, y de pie permaneció mientras ella colocaba la bandeja en una mesita entre los dos hombres. «Ah, muchas gracias. Muchas gracias —sonrió Mandela, aún de pie—. Ah, y éste es François Pienaar... Lenoy Coetzee.» Pienaar le dio la mano a la mujer y, antes de que ella se fuera, Mandela volvió a darle las gracias; no se sentó hasta que la afrikaner salió de la sala.

Pienaar contempló el despacho, grande y revestido en madera, y notó vagamente una decoración mezcla de la vieja y la nueva Sudáfrica; acuarelas de carretas junto a escudos de cuero y esculturas africanas de madera. Mandela le interrumpió: «¿Quiere leche, con su café, François?»

En menos de cinco minutos, el humor de Pienaar se había transformado. «No es sólo que uno se sienta cómodo en su presencia —recordaba Pienaar—. Tienes la sensación, cuando estás con él, de sentirte seguro.» Tan a salvo que Pienaar tuvo la osadía de preguntarle, medio en broma, si iba a acompañar a los Springboks en una gira a Nueva Zelanda el mes siguiente. «¡Nada me gustaría más, François! —sonrió—. ¡Pero, por desgracia, tengo gente en este edificio que me hace trabajar muchísimo, y sé que ellos ordenarán que me quede y trabaje!»

Para alivio de Pienaar, a partir de ese momento, Mandela se hizo cargo y se lanzó a una serie de recuerdos e historias que hicieron sentirse al jugador, en palabras suyas, como un niño pequeño sentado a los pies de un sabio anciano. Una de las historias hablaba del robo de unos pollos en Qunu, la aldea del Transkei en la que Mandela se había criado y a la que todavía regresaba a cumplir sus deberes tradicionales de jefe. Un día, cuando estaba allí Mandela, una mujer se acercó a su casa para decirle que un vecino le había robado sus pollos. Según lo relataba Pienaar: «Mandela convocó al vecino, que confesó que lo había hecho, pero sólo porque su familia estaba hambrienta. Entonces, Mandela llamó a los dos a su casa y dictó que el hombre tenía que pagarle a la mujer dos pollos. Pero ella discutió, negoció, porque quería más, y acordaron una cantidad mayor. Sin embargo, eso era demasiado para el hombre, así que Mandela le ayudó a pagarlo.»

Mandela se reía mientras contaba la anécdota, una historia curiosa para contarle al capitán Springbok en una reunión que había convocado con el claro propósito de forjar una relación con él para prepararse para la Copa del Mundo de rugby del año siguiente. Era una historia especialmente ligera e insustancial dada la solemnidad del entorno, un despacho en el que, como había dicho Mandela en una entrevista unos días antes, «se fraguaron los planes más diabólicos». Pero la historia de los pollos robados fue útil, porque ayudó a crear precisamente el tipo de intimidad y complicidad que el presidente quería establecer con el joven. Al contarle lo que era una especie de confidencia privada, una historia que Pienaar no podía leer en los periódicos, Mande-

la encontró una forma de llegar al corazón del abrumado capitán de rugby, de hacerle sentir como si estuviera
en compañía de su tío abuelo favorito. Pienaar no podía
saberlo entonces pero, para Mandela, ganarse su confianza —y, a través de él, conquistar al resto del equipo
Springbok— era un objetivo importante. Porque lo que
Mandela había deducido, con ese estilo medio instinti-
vo y medio calculador que tenía, era que la Copa del
Mundo podía ayudar a afrontar el gran reto de la unificación nacional que aún quedaba por hacer.

Mandela nunca dijo claramente cuál era su propósito en aquella primera reunión con Pienaar, pero sí se
aproximó al tema cuando empezó a hablar sobre sus recuerdos de los Juegos Olímpicos de Barcelona, a los que
había asistido en 1992 y que evocaba con gran entusiasmo. «Habló del poder que tenía el deporte para emocio-
nar a la gente y cómo lo había comprobado poco después de su liberación en los Juegos de Barcelona, que recordaba en especial por un momento concreto en el que,
contaba, se puso de pie y sintió cómo retumbaba todo el
estadio», contaba después Pienaar. La intención de Mandela era plantar en su mente las primeras semillas de una
idea política; Pienaar no se dio cuenta de que eso era lo
que estaba pasando, pero, en la versión que contaba
Mandela después, junto a toda la calidez del encuentro,
el mensaje subliminal estaba clarísimo.

«François Pienaar era el capitán de rugby y, si yo
quería utilizar el rugby, tenía que contar con él —explicaba Mandela—. En nuestra reunión me concentré en
felicitarle por el papel que desempeñaba y podía desempeñar. Y le conté lo que estaba haciendo a propósito del deporte y por qué. Me pareció una persona muy
inteligente.» Había llegado el momento, explicó Mande-

la a su invitado, de abandonar la vieja percepción del equipo de rugby de los Springboks como los «enemigos» y considerarlos compatriotas y amigos. Su mensaje fue: «Vamos a usar el deporte para la construcción nacional y para promover todas las ideas que creemos que conducirán a la paz y la estabilidad en nuestro país.»

Pienaar había pasado a ser otro más de los afrikaners «envueltos» —como decía él— en el aura de Mandela; pero no se convirtió en apóstol de la noche a la mañana. Era un hombre dedicado en cuerpo y alma al rugby para el que las palabras grandilocuentes como «construcción nacional» significaban poca cosa. El mensaje que se llevó de la reunión estaba muy claro: sal a ganar, lleva esa camiseta con orgullo, no tengas duda de que yo te apoyo. Mandela se despidió de Pienaar como si fueran ya íntimos amigos.

Mandela volvió a su trabajo y Pienaar al suyo, sin que ninguno de los dos advirtiera la extraordinaria semejanza entre las tareas que les aguardaban. Pienaar, recién llegado al puesto de capitán, visto con ciertas reservas por un sector de la fraternidad del rugby que ponía en tela de juicio su carácter y su capacidad, tenía un trabajo difícil: consolidar su autoridad y unir a la selección de rugby. Para ello era necesaria una buena dosis de habilidad política, porque los Springboks eran hombres grandes con grandes egos, que procedían de equipos de provincias y estaban acostumbrados a verse unos a otros como feroces enemigos en la gran competición nacional, la liga sudafricana, la Currie Cup.

La división entre afrikaners e ingleses era otro inconveniente. Una prueba inmediata de la capacidad de liderazgo de Pienaar fue su forma de manejar a James Small, uno de los «ingleses» de más talento en el rugby sudafricano. Small, un jugador relativamente bajo y menudo, de 1,80 metros y 100 kilos de peso, era uno de los corredores más rápidos del equipo y uno de los caracteres más volátiles. La alegría de Pienaar por haber vencido a Inglaterra la semana antes de conocer a Mandela se había visto empañada por una cosa que le había dicho Small en el terreno de juego durante el partido. Un desliz de Small había hecho que concedieran un penalti a Inglaterra. Pienaar le regañó con un brusco «¡Pero hombre, James!», a lo que Small replicó: «¡Vete a la mierda!» Pienaar se quedó asombrado. En otros deportes, el papel del capitán, muchas veces, es meramente simbólico o ceremonial, pero en el rugby tiene auténtico peso. El capitán no sólo ejerce mucha autoridad táctica durante un encuentro, ordenando jugadas que, por ejemplo, en el fútbol, indican los entrenadores desde las bandas, sino que, por tradición, tiene un gran componente místico. Se supone que el resto del equipo le trata con un respeto similar al de los alumnos de un colegio por el director o el de los soldados por su oficial al mando. El «vete a la mierda» de Small era un acto de insubordinación tan grave que, de haberlo dejado pasar, podía haber acabado erosionando la influencia de Pienaar con todo el equipo. Después del partido, François, que era mucho más alto que Small, se lo llevó aparte y le dijo con firmeza que nunca, nunca, debía volver a hablarle de esa forma en el campo. Small tenía fama de participar en peleas de bares y era más agresivo que Pienaar, pero comprendió a la perfección lo que le decía su capitán. Nunca volvió a increparlo.

Sudáfrica estaba compensando los años perdidos por el aislamiento con una repentina avalancha de partidos internacionales, y viajó a Nueva Zelanda por primera vez en trece años en julio de 1994; perdió por la mínima un partido y empató otro contra los All Blacks neozelandeses, considerados por todos los favoritos para la Copa del Mundo del año siguiente. En octubre, los Springboks jugaron dos partidos en casa contra Argentina, otra selección fuerte, y ganaron ambos. Small fue la estrella del segundo encuentro, pero las celebraciones de esa noche acabaron con él en otra pelea de borrachos. El incidente, que comenzó cuando una mujer en un bar pellizcó el trasero del jugador, recibió gran cobertura en los medios. Le prohibieron que fuera a una gira por Gran Bretaña el mes siguiente, en la que los sudafricanos derrotaron de forma convincente a Escocia y Gales e intimidaron a todos los que les vieron con la implacable ferocidad de su juego.

Los Springboks estaban ya centrados en una sola cosa. Lo único que les preocupaba era la Copa del Mundo, que iba a comenzar a finales de mayo del año siguiente. Ni Pienaar, ni Small, ni ningún otro jugador prestaba la menor atención a la política sudafricana, en la que estaban sucediendo muchas cosas.

Noviembre de 1994 había sido el mes de mayor incertidumbre del medio año que llevaba Mandela en el poder. Había dejado en manos de sus ministros la dura tarea de proporcionar viviendas y servicios públicos a aquellos a los que el apartheid había negado deliberadamente los elementos básicos de una vida moderna digna. Él tenía que trabajar para convertirse en el padre de toda la nación, hacer que todo el mundo tuviera el sentimiento de que él simbolizaba su identidad y sus valores. Ése era el motivo por el que una parte de él siempre observaba con cautela a los miembros más recalcitrantes de la nueva familia que estaba tratando de crear, la derecha afrikaner. Y eso significaba preocuparse también por la policía. Mandela estaba bastante tranquilo respecto a la Fuerza Sudafricana de Defensa, a cuyos generales afrikaner se habían unido, en las altas instancias, antiguos jefes de Umkhonto we Sizwe. Los generales de la FSAD eran disciplinados. La policía era más incontrolable, y casi todos los mandos de la era del apartheid continuaban en sus puestos. Los servicios de inteligencia del gobierno, hasta entonces utilizados para vigilar a la izquierda, habían empezado a concentrar sus energías en ese 50 % de los antiguos partidarios del general Viljoen que no había participado en las elecciones de abril y de cuyas filas descontentas habían surgido los terroristas que colocaron las bombas antes de los comicios.

La sensación predominante entre los sudafricanos blancos, tras la toma de posesión de Mandela, era de alivio. El apocalipsis se había ido por donde había venido y la vida seguía como siempre. No se habían erigido las guillotinas y los funcionarios, en general, seguían en sus puestos. Pero los blancos no se libraron de su mezcla inherente de culpa y miedo de la noche a la mañana. Empezó a preocuparles si aquello no sería la calma antes de la tormenta, si podía haber un cambio repentino de política sobre los puestos en la administración para los blancos, precipitados por el inevitable clamor que esperaban oír entre los negros exigiendo una gratificación económica inmediata. Como muestra de hasta qué punto los blancos seguían subestimando la inteligencia de sus vecinos negros, empezaron a circular historias sobre «chicas de la limpieza» y «chicos del jardín» negros que entraban en los cuartos de estar de sus «señoras» y sus «señores» y les exigían las llaves de sus hogares.

En realidad, los sudafricanos negros eran, en su mayor parte, suficientemente astutos y pacientes para saber que Roma no se construiría en un día. Confiaban en que su gobierno acabaría por cumplir sus promesas, pero eran conscientes de que arrojar a los blancos al mar no era bueno para nadie. Por eso habían votado por el CNA, y no por el CPA.

La generosidad que había supuesto esa elección se escapaba a la comprensión de un gran sector de la población blanca, entre la que pocos miembros tenían la menor idea de lo que pensaban los negros. El general Viljoen, el político accidental, también seguía preocupado, todavía con dudas sobre si había hecho bien, desde el punto de vista de su gente, al abandonar la opción del *Boerestaat* y sumarse a la buena fe del CNA de Mandela. Le inquietaban también las posibilidades de violencia que podían representar sus antiguos aliados, fuertemente armados y, en algunos casos, no del todo en su sano juicio. Mandela, que hablaba de estas cuestiones con Viljoen, con quien tomaba el té de forma habitual, vio sus temores confirmados la noche del 5 de noviembre.

Ese día, los Springboks habían aniquilado a un equipo galés con tal estilo y tanta pasión que el entrenador, Kitch Christie, proclamó convencido que podían ganar la Copa del Mundo. Seguramente, Johan Heyns, como otros muchos afrikaners, se había formado la misma opinión. Pero no vivió para verlo. Esa noche, cuando estaba sentado en su casa de Pretoria, jugando a las cartas con su mujer y sus dos nietos, de ocho y once años, le mataron de un disparo. Un pistolero le asesinó desde el exterior de un balazo en la nuca.

El profesor Johan Heyns, que tenía sesenta y seis años, había sido un pilar del sistema del apartheid en su cargo de moderador de la Iglesia Reformada Holandesa entre 1986 y 1990. Pero también había sido un motor del cambio político y había puesto fin a treinta años de conflicto con Braam Viljoen y el pequeño grupo de teólogos disidentes que pensaban como él, al reconocer que era un error creer que el apartheid tenía su justificación en la Biblia. Eso fue en 1986. Su última acción como jefe de la mayor Iglesia afrikaner había sido atreverse a declarar en 1990, poco después de que Mandela saliera en libertad, que el apartheid era un pecado. Había vivido su propia conversión durante una estancia prolongada en Europa a principios de los años ochenta. «Me había educado en la idea de que los negros eran culturalmente inferiores a los blancos —confesó en una ocasión Heyns—. El contacto con negros de gran nivel académico en Europa tuvo un profundo efecto sobre mí.»

En 1990, cuando empezaban a sentirse los primeros espasmos de la resistencia de la derecha, Heyns dijo: «Lo que estamos experimentando ahora son los dolores de parto de la nueva nación. Y no tengo duda de que la nueva nación nacerá. Pero el nacimiento suele ir acompañado de dolor, e incluso de muerte.»

El asesinato de Heyns no podía compararse al de Chris Hani en cuanto a los peligros inmediatos que representaba, pero sí llenó a la gente de aprensión. ¿Quién lo había hecho y quién podía ser el próximo? ¿Podía haber sido un antiguo miembro de la vieja policía o de los escuadrones de la muerte del ejército? Desde luego, había sido un trabajo de profesional. El arma asesina era un fusil de gran calibre, disparado a través de una ventana, desde unos siete metros de distancia. Nadie dudaba de que había sido un acto de la extrema derecha. Pero nadie sabía quién lo había hecho, ni por qué.

Mandela estaba indignado. Heyns, con quien se había reunido en muchas ocasiones, era el tipo de afrikaner que más le gustaba. Moral y físicamente valiente, honrado hasta la médula, había tenido el valor, ya mayor, de reconocer que se había equivocado. Mandela lamentó su «pérdida para la nación sudafricana en su conjunto, tanto negra como blanca». Pero luego, tres días después de la muerte de Heyns, pasó a la ofensiva. Anunció enérgicas medidas contra la extrema derecha y acusó al gobierno anterior de no haber hecho en absoluto lo suficiente para disipar la amenaza de los extremistas. Y empezó esas medidas por la policía, entre cuyas filas sospechaba que había connivencia con los asesinos de Heyns, además de una falta de voluntad de descubrir verdaderamente a los culpables. Hasta ese momento, Mandela había andado con pies de plomo en sus relaciones con la policía. No había querido hacer lo que le pedía su instinto, que era cortar las cabezas más altas. Ahora lo hizo.

Uno de los hombres que permanecía en su puesto, seis meses después de que Mandela asumiera la presidencia, era el jefe supremo de la policía del país, el comisario Johan van der Merwe, un antiguo jefe de la Policía de Seguridad que había sido sospechoso de complicidad en operaciones sucias contra el CNA, incluidos asesinatos. Mandela estaba dispuesto a tragar muchas cosas en nombre de la paz e incluso había nombrado al líder de Inkatha, Mangosuthu Buthelezi, ministro del Interior. Pero la muerte de Heyns agotó su paciencia. «No podemos consentir que se desarrolle una fuerza de policía en oposición al gobierno», afirmó, e inclusó llegó a acusar a sectores de la policía de «declarar la guerra» al CNA. Destacó personalmente a Van der Merwe y le acusó de no apoyar al gobierno democrático. Unos días después, hizo realidad sus amenazas y lo destituyó.

Dos meses después, Mandela, que esperaba alguna reacción en contra, recibió informes sobre lo que parecía una conspiración seria contra su gobierno. «Descubrí que entre la derecha existía un plan para unirse el Partido de la Libertad Inkatha y atacar juntos al CNA. Entonces fui a Pretoria. Ni siquiera lo dije en el CNA. Fui a Pretoria porque el debate se estaba produciendo allí. Después de verificar y volver a verificar los datos con la gente de los servicios de inteligencia, averigüé que un grupo de derechistas decía: "Vamos a unirnos a Inkatha y atacar al CNA. Naciones Unidas no se inmiscuiría porque serían unos negros contra otros. No se inmiscuirán. Y tenemos que derribar este gobierno porque es un gobierno comunista." Pero otros derechistas decían: "¡No, no podéis hacer eso! Mirad lo que han hecho por el rugby, mirad el rugby internacional que nos han dado."»

El periódico conservador *Rapport* publicó poco después un artículo que confirmaba lo que las fuentes de Mandela le habían dicho a él. La coalición de derechas estaba preparando un plan para matar al rey zulú, con la esperanza de que eso desatara una rebelión negra contra el CNA. Mandela se apresuró a asignar el caso a su gente en los servicios de inteligencia y sus oficiales de policía más leales. Además emprendió una ofensiva política, de nuevo con el rugby como instrumento, como zanahoria. Pero entonces surgió otro problema.

En la dirección del CNA, el partido mayoritario, con gran diferencia, en el gobierno de coalición que presidía Mandela, todos se habían convencido ya de que acoger la Copa del Mundo de rugby en Sudáfrica era algo positivo. Sin embargo, muchos no podían soportar la idea de conservar el nombre de Springbok. Se habían deshecho de la vieja bandera, se habían medio deshecho del viejo himno y no podía permitirse que ese nombre, el tercer gran símbolo del apartheid, siguiera siendo la enseña de un equipo que representaba a la nueva Sudáfrica. Se filtró el rumor de que la ejecutiva nacional del CNA quería cambiar el nombre, y la fraternidad afrikaner del rugby se levantó en armas.

Mandela contó posteriormente que, al principio, había estado de acuerdo en eliminar el nombre de Springbok. Pero las tensiones precipitadas por la muerte de Heyns y el despido de los jefes de policía, más las noticias sobre la conspiración derechista, le hicieron dudar. Tuvo en cuenta la situación general y decidió que debía hacer algo para apaciguar a la agitada derecha.

«Decidí actuar. Hice una declaración. Sugerí que debíamos conservar el nombre de Springbok.»

Un año antes, la dirección del CNA había respondido dócilmente a la reprimenda a propósito del himno, pero esta vez la reacción fue abiertamente rebelde.

«¡Fue increíble! ¡Gente como Arnold Stofile! ¡Empezaron a atacarme! Así que les llamé uno por uno y hablé con ellos. Les expliqué la situación.» Para Mandela, el nombre de Springbok era una cuestión superficial; para personas como Stofile, era algo que llevaban en el corazón, un motivo de mucha indignación acumulada. No podían verle la gracia, como hacía Mandela. Este último telefoneó a Stofile y le pidió que pasara por su casa. «Me gustaría que hablásemos sobre este animal», le dijo.

«No le entiendo», replicó Stofile.

«Ya sabe, este animal del deporte.»

Se entrevistaron al día siguiente y, después de algunos nervios, Stofile, al saber por Mandela que había un problema de seguridad nacional por medio, cedió. «Al final —contó Stofile—, estuvimos de acuerdo en no estar de acuerdo.» Como hicieron los demás rebeldes del rugby del CNA. Mandela había vuelto a imponer su voluntad. El Springbok estaba a salvo, justo a tiempo para la Copa del Mundo.

Capítulo XIII
SERENATA SPRINGBOK

La cuestión, ahora, era saber si los Springboks iban a salvar a Mandela. Él había arriesgado mucho por la gente del rugby, y ahora ellos debían pagarle con la misma moneda. Stofile y otros miembros del Comité Ejecutivo Nacional del CNA aún se resentían al recordar la reacción de las autoridades del rugby, tres años antes, ante su decisión de permitirles volver a jugar partidos internacionales. En el encuentro frente a Australia en 1992, Louis Luyt, presidente de la Unión Sudafricana de Rugby, había animado deliberadamente a la multitud a desobedecer las condiciones impuestas por el CNA, a ondear la vieja bandera y cantar el viejo himno. Luyt, un ex jugador gigantesco, había salido de una relativa pobreza durante su niñez para convertirse en un magnate de los fertilizantes y la cerveza, una persona tremendamente rica. La humildad no era el rasgo más visible de aquel hombre hecho a sí mismo. Tenía sesenta y dos años y era descarado, ruidoso y mandón. Odiaba que alguien le dijera lo que tenía que hacer, y mucho más si ese alguien era negro. De ahí su reacción a las normas que el CNA había tratado de imponerle en 1992.

Pero en ese breve periodo habían cambiado muchas cosas en Sudáfrica, y también había cambiado Luyt. Ablandado gracias a Mandela, como parecía ocurrirles a todos los afrikaners («Se mostró muy simpático, respetuoso y encantador la primera vez que nos vimos», contaba), Luyt había adquirido un nuevo sentido de la responsabilidad política a instancias de las autoridades internacionales de rugby, que no querían que la Copa del Mundo se convirtiese en un desastre mundial por problemas raciales. Ante esa necesidad, Luyt hizo dos nombramientos muy inteligentes. Designó a Edward Griffiths, un ex periodista de mentalidad liberal, como consejero delegado de la federación de rugby, y a Morné du Plessis, el ex capitán Springbok que había ido a ver a Mandela en la Parade de Ciudad del Cabo el día de su liberación, como mánager del equipo para la Copa del Mundo. Griffiths se ganó muchos elogios por la habilidad con la que dirigió las operaciones de la Copa del Mundo, pero su contribución más valiosa y duradera fue el eslogan que inventó para la campaña de los Springboks. «Un equipo, un país» no sólo capturaba la imaginación de los sudafricanos, sino que transmitía el propósito de Mandela a la perfección.

Si Griffiths era el cerebro entre bastidores, Morné du Plessis era el espíritu conductor, con la misión de convertir la teoría en práctica, hacer que el comportamiento del equipo convenciera al país en general, y a la Sudáfrica negra en particular, de que el eslogan no eran palabras huecas. Además, ser mánager significaba muchas otras cosas. El trabajo era distinto del del entrenador, Kitch Christie, que estaba a cargo de todo lo relacionado propiamente con lo deportivo, con lo que ocurría en el terreno de juego, empezando por escoger a los integrantes del equipo. Las tareas de Du Plessis abarcaban todo lo que ocurría fuera del campo, como una especie de administrador: asegurarse de que estuvieran a punto todos los preparativos de viaje, que el equipamiento necesario estuviera a mano, que las cuentas estuvieran pagadas. Pero en este caso, en aquel momento de la historia de Sudáfrica, el cargo tenía un significado mucho mayor. Era para Du Plessis la oportunidad, no sólo de construir un equipo ganador, sino de hacer penitencia por lo que cada vez más consideraba que había sido su gran fallo («Una de las cosas de las que más me arrepiento en mi vida», confesó más tarde), no haber estado a la altura de las circunstancias, cuando era capitán Springbok, y no haber dicho o hecho alguna cosa que hubiera podido ayudar a mejorar la situación de los sudafricanos negros.

Du Plessis pensaba que su nuevo papel no debía limitarse a la logística. Quería que su equipo estuviera en sintonía con la nación, que captara bien la atmósfera política, quería que los jugadores comprendieran que estaban jugando no sólo para la Sudáfrica blanca sino para todo el país. Lo mejor que tenía a su favor era su credibilidad. Aquel gigantón seguía siendo una leyenda entre los sudafricanos blancos, que no habían olvidado su historial como capitán Springbok, en especial el mando y el talento desplegados en una famosa victoria contra el viejo enemigo, Nueva Zelanda, en 1976. El hecho de que Luyt escogiera a Du Plessis impresionó al CNA, porque eran conocidas las tendencias políticas liberales del segundo. No obstante, lo que le aguardaba era una tarea delicada, y él lo sabía. «Comprendí casi de inmediato, al asumir el cargo, con qué facilidad se podía sufrir un traspiés, cómo se podía arruinar todo con un error tonto, si se decía algo equivocado, si se enviaba una mala señal.»

Fue precisamente su deseo de dar con el tono apropiado lo que sugirió a Du Plessis la idea de enseñar a los Springboks a cantar la parte «negra» del nuevo himno nacional, el *Nkosi Sikelele*. Mandela y él tenían una misma misión imposible: convencer a los negros de que ejecutaran un vuelco histórico y apoyaran a los Boks. Mandela estaba realizando la labor que le correspondía dentro del CNA, transmitiendo el mensaje a su gente que «ellos» eran ya «nosotros». Du Plessis, por su parte, instó a sus jugadores a comportarse de forma respetuosa en público. Sabía que las consecuencias podían ser terribles si, antes de cada partido de la Copa del Mundo, la gente veía a los Springboks cantando la letra de *Die Stem* en afrikaans y en inglés con entusiasmo pero no la del *Nkosi Sikelele*. Si ocurría eso, el empeño de Mandela y Du Plessis estaría condenado al fracaso; la noción de «un equipo, un país» sería el hazmerreír de todos. Du Plessis tenía claro lo que había que hacer. Tenía que verse a los jugadores cantando el viejo himno de protesta y liberación. Esa imagen trastocaría la idea convencional de los negros de que los Springboks eran unos patanes afrikaner que cantaban canciones racistas y violentas.

Du Plessis no había hablado de política con ninguno de los jugadores, pero no tenía motivos para creer que fueran otra cosa que los típicos votantes del Partido Nacional, con la ignorancia y los prejuicios que eso entrañaba. «Teníamos a algunos afrikaners de pura cepa, y eso [el *Nkosi Sikelele*] estaba en xhosa, que era la lengua del que, para muchos sudafricanos blancos, había sido el enemigo. Era duro pedir a estos chicos que cantaran una canción que tenía esas connotaciones.» Y era duro enseñarles a pronunciar las palabras en xhosa. En el equipo sólo había dos jugadores que hablaran el idioma. Mark Andrews, de 1,97 metros y 120 kilos de peso, se había criado en la zona rural del Cabo Oriental, la región xhosa, y había tenido contacto con la lengua de Mandela desde que nació. Hennie le Roux, más menudo y más rápido y también de aquella parte del país, hablaba asimismo un poco de xhosa. Los 24 jugadores restantes no tenían ni idea.

Por suerte, Du Plessis tenía una amiga que podía ayudar, una vecina suya en Ciudad del Cabo llamada Anne Munnik. Era una mujer blanca de treinta y tantos años, esbelta, atractiva y llena de vida, de habla inglesa, que se ganaba la vida enseñando xhosa. Había aprendido la lengua de niña, también en la zona del Cabo Oriental, y la había perfeccionado en la Universidad de Ciudad del Cabo, donde ahora daba clases. Se quedó estupefacta cuando Du Plessis le sugirió que diera una clase a los Boks para enseñarles a cantar el *Nkosi Sikelele* y luego, cuando lo pensó un poco, dubitativa sobre el tipo de reacción que podrían tener aquellos bóers gigantescos. Pero Du Plessis insistió y ella, con algunas reservas, aceptó.

Quedaron una tarde de la tercera semana de mayo de 1995 en el hotel de Ciudad del Cabo en el que se alojaba el equipo durante los preparativos para el primer partido de la Copa contra los campeones del mundo, los australianos, para el que faltaban pocos días. Se ordenó a los jugadores que se reunieran después del entrenamiento en lo que habían empezado a llamar la sala del equipo, un espacio anodino en el que bancos y empresas de marketing locales solían celebrar seminarios para su personal, y en el que, en esos días, Kitch Christie adoctrinaba a sus jugadores sobre táctica y estrategia. En esa ocasión, les aguardaban al fondo de la sala Du Plessis y Anne Munnik.

Du Plessis, mucho más alto que la directora del coro, la presentó a los Springboks recién salidos de la ducha como una vieja amiga a la que conocía desde hacía veinte años. Los jugadores reaccionaron como adolescentes. Codazos, guiños, gestos de complicidad. «Cuando Morné dijo que había estado en mi granja varias veces, no hubo más que hablar —recordaba Anne Munnik—. Todo fue "Oh", y "Ah", y risitas, y carcajadas, e insinuaciones, y empezaron a tomarnos el pelo.»

Pero con buena intención. Se calmaron cuando Du Plessis se puso serio y dijo: «Vamos, chicos, si cantáis el himno en voz alta y con orgullo, estaréis dando vida al lema "Un equipo, un país".» Anne Munnik miró boquiabierta el espectáculo. Era aficionada al rugby, pero nada de lo que había visto en televisión la había preparado para el tamaño de aquellos hombres en carne y hueso. Grandes y musculosos, parecían escogidos por un exageradamente entusiasta director de reparto de Hollywood para cubrir 26 papeles de gladiadores romanos. Había visto sus nombres guturales típicos del afrikaans en una lista que le había dado Du Plessis —Kobus Wiese, Balie Swart, Os du Randt, Ruben Kruger, Hannes Strydom, Joost van der Westhuizen, Hennie le Roux— y tenía la sensación de que, desde el punto de vista político, también debían de tener más en común con la extrema derecha que con el CNA, con *Die Stem* que con el *Nkosi Sikelele*. Pero empezó su clase: dio a cada jugador una hoja de papel con la letra de la canción y les hizo leerla, repitiendo las palabras más difíciles e intentando reproducir los sonidos chasqueantes del xhosa, casi imposibles para personas que no los hubieran aprendido desde niños. «Luego, cuando llegó el momento de cantar —contaba, aún sorprendida, años más tarde—, lo hicieron con mucho sentimiento.»

Algunos más que otros. Kobus Wiese, Balie Swart y Hannes Strydom tenían talento natural. Wiese y Strydom medían 1,93 metros y pesaban 125 kilos; Swart media casi ocho centímetros menos, pero era tan ancho como la puerta de un establo. Todos estaban extraordinariamente en forma, como debía ser para jugar el rugby tan brutal por el que eran famosos los Boks. Y les gustaba mucho cantar. Wiese (pronunciado «Vise») era uno de los payasos del equipo y un hombre cuya agudeza mental parecía impropia de su tamaño, pero nadie habría podido acusarlo nunca de ser progresista. La liberación de Mandela había emocionado a Du Plessis, había inspirado a su compañero de equipo Joel Stransky, había supuesto un vuelco para Pienaar, pero a Wiese, según reconocía él mismo, le había dejado frío. Swart era uno de los miembros más discretos del equipo, pero, como era más viejo que la mayoría, y más fornido, exigía e inspiraba respeto. Wiese y Swart eran muy buenos amigos. No sólo eran ambos delanteros, unidos entre sí de forma casi diametral durante los frenéticos amontonamientos humanos que el rugby dignifica con nombres como *ruck*, *maul* y *melé*, sino que cantaban juntos en un coro desde hacía años.

Wiese se asombró al ver con qué rapidez la música del *Nkosi Sikelele*, desde la primera vez que cantó el himno, había eliminado de un plumazo los escrúpulos políticos. «Había oído la canción, por supuesto —contaba—. Había visto en televisión a esas masas enormes de negros desfilando, cantando y bailando por las calles con palos y neumáticos en llamas; les había visto arrojar piedras e incendiar casas. Y siempre se oía el *Nkosi Sikelele iAfrika* de fondo. Para mí, y prácticamente para todos los que conocía, el himno era sinónimo de *swart gevaar*, el peligro negro. Pero el caso es que me gusta mucho cantar. Siempre me ha gustado. Y de pronto descubrí, para mi asombro, que estaba atrapado en el canto, que era una melodía preciosa.»

Os du Randt, el más joven del equipo con veintidós años, pero el más pesado, con 1,88 metros y 130 kilos, cantaba con timidez, como si no quisiera que lo vieran. Llamado «el Buey», había servido en el ejército en un regimiento de carros de combate, aunque era un misterio para todos cómo había conseguido meterse en un vehículo tan cerrado. Ruben Kruger, de 1,85 y sólo 112 kilos, era uno de los jugadores más menudos en la delantera, pero fuerte como un ñu, con unos músculos cultivados desde muy pequeño en un negocio familiar en el que su principal ocupación era acarrear grandes sacos de patatas sobre los hombros. Pienaar, como siempre, trató de dar ejemplo y se unió lleno de buena voluntad, pero le costaba muchísimo la pronunciación de las palabras y tenía la canción en sí mucho menos presente —«pocos de nosotros conocíamos ni siquiera la melodía, la verdad»— que Wiese, con toda su falta de progresismo.

Wiese, Swart, Kruger, Pienaar, Du Randt y Mark Andrews eran algunas de las estrellas en el «pack» de la delantera. Los jugadores que ocupaban las veloces posiciones de «tres cuartos» casi parecían, a primera vista, pertenecer a una especie diferente. A Anne Munnik le llamó la atención el contraste. No sólo tenían un tamaño más normal, sino que sus rostros eran menos temibles, sus narices estaban menos torcidas y sus orejas no estaban deformadas por horas y horas de frotarlas contra gruesos muslos peludos en la sudorosa y jadeante fábrica de carne de las melés. Eran los galanes de los Springboks, los David Beckham del rugby.

James Small, que, cuando no jugaba al rugby, era modelo, era el chico malo, el que había estado proscrito de la gira del año anterior por Gran Bretaña después de una pelea de bar. Sin embargo, Munnik advirtió que nadie cantaba la canción con tanto sentimiento como él. «Estuvo todo el tiempo a punto de llorar», decía. Al sudafricano corriente aficionado al rugby, conocedor de sus líos fuera del terreno de juego, le habría resultado difícil creerlo, pero a sus compañeros de equipo, no. Todos los que le conocían tenían la sensación de que vivía al límite, de que, si no hubiera sido por la válvula de escape que el rugby proporcionaba a sus emociones desmesuradas, su personalidad descontrolada y violenta habría podido enviarle detrás de las rejas. Él era el primero en decirlo. «Soy muy afortunado —explicaba—. Yo era un tipo duro, podía haber acabado en la cárcel. Iba a los clubes más siniestros de Johanesburgo por la noche. Muy fácilmente podría haber acabado recibiendo un disparo.»

Pero había otro motivo por el que se emocionó tanto cuando empezó a cantar el viejo himno negro. Él sabía lo que significaba vivir marginado. El apartheid también existía en el rugby, entre los blancos. «Sé lo que es estar en la parte perdedora —decía—. Yo era un inglés que practicaba un deporte de holandeses. Cuando empezé a nivel provincial, los jugadores afrikaners me hacían muchas faenas. Tanto mi equipo como los rivales me hacían sentir que no era bienvenido. Algunos jugadores de mi propio equipo trataban de que seleccionaran a sus compañeros afrikaner antes que a mí. Me hacían el vacío, y recibí muchas palizas. Cuando me seleccionaron para los Springboks, al principio, me hicieron tanto daño que mi padre quiso denunciarlo a la policía. Lo que querían dejar claro es que éste era un deporte de afrikaners, y no había sitio para un inglés. El inglés era un intruso.» Ésa era precisamente la opinión que había tenido Pienaar de «los ingleses» cuando era adolescente, como lo demuestra el orgullo que sentía de que su equipo nunca hubiera perdido contra otro de un colegio «inglés». «Pero usé todo eso como estímulo —decía Small—, y, al final, me salí con la mía. Me convertí en un Springbok. Toda aquella experiencia me enseñó a valorar al de fuera, a simpatizar con quienes no habían tenido, en mi país, las oportunidades que yo había tenido.»

Un afrikaner que nunca mostró a Small más que amabilidad y respeto era Morné du Plessis. Su influencia también se vio en la reacción de Small cuando tuvo que aprender el himno negro. «Veía las cosas de forma muy distinta que un año antes. A medida que nos acercábamos a las elecciones de 1994, me dejé arrastrar por el miedo que tenían muchos blancos de que fuera a haber caos, violencia, venganza. Por eso compré un arma por primera vez en mi vida. Tenía miedo. Y, sin embargo, un año después... ¡estaba cantando el *Nkosi Sikelele*! Pero no habría sido posible sin Morné. Él fue el que nos convenció de que debíamos representar a Sudáfrica como colectivo, que teníamos que comprender de verdad lo que significaba ser sudafricano en una Sudáfrica que no tenía más que un año de edad. Fue gracias a él como entendí que aprender el *Nkosi Sikelele* era parte de eso.»

Chester Williams no se sintió tan conmovido como Small por el canto de liberación. Como Small, Williams era un jugador fornido y rápido que jugaba en el ala. A diferencia de Small, era un hombre discreto, cuya timidez le hacía parecer frío. Williams era el único jugador no blanco en el equipo, pero eso no quería decir que tuviera más facilidad que Small para el xhosa o el zulú. Era un «mestizo», según las normas de la Ley de Inscripción de la Población, difunta desde hacía poco. Los «mestizos» —o, como decía la apelación políticamente correcta, «los llamados mestizos»— eran el subgrupo menos comprometido políticamente de los cuatro principales del apartheid; los otros eran negros, blancos e indios. Como eran una mezcla de razas, también eran los que contenían más diversidad física. En su mayoría coincidían más con la idea habitual del negro africano que con el blanco europeo, pero el grupo étnico al que los mestizos solían sentirse más próximos eran los afrikaners, sobre todo porque en casa hablaban la misma lengua que ellos. A esa categoría general pertenecía Chester Williams: de aspecto africano, de lengua afrikaans, apolítico.

No es que los afrikaners mostrasen ningún respeto especial por los mestizos. La esposa de F. W. de Klerk, Marike, hizo unas celebradas declaraciones sobre los «mestizos» en 1983 que le pasaron factura más tarde, cuando su marido trataba de asumir cierto grado de respetabilidad «no racial». «Son un grupo negativo, ¿sabe?

—había dicho la futura primera dama—. La definición de mestizo en el registro de la población es alguien que no es negro, no es blanco y no es indio, en otras palabras, una no persona. Son los restos. Son la gente que quedó cuando se repartieron las naciones. Son los demás.»

La evolución en el trato que recibía Williams de sus compañeros Springboks entre el momento de incorporarse al equipo, en 1993 —el año en el que se formó el Volksfront—, y la Copa del Mundo, dos años más tarde, fue un reflejo del cambio radical en la relación de la gente blanca en general, y los afrikaners en particular, con sus compatriotas de piel oscura. «Fue una época difícil para mí —decía Williams, hablando de sus primeros días como Springbok—. La gente no me aceptó. Yo intentaba entablar conversación, pero me dejaban solo.»

En un libro coescrito por él, Williams fue más lejos y llegó a afirmar que James Small, entre otros, le llamaba *kaffir* y sugería que estaba en el equipo, no por mérito, sino porque era «el negro simbólico». Small se sintió herido por esas afirmaciones, y Williams, hasta cierto punto, se desdijo. Según Small, Williams se disculpó posteriormente delante de todo el equipo y ambos hicieron las paces. En una entrevista realizada poco después de que hubiera pasado la tormenta, Williams pareció un poco avergonzado por algunas de las cosas que aparecían en el libro y reconoció que quizá había habido algunas exageraciones. Pero insistió en que se había sentido discriminado. «Sólo con el paso del tiempo vi que la gente cambiaba, que cada vez me aceptaban más; en 1995, ya me habían aceptado por completo como miembro del equipo, por mis propios méritos.»

El equipo, en cierto modo, tenía poca elección,

puesto que los responsables de márketing del rugby sudafricano habían escogido a Chester Williams como el
rostro evocador de la Nación Arcoiris en el torneo. Para
él era una situación extraña, dado su carácter retraído,
pero, para su asombro y el de sus compañeros, cada vez
que iban a algún lugar del país, su rostro les contemplaba desde enormes carteles publicitarios. También debía
de ser un poco confuso, y no totalmente convincente,
para los sudafricanos negros, no sólo porque Williams
era «mestizo» (gustara o no, y al CNA no le gustaba, las
etiquetas, muchas veces, seguían existiendo), sino porque era sargento en la Fuerza Sudafricana de Defensa,
una institución en la que había servido durante el
apartheid. Williams, cuya relación con los negros había
sido mínima, cuyas lenguas no hablaba, seguramente
entendió esa reacción mejor que la gente de márketing,
cuyas ideas tenían más impacto entre los blancos que
entre los negros, entre los visitantes extranjeros que entre los sudafricanos en general. En una subasta llevada a
cabo a principios de mayo, Williams miró asombrado
cómo un retrato de él se vendía por lo que entonces
equivaldría a 5.000 dólares. Sudáfrica estaba vendiendo
al mundo una imagen de sí misma que el mundo quería comprar.

El sueño que había tenido Joel Stransky al ver en un bar
francés, por televisión, la salida en libertad de Mandela,
de que el mundo volviera a aceptar a Sudáfrica, se había
hecho realidad e incluso se había visto superado. No
sólo iba a jugar al rugby por su país, sino que lo iba a
hacer en una Copa del Mundo. E iba a ocupar el puesto fundamental de medio apertura, que, en su caso, in-

cluía también la enorme responsabilidad de lanzar los penaltis, de los que tantas veces dependía el resultado de los grandes encuentros. Para sus obligaciones necesitaba nervios de acero además de una gran audacia física, porque, con 1,75 metros de altura y 95 kilos de peso, tenía que soportar las cargas más brutales de hombres mucho más voluminosos que él. Sin embargo, al empezar la clase de canto, estaba nervioso y habría preferido estar en otro sitio. «Soy una de esas personas que odian cantar —explicaba—. Es casi una fobia.» Pero se sorprendió a sí mismo. «Todos sabíamos el contenido político de aquella canción, y habíamos oído hablar mucho de ella y, de pronto, allí estaba, aprendiendo la letra, y era algo verdaderamente especial.»

Hennie le Roux, uno de los miembros más serios del grupo e íntimo amigo de François Pienaar, se dedicó con gran aplicación a las lecciones de Anne Munnik. Con un gran talento para correr sorteando al contrario y el más versátil de los tres cuartos del equipo, Le Roux era tan poco político como los demás, pero tenía ya muy clara la necesidad nacional de aprender el *Nkosi Sikelele*. Lo había comprendido, como otros Springboks, a su llegada al hotel de Ciudad del Cabo unos días antes, cuando el personal, en su mayoría negro, salió a recibirles en el vestíbulo. «Nos recibieron cantando, bailando y celebrando, felices de vernos, muy acogedores. Fue algo que no habíamos visto nunca en nuestras carreras, unos negros ahí delante, saludándonos con tanto entusiasmo como el que nos mostraban las muchedumbres de aficionados blancos más enloquecidos. Fue un gran momento para todos nosotros.» James Small lo decía de forma más directa. «Nos miramos entre nosotros y pensamos: "¡Joder, aquí está pasando algo!"» Para Le Roux, ése fue el momento en el que comprendió que tenía que poner algo de su parte. «Si ellos estaban tan dispuestos a estar a nuestro lado, lo menos que podíamos hacer nosotros era un esfuerzo para aprender su canto. El recuerdo de aquellas escenas de nuestra llegada mientras estábamos aprendiendo la canción hizo que me resultara mucho más emocionante.»

Pienaar estaba tan emocionado como su amigo, pero su motivación era todavía más personal. Era el único Springbok que había hablado cara a cara con Mandela y estaba especialmente ansioso de que su equipo proyectase una imagen que agradase al presidente. Pero también pensaba, como hacía siempre con una minuciosidad implacable, que lo que el equipo hiciera fuera del terreno de juego podía mejorar su actuación en él. Y, mientras se oía a sí mismo y a sus compañeros cantando, su cerebro de rugby se puso en marcha. Comprendió que la victoria en un partido de rugby de primera categoría era en un 50 % cuestión de psicología, y vio en la canción un valor deportivo, más allá de la política. «En aquel mismo instante decidí que aquello era una ventaja inesperada que nos había proporcionado Morné; que podía aportarnos algo especial antes de empezar a jugar, si lo respetábamos y sentíamos su energía —explicó después Pienaar, que añadió, sonriendo y meneando la cabeza—: Ahora... es asombroso, si se piensa. ¡Los chicos afrikaners cantando aquel himno!»

Anne Munnik estaba a punto de acabar la clase cuando los tres jugadores más grandes del equipo, Kobus Wiese, Hannes Strydom y Balie Swart, alzaron la mano: ¿podían cantar el himno una vez más, ellos tres solos? «Dije: "¡Por supuesto!" Y empezaron a cantar, como tres niños de coro gigantes, primero en voz baja, subiendo hasta las notas más altas. ¡Lo cantaron de forma tan hermosa! Los demás jugadores se quedaron boquiabiertos. No hubo risas ni bromas. Simplemente los miraron.»

Para los tres gigantes, cantar aquella canción tuvo el poder de una epifanía. «¡Allí se quedó mi inocente ignorancia, hecha añicos! —exclamaba Wiese—. Cuando aprendí la letra de aquel canto, se me abrieron las puertas. Desde entonces, cada vez que oigo a un grupo de negros cantando el *Nkosi Sikelele...*, es deslumbrante, tío. Es precioso.»

Uno podía tener tantas dudas sobre los Springboks como Justice Bekebeke o verlos con tanta generosidad como Mandela, pero cualquier sudafricano negro que hubiera entrado en aquella sala mientras el trío de bóers rompía a cantar también se habría quedado deslumbrado.

Capítulo XIV
SILVERMINE

El 25 de mayo de 1995, los Springboks iban a enfrentarse a los vigentes campeones del mundo, Australia, en el primer partido de la Copa del Mundo en Ciudad del Cabo. El día anterior, el equipo estaba reunido en Silvermine, una vieja base militar dentro de una reserva natural montañosa en la península de El Cabo, donde habían establecido un campo de entrenamiento temporal. Silvermine, situado en la mitad oriental de la estrecha cintura de la península, es uno de los lugares más hermosos de Sudáfrica. Hacia el norte, se ve el simbólico monolito de Table Mountain. Hacia el sur, el extremo rocoso en el que se unen el Océano Índico y el Atlántico. Por todas partes hay acantilados, bosques, valles y el mar.

Los jugadores acababan de terminar una sesión de tarde de entrenamiento cuando levantaron la vista y vieron un gran helicóptero militar que bajaba desde el cielo. Morné du Plessis, al que habían avisado de la visita, se había puesto chaqueta y corbata. Mientras los demás miraban boquiabiertos la máquina voladora que descendía hacia el suelo, les anunció que era Mandela, que venía a verlos. Siguieron mirando cómo salía Mandela del aparato, debajo de la hélice, vestido con una reluciente camisa suelta roja y naranja, con el estilo que se había convertido en la imagen de marca de su presidencia. Se aproximó con una sonrisa hacia los jugadores, y ellos se apelotonaron y empezaron a darse codazos unos a otros como fotógrafos en una rueda de prensa, estirando el cuello para ver mejor.

Mandela hizo varios comentarios casuales que despertaron las risas, y luego Du Plessis pidió silencio para que el presidente pudiera dirigir unas palabras al equipo.

Para su sorpresa, Mandela comenzó abordando los mismos temas serios que solía tocar cuando hablaba con blancos (aquel día, todo su público era blanco, porque Chester Williams estaba ausente, recuperándose de una lesión). Les recordó que el CNA había prometido que el nuevo gobierno iba a mantener al jefe del ejército, el comisario nacional de policía, el gobernador del Banco de la Reserva y el ministro de Finanzas, y que, un año después de las elecciones, el gobierno había cumplido su palabra. Como afrikaners, no tenían nada que temer del CNA. Ni tampoco, añadió Mandela con una sonrisa, de sus rivales del día siguiente.

«Os enfrentáis a los campeones del mundo, Australia. El equipo que gane este partido seguirá hasta la final —predijo, antes de recuperar un tono solemne—. Ahora tenéis la oportunidad de servir a Sudáfrica y unir a nuestro pueblo. En cuestión de mérito, sois iguales a cualquier otro en el mundo. Pero jugáis en casa, y eso os da ventaja. Recordad, todos nosotros, blancos y negros, estamos con vosotros.»

Los jugadores vitorearon y aplaudieron, y luego

Mandela se detuvo a charlar con todos uno por uno. «Me preguntó por qué me había vestido con tanta formalidad para recibirle —recordaba Du Plessis—. Pero lo más asombroso fue la química. Los jugadores se sintieron atraídos hacia él inmediatamente.» Kobus Wiese reconoció: «No puedo recordar por qué nos reíamos, pero recuerdo que nos reímos con Mandela todo el rato que estuvo allí.»

De pronto, Hennie Le Roux, el corpulento centro tres cuartos, decidió ofrecer a Mandela una señal de agradecimiento por haberse molestado en ir a visitarles. Cuando el presidente llegó donde estaba él, le entregó su gorra verde de Springbok y le dijo: «Por favor, tómela, señor presidente, es para usted. —Hizo una pausa y añadió—: Muchas gracias por estar aquí. Significa mucho para el equipo.»

Mandela la cogió, sonrió y dijo: «Muchas gracias. ¡La voy a llevar!» Se puso la gorra allí mismo.

François Pienaar puso el sello a la ceremonia de la montaña con un breve mensaje de despedida a Mandela. Se refirió al partido del día siguiente y declaró: «Hay una persona para la que ahora sabemos que tenemos que jugar, y es el presidente.»

El encuentro de Silvermine redefinió los sentimientos de los Springboks respecto a su presidente y su país. Cuando intentó describir el momento en el que Mandela subió al helicóptero y se alejó, a Du Plessis casi le faltaban las palabras. «Miré a los jugadores mientras contemplaban el helicóptero y estaban como niños, saludando, llenos de... entusiasmo. Aquellos chicos habían visto un millón de helicópteros, pero Mandela... se había ganado sus corazones.»

Y les hizo bien como equipo de rugby. Pienaar había

estado preocupado por la tensión entre sus compañeros de equipo la víspera del comienzo del campeonato. Normalmente, habría tratado de romperla con una canción o una película, pero, en esta ocasión, Mandela lo había hecho por él. Un año antes, Mandela había conseguido que Pienaar se encontrara a gusto en el despacho presidencial. Ahora había hecho lo mismo con el equipo entero. «Relajó a los chicos. Su trato con el equipo fue jovial, siempre sonriente, siempre con pequeñas bromas. Y siempre tiene tiempo para todos. Se detiene a hablar, y aquella vez hizo que los jugadores se sintieran cómodos. Fue una cosa muy especial antes del partido inaugural.»

Mandela tal vez rebajó el estrés de los Springboks, pero no pudo eliminarlo por completo. Hay pocos jugadores que mueran en un campo de rugby, pero, por lo demás, ningún otro deporte es más parecido —por el dolor soportado y la brutalidad de los choques— a la guerra. Los jugadores de rugby dan y reciben golpes tan duros como los de fútbol americano, pero sin cascos, hombreras ni otros elementos de protección. Y el rugby exige mucha más capacidad de resistencia que el fútbol americano. Cada partido de rugby consiste en dos mitades de 40 minutos con un único intermedio de 10 minutos entre ellas y ningún tiempo de descuento salvo en caso de lesiones. Pero el miedo físico no dominaba tanto la mente de los jugadores como el peso de la expectación nacional. En menos de 24 horas iban a enfrentarse a los Wallabies australianos, uno de los cinco equipos con serias posibilidades de ganar la Copa, junto con Francia, Inglaterra, Nueva Zelanda y Sudáfrica. Mandela les había hecho sentirse especiales, pero todavía estaba por ver si los Springboks podían canalizar esa presión a su favor durante el partido o caer aplastados bajo su peso.

También estaba por ver cuánto apoyo iban a dar verdaderamente los negros a los Springboks, hasta qué punto habían triunfado los esfuerzos de Mandela para convencer a su gente de que la vieja camiseta verde y oro ahora era también la suya.

La Unidad de Protección Presidencial era un barómetro tan bueno como cualquier otro para medir el ambiente nacional. Era un grupo de sudafricanos que, la noche antes del partido contra Australia, se fueron a la cama tan tensos como los propios Springboks. Pero por diferentes motivos. «La preocupación por la seguridad en aquel primer partido contra Australia era enorme y las medidas tomadas, muy numerosas», explicaba después Linga Moonsamy, ex guerrillero del CNA y miembro de la UPP desde la toma de posesión de Mandela. «Pasamos semanas preparándonos para aquel día. Examinamos repetidamente cada rascacielos alrededor del estadio. Colocamos francotiradores en las azoteas en puntos estratégicos, pusimos gente en los puntos más débiles dentro del estadio.»

La UPP se sentía unida en su misión pero dividida en dos entre negros y blancos, entre antiguos miembros de Umkhonto we Sizwe, como Moonsamy, y antiguos miembros de la Policía de Seguridad. «Los tipos de Umkhonto y los policías habíamos sido enemigos mortales, literalmente, habíamos querido matarnos mutuamente durante años —contaba Moonsamy—, aunque hay que decir que ellos lo consiguieron mucho más que nosotros.»

Y esa división se extendía al rugby. El hecho de estar acompañando a Mandela un día sí y otro no durante un año había suavizado el aspecto más duro de Moonsamy. Pero todavía no llegaba a apoyar de corazón a los Springboks ni, en realidad, a entender verdaderamente de qué iba el rugby.

«Habían corrido muchos rumores de que la extrema derecha iba a utilizar la competición para preparar un acto terrorista contra la nueva democracia, contra el propio Mandela —recordaba Moonsamy—. Nuestros colegas blancos eran tan conscientes de esa posibilidad como nosotros y estaban tan preparados como nosotros, pero la gran diferencia era que estaban todavía más nerviosos por el resultado del partido. Nosotros les mirábamos, sonreíamos y meneábamos la cabeza. No lo entendíamos.»

Llegado el momento, la preparación de la UPP valió la pena. El partido entre Sudáfrica y Australia se desarrolló sin incidentes. Mandela llegó en helicóptero desde la residencia presidencial en Ciudad del Cabo hasta un edificio alto próximo al estadio. Desde allí se trasladó en un BMW blindado de color gris metalizado con Moonsamy, que aquel día era el guardaespaldas número uno e iba sentado en el asiento del copiloto, delante de él. En medio de toda la emoción, Mandela no había olvidado la gorra de Hennie Le Roux. Se la puso en la ceremonia de inauguración del torneo, donde los 16 equipos que participaban desfilaron en el estadio de Newlands, al lado de 1.500 bailarines (o 1.501, porque el propio Mandela se unió y se puso a brincar), antes de dar paso al partido. Y se la puso cuando salió al campo a dar la mano a los dos equipos, en medio de los cálidos vítores de una muchedumbre abrumadoramente blanca, 50.000 personas, entre las que se veían abundantes banderas sudafricanas nuevas. Siguió con la gorra puesta cuando los Springboks cantaron los dos himnos nacionales con la misma emoción, aunque todavía fuera evidente que se sabían mejor la letra de *Die Stem*.

El partido fue un triunfo para los Springboks. Toda la tensión les había favorecido y, al final, derrotaron a Australia, que llevaba invicta 14 meses, con más comodidad de la que sugería el resultado: 27-18. Joel Stransky fue la estrella del partido, al marcar 22 puntos, 17 de ellos de chut y uno con un ensayo sobre la línea. Cuando el partido estaba acabando, apareció en medio de la multitud una pancarta pintada a toda prisa que decía: «Olvidémonos del rinoceronte. ¡Salvemos al Wallaby!» Los australianos, feroces competidores en todos los deportes que practicaban, aceptaron la derrota con elegancia. «No hay duda de que ha ganado el mejor equipo —dijo Bob Dwyer, su entrenador—. Cualquier otro resultado, si lo hubiéramos logrado colar, habría sido injusto.»

Esa noche, los Springboks lo celebraron como suelen hacerlo los jugadores de rugby, bebiendo hasta las cuatro de la mañana y llevados en hombros por todas partes. A la mañana siguiente, Kitch Christie, el entrenador, no les perdonó la carrera diaria a las nueve, desde el centro de la ciudad hasta la orilla del mar, pero el dolor de la resaca se vio aliviado por todos los transeúntes que les felicitaron por el camino.

Un día después, con las cabezas todavía doloridas, se encontraban en un ferry que se dirigía a Robben Island. Fue una idea de Morné du Plessis, que había visto el enorme impacto que iba a tener el «Un equipo, un país», no sólo por lo positivo que podía ser para la nación, sino por lo que podía beneficiar al equipo.

«Había una relación causa-efecto entre el factor Mandela y nuestra actuación en el campo —decía Du Plessis—. Causa y efecto en mil frentes. En cómo superaban los jugadores la barrera del dolor, en un deseo superior de ganar, en tener la suerte de tu lado porque tú te fabricas tu propia suerte, en todo tipo de detalles mínimos que, juntos o por separado, marcan la diferencia entre ganar y perder. Aquel día todo convergió a la perfección. Nuestro deseo de ser el equipo de la nación y el deseo de Mandela de convertir el equipo en el equipo nacional.»

Robben Island todavía se usaba como cárcel, y todos los presos eran negros o mestizos. Parte de la jornada consistió en conocerlos, pero antes los jugadores vieron, por turnos, la celda en la que Mandela había pasado dieciocho de sus veintisiete años en cautividad. Los jugadores entraron en la celda de uno en uno o de dos en dos; no cabían más. Como acababan de conocer a Mandela, sabían que era un hombre alto como casi todos ellos, aunque no tan corpulento. No hacía falta gran imaginación para comprender los problemas, físicos y psicológicos, de estar tanto tiempo encerrado en un sitio tan pequeño. Pienaar, que había leído algo sobre el pasado de Mandela, sabía también que de aquella celda, o al menos de aquella prisión, era de donde había surgido gran parte de la energía y la planificación del boicot a las giras internacionales de los Springboks. Morné du Plessis hizo una reflexión similar, mucho más intensa aún porque él había sido uno de los jugadores directamente afectados. Steve Tshwete, ahora ministro de Deportes, le había dicho a Du Plessis que en aquellas celdas escuchaban los partidos de los Springboks contra los Lions británicos en 1980, y que los guardias les gritaban a los presos que dejaran de animar a los rivales, pero que ellos seguían. «¿Y sabe qué? —me decía Du Plessis—, mirando aquellas celdas, viendo lo que les hicimos sufrir, yo también habría animado a los Lions.»

Después de la celda de Mandela, los jugadores salieron al patio en el que, en otro tiempo, Mandela había tenido que picar piedra. Allí les esperaba un grupo de presos.

«Estaban felices de vernos —contaba Pienaar—. A pesar de estar encerrados allí, estaban claramente orgullosos de nuestro equipo. Hablé con ellos sobre el sentimiento que teníamos de representar a todo el país, ellos incluidos, y nos cantaron una canción. James Small —nunca lo olvidaré— estaba de pie en un rincón, llorando a lágrima viva. James vivía siempre al límite, y supongo que debió de pensar: "Yo podía haber estado aquí." Es verdad, su vida podía fácilmente haber seguido otro camino. Pero la mía también, ¿eh? —añadió Pienaar, recordando las peleas en las que se había enzarzado de joven, la vez que mató a un hombre—. Yo también podía haber acabado allí.»

Small recordaba el episodio. «Los presos no sólo nos cantaron, sino que nos vitorearon y yo... rompí a llorar —dijo, con los ojos enrojecidos al recordarlo—. Allí fue donde verdaderamente tuve la sensación de que pertenecía a la nueva Sudáfrica y donde comprendí mi responsabilidad como Springbok. Allí estaba, oyendo los aplausos que me daban y, al mismo tiempo, pensando en la celda de Mandela y en que él había pasado veintisiete años en la cárcel y había salido lleno de amor y amistad. Todo aquello me abrumó, fue una iluminación tremenda, y las lágrimas corrieron por mi rostro.»

Capítulo XV
VER PARA CREER

«¡Mis propios seguidores me abuchearon! ¡Me abuchearon cuando les dije: estos chicos son ahora de los nuestros, vamos a apoyarlos! —Mandela fruncía al ceño al recordarlo—. Fue muy difícil...»

Estaba recordando un incidente concreto hacia el final de la Copa del Mundo, una concentración del CNA en el corazón del KwaZulu rural que representó para él las enormes dificultades a las que tenía que hacer frente para convencer a los sudafricanos negros de que apoyaran a los Springboks. Convencerles para que apoyaran un símbolo tan evocador del sufrimiento y las indignidades que había soportado durante tanto tiempo era un ejercicio de persuasión política casi tan inverosímil como el que habían llevado a cabo con Constand Viljoen. Justice Bekebeke, por ejemplo, no iba a ceder fácilmente en este aspecto. Como decía él, «esos afrikaners del rugby eran precisamente los que peor nos trataban. Ésos eran los que nos echaban a patadas de las aceras. Ésos —los blancos matones y grandullones— eran los que nos decían "quítate, *kaffir*"».

Pero sus circunstancias en ese momento, como correspondía al nuevo espíritu imperante en el país, habían cambiado. Después de haber evitado la horca, en mayo de 1995 estaba a punto de obtener su licenciatura en Derecho, a finales de ese año. Estaba de acuerdo con el compromiso histórico que había elaborado Mandela, estaba a favor de que blancos y negros compartieran el gobierno; sin embargo, había un límite.

«Yo era un miembro leal del CNA —explicaba posteriormente—, creía en la filosofía del no al racismo y era admirador de Mandela. El ejemplo que me había dejado Anton Lubowski era una garantía inamovible de que nunca sería racista. Pero los Springboks, el emblema Springbok del que tanto se enorgullecía aquella gente, lo odiaba. Para mí seguía siendo un potente y detestable símbolo del apartheid.»

Ese símbolo fue exactamente lo que los partidarios del CNA en la concentración de KwaZulu vieron ponerse a Mandela sobre la cabeza a mitad de su discurso. Era la gorra Springbok que le había regalado Hennie le Roux. Mandela había llegado al pueblo a celebrar el aniversario del suceso que desencadenó la revolución sudafricana, el día de 1976 en el que los niños de Soweto se alzaron contra sus maestros del apartheid. Sin embargo, le abuchearon.

Al escoger aquel lugar, Ezakheni, para realizar su gesto, Mandela quizá estaba tentando la suerte. Primero porque, como señaló en su discurso aquel día, era en los lugares más atrasados, como Ezakheni, donde la gente había experimentado lo peor del viejo sistema. «Aquí —dijo Mandela— el apartheid dejó comunidades en condiciones que escapan a toda descripción.» Segundo, la violencia que durante una década se había desatado entre los zulúes partidarios del CNA y los zulúes partidarios de Inkatha había continuado a pesar de la llegada del nuevo gobierno, y Mandela tuvo que declarar: «La muerte de zulúes a manos de otros zulúes debe acabar.» Tercero, la muchedumbre odiaba a los granjeros blancos locales, que, en su mayoría, habían simpatizado con Inkatha.

Buthelezi, el líder de Inkatha, era ahora ministro del gobierno de Mandela. La generosidad de este último hacia él era un ejemplo de pragmatismo político llevado al extremo moral. Pero en Ezakheni las heridas seguían abiertas y la confraternización con el enemigo no estaba bien vista. Pedirles que tuvieran cariño a los Springboks era casi una grosería. Sin embargo, eso fue lo que hizo Mandela. «Ved esta gorra que llevo —dijo a su público—, es en honor de nuestros chicos, que juegan contra Francia mañana por la tarde.»

Aquello fue lo que despertó los abucheos de la gente. Y Mandela no lo consintió. «Mirad —les amonestó—, entre vosotros hay líderes. No seáis cortos de miras, no os dejéis llevar por las emociones. La construcción nacional significa que hay que pagar un precio, del mismo modo que los blancos tienen que pagar un precio. En su caso, abrir los deportes a los negros es pagar un precio. Para nosotros, decir que ahora debemos apoyar a la selección de rugby es pagar un precio. Eso es lo que tenemos que hacer. —Mientras los abucheos se callaban poco a poco, prosiguió—: Quiero ver a líderes entre vosotros, hombres y mujeres, que se levanten y promuevan esta idea.»

Cuando Mandela recordaba aquella concentración, hablaba como un cazador de su presa. «Al final —decía con una sonrisa victoriosa—, al final me gané a la gente.» Ya había pasado por ello, ya le había sucedido estar aparentemente a punto de perder a una muchedumbre y ganársela en el último momento. Una vez le había ocurrido en un territorio en el que Inkatha había causado una pérdida terrible de vidas humanas. Ante el comprensible deseo de venganza de la muchedumbre, les pidió que adoptaran una visión más amplia, que «arrojaran sus armas al mar». En otra ocasión, en un distrito negro a las afueras de Johanesburgo llamado Katlehong, en el que Inkatha también había atacado a la población civil, calló a 15.000 personas indignadas por su negativa a darles armas cuando les preguntó si querían que siguiera siendo su líder. Porque, si no hacían lo que les estaba pidiendo, que era el esfuerzo de hacer las paces con individuos que, según él, más que ser malos, estaban equivocados, presentaría su dimisión. La gente no deseaba llegar a eso, y, al terminar su discurso, todos cantaron su nombre y bailaron victoriosos, celebrando el éxito del llamamiento que Mandela había hecho a la parte más sabia de sus naturalezas.

Casi igual de difícil fue convencer a la gente de que los Springboks podían verdaderamente ganar la Copa del Mundo. Todos los expertos estaban de acuerdo en que era una esperanza vana. «Cuando fui a ver a los jugadores en Silvermine y les dije que estaba seguro de que iban a ganar, no quería que luego resultase que me había equivocado —contaba Mandela—. Personalmente, era muy importante para mí, porque sabía que la victoria movilizaría a los incrédulos que, como Santo Tomás, necesitan ver y tocar para creer. ¡Por eso tenía tantas ganas de que Sudáfrica venciera! Sería la recompensa por todo el duro trabajo, todo el recorrer el país, todos los abucheos...»

Hablaba de «duro trabajo» y antes había empleado la palabra «campaña»; prueba de que se había fijado deliberadamente el objetivo de utilizar el rugby como instrumento político. Nicholas Haysom, asesor legal de Mandela en la presidencia, era un antiguo jugador, y aficionado al rugby de toda la vida, que se convirtió en el experto residente en Union Buildings. Haysom decía que Mandela había visto con mucha claridad el instrumento tan poderoso que podía ser la Copa del Mundo para «el imperativo estratégico número uno de sus cinco años de mandato». Pero no era sólo eso. Una vez más, el elemento político y el personal, el cálculo y la espontaneidad, se fundían en uno. «Cuando la Copa del Mundo estaba empezando —recordaba Haysom—, me hablaba de "los chicos", cosas como "los chicos están animados", o "los chicos van a ganar". Al principio, le preguntaba: "¿Qué chicos?" Y él me miraba como si le hubiera hecho una pregunta increíblemente tonta y respondía: "*Mis* chicos", que enseguida entendí que quería decir los Springboks.» Aunque Mandela no empezó la Copa del Mundo como un hombre con un gran conocimiento histórico del rugby, se fue informando y apasionando más a medida que avanzaba el torneo. «Vio la oportunidad política, es verdad, pero no fue un cálculo frío, porque él también se vio arrastrado por el fervor y se convirtió en otro aficionado patriota y enloquecido.»

A la mitad negra del cuerpo de guardaespaldas de Mandela le costó más que a él entrar en el espíritu del campeonato. Aquel primer partido contra Australia, recordaba Moonsamy, había sido una experiencia espeluznante desde el punto de vista de su responsabilidad profesional de mantener al presidente con vida. Pero, desde el punto de vista deportivo, el partido les había dejado indiferentes.

«Cuando sonó el pitido que marcaba el final, los blancos se volvieron locos. Nosotros nos quedamos mirándoles entre risitas, confundidos. No entendíamos el juego, no nos interesaba, no estábamos nada impresionados. Los Springboks eran todavía su equipo, no el nuestro.» Moonsamy contó después que la campaña de Mandela para desdemonizar a los Springboks le había hecho pensar, pero que todavía tenía que pasar de la indiferencia al apoyo claro. Su evolución durante las cuatro semanas de la Copa del Mundo, como la del resto de los miembros negros de la UPP, fue un reflejo del cambio en la relación de los sudafricanos negros con el viejo enemigo verde y oro.

«Cuando los Springboks ganaron su segundo partido, empezamos a sentir un poco de curiosidad —dijo Moonsamy, refiriéndose a un encuentro relativamente fácil contra Rumanía—. El entusiasmo de nuestros colegas blancos nos intrigó sin poderlo remediar, así que empezamos a preguntarles cosas sobre el rugby. Para nuestro asombro, se convirtió en un tema de conversación entre nosotros.» Cada dos semanas, la UPP salía de la ciudad para una sesión de entrenamiento con el fin de refrescar los procedimientos y mantenerse en forma. Practicaban tiro, combate cuerpo a cuerpo y otras habilidades. En la sesión posterior al partido de Australia, un miembro de la unidad blanco y corpulento, llamado Kallis, les enseñó a jugar a rugby sin contacto. Es decir, con menos violencia física, sin la ferocidad habitual en los choques. «A través de aquellas sesiones —contaba

Moonsamy—, los guardaespaldas negros aprendieron los detalles del rugby.»

Se enteraron de que había 15 jugadores en cada equipo; que ocho de ellos eran delanteros y que siete formaban la línea de tres cuartos; que se ganaban cinco puntos por un ensayo, lo cual quería decir apoyar el balón tras cruzar la línea de marca, que se ganaban dos puntos por una transformación —es decir, chutar el balón para pasarlo entre los dos palos—, que se ganaban tres puntos por un penalti entre los palos y tres si se conseguía eso mismo en el transcurso del juego, chutando un «drop», es decir chutando el balón a bote pronto. «Pero, sobre todo, empezamos a entender el sentido del rugby. Jugábamos sin contacto pero entrábamos con fuerza. Así empezamos a comprender el rugby y, de nuevo para nuestro gran asombro, empezó a gustarnos.»

Las imágenes emitidas en la televisión sudafricana el día antes de un partido contra Canadá hicieron pensar a Moonsamy que quizá también tenían que empezar a gustarle a él los Springboks. Todo el equipo había visitado un pequeño distrito negro llamado Zwide, a las afueras de la gran ciudad de Port Elizabeth, en Cabo Oriental. Las escenas de aquellos gigantes blancos charlando y jugando con los niños negros entusiasmados conmovieron a Moonsamy y a cuantos las vieron.

Aproximadamente 300 niños se reunieron en un campo polvoriento para recibir una lección impartida por Morné du Plessis, que separó a los chicos en grupos de 15, aunque fue Mark Andrews quien acaparó toda la atención, porque era inmenso y porque hablaba xhosa. También estaba allí Balie Swart, enseñando a los niños a pasar y mostrando a los atónitos adultos que los bóers grandullones también podían ser amistosos. Esa misma noche, Du Plessis llevó a un grupo de jugadores a un estadio destartalado en el que jugaban los equipos negros locales. Se estaba jugando un partido, y a Du Plessis le pareció que les gustaría que fueran a verlos los Springboks. Así fue, gracias, entre otros, a James Small, cuyo talento y cuya fama hacían que fuera el rostro más reconocible del equipo. Small pasó hora y media firmando autógrafos, tanto a niños como a adultos.

Cuando Sudáfrica venció a Canadá 20-0 en el estadio Boet Erasmus de Port Elizabeth, todo Zwide lo celebró, y también lo celebró Linga Moonsamy. El siguiente partido, un encuentro de cuartos de final contra los duros y brillantes jugadores de Samoa Occidental, unos isleños grandotes y fanáticos del rugby, parecía un reto más difícil. Además, el partido habría podido representar una forma de comprobar las lealtades de los sudafricanos negros, porque Samoa era un equipo de piel oscura al que habrían apoyado en los viejos tiempos. Chester Williams se encargó de ello y estuvo a la altura de lo que, hasta entonces, había parecido una fama un poco inflada; marcó cuatro ensayos, o 20 puntos, en una victoria por 42-14. «Todas las dudas que podía haber tenido sobre mí mismo o el resto del equipo, o que cualquier otra persona podía haber tenido sobre mí, desaparecieron ese día, sin más —recordaba Williams—. Recibí un inmenso apoyo, dentro y fuera del terreno de juego, de François y Morné, y, a partir de entonces, fui para todos un miembro del equipo plenamente aceptado y respetado. La historia dio un vuelco aquel día. El hecho de que no fuera blanco había pasado a ser completamente irrelevante.»

Una semana más tarde se jugó la semifinal, la que

Mandela había mencionado en Ezakheni, contra una de las selecciones que habían partido como favoritas, Francia. El campo iba a ser el estadio King's Park de Durban, donde Pienaar había debutado con los Springboks dos años antes, el mismo día del asalto del Volksfront al World Trade Centre. La atmósfera política en vísperas del partido no podía ser más distinta. Cuando el equipo iba y venía del hotel al entrenamiento, las calles estaban llenas de gente, cada vez con más negros, a medida que pasaban los días. James Small recordaba que «nos mirábamos y pensábamos: ¡Joder!, el presidente Mandela no estaba bromeando; quizá era verdad que todo el país estaba con nosotros».

Hennie le Roux se hizo eco de lo que había dicho Mandela de que la victoria movilizaría a los incrédulos. «Podíamos ver que el país estaba uniéndose detrás de nosotros pero que, si ganábamos, haríamos que ese vínculo fuera más fuerte. Cuanto mejor lo hiciéramos en el campo, mayor sería la onda expansiva.»

La adversidad y las emociones patentes antes y durante el partido contra Francia también ayudaron. Había una clara posibilidad de que el encuentro se suspendiera y se diera la victoria a Francia. La agradable ciudad índica de Durban había experimentado una de sus periódicas lluvias semitropicales y el terreno de King's Park estaba inundado. Si no se jugaba ese día, las normas de la Copa del Mundo decretaban que se declarase ganador a Francia, porque Sudáfrica tenía peor historial disciplinario hasta ese momento en el campeonato (un jugador había sido expulsado por juego duro en el muy disputado partido contra Canadá). Todo el país prestó atención, angustiado, mientras las autoridades de rugby e incluso las fuerzas armadas emprendían una carrera de-

sesperada para arreglar el campo a tiempo. Se recluta-
ron helicópteros militares para ventilar el terreno desde
arriba, pero la situación, al final, se resolvió gracias a un
batallón de mujeres negras armadas con cubos y frego-
nas, cuyos heroicos esfuerzos convencieron al árbitro
para que permitiera que se celebrase el partido.

A pesar de la labor de las limpiadoras, el encuentro
fue un baño de barro con un resbaloso balón ovalado
que circulaba por allí y sobre el que se peleaban violen-
tamente unos hombres grandes y sucios. Cuando faltaban dos minutos y Sudáfrica resistía con un 19 a 15, un
francés de origen marroquí, tan enorme como Kobus
Wiese, llamado Abdelatif Benazzi, pensó que había plantado el balón al otro lado de la línea, lo que habría supuesto el ensayo de la victoria. En lugar de ello, el árbitro concedió a los franceses una melé, los ocho jugadores
más grandes de cada equipo enfrentados uno contra otro
en formación de tortuga, a cuatro metros y medio de la
línea sudafricana. Si los exhaustos Bleus empujaban a los
exhaustos Springboks al otro lado de la línea, el partido
estaría acabado. Francia estaría en la final. El torneo habría acabado para la Nación Arcoiris. Los Springboks estaban a punto de ir a asumir sus posiciones en la melé
cuando Kobus Wiese, con sus 1,93 metros de estatura en
la segunda fila de la sala de máquinas de la melé, lanzó
un grito de guerra que espoleó a sus compañeros. Se dirigió a su mejor amigo, Balie Swart, el delantero base en
primera fila, y le dijo: «Mira, Balie, en esta melé, no
puedes retroceder. Puedes ir hacia adelante, puedes ir
hacia arriba, puedes ir hacia abajo o puedes caer. ¡Pero
no vas a retroceder!»

Los Springboks no retrocedieron y Sudáfrica pasó a
la final. «Fue un combate de voluntades, más que otra

cosa —explicó Morné du Plessis—. Fue el partido en el que verdaderamente sentimos que la magia de Mandela había surtido efecto en nosotros a la hora de jugar. Porque nos habíamos enterado del discurso de Mandela el día anterior en KwaZulu. Habíamos oído que, en un lugar en el que la gente se moría, él había dicho que había llegado la hora de que toda Sudáfrica apoyase a los Springboks, y lo había dicho con su gorra Springbok puesta. Aquello emocionó verdaderamente al equipo.»

Linga Moonsamy se conmovió más de lo que podía imaginarse. «Estábamos muy tensos durante el partido —recordaba—. Estábamos muy unidos al final. Los negros y los blancos de nuestra unidad, todos indistinguibles. Todos absolutamente locos de alivio y alegría.»

Varios años más tarde, Morné du Plessis se encontró con Benazzi, el gran delantero francés que había estado a punto de dar la victoria a su equipo. Como era inevitable, hablaron de aquel partido, y Benazzi insistió en que la polémica jugada había sido un ensayo, que el balón había cruzado la línea. Ahora bien, también le dijo a Du Plessis: «Lloramos desconsolados cuando perdimos con vosotros. Pero, cuando fui a ver la final el fin de semana siguiente, volví a llorar, porque sabía que era más importante que no estuviéramos allí, que lo que estaba ocurriendo ante nuestros ojos era más importante que una victoria o una derrota en un partido de rugby.»

Capítulo XVI
LA CAMISETA NÚMERO SEIS

24 de junio de 1995, por la mañana

La víspera de la final de la Copa del Mundo de rugby contra Nueva Zelanda, justo después de que los Springboks terminaran su último entrenamiento, François Pienaar estaba en el vestuario, a punto de quitarse las botas, cuando sonó su teléfono móvil dentro de la bolsa. «Hola, François, ¿cómo estás?» Era Mandela, que llamaba para desear buena suerte al equipo. Morné du Plessis se aseguró de informar de ello a la prensa. A Mandela le encantó leer en los periódicos, la mañana de la final, cómo contaba Du Plessis la historia de la llamada telefónica. «El señor Mandela le dijo a François que estaba casi más nervioso que el equipo», citaban todos los periódicos. «Estas llamadas prueban que forma ya parte de nuestro equipo y nuestra campaña.»

Todo indicaba que aquél iba a ser un buen día, que los sudafricanos habían pasado página, que se avecinaba una nueva era de madurez política; pero nunca se sabía. Si hubiera hablado con Niël Barnard, el viejo jefe de

257

espías bóer le habría dicho que, en junio de 1995, «la situación política estaba todavía muy verde: muchos blancos se sentían ajenos, fuera de los acontecimientos». Era difícil saber cómo podían reaccionar esos blancos distanciados, muchos de los cuales, sin duda, estarían presentes en el estadio. Quizá por eso Mandela, al recordar la tensa víspera del partido, hizo una observación sorprendente: «Nunca se me ha dado muy bien predecir cosas.» Era su forma de confesar los recelos que tenía. ¿Y si, a pesar de todos sus esfuerzos, había juzgado equivocadamente la actitud de los afrikaners? ¿Y si algunos aficionados abucheaban durante el canto del *Nkosi Sikelele*? ¿Y si la gente empezaba a desplegar las banderas de la vieja Sudáfrica, como había hecho en el fatídico partido contra Nueva Zelanda tres años antes?

Esas preguntas flotaban en su mente cuando se sentó ante el desayuno de papaya, kiwi, mango, gachas y café que siempre tomaba en su casa de Houghton. Estaba preocupado, pero tampoco estaba exactamente consumido por la ansiedad. Las buenas noticias pesaban más que los malos augurios. Uno de los motivos por los que Mandela renunció a su paseo de las 4:30 de la mañana el día de la final de rugby fue que quería dedicar más tiempo a los periódicos matutinos. Normalmente, devoraba la sección de política y miraba por encima la sección de deportes. Esta vez, prestó atención a ambas. Nunca había disfrutado tanto con la prensa de la mañana como aquel día. El consenso nacional que tanto se había esforzado en forjar en torno a los Springboks se reflejaba en el tono unánime de celebración de los editoriales y los analistas políticos. Sudáfrica se daba una gran palmadita en la espalda. Y, aunque se notaba cautela en cuanto al resultado del partido, y un enorme respeto por los rivales, los All Blacks de Nueva Zelanda (*Die Burger* decía: «Los All Blacks se alzan como Himalayas ante los Boks»), había una tranquila confianza en que el destino iba a jugar en favor de Sudáfrica. El titular en el principal periódico de Ciudad del Cabo, el *Argus*, proclamaba a los cuatro vientos el entusiasmo nacional. «¡Viva los Boks!», decía. «Viva», en este caso, era un grito de guerra de las protestas negras que se usaba desde hacía muchos años, tomado en algún momento de la revolución cubana.* Incluso mejor que el titular era el artículo que figuraba a continuación, firmado por el «equipo político» del periódico.

«La Copa del Mundo de rugby ha reforzado de forma espectacular la reconciliación nacional entre todas las razas en Sudáfrica, han dicho esta semana varios investigadores y sociólogos.» El artículo citaba a un conocido profesor afrikaner llamado Willie Breytenbach, que decía que la amenaza del terrorismo de extrema derecha había quedado «prácticamente aniquilada» y que el clamor por un Estado afrikaner independiente había disminuido sustancialmente. «Al mismo tiempo, las calles predominantemente negras de Johanesburgo se vacían de forma extraordinaria cada vez que juegan los Springboks. Los habitantes de los distritos negros vuelven corriendo a sus casas para ver los partidos por televisión... El rugby, el asombroso nuevo fenómeno de construcción nacional, ha sorprendido a los analistas, que ven cómo todas las razas se han aferrado, encantadas, a un acontecimiento que ha desatado una ola de patriotismo latente a través de un deporte tradicionalmente asociado en Sudáfrica a varones blancos afrikaner.»

* Ver nota de página 121.

Después, el *Argus* enumeraba los cinco «factores clave» que hacían que el rugby pudiera ser «un catalizador de unidad»: el ruidoso apoyo de Mandela a «nuestros chicos» y sus apariciones con la gorra Springbok; el respaldo público del arzobispo Tutu; la actuación del equipo en consonancia con el lema «Un equipo, un país»; los éxitos del equipo en el terreno de juego; el canto del nuevo himno combinado y la exhibición de la nueva bandera.

Ése era el fruto de todas las orquestaciones de Mandela entre bastidores, y él estaba feliz de ver que había variaciones patrióticas sobre los mismos argumentos en todos los periódicos. Le gustó ver que los diarios negros se unían al espíritu reinante. El *Sowetan,* de gran difusión, fue especialmente memorable, porque acuñó una nueva palabra sudafricana que iba a capturar la imaginación de todos los negros del país: «AmaBokoBoko», un nuevo término para designar a los Springboks, que daba por fin a los negros cierto sentido de empatía con el equipo. Pero lo que más satisfizo a Mandela fueron los periódicos afrikaans, que apenas podían contener la euforia por la manera en que la Sudáfrica negra había decidido apoyar a los Springboks. *Die Burger* citaba una frase de la Liga Juvenil del CNA, famosa por su radicalismo, que decía: «¡Traed la copa a casa, Boks! ¡Os esperamos!» *Beeld* contaba que el negociador principal del CNA en las conversaciones constituyentes, el ex responsable sindical Cyril Ramaphosa, había declarado: «Estamos orgullosos de nuestro equipo nacional, los Springboks.» A Mandela le gustó especialmente verse citado en las primeras páginas de *Beeld* y *Die Burger*. «Nunca he estado tan orgulloso de nuestros chicos —decía su propia cita que leyó—. Espero que todos sigamos animándolos hasta la victoria. Jugarán en nombre de toda Sudáfrica.»

Esa palabra, «espero», revelaba un atisbo de preocupación. La multitud con la que se iba a encontrar hoy era la más aterradora de su vida. En el estadio Newlands de Ciudad del Cabo, para el primer partido contra Australia, había sido otra cosa. El Cabo era el bastión blanco liberal de Sudáfrica. Allí los afrikaners eran más blandos, más moderados. Eran los descendientes de los bóers que habían decidido no emprender la Gran Marcha hacia el norte, que no se habían ofendido tanto por la decisión del Imperio británico de abolir la esclavitud. En cambio, la gente del Transvaal en Ellis Park tenía a Piet Retief y la Batalla del Río Sangriento grabados en su ADN. Eran seguramente, en muchos casos, de los que habían gritado de júbilo ante el asalto al World Trade Centre, los que, como había observado amargamente Bekebeke, habían visto la expresión «¡Quítate, *kaffir*!» como una cosa normal toda su vida. Eran los que habían «votado Nacional» siempre y los que, en algunos casos, se habían pasado después a la extrema derecha. De los 62.000 espectadores que iba a haber esa tarde en Ellis Park, muchos, si no la mayoría, parecerían recién salidos de una manifestación de desafío bóer. Llevarían sus uniformes de guardias forestales de color caqui, sus calcetines largos de lana y sus enormes barrigas, forjadas a base de innumerables cervezas Castle y salchichas *boerewors*. Mandela había sido el centro de atención de más concentraciones de masas que ninguna otra persona, pero nunca se había atrevido con una multitud semejante.

Mandela miró por la ventana de su salón y vio fuera a sus guardaespaldas, unos hombres musculosos, 16 en total, que estaban comprobando sus armas, rellenando papeles, examinando los motores de los coches y charlando amigablemente entre sí. Se dio cuenta de que, hasta hacía unas semanas, sus guardaespaldas blancos y negros habían ofrecido una triste imagen de separación digna del apartheid. Ahora les veía charlar todos juntos, haciendo gestos enfáticos, sonriendo, riéndose.

«Estábamos hablando de qué había que hacer para parar a los All Blacks, algunos decían que no teníamos posibilidades, otros que jugaríamos mejor ese día —explicaba Moonsamy—, cuando, en plena conversación, surgió la idea de que sería estupendo que el presidente llevara la camiseta verde y oro de los Springboks al estadio.» Al insistirle, Moonsamy reconoció que era él quien había tenido la idea. El impacto en sus colegas, continuó, había sido como una descarga eléctrica. «Nos sumamos todos a ello. Nos pusimos de acuerdo en que, cuando yo entrara en la casa a repasar las instrucciones de seguridad, que era siempre tarea del que estaba de "número uno" cada día, se lo mencionaría.»

Estaba previsto que salieran hacia el estadio a la una y media. A las 12, Moonsamy entró en la casa para informar a Mandela. Terminadas las formalidades de seguridad, le dijo: «*Tata* —el apodo afectuoso que utilizaban los guardaespaldas negros con él, y que quería decir abuelo—, estábamos pensando, ¿por qué no lleva hoy la camiseta de los Springboks?»

Mandela, cuando alguien le proponía una cosa completamente nueva, sobre todo una cosa que acarreaba repercusiones políticas y afectaba a algo que le importaba siempre tanto como su imagen pública, solía adoptar su rostro pensativo, de esfinge. Pero esta vez no dudó ni un instante. Por el contrario, mostró una sonrisa de oreja a oreja. «Se le iluminó —decía Moonsamy—. Le pareció una idea magnífica.»

Mandela había comprendido el valor del gesto inmediatamente. «Decidí llevar la camiseta —explicaba después— porque pensé: "Cuando los blancos me vean llevando la camiseta de rugby de los Springboks, verán que aquí hay un hombre que apoya por completo a nuestro equipo."»

Pero había un problema. No tenía esa camiseta, y faltaba sólo hora y media para la salida hacia el estadio. Fue directo de Moonsamy a su secretaria, Mary Mxadana, y le ordenó que llamara de inmediato a Louis Luyt, el responsable de la Unión Sudafricana de Rugby. Le pidió que le dijera que no quería cualquier camiseta, sino —y esto fue idea suya— que debía tener el número 6 de Pienaar en ella, y que quería también una gorra Springbok (había dejado la de Le Roux en su residencia de Ciudad del Cabo).

Una hora después de que Moonsamy le hubiera propuesto la idea, la camiseta estaba en casa de Mandela y su ama de llaves, a petición de él, estaba planchándola. Entonces, Mandela centró toda su atención en el propio partido. Su principal preocupación, como la de todos los aficionados y jugadores de los Springboks, era un negro grandullón llamado Jonah Lomu.

Nueva Zelanda tenía un equipo formidable, uno de los mejores de la historia. Su capitán, Sean Fitzpatrick, y los veteranos Zinzane Brooke, Frank Bunce, Walter Little e Ian Jones eran jugadores que no sólo eran famosos allí donde se jugaba al rugby, sino que eran los mejores del mundo en sus respectivos puestos. Pero su arma secreta, el hombre del que ya se decía que era el mejor jugador de rugby de toda la historia, era el veinteañero Jonah Lomu. Originario de Tonga, con la piel tan oscura como Mandela, medía 1,90 y pesaba 130 kilos. Era tan grande como el más corpulento de los Springboks, Kobus Wiese, y podía correr más deprisa que Williams y Small, 100 metros en menos de 11 segundos. Un periódico le llamaba «un rinoceronte con zapatillas de ballet». En la semifinal que enfrentó a los All Blacks contra Inglaterra, una de las selecciones favoritas, se había mostrado prácticamente imparable. Fue capaz de atravesar las líneas cuatro veces y marcó un total de 20 puntos. Como decían los diarios londinenses, hizo que los del equipo inglés parecieran niños pequeños.

El puesto de Small en los Springboks hacía que fuera él quien iba a tener que ocuparse de controlar a Lomu. Los periódicos publicaron gráficos comparando las estadísticas vitales de ambos jugadores, como si fueran boxeadores a punto de saltar al ring. Small —que, por una vez, hacía honor a su apellido, «pequeño»— era 10 centímetros más bajo y pesaba 30 kilos menos que su oponente.

En los periódicos, Mandela leyó su opinión sobre qué hacer con el coloso de los All Blacks. «Estratégicamente sería un error concentrarse en él, porque deben concentrarse en todo el equipo —había dicho, antes de añadir, como sorprendido por su audacia al aventurarse en un terreno poco conocido—, pero estoy seguro de que los Springboks lo tienen completamente resuelto.»

Pocos compartían su optimismo, sobre todo entre los neutrales. El entrenador australiano, Bob Dwyer, ocupaba todas las páginas de deportes con su confiada predicción de que los All Blacks, «rápidos y en forma», iban a tener a los pesados delanteros Springboks persiguiendo fantasmas toda la tarde; el *Sydney Morning Herald* había dicho que los Boks, a punto de caer en la trampa, «no podían ni soñar con ganar»; un ex jugador All Black, Grant Batty, parecía resumir todas las opiniones de los expertos sobre el partido cuando dijo que «sólo un rifle para elefantes» podía impedir a Lomu y compañía la victoria.

Un rifle para elefantes... o un esfuerzo sobrehumano de voluntad colectiva. Y algo parecido es lo que los Springboks descubrieron que tenían a su alcance cuando se levantaron esa mañana en el Sandton Sun and Towers Hotel, un moderno complejo hotelero de cinco estrellas en una zona comercial y acomodada de Johanesburgo, a unos diez minutos en coche al norte de la casa de Mandela.

Kobus Wiese compartía habitación con su colega y compañero de coro Balie Swart. Wiese era el que había lanzado el espeluznante grito de guerra en la melé durante la semifinal contra Francia, pero ahora estaba callado. «La presión —contó posteriormente— era absolutamente insoportable. Era inmensa. La noche anterior había llamado a mi madre. Nada concreto, sólo para oír su voz, que me ayudaba a desconectar. Pero ahora tenía miedo, miedo de decepcionar a todos aquellos millones de aficionados. Teníamos esa expectación de saber, por primera vez, que el país entero estaba con nosotros, y era algo abrumador. Era aterrador, pero también nos daba energía. Tenía la profunda sensación de que todo lo que había hecho en mi vida estaba llegando a su momento decisivo.»

Los jugadores desayunaron en un ambiente de tensión, presión y expectación insoportables. Sentían que estaban dentro de una burbuja, suspendida en el tiempo. O como unos austronautas a punto de despegar. Necesitaban desahogarse o iban a explotar. Y para eso sirvió la «carrera del capitán». A media mañana, se reunieron en el vestíbulo del hotel y, con Pienaar a la cabeza, corrieron dos kilómetros por las inmediaciones del complejo. Según recordaba François Pienaar, «había mucho nerviosismo entre los chicos, pero entonces, cuando giramos hacia la izquierda al salir del hotel, en un grupo apretado, oí ruidos y gritos, y cuatro niños negros que vendían periódicos nos reconocieron y empezaron a perseguirnos y a llamarnos por nuestros nombres —conocían prácticamente a todos los del equipo—, y se me pusieron los pelos de punta. No sé si los niños sabían leer siquiera, pero nos reconocieron y, para ellos, éramos su equipo. En aquel momento vi con más claridad que nunca que aquello era mucho más serio y más importante de lo que podíamos haber imaginado».

Mandela se miró en el espejo con su nueva camiseta verde, se puso la gorra, y se gustó. Poco antes de la una y media, salió por la puerta de casa para subirse a su Mercedes-Benz blindado de color gris metalizado e ir al estadio. El partido empezaba a las tres en punto. Normalmente, no se tardaba mucho más de 15 minutos en llegar a Ellis Park, pero, dado que iba a haber mucho tráfico, prefirieron salir pronto. Los guardaespaldas eran un modelo de eficacia rápida, callada y ágil. A medida que avanzaba el día estaban cada vez menos habladores, más ocupados y solemnes, estudiando su ruta en el plano, como habían hecho una docena de veces en la semana anterior, atentos a cualquier posible punto vulnerable. Estaban en contacto permanente con la policía, comprobando que los francotiradores estaban en sus puestos alrededor del estadio, que todo estaba bien con los escoltas en motocicleta y, con la gente de seguridad en Ellis Park, que la entrada estaría despejada para la llegada de la caravana presidencial.

Sin embargo, cuando Mandela salió de la casa, los 16 guardaespaldas se quedaron helados y rompieron sus intensos preparativos para mirar, atónitos, su nueva camiseta verde. «¡Wow!», se oyó Moonsamy decir a sí mismo entre dientes. Mandela sonrió al ver su sorpresa y les dio su acostumbrado y alegre buenos días, a lo que ellos mascullaron otro «buenos días» en respuesta; después recuperaron de golpe su actitud de UPP, introdujeron rápidamente al presidente en el coche, cerraron las puertas con fuerza y ocuparon sus puestos en los cuatro coches que formaban la caravana. El sitio de Moonsamy, como «número uno», estaba en el Mercedes gris, erguido y alerta, en el asiento del pasajero de enfrente. A lo largo del día, nunca estaría a más de un paso de distancia del presidente. Las motos de la policía aguardaban fuera. Emprendieron camino entre el chirrido de las ruedas sobre el pavimento de la entrada de vehículos. Los hombres de la UPP exhibían los rostros serios de guardaespaldas, pero, por dentro, estaban felices. «Le veíamos con aquella camiseta verde de rugby —explicaba Moonsamy—, y nos sentíamos muy orgullosos, porque él se sentía muy orgulloso.»

Mandela no fue el único hombre negro que llevó una camiseta de los *AmaBokoBoko* aquel día. En toda Sudáfrica se veía a negros llevando alegremente el símbolo de los viejos opresores, como descubrió Justice Bekebeke, estupefacto, la mañana de la final.

Si Mandela se había despertado pensando que tenía el apoyo de los negros a los Springboks en el bote, no había contado con el hombre al que había estado a punto de conocer en el Corredor de la Muerte cinco años antes. Mandela estaba preocupado por los del final amargo, los resentidos blancos, y no era consciente de que también existían resentidos negros.

«Al principio de la Copa del Mundo, yo apoyaba a los All Blacks con tanta pasión como lo había hecho de niño, cuando les apoyé aquella vez que vinieron a Upington —explicaba Bekebeke—. Me alegraba de que hubiéramos llegado al acuerdo político que teníamos con los blancos. Aceptaba que, por ahora, teníamos que tener un gobierno compartido, con gente como De Klerk en el gabinete. Muy bien. Lo comprendía. Me parecía bien. Pero mi posición era: "¡No me pidáis que apoye a los Springboks!" No tenía intención de ceder. Ya había perdonado suficientes cosas.»

Lo que tenía a Bekebeke confundido era que no parecía que hubiese mucha gente en Paballelo que compartiese su opinión. Ni siquiera Selina, su novia, que había seguido a su lado mientras estaba en la cárcel, que había ayudado a financiar sus estudios. Sobre el papel, ella era más radical políticamente que él. Pertenecía no sólo al CNA, sino a su aliado ideológico de la línea dura, el Partido Comunista Sudafricano. Pero ella había hecho lo que pedía Mandela, había abandonado los justificados prejuicios de toda una vida y había decidido considerar a los Springboks «nuestro equipo». Los jugadores podían ser, prácticamente todos, blancos, en su mayoría bóers, pero ella iba a apoyarlos en el partido de esa tarde con tanto entusiasmo patriótico como si hubieran sido todos negros, como ella.

Lo cual suponía un dilema para Bekebeke: cómo pasar el resto del día. Selina estaba totalmente empeñada en ver el partido, pero él no estaba seguro de qué hacer. Podía hacer lo que había hecho toda su vida: apoyar al equipo visitante, en este caso, Nueva Zelanda. O quizá podía hacer una excepción, por esta vez, y que le diera igual.

«A medida que discurría la mañana, a medida que vi los periódicos, oí la radio, vi cómo mi novia estaba cada vez más emocionada, empecé a sentirme dividido. Una parte de mí pensaba que era mejor no ver el maldito partido. Pero luego pensé que todo el mundo iba a verlo. Mi novia iba a verlo. Todos mis amigos. Incluso los camaradas que habían estado en la cárcel conmigo. No podía perdérmelo.»

Una cosa que Bekebeke tenía clara era que no debía ver el partido a solas con Selina. «Me preocupaba que, si lo hacíamos, nos pusiéramos muy tensos y acabásemos peleándonos —explicaba—. Así que, por suerte, surgió la oportunidad de ver el partido en casa de unos amigos. Habían organizado una *braai* [una barbacoa] para la ocasión, y pensé que, si tenía que aguantar el partido, al menos habría alguna compensación con la comida.» En la *braai* iban a estar cuatro parejas, incluidos ellos. Los otros tres hombres habían estado en prisión con Bekebeke; uno de ellos —Kenneth Khumalo, el «acusado número uno»— había estado en el Corredor de la Muerte con él. Bekebeke se sintió animado por ello, convencido de que no estaría solo en sus dudas respecto a todo aquel lío de los Springboks y seguro de que el entusiasmo de Selina iba a llamar la atención en el grupo. Ella había ido por delante para ayudar con los preparativos, así que él llegó solo, más o menos a la misma hora que Mandela salía de casa hacia el estadio.

«No he sentido tanto asombro como aquel día en mi vida —contó despúes Bekebeke—. Se abre la puerta, entro en la casa y ¿qué veo? ¡Los siete vestidos con la camiseta verde de los Springboks!»

Capítulo XVII
«¡NELSON! ¡NELSON!»

24 de junio de 1995, por la tarde

En los 60 minutos que mediaron entre la llegada de Mandela a Ellis Park y el inicio del encuentro a las tres en punto hubo de todo. Primero se cantó una canción, luego pasó volando un *Jumbo* y, por último, se oyó un clamor que conmocionó el mundo.

La canción se llamaba *Shosholoza*. Mandela la conocía muy bien, como prácticamente todos los negros en Sudáfrica. Históricamente la cantaban los trabajadores negros que emigraban desde las zonas rurales del sur de África a las minas de oro en torno a Johanesburgo, y era una melodía alegre y llena de energía que parecía imitar el ritmo del tren de vapor. «Shosholoza» se traducía a veces como «abrirse paso», a veces como «avanzar», a veces como «viajar deprisa». Era, además, una canción dinámica, enormemente popular en los partidos de fútbol entre los aficionados a este deporte, casi exclusivamente negros. Mandela solía cantarla con Walter Sisulu y otros presos cuando trabajaban en la cantera de cal de

Robben Island. Había vuelto a cantarla hacía sólo cuatro meses cuando, con otros cien ex presos, había regresado a la cárcel para llevar a cabo una alegre ceremonia. Pero ahora, en otra señal del rápido cambio que estaba experimentando Sudáfrica, la Unión de Rugby de Louis Luyt había escogido *Shosholoza* como canción oficial de la Copa del Mundo, y los aficionados blancos la habían adoptado alegremente como propia.

No obstante, necesitaban un poco de ayuda con la música y con la letra. Necesitaban, como los Springboks con el *Nkosi Sikelele*, a alguien que les enseñara a cantar. Y ahí es donde entró Dan Moyane. Moyane nació en Soweto en 1959 y se crió sin ningún interés por el rugby, «salvo para darme cuenta —decía— de que era un símbolo de la dominación afrikaner». Tras los disturbios estudiantiles de 1976, la mayoría de sus amigos fueron al exilio o a la cárcel. Él, acosado por la Policía de Seguridad, huyó del país y consiguió pasar la frontera a Mozambique, donde, en 1979, se incorporó al CNA. Allí trabajó como periodista para BBC Radio y Reuters, entre otros; sobrevivió a las incursiones de los comandos de las fuerzas especiales del general Constand Viljoen al otro lado de la frontera a principios de los ochenta y volvió a su país en 1991, un año después de que se levantara la prohibición sobre el CNA. Casi de inmediato obtuvo trabajo en la emisora de Johanesburgo Radio 702 (donde Eddie von Maltitz tendría posteriormente su conversación telefónica con Mandela), y pronto empezó a presentar un *talk-show* de seis a nueve de la mañana en colaboración con un ex jugador de rugby nacido en Irlanda, John Robbie, que había jugado con los Lions británicos contra los Springboks en 1980. Formaban un dúo muy popular, y su mezcla de conversación ligera y discusión seria sobre temas políticos fue una de las aportaciones más palpables de la sociedad civil al impulso de los cambios políticos en Sudáfrica. En su programa, incitaban suavemente a sus oyentes —especialmente los blancos— a tener una actitud más generosa respecto a las nuevas realidades del país.

La Copa del Mundo de rugby les dio mucho de lo que hablar. Para Robbie, era un sueño hecho realidad, una oportunidad de conciliar sus dos pasiones, el rugby y la reconciliación racial en Sudáfrica. Moyane, al principio, no estaba tan seguro. Sacudirse de encima las connotaciones que tenían los Springboks era para él tan difícil como para cualquier otro negro. Robbie y él discutían de rugby ante los micrófonos. Hasta que llegó el partido inaugural contra Australia.

«Cuando oí que Nelson Mandela iba a estar presente, tuve que hacer esfuerzos para creérmelo —dijo Moyane—. Pero pusimos la televisión en casa y allí estaba él, y mi esposa me dijo: "Bueno, si Mandela está allí apoyando a los Springboks, supongo que nosotros también tendremos que hacerlo. ¡Vamos a tener que ver el rugby!" Era una idea asombrosa, pero así fue, y creo que la misma conversación, con más o menos variaciones, se repitió en los hogares negros de todo el país.»

A lo largo del mes siguiente, gran parte del programa matutino consistió en Moyane haciendo de ingenuo interrogador y Robbie de hombre de rugby experto y sabio. Un día pusieron *Shosholoza*, en una versión que acababa de grabar el sudafricano grupo coral masculino, mundialmente famoso, Ladysmith Black Mambazo. Era una versión muy bella, pero, cuando Robbie le pidió a Moyane su opinión, éste respondió que, a su juicio, la canción debía tener un espíritu más descarnado. «Era una canción de ánimo, de esperanza, cantada por hombres que estaban lejos de sus familias, que estaban trabajando duramente pero que pronto iban a coger el tren para volver a casa.» Moyane le dijo a Robbie que, en su opinión, no era una canción pensada para arreglos corales muy elaborados. «Me parecía una canción que había que cantar con entusiasmo, con una pasión de gente de la calle, con corazón y con agallas.» Robbie respondió: «Muy bien, ¿por qué no la cantas tú entonces, Dan? Muéstranos cómo hay que hacerlo.» Y eso hizo Dan Moyane. Entonó un par de compases. «Era la primera vez que cantaba así ante el micrófono, y, en unos segundos, las líneas de teléfono del estudio se saturaron. Blancos y negros llamaron para decir que les había encantado.»

Pronto llamaron también productores de música locales. Al cabo de diez días, Moyane había grabado y producido su propia versión de *Shosholoza*, con un coro de Soweto. «De pronto me vi firmando autógrafos en tiendas. La canción fue un éxito inmediato.» Todo aquello era bastante asombroso, pero no podía compararse con lo que estaba por venir. Una semana antes de la final, después de que Sudáfrica derrotara a Francia, los organizadores de la Copa del Mundo le invitaron a dirigir a los aficionados cantando una hora antes del partido contra los All Blacks.

A primera vista, Moyane no parecía una elección natural para una ocasión tan ruidosa. De mediana altura y constitución delgada, tenía unos rasgos suaves y redondeados y unas maneras frágiles que contrastaban con la fisionomía y la actitud del aficionado blanco al rugby en general. Sin embargo, estuvo a la altura de la ocasión como si hubiera nacido para ello.

A las dos en punto, salió al terreno de juego. Su

versión de *Shosholoza* se había oído por los altavoces del estadio mientras los aficionados iban entrando; ahora iban a cantarla todos juntos. Moyane se acercó al micrófono y preguntó: «¿Me oís?»

Sesenta y dos mil aficionados rugieron: «¡SÍ!»

«Muy bien, para estar seguros de que me oís verdaderamente, ¿podemos tener un poco de silencio ahora?» Ellis Park se calló de pronto. Entonces apareció en las dos grandes pantallas a los lados del estadio la letra de la canción en lengua zulú.

En medio del silencio, Moyane gritó: «¡Vamos a cantar la canción hasta echar a los All Blacks del estadio!», y se oyeron enormes vítores. Primero, leyó la letra en voz alta con el público, y luego todos empezaron a cantar.

Dirigió a aquellas masas de herederos de Piet Retief en dos sonoras interpretaciones de la canción zulú. «Mi cabeza se vio inundada de emociones e ideas —explicaba Moyane—. Me vinieron a la mente imágenes de 1976, de amigos encarcelados, de personas a las que conocía y a las que aquellos que estaban allí —o, por lo menos, otros próximos a ellos— habían torturado y asesinado. Pero al mismo tiempo pensé, ¡qué gesto por parte de esta gente! Estaban devolviéndonos el favor de haberles dejado conservar la camiseta verde. Era una canción negra callejera, una canción de fútbol, una canción de emigrantes, una canción de presos. Aquél fue un ejemplo maravilloso de que se habían cruzado las líneas, de que los ánimos estaban cambiando.»

Y de que la gente estaba cogiendo velocidad para el gran partido. Lo siguiente elevó aún más el nivel de decibelios. El culpable fue el protagonista del segundo acto del espectáculo, un piloto de South African Airways llamado Laurie Kay. Nacido en Johanesburgo en 1945, Kay creció completamente protegido del mundo en el que vivía Dan Moyane. Era un blanco de habla inglesa que, por un capricho de circunstancias familiares similares al que había afectado a otros dos millones de personas como él, acabó viviendo en la punta meridional de África. Estaba obsesionado con volar desde la niñez, pero no entró a formar parte de las fuerzas aéreas sudafricanas, sino de la Royal Air Force británica, no por convicción política, sino por sentido práctico. Le resultó más fácil entrar en la RAF. «Ahora no me enorgullezco de contarlo —decía años después—, pero la verdad es que yo era una persona blanca, completamente apolítica, que votaba al Partido Nacional.»

Las primeras semillas de conciencia política se plantaron en Kay poco después de que Mandela saliera de la cárcel. Se encontraban ambos en un vuelo de SAA de Río de Janeiro a Ciudad del Cabo. Era un Boeing 747 y Kay era el capitán. «Fue mi primer y último encuentro cara a cara con Nelson Mandela. Me pasaron un mensaje diciendo que quería verme. Así que salí de la cabina y vi que estaba con su mujer, Winnie. Estaban en los asientos 1D y 1F; nunca lo olvidaré —contaba Kay—. En cuanto me vio, se levantó. Yo le dije: "No, por favor", pero él insistió, se levantó, me saludó y me dio la mano. No me había ocurrido ni ha vuelto a ocurrirme jamás con un pasajero. Para mí, la cortesía y el respeto de aquel gesto fueron reveladores.» Mandela había dejado boquiabiertos a Kobie Coetsee y a Niël Barnard desde el primer instante, como le pasaría después con el general Viljoen. Pero esos hombres tenían cierta preparación política, cierta idea de qué esperar. El capitán Kay era una página en blanco. Sin embargo, el efecto fue, una vez más, automático. «Se levantó y me conquistó. Me di cuenta de que era una clase distinta de hombre. Hasta entonces, era un rostro y un nombre más de negro que quizá representaba una amenaza contra mi forma de vida. Yo me había criado en la mentalidad afrikaner y, aunque me preocupara poco por la política, aquélla era la influencia que me había llegado.»

A menudo, Mandela se mostraba encantador porque sí. En muchas otras ocasiones, su intención era lograr algo a cambio. Algunas veces, era puramente personal; otras, era político. En aquel caso, Mandela quería pedir un favor específico. «Me explicó que el resto de su delegación viajaba en clase turista y que quería saber si se les podía subir de categoría.» Kay no lo dudó. «Inmediatamente di la orden de que los llevaran al piso de arriba, a primera.»

Era evidente que Mandela le había manipulado. Pero, aunque Kay se dio cuenta de ello, no por eso disminuyó su admiración, en parte porque, como decía después, «¡Debería ver a algunos de los tipos fríos y arrogantes que viajan en primera! Pero fue más que eso. A partir de ese día, cambié para siempre. Es un mago, no cabe duda. Yo creo que ciertas personas tienen un aura. Eugene Terreblanche, por ejemplo. Una vez fui andando hasta un avión a su lado: tenía un aura malvada. Mandela posee un aura de bondad.»

Los caminos de Kay y Mandela volvieron a cruzarse —o estuvieron a punto de hacerlo— el día de la final de la Copa del Mundo de rugby.

South African Airways había iniciado conversaciones con la Unión de Rugby, unas semanas antes, para ver si podían sacar algún provecho comercial al gran acontecimiento. Al principio, las discusiones se centraron en la idea de que un pequeño avión controlado con mando a distancia, con los colores de SAA, sobrevolara el estadio. Sin embargo, a medida que avanzaban las negociaciones, los planes se volvieron más ambiciosos, hasta que Kay recibió una llamada de un directivo de SAA que quería convencerlo de pilotar un *Jumbo* en la tarde del partido, con las palabras «Go Bokke» (el plural de Bok en afrikaans) pintadas en la parte inferior del aparato. Kay no se lo pensó dos veces. Si Mandela había estado toda su vida preparándose para este momento, él también. No sólo era el piloto con más experiencia en 747 de la compañía, sino que había sido durante treinta años piloto acrobático. Había hecho espectáculos de acrobacia e incluso, en una ocasión, había trabajado en una película del actor Jackie Chan.

La diferencia, esta vez, era que podía representar un grave peligro, y no sólo para sí mismo y las 62.000 personas dentro del estadio, sino para muchísimas más fuera. Porque Ellis Park se encontraba en plena hondonada dentro de Johanesburgo. Estaba rodeado de edificios residenciales y de oficinas.

Laurie Kay pasó la semana previa a la final preparándose con diligencia para el que iba a ser el vuelo rasante más espectacular de la historia. Mantuvo numerosas reuniones con la gente de aviación civil y las autoridades de la ciudad, ahora bajo el mando del nuevo primer ministro de la provincia, el carismático ex preso de Robben Island Tokyo Sexwale. «Instalamos un control militar de tráfico aéreo en la cubierta de Ellis Park y declaramos una franja de cinco millas náuticas de cielo alrededor del estadio zona «estéril», es decir, sin tráfico aéreo, durante el día del partido», explicaba después Kay. Sus colegas de South African Airways y él tuvieron que reunirse asimismo con la SABC, que iba a emitir el partido en directo a todo el mundo, para asegurarse de que el vuelo se hiciera justo en el momento de máxima audiencia televisiva. «Dijeron que querían que pasara exactamente a las 14:32 y 45 segundos. Eso podía hacerlo. Pero luego dijeron que tenía que volver a pasar una segunda vez, 90 segundos después. Aquello me dejó perplejo, porque no sabía si podía maniobrar un avión tan grande en tan poco tiempo. Pero practiqué en el simulador y descubrí que sí podía hacerlo.»

Sin embargo, el simulador no tenía ningún programa que pudiese prepararle para la maniobra concreta que tenía prevista. Para ello tuvo que salir y hacer un poco del viejo trabajo de preparación sobre el terreno. «Pasé mucho tiempo sobre la cubierta de Ellis Park y en las colinas que lo dominaban, para decidir la mejor aproximación y hacerme una idea de lo que iban a ver los aficionados. Ellis Park está en una depresión, y es difícil acercarse. Comprendí que iba a necesitar alguna maniobra agresiva.»

En aquella época, Sudáfrica tenía algo del salvaje oeste. Con todos los cambios radicales que estaba experimentando, era un país temerario, vibrante y lleno de posibilidades. Con ese ánimo afrontó Laurie Kay el reto profesional más peligroso de su vida.

«La Autoridad de Aviación Civil tiene normas para sobrevolar áreas habitadas y concentraciones públicas. Creo que la altitud mínima es de 600 metros. Por supuesto, esas normas quedaron provisionalmente anuladas. Era responsabilidad mía decidir hasta dónde debía bajar.» Kay, su copiloto y su mecánico de vuelo despegaron y se dirigieron, como en un bombardero de la Segunda Guerra Mundial, hacia su objetivo.

«Íbamos tres en la cabina, pero, cuando nos preparábamos para nuestra aproximación final, les dije: "Muy bien, chicos, a partir de ahora asumo plena responsabilidad." Porque no servía de nada, en una ocasión como ésta, volar tan alto que la gente casi no pudiera oírte. Así que me aproximé a un ángulo bajo para asegurarme de que los espectadores pudieran leer las palabras escritas en la parte inferior del aparato, y la velocidad más lenta posible sin llegar a detenerme. A 259 kilómetros por hora. Fui despacio para que pudiéramos generar suficiente fuerza para subir en cuanto pasáramos el estadio. Así que, cuando llegamos allí —el tiempo que estuvimos sobre nuestro objetivo fue de entre dos y tres segundos—, aceleramos los motores, los forzamos para que transmitieran al estadio todo el ruido y toda la potencia posibles.»

Kay voló tan bajo que habría acabado en la cárcel si la AAC no hubiera aceptado suspender las normas. Voló a sólo 60 metros de altura sobre los asientos superiores del estadio, la misma distancia que la de la envergadura del aparato. «Y volvimos perfectamente a tiempo para la segunda pasada, en menos de 80 segundos —contaba Kay, que añadía, con modestia—: Hubo algunos factores que jugaron a nuestro favor. La visibilidad era excelente. No había viento. Pero, sobre todo, yo quería que transmitiéramos al estadio el mensaje de que éramos fuertes e íbamos a ganar. De modo que, sí, vaciamos toda la potencia que pudimos en el estadio.»

La primera reacción de la multitud, que, en su mayoría, no había visto venir el avión, fue de auténtico terror. Fue como si hubiera estallado una gran bomba dentro del estadio. El impacto de los cuatro motores rugientes del Boeing 747 ensordeció a todo el mundo e hizo vibrar las paredes. Louis Luyt estaba en la suite presidencial, con Mandela a su lado.

«¡Qué salto di! —exclamaba Luyt—. ¡Y Mandela también saltó!» Como todo el mundo en el estadio. «¡Qué cabrón! —sonreía Luyt, refiriéndose al capitán Kay—. No nos había dicho que iba a volar tan bajo. ¡A 60 metros! ¡Qué susto me pegué! Podía haber rozado la cubierta del estadio.»

La sorpresa y el susto dieron paso a un entusiasmo atronador. La potencia que el capitán Kay vertió sobre el estadio electrizó a todos los presentes y mantuvo a la muchedumbre ronroneando hasta el final del partido.

Cinco minutos antes del inicio, Nelson Mandela salió al campo para dar la mano a los jugadores. Llevaba la gorra verde y la camiseta verde de los Springboks, abotonada hasta el cuello. Cuando el público le vio, se quedó en silencio. «Fue como si no pudieran creer lo que estaban viendo», explicaba Luyt. Entonces empezó a oírse un clamor, primero en voz baja pero enseguida subiendo en volumen e intensidad. Morné du Plessis lo oyó al salir del vestuario y pasar por el túnel hacia el campo. «Salí a aquel sol frío y brillante de invierno y, al principio, no entendía lo que pasaba, qué gritaba la gente, por qué había tanta excitación cuando los jugadores todavía no habían saltado al campo. Entonces descifré las palabras. Aquella multitud de blancos, afrikaners, gritaban, como un solo hombre, una sola nación: "¡Nel-son! ¡Nel-son! ¡Nel-son!" Una y otra vez, "¡Nel-son! ¡Nel-son!", y fue algo...» Los ojos de este ex jugador de rugby se le llenaban de lágrimas mientras intentaba encontrar las palabras para describir el momento. «No creo —prosiguió—, no creo que vuelva a vivir nunca un instante como aquél. Fue un momento mágico, un momento maravilloso. Fue cuando comprendí que realmente había una posibilidad de que este país saliera adelante. Aquel hombre estaba demostrando que era capaz de perdonar por completo, y ellos —la Sudáfrica blanca, la Sudáfrica blanca aficionada al rugby— estaban probando, con aquella reacción, que también querían devolverle el favor, y eso es lo que hicieron al gritar "¡Nelson! ¡Nelson!"». Fue maravilloso. Fue digno de un cuento de hadas. Fue Sir Galahad: mi fuerza es la fuerza de diez porque mi corazón es puro.

«Entonces vi a Mandela con aquella camiseta, agitando la gorra en el aire, con aquella sonrisa enorme y especial que tenía. Estaba tan contento. Era la viva imagen de la felicidad. Se reía sin parar, y pensé, sólo con que le hayamos hecho feliz en este momento, ya es suficiente.»

Rory Steyn, uno de los miembros del equipo de guardaespaldas presidenciales de Mandela, tuvo también asiento de primera fila. Le habían asignado la responsabilidad de la seguridad de los All Blacks, por lo que estaba en el campo con ellos, al lado de su banquillo. «Con aquel acto de generosidad, Mandela transformó a toda Sudáfrica en una nación nueva —dijo después Steyn, un ex Policía de Seguridad que, durante años, se había dedicado a perseguir al CNA y sus aliados—. Recibimos el mensaje de la población negra con gratitud y alivio. Compartimos vuestro júbilo, nos decían; os perdonamos por el pasado.»

El perdón iba acompañado de la expiación. Eso era

también lo que querían decir los gritos de «¡Nelson! ¡Nelson!» Al rendir homenaje al hombre cuya pena de cárcel había sido una metáfora del cautiverio de la Sudáfrica negra, estaban reconociendo su pecado, descorchando la botella en la que estaba encerrada su culpa. Linga Moonsamy, situado en el césped un paso detrás de Mandela, absorbiéndolo todo, se sintió completamente abrumado. Por un lado, estaba saboreando el sueño al que había dedicado su vida como joven luchador del CNA; por otro, tenía una misión que debía cumplir con frialdad. «Allí estaba, casi pegado a su espalda, escuchando aquel rugido, y los gritos de "¡Nelson! ¡Nelson!" y, aunque estaba muy emocionado, más conmovido de lo que había estado en toda mi vida, también tenía que cumplir un deber, y estaba totalmente alerta, vigilando a la muchedumbre. Y entonces, hacia la esquina derecha del campo, vi que ondeaban unas cuantas banderas sudafricanas antiguas y eso despertó en mí una reacción completamente contraria. Me entraron escalofríos. De pronto había una alerta de seguridad alarmante. Sabía que debíamos vigilar cuidadosamente a aquel sector del público y me propuse mencionarlo en cuanto pudiera al resto del equipo. Pero me sentí dividido, porque me sorprendió comprender lo que significaba desde el punto de vista político.»

El simbolismo era alucinante. Durante décadas, Mandela había representado todo lo que más temían los blancos; durante más años todavía, la camiseta Springbok había sido el símbolo de todo lo que más odiaban los negros. Ahora, de pronto, ante los ojos de toda Sudáfrica y gran parte del mundo, los dos símbolos negativos se habían fundido para crear uno nuevo que era positivo, constructivo y bueno. Mandela era el responsable de esa transformación y se había convertido en la encarnación, no del odio y el miedo, sino de la generosidad y el amor.

Dos años antes, Louis Luyt no habría sabido cómo interpretar todo aquello, pero ahora sí. «Mandela sabía que aquélla era la oportunidad política de su vida, y ¡Dios mío, cómo supo aprovecharla! —dijo posteriormente—. Cuando la muchedumbre estalló, pudimos verlo: aquel día era el presidente de Sudáfrica sin un solo voto en contra. Sí, la toma de posesión, un año antes, fue estupenda, pero era la culminación de unas elecciones en las que unos habían ganado y otros perdido. Aquí estábamos todos en el mismo bando. Ni un voto en contra. Aquel día fue nuestro rey.»

Ése era el objetivo. Mandela había sabido valorar el poder de su gesto cuando había dicho que el hecho de que se pusiera la camiseta «tendría un efecto magnífico entre los blancos». Aquel día fue el rey de todos. Ya había tenido una coronación, en el estadio de fútbol de Soweto, al día siguiente de su liberación. Entonces, había sido coronado rey de la Sudáfrica negra. Cinco años más tarde, se producía su segunda coronación en el *sancta sanctorum* de los afrikaners, el estadio nacional de rugby.

Van Zyl Slabbert, que había inspirado a Morné du Plessis en su juventud y era jefe de Braam Viljoen en el *think-tank* de Pretoria, estaba en el estadio. «No se puede hacer idea de lo que significó para mí ver a aquellos bóers típicos a mi alrededor, con sus barrigas cerveceras, sus pantalones cortos y sus calcetines largos, típicos simpatizantes del AWB, bebiendo coñac con coca cola, ver a aquellos norteños reaccionarios del Transvaal cantando *Shosholoza*, dirigidos por un joven negro, y vitoreando a Mandela —decía Slabbert, perplejo al recordar la escena—. Podíamos haber esperado que, cuando llegara a la presidencia, dijera: "¡Voy a acabar con vosotros...!" Pero no, él contradice todos los estereotipos de venganza y castigo.»

El arzobispo Tutu, que, de niño, iba andando a Ellis Park a ver los partidos con sándwiches que le hacía su madre, tuvo que vivir con la cruel ironía de no poder acudir al estadio porque tenía un compromiso fijado con anterioridad en Estados Unidos. Pero no estaba dispuesto a perderse el partido. Lo vio, a primera hora de la mañana, en un bar de San Francisco.

«Nelson Mandela tiene el don de hacer lo más apropiado y ser capaz de hacerlo con aplomo —dijo Tutu—. Otro líder político, otro jefe de Estado, si hubiera intentado hacer algo así, se habría dado de bruces. Pero era lo que había que hacer. No es una cosa que uno pueda inventarse... Creo que fue un momento definitorio en la vida de nuestro país.»

Nadie capturó el cambio trascendental que había llevado a cabo Mandela mejor que Tokyo Sexwale, que había pasado trece años en Robben Island condenado por terrorismo y conspiración para derrocar el gobierno; que, al salir de prisión, se había convertido en el mejor amigo del asesinado Chris Hani; que, como primer ministro de la provincia de Gauteng (antes Transvaal), se había convertido en uno de los seis o siete personajes más destacados del CNA.

«Aquél fue el momento en el que comprendí con más claridad que nunca que el fin de la lucha de liberación de nuestro pueblo no era sólo liberar a los negros del cautiverio —decía Sexwale, teniendo muy en cuenta la principal lección que había aprendido de Mandela en la cárcel—, sino, todavía más, liberar a los blancos del miedo. Y allí estaba. "¡Nelson! ¡Nelson! ¡Nelson!" El miedo que se disipaba.»

¿Y qué pasó con el último Santo Tomás? ¿Qué pasó con Justice Bekebeke, el único del grupo de ocho en la barbacoa de Paballelo que no llevaba camiseta Springbok? Para él también fue un momento definitorio. Por fin capituló, impotente ante la marea del nuevo sentimiento sudafricano que había desencadenado Mandela.

«Una hora antes de que empezara el partido, seguía indeciso y confuso —explicaba—. Pero entonces encendimos el televisor y vimos a aquella gente cantando *Shosholoza*, y luego aquel vuelo rasante asombroso, y después el anciano, mi presidente, con la camiseta Springbok. Yo me debatía. Todavía no acababa de sacudirme el viejo resentimiento, el odio, pero me estaba pasando algo, y comprendí que estaba cambiando, me estaba ablandando, hasta que tuve que ceder, tuve que rendirme. Y me dije, bueno, ésta es la nueva realidad. No hay vuelta atrás: el equipo sudafricano es ya mi equipo, sean quienes sean, sea cual sea su color.

»Fue todo un hito para mí. Para toda mi relación con mi país, con los sudafricanos blancos. A partir de aquel día, todo cambió. Todo se redefinió.»

CAPÍTULO XVIII
EL SABOR DE LA SANGRE

«No pude cantar el himno —reconocía François Pienaar—. No me atreví.» Había querido desesperadamente estar a la altura de la ocasión, ser un ejemplo, no decepcionar a Mandela. Había visualizado la escena una y otra vez en su cabeza. Sin embargo, cuando llegó el momento, cuando los dos equipos se pusieron en fila a un lado del campo, antes del partido, y la banda tocó los primeros compases del *Nkosi Sikelele*, no fue capaz de abrir la boca.

«Sabía que, si lo hacía, me iba a venir abajo. Me iba a deshacer en lágrimas allí mismo. Estaba tan emocionado —contaba el capitán Springbok—, que quería llorar. Sean Fitzpatrick [el capitán de los All Blacks] me dijo después que me había mirado y había visto cómo me caía una lágrima por la mejilla. Pero eso no era nada comparado con lo que sentía por dentro. Era un momento de mi vida de tanto orgullo, y yo estaba allí, y todo el estadio retumbaba. Era demasiado. Traté de localizar a mi novia, fijar mi atención en ella, pero no pude. Así que me mordí el labio. Me lo mordí con tanta fuerza que sentí el sabor de la sangre.»

Lo que había hecho que Pienaar estuviera a punto de venirse abajo de la emoción había sido la visita de Mandela al vestuario de los Springboks diez minutos antes. Entre el sobrevuelo del *Jumbo* y su salida al campo vestido con la camiseta, Mandela había pedido a Louis Luyt que le llevara a las entrañas del estadio para decir unas palabras a los jugadores.

Pienaar recordaba la escena. «Acababa de ponerme los vendajes y estábamos todos allí, en un estado de tensión como no habíamos vivido jamás, y por la cabeza me pasaban un montón de cosas, consciente de que aquello era lo más grande que había hecho nunca; una oportunidad de lograr todo lo que siempre habíamos deseado. Y estaba pensando en todo eso pero, al mismo tiempo, con toda la atención puesta en los detalles del partido, cuando, de pronto, apareció él. No sabía que iba a venir, y todavía menos que iba a llevar la camiseta Springbok. Dijo "Buena suerte", se dio la vuelta y vi en la espalda el número 6, que era yo...

»Los hinchas más apasionados, sabe, son los que llevan la camiseta de su equipo. Y allí estaba yo viéndole entrar en el vestuario, precisamente en aquel instante, vestido como otro hincha más, pero resulta que era mi camiseta la que llevaba. No hay palabras para describir las emociones que me embargaron.»

Como un mes antes en Silvermine, Mandela sorprendió a los Springboks. Según recordaba Morné du Plessis, antes de que entrara en la sala, el silencio era absoluto. «De pronto, los jugadores le vieron y todo el mundo empezó a reírse, a sonreír, a aplaudir. La tensión se disipó.» En esta ocasión, el discurso de Mandela fue más breve, más cercano y más directo que el de la víspera del partido contra Australia. «Mirad, chicos —dijo—, jugáis contra los All Blacks. Son uno de los equipos más potentes en el mundo del rugby, pero vosotros sois todavía más potentes. Y sólo tenéis que recordar que toda esta multitud, tanto negros como blancos, está con vosotros, y que yo estoy con vosotros.» Luego se paseó por la sala, dando la mano y diciendo unas palabras a cada jugador. Cuando salía por la puerta, François Pienaar le dijo en voz alta: «Me gusta la camiseta que lleva, señor.»

Mandela era consciente de que su visita podía elevar más aún la presión sanguínea de los Springboks, que ya estaba en un nivel peligroso. Pero luego dijo que sus palabras habían estado «calculadas para animarles».

Sus cálculos, una vez más, eran acertados. Stransky, que, en su puesto de medio apertura, iba a ser seguramente el que más tensión iba a soportar aquel día, confirmó posteriormente que «supo dar exactamente con el tono adecuado. Fue una auténtica inspiración. Yo habría pensado que era completamente imposible hacer más intensos los sentimientos que teníamos antes del encuentro, pero Mandela lo consiguió. Nos "aceleró" todavía más».

Louis Luyt, que había acompañado a Mandela al vestuario, estaba de acuerdo. «Les cargó las baterías con aquellas palabras, cuando dijo que todo el país estaba con ellos. Fue un discurso breve pero que, Dios mío, ¡iba a hacer que los chicos jugaran como demonios!»

Tres minutos después, mientras los clamores de «¡Nelson! ¡Nelson!» todavía recorrían el estadio, les tocó a los jugadores salir al campo. A partir de ese momento, era cosa suya. La responsabilidad del bienestar del país quedó depositada en manos de los jugadores. No iba a haber nada más importante durante la hora y media siguiente. Si Sudáfrica perdía, todavía habría cosas que podían salvarse. Era un honor haber llegado a la final. La nación estaba unida como nunca. «Un equipo, un país» había dejado de ser un astuto lema de márketing. Pero, si Sudáfrica perdía, todo acabaría en un mustio anticlímax, un recuerdo agridulce que más valdría olvidar. El gran instante de «¡Nelson! ¡Nelson!» seguiría vivo, pero sin las alegres connotaciones de trompetas y la Novena de Beethoven que podía evocar la victoria.

Para marcar el día, para hacerlo histórico, los Springboks tenían que vencer los pronósticos y ganar. Para ello, tenían que detener a Jonah Lomu. Le vieron por primera vez cara a cara cuando salieron del vestuario hacia el túnel, en preparación para la salida paralela de los dos equipos al campo. Los All Blacks tenían un equipo temible, lleno de nombres famosos. Pero todas las miradas estaban puestas en Lomu, como lo habían estado la mayoría de los pensamientos de los Springboks desde que, una semana antes, habían visto al inmenso corredor dejar el orgullo de Inglaterra reducido a un montón de golfillos desconcertados.

«Era enorme —decía Stransky—. Era imposible no admirarlo. En el túnel, no podía apartar mis ojos. Parecía una montaña. ¡Una montaña que teníamos que escalar!»

Para ser más específicos, una montaña que tenía que escalar James Small. «Recuerdo que vi a Jonah y pensé: "¡Joder!"», explicaba Small, con su típica concisión. Todo el equipo era consciente de la carga sobre los hombros del «inglés», el designado para marcar a Lomu, y todos habían notado que estaba más callado que de costumbre en el autobús hacia el estadio. «Era prácticamente lo único en lo que pensaba. Sabía que, si él conseguía sacar dos o tres yardas de diferencia, no había nada que hacer. Pero los demás jugadores estaban conmigo y me dejaron claro que iban a apoyarme en cuanto Jonah se hiciera con el balón.» Chester Williams, cuyas diferencias anteriores con Small quedaron sumergidas en la solidaridad del momento, fue el primero en acercarse a tranquilizarlo: «Lo único que tienes que hacer es contenerlo, y nosotros acudiremos. No te preocupes. Yo estaré cubriéndote las espaldas.»

Durante la semana anterior, la prensa sudafricana había visto la aparición de un nuevo tipo de experto en rugby, el *Lomúlogo*. Todos tenían sus teorías sobre cómo pararle. Una de ellas era la estrategia directa propuesta por Chester Williams. Si Small lograba retenerlo durante un segundo, hacerle perder el paso, el resto del equipo se abalanzaría sobre él. Otras teorías decían que Lomu no tenía tanta fuerza mental como física. Quizá tenía algo de Sonny Liston, el temible campeón de los pesos pesados al que Mohamed Alí derrotó no castigándole el cuerpo, sino jugando con su mente, sacudiendo su frágil autoestima. Dos días antes del partido, los periódicos sudafricanos habían citado con profusión las palabras de un ex capitán de rugby australiano que decía que la clave para neutralizar a Lomu era «intentar quebrar su confianza desde el principio del partido». La idea era que Lomu era imparable si estaba convencido de que era imparable. Si perdía esa convicción, se derrumbaría. El australiano decía que sería útil, por ejemplo, que Stransky pateara unos cuantos balones altos y difíciles en su dirección, para que tuviera que ir en su busca, o, lo mejor de todo, arrojarlo al suelo una o dos veces en los primeros diez minutos. Desde el primer instante, el objetivo de los Springboks tenía que ser «confundir al grandullón», «proporcionarle uno o dos reveses mentales».

Hay pruebas de que Mandela también intentó proporcionarle alguno. Según contó más tarde Linga Moonsamy, antes de ir al vestuario Springbok, Mandela visitó el de los All Blacks. «Jonah Lomu, de cerca, era gigantesco —recordaba Moonsamy—. Pero se podía ver inmediatamente que era tímido. Estaba como atemorizado por Mandela. Los chicos de Nueva Zelanda estaban todos sin camiseta y, cuando Mandela se acercó a Lomu, le oí decir: "¡Uff!"» Dio la mano a todos los jugadores y les deseó suerte. Mandela no había sido tan poco sincero en toda su vida, y los All Blacks lo sabían. «Hubo un detalle que los neozelandeses no tuvieron más remedio que advertir —decía Moonsamy entre risas—. ¡Llevaba la camiseta de los Springboks! Luego me pregunté si, en realidad, el hecho de haber entrado a verlos era una forma de transmitirles un mensaje deliberadamente ambiguo.»

Quince minutos después, Mandela estaba en el campo, recorriendo la fila de jugadores de Nueva Zelanda, dándole la mano a cada uno. Cuando llegó a Lomu, saludó al hombre al que acababa de conocer como si fuera un amigo al que no veía desde hacía tiempo. «¡Ah, hola, Jonah! ¿Cómo estás?», sonrió. Según un periodista de televisión que estaba cerca: «¡Lomu tenía pinta de ir a cagarse encima!»

El ultimo número del espectáculo antes de que empezara el partido era el tradicional Haka de los All Blacks. El equipo ejecutaba este rito antes de los partidos internacionales desde hacía más de cien años. Era una danza de guerra maorí cuyo propósito era infundir terror a las filas enemigas. Los 15 All Blacks se colocaban en el centro del terreno de juego, en amplio despliegue, cada uno con las piernas separadas y medio en cuclillas. A un grito del capitán, comenzaba la danza. Entre mucho gruñido y mucho sacar la lengua, grandes pisotones, palmadas en los muslos, pechos hinchados y gestos amenazadores, los All Blacks entonaban un canto que era mucho más alarmante en los gritos originales en maorí que traducido y por escrito. El enardecedor final decía:

Tē-nei te tangata pū-huruhuru
Nā-na nei i tiki mai whakawhiti te rā
Ā upane, ka upane
Ā upane, ka upane
Whiti te rā, hī!

Éste es el hombre peludo que aquí se yergue.
Que trajo el sol y lo hizo brillar.
Un paso hacia arriba, otro paso hacia arriba.
¡Un paso hacia arriba, otro paso hacia arriba! ¡El sol brilla!

Por suerte para los All Blacks, sus rivales no suelen tener a mano la traducción. Lo que suelen hacer es tratar de amilanarlos con la mirada, o sonreír con aparente desprecio, o fingir indiferencia. Pero ninguna de esas cosas resulta nunca del todo convincente, por lo hipnótico y amenazador del canto. En esta ocasión, sin embargo, hubo una ligera pero significativa ruptura del protocolo. A mitad de la interpretación, que dura aproximadamente un minuto y 20 segundos, Jonah Lomu se salió de la pauta y empezó a aproximarse, despacio pero con decisión, sin dejar de mirarlo, a James Small. Pero entonces ocurrió algo de lo que pocos de los que veían el partido en el estadio y en televisión se dieron cuenta, pero que sí registraron todos los jugadores en el campo. Kobus Wiese, que estaba al lado de Small, rompió también el protocolo y dio dos o tres pasos hacia Lomu, interponiéndose delante de Small. «Kobus rompió la fila como para decir a Lomu: "Para llegar hasta él, tienes que enfrentarte primero a mí», recordaba Pienaar. Fueron pequeños gestos de dos hombres gigantescos, unos gestos infantiles en medio de todos los acontecimientos del día, pero que surtieron efecto. Antes de que el silbato del árbitro señalara el comienzo del partido, el marcador era ya Springboks 1, Lomu 0.

Si la atención de los aficionados estaba centrada en James Small, la máxima presión la sufría Stransky. Debido al puesto en el que jugaba, era el pateador del equipo, las miradas iban a estar puestas en él más que en ningún otro jugador. François Pienaar y Kobus Wiese podían, hasta cierto punto, esconderse tras el tumulto de gruñidos de la melé. Si cometían un error, pocos fuera del equipo o de la esfera de los expertos tenían por qué darse cuenta. Lo malo era que, por eso mismo, pocas veces se les daba todo el mérito que les correspondía. Por el contrario, nadie podía perderse lo que hiciera o dejase de hacer Stransky. Su puesto de medio apertura era el más visible del equipo y, además, de su puntería dependía muchas veces el resultado del partido. Era el encargado de chutar los *drops*, las transformaciones de los ensayos y los penaltis, con los dos o tres puntos que eso suponía. Si el chut salía bien, el jugador era un héroe. Si no, corría el riesgo de la ignominia eterna o, en el mejor de los casos, de reprochárselo a sí mismo eternamente, como un futbolista que falla un penalti. Y, como un futbolista en esas circunstancias, muchas cosas dependían de una minucia. La diferencia entre la gloria y el desastre residía en un cambio sutil en la dirección del viento, unos movimientos casi microscópicos de los músculos, tendones y nervios en el tobillo, la rodilla, la cadera, el dedo gordo del pie.

El rugby puede ser un deporte espectacular de ver, incluso para personas que no conocen todas sus complejidades. Combina la táctica, la fuerza y la velocidad del fútbol americano con la fluidez, la amplitud, el esfuerzo colectivo y el talento individual del fútbol. Para jugar en la máxima categoría hay que tener la fuerza necesaria en el primero y la agilidad necesaria en el segundo. Cuando se juega bien, con ritmo y habilidad, el espectáculo es como una pelea de gladiadores y, al mismo tiempo, un placer para los sentidos. Si el partido está muy igualado, todavía mejor, porque entonces se mezclan el arte y el teatro.

La final de la Copa del Mundo de rugby de 1995 produjo más teatro que arte. Fue un partido agotador. Fue puro desgaste. Fue una guerra de trincheras, no demasiado grato como espectáculo. Pero, como muestra de dramatismo, fue inigualable.

Toda Sudáfrica estaba pendiente; todas las razas, religiones, tribus estaban pegadas a sus televisores. Desde Kobie Coetsee, que encontró un bar abarrotado cerca de su casa de Ciudad del Cabo en el que ver el partido, pasando por Constand Viljoen, que lo vio con unos amigos, también en Ciudad del Cabo, Tutu, que lo vio con desconocidos en California, Niël Barnard que lo vio en su casa de Pretoria con su mujer y sus tres hijos, y Justice Bekebeke con sus viejos amigos y camaradas en Paballelo, hasta el juez Basson, el hombre que les había

condenado a muerte, que lo vio en su casa de Kimberley. Todos pertenecían, por fin, al mismo equipo. Como
Eddie von Maltitz, que lo vio con sus viejos *kommandos*
bóer en la granja, en el Estado Libre de Orange. Estaba
ya tan comprometido con la causa de los Springboks y
Nelson Mandela como lo había estado con la del AWB
de Eugene Terreblanche.

«Todos rezábamos aquel día, tío —contaba—. Estábamos tensos. Rezando, rezando. Si podíamos ganar al
equipo de Nueva Zelanda, podríamos hacer muchas cosas como nación. Estábamos muy unidos, y ahora teníamos la oportunidad de estar más unidos todavía. Era
muy importante ganar para Sudáfrica.»

Tan importante que las calles estaban desiertas,
como sólo pudieron atestiguar el piloto Laurie Kay y los
miembros de su tripulación. El avión aterrizó antes de
que empezara el partido, pero en el aeropuerto no había nadie del personal de tierra para recibirlos. Salvo
que recurrieran a alguna medida extrema como desplegar el tobogán de emergencia, estaban atrapados en el
aparato. Por fin, apareció su chófer, que encontró unas
escalerillas y las llevó rodando hasta el avión. «No había
nadie en las calles. Parecía una escena de aquella novela
postapocalíptica, *La hora final*. Llegué a casa en diez minutos justos.» Lo cual quiere decir que debió de ir por
las calles más deprisa que en el vuelo que había hecho
sobre Ellis Park.

El partido en sí fue flojo. No fue fluido en ningún
momento, en parte porque Sudáfrica no dejó a Jonah
Lomu que jugara como sabía. James Small no tenía que
haberse preocupado; todo el equipo se encargó de
Lomu. Si el primer placaje no podía con él, el segundo,
o el tercero, o el cuarto lo conseguirían. Hubo momen-

tos en los que Lomu parecía un búfalo atacado por una manada de leones. Antes de que perfeccionaran el placaje en grupo, hubo un par de acciones de valor individual. La primera vez que Lomu recibió el balón, uno de los jugadores más menudos de Sudáfrica, el medio melé Joost van der Westhuizen, lo derribó con un placaje bajo, justo por debajo de las rodillas («*Aquello marcó el tono del partido*», contaba Pienaar). Un poco después, cuando parecía que Lomu había encontrado el tiempo y el espacio para acumular energía, lo derribó con el mismo aplomo Japie Mulder, el centro tres cuartos que formaba pareja con Hennie le Roux. Mientras el gigante se levantaba, Mulder —un pigmeo en comparación— le aplastó el rostro contra el cesped de Ellis Park.

«Fue bastante poco elegante por parte de Japie hacer eso —decía Morné du Plessis, sin una pizca de desaprobación—. Pero fue un mensaje a Lomu y a todos los All Blacks: Nadie va a poder hoy con nosotros.»

Y nadie pudo. Los All Blacks se habían emborrachado de tantos marcados en ensayos durante el torneo, pero no consiguieron ni uno contra los Springboks. John Robbie, el ex jugador de rugby y presentador de radio, lo resumió muy bien. «Los Springboks cerraron el juego, lucharon por cada centímetro de terreno y placaron como demonios. Contra aquel equipo, era la única forma de tener alguna posibilidad de ganar.»

Lo malo era que los sudafricanos tampoco estaban marcando ningún ensayo. La defensa de los All Blacks era tan firme como la de los Springboks. Era el equivalente deportivo de la Primera Guerra Mundial: ningún avance, líneas defendidas con obstinación, proyectiles que volaban entre un bando y otro. Fue un partido que se decidió en los chuts. Todo el tanteo del partido salió de los penaltis y los *drops*, que valían tres puntos cada uno.

Al llegar al descanso, Joel Stransky había chutado a palos con acierto tres veces, mientras que Andrew Mehrtens, el medio apertura de los All Blacks, lo había hecho en dos ocasiones. Cuando se detuvieron, al terminar los primeros 40 minutos, para el obligatorio descanso de 10, el marcador indicaba 9-6 a favor de Sudáfrica. Pero Mehrtens igualó en la segunda mitad, y el partido terminó, en un ambiente de tensión insoportable, en el que la situación podía variar en cualquier momento en un sentido u otro, con un tanteo de 9-9. Por primera vez en una Copa del Mundo de rugby, había que jugar una prórroga, dos mitades de 10 minutos cada una. Ningún jugador de los que estaban en el campo había cruzado nunca ese umbral. Estaban física y mentalmente exhaustos. Pero los aficionados estaban sufriendo aún más, entre ellos Mandela, pese a que —como la mayoría de los recientes conversos negros de todo el país— se había perdido algún detalle que otro. «No entendía mucho, pero sí lo suficiente para seguir el partido —recordaba el brusco Louis Luyt, que estaba sentado junto a él—. Me hacía preguntas: "Ese penalti, ¿por qué ha sido?" ¡Eso sí, qué nervioso estaba! ¡Increíblemente tenso! ¡Sobre el filo de una navaja!»

Mandela no dudaba en corroborar la impresión que había sacado Luyt. «¡No sabe lo que sufrí aquel día! ¡No lo sabe! —decía después, identificándose con todos sus compatriotas—. No había visto nunca un partido de rugby en el que no se hubiera logrado ningún ensayo. Todo penaltis o *drops*. No había visto nunca nada igual. Pero, cuando decidieron darnos diez minutos más, sentí que me desmayaba. Francaménte, no he estado nunca tan nervioso.»

Morné du Plessis, veterano de cien batallas, también se sintió desmayar cuando se imaginó en el lugar de los jugadores. «Era mucho más que un partido de rugby, recuerde, y todos lo sabían; era como tener a un grupo de soldados que acaban de vivir el trauma del campo de batalla y volverlos a enviar inmediatamente al frente.»

Pienaar, el general, de veintiocho años, recordó a sus compañeros el gran objetivo que tenían en el intervalo antes de que se reanudara el juego. «Mirad a vuestro alrededor —dijo a sus cansadas tropas—. ¿Veis esas banderas? Jugad para esa gente. Ésta es nuestra oportunidad. Tenemos que hacerlo por Sudáfrica. Vamos a ser campeones del mundo.»

Su elocuencia no impidió que los All Blacks se adelantaran con un *drop* de Mehrtens al minuto de haber empezado. Nueva Zelanda ganaba 12-9, pero, a medida que se aproximaba el minuto 10, cuando estaba a punto de sonar el pitido del descanso, Stransky colocó otro penalti alto y directo entre palos. Estaban 12-12. Sonó el silbato y, cinco minutos después, los jugadores, con piernas de plomo, reanudaron la batalla por última vez. Los últimos 10 minutos del partido.

«Unos días antes de la final, Kitch Christie [el entrenador] me había dicho: "No te olvides de los *drops*" —recordaba Joel Stransky—. Y estuve practicando marcar *drops* durante los dos días anteriores al gran encuentro. Menos mal que lo hice.

»Sólo recuerdo tres de los cinco chuts entre palos que metí aquel día. La última es una de ellas. Faltaban siete minutos y el marcdor seguía 12-12. Tuvimos una melé a 25 yardas de su línea. François ordenó una jugada de la fila posterior, que habíamos practicado una y otra vez.» Eso quería decir que los delanteros intentaban atravesar corriendo las densas filas de los All Blacks para hacer un ensayo. «Pero Joel anuló mi orden —recordaba Pienaar—. Dijo que quería el balón de inmediato.» Así que eso es lo que hicieron. Según recordaba Wiese, «Joel nos pidió que la melé girase en una dirección concreta para que pudiera marcar su *drop*. Estábamos muy cansados, pero lo intentamos y salió».

El balón emergió de la masa humana de la melé y Joost van der Westhuizen, el medio melé, el nexo entre los delanteros y los tres cuartos, lanzó el balón a Stransky. Éste dispuso de 30 segundos desde que dio su orden hasta que recibió el balón para ser completamente consciente de que aquél era el momento más importante de su vida y de las vidas de muchas otras personas. La presión mental, la enorme responsabilidad y la dificultad física de dejar caer el balón e impactarlo limpiamente con el pie en cuanto toca el suelo, de forma que vuele alto y directo, sabiendo a la perfección que dos o tres gigantes se dirigen hacia ti con ganas de asesinarte... Stransky se había ofrecido a cumplir uno de los deberes más peligrosos en cualquier deporte.

«Recibí el balón limpiamente, y ejecuté un chut perfecto —decía Stransky, reviviendo el momento más feliz de su vida—. Mantuvo su trayectoria. Giró como debía, sin desviarse. Y ni siquiera miré para ver si iba a atravesar los palos. Sabía, en cuanto se alejó de mi bota, que era un golpe demasiado bueno para fallar. Y me sentí absolutamente exultante.»

Él y todos los demás sudafricanos que estaban viendo el partido: Justice Bekebeke, Constand Viljoen, Arnold Stofile, Niël Barnard, Walter Sisulu, Kobie Coetsee,

Tokyo Sexwale, Eddie von Maltitz, Nelson Mandela; todos. Pero aún quedaban seis minutos. Y Lomu seguía allí. Y allí seguían los otros 14 All Blacks, según el *Daily Telegraph* de Londres, la alineación de rugby «de talento más asombroso» que nadie podía recordar.

Pienaar dijo a sus hombres que aguantaran, que aguantaran e hicieran todo lo posible para tratar de mantener el balón en el campo de Nueva Zelanda, inmovilizarlos, no dejarles ver ni un atisbo de luz.

«Cuando Joel Stransky lanzó aquel *drop*, había un británico que estaba cerca de mí y que me dijo: "Estoy seguro de que ése ha sido el tanto decisivo" —recordaba Mandela—. Pero yo no me atrevía a creerlo del todo. ¡Y la tensión, qué nervios! ¡Le digo que fueron los seis minutos más largos de mi vida! Miraba sin cesar mi reloj, todo el tiempo, y pensaba: "¿Cuándo va a sonar el silbato?"»

Los seis minutos pasaron, los Springboks resistieron, y el silbato sonó. François Pienaar salió disparado de una melé y saltó con las manos levantadas. De pronto se arrodilló y se ocultó el rostro con el puño, y los demás jugadores se arrodillaron a su alrededor. Rezaron y luego se levantaron, saltaron y se abrazaron, que era lo que estaba haciendo todo el mundo en el estadio, incluido Nelson Mandela, que no era muy dado a abrazos.

«Estaba en el séptimo cielo —decía Moonsamy—. Estuve con Nelson Mandela cinco años, toda su presidencia, y nunca le vi tan feliz como entonces. Estaba entusiasmado, extático. Cuando sonó el silbato, toda la suite estalló. Si la gente cree que los guardaespaldas son robots, deberían habernos visto cuando sonó el silbato. Nosotros también nos abrazamos, y algunos lloramos.»

Mandela se reía tanto al recordar el momento que

casi no podía hablar. «Cuando sonó el silbato, Luyt —decía—, Louis Luyt y yo... de pronto nos encontramos... ¡abrazándonos! ¡Sí, abrazándonos!» Luyt lo confirmó. «Cuando sonó el silbato y los jugadores se arrodillaron, nos abrazamos. Y él me dijo: "¡Lo hemos conseguido! ¡Lo hemos conseguido!" Nos abrazamos con tal fuerza —seguro que él no mencionó este detalle— ¡que le levanté del suelo!»

En las gradas, 62.000 rostros exultantes volvieron a gritar: «¡Nel-son! ¡Nel-son!» La emoción de la victoria hacía que su grito fuera más alto, más visceral que antes. En el campo, envuelto en el éxtasis del público, de sus compañeros de equipo y del suyo propio, Kobus Wiese digería la enormidad del momento. «Era muy consciente de que sólo unos pocos pueden tener ese sentimiento y ser parte de una cosa así. Vertí lágrimas de alegría. Creo que todos lloramos. En esos momentos, tras la victoria, absorbes toda la emoción, y no hablas. Te abrazas con todos y nadie tiene que decir nada. En aquel terreno nos dimos cuenta, con toda la emoción que sentíamos, de que habíamos pasado a formar parte de la historia.»

«Era imposible decir nada que expresase lo que sentíamos. Nos limitamos a saltar y saltar, y sonreír y sonreír —decía Joel Stransky, sonriente—. Sonreí durante toda una semana. No he dejado de sonreír.»

Capítulo XIX
AMA A TU ENEMIGO

«Cuando terminó el partido —contaba Morné du Plessis—, di la vuelta y empecé a correr hacia el túnel, y allí estaba Edward Griffiths, el creador del eslogan "Un equipo, un país", y me dijo: "Las cosas nunca volverán a ser igual." Comprendí inmediatamente que tenía razón, porque me di cuenta, allí mismo, de que lo mejor había quedado ya atrás, que la vida no podía ofrecer nada mejor. Le dije: "Hoy lo hemos visto todo."»

Pero Du Plessis se equivocaba. Quedaba más. Quedaba Mandela bajando al campo, con la camiseta puesta, la gorra en la cabeza, para entregar la copa a su amigo François. Y quedaba el público embelesado de nuevo —«¡Nelson! ¡Nelson! ¡Nelson!»— cuando Mandela apareció en la línea de banda, sonriendo de oreja a oreja, saludando a la muchedumbre, mientras se disponía a acercarse al pequeño podio colocado en el campo en el que iba a a entregar el trofeo de la Copa del Mundo a François Pienaar.

Van Zyl Slabbert, el afrikaner liberal, rodeado en el estadio —según palabras suyas— de tipos barrigudos

303

con pinta de pertenecer al AWB, se quedó asombrado ante la pasión por la Nueva Sudáfrica de sus compatriotas renacidos. «Tendría usted que haber visto las caras de esos bóers a mi alrededor. Recuerdo ver a uno al que le corrían las lágrimas por el rostro y que no paraba de decir, en afrikaans: "Ése es mi presidente... Ése es mi presidente..."»

Y hubo más aplausos y más lágrimas cuando Pienaar ofreció el que iba a ser el primero de dos ejemplos memorables de elocuencia improvisada. Un periodista de la cadena de televisión SABC se le acercó en el campo y preguntó: «¿Qué ha sentido al tener a 62.000 aficionados apoyándoles aquí en el estadio?»

Sin dudarlo un instante, respondió: «No teníamos a 62.000 aficionados con nosotros. Teníamos a 43 millones de sudafricanos.»

Linga Moonsamy, que salió al terreno de juego un paso por detrás de Mandela, miró a la multitud, al viejo enemigo que coreaba el nombre de su líder, y luchó para recordar que estaba trabajando, que, mientras todos los que le rodeaban perdían la cabeza, él tenía que conservar la suya. Mantuvo la suficiente sangre fría para recordar que, antes del partido, había visto en la esquina derecha del estadio aquellas viejas banderas sudafricanas. Así que volvió a mirar hacia allí. «Pero no —contaba—, las viejas banderas habían desaparecido. Sólo había banderas nuevas. Y la gente en aquel sector del público estaba llorando y abrazándose, como todos los demás. Así que me relajé un poco y me permití pensar que aquél era un momento inmenso para el país, que yo había hecho lo que había hecho cuando era joven, había corrido riesgos, había luchado por esto, y nunca había imaginado que podía manifestarse con tales dimensiones.»

Tokyo Sexwale, que estaba en el estadio, compartía los sentimientos de Moonsamy. «Te sientas allí y sabes que ha valido la pena. Todos los años en la clandestinidad, en las trincheras, de abnegación, de estar lejos de casa, en la cárcel, todo valió la pena. Aquello era todo lo que queríamos ver. Y otra vez, "¡Nelson! ¡Nelson! ¡Nelson!" Estábamos allí de pie y no sabíamos qué decir. Yo me sentía orgulloso de encontrarme junto a aquel hombre con el que había estado en la cárcel. ¡Qué arriba estaba en aquel momento! Me sentí tan orgulloso, tan orgulloso de haberme codeado con los dioses...»

Los dioses, en aquel momento, eran Mandela y Pienaar, el anciano vestido de verde, coronado rey de toda Sudáfrica, que entregaba la copa a Pienaar, el joven vestido de verde, designado, aquel día, jefe espiritual de la nueva *afrikaneidad*.

Mientras el capitán sostenía la copa, Mandela le puso la mano izquierda en el hombro derecho, le miró con afecto, le dio la mano y dijo: «François, muchas gracias por lo que has hecho por nuestro país.»

Pienaar miró a Mandela a los ojos y respondió: «No, señor presidente. Gracias a *usted* por lo que ha hecho por nuestro país.»

Si se hubiera estado preparando toda la vida para aquel instante, no habría podido ser más certero. Como dijo Desmond Tutu: «Aquella respuesta fue una inspiración divina. Los seres humanos hacemos todo lo que podemos, pero aquellas palabras en aquel momento... nadie habría podido escribirlas.»

Tal vez un guionista de Hollywood habría hecho que se dieran un abrazo. Fue un impulso que Pienaar confesó haber reprimido a duras penas. Pero no, los dos se miraron y se rieron. Morné du Plessis, que estaba al lado, miró a Mandela y al afrikaner pródigo, vio a Pienaar que levantaba la copa sobre los hombros, mientras Mandela, riendo, alzaba los puños, y le costó creer lo que veían sus ojos. «No he visto jamás una alegría tan completa —dijo Morné du Plessis—. Mandela miraba a François y no paraba de reír... y François miraba a Mandela y... ¡qué afecto se palpaba entre ellos!»

Todo aquello resultó abrumador para el duro Slabbert, veterano de mil batallas políticas. «Cuando François Pienaar dijo aquello en el micrófono, con Mandela escuchando, riéndose y saludando a la multitud y agitando la gorra —contaba—, *todos* lloraron. No quedó un ojo seco en el estadio.»

No quedó un ojo seco en el país. El viejo ministro de Justicia y Servicios Penitenciarios del *groot krokodil*, en su atiborrado bar de Ciudad del Cabo, sollozaba como un niño. Kobie Coetsee no podía dejar de pensar en su primer encuentro con Mandela, diez años antes. «Superó los demás logros. Fue el momento en el que mi gente, sus adversarios, aceptó a Mandela. Fue un momento comparable, pensé entonces, a la creación de Estados Unidos. Fue el mayor triunfo de Mandela. Les vi a él y a Pienaar y lloré. Me dije a mí mismo: "Ha valido la pena. Todo el sufrimiento, todo lo que he vivido, ha valido la pena. Esto refuerza el milagro." Eso es lo que sentí.»

Lejos de allí, en el polvoriento Paballelo, Justice Bekebeke sentía lo mismo. Cinco años antes estaba en el Corredor de la Muerte, enviado allí por uno de los jueces de Coetsee, pero, de pronto, todo aquello le pareció muy remoto. «¡Me sentí en el séptimo cielo! —explicaba—. Cuando Joel Stransky metió el *drop*, mis amigos empezaron a celebrarlo y a gritar como locos, y este Santo Tomás incrédulo también. Me sentí cien por cien sudafricano, más sudafricano que nunca. Estaba tan eufórico como todos los demás. Nos volvimos completamente locos. Y después de que sonara el silbato, después de que Mandela entregara la copa a Pienaar, salimos a la calle. Como todo el mundo en Paballelo. Las bocinas sonaban y todo el distrito salió a bailar, cantar y celebrarlo.»

Eran las mismas calles en las que Bekebeke había matado al policía que había disparado contra un niño; donde los antidisturbios habían enloquecido la noche antes de que se dictaran las penas de muerte para los 14 de Upington y habían golpeado a todos los que veían, hasta enviar a veinte personas al hospital.

«Era irreal. Y pensar que esas escenas estaban repitiéndose en toda Sudáfrica sólo cinco años después de la liberación de Mandela, dos años después del asesinato de Chris Hani. Entonces me habría resultado lo más improbable del mundo imaginar que iba a celebrar una victoria de los Springboks. Sin embargo, viéndolo ahora, no puedo creer la indiferencia que sentía aquella mañana antes de la final, no puedo creer que no me importara. Porque sólo había una manera de describir lo que sentía en aquel instante: una euforia desatada.»

En Paballelo, en Soweto, en Sharpeville y en otros mil distritos negros, grupos de jóvenes recorrían las calles sin árboles interpretando su propia Haka, su propia danza de guerra, el Toi Toi. Pero ahora no marchaban desafiantes; rebosaban orgullo nacional multicolor y celebraban la victoria de los *AmaBokoBoko*.

Llegaban noticias de las zonas residenciales acomodadas de Ciudad del Cabo, Durban, Port Elizabeth y

Johanesburgo de que las señoras blancas estaban deshaciéndose de generaciones de prejuicios y contención y abrazando a sus criadas negras, bailando con ellas en las calles arboladas de pulcros barrios como Houghton. Por primera vez, los mundos paralelos del apartheid se habían fundido, las dos mitades se habían unido en un todo, pero en ningún sitio como en la propia Johanesburgo y, sobre todo, en torno a Ellis Park, donde el carnaval de Río se confundió con la liberación de París en un tumulto de verde Springbok. Un anciano negro estaba en mitad de la calle, delante del estadio, ondeando una bandera sudafricana y gritando una y otra vez; «Sudáfrica ya es libre. Los Boks nos han permitido ser libres y estar orgullosos.»

Enfrente de Ellis Park se encontraban las oficinas del periódico dominical negro, *City Press*. Khulu Sibiya, el director del periódico, miraba estupefacto el espectáculo desde su ventana. «Nunca he visto a tantos negros celebrando en las calles. Nunca. Es más, nuestras páginas, al día siguiente, hablaron más de lo increíble que era ver a los negros festejando que sobre Pienaar y la copa en sí. Fue asombroso.»

El arzobispo Tutu, que también tenía mucho olfato periodístico, estaba de acuerdo. La noticia *fueron* las celebraciones de los negros. «Lo que vimos aquel día fue una revolución», decía, encantado de haber vivido para ver cómo su país engendraba un modelo nuevo de revolución, en el que no se eliminaba al enemigo, sino que se le acogía; que, en vez de dividir a la gente, la unía. «Si se hubiera profetizado sólo un año —sólo unos meses— antes que en las calles de Soweto la gente iba a bailar para celebrar una victoria de los Springboks, casi todo el mundo habría dicho: "Has tomado demasiado sol sudafricano y te ha afectado al cerebro." Aquel partido hizo por nosotros lo que no habían podido los discursos de los políticos ni los arzobispos. Nos electrizó, nos hizo comprender que era verdaderamente posible estar todos en el mismo bando. Nos dijo que era posible convertirnos en una sola nación.»

La inevitable histeria patriótica en los periódicos sudafricanos al día siguiente, la sensación de que el país había cambiado para siempre, quedó resumida en el titular de primera página, a ocho columnas, de un diario que tuvo la buena fortuna de nacer precisamente aquel día, el *Sunday Independent*. «Triunfo de los Guerreros del Arcoiris», clamaba el primer número del periódico. La prensa extranjera se sumó a la fiesta y hasta los cronistas deportivos casi se olvidaron de escribir sobre el partido propiamente dicho, como el especialista en rugby del *Sydney Morning Herald*, que comenzaba su información de esta forma: «Sudáfrica se convirtió ayer rotundamente en "un equipo, un país", mientras la nación arcoiris caía rendida en éxtasis.» Y añadía, en referencia al final de la Segunda Guerra Mundial, «fue como una repetición del Día de la Victoria, con oleadas de pasión similares, y el sentimiento de que acababa de suceder algo trascendental e inolvidable».

Van Zyl Slabbert, que era un hombre corpulento, un típico bóer, se encontró en medio de la histeria posterior al partido. «Salí a las calles, que estaban repletas de negros bailando, y tenía que llegar hasta casa, así que me metí en un taxi negro.» Un «taxi negro» es un híbrido de taxi tradicional y autobús, un vehículo que se para cuando uno lo llama pero que sigue una ruta concreta y que tiene una capacidad de alrededor de una docena de personas. Es «negro» porque en Sudáfrica era siempre una forma de transporte que usaban los negros; los blancos, casi invariablemente, tenían coche propio. Lo que hizo Slabbert, parar uno y subirse, era prácticamente inaudito, sobre todo para los habitantes del elegante barrio del norte de la ciudad, no lejos de Houghton, en el que vivía. «Me metí, y la gente estaba dando gritos y celebrando con tanta pasión como los bóers en Ellis Park. Le dije al conductor que me podía dejar en el Centro Cívico, en la ciudad, pero me preguntó cuál era mi destino. Le dije que mi casa estaba en un barrio a las afueras, pero que el Centro Cívico bastaba porque suponía que seguramente le pillaba de camino. Pero el conductor se mostró muy insistente. Me dijo que no, que me iba a llevar hasta casa, pese a que le supondría una demora de más o menos media hora y, con el caos de tráfico de aquel día, seguramente más. Así que le dije que muy bien, pero qué pasaba con las otras personas que estaban en el taxi, que iba completamente lleno. Todos gritaron que no había inconveniente. Se lo tomarían como un paseo. Estaban tan contentos. Por fin llegamos a casa y, al salir, le pregunté al conductor: "¿Cuánto?" Me sonrió y dijo: "No. Hoy, nadie paga."»

Slabbert suponía que nadie de los que iban en el taxi tenía más que vagos conocimientos sobre rugby, pero eso no aguó la fiesta general en Johanesburgo, como tampoco a 750 kilómetros de distancia, en Paballelo. «En mi distrito, entre mi gente, no había ni un solo aficionado al rugby —contaba Bekebeke—. Pero aquel día... hasta mi madre ululaba en celebración. Lo celebrábamos como sudafricanos, como una nación. Y sabíamos, en el fondo, que los Springboks habían ganado porque nos habíamos propuesto que ganaran. ¡Fue un día increíble! Una democracia joven, recién nacida, y allí estaba el símbolo de nuestra transformación, Mandela. Cuando levantó la copa, aquélla fue nuestra victoria. Supimos, al fin, que éramos una nación triunfadora.»

Arrie Rossouw, el periodista afrikaner que conoció a Mandela en Soweto al día siguiente de su liberación, estaba de acuerdo, pero lo sentía incluso con más intensidad porque, como sudafricano blanco, se había sentido un perdedor, un paria a los ojos del mundo. «Habíamos dejado de ser los malos —decía—. No sólo ganamos, sino que el mundo quería que ganáramos. ¿Se da cuenta de lo que significó aquello para nosotros? ¿Qué alegría? ¿Qué inmenso alivio?»

Tokyo Sexwale dijo que Mandela había liberado a los blancos del miedo. Era verdad, pero no era sólo eso. Los liberó en más sentidos. Los redimió ante sus propios ojos y ante los ojos del mundo.

Y entonces les hizo campeones del mundo. Kobus Wiese, François Pienaar, Hennie le Roux, Chester Williams, James Small, todos estaban de acuerdo en que el factor Mandela había sido decisivo. Habían ganado el partido por él y gracias a él. «Los jugadores sabíamos que el país tenía un rostro y un nombre —explicaba Le Roux—. Jugamos por Sudáfrica, pero también jugamos para no decepcionar al viejo, que venía a ser lo mismo.»

«Se conjugó todo a la perfección: nuestro deseo de ser el equipo de toda la nación y su deseo de convertir el equipo en el equipo nacional —explicaba Morné du Plessis—. Coincidió en el momento justo. Y estoy convencido de que ésa fue la razón por la que ganamos la Copa del Mundo.»

El propio Louis Luyt estaba también de acuerdo. «¡No habríamos ganado sin Mandela! Cuando bajé con él a ver a los jugadores en el vestuario, antes del partido, pude verlo: les levantó la moral un cien por cien. Ganaron en su nombre, tanto como por todo lo demás.»

Morné du Plessis tuvo la sensación de que iba a ser el gran día de Sudáfrica en cuanto vio a Mandela al borde del campo con la camiseta verde, recibiendo las aclamaciones del público. «Lo digo con todo el respeto a un equipo All Black verdaderamente memorable, pero, con la inmensidad del hombre que nos apoyaba, y el poder que emanaba de él y a través de él, me pareció un poco injusto.» Sean Fitzpatrick, el temible capitán All Black, reconoció mucho después que Du Plessis tenía razón, que se había sentido sobrecogido, en cierto modo, al oír la reacción del público ante Mandela. «Les oímos corear su nombre —explicaba—, y pensamos: ¿Cómo vamos a derrotar a estos cabrones?»

Demasiado tarde, Fitzpatrick comprendió que su equipo podía tener a Jonah Lomu, pero los otros jugaban con un hombre más; disponían de un arma secreta contra la que el mejor equipo de rugby de la historia no tenía respuesta. Joel Stransky habría podido atribuirse el mérito del triunfo, pero se lo cedió al decimosexto hombre de los Springboks. «El efecto que causó en los jugadores fue inconmensurable. Aquel día fue un cuento de hadas hecho realidad, con Mandela en el centro. Él nos dio la victoria.»

Y, aquel día, disfrutó enormemente con ella. El camino de vuelta a casa desde el estadio duró tres veces más de lo previsto, pero, como decía Moonsamy, podría haber durado seis veces más y Mandela habría pedido más. «Todos nuestros planes se vinieron abajo. Nuestra ruta estaba completamente atascada. Toda la ciudad se había transformado en una gigantesca fiesta callejera. Pero Mandela disfrutó de cada minuto.»

Moonsamy seguía alerta, pero la idea de que alguien pudiera querer asesinar a Mandela en aquel momento le parecía descabellada incluso a él. Cuando los cuatro coches que formaban la caravana llegaron, por fin, a Houghton, había una pequeña muchedumbre reunida delante de su casa, celebrándolo. Mandela salió del Mercedes para saludarlos y una anciana se le acercó. Moonsamy vio, asombrado, que le soltaba un pequeño discurso a Mandela para declarar que, hasta esa tarde, había sido del AWB, pero que ahora, dijo, «renuncio a seguir siendo miembro».

Estaba anocheciendo, eran alrededor de las seis y media. Mandela dejó marchar a sus guardaespaldas. «Chicos —dijo—, id a divertiros.»

Le tomaron la palabra. «Llegué a casa, a través de las masas ruidosas —recordaba Moonsamy—, y entonces, mi cuñado, su mujer y sus hijos, y mi familia y yo fuimos al lago, a Randburg Waterfront, donde todo el mundo estaba reuniéndose para celebrar la victoria, y allí vi una Sudáfrica unida. Blancos y negros abrazándose, riendo y llorando, hasta altas horas de la noche.»

Mandela prefirió quedarse tranquilamente en casa. «Volví del rugby y me quedé en casa, feliz, reflexionando», y siguiendo sus rutinas inviolables. Vio el informativo en inglés a las siete y en xhosa a las siete y media. A las ocho menos diez se sentó para tomar su habitual cena ligera: muslo de pollo con piel, batata y zanahorias. Nada más. Antes de irse a la cama, una hora después, se sentó a solas en el salón para recapitular, como hacía en su celda cada noche antes de dormir. Lo que le había sorprendido y satisfecho era hasta qué punto había acabado siendo el centro de atención. Porque era consciente de que, detrás de aquel clamor espontáneo de los blancos en Ellis Park —aquel «¡Nelson! ¡Nelson!»—, había pruebas elocuentes y convincentes de que sus duros esfuerzos habían surtido efecto. Al rendirle tributo a él, estaban rindiendo tributo al gran valor del «no racismo» por el que había soportado veintisiete años de cárcel. Estaban pidiendo perdón y aceptando el generoso abrazo que él, y a través de él la Sudáfrica negra, les estaba ofreciendo. Había empezado con Kobie Coetsee aquel día de noviembre de 1985 en el hospital, el primero de sus enemigos al que conquistó. Luego Niël Barnard, luego P. W. Botha, luego los medios afrikaans, De Klerk y sus ministros, el alto mando de la FSAD, Constand Viljoen y los demás generales del final amargo, del Volksfront afrikaner, Eddie von Maltitz, John Reinders y el resto del personal en los Union Buildings, Morné du Plessis, Kobus Wiese, François Pienaar: uno tras otro habían sucumbido a medida que él ampliaba cada vez más su abrazo, hasta el día de la final de rugby, en el que abrazó a todos.

John Reinders, el jefe de protocolo de la presidencia, lo comprendió perfectamente: «La final de la Copa del Mundo de rugby mostró lo mejor de él; fue todo él —decía—. Fue el día en el que todo el país vio en público al hombre que nosotros habíamos visto en privado. Fue el día en que todo el mundo, especialmente la Sudáfrica blanca, pudo verle como era de verdad.»

«Fue un día memorable —dijo Mandela años después, con una sonrisa que iluminaba el mismo salón en el que se había sentado a saborear la victoria aquella noche del 24 de junio de 1995—. Nunca imaginé que ganar la Copa del Mundo pudiera tener tanto impacto en una persona. Nunca me lo esperé. Todo lo que hacía era seguir adelante en mi tarea de movilizar a los sudafricanos para que apoyaran el rugby e influyeran en los afrikaners, sobre todo con vistas a la construcción nacional.»

«Influir» era una forma de llamarlo. La gran tarea de su presidencia, asegurar los cimientos de la nueva nación, «hacer sudafricanos», se había completado no en cinco años, sino en uno. De un plumazo, había eliminado la amenaza de la derecha. Sudáfrica no había tenido tanta estabilidad política en ningún momento desde la llegada de los primeros colonos blancos en 1652.

Die Burger lo resumió bien. El periódico destacaba que «el aislamiento deportivo fue una de las principales presiones que precipitó el cambio político» y decía: «¿No es irónico que el rugby sea una fuerza unificadora de tal calibre cuando, durante tanto tiempo, sirvió para aislarnos del mundo? Porque ya no cabe duda de que el equipo Springbok ha unido al país más que cualquier otra cosa desde el nacimiento de la nueva Sudáfrica.»

También lo supo, cosa más importante, Constand Viljoen. Las preocupaciones que le habían atormentado, la idea de que se había equivocado al optar por las elecciones en vez de una guerra de liberación bóer, o de que todavía podía estallar esa guerra sin él, se habían desvanecido. «Aquel partido de rugby me convenció de que había acertado con mi decisión», dijo. El alivio del general Viljoen derivaba de la seguridad de que, cuando las hordas gritaban «¡Nelson! ¡Nelson!», se le había quitado un gran peso de encima. Con aquel gesto, los afrikaners estaban asumiendo la responsabilidad del general sobre sus propios hombros, estaban apropiándose de la devoción que sentía él por Mandela.

«Verlo a él, el icono de los negros, tan feliz con su camiseta Springbok, me resultó tremendamente tranquilizador. Me había resultado muy difícil tomar la decisión y nunca imaginé que iba a verme reafirmado de forma tan espectacular.»

En este sentimiento, su hermano Braam, el gemelo «bueno», encontró por fin algo en común con Constand. «He conocido la ira de la política afrikaner toda mi vida, y que pudiera ocurrir aquello me pareció un milagro —reflexionaba—. ¡Qué carisma tenía aquel hombre! ¡Qué líder era Mandela! Cogió del brazo a mi hermano y no lo soltó.»

¿Tenía Mandela algún defecto? Sisulu lo conocía mejor que nadie. Su respuesta era que su viejo amigo tenía tendencia a confiar demasiado en la gente, a creerse a la primera sus buenas intenciones. «A veces desarrolla demasiada confianza en una persona —dijo—. Cuando confía en una persona, va a por todas.» Pero luego Sisulu pensó un momento en lo que había dicho y añadió: «Claro que eso quizá no es un defecto... Porque la verdad es que no nos ha decepcionado con esa confianza que tiene en la gente.»

La debilidad de Mandela era su mayor virtud. Triunfó porque prefirió ver el bien en personas a las que el 99 % de la gente habría considerado imposibles de redimir. Si Naciones Unidas decretó que el apartheid era un crimen contra la humanidad, ¿qué mayores criminales que el ministro de Justicia del apartheid, el jefe de los servicios de inteligencia del apartheid, el jefe militar supremo del apartheid, el jefe de Estado del apartheid? Sin embargo, Mandela apuntó directamente a la semilla oculta que albergaba a sus «ángeles buenos» y supo sacar la bondad que yace en el fondo de todas las personas. No sólo Coetsee, Barnard, Viljoen y P. W. Botha, sino los esbirros del apartheid —los guardias de prisiones, Badenhorst, Reinders— y sus cómplices inconscientes: Pienaar, Wiese, Luyt. Con su empeño en despertar e incitar lo que había de mejor en ellos, y en todos los sudafricanos blancos que vieron el rugby aquel día, les ofreció un regalo de valor incalculable: hizo que pudieran sentirse mejores personas y, en algunos casos, los transformó en héroes.

Su arma secreta era que daba por supuesto no sólo que le iban a caer bien las personas a las que conociera, sino que él les iba a gustar a ellas. Esa enorme seguridad en sí mismo, unida a la sincera confianza que tenía en otros, era una combinación tan irresistible como encantadora.

Era un arma tan poderosa que engendró un nuevo tipo de revolución. En vez de eliminar al enemigo y partir de cero, incorporó al enemigo a un nuevo orden deliberadamente construido sobre los cimientos del viejo. Al concebir su revolución, no sólo como la destrucción del apartheid, sino, a largo plazo, como la unificación y reconciliación de todos los sudafricanos, Mandela rompió el molde histórico.

Pero, como mostró su reacción a la actitud del público en Ellis Park, se sorprendió incluso a sí mismo. No había valorado lo suficiente el poder de su encanto.

Un domingo, pocas semanas después de la victoria de los Springboks, Nelson Mandela visitó una iglesia en Pretoria. Era un templo de la Iglesia Reformada Holandesa, la confesión que en otro tiempo había tratado de encontrar justificación bíblica para el apartheid; que había convencido a Constand Viljoen de que había Cielos separados para blancos y negros; que había exiliado a su hermano Braam por decir que aquella doctrina era una herejía. «Aquélla fue la ocasión —contaba Mandela, con los ojos chispeantes— en la que vi que los efectos del partido de rugby iban a durar, que la actitud de los afrikaners hacia mí había cambiado verdaderamente por completo.» Durante el servicio, se dirigió a los fieles en afrikaans, y después le rodearon ante la iglesia, como si estuvieran en una melé. Era exactamente lo que le había sucedido en cientos de concentraciones del CNA en los distritos negros de todo el país. En cualquier sitio al que iba, los negros le trataban como si fuera una combinación de David Beckham, Evita Perón y Jesucristo. Ahora, los blancos estaban haciendo lo mismo. «De la masa salían manos que trataban de estrechar la mía. Y las mujeres: ¡querían besarme en la mejilla! Eran espontáneos, entusiastas. Se desvivían por acercarse, y a mí me llevaban de un lado a otro. Y perdí un zapato. ¿Puede creerlo? ¡Perdí un zapato!»

Mandela estaba casi doblado de risa mientras contaba la historia. Se reía porque era divertida, pero también porque estaba describiendo la culminación del sueño de su vida, el momento en el que comprendió que Sudáfrica, por fin, era un país.

EPÍLOGO

Doce años después de la final de la Copa del Mundo de rugby, en agosto de 2007, se descubrió una estatua de bronce de Nelson Mandela en la Plaza del Parlamento de Londres, junto a las de Abraham Lincoln y Winston Churchill. En su información del acto, un periódico nacional británico calificó a Mandela de «líder negro». No pretendía ofender, seguramente, pero, aun así, parecía un poco insultante verlo descrito en esos términos. Como lo habría sido ver a Lincoln y a Churchill descritos meramente como «líderes blancos».

Identificar a Mandela por su raza es disminuirlo. Tony Benn, un veterano parlamentario británico, se aproximó más a la verdad cuando, en la ceremonia, llamó a Mandela «presidente de la humanidad».

Pero Mandela, que entonces tenía ochenta y nueve años, no era una especie de aberración de la naturaleza. Como dijo él en su turno de intervención, frágil pero con voz firme, «aunque esta estatua representa a un hombre, en realidad debería simbolizar a todos los que se resistieron a la opresión, especialmente en mi país».

La modestia de Mandela podía, a veces, ser un poco artificial, pero en esa ocasión no lo era. Mandela era la encarnación de las mejores cosas que podía ofrecer su país. Lo vi personalmente, en repetidas ocasiones, durante los seis años que estuve destinado en Sudáfrica, entre 1989 y 1995, una época en la que, en medio del esperanzado movimiento hacia delante, se desató una violencia terrible en los distritos negros, sobre todo los de alrededor de Johanesburgo, donde yo vivía. Lo mejor de Sudáfrica no era Mandela, sino que el país estaba repleto de mini-Mandelas, de gente como Justice Bekebeke, su novia, Selina, o *Terror* Lekota, el primer ministro del Estado Libre de Orange que invitó a Eddie von Maltitz a su fiesta de cumpleaños.

La primera vez que entrevisté a Mandela, a principios de 1993, le pregunté cómo era posible que el mensaje de «no racismo» del CNA hubiera capturado la imaginación de los negros sudafricanos, en detrimento del vengativo «un colono, una bala» del CPA. Me respondió que la historia había enseñado a su pueblo a ser cálido, amable y generoso, incluso con sus enemigos. «El rencor no se concibe —dijo—, ni siquiera cuando luchábamos contra algo que nos parecía que estaba mal.» El mensaje del Congreso Nacional Africano, dijo, «no había hecho más que consolidar ese modelo histórico».

Esa verdad quedó demostrada por mi experiencia, pero no era toda la verdad. Otro tipo de líder del CNA habría podido escoger la opción, más fácil, de apelar a la indignidad y el dolor que había sufrido la Sudáfrica negra y convertirlos en un enfrentamiento violento. Hacía falta una sabiduría poco frecuente para que Mandela dijera a su gente, como me parafraseó en aquella misma entrevista: «Entiendo vuestra ira. Pero, si estáis construyendo una nueva Sudáfrica, debéis estar preparados para trabajar con gente que no os gusta.»

Su generoso pragmatismo era todavía más extraordinario si se tenía en cuenta la trayectoria histórica de su propia vida. Albert Camus escribió en su libro *El hombre rebelde*: «Veintisiete años en prisión no engendran una forma muy conciliadora de inteligencia. Un encierro tan prolongado hace que un hombre se convierta en un pelele, o un asesino, o a veces ambas cosas.» En defensa del filósofo francés, hay que decir que murió en 1960, antes incluso de que Mandela entrara en la cárcel. Pocos habrían discutido la lógica de esas palabras cuando las escribió Camus. Mandela fue un primer caso y seguramente un último. Fue para Sudáfrica lo que George Washington fue para Estados Unidos, el hombre indispensable. Como me dijo el arzobispo Tutu: «No habríamos podido hacerlo sin él.»

Mandela impidió que estallara una guerra pero eso no significó que dejara a Sudáfrica un estado de paz y armonía perfectas, como Washington tampoco lo logró en Estados Unidos. Después del apartheid, Sudáfrica se libró de su singularidad en el mundo, dejó de ser el parangón de la injusticia y el chivo expiatorio (totalmente merecido) de la incapacidad humana de superar los antagonismos raciales, tribales, nacionalistas, ideológicos y religiosos. Se convirtió en un país con los mismos retos que otros en parecidas circunstancias económicas: cómo proporcionar viviendas a los pobres, cómo combatir los crímenes violentos, cómo luchar contra el sida. Y hubo corrupción, hubo ejemplos desagradables de clientelismo político, hubo dudas sobre la eficacia del CNA en el gobierno. Y la eterna cruz de la humanidad, el retrógrado problema del color de la piel, tampoco desapareció por arte de magia, aunque, al comenzar el siglo XXI, la transformación era tal que no había muchos países cuyos ciudadanos blancos y negros se relacionasen con tanta naturalidad como en Sudáfrica.

También era cierto que los fundamentos políticos siguieron siendo tan sólidos como los había dejado Mandela al acabar sus cinco años de mandato presidencial: el país siguió siendo un modelo de estabilidad democrática y el imperio de la ley permaneció firme.

¿Permanecería así para siempre? ¡Quién podía saberlo! Lo que sí perduraría es el ejemplo de Mandela, y aquel atisbo de utopía que su pueblo vio desde la cima de la montaña a la que les llevó el 24 de junio de 1995. Cuando pregunté a Tutu cuál era el valor más perdurable de aquel día, replicó: «Es fácil. Un amigo de Nueva York me dio la respuesta cuando me dijo: "¿Sabes qué? Lo mejor de todo lo bueno que ha ocurrido es que puede volver a ocurrir."»

¿DÓNDE ESTÁN HOY?

NIËL BARNARD: ocupó un alto cargo del Partido Nacional en el gobierno de coalición de Mandela hasta su retirada en agosto de 1996; Mandela organizó un banquete de despedida en su residencia oficial de Pretoria para rendir homenaje a su contribución al cambio pacífico. Hoy trabaja como consultor y emplea su «experiencia y conocimientos», según sus palabras, en asesorar a líderes africanos de todo el continente «sobre el gobierno y la forma de gobernar».

JUSTICE BEKEBEKE: fue responsable electoral de la Provincia del Cabo Norte en Sudáfrica y en 2004 formó parte de un equipo de observadores internacionales independientes que viajó a Estados Unidos para ayudar a certificar que las elecciones presidenciales de ese año eran libres e imparciales.

P. W. BOTHA: murió de un ataque al corazón a los noventa años, en 2006. Mandela transmitió sus condolencias a la familia y dijo: «Aunque, para muchos, el señor Botha seguirá siendo un símbolo del apartheid, también le recordamos por los pasos que dio para abrir camino hacia una solución negociada y pacífica en nuestro país.»

CHRISTO BRAND: lleva la tienda oficial de recuerdos en Robben Island. Su hijo Riaan, el que Mandela abrazó secretamente en la cárcel cuando tenía ocho meses, murió en un accidente de coche en 2005. Mandela, cuyo hijo murió a una edad parecida en otro accidente mientras él estaba en Robben Island, voló hasta Ciudad del Cabo para consolar a su viejo carcelero.

KOBIE COETSEE: murió de un ataque al corazón a los sesenta y nueve años, en 2000. Mandela dijo: «Siempre cultivaremos y valoraremos el recuerdo de Kobie Coetsee como uno de los grandes arquitectos de la transformación hacia una Sudáfrica democrática. Nos entristece que haya fallecido antes de que nosotros, y el país, pudiéramos rendir el homenaje apropiado a este hombre discreto y modesto por sus contribuciones pioneras, cuyos frutos estamos disfrutando ahora.»

NICHOLAS HAYSOM: trabajó para Naciones Unidas en la resolución de conflictos y la construcción nacional en Líbano, Nigeria, Indonesia, Filipinas, Timor Oriental, Sudán, Somalia, Sri Lanka, Lesotho, Colombia, Congo, Tanzania, Zimbabue, Kenia, Nepal, Myanmar e Irak, antes de ser nombrado director de asuntos políticos en la Oficina Ejecutiva de la Secretaría General de la ONU.

NELSON MANDELA: unas semanas antes de cumplir ochenta y seis años, convocó una rueda de prensa para anunciar su retirada y al final dijo: «Muchas gracias por su atención y muchas gracias por su amabilidad con un anciano, por permitirle que descanse, aunque muchos de ustedes puedan pensar que, después de vaguear en una isla y algunos otros lugares durante 27 años, el descanso realmente no es merecido.» Desde entonces, se ha dedicado a sus tres organizaciones benéficas personales: la Fundación Mandela Rhodes, la Fundación Nelson

Mandela y el Fondo Nelson Mandela para la Infancia, dedicadas, respectivamente, a promover la educación, luchar contra la pobreza y combatir el sida.

LINGA MOONSAMY: es jefe de seguridad corporativa en South African Airways, pero sigue siendo amigo de Mandela. Está casado con una sobrina de la esposa de Mandela, Graça Machel, y va muchas veces a comer los domingos a su casa.

EDDIE VON MALTITZ: sigue viviendo en su granja del Estado Libre de Orange, todavía va vestido de camuflaje, lleva un arma y llama por teléfono a las emisoras de radio sudafricanas para denunciar injusticias.

MORNÉ DU PLESSIS: dirige el Instituto de Ciencias del Deporte de Sudáfrica y es miembro de la Academia Mundial del Deporte, un organismo de antiguos grandes del deporte entre los que están Jack Nicklaus, Dan Marino, Martina Navratilova y sir Bobby Charlton. Cada año se reúnen para seleccionar a los ganadores de los Premios Mundiales Laureus, el equivalente en el mundo del deporte a los Oscars de Hollywood.

CONSTAND VILJOEN: dirije una granja en lo que ahora se denomina la Provincia de Mpumalanga (cuando era niño, era el Transvaal Oriental) y de vez en cuando pasa sus vacaciones en Ciudad del Cabo, donde se aloja con su mujer en una casa en la costa para militares retirados, llamada *El Alamein*.

BRAAM VILJOEN: dedica su jornada de trabajo a su granja al norte de Pretoria. Su hermano y él tienen una relación más estrecha que nunca desde su niñez. Disfrutan hablando de política.

FRANÇOIS PIENAAR: trabaja como alto ejecutivo en el First National Bank de Ciudad del Cabo. Mandela, que es padrino de su hijo mayor, Jean, les ha invitado en varias ocasiones a su casa a él, su mujer, Nerine, y sus hijos. Mandela dio al hijo pequeño de Pienaar, Stephane, el apodo de *Gora*, que significa «el valiente» en xhosa.

EUGENE TERREBLANCHE: el líder del Movimiento de Resistencia Afrikaner (AWB), de extrema derecha, fue encarcelado en 1997 por lesiones graves e intento de asesinato, en ambos casos de unos hombres negros indefensos. Quedó en libertad de 2004 y hoy predica sermones que invitan al arrepentimiento y la redención.

AWB: un editorial en el boletín de la organización, *Storm*, publicado en 2002, decía: «Desde las elecciones de 1994, las organizaciones patrióticas afrikaner se han visto debilitadas por la incertidumbre entre sus partidarios sobre si votar o no. La unidad que existía antes de las elecciones de 1994 ha quedado destruida. Nuestra gente está decepcionada por el hecho de que el CNA se haya hecho con el poder, y nos invade un sentimiento de impotencia. Desde entonces, la actitud reinante es de "sálvese quien pueda", y todo el interés por la política ha desaparecido.»

LOS SPRINGBOKS: volvieron a ganar la Copa del Mundo de rugby en 2007, derrotando a Inglaterra en la final, y todavía visten la camiseta verde y oro. Una vez más, el país estalló de júbilo, negros, blancos y todos los colores intermedios.

AGRADECIMIENTOS

Ante todo, mil gracias a los numerosos actores del drama sudafricano que se molestaron en hablar conmigo para este libro.

Gracias a Pearlie Joubert, por concertarme citas con ellos y simplemente por ser tan estupenda.

Gracias a Stephen Glover, así como a Andreas Whittam Smith, por nombrarme corresponsal en Sudáfrica del *Independent* de Londres. Si no hubieran tenido tanta fe en mí en 1989, este libro nunca habría visto la luz.

Y gracias a Javier Moreno, mi jefe actual en *El País*, por concederme el tiempo necesario para escribirlo.

Un afectuoso agradecimiento a mi editora Elena Ramírez, la directora de Seix Barral, cuya mezcla de rigor, inteligencia y apoyo me han ayudado de forma inconmensurable. Mil gracias a Nahir Gutiérrez y el resto del equipo de Seix Barral, y a Marisa Rodríguez, mi traductora, por su empeño, perseverancia y sensibilidad. Tampoco olvido que Adolfo García Ortega fue uno de los primeros en animarme a escribir este libro.

Zelda la Grange (junto con Pearlie, una fuerte aspirante al título de la mejor mujer sudafricana viva) fue muy amable. También lo fueron Moegsien Williams y

Kathy Macfarlane en el *Star* de Johanesburgo, y Amanda Oosthuizen en *Die Burger*. Asimismo, Marietta Van Wyk.

Indra Delanerolle, David Fanning, Sara Blecher, Sharon Cort, Cliff Bestall, Lindy Wilson y el resto del grupo del documental sobre Mandela que hicimos para televisión: muchas gracias a todos.

Entre los amigos y conocidos que me han brindado su apoyo, sus sugerencias y ánimos, y a los que debo enorme gratitud, están (y que aquellos de los que me he olvidado me perdonen) Daniel Tanzer, James Lemoyne, Peter Ettedgui, Mark Phillips, Wim Trengrove, Stephen Robinson, Jorge Valdano, Jeremy Thompson, Tony O'Reilly, Teresa Rioné, Morgan Freeman, Sebastian Spear, Jayendra Naidoo y Tony Peckham.

Un agradecimiento especial a Lauren Jacobson y Keith Coleman, Michael Shipster, Joaquín Villalobos y Kobus Jordaan, magníficos amigos, tan generosos con su tiempo, sus conocimientos y su agudeza mental.

Gail Behrman hizo un gran trabajo recopilando las fotografías para este libro. La sensibilidad y los ánimos de Sue Edelstein fueron un impulso tremendo a lo largo de todo el proceso.

Anne Edelstein (nada que ver), mi agente en Barcelona y Nueva York, fue decisiva. La idea de este libro llevaba rondándome la cabeza desde hacía años. Sin su impulso entusiasta, quizá nunca habría nacido y, desde luego, no habría nacido ahora. Su devoción al empeño, como libro y como causa, ha sido muy valiosa y una fuente de inspiración.

Gracias a Anne, conocí a mi editor, Eamon Dolan. Él es (junto con Anne) la confirmación de lo que siempre he pensado: que los mejores estadounidenses son la mejor gente. Si este libro tiene algún valor, gran parte del mérito corresponde a Eamon, un artesano de la palabra brillante, exhaustivo y apasionado. Todavía no acabo de creerme mi suerte.

Por último, gracias a Sudáfrica por haber compartido sus secretos y su genio conmigo. Gracias a Nelson Mandela y a los miles de Mandelas menos famosos, a los que tuve la inmensa fortuna de conocer durante mi estancia allí, y cuyo espíritu generoso late en lo que de bueno pueda tener este libro. Pienso en Justice Bekebeke, pienso en Walter Sisulu y Ahmed Kathrada, pienso en mi viejo amigo Mandla Mthembu (que salvó mi vida al menos en una ocasión), pienso en Kader Asmal, *Terror* Lekota, John Battersby, Dudu Chili, Cyril Ramaphosa, Shaun Johnson, Ronnie Kasrils, Jacques Pauw, Gill Marcus, Debora Patta, Carl Niehaus, Max du Preez, Henrietta Mqokomiso, Halton Cheadle, Aziz Pahad, Ali Bacher, Anton Lubowski, Andy Durbach, Brian Currin, Desmond Tutu, Tim Smith, John Allen, Helen Suzman, y pienso en el difunto, gran Bheki Mkhize, el hombre más bueno, valiente y noble que he conocido jamás en ningún sitio. Él iluminó Sudáfrica para mí como el sol.

UNA NOTA SOBRE LAS FUENTES

Prácticamente todo el material de este libro está extraído de entrevistas que hice esepecíficamente para él entre 2000 y 2007, o a lo largo de mi trabajo periodístico general desde que fui a vivir a Sudáfrica, en 1989. Un proyecto en el que participé de cerca, un documental televisivo sobre Mandela, emitido en PBS (*The Long Walk of Nelson Mandela*), SABC (*The First Accused*) y otros lugares en 1999, resultó especialmente valioso. También me resultaron útiles varios libros, entre ellos: la autobiografía de Nelson Mandela, *Long Walk to Freedom* [*El largo camino hacia la libertad*]; el libro de Anthony Sampson *Mandela: The Authorized Biography*; *Rainbow Warrior*, de François Pienaar; *Days of the Generals*, de Hilton Hamann; *One Team, One Country*, de Edward Griffiths; *Anatomy of a Miracle*, de Patti Waldmeir; *One Step Behind Mandela*, de Rory Steyn y Debora Patta; *Apartheid: The Lighter Side*, de Ben Maclennan; *The Other Side of History*, de Frederik van Zyl Slabbert; y *A Common Purpose: The Story of the Upington 25*, de Andrea Durbach.

ÍNDICE

333